WORD
COMPANION

WORD COMPANION

The definitive guide
to Microsoft® Word 3
for the Macintosh™

Judy Mynhier
Gena B. Cobb

With:
Amy R. Willard

COBB

WORD COMPANION

Published by
The Cobb Group, Incorporated
301 North Hurstbourne Lane
Louisville, Kentucky 40222

Library of Congress Catalog Card Number: 87-70443

ISBN 0-936767-05-7

Editing:
Marjorie Maddox
Linda Baughman
Mary Welp

Production:
Maureen Pawley
Elayne Noltemeyer

Design:
Julie Baer Tirpak

Word Companion is based on Microsoft Word Version 3.01 for the Apple Macintosh. Any problems with this original version that are mentioned in this book may be corrected in future releases of Microsoft Word.

Printed in the United States of America

HL 0 9 8 7 6 5 4 3

TABLE OF CONTENTS

Dedication

To Art, for keeping it all in perspective.
JLM

To the Bear, my happy helper.
GBC

To Charles, who always says yes.
ARW

Acknowledgments

No project of this magnitude can be carried out successfully without the help and encouragement of dozens of people. We'd like to take this opportunity to thank a few of them:

Douglas Cobb, publisher, head cheerleader, slavedriver, and surgeon; Tom Cottingham, for setting up the contacts and making the sale.

Maureen Pawley, for going the extra mile, and then some; Elayne Noltemeyer, for jumping in when the going got tough; Julie Baer Tirpak, for "the look"; Margie Maddox, Linda Baughman, and Mary Welp, for all of those marathon editing (and re-editing!) sessions; Amy Willard, whose remarkable versatility and positive attitude have been invaluable.

Steve Cobb, for giving up his Mac Plus; Barbara Wells, for keeping the group under control; All the folks who keep the wheels turning—Denise Rogers and Andy Spurgeon (our bodyguards), Brenda Bankston, Shannon Portman, Grand Britt and Kevin Fuqua (thanks for lunch), Theresa Martin, Teresa Poole, and Franny Corrigan; Eric Schlene, for the water trick.

Mike Slade and Valerie Houchens at Microsoft, for their continued support; Sylvia C. Hayashi and David Dressler, Microsoft's technical support specialists, who handled our barrage of long-distance questions with the utmost patience and good cheer.

Dave Parks and all the folks at Printer's Type Service, for the supersonic turnaround; Wayne Masters at Arcata Graphics, for finding us a slot; George Reichler, from the Computer Shoppe, for going out of his way to be helpful.

Linda Baughman again, for her thesis; Bert Baker, for the dense documents; Courtenay Penick, for the clean-up; Art Penick, remember me?; Wes and Tim, for making us smile; Michelle Cobb, for taking care of a little boy who was missing his mommy; Theresa Wheatley, for the extra hours and trips to the office; Sara Ford (Nanny), thanks for understanding.

Preface

There's no doubt about it—Microsoft Word 3 is the most powerful word processor ever for personal computers. From the first time we saw the new version of Word, in the fall of 1986, we knew that it was going to be a big hit. We also knew that Word was a product we wanted to write about.

Word 3 offers capabilities that were beyond imagination a few years ago. Not only does it have all of the editing features you would expect from a top-flight word processor, it also boasts a built-in outliner to help you organize your thoughts, a spelling checker, style sheets that help you format your text, a hyphenation dictionary to help you polish your finished documents, sophisticated multicolumn formatting capabilities (including independent side-by side columns), the ability to use borders and other graphic elements, tables of contents and indexes, automatic line and paragraph numbering, sorting, and much more. These features give Word the depth and sophistication that you need to create every kind of document imaginable—from letters, memos, and reports to professional-quality newsletters and books.

However, all of this power is not without a price. If you've ever spent two hours trying to develop a multicolumn page design or cursing because a page of tabular data keeps jumping from place to place, you know that Word is a complex and challenging tool. While Word's powerful word processing, formatting, editing, and design tools are intuitive and easy to use, you may find that it takes you months to explore all the nooks and crannies of this powerful program. Even with the user-friendly features of the Macintosh, learning Word is a big job.

ABOUT THIS BOOK

We wrote the *Word Companion* to help make Word easier to learn and use. No matter what your level of expertise, we think you'll find a great deal of useful information on the following pages. If you are brand new to word processing and desktop publishing, you can use this book as a tutorial to help you get started. If you are an experienced user of word processing, you can use it as a reference guide to help you solve specific design and technical problems. If you've used previous versions of Microsoft Word, you can use the book to come up to speed quickly on the new features of Word 3.

We had three goals in mind as we created the book. First, we wanted to help you learn to use Word efficiently—after all, a productivity tool is supposed to save—not cost—time. Second, we wanted to provide an indepth source of reference information that you will return to time and time again, whether you're a Word novice or expert. Third, we wanted to introduce you to some of the theories of word processing, typography, and design so that you can begin to use those theories to create your own professional publications. We think we've achieved all of these goals.

Word Companion has three sections. Section One offers a basic overview of Microsoft Word and the Macintosh environment. If you are new to the Macintosh or new to Word, you'll want to read this section carefully before you dive into the more complex aspects of the program. If you have been using Word for awhile, we suggest that you skim this section to familiarize yourself with our terminology and approach before you move on to Sections Two and Three. In Section Two, we cover the basics—creating documents, editing, formatting, printing and page design. Then, in Section Three, we explain the special features that make Word more than a word processor. Here, you will learn about style sheets, outlining, and the merge facility.

About Carts and Horses

Most software manuals provide an abundance of technical information about their products. Every command, every option, every syntax rule is presented in laborious detail. Unfortunately, none of this encyclopedic information is geared toward helping you do your job. Until you become familiar with the program, you'll have no way of looking up the information you need.

On the other hand, most of the books we've seen on word processing packages go to the opposite extreme—they are almost completely tutorial in nature, offering little or no reference information to help you apply technical concepts to your own work. Instead, the author walks you through the development of a standard business letter or the design of a prefab two-column newsletter.

We've tried to strike a balance with *Word Companion*—to give you the technical information you need to use Microsoft Word effectively and to teach by example. For that reason, the book is organized functionally, rather than by command name. We try to walk you through the steps you need to develop a document, introducing new commands and concepts as they logically arise.

About Word 3

This book covers Word Version 3.0 and 3.01. Since there are very few differences between the two, we use the term Word 3 to describe both versions. We point out in the text any important differences between the two versions.

If you have not yet upgraded from Word 3.0 to Word 3.01, we advise you to do so immediately. For more information on the mechanics of upgrading, contact your computer dealer or call Microsoft at 1-206-882-8080.

ABOUT THE COBB GROUP

The Cobb Group is a leading publisher of books and journals about business software for personal computers. Bestselling Cobb Group books include *Excel in Business*, currently the number one Macintosh bestseller, *Doug Cobb's Tips for Microsoft Excel*, *Douglas Cobb's 1-2-3 Handbook*, *Mastering Symphony*, and *Understanding OverVUE*. Cobb Group journals include *Inside Word*, a monthly journal for users of Microsoft Word 3 on the Macintosh, and *Excellence: The Microsoft Excel User's Journal*. Douglas Cobb, President of The Cobb Group, is the author and coauthor of many bestselling computer books, including *Excel in Business*, *Using 1-2-3*, and *Mastering Symphony*.

ABOUT THE AUTHORS

Judy Mynhier is an author with The Cobb Group, Incorporated. She is Editor-in-Chief of *Inside Word* and *Excellence: The Microsoft Excel User's Journal*. Judy is the coauthor of *Excel in Business*, the *Hands-On Excel* workbook, *Doug Cobb's Tips for Microsoft Excel*, and the *Microsoft Excel Functions Library*. She holds a B.A. from the Indiana University School of Journalism.

Gena B. Cobb is Vice President of The Cobb Group, Incorporated, where she serves as an author and technical editor. She is the coauthor of several books, including *Douglas Cobb's 1-2-3 Handbook*, *Doug Cobb's Tips for Microsoft Excel*, and *Mastering Symphony*. She received her B.S. from the University of Virginia and her M.B.A from the Harvard Business School.

Amy Willard is an author at The Cobb Group, Incorporated. She is a graduate of the University of Pittsburgh, and her background includes scientific writing, with specialization in the fields of cancer and psychiatry.

THERE'S MORE!

In developing *Word Companion*, we spent months exploring every feature of Word—poking, prodding, and putting the program through its paces. We came up with more material than we could conceivably include in one book—tips, shortcuts, advanced techniques, and unique applications. Even as we go to press, we continue to discover new nooks and crannies.

If you're interested in learning more about Microsoft Word, we urge you to subscribe to our newest monthly technical journal: *Inside Word*. This journal lets us keep you up to date on the newest developments in Word and lets us pass along to you all of the exciting capabilities and techniques that we continue to uncover. You can receive a free issue of *Inside Word* by sending us the card at the back of this book.

THE SECTION ONE PRELIMINARIES

Section One lays the groundwork for using Microsoft Word 3. In this brief section, we'll introduce you to Word 3 on the Macintosh, and we'll show you how to get started with the program. You'll find it well worth the time to familiarize yourself with the concepts presented here before you launch into a full-scale assault on Word, particularly if you are new to the program.

We will assume through the course of this book that you are familiar with the Macintosh basics that are common to all programs — how to use the mouse, how to select icons and menu commands, and so forth. If you are not comfortable with these basics, we suggest that you review your Macintosh owner's guide before you proceed. You'll find it much easier to come up to speed on Microsoft Word if you have a feel for the general workings of the Mac first.

Though we do not presume to give you a full-length course on the Macintosh in this section, we will review a few Mac basics as they relate directly to using Word. In Chapter 1, we'll discuss the hardware you need to use Word, then we'll show you how to create backup copies of your Word disks and customize your software. In Chapter 2, we'll introduce you to the Word environment and show you some of the tools at your disposal. In Chapter 3, we'll discuss file-handling in Word.

BEFORE YOU BEGIN 1

Before you begin working with Word, you must attend to a few housekeeping chores: You should be sure that you have the hardware required to use the program, and you should familiarize yourself with the "layout" of your Word disks. Then you can create backup disks and customize your copy of the Word software to suit your needs. We'll cover those preliminaries in this chapter.

HARDWARE REQUIREMENTS

To use Microsoft Word 3, you must have an Apple Macintosh with at least 512K of memory. You must also have at least one double-sided (800K) disk drive, two single-sided (400K) disk drives, or a hard disk accompanied by one single-sided or one double-sided disk drive. Other possible configurations include one 400K and one 800K disk drive, or two 800K disk drives.

Currently, the optimal configuration for using Word is a Mac Plus or a Mac SE with an 800K internal drive plus an additional 800K external disk drive, or a Mac installed with a hard disk plus one external 800K drive. You'll find that the Mac Plus and the Mac SE (or a Mac installed with a hard disk) are much faster than the 512K Mac. Because of their expanded memory capacity, the Mac Plus and Mac SE can load much more program information and data into memory at one time. This means that your data can be processed much more quickly, with less need to read back and forth to disk and less disk-swapping on your part.

Though you can run Word with one 800K internal disk drive, we strongly recommend that you use two disk drives. Otherwise, you'll find yourself performing a great deal of time-consuming and frustrating disk-swapping. You also may find yourself limited as to the number of desk accessories, fonts, and other tools that you can fit onto one disk.

Through the course of this book, we will address two of the most common Macintosh configurations: a Mac Plus with two 800K drives and a 512K Mac with two 400K drives. If you use a Mac SE or a Macintosh installed with a hard disk, see Appendix 3. If you have another configuration, please refer to your owner's manual for more specific information about your hardware.

The expanded keyboard that comes with the Macintosh Plus can help speed your work in Word. As you'll see through the course of the book, the numeric keypad on the right side of the keyboard serves as a navigational device. You can also use an add-on numeric keypad to navigate in Word if you have a standard Mac keyboard.

Because Version 3 of Word uses the new hierarchical file system (HFS), users with 512K Macs should know whether their computers have old or new ROM chips. (ROM stands for read-only memory—a permanent part of the Mac's internal memory that tells the computer how to handle basic functions, like startup procedures and other operating system duties.) Many 512K Macs have been enhanced with new ROM chips that can take advantage of Microsoft's new HFS structure.

Though you can still use Word quite effectively with the old ROM chips, you will not be able to take advantage of some of the more sophisticated document-handling features that are available on the newer Macs. For example, you will not be able to work with folders from within the Word program, and you will not see a zoom box in your Mac window displays. We'll point out these minor differences as they arise.

Choosing a Printer

Chances are, you'll also need a printer so that you can view the results of your work in hard-copy form. The two most common printers for the Mac are the Apple LaserWriter (or the newer, enhanced LaserWriter Plus) and the Apple ImageWriter. Though you can use other printers with your Macintosh, you may run into some compatibility problems. For instance, you may find that many of the fonts available for Macintosh programs cannot be reproduced on other printers. In addition, many printers support only fixed-pitch fonts and cannot handle proportionally spaced fonts.

Before you can use any printer, you must have a resource file for that printer on the disk that contains your Word System files. In addition to the ImageWriter and LaserWriter printer resources, Microsoft has provided you with resource files for the Brother, Diablo630, NEC7710, AppleDaisy, and Typewriter printers. There is also a serial printer resource. If your printer is not listed here, don't panic; you may still be able to use that printer with the Mac. See your printer owner's manual for more information about configuring your printer to communicate with the Macintosh.

Before you decide to use a printer other than the LaserWriter or ImageWriter, we suggest that you ask your local dealer for more information (and a demonstration!) concerning the printer's compatibility and performance.

The ImageWriter is the default printer installed on your Word system disk. However, because the ImageWriter's dot matrix output does not lend itself well to reproduction, we will use an Apple LaserWriter printer to produce our sample output in this book. We recommend the LaserWriter (or the LaserWriter Plus) for any user who requires high-quality print. Next to phototypesetting, the LaserWriter is the best output device available for the Mac. In Chapter 7, we will show you how to install and choose a printer resource, and we'll offer instructions for using both the ImageWriter and LaserWriter printers.

THE SOFTWARE

If your Mac uses one or more 800K disk drives, you should have received two double-sided disks in your Microsoft Word 3 package: the program disk and a utilities disk. Your program disk contains the Word and Switcher applications, the System folder, a Standard Glossary file, and a Release Notes file, which contains updates to the Word documentation.

Your utilities disk contains your Help file, a Hyphenation file, the Main Dictionary (US) and United Kingdom Dictionary files, a Switcher Sets folder (including the new QuickSwitch facility, which lets you create dynamic links between your Word files and files created in other application programs), a set of printer resources, a set of Sample Documents and LaserWriter Output files, a PostScript Glossary, and a DCA Conversion application file.

If your Mac has 400K drives, you should have received three single-sided disks: the program disk, a system disk, and a utilities disk. Because there is not enough room on one single-sided disk for the 331K Word program application in addition to your System file and other application files, the program disk contains the Word program, Hyphenation file, Release Notes, and Sample Documents, while the System folder, Switcher application, Switcher Sets, and QuickSwitch are located on the system disk. Your utilities disk contains the Help file, the Main and UK Dictionaries, your printer resources, the Standard Glossary file, the PostScript Glossary, and the DCA Conversion application. No LaserWriter printer resource and no LaserWriter Output files are included with the 400K Word package.

The System Folder

Inside the System folders on both versions of the program are the ImageWriter printer resource and the System and Finder applications. You'll also see a Clipboard file and—after you load Word for the first time—a file called Word Settings. We've already talked about the ImageWriter printer resource file. Now let's look briefly at the other System folder files.

Much like the ROM chips that we mentioned earlier, the System controls the startup procedures and provides operating information to the Mac. (System file information is stored in RAM or random-access memory—the part of your computer's memory that can be altered or updated so that you can customize it to fit your personal needs.) The System also keeps track of the desk accessories, fonts, and printer resources that you have installed. Throughout this book, we'll address version 3.2 of the System, which is delivered with the Word program. If you're using a later version of the System, you may notice some minor differences, such as new symbols in your alert boxes and changes in the desk accessories. In Appendix 3, we've addressed some of the differences between System 3.2 and later versions.

Your System file is already installed with six desk accessories: the Chooser, the Control Panel, the Scrapbook, Key Caps, the Alarm Clock, and the Calculator. A set of twelve Macintosh fonts is also built into your System application: Chicago, New York, Geneva, Monaco, Venice, Boston, Times, Helvetica, Courier, Symbol, Dover, and Dover PS. Each font is available in a range of sizes. We'll talk more about fonts and desk accessories in a few pages.

No matter what programs you use, you've probably seen the terms "Finder level" and "DeskTop" in every book or reference manual written about the Macintosh. When you insert the Word disk(s) into your machine and boot up your computer, you are initially at the Finder level. The Finder application is a part of the Mac system that controls disk procedures and manages documents. It keeps track of where documents are stored and controls the display of all of those icons and windows that appear on your screen.

Another file in your System folder, called DeskTop, handles the display of the menu bar and the background area of your screen. The DeskTop file, which is invisible, works in conjunction with the Finder application.

The Clipboard is a temporary holding area in which Word stores text and graphics when you copy or move a selection in your Word document. We'll show you how the Clipboard works in Chapter 6.

Word automatically creates the Word Settings file to keep track of certain environmental settings such as special markup character displays, the ruler display, and your menu configuration. We'll talk more about the Word Settings file when we discuss Word's default settings in Chapter 17.

BACK IT UP!

We cannot stress strongly enough the importance of making backup copies of your Word disks before you begin working with the program. Because Microsoft has removed copy-protection from Version 3 of the program, creating and using backup disks is easier than ever! You should always use these backup disks as your working copies.

If you've used previous versions of Word, you know that you once had to insert your Word master disk each time you started your Mac with a backup copy of the program. Many users neglected to use copies of their master disks because this disk-swapping routine was such a hassle. With Version 3, you no longer have to use your master disk to load the program. The removal of copy-protection also makes it easier for hard-disk owners to install the Word program.

More important, your Word disks are extremely vulnerable. A misguided magnetic force (your telephone, for example), an errant cup of coffee, or even a serious system error could mean that your software investment is gone forever. Why risk it? Backing up your Word disks takes only a few minutes and could help you to avoid catastrophe.

Finally, by making backup copies of Word, you can customize your disks—without altering your originals. You may even want to create several copies of Word with different desk accessories, fonts, and other features to suit various project needs. We urge you never to make changes to your master disks. Instead, duplicate these disks and make your changes to the disk copies.

Personalizing Your Program Disk

Before you begin the backup procedure, you should personalize your copy of the Word program disk. As far as we are concerned, this is the only time you should ever use the master copy of your Word program disk to load Word. If you have the 800K version of Word, boot your Macintosh with the master Word program disk in the internal disk drive. If you're using 400K disks, start up your Macintosh with the master system disk in the internal drive and the Word program disk in your external drive. Double-click the icon for the Word program disk to view its contents, then double-click the Word application icon. Word will display a dialog box with edit bars where you can enter your name and the name of your company or organization. Type the appropriate information in each of the edit bars, then click OK. When you click OK, Word will "stamp" the disk with your name and your company name. This information will appear on the screen every time you load Word, and it will be transferred to each copy that you make of the Word program disk.

After you've personalized the Word program disk, you'll see a new blank document window. Although you could begin working with Word at this point, we recommend that you choose Quit from the File menu to return to the Finder level and make backup copies of your master disks.

At the Finder level, there's one detail to attend to before you make your backup copies. Eject your Word master disk(s) and place the write-protection tabs at the top-right corner of each disk in the up position. You should be able to see through the small square hole near the corner of each disk. This ensures that you will not inadvertently alter your master disks as you duplicate them.

Backing up Your Disks on a Mac Plus

If you use the 800K version of Word, follow these simple steps to make backup copies of your Word disks:

1. If you have started your Macintosh with another program, select Shut Down from the Special menu to reboot your computer. Place your master Word program disk in the Mac's internal drive. In a few seconds, you'll see the *Word Program* master disk icon in the upper-right corner of your screen.
2. Place a blank, 800K disk into your external drive. When you see the message *This disk is unreadable. Do you want to initialize it?*, click the Two-Sided button.
3. When you see the message *Please name this disk*, type a name for your new disk. If this is to be a customized disk, you'll want to use a descriptive name to remind yourself of any special features that you plan to add to the disk. Otherwise, a name like *Word3 Copy* will do. Click OK to lock in your new disk name. Notice that the *Word3 Copy* disk icon appears just below the icon for the master Word program disk on the Mac DeskTop. To

make a copy of the master Word program disk, drag the icon for that disk over the icon for the new disk. You'll see the message *Completely replace contents of "Word3 Copy" (external drive) with contents of "Word Program" (internal drive)?* Click OK to proceed. You'll see a status message at the top of your screen as the master files are copied to your new disk.

4. When the status box at the top of your screen disappears, press Shift-⌘-2 to eject the newly created Word program disk from the external drive. Insert another new blank disk in the external drive and initialize it as described in Step 2 above. Use a name like *Utilities Copy* to name this new disk.
5. Now, press Shift-⌘-1 to eject the master Word program disk from your internal drive and insert the master copy of your utilities disk into the internal drive.
6. Drag the icon for the master utilities disk over the icon for the utilities copy disk, and click OK when you see the message *Completely replace contents of "Utilities Copy" (external drive) with contents of "Word Utilities" (internal drive)?*

Backing up Your Disks on a 512K Mac

If you use the 400K version of Word, use this procedure to make backup copies of your Word disks:

1. If you have booted your Macintosh with another program, eject any disks currently in your disk drives and turn the Mac's power off. (You can also use the Shut Down command to reboot your Mac if that command is available on your Special menu.) Place your master system disk in the Mac's internal drive. In a few moments, you'll see the *400K System* disk icon in the upper-right corner of your screen.
2. Place a blank, 400K disk in your external drive. When you see the message *This disk is unreadable. Do you want to initialize it?*, click the OK button.
3. When you see the message *Please name this disk*, type a name for your new disk. If this is to be a customized disk, you'll want to use a descriptive name to remind yourself of any special features that you plan to add to the disk. Otherwise, a name like *Word3 System Copy* will do. Click OK to lock in your new disk name. Notice that the *Word3 System Copy* disk icon appears just below the *400K System* disk icon on the Mac DeskTop. To make a copy of the master system disk, drag the icon for this disk over the icon for the new disk. You'll see the message *Completely replace contents of "Word3 System Copy" (external drive) with contents of "400K System" (internal drive)?* Click OK to proceed.
4. Press Shift-⌘-2 to eject the newly created system disk from the external drive. Insert another new blank disk in the external drive and initialize it as described in Steps 2 and 3 above. Use a name like *Word3 Program Copy* to name this new disk.
5. Now, press Shift-⌘-1 to eject the master Word system disk from your internal drive and insert your master Word program disk in the internal drive.

6. Drag the *Word Program* disk icon over the icon for the new disk and click OK when you see the message *Completely replace contents of "Word3 Program Copy" (external drive) with contents of "Word Program" (internal drive)?*
7. Repeat Steps 2 through 6 to copy your utilities disk. As you perform this copy procedure, the Mac may eject the disk in your internal drive and ask for the master system disk. Just follow the Mac's instructions and swap disks as needed.

That's all there is to it! If you want to begin working with your new copy of Word, just select Shut Down from the Special menu, then reboot your Mac as described below. Remember to tuck the master disks away in a safe place.

If you use a hard disk, or some other Macintosh hardware configuration not covered here, please refer to your hardware user's manual for more information on how to back up your software.

Throughout this book, we'll often use the term "startup disk" to refer to the disk that contains your System folder. If you're using the 800K version of Word, then the startup disk will likely contain both the Word program and the System folder. If you're using Word with 400K disks, your startup disk will be the system disk that you created by copying the master 400K System disk.

LOADING WORD

You load the Word program as you load any Macintosh application. If you are using 800K disks, you'll begin by placing your program disk in the internal disk drive. If you'll be storing documents on a separate data disk, you'll want to insert that disk in your external drive, or, if you'll be using one of the files on the utilities disk, you can place that disk in your external drive instead. (To prevent overcrowding, you'll generally want to avoid storing documents on your startup disk—the disk that contains your System files. We suggest that you keep at least 20K free on this disk so that Word can back up your work when you are editing a document.)

If you are using 400K disks, you'll place your system disk in the internal drive and your Word program disk in the external drive. (The Mac always looks first for the startup disk in the internal drive of your computer).

After inserting your disks, the next step is to double-click the icon for the disk that contains your Word program to open that disk (if it is not already open). Then double-click the Word application icon. In just a few seconds, Word will present you with a new blank document window called Untitled1.

If you want to simultaneously load the Word program and open an existing Word document (more about creating and saving documents in Chapter 3), you can double-click any Word document icon at the Finder level. If the document that you want is located in a folder, double-click the folder icon to open the folder, then double-click the icon that represents the document you want to work with. The Word program and the selected document will be loaded simultaneously. If the document you select is very long, it may take a few moments for the file to be loaded.

To open the Word program and two or more Word files simultaneously, press the Shift key and click on the icons for the files you want. Then select the Open command from the File menu or double-click on one of the icons.

If you are using the 400K version of Word, opening a document from the Finder level can get a bit complicated. If the document you want to open is located on a third data disk, you must eject the startup disk from your internal drive and place your data disk in that drive. (You can eject the Word program disk from the external drive instead, but you'll find that this slows down the loading process substantially.)

Once you've inserted your data disk, double-click on the icon for the document that you want to open. You may have to do a little disk-swapping as the Mac loads the Word program and opens your document for you. (We offer a few suggestions to help you minimize this hassle in the section on customizing your Word disks later in this chapter.)

Other Loading Techniques

If you commonly need to transfer data from other programs into your Word documents, you'll definitely want to take advantage of the Switcher when you load Word. Switcher lets you simultaneously open two or more applications and move back and forth between them without returning to the Finder level. You can also attach documents to your Switcher routines so that those documents are opened automatically when you use the Switcher. Microsoft has provided five common Switcher combinations for you on your utilities disk: Word/Draw, Word/Paint, Word/Excel, Word/File, and Word/Works. Of course, you can also create your own Switcher combinations. We'll talk more about using the Switcher (and the new QuickSwitch application) in Chapter 16.

You can also use the MiniFinder to load your Word program and open one or more Word documents at the same time. The MiniFinder, which is described in your Macintosh owner's manual, lets you bypass the Finder to quickly access those documents and applications you use most often.

Finally, if you use an add-in macro application, like Tempo, you can create a macro routine to load the Word program automatically—and any needed Word documents, if you like.

Though it is not within the scope of this book to explore applications like the MiniFinder and Tempo, we urge you to read up on those applications and take advantage of these timesaving techniques.

CUSTOMIZING YOUR WORD SOFTWARE

You'll almost certainly want to customize your Word software to meet your special project needs. For example, you may want to customize the desk accessories that are available on the menu and add some additional fonts to your current collection.

Even if you use a Mac Plus with two 800K disk drives, you'll find that there is precious little room left on your startup disk to add any other items. Thus, you'll also want to delete those tools that you don't use often. So many fonts, desk accessories, and other tools are available for Word that you'll never fit them all on one disk. By making several copies of Word, however, you can customize different disks for different purposes.

For example, you might fill one disk with special fonts just for doing display-type projects. You might add Switcher to one disk so that you can use it with other programs. You might want to put Word and Paint together on a disk so that you can easily transfer data from one program to another.

A reminder: *Never* make changes to your master program, system, or utilities disks. Customize your working copies of the Word program, system, and utilities disks only. In fact, we recommend that you lock your master disks so that you cannot inadvertently alter your originals. (To lock a disk, just place the write-protection tab in the up position so that you can see through the small square hole in the upper-right corner of the disk.)

For the remainder of this chapter, we'll look at some of the tools available to you and offer some suggestions as to how you can make your Word system operate as efficiently as possible. Because most of these elements are common to all Macintosh programs, much of this information should be review. If you are unfamiliar with any of the concepts presented in the next few pages, please review your Macintosh owner's guide.

If you want more information about the Macintosh, we suggest the *Apple Macintosh Book*, an excellent reference guide written by Cary Lu and published by Microsoft Press.

The Menu

The menu contains a special set of commands that let you access handy desk accessory features and tailor the Word environment to your needs.

When you are at the Finder level, the first command on your menu is About the Finder.... You can choose this command to find out which version of the Finder you are using. Once you have loaded Word, however, this command changes to About Microsoft Word.... As you'll see in Chapter 2, you can use the About Microsoft Word... command to access Word's Help menu.

Desk accessories

The bottom portion of the menu is devoted to desk accessories. These handy tools are available at all times—both at the Finder level and from within Word. Let's take a brief look at the desk accessories that are available on your startup disk, then we'll describe some of the other accessories that are available for Macintosh users.

The three most important desk accessories are the Control Panel, the Chooser, and the Alarm Clock. We recommend that you keep these desk accessories on all of your startup disks.

The Control Panel

The Control Panel desk accessory contains vital settings information that the Macintosh system uses to format your DeskTop, to program your keyboard, and to control other important "environmental conditions." When you select the Control Panel command from the menu, you'll see a dialog box like the one in Figure 1-1.

FIGURE 1-1

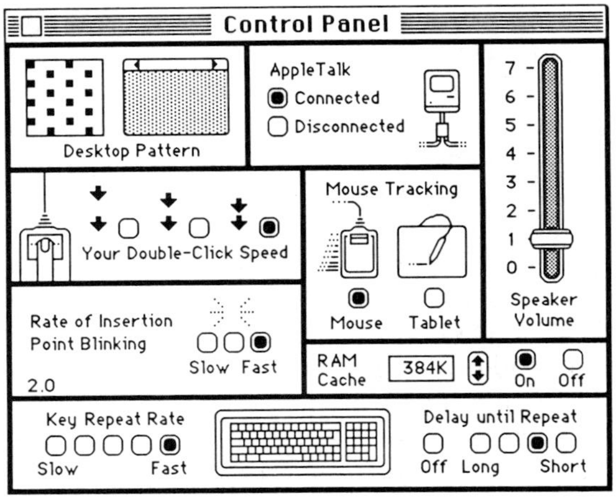

You'll use the Control Panel desk accessory to personalize your Mac environment.

As you can see, you can use this dialog box to control the repeat rate for your keyboard, set your double-click speed, and change your DeskTop pattern, among other things.

Another very important Control Panel option is the AppleTalk setting. As you'll learn in Chapter 7, if you are using AppleTalk to communicate with your printer, you must enable this setting by selecting the Connected option in the Control Panel window.

The Chooser

The Chooser lets you select the printer you want to use once you have installed the appropriate printer drivers on your startup disk. The contents of this dialog box will change, depending on the type of printer resource files you have installed. We'll look at the various Chooser options that are available to you in Chapter 7.

The Alarm Clock

Though the Alarm Clock desk accessory may seem like a simple convenience item, it is important that you set the System Clock and ensure that it maintains the correct date and time. The Macintosh is supplied with a battery and keeps track of the current time and date, even when your Mac's power is off.

Whenever you create or save a file, the Mac system records the date and time at which that document was last modified. This information can be critical when you need to locate the most recent version of a file. (By the way, when you are at the Finder level, you can find out when a file was created by choosing Get Info from the File menu, or you can choose the commands by Date, by Name, by Size, or by Kind from the View menu.)

When you select Alarm Clock from the menu, you'll see a small window like the one in Figure 1-2. To provide the Macintosh with the correct time, begin by clicking on the lever icon that appears on the right side of the window. The window will expand to reveal a settings area, as shown in Figure 1-3. Click on the clock, calendar, or alarm icons to change the Alarm Clock settings. A set of arrows will appear. You can make any needed adjustments by clicking one of these arrows or simply by typing the correct settings.

FIGURE 1-2

Select Alarm Clock from the menu to see the current time.

FIGURE 1-3

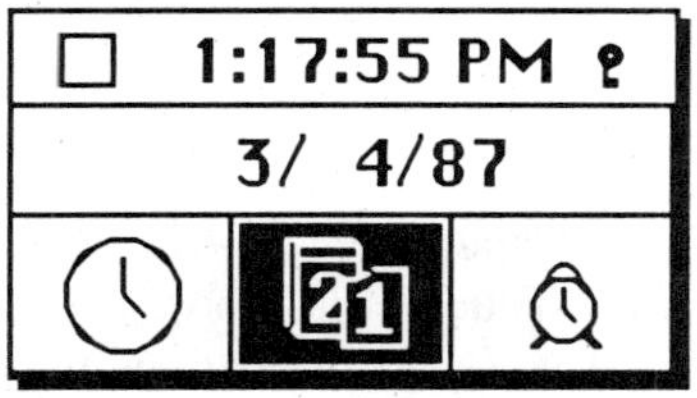

To set the date and time, click on the lever on the right side of the alarm window.

Key Caps

The Key Caps desk accessory is another handy tool that lets you see how the character keys on your keyboard are defined. When you choose Key Caps from the menu, you'll see a dialog box, like the one in Figure 1-4.

FIGURE 1-4

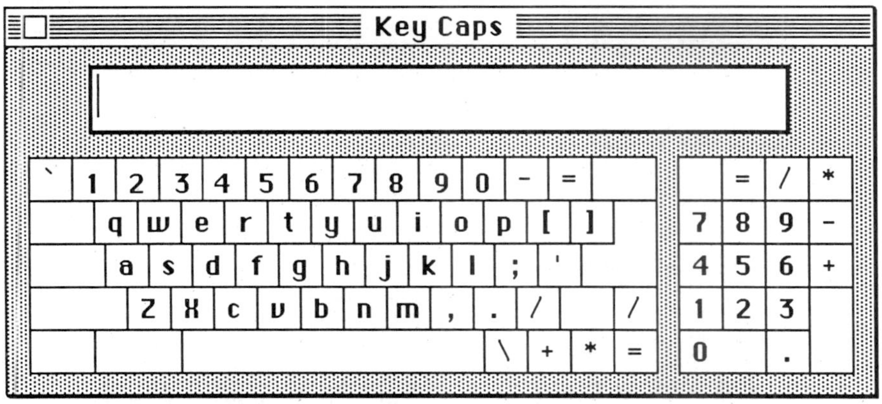

You can use Key Caps to see how your character keys are defined.

Obviously, this screen doesn't tell you much that you couldn't see by looking at your own keyboard. However, if you press the Shift or Option keys (or both) while the Key Caps dialog box is active, you'll see many of the special characters that are available from your keyboard.

When you issue the Key Caps command, you'll also see a special Key Caps menu on your menu bar. This menu lists all of the fonts available on your startup disk, which is quite convenient if you are at the Finder level and want to know what fonts you have installed in your Word System file. In addition, you can select a font name from the Key Caps menu to display the special characters available in each font.

The Scrapbook

The Scrapbook is a storage bin where you can keep text and graphics for later use. As you'll learn in Chapter 5, you can even transfer your Scrapbook desk accessory from one startup disk to another so that you can trade information with other programs.

The Calculator

When you choose Calculator from the menu, you'll see a four-function "pocket" calculator, like the one in Figure 1-5. Though the Calculator is convenient for performing quick calculations while you are in Word, it will probably be one of the first desk accessories to go if you need to open up more space on your startup disk.

FIGURE 1-5

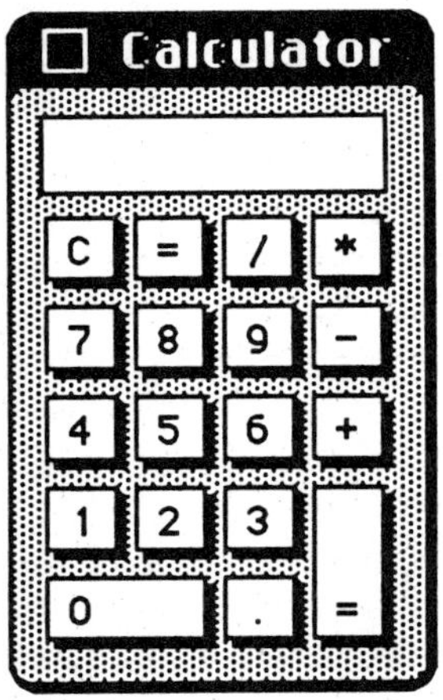

You can use the Calculator desk accessory to perform simple calculations.

Fonts

As we mentioned earlier, your System file is initially installed with a number of fonts, each of which is available in a range of sizes. Table 1-1 on pages 16-17 shows all of the fonts available in Word and the type sizes available for each.

Of course, as you'll learn in Chapter 5, you can also format each of these fonts in a variety of ways to achieve different effects. For example, you can use boldfacing, italics, outlining, shadows, and underlining to change the appearance of any of these type faces.

Though this range of fonts, sizes, and styles may suit your needs perfectly, you'll probably decide to add some, or delete those fonts that you won't use often, in order to make more room on your startup disk.

Rearranging Your Disks

Obviously, there are as many possible configurations of Word disks as there are Word users. Although we cannot offer you any hard and fast rules for customizing your Word disks, we can offer a few recommendations to help you on your way.

As you create your own customized system of Word disks, you need to decide which applications you'll be using most often and how those applications can best be grouped to work most efficiently. As we mentioned earlier, you may want to create several sets of Word disks to meet different needs.

One of the first things you can do is use the Font/DA mover to customize the System file on your Word startup disk. Remove any desk accessories and fonts that you don't plan to use, and add any others that you need. A copy of the Font/DA Mover application is located on the System Tools disk that came with your Macintosh, and your Macintosh owner's guide offers step-by-step instructions for using that facility.

You may also want to juggle some of the application files that came with your Word package to take better advantage of disk space. For example, if you plan to use Word's spelling facility, you may want to place the Main Dictionary file and any of your own custom dictionary files on the same disks that you plan to use to store your data files. Then you won't have to pause to insert your utilities disk when you want to check your spelling.

Similarly, if you want to use the Switcher so that you can run two or more applications concurrently, you'll need to make room for all of the programs you want to use. For example, on a Mac Plus you might have the Word program and System files on one disk, and the Microsoft Excel application along with your data files on another disk. Since both program files practically fill up a 400K disk, you can guess that this technique is not likely on a 512K Mac.

To avoid the disk-swapping hassles associated with storing documents on a third data disk, many 400K Word users prefer to copy their System folders to each of their data disks. (To copy your System folder to another disk, just open both disk icons and then drag the System folder icon from your startup disk to your data disk.) In effect, you can make each of your data disks a startup disk. Though this technique limits the amount of document space available on each data disk, it is much more convenient than swapping disks every few minutes.

In planning your configuration, you'll find it helpful to use the Get Info command at the Finder level to determine how much disk space each of the files you want to use will require. Just click on the icon for the file that you want to

TABLE 1-1

New York	
9	The quick brown fox jumps over the lazy dog.
10	The quick brown fox jumps over the lazy dog.
12	The quick brown fox jumps over the lazy dog.
14	The quick brown fox jumps over the lazy dog.
18	The quick brown fox jumps over the l
20	The quick brown fox jumps over
24	The quick brown fox jumps
Geneva	
9	The quick brown fox jumps over the lazy dog.
10	The quick brown fox jumps over the lazy dog.
12	The quick brown fox jumps over the lazy dog.
14	The quick brown fox jumps over the lazy dog.
18	The quick brown fox jumps over the laz
20	The quick brown fox jumps over the
24	The quick brown fox jumps o
Boston	
9	The quick brown fox jumps over the lazy dog.
10	The quick brown fox jumps over the lazy dog.
12	The quick brown fox jumps over the lazy dog.
18	The quick brown fox jumps
20	The quick brown fox jum
24	The quick brown fox jum
Dover	
8	The quick brown fox jumps over the lazy dog.
10	The quick brown fox jumps over the lazy dog.
12	The quick brown fox jumps over the lazy dog.

Font / Size	Sample
Dover PS	
12	The quick brown fox jumps over the lazy dog.
Times	
9	The quick brown fox jumps over the lazy dog.
10	The quick brown fox jumps over the lazy dog.
12	The quick brown fox jumps over the lazy dog.
14	The quick brown fox jumps over the lazy dog.
18	The quick brown fox jumps over the lazy dog.
24	The quick brown fox jumps over th
Helvetica	
9	The quick brown fox jumps over the lazy dog.
10	The quick brown fox jumps over the lazy dog.
12	The quick brown fox jumps over the lazy dog.
14	The quick brown fox jumps over the lazy dog.
18	The quick brown fox jumps over the lazy dog.
24	The quick brown fox jumps over th
Courier	
10	The quick brown fox jumps over the lazy dog.
12	The quick brown fox jumps over the lazy dog.
Symbol	
9	Τηε θυιχκ βροων φοξ φυμπσ οϖερ τηε λαζψ δογ.
12	Τηε θυιχκ βροων φοξ φυμπσ οϖερ τηε λαζψ δογ.
18	Τηε θυιχκ βροων φοξ φυμπσ οϖερ τηε λαζ
24	Τηε θυιχκ βροων φοξ φυμπσ οϖε
Chicago	
12	The quick brown fox jumps over the lazy dog.
Monaco	
9	The quick brown fox jumps over the lazy dog.
12	The quick brown fox jumps over the lazy dog.
Venice	
14	The quick brown fox jumps over the lazy dog.

A number of fonts and font sizes are available in Word.

use, and select Get Info from the File menu. You'll see an Information dialog box like the one in Figure 1-6. Make a note of the size of each file you want to use, and then you can calculate how many files will fit on each of your disks.

FIGURE 1-6

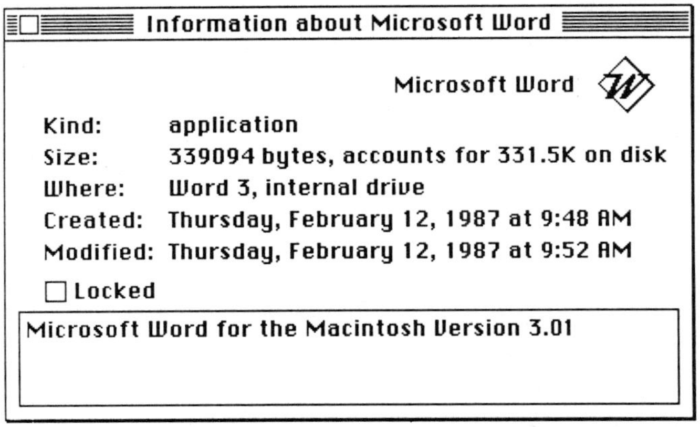

Use the Get Info command to determine how much disk space is required by the files that you want to use.

Similarly, you can find out how much space the fonts and desk accessories will require by using the Font/DA mover on the System Tools disk. When you click on a font or desk accessory name in the Font/DA mover dialog box, the size of the selected item appears, as shown in Figure 1-7.

FIGURE 1-7

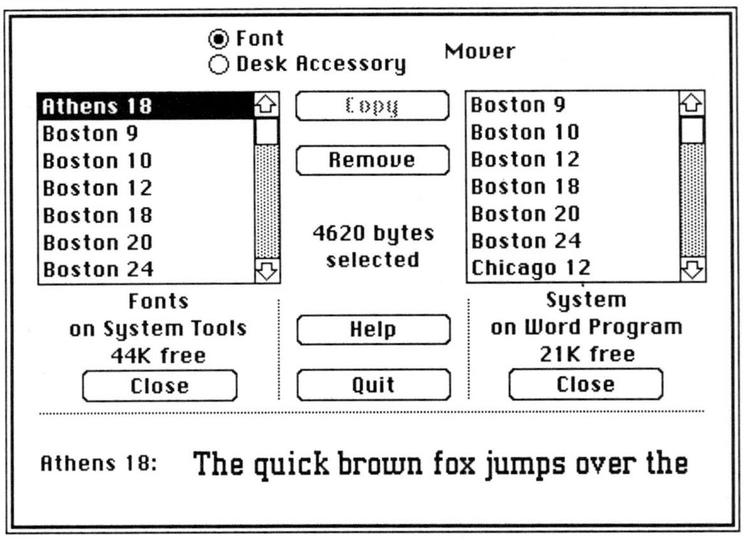

Use the Font/DA Mover to determine how much disk space is required by the fonts and desk accessories that you want to use.

Other Desk Accessories and Tools

You can also customize your Word disks by adding your own desk accessories and add-in applications. For example, if you commonly incorporate Paint graphics into your Word documents, you may want to use the ArtGrabber desk accessory to speed up your work. ArtGrabber lets you open Paint files and copy pictures directly into Word, without using the Switcher or the Scrapbook.

There are also many advanced add-in applications, like macro programs, print spoolers, and personal productivity tools, that you can add to your Word system. Though many of these programs are full-blown applications in their own right, they "coexist" with Word by residing on your menu, where you can access them at any time without leaving Word.

If the range of fonts available on the Macintosh doesn't suit your needs, you can purchase special fonts packages with custom display types created especially for the Macintosh. In fact, you can even use applications like Fontastic to create your own custom fonts to use in Word.

Your software dealer can give you more information about the variety of fonts, desk accessories, and add-in applications available for Macintosh users.

A BRIEF TOUR 2

In this chapter, we'll take a tour of the Microsoft Word workspace or DeskTop and introduce some key concepts and terms that you'll need throughout the rest of the book. If you are new to Word, please read this chapter carefully. It lays the groundwork for everything to follow. If you've been using Word 3 for a while, we suggest that you skim this chapter just to be sure that you're familiar with our terminology. If you've used earlier versions of the program but are not familiar with Word 3, this chapter will highlight many of the new features of the program and give you an idea of the variations you should be looking out for.

We'll be covering a lot of topics at a very general level in this chapter. If you do not understand all of the concepts presented here, don't worry about it. We'll be returning to each of these points in much more detail through the course of the book.

THE WORD DESKTOP

When you double-click the Word icon on the Macintosh DeskTop, Word will present a screen like the one shown in Figure 2-1. The Word screen is divided into two major areas: the menu bar at the top of the screen and the document window—your workspace—below the menu bar. The document window, which occupies the bulk of the screen, is the basis of your creations in Microsoft Word—your *tabula rasa*, so to speak. Through this window you will create, edit, format, and view your documents.

FIGURE 2-1

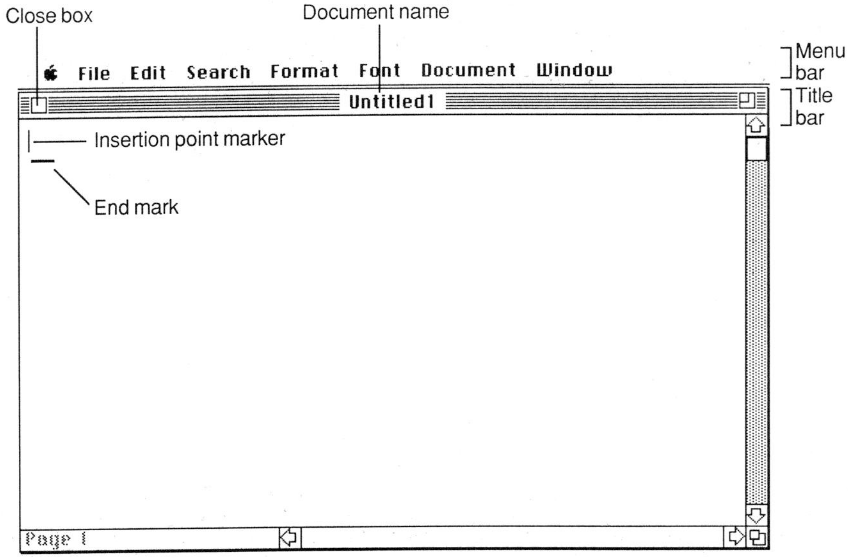

When you load the program, an empty Word document appears.

At this point, your document window will be empty except for a blinking vertical bar called the insertion point marker and a dark horizontal line called the end mark. As you might have guessed, the end mark signals the end of the document. The insertion point marker represents your position in the Word document. As you'll see when we begin working with text, this blinking bar moves one character to the right each time you type a character in your document. You'll also use the insertion point marker to specify the point at which you want to edit text. If you have worked with PC-based word processors, the insertion point marker is similar to the cursor that you have seen in those programs.

At this point, the insertion point marker occupies the first character space in your document window since you have not yet entered any text. Similarly, the end mark appears beneath the first line in the document window since the file Untitled1 is empty.

THE MENU BAR

At the top of the screen is the menu bar. From this menu bar, you will issue instructions to Word. In addition to the menu, which contains your desk accessories, Word offers seven menus to choose from: File, Edit, Search, Format, Font, Document, and Window. (In Chapter 11 you will see a new custom menu, called Work, which you can use to create your own Word commands and shortcuts.)

Each of these menus contains a different set of commands—a different group of tools to work with. The File menu contains document-handling and printing commands. On the Edit menu, you'll find a series of commands that let you copy and move text, specify your type measurement preferences, and control the content of the menus themselves. The Search menu lets you search for text, change text, and go to a specified page in your document. The Format and Font menus let you control the appearance of the text in your document. From the Document menu, you can take advantage of Word's sophisticated features like variable headers and footers, spelling and hyphenation, outlining and indexing, and other tools for designing complex documents. Finally, the Window menu lets you create new windows to view different parts of your document. You can also move between document windows and see the contents of the Clipboard via the Window menu.

Issuing a Command

As you should already know, to select a command from a menu, all you have to do is point to that menu and press the mouse button. When the list of available commands appears below the menu name, hold down the mouse button and drag downward until the command you want is highlighted, then release the mouse button.

⌘-key shortcuts

As you glance through the Word menus, notice the ⌘ characters and letters that appear to the right of many commands. This notation indicates that you can press the ⌘ key and a letter key to issue that command without using the mouse. For example, to save a document, you can press ⌘-s rather than selecting Save from the File menu. Similarly, you can press ⌘-x to issue the Cut command rather than selecting Cut from the Edit menu. You can also use the ⌘ key to perform many actions that are not listed on the Word menus. For example, you can use the ⌘ key to split windows into panes and to cancel any command or operation.

Using the keypad

If you have a numeric keypad, you can browse through the menus without using your mouse. To "pull down" the desired menu, just press the decimal point key on your numeric keypad and type the first letter of the menu whose contents you want to see. For example, to see the contents of the File menu, begin by pressing the decimal point key. The menu bar will appear in reverse video for about five seconds, then it will return to normal if you don't select a menu. To activate the File menu, type an *f*. Figure 2-2 shows the results.

After you have activated a menu, the menu display will remain on your screen until you issue a command or click in another area of the screen. You can also close a menu by pressing the Backspace key or by pressing the ⌘ and period keys (⌘-.)

FIGURE 2-2

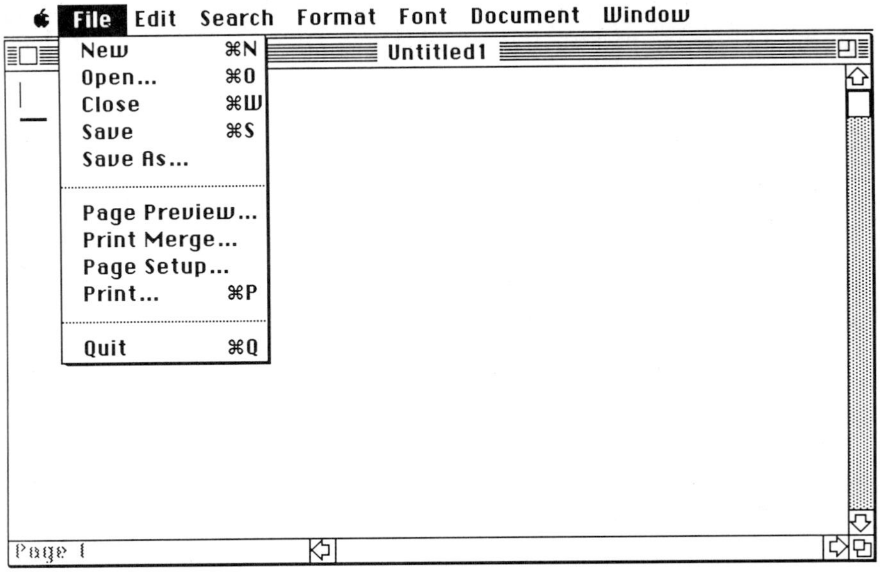

To see the contents of a menu, you can press the decimal point character on the numeric keypad, then type the letter or number that represents the menu you want to see.

Alternatively, you can activate a menu by pressing the decimal point key on the numeric keypad and typing a number from 0 through 8—0 for the menu, 1 for the File menu, 2 for the Edit menu, and so forth. (This technique is particularly handy since three of the menu names begin with an *F* and since there is no letter equivalent for the menu.)

In addition, you can press the decimal key and then press the ← or → keys to access the first or last item on the menu bar. The first menu, of course, is the menu. The last item on the menu bar may be either the Window menu or the Work menu, if you have created your own custom commands. Once you have activated a menu, you can also press the → and ← keys to move from one menu to the next.

To select a command from a menu that you have displayed on the screen, you can use the ↓ and ↑ keys to move through the list of commands and highlight the one you want. Once the command is highlighted, press Return or Enter to issue the command.

You can also select a command by typing the first letter of the command you want. If more than one command on a menu begins with the same letter, Word will move to the next command that begins with that letter. For example, to select the Save command from the open File menu shown in Figure 2-2, just type an *s*. To select the Save As... command, type *s* again. If you type *s* a third time, Word will cycle back to the Save command again.

Incidentally, the 4, 6, 8, and 2 keys on the numeric keypad serve the same functions as the ←, →, ↑, and ↓ keys respectively after you display a menu on the screen. Use the 4 and 6 keys to move from one menu to the next and the 2 and 8 keys to select commands from an open menu.

Short Vs. Full Menus

When you first open Word, you will see only some of the commands that are actually available to you. Word is initially loaded in the Short Menus mode. When the Short Menus setting is in effect, Word displays only the most common commands and options. To see all of the commands available in Word, point to the Edit menu and select the Full Menus command. Now, if you point to the various menu names, you'll see the expanded menus.

By the way, Full Menus is a toggle command. That means that the command changes each time you issue it. When you select Full Menus from the Edit menu, that command changes to read Short Menus. If you issue the Short Menus command, Word will again display the condensed form of each menu and change the command to read Full Menus again.

Figure 2-3 on the next page shows the commands available on the short and full versions of the Word menus.

The Short Menus/Full Menus toggle also affects the appearance of your status box, ruler display, horizontal scroll bar, and many dialog boxes. Let's look at the style status box first, then we'll look at dialog boxes and the ruler.

The Style Status Box

Another change takes place on your screen when you select Full Menus from the Edit menu: The status box at the bottom of your screen is split into two portions. As you can see in Figure 2-4, the word *Normal* appears on the right side of the status box. This is a style notation. The *Normal* style notation means that any text that you enter into your document at this point will appear in Word's default text format: 12 point, New York, Plain.

FIGURE 2-4

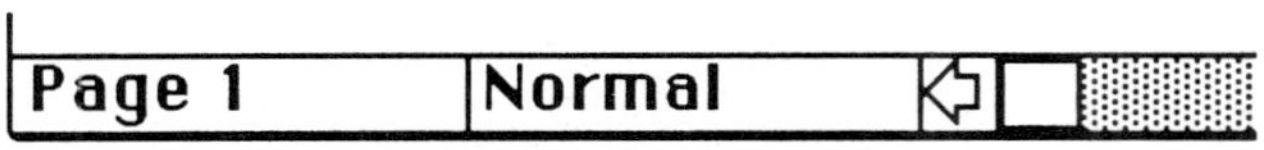

When you choose Full Menus, a style notation will appear in a status box in the bottom-left corner of your screen.

When you begin changing the formats of your document, you'll see the phrase *Normal+...* in this status box. We'll talk about this notation and other style sheet concepts in Chapter 9.

Dialog Boxes

You'll notice that many of the command names on the Word menus are followed by an ellipsis (...). The ellipsis tells you that a second level of options appears "below" that command. These options appear in a special kind of window called a dialog box.

FIGURE 2-3

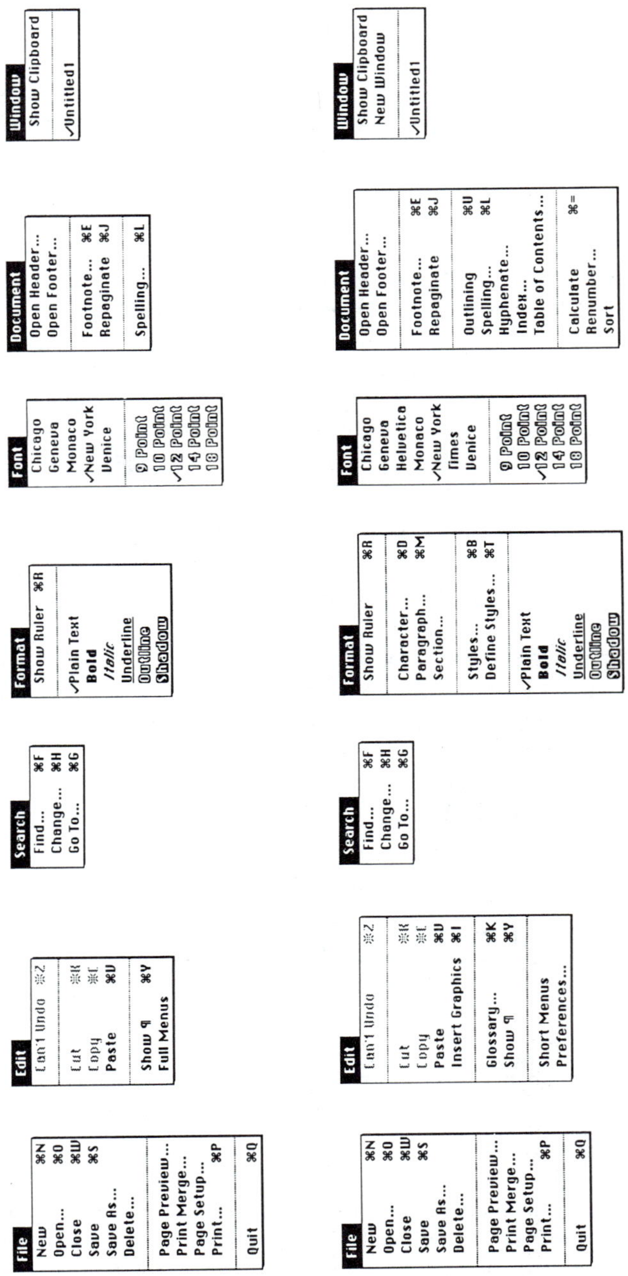

The contents of your menus vary when you use the Short Menus and Full Menus toggle command.

For example, if you select the Character... command from the Format menu (this command is available only when the Full Menus setting is in effect), you'll see a dialog box like the one in Figure 2-5.

FIGURE 2-5

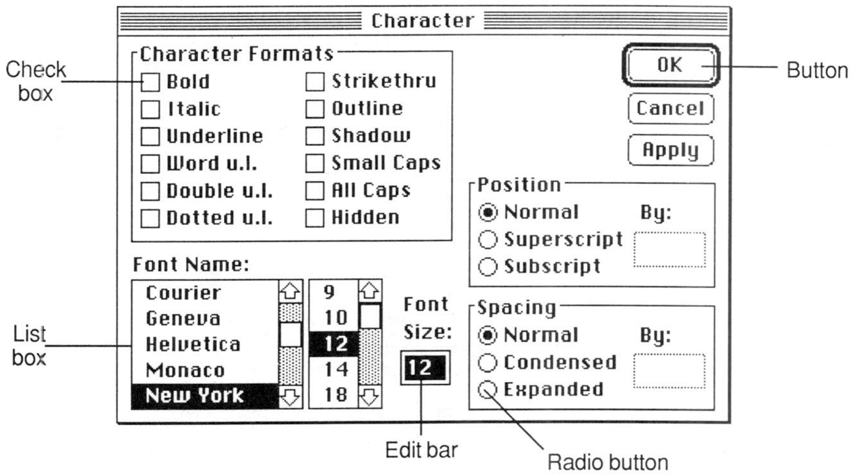

The Character dialog box appears when you choose the Character... command from the Format menu.

Selecting options

There are several ways to issue instructions from within a dialog box. The small circles that appear to the left of the Position and Spacing options are called radio buttons. To select an option, just click on the radio button next to the option you want. You can also click on the option name itself to fill in the circle and select that option. For example, to assign the Superscript Position format to text in your document, you would click on the word Superscript or click on the radio button that appears next to the word.

In most dialog boxes, only one radio button that pertains to a particular group of options can be turned on at a time. That is, radio button options are generally mutually exclusive. For example, when you select the Superscript option, Word will fill in the circle next to the Superscript option and deselect the Normal option. Obviously, your text cannot appear in the normal and superscript positions at the same time.

Other options are selected via check boxes, like the ones next to the Character Formats options in Figure 2-5. (Actually, an x will appear in one of these boxes when you select it—Microsoft evidently felt that the term *check box* is easier on the tongue than x-box.) Usually, check boxes represent options that can be activated simultaneously. For example, if you want to display your text in bold, italic type, and you want all of the characters to appear in upper-case letters, you can check the Bold, Italic, and All Caps options in the Character dialog box. Word will not usually deselect one option when you select another.

This also means that you must manually deselect most check-box options when you want to change them; selecting another option won't do it. Thus, if you decide that you want your text to appear in small capital letters with an outline around each character, you must click on the Bold, Italic, and All Caps options to deselect them, then click on the Small Caps and Outline options to assign your new formats.

There are a few occasions where check-box options are mutually exclusive. For example, in the Character dialog box you can choose only one underline format at a time. If you click on the Underline option, then click on the Word u.l. option, Word will deselect the Underline setting.

Edit bars

Of course, not every Word setting can be specified with a simple on or off selection. For more precise definitions, you have edit bars like the By and Font Size options in the Character dialog box. In these edit bars, you can type the value or text that you want to use.

For example, the number *12* currently appears in the Font Size edit bar in Figure 2-5. To change the contents of this edit bar, just drag through the characters that you want to change and overwrite them. You can also double-click in the edit bar to select all of the characters at once, or you can click in the spot where you want to make your changes and insert new characters. You also can use the Backspace key to delete characters.

In some cases, the edit bar may not be large enough to display all of the characters that you want to enter. If this is the case, the characters will scroll out of view as you type. You can scroll these hidden characters back into view by clicking in the edit bar and dragging to the left or right.

You can move quickly from one edit bar to the next by pressing the Tab key. When you press the Tab key, Word will automatically select the contents of the next edit bar for you so that you can overwrite the existing entry without pausing to drag through the characters first. To move back to the previous edit bar, press Shift-Tab.

List boxes

The Character dialog box also contains two list boxes—one for font names and one for font sizes. To use a list box, just point to the name of the option you want in order to select it.

For example, in addition to typing a value in the Font Size edit bar, you can also select a font size by clicking on the size that you want in the Font Size list box. Similarly, to select a font name, you can click on one of the names in the Font Name list box shown in Figure 2-5.

If the option you want is not visible in the list box, you can click in the gray scroll area to bring new options into view. You can also click on the arrow icons at either end of the scroll bar to bring new options into view.

In addition, if you have a Mac Plus keyboard, you can move through the options in a list box by pressing the ⬆ and ⬇ keys. Alternatively, you can press the 8 and 2 keys on your numeric keypad to select a list box item. Word will simultaneously scroll new options into view and highlight them for you.

Implementing your selections

The large rectangular objects in the upper-right corner of the Character dialog box are called buttons (not to be confused with radio buttons). Generally, these large buttons are the last options you'll click to lock in your dialog box selections and direct Word to carry out your instructions. For example, if you click the OK button in the Character dialog box, Word will apply the Character settings that you have chosen and remove the dialog box from your screen. If you click the Cancel button, Word will remove the dialog box from your screen without implementing your changes.

The Apply command—a new Word 3 feature—allows you to preview the effects of your dialog box selections. If you click the Apply button, Word will implement your character format selections but will not remove the dialog box from your screen. Thus, you can see the effects of an option or setting in your document before you close the dialog box.

More dialog box shortcuts

Once you become accustomed to using dialog boxes, you'll find that there are lots of ways to streamline your work. For example, you can use ⌘ and letter key combinations to select many dialog box options and buttons, much as you do when selecting commands from Word menus.

For example, in the Character dialog box shown in Figure 2-5, rather than clicking OK, you can press ⌘-o. Similarly, ⌘-c is equivalent to clicking the Cancel button. You can also use the ⌘ and period keys (⌘-.) to cancel any dialog box selections and return to your document. The ⌘-b, ⌘-i, and ⌘-u key combinations let you select the Bold, Italic, and Underline options, respectively. We'll show you more dialog box shortcuts as we introduce each command in subsequent chapters.

On the Macintosh Plus keyboard, you can move from one group of options to the next by pressing the ⬅ and ➡ keys. You can also use the 4 and 6 keys on the numeric keypad to move from one group of options to the next. When you "activate" a group of options, Word will display a flashing gray bar in that portion of the dialog box. Once you have activated a group of options, you can press the ⌘-Tab or Shift-⌘-Tab key combinations to select individual options from within that group.

For example, in the Character dialog box in Figure 2-5, you might press the ➡ or 6 key to activate the Position options. Then you could press ⌘-Tab to move the flashing gray bar under the Subscript option.

If you press ⌘-Tab while the flashing gray bar appears under the last option in a group, Word will move to the first option in the next group. If you have a numeric keypad, you can also press the decimal point key to move from the last option in a group to the next group of options in a dialog box. Similarly, if you press Shift-⌘-Tab while the flashing gray bar appears under the first option in a group, Word will move to the last option in the previous group.

Once the option you want is underlined with the flashing gray bar, you can press ⌘-Spacebar to "click on" that item. You can also select an underlined item by pressing 0 on the numeric keypad.

When you see a group of radio buttons or check boxes under one heading—like the Position, Spacing, and Character Formats options shown in Figure 2-5—you can often cancel the selections pertaining to a particular option by clicking on the heading itself. For example, suppose you have selected the Superscript, Expanded, Bold, and Italic options in the Character dialog box. At this point, the dialog box will look like the one in Figure 2-6.

FIGURE 2-6

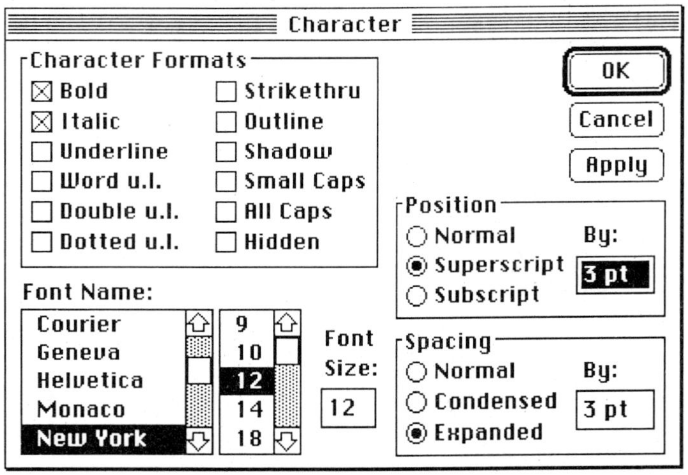

The Superscript, Expanded, Bold, and Italic options have been selected.

Now, suppose you decide that you really did not mean to select the Superscript format. You can click on the Position heading above that group of options to cancel your Position selection, without altering the remaining selections in the dialog box. When you use this technique, Word will revert to the setting that was selected when you opened the dialog box—not necessarily to the default setting for that group of options.

All of these dialog box options may seem a bit confusing if you are new to Word. However, once you become proficient with the program, you'll find that these simple shortcuts can speed up your work considerably. We suggest that you experiment with these techniques in a sample document to get a feel for the various keyboard shortcuts.

Dialog box options and the Full/Short Menus command

When the Short Menus setting is in effect, Word also changes the format of many of your dialog boxes. For example, when you issue the Page Setup... command while Short Menus is in effect, you'll see a dialog box like the one in Figure 2-7. However, if the Full Menus setting is in effect when you select Page Setup... from the File menu, you will see a dialog box like the one in Figure 2-8.

FIGURE 2-7

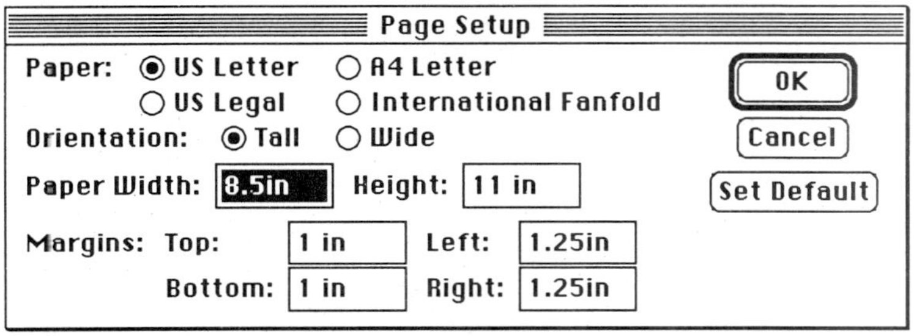

When you use Short Menus, an abbreviated version of the Page Setup dialog box appears.

FIGURE 2-8

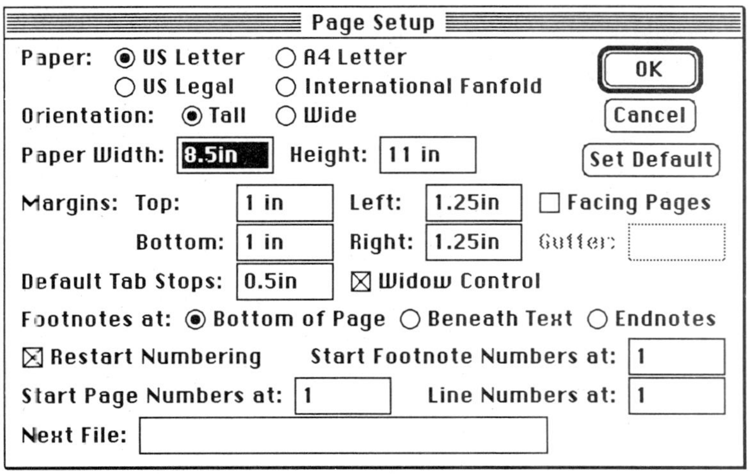

When the Full Menus setting is in effect, the Page Setup dialog box contains more options.

As you can see, the Page Setup dialog box options grow substantially when the Full Menus setting is in effect. If you are working on a fairly simple document and don't need all of these options, you may want to use the Short

Menus command to reduce clutter from your screen. If you are working with a complex document with multicolumn formatting, custom menus, or multiple headers and footers, however, you'll want to use the Full Menus setting.

WINDOWS

Since your Macintosh screen measures only nine inches diagonally, it is obvious that you cannot view the contents of an entire file on just one screen—unless you create only very short documents! That is why you need document windows. A window is like a porthole through which you can view a limited portion of your document.

To illustrate, suppose you cut a small square hole in a piece of cardboard and you then place the cardboard over this page. At any given time, you can see only a portion of the page through the square. By moving the cardboard around on the page, however, you can eventually read the entire page through the "window" in your piece of cardboard.

Everything you see on your Macintosh screen is actually viewed through a window of one type or another—dialog boxes, alert boxes, even disk and folder windows at the Finder level. In fact, there are two different types of document windows in Word: the standard document workspace, shown in Figure 2-1, and an outlining window, which we'll introduce in Chapter 12.

At the top of the document window is the title bar. At this point, Word has assigned the generic name Untitled1 to our document. (We'll show you how to assign names to your documents in Chapter 3.)

The title bar does much more than display the name of your document, however. Notice the two small boxes at either end of the title bar. The one on the left is called the close box. To remove your document from the screen, you can click in this close box. As you'll see in Chapter 3, clicking in the close box is equivalent to selecting the Close command from the File menu.

Resizing Windows

On the right side of the title bar is a zoom box. You can click in this zoom box to change the size of your document window from full-screen to half-screen size. (The zoom box is available only on the Mac Plus and on 512K Macs that have been enhanced with new ROM chips. If you use a 512 Mac with old ROMs, you'll have to rely on the size box, described below.)

For example, if we click the zoom box in the document window shown in Figure 2-1, our screen will look like the one in Figure 2-9. If we click the zoom box again, our screen will return to full-screen size. If you prefer, you can press Option-⌘-] to access the zoom feature from the keyboard.

FIGURE 2-9

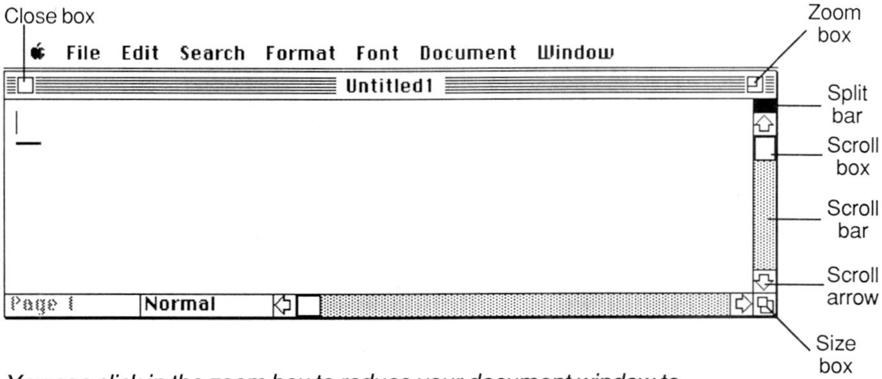

You can click in the zoom box to reduce your document window to half-screen size.

You can also use the size box at the lower-right corner of the document window to change the height and width of your window. For example, if you point to the size box on a full-screen window and drag up and to the left, you can create a window like the one in Figure 2-10.

FIGURE 2-10

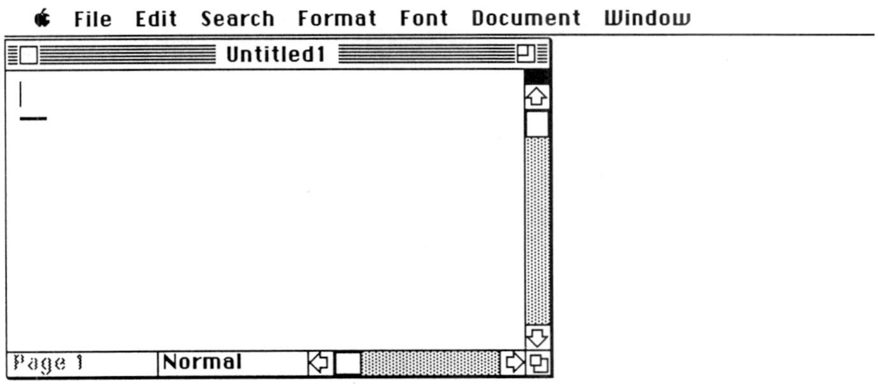

To manually resize a window, drag the size box.

Once you have manually resized a window, you can use the zoom box at the top-right corner of the screen to toggle between the full-screen view and the size that you set manually. Thus, if we click in the zoom box in Figure 2-10, our window will look like the one in Figure 2-1 again. If we click the zoom box again, our screen will return to the size that we set manually in Figure 2-10, rather than to full-screen size. By the way, whenever you open a document,

Word will initially display that document in full-screen size—even if you have previously used the zoom box or size box to resize the window.

Resizing windows is not generally necessary unless you have two or more windows open on your DeskTop at the same time. In that case, you may want to create nonoverlapping document windows so that you can see the contents of both windows at the same time. Interestingly, when you have two or more document windows open at the same time, Word 3 makes it easy to create nonoverlapping windows by automatically repositioning the windows when you click in the zoom box.

For example, suppose you have two document windows open on your screen at the same time: Untitled1 and Untitled2. Currently, Untitled1 is hidden behind Untitled2, but you want to view the contents of both windows at the same time. Begin by clicking in the zoom box in the title bar of Untitled2. Your screen will look like the one in Figure 2-11. Notice that Word has not only reduced that window to half-screen size, but has moved the window to the bottom of the screen as well.

FIGURE 2-11

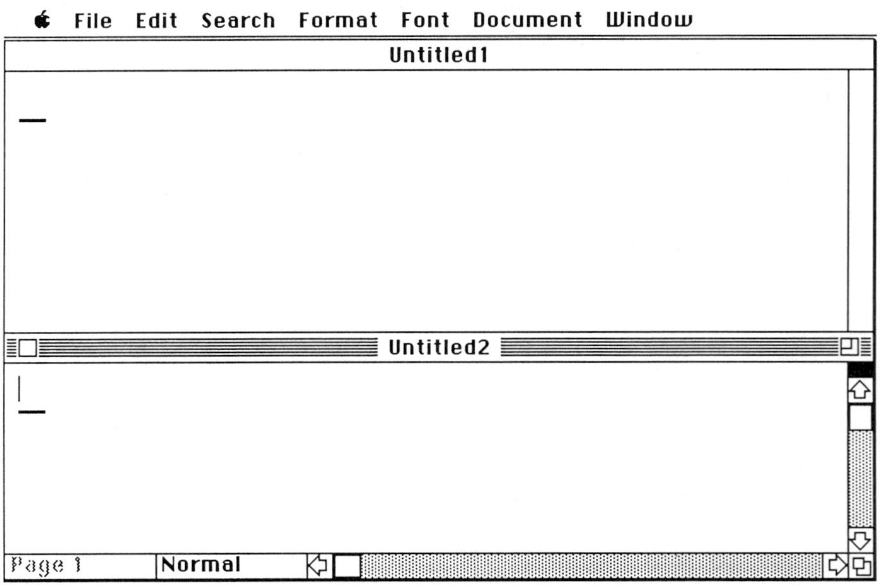

The bottom window has been reduced to half-screen size.

Next, click on the Untitled1 window to activate it. Untitled 1 will now completely cover Untitled2. However, if you click in the zoom box in the Untitled1 title bar, Word will reduce that window to half-screen size and position it at the top of the screen, as shown in Figure 2-12

FIGURE 2-12

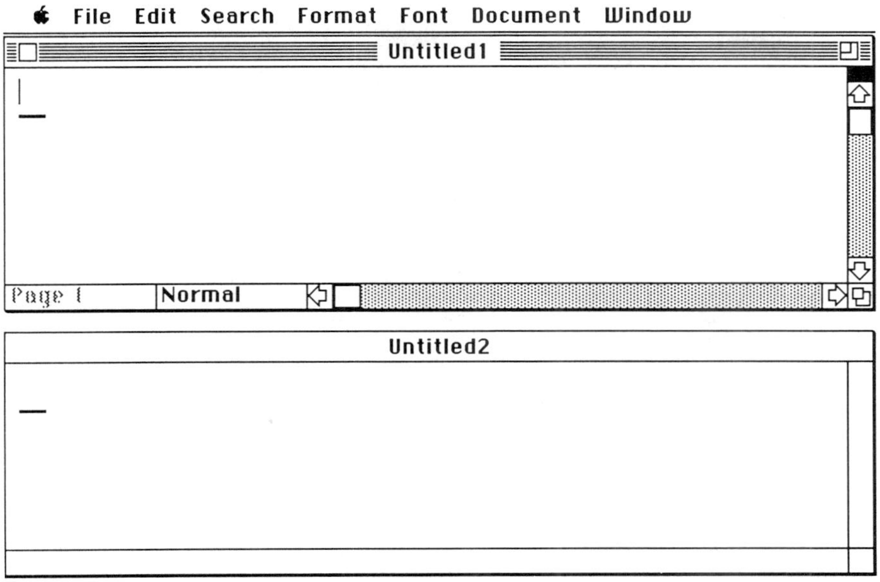

The first window is now stacked above the second.

If you open a third document window and click in its zoom box, Word will automatically reduce that window to quarter-screen size, as shown in Figure 2-13 on the next page. Likewise, if you have four or more windows open at the same time, Word will continue to resize and reposition the windows when you click in the scroll box to make each window as easy as possible to view and access.

If you want to display two windows side-by-side rather than stacked, you'll need to drag the windows to the desired position on the screen—which brings us to another topic: Whenever you see horizontal stripes at the top of a window (at the Finder level or in a dialog box as well as in a document window), you can drag that window around on the screen. To move a window, just point anywhere on the title bar (except the close or zoom boxes) and drag.

For example, Figure 2-14 on the next page shows two document windows arranged side-by-side on the screen. To create these windows, you would begin by dragging the size box for the window Untitled1 to the left until it fills half the screen vertically. Next, click in the window Untitled2 and use the same technique to reduce that window to half-screen size vertically. At this point, the two windows will overlap exactly. Finally, point to the title bar of Untitled2 and drag to the right until the two windows appear side by side.

FIGURE 2-13

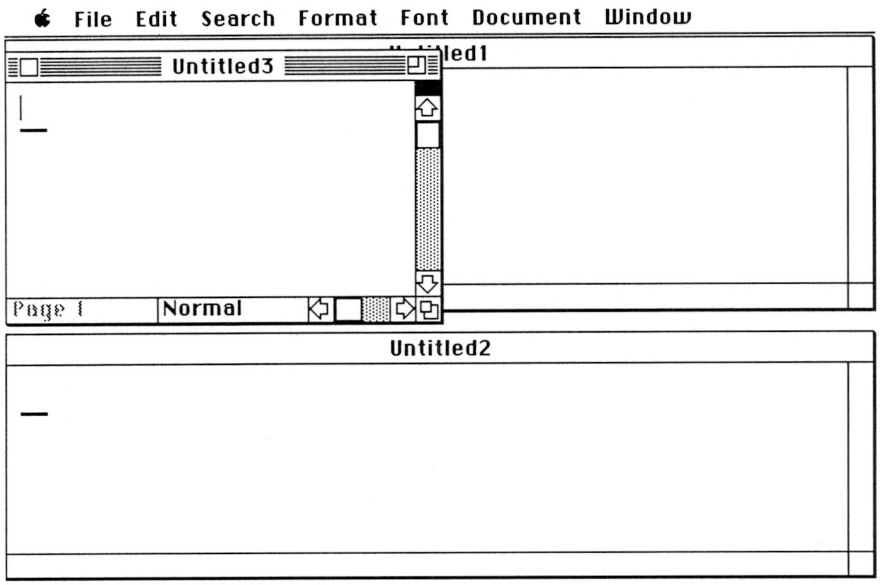

The third window appears in quarter-screen size.

FIGURE 2-14

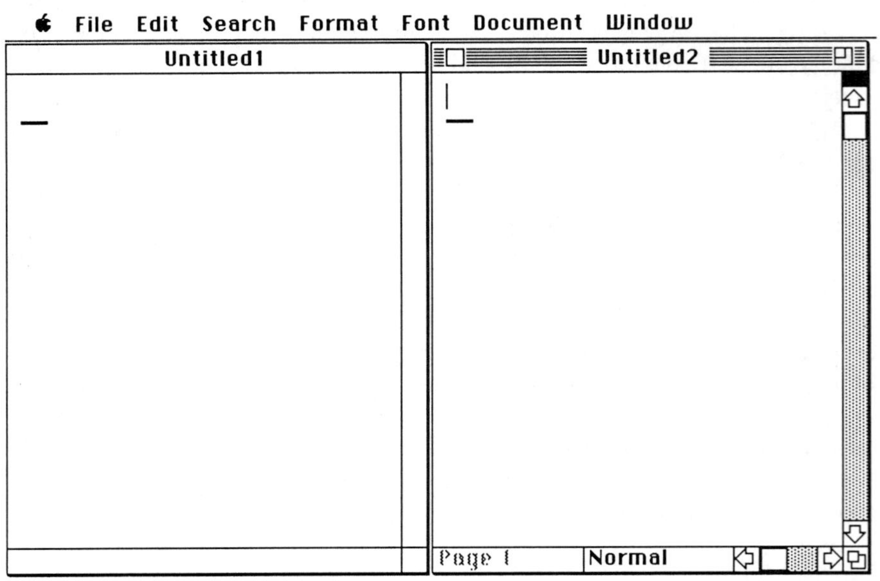

You can create nonoverlapping windows by resizing and dragging the windows manually.

The active window

We mentioned that the horizontal lines that appear at the top of your document window indicate that you can drag that window around by its title bar to reposition it. Actually, the horizontal lines mean much more than that. These lines also tell you whether or not the window is active. The active window on your screen is the one that you currently are working in—that is, any commands you issue will apply to the window that is active at the time.

For example, notice that the window Untitled1 in Figure 2-14 does not display horizontal lines (or close and zoom boxes). This window is inactive. In order to edit or make any other changes in this window, you must click on it to reactivate it. (You can also use the Window menu to activate a window, as you'll see in Chapter 4.)

By the way, if you want to move a window around on the screen without deactivating the current window, just press the ⌘ key as you drag the title bar of the second window. The partially active window will "slide behind" the active window, rather than coming to the top of the stack. If you click anywhere else on the window, however, Word will activate that window and bring it to the top of the stack. To reactivate the window you were working in, you must select it from the Window menu or click on it again.

Moving between windows

Moving between document windows is much like shuffling a stack of playing cards. To move from one window to another, you can click on the window you want; select the window name from the Window menu; or press Option-⌘-w. When you press Option-⌘-w, the next window in the stack comes into view, and the previous window moves to the bottom of the stack.

Other Window Features

The gray bars at the right and bottom of the screen are called scroll bars. (The horizontal scroll bar shows up only in Full Menus.) Once you've entered some text into your Word document file, you'll use these scroll bars to move through your document. (More on scrolling and other navigational techniques in Chapter 4.)

To the left of the horizontal scroll bar at the bottom of your screen is a status box that currently displays a page number. Since we are viewing an empty document window right now, we see the notation *Page 1*. When you begin learning about outlining, formatting, and using the glossary, you'll see other messages in this area as well.

Using the split bar

If you are using Word's Full Menus setting, you can also split a window into panes to see two different portions of your document at the same time. For example, suppose you are writing a sales report and you have presented a table of statistics at the beginning of the document. If you want to refer to these statistics later in the document, rather than scrolling back and forth to check the contents of your table, split your document window into two panes. In this way you can keep the table in view as you write the body of your report. You can even copy data from one portion of the window to the other.

To split a window into panes, point to the black bar that appears above the vertical scroll bar on the right side of the document window. Drag this split bar downward to the desired position. As you can see in Figure 2-15, Word now gives you two sets of vertical scroll bars so that you can move through the two window panes independently.

FIGURE 2-15

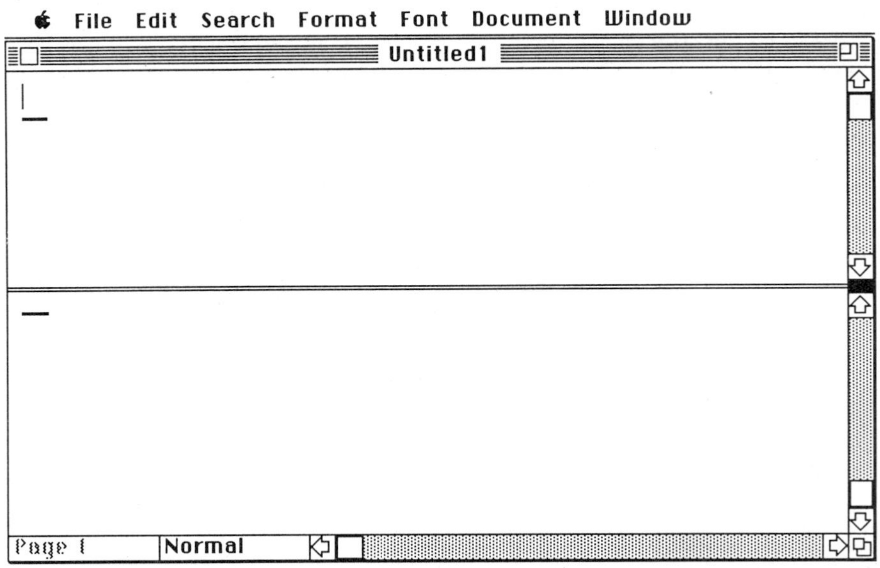

To split a window into panes, you can just drag the split bar toward the middle of the screen.

To remove the split pane from your window, just point to the black bar again and drag it past either end of the vertical scroll bar. You can also toggle the split feature on and off by pressing Option-⌘-s.

The New Window command

In addition to the split screen technique we just described, Word 3 offers a new Window feature that those of you who have used previous versions of the program will be happy to see: multiple windowing capabilities for a single document. By creating multiple windows, you can see different parts of the same document at the same time. This is particularly convenient when you are working with very large documents and you want to see several blocks of text simultaneously. When you begin working with outlines in Chapter 12, you may also want to use multiple windows to view your outline and your main document at the same time.

To create a new document window, just select New Window from the Window menu. For example, if we select New Window while the document Untitled1 is active, Word will display a new window called Untitled1:2. It will also rename our original window Untitled1:1. Subsequent windows will be named Untitled1:3, Untitled1:4, and so forth.

Keep in mind that each of these windows is just another porthole through which you view a single document. Any changes you make in one window will affect the entire document—not just the version you see in the active window.

To remove a window from your screen, click the close box or press ⌘-w. Word will automatically renumber the remaining document windows, if necessary. If you click the close box of the only window that is open for a particular document, however (you can easily tell if only one window is open for a document since the colon and number that identify multiple windows will not appear), Word will assume that you want to close your document altogether and will ask if you want to save any changes before it removes the window from your screen. We'll talk more about closing and saving files in Chapter 3.

THE RULER

You can specify formatting features such as line lengths, paragraph indentations, paragraph justification, line spacing, and tab settings in Word by using the ruler. The ruler does not automatically appear on your screen when you open a new document. To access the ruler, select Show Ruler from the Format menu or press ⌘-r.

The appearance of the ruler depends on whether the Short Menus or Full Menus setting is in effect. If you're using Short Menus, your ruler will look like the one in Figure 2-16. If you're using Full menus, you'll see a ruler like the one in Figure 2-17. As you can see, several additional ruler icons are available when the Full Menus setting is activated.

FIGURE 2-16

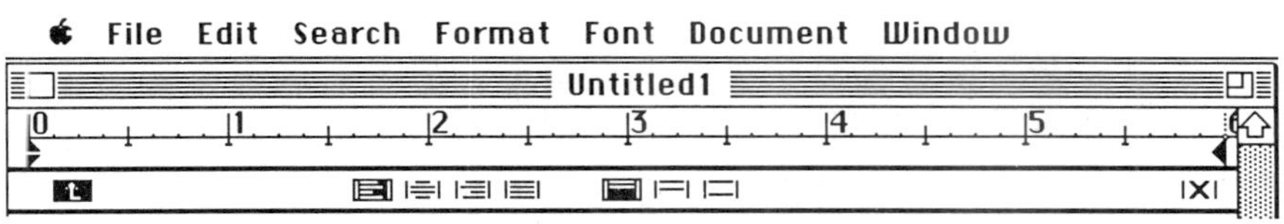

If you're using Short Menus, you'll see this ruler when you select Show Ruler from the Format menu.

FIGURE 2-17

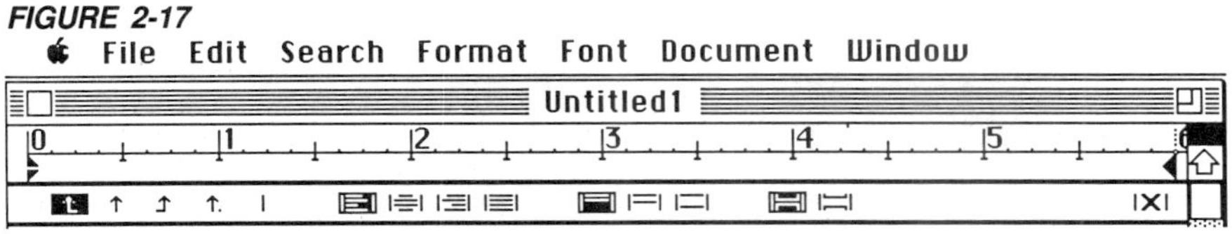

If you're using Full Menus, you'll see this ruler when you select Show Ruler from the Format menu.

Show Ruler is another toggle command that changes when issued. When you select Show Ruler from the Format menu, that command changes to Hide Ruler. Once you've specified your ruler settings, you may prefer to suppress the ruler display so that more of your document is visible on the screen. You can select the Hide Ruler command (or press ⌘-r again) to suppress the ruler display. Your ruler specifications will remain in effect even when the ruler is not visible on the screen.

Though you can see only about 6.5 inches of the ruler on your screen at a time, your ruler actually extends from -11 to 21.75 inches. You can see the remainder of the ruler by clicking on the right and left scroll arrows at the bottom of your screen. To see the negative values on your ruler, you must press the Shift key and then click on the left scroll arrow.

We'll talk more about formatting with rulers in Chapter 5.

THE POINTER

As you may have noticed, your mouse pointer takes on a number of different shapes as you move around the screen in Word. Table 2-1 shows the various pointer icons that you'll be seeing as you work in Word.

TABLE 2-1

Pointer
I-beam
Left arrow
Right arrow
Crosshair
Magnifying glass
Question mark
Plus sign
Minus sign
Page number
Watch

Word has ten distinct pointer shapes.

You'll use the I-beam pointer to select text and to move the blinking insertion point marker around on your screen. The I-beam will probably be the most commonly used pointer shape as you edit and format text.

Do not confuse the I-beam pointer with the blinking insertion point marker. You use the I-beam pointer to select an insertion point, but your selection does not go into effect until you actually click the mouse button to place the insertion point marker in your text. In fact, if you use the scroll bars to move through your document, your insertion point marker might be in a completely different part of the document from the part you are viewing on your screen. Make sure the insertion point marker is in the correct spot before you begin typing or editing text.

The arrow that points to the left appears whenever you point to the menu bar, title bar, or scroll bars. It also appears when you point to options in a Word dialog box. You'll use this arrow to select commands and options and to move through your document via the scroll bars.

The arrow that points to the right appears only when you point to the far-left side of your window. There is an invisible selection bar in this area. When your pointer takes on this shape, you know that you are in the selection bar. Then you can use the right-arrow pointer to select blocks of text quickly.

The magnifying glass, page number, and crosshair pointers appear when you use the Page Preview... command to see what your document will look like when it's printed. The magnifying glass lets you zoom in on various parts of the page to enlarge them to actual size. The crosshair pointer lets you reposition items on the page, and the page number pointer lets you insert and position a page number on each page of your document. We'll show you all three of these techniques in Chapter 7.

The watch shape indicates that Word is working to execute your last command. While this watch appears, you cannot use these pointers to issue any other commands or to select text in Word. However, you can use the keyboard while the watch is visible. You can type text or even get a jump on Word by using ⌘-Key options to issue commands and select options. Word will catch up to you once it has finished the current task.

The question mark pointer appears when you press ⌘-? to access Word's Help facility. We will take a look at the Help facility at the end of this chapter.

Finally, the plus and minus sign pointers appear when you are creating custom menus in Word. As you'll learn in Chapter 11, you'll use these pointers to select commands and options that you want to add to or delete from menus.

THE KEYBOARD

As you've no doubt guessed by now, your Macintosh keyboard is much more than a standard typewriter keyboard. The Mac keyboard has a number of extra keys that let you perform special functions. The Return, Option, and ⌘ keys are the most obvious differences. If you use a Mac Plus, you have a numeric keypad and a set of arrow keys at your disposal as well. Figures 2-18 and 2-19 show diagrams of the 512K and Macintosh Plus keyboards.

FIGURE 2-18

A 512K Macintosh keyboard looks like this.

FIGURE 2-19

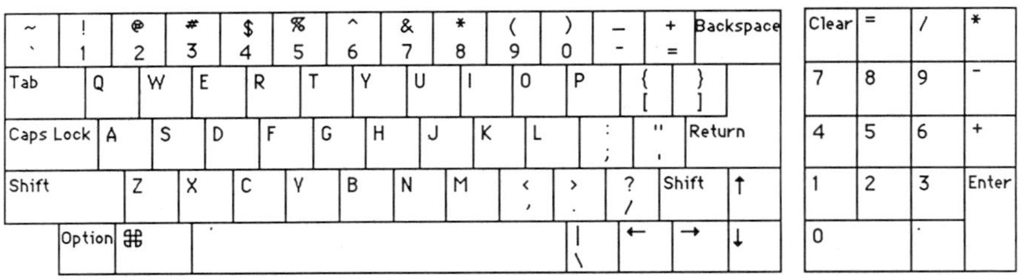

The Macintosh Plus keyboard has a numeric keypad and arrow keys.

The Option and ⌘ keys are special function keys that let you issue commands and perform tasks quickly—without the aid of your mouse. Generally, these keys are used in conjunction with the alphabetic keys.

The Spacebar works just like the Spacebar on a standard typewriter. Use it to enter blank spaces into your document.

You'll use the Tab key to set up columnar tables of data and to control the positioning of text in your document.

As you might have guessed, the Shift key's primary purpose is to let you type in upper-case characters. The Shift key also serves as a special function key when used in conjunction with the Option and ⌘ keys.

The Caps Lock key on your Mac keyboard is quite similar to the Caps Lock key on a standard typewriter—it allows you to type in all upper-case letters, without pressing the Shift key. Keep in mind that Caps Lock does not apply to the numeric keys along the top of your keyboard. In order to use the top-row characters like *!*, *@*, and *#*, or punctuation marks like *:*, *"*, and *?*, you must still press the Shift key.

The Backspace key is primarily an editing key that lets you back up over typographical errors or delete blocks of text. As you'll learn in Chapter 10, you also use the Backspace and ⌘ keys to make glossary entries in your document.

Among other things, the Return and Enter keys let you lock in dialog box selections and signal the beginning of a new paragraph in your Word documents.

Do not confuse the Return and Enter keys with the carriage return on a standard typewriter! You do not have to press the Return key at the end of each line to move to the beginning of the next line. Word offers a special feature called WordWrap that automatically moves the insertion point marker from one line to the next for you. Press Return or Enter only when you want to end one paragraph and start a new one.

If you have a Mac Plus keyboard (like the one shown in Figure 2-19), you can use the numeric keypad and the ←, →, ↑, and ↓ keys as navigational tools to move quickly through your Word documents.

You must press the Clear key before you can use the numeric keypad for entering text into your document. Otherwise, you will find yourself zooming around the screen instead of typing numeric characters into your document! Though the numeric keypad is designed for quick numeric entry for spreadsheet and other business software users, Microsoft has turned it into a navigational tool for Word users. When you press the Clear key, however, Word will allow you to use the keypad for entering numbers. In effect, the Clear key serves as a NumLock key in Word. When you are using the keypad to enter numbers, *Num. Lock* will appear in the status box in the lower-left corner of your screen. To use the keypad for navigation again, just press the Clear key one more time.

In addition to the special function keys described above, many of the standard typewriter keys also serve special functions in certain circumstances. As we mentioned earlier, you can use the ⌘ and Option keys in conjunction with certain letter keys to issue Word commands and perform other tasks. We'll introduce these special functions and techniques as we discuss Word's various features throughout the course of the book.

GETTING HELP

The Help file that is located on your utilities disk contains quick-reference information about all of Word's commands and options. You can access the Help facility from within Word at any time by choosing About Microsoft Word... from the menu. You also can access Help from the Finder level by inserting your utilities disk in one of the disk drives and double-clicking the *Word Help* file icon.

When you load the Help facility from within Word, you'll see a screen like the one in Figure 2-20. Among other things, this dialog box tells you which version of Word you are using.

FIGURE 2-20

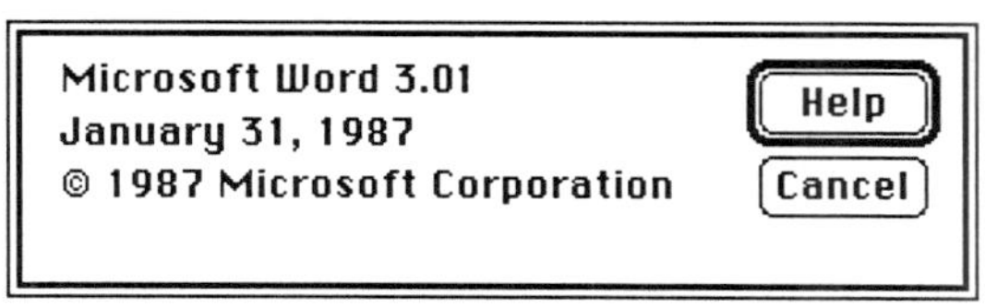

When you select About Microsoft Word... from the menu, Word presents the Help dialog box.

As you might have guessed, to see Word's Help screens, you need to click the Help button. If the disk that contains your Help file is not in one of your disk drives, Word will present a dialog box like the one in Figure 2-21. Just eject the disk currently in one of your drives and insert the utilities disk (or whichever disk happens to hold your Help file). Now, click on the file name Word Help, as shown in Figure 2-22, and click the Open button or press Return or Enter. In a moment, you'll see a dialog box like the one in Figure 2-23.

FIGURE 2-21

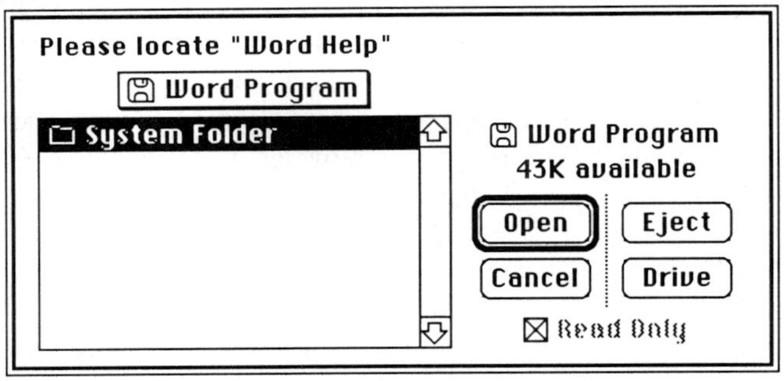

Word will ask you to locate the Help file if it is not currently in one of your disk drives.

FIGURE 2-22

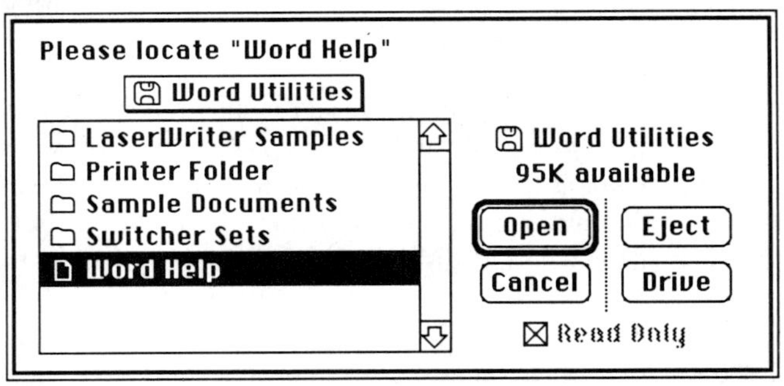

When you locate the Help file, use the Open option to access the Help facility.

FIGURE 2-23

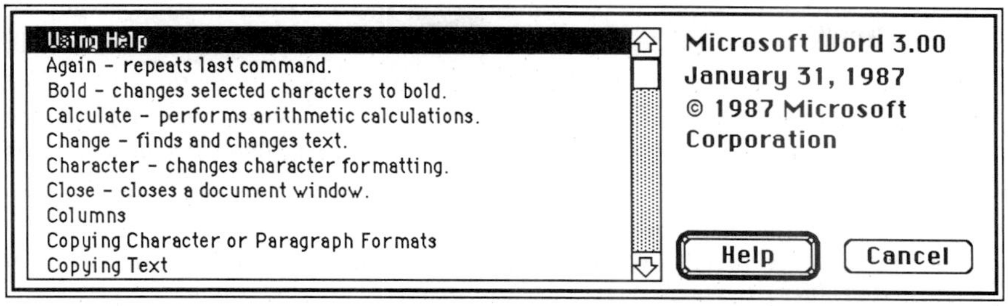

When you select the Help file, Word will present you with a list of topics.

Scroll though the list box until the topic you are interested in comes into view. Then click on the topic name and click the Help button or press Return or Enter. For example, if you select the topic Using Help, you'll see a window like the one in Figure 2-24. To get back to the main list of topics shown in Figure 2-23, click the Topics button. To see the next Help screen in the sequence, click Next. To move back to the previous topic in the sequence, click Previous. Finally, to remove the Help window from your screen and return to your document, just click Cancel. If you have inserted the utilities disk, Word will ask you to reinsert the disk that was originally in the drive.

FIGURE 2-24

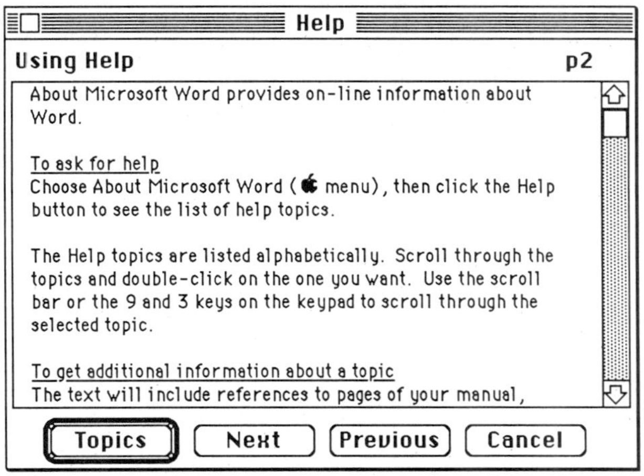

If you select Using Help, you'll see this screen.

Context - Sensitive Help

Word's Help facility is also context-sensitive, making it easy for you to look up information about a particular command or option. For example, suppose you want to learn more about the Character... command on Word's Format menu. Rather than scrolling through the lists of general topics, just press ⌘-?. When your pointer takes on the question mark shape, choose the Character... command. Rather than presenting a list of topics for you to choose from, Word will go directly to the Help screen that explains the Character... command, as shown in Figure 2-25. (Again, if your Help file is not currently in one of your disk drives, Word will ask you to locate the Help file before it displays the Help screen.)

FIGURE 2-25

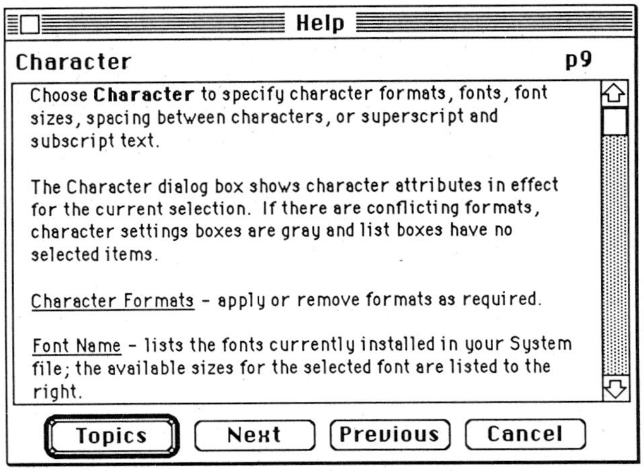

To get context-sensitive help, just press ⌘-? and select a command or option.

FILE HANDLING 3

In Section 2, we'll be showing you how to create, edit, and format documents. Before you invest your time and energy in building a document, however, you should be familiar with the procedures for opening, closing, deleting, and saving files in Word. In this chapter, we'll show you seven of the commands on Word's File menu: New, Open…, Close, Save, Save As…, Delete…, and Quit. In Chapters 14 and 16, we'll be showing you some additional file-handling techniques for working with the Print Merge and Switcher facilities.

CREATING AND OPENING FILES

As we explained in Chapter 1, when you click the Word icon at the Finder level to load the Word program, Word will automatically create a new blank file for you. The document name *Untitled1* will appear in the title bar. Similarly, you can simultaneously load Word and open one or more existing files from the Finder level by selecting the icons for the files that you want to work with and issuing the Open command. You may also double-click on one of the highlighted file icons.

If you need to open a new, blank document while you are in Word, you can always select the New command from the File menu. If you have already opened one untitled document, your new document will be called Untitled2. As you open new files during a session, Word will number those files sequentially—Untitled3, Untitled4, and so forth.

Retrieving Existing Files

If you have already created a file and you want to retrieve it from disk while you are working in Word, choose the Open... command from the File menu. Word will present a dialog box like the one in Figure 3-1. If you use a 512K Mac with old ROMs, your dialog box will look like the one in Figure 3-2.

FIGURE 3-1

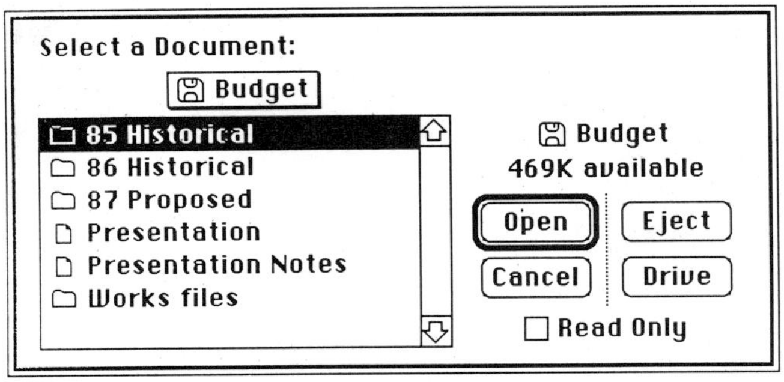

When you issue the Open... command, Word presents you with a list of files on the active disk.

FIGURE 3-2

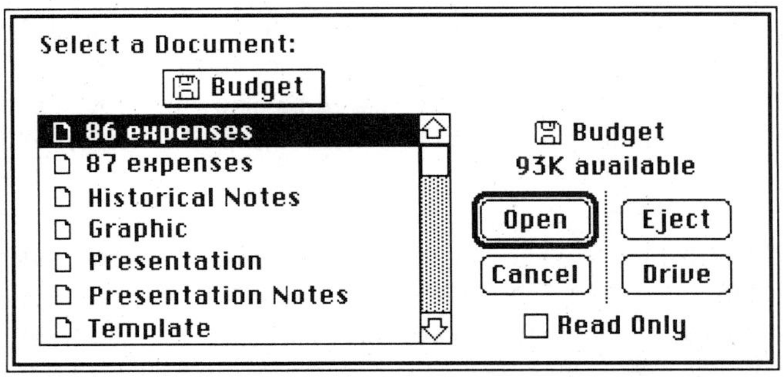

A slightly different version of the Open dialog box appears if you use a 512K Mac that has not been enhanced with new ROMs.

On the right side of the Open dialog box, Word presents the name of the disk in the active disk drive. The amount of space available on the disk appears below the disk name, just above the Open, Eject, Cancel, and Drive buttons.

On the left side of the dialog box is a list box that contains the names of all of the Word files on the active disk. Initially, a disk icon and the disk name also appear above the list box. Documents created in other applications will not appear in the list box unless they have been stored in a format that Word can read. (More on opening files created in other programs in Chapter 16.)

If you use a Mac Plus or an enhanced 512K Mac with new ROMs, you will be able to view and open all of the folders on the active disk as well. As you can see in Figure 3-1, the small icons on the left side of each item of the list box show whether an item is a folder or a document.

If you use a 512K Mac with old ROMs, you will see only the Word files on the active disk, as shown in Figure 3-2. Though you can access documents that are stored in folders, you cannot see the folder icons in the Open dialog box. The ability to work with folders from within an application is a product of the new hierarchical file structure (HFS), which depends on the updated ROMs.

The document and folder names appear in alphabetical order in the Open dialog box list box. If your disk contains more than seven files and folders, you can click on the scroll arrows or in the gray area of the scroll bar to bring additional names into view. If you have a Mac Plus keyboard, you can also use the ↑ and ↓ keys to move through the list of document and folder names.

You can move quickly to the file you need by typing the first letter of the file (or folder) name. Word will immediately scroll through the lists of files and folders and highlight the first name that begins with the letter you typed. If you're quick, you can narrow your selection even further by typing the first two or three letters of the name. For example, in the Open dialog box shown in Figure 3-2, if we type *t*, Word will highlight the document name *Template*.

To open a folder, simply highlight the folder name and press Return or Enter or click the Open button. If you have a Mac Plus keyboard, you can also press ⌘-↓ to open a folder. When you open a folder, your dialog box will look like the one in Figure 3-3. Notice that an open folder icon replaces the disk icon above the list box. Inside the folder, you'll see another list of Word files—and additional folders, if you have placed one folder inside another at the Finder level.

FIGURE 3-3

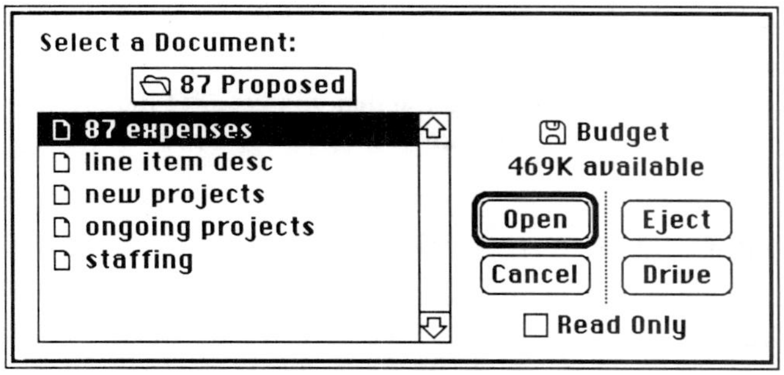

If you use a Mac Plus or a 512K Mac with new ROMs, you can see the contents of folders in the Open dialog box.

To close a folder and move back up to the next "level" in the list box, point to the folder title above the list box and drag down to select the disk icon again. If you have a Mac Plus keyboard, you can also press ⌘-⬆ to move back up to the next level.

If the file you want to see is on a disk that is located in another drive, just click the Drive button to see a list of the files and folders on the disk in that drive. You can also press ⌘-d or Tab to activate another disk drive. If you have only one disk drive, or if the second disk drive is empty, the Drive button will be dimmed.

If the document that you want is not on one of the disks currently in your disk drive(s), click the Eject button or press ⌘-e to eject the disk in the active drive. Then place the disk that contains the needed file in the disk drive.

Finally, once you have selected the file you want, press either the Return or Enter key, click the Open button, or press ⌘-o to display the document on your Word DeskTop.

The Read Only option

The Read Only option is designed primarily for Macintosh networks, where two or more users may have access to the same files. To ensure that no one alters the master version of a file, you can apply the Read Only option. (As you'll see in Chapter 6, Word also applies the Read Only option to your Main Dictionary file, to protect it from revisions.)

Even if you are a solo Mac user, if you want only to see the contents of a file without making changes to it, you can click the Read Only option before you open the file. When you use the Read Only option, Word will let you scan the file and even make changes to it, but it will not let you save that file under the same name that was originally assigned to it. In other words, if you want to keep any changes you have made to a file that was opened with the Read Only option in effect, you must save that file under a new name.

If you issue the Save command to save a file that you opened with the Read Only option, Word will automatically present the Save As dialog box. If you attempt to assign the same name to the altered file that you used for the original, Word will present the alert box shown in Figure 3-4.

FIGURE 3-4

If you use the Read Only option, Word will not let you save a file under the same name as the original.

In order to save your changes to the file, you must click OK in this alert box, then assign a new name to the document. (More on saving files in a moment.) Though the Read Only option is hardly a foolproof security device, you may find it a convenient way to protect your files from inadvertent changes.

SAVING YOUR WORK

Word gives you several ways to save a file. As you might have guessed, to save a document you need to select the Save or Save As… command from the File menu. The first time you save an untitled document, you'll see the Save As dialog box shown in Figure 3-5. This dialog box appears whether you select Save or Save As… from the File menu. Once you have assigned a name to a document, however, you can bypass this dialog box by issuing the Save command rather than choosing Save As….

FIGURE 3-5

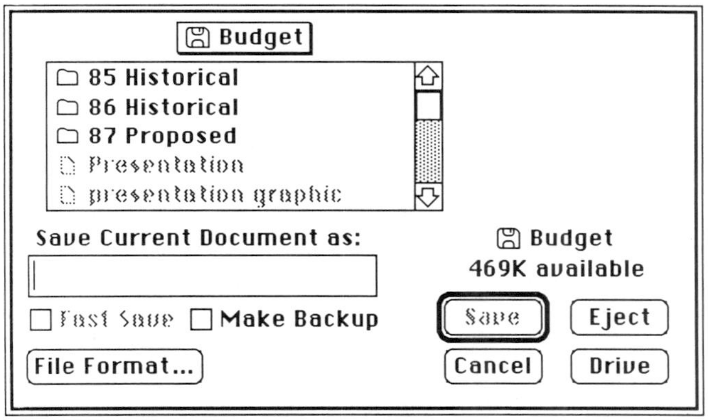

The Save As dialog box appears when you issue the Save As… command or when you issue the Save command to save a file for the first time.

The first thing you need to tell Word is where you want the file to be stored. Use the Drive and Eject buttons, described above, to access the needed disk. Notice that the names of the documents already stored on the active disk are dimmed in the list box. You cannot select any of the documents from this list box; they appear only as a reminder of the names you have already used.

If you use a Mac Plus or an enhanced 512K Mac, you'll also see the folders on the active disk in the Save As dialog box list box. Unlike the file names, folder names are available for selection in the Save As dialog box. If you want to place a document into a folder, just double-click the folder icon to open it. When you return to the Finder level, you'll see that the document has indeed been tucked into the selected folder.

Word also tells you how much room is on the active disk. As you work with documents of various lengths, you'll soon get a feel for the amount of space required to store documents of various lengths and various levels of complexity. In general, a ten-page document requires about 30K of disk space, depending on its complexity.

If there is not enough room on the active disk to save your document, you'll see an alert box like the one in Figure 3-6. At this point, you can either cancel the Save procedure and delete some of the documents on the disk (we'll talk about the Delete... command in a few pages), or you can eject the current disk and save your document on another disk.

FIGURE 3-6

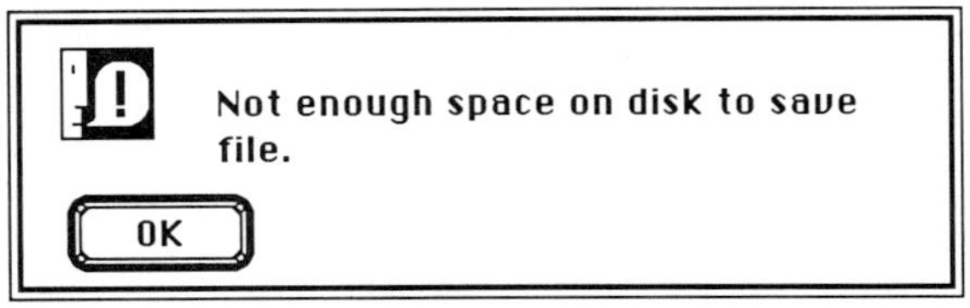

You'll see this alert message if there is not enough room for your document on the active disk.

Once you decide where you want to store your document, you must provide Word with a name for the file. (The Save button will remain dimmed until you provide a name.) If this is the first time you have saved the document, the Save Current Document as edit bar will be empty. Just type the name you want to use. If you have saved the document before, Word will display the current document name in the Save Current Document as edit bar. You can leave that entry intact, or you can type a new name for your document.

After you have entered the name you want to use in the Save As dialog box, click the Save button, press ⌘-s, or press the Return or Enter keys.

If you have entered a name in the Save Current Document as edit bar that has already been used on the active disk, you'll see an alert box like the one shown in Figure 3-7. If you want to replace the existing file with the document that is currently open on your screen, click Yes; otherwise, click No. If you click No, Word will redisplay the Save As dialog box and allow you to enter a new document name in the Save Current Document as edit bar.

FIGURE 3-7

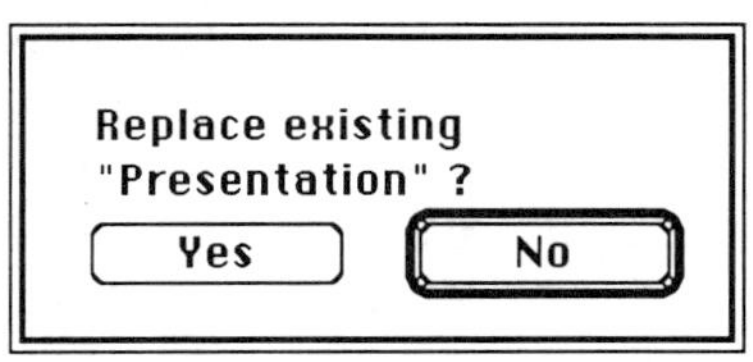

Word asks you to verify your file name when you assign the same name to two documents.

By the way, Word will not display the alert message in Figure 3-7 if the existing file on your disk is stored in an unopened folder. In other words, Word will allow you to create files with identical names on the same disk, as long as those files are in separate folders. However, we strongly recommend that you avoid duplicate file names.

The Close and Quit commands

Of course, you can issue the Save or Save As... command at any time during a Word session to save your revisions to a document. If you issue the Save command to save a document that has already been named, Word will assume that you want to save the revised document under the existing name. In other words, Word will replace the version of the document that is stored on disk with the current document.

If you issue the Close command after you have made changes to a document (this includes entering data into a new, blank file), you'll see an alert box like the one in Figure 3-8.

FIGURE 3-8

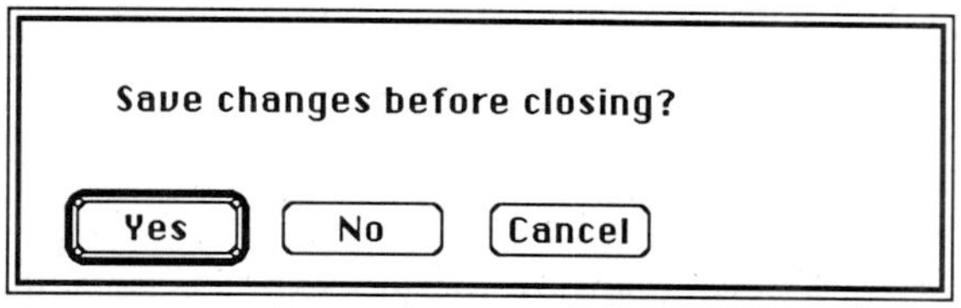

The Close alert box appears when you issue the Close command without saving your changes.

If you click No in the Close alert box, Word will close the current document window without saving your changes. If you click Yes and the current document has previously been saved, Word will automatically save the document under its current name. If the document has never been saved before, Word will present the Save As dialog box shown in Figure 3-5.

Similarly, if you issue the Quit command after you have made changes to a document, you'll see a Save Changes alert box like the one shown in Figure 3-9 on the next page. Keep in mind that the Quit command tells Word to close all documents that are open on the Word DeskTop and return to the Finder level. Therefore, when you choose Quit, Word will present the Save Changes alert box for each file that has been changed since your last save (including dictionary and glossary files, which we'll discuss in Chapters 6 and 10). You may elect to save or discard your changes to each file.

FIGURE 3-9

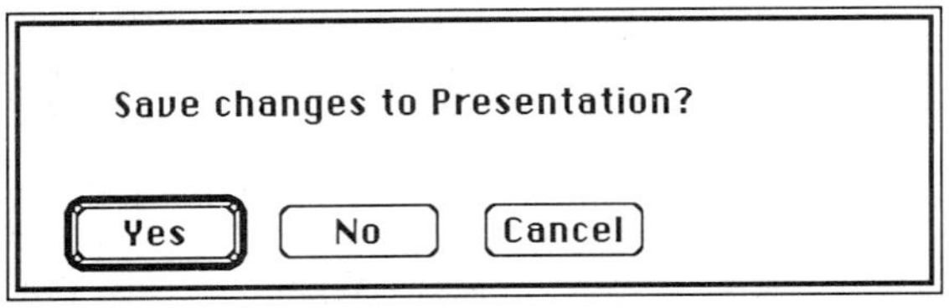

When you issue the Quit command without saving your changes, Word will display this alert box for each open file.

Backing up your work

If you want to make sure that you have a backup of your document, use the Make Backup option in the Save As dialog box. When you use the Make Backup option, Word duplicates the last version of the document that you saved. Any changes that you have made since your last save will not be reflected in the backup file because Word duplicates the last saved version of the file before it saves your most recent round of changes to the document that is currently open on the DeskTop.

When you use the Make Backup option, Word will add the prefix *Backup of* to the document name that appears in the Save Current Document as edit bar. For example, if your main file is named *Presentation*, your backup file will be named *Backup of Presentation.*

To use the Make Backup option, you must use the Save As… command to save a previously saved file. Word will not make a backup copy of an untitled document or a document whose name you have changed; the document name must already be recorded on disk so that Word can duplicate the original document before it implements your Save As… command to record your changes to the file. Thus, you should leave the existing document name in the Save Document as edit bar, click the Make Backup option, then click Save, press ⌘-s, or press Return or Enter to save the document under the same name. Click Yes when Word asks if you want to replace the existing file that is stored under that name.

Keep in mind that Word will never update the backup copy of your document unless you specifically instruct it to do so. If you want to update your backup copy to reflect the status of your document as of the last time you saved, you must reissue the Save As… command and save the document again with the Make Backup option in effect.

Some precautions

We recommend that you save each of the open documents on your DeskTop *at least* every half hour to ensure that any changes you have made to those files are recorded on disk. As you may have learned the hard way, a momentary power outage or an undoable editing command can mean the loss of a lot of hard work. By saving your files regularly, you can ensure that you will not lose hours' worth of work.

For important documents, you should also copy the file to a separate backup disk. Though the Make Backup option is a handy way to create backup copies of your files, it will not help you if the disk on which your documents are stored becomes unreadable for some reason. By regularly copying your files to a separate disk, you decrease the chances of losing important work.

By the way, whenever you save a file, Word will replace the page number in the lower-left corner of your window with a character count. This change is temporary; as soon as you click anywhere in your document, type a character, or issue a command, the page number will reappear.

Making a fast save

To make it easier for you to save your changes to long documents, Word 3 offers a new feature called Fast Save. If you click the Fast Save option in the Save As dialog box, Word will be able to shorten substantially the amount of time needed to save your documents.

Here's how it works: Word maintains a set of pointer tables to keep track of the changes that you make to your document. Normally, when you issue the Save command, Word updates all of the pointer tables and completely rewrites your document on the disk. When you use Fast Save, Word does not update the pointer tables. Instead, it appends your changes to the last saved version of the document. As a result, when you use Fast Save, your files will get longer and longer each time you issue the Save command to record your changes to a file. To keep your document from getting too long, Word will occasionally perform a full-fledged Save procedure to consolidate your changes and restructure the pointer table. Of course, Word always updates all of the pointer tables and rewrites your entire file to disk when you issue the Close or Quit command and save your changes.

You cannot use the Make Backup and Fast Save options simultaneously. However, you can switch options at any time by issuing the Save As... command rather than the Save command. For example, suppose you have been using the Fast Save option to save your revisions to a document as you work, then you decide that you would like to make a separate backup file to ensure that the last saved version of your file is kept safe while you make some changes to the current version on your screen. You can issue the Save As... command and select the Make Backup option, as described earlier. Then, the next time you want to save your work, you can issue the Save As... command again and reselect the Fast Save option so that you can continue to make quick saves as you continue with your work.

Duplicating a file

Occasionally, you may find it necessary to duplicate a file while you are working in Word. You can accomplish this task by issuing the Save As... command and typing a new name in the Save Current Document as edit bar. For example, suppose you want to create two very similar versions of a report. After creating and formatting the first report, save it under an appropriate name (let's say *Report1*). Then, to duplicate the file without returning to the Finder level, issue the Save As... command and type a new name (like *Report2*) in the Save Document as edit bar. The document on your screen will now carry the name *Report2*, and the original *Report1* will be filed away safely on disk. Now you can make any needed changes to the second report, without altering the first.

As you'll learn in Chapter 17, you can use this technique to create permanent template files so that you can create similar sets of documents quickly and easily. When you use the Save As... command to duplicate a file, Word also remembers the print settings, styles, and other formats that you have assigned to that file.

DELETING A DOCUMENT

The Delete... command is a new addition to Word 3. In earlier versions of the program, you could delete files from a disk only by dragging them into the Trash at the Finder level. By adding the Delete... command to Word's File menu, Microsoft has made it much easier for you to make room on your data disks when you are running short on space.

To delete a file from within Word, select the Delete... command from the File menu. Word will display a dialog box like the one in Figure 3-10. This dialog box should look familiar by now. As with the Open... and Save As... commands, you can use the Drive button to see the contents of either disk drive, and you can use the Eject button to access another disk.

FIGURE 3-10

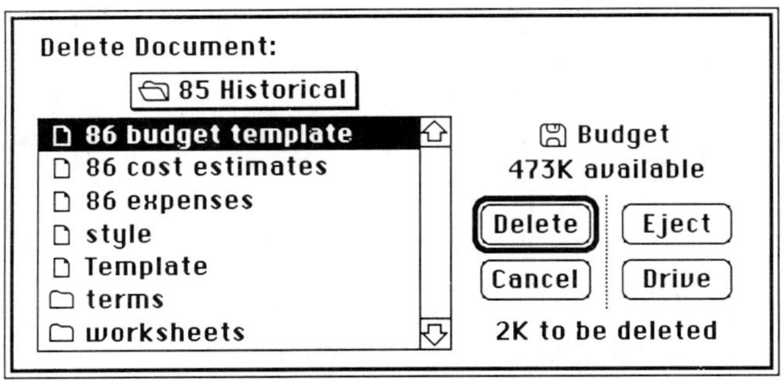

The Delete dialog box is similar to the Open and Save As dialog boxes.

Notice that Word displays the names of all files—not just the Word files—on the current disk in the Delete dialog box. You may delete a file created in any application to make room on the active disk. The only file names that will not appear in the list box are certain protected files, like the System, Finder, and Word applications, and any files that are currently open on the Word DeskTop.

Notice also that Word displays the size of the selected file at the bottom-right side of the Delete dialog box. This feature is helpful when you are trying to make enough room on a data disk to save a file. If you can estimate the length of the file you need to save, you may be able to select one or two unneeded files that consume approximately the same amount of space on the disk. As usual, the amount of available space on the disk appears just below the disk name. Word will update this value after each deletion to let you know how much disk space you have recovered.

To delete a file, simply point to the name of the file that you want to delete and click the Delete button. Word will display an alert box like the one in Figure 3-11. If you're sure you want to delete the file, click Yes. Otherwise, click No or Cancel. If you click No, Word will present the Delete dialog box again. If you click Cancel, Word will return you to the Word DeskTop.

FIGURE 3-11

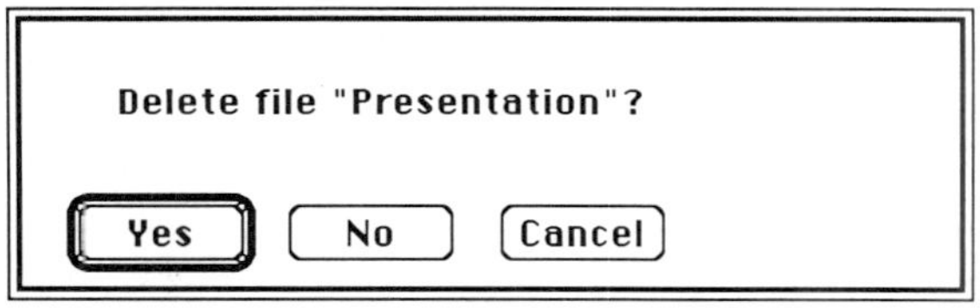

Word asks you to verify a Delete... command.

Once the file has been deleted, Word will redisplay the dialog box shown in Figure 3-10. At this point, you can select another file to delete, or you can click Cancel to remove the Delete dialog box from your screen.

Temporary Files

Word periodically creates special temporary files with names like *Word Temp 1* and *Word Temp 2* to back up your work. These temporary files often appear in the System folder on your startup disk. For this reason, if you store documents on your startup disk, you'll want to make sure that you leave about 20K of space open on that disk so that Word can keep track of your actions. If you fail to leave adequate room on your startup disk for the temporary files, Word may present you with a warning that it is running low on space.

We recommend that you never use the Delete... command to delete these temporary files while you are working in Word. You may create a system error and lose a great deal of work. However, if need be, you can drag these temporary files into the Trash at the Finder level after you have finished a Word session.

A tip on naming files

When you use the Delete... command, keep in mind that Word will display the names of every file located on the selected disk—not just the names of Word documents. It is impossible to tell what type of document you are selecting when you click on a file name in the Delete dialog box. If you commonly store files of different types on the same disk, you may want to store each type of file in a separate folder or identify each file by adding a type code. For example, you might want to use a *W* suffix for Word files, a *C* suffix for Microsoft Chart files, an *E* or *X* suffix for Microsoft Excel files, and so forth. Thus, an Excel budget worksheet might be called *Budget.X*, while your budget proposal text created in Word might be called *Budget.W*.

OTHER TOPICS

In this chapter, we've reviewed the basics of opening, closing, and saving files in Word. However, we've not yet explored the structure or format of those files. If you commonly need to transfer information from one program to another, you need to understand the basic characteristics of the files created in each program so that you can effectively communicate with other applications.

For example, the File Format... option in the Save As dialog box lets you save your documents in different formats so that you can access them from within other programs. Similarly, programs like Microsoft Works and Microsoft Excel let you save files in a text format that is readable by Word. In addition, the QuickSwitch application lets you set up links between files created in different programs. We'll talk more about these topics in Chapter 16, "Sharing Data with Other Programs."

2

SECTION TWO

WORKING WITH WORD

Now that we've been through the rather laborious process of learning the Word environment and getting geared up for production, let's get some work done! Your first step, of course, will be to enter some text into a Word file, then you can use Word's formatting and editing tools to create a finished document.

Once you complete this section, you will have mastered the basic tools you need to use Word. In Chapter 4, we'll show you how to enter text into a new document window, then we'll show you how to select and view that text and perform some basic editing tasks. In Chapter 5, we'll explore some formatting techniques. Next, in Chapter 6 we'll take a look at some of Word's more powerful editing facilities. Finally, in Chapters 7 and 8 we'll show you how to design a page layout and print your Word documents.

WORD BASICS 4

Presumably, your first task upon opening a new Word document will be to enter some text. Then you can format and edit the document to suit your needs. In this chapter, we'll show you how to enter text in Word, then we'll show you some navigational and selection techniques that you'll need in order to view, edit, and format that text. We'll wrap up the chapter with some basic manual editing techniques before we launch into Word's formatting and editing commands in Chapters 5 and 6.

On the following pages, you'll find dozens of keyboard shortcuts and special tools for moving around in your document window, selecting text, and editing your Word files. We urge you to practice these techniques; they will help you to work more efficiently in Word. For easy reference, Appendix 1 offers a summary of these keyboard shortcuts.

ENTERING TEXT

Entering text in Word is actually easier than typing text on a typewriter. A special facility called WordWrap lets you type a constant stream of characters without the need for carriage returns at the end of each line. If you are new to word processing, you may be tempted to press the Return or Enter key as you near the end of a line of text in order to move to the next line. Not to worry—if there is not enough room for the word you are typing on the current line, Word will move that word to the beginning of the next line automatically.

In fact, the only time you need to press the Return or Enter keys as you enter text in Word is when you want to start a new paragraph. You can significantly hinder your editing and formatting capabilities by placing carriage returns at the end of each line. If you decide later to insert or delete text or change the widths of your margins, you'll have to edit each line manually in order to reset your line breaks. If you let WordWrap handle this task for you, you can easily change the content, format, and layout of your document and have Word automatically reflow the text for you.

A Sample Document

To illustrate some basic entry, selection, and editing techniques in Word, we'll enter the sample document shown in Figure 4-1 into a new Word file. If you would like to follow along with our example, load Word and open a new Word document by double-clicking the Word program icon at the Finder level. If you are already in Word and need to open a new blank document, select the New command from Word's File menu. You'll see a blank document window with a name like Untitled1 or Untitled2.

FIGURE 4-1

Poofreader software package now available ¶

Newspeak Software announced today that the long-awaited Poofreader online editing package is now being shipped to dealers across the country. Poofreader, which has been under development for more than three years, is touted as the most sophisticated editing software on the market today. ¶

"Poofreader is much more than a common spelling checker," according to Newspeak's president, "Poofreader will make paper shredders obsolete!" ¶

Industry analysts predict that Poofreader will revolutionize the word processing industry and make highly paid copy editors a thing of the past. Now, users with no editing experience whatsoever can turn a perfectly sensible document into gibberish in minutes. Complete randomization of text and elimination of any logical sentence structures are only a few of the program's features. ¶

Poofreader also sports a set of three style sheets, called Journalese, Computerese, and Bureaucratese, that automatically convert your document to the appropriate level of incomprehensibility. All three style sheets ensure that at least 73 percent of the sentences in your document use the popular passive voice construction. ¶

The standard spelling checker available for so many word processing packages has been replaced by a revolutionary new facility called Anagram. With lightning speed, Anagram will locate all of the words in your document that are not recorded in its mammoth random-entry dictionary and suggest dozens of possible permutations that bear absolutely no resemblance to your original text. ¶

If you find that your document is in need of more work than it's worth, you'll appreciate another feature of the program called Clean Slate. The Clean Slate facility lets you wipe out your entire document and start again from scratch. Developers project that Clean Slate will be one of the most popular features of the program. ¶

We'll use this sample document to illustrate Word's selection, navigation, and editing facilities.

Begin by typing the first line of text shown in Figure 4-1. As you type, keep your eye on the blinking vertical insertion point marker. The marker will move one space to the right as you type each character, indicating your position in the document.

If you make an error as you are typing, just press the Backspace key to move the insertion point marker back one space at a time and erase the offending characters. Then you can resume typing as usual. If you don't notice an error until you're several words along, don't worry about it at this point. We'll show you how to correct those mistakes in a few pages.

When you reach the end of the first one-line paragraph shown in Figure 4-1 (this will become a headline when we begin formatting the text in Chapter 5), press the Return or Enter key to begin a new paragraph. Continue typing the sample text, pressing Return or Enter only when you need to begin a new paragraph. We have included ¶ symbols in our sample document to indicate where paragraph breaks are needed. You will not see these symbols in your Word document at first.

Don't worry if some of the text disappears from view as you type. As you'll see in a moment, you can use Word's scrolling features to bring that text back into view.

By the way, we used Word's default type formats—New York, 12-point, Plain—to create the sample document in Figure 4-1. If you are using another type style or size, your line breaks may look a bit different from ours. (More on fonts and formatting in Chapter 5.)

MARKING UP YOUR DOCUMENT

One of Word's strongest selling points is that you can see on the screen exactly what your text will look like when it's printed (with a few exceptions in the case of multicolumn text and formulas). You don't have to litter the online version of your document with hard-to-read codes every time you want to begin a new paragraph, change margin widths, or assign a special format to some element of your text. This online display is whimsically referred to as the WYSIWYG feature—what you see is what you get.

Without being aware of it, however, you do enter special coding information every time you create a new paragraph or make some formatting change to your document. Word does a lot of work behind the scenes as it implements your editing and formatting instructions. Some of this work is evident in a set of special markup characters that indicate where paragraph breaks, line breaks, blank spaces, optional hyphens, and so forth, occur in your document.

To see these symbols, choose Show ¶ from the Edit menu. Immediately, you'll see a series of ¶ and • markers in your document window, as shown in Figure 4-2 on the next page. These symbols do not appear when you print your document; they appear on the screen only for your information.

When you Choose Show ¶ from the Edit menu, Word will change that command to read Hide ¶. As you might have guessed, you can choose the Hide ¶ toggle to suppress the display of all special markup characters again. (Normal hyphens will remain in view at all times.) You can toggle between the Show ¶ and Hide ¶ commands at any time during a Word session by pressing ⌘-y.

FIGURE 4-2

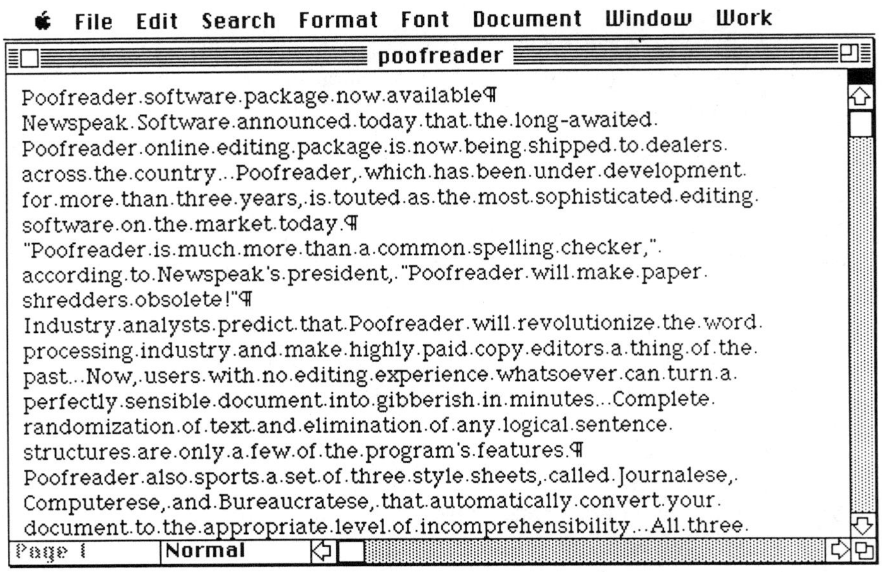

When you use the Show ¶ command, Word displays special markup characters on your screen.

We'll generally leave the marker symbol displays on in our sample screen displays throughout this book to help you interpret the content and design of our sample documents. We think you'll find these displays helpful as you begin editing and formatting text in Word for selecting blocks of text and seeing the effects of your changes in the document window.

As you already know, the ¶ symbol represents the end of a paragraph in your Word document. Among other things, it tells Word that you want to begin a new line of text. As you'll learn when we begin formatting text in Chapter 5, the paragraph marker also "stores" the formatting characteristics that you have assigned to your text.

The dots (·) that appear between the words and sentences in Figure 4-2 represent blank spaces. It's a little difficult at first to distinguish the blank space markers from period characters, but if you look closely, you'll see that the · markers sit slightly higher than the periods.

Table 4-1 lists some of the other markup characters that Word displays on your screen when you use the Show ¶ command.

In addition to these special markup characters, the Show ¶ command affects the display of graphics, dates, times, page numbers, and footnote entries in your Word documents. We'll discuss each of these topics as they arise through the course of the book. For now, let's explore some of the effects of the · and ¶ markers on your Word document.

TABLE 4-1

Symbol	Name	To enter type
¶	Paragaph mark	Return or Enter
↵	End-of-line mark	Shift-Return
. . .	Normal blank space	Spacebar
~ ~ ~	Nonbreaking space	⌘-Spacebar
➧	Tab mark	Tab
- - -	Normal hyphen	Hyphen (-) key
≂ ≂ ≂	Nonbreaking hyphen	⌘-~
‐ ‐ ‐	Optional hyphen	⌘-hyphen (-)

When you issue the Show ¶ command, Word displays markup characters on your screen.

DEFINING THE BASIC ELEMENTS OF A DOCUMENT

Now that we've entered some text and have seen how Word helps us to mark up our document, let's review some basic definitions. As you begin selecting, editing, and formatting text in your document, you'll need to understand how the Word program defines elements like characters, words, sentences, and paragraphs. While these concepts are not difficult to grasp, they can be quite different from the definitions you may have become accustomed to in writing or typing text. Many new users find themselves extremely frustrated as they begin editing and formatting documents because they've never been exposed to this new mindset.

Characters

The most basic element of text in your Word document is a character. A character can be any element that you enter onto the screen. It can be a blank space, letter, number, punctuation mark, or any other special symbol. Words, sentences, and paragraphs are nothing more than predefined combinations of characters. Simple enough so far?

Words

The Word program, of course, does not look at words in your document as nouns, verbs, adjectives, and so forth. To Word's way of thinking, a word is any group of alphabetic and/or numeric characters set apart by one or more blank spaces, or by a period, comma, hyphen, colon, semicolon, question mark, exclamation point, or quotation mark. Other characters that can serve as word separators include parentheses, braces, brackets, greater than or less than signs, the pound sign, the @ symbol, the dollar sign, the ampersand, left and right slash marks, and the asterisk.

Oddly enough, characters like <, ?, >, !, @, -, + and = mark the end of a word only when they are mixed with alpha or numeric characters—not when they are grouped together. For example, the character string =-+ would be interpreted as one word, but the character string *abc+=-def* would be considered as three words: *abc*, +=-, and *def*.

In short, all of the characters below serve as word delimiters, except when they are grouped together:

! @ # $ % & * ( ) - = + [ ] { } ; : " , . < > \ | / ?

Keep in mind that a blank space always marks the end of a word, even when it is used in conjunction with the characters above.

Unlike most punctuation marks, an apostrophe doesn't end a word since that character is commonly used in contractions and in creating the possessive form of a noun. Likewise, the ^, `, _, and ~ characters don't mark the end of words. Word treats these characters exactly as it does alphabetic characters and numbers.

With all these definitions in mind, how many words would you say make up the quote *"Poofreader will make paper shredders obsolete!"* at the end of the third paragraph in Figure 4-2? You might be tempted to answer six, but by Word's definition, there are actually eight distinct words in this sentence, as shown by the vertical lines below

|"|Poofreader·|will·|make·|paper·|shredders·|obsolete|!"|

The ¶ symbol at the end of the sentence also counts as a word, but Word does not consider the paragraph marker as part of the sentence.

As you know by now, Word always tries to keep words together in your document. That is, if a word is too long to fit at the end of a line, the WordWrap feature will push that word forward to the beginning of the next line. There are two exceptions to this. In keeping with our definitions above, if a word contains a hyphen, Word will treat it as two words. Thus, if a hyphenated word will not fit on one line, all of the characters up to and including the hyphen will appear at the end of the first line, while the remaining characters will drop down to the beginning of the next line. You can control these breaks to some extent with Word's special hyphenation features, which we'll cover in Chapters 5 and 6.

The only other time that WordWrap will not keep all the characters in a word together is when the word is simply too long to fit on a single line. This most likely will be a problem when you are working with very narrow columns. For example, in Figure 4-3 we typed the word *supercalifragilisticexpialidocius* into an empty Word document with a 1 inch column width (more on column widths in Chapters 6 and 8). As you can see, Word included as many characters in the first line as possible, allowing the remaining characters to flow to the next two lines.

FIGURE 4-3

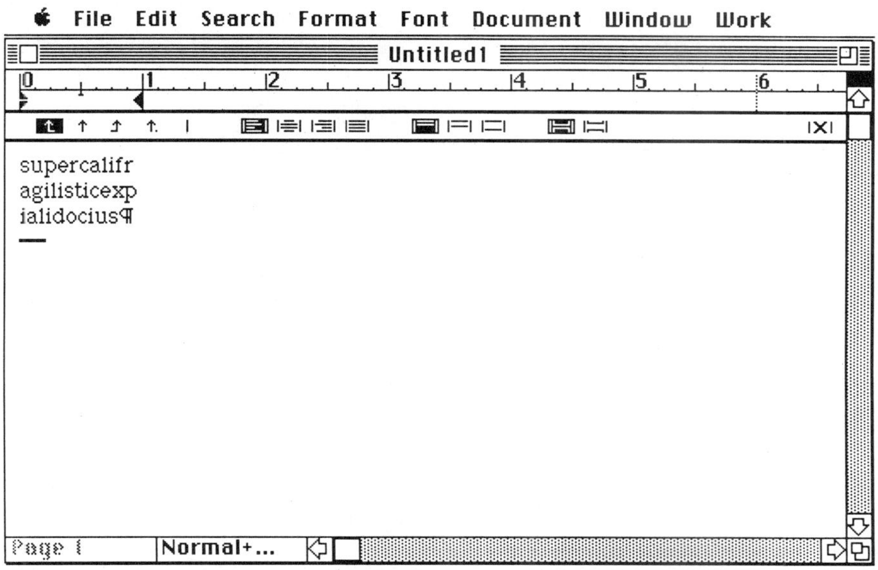

If all of the characters in a word will not fit on one line, Word will allow the characters to flow from one line to the next.

Sentences

A sentence is a group of characters and words set apart by a period, exclamation point, or question mark. A forced line break (which is represented by the ↵ symbol and entered into the document by pressing the Shift and Return keys) or a ¶ marker may also mark the end of a sentence. Of course, as you may have guessed from our discussion of words, any character that marks the end of a sentence also marks the end of the last word in that sentence.

For example, consider the sentence *Poofreader...is touted as the most sophisticated editing software on the market today.* in the second paragraph of our sample document. The period at the end of this series of characters marks the end of the sentence, as well as the end of the word *today*.

Paragraphs

Finally, a paragraph can be any combination of characters, words, and symbols, set apart by a ¶ symbol. Keep in mind that the ¶ symbol at the end of a paragraph is considered part of that paragraph. In fact, the ¶ symbol is treated as an individual word, which marks the end of the last word and the last sentence in a paragraph. And, as you might have guessed, the first sentence at the beginning of a paragraph is delimited by the ¶ symbol at the end of the previous paragraph. Similarly, the first word in a paragraph is delimited by the ¶ symbol from above.

For example, in the sample document shown in Figure 4-2, the first line of the document ends with a ¶ symbol which marks the end of the first sentence, as well as the first paragraph. It also marks the end of the word *available* and the beginning of the first word and sentence in the next paragraph, *Newspeak*.

These definitions may seem a bit esoteric at this point, but they will become important to you when you begin selecting text blocks and editing your document. As you will learn in Chapter 6, a thorough understanding of these definitions is also critical to using Word's Find... and Change... commands effectively.

SELECTING TEXT

Now that you know how Word defines the basic elements of your document, you can learn how to "get hold" of these elements so that you can edit and format them. Before you can edit or format any of the text you have created in Word, you must select the text you want to work with.

When you select text in Word, that block of characters will appear in reverse video—that is, you'll see white type on a black background rather than the normal black on white. Through the course of this book, you'll see this reverse-video text referred to as highlighted or selected text.

Selecting Text with the Mouse

If you've used previous versions of Word, or if you've used other word processing software on the Macintosh, you know that most of your text selection and navigation is done with the mouse. However, Microsoft has also added several very nice keyboard shortcuts to help you select text and move around your document quickly. Let's begin with the standard mouse selection techniques, then we'll explore Word's many keyboard selection techniques.

Click and drag

The most basic mouse selection technique is the click and drag method. For example, suppose you want to select the words *common spelling checker* in the third paragraph. Begin by clicking just to the left of the letter *c* in the word *common*. Now, without releasing the mouse button, drag to the right until the desired characters are highlighted, as shown in Figure 4-4.

You can use this dragging technique to select any size block of text, from a single character to an entire document.

The click/Shift-click method

Of course, if you need to select a large block of text, you might find it tiresome to drag through line after line of text. Another technique for selecting text is the click/Shift-click method. For example, suppose you want to highlight all of the text beginning with the words *Now, users with no editing experience* and ending with *program's features*. Begin by clicking just to the left of the word *Now*, then press the Shift key and click just to the right of the period that follows the word *features*. Figure 4-5 shows the results.

FIGURE 4-4

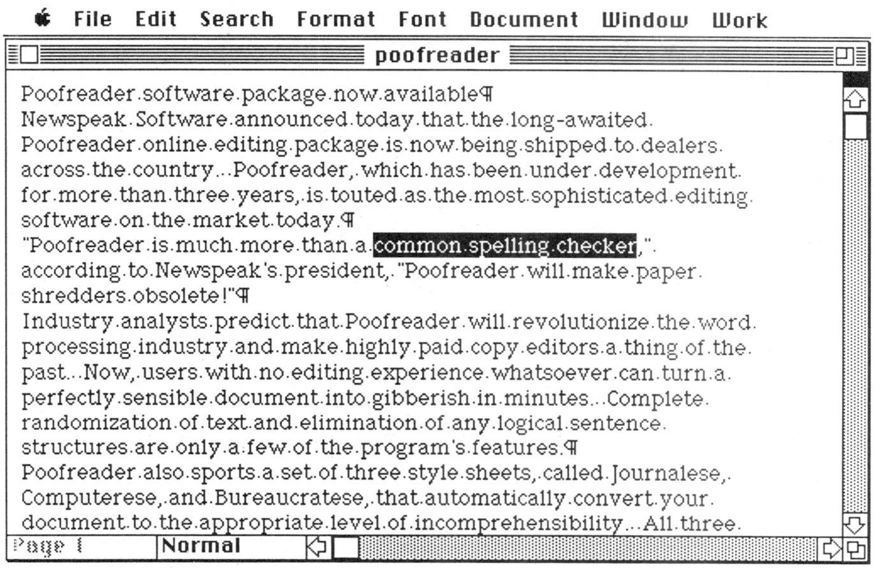

Use the click and drag method to select a block of text.

FIGURE 4-5

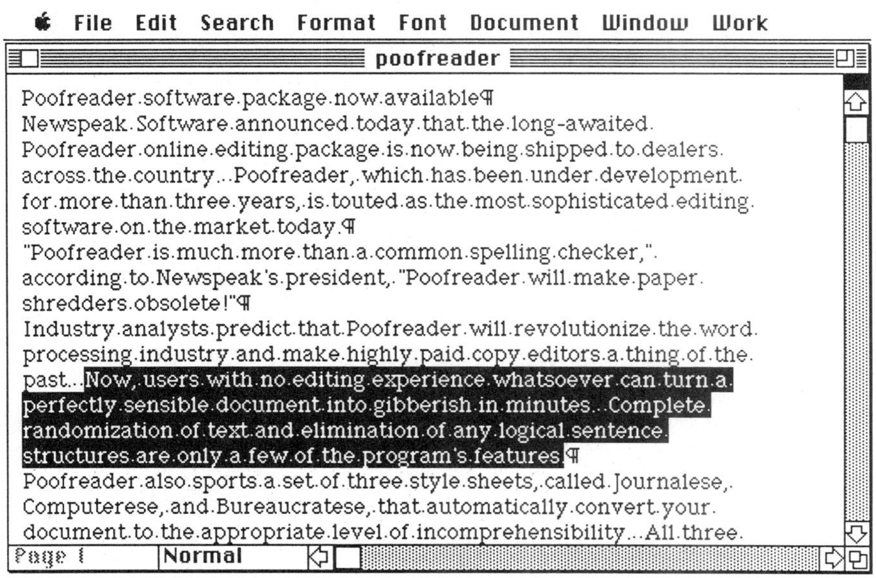

You can select any size block of text by clicking at the beginning of the block, then pressing the Shift key and clicking at the end of the block.

Double-clicking

You can select an entire word by double-clicking anywhere on that word. For example, to select the word *software* in the first line of our sample document, just place the I-beam pointer over that word and double-click. As you can see in Figure 4-6, Word will highlight the entire word, as well as any blank spaces that appear to the right of the word.

FIGURE 4-6

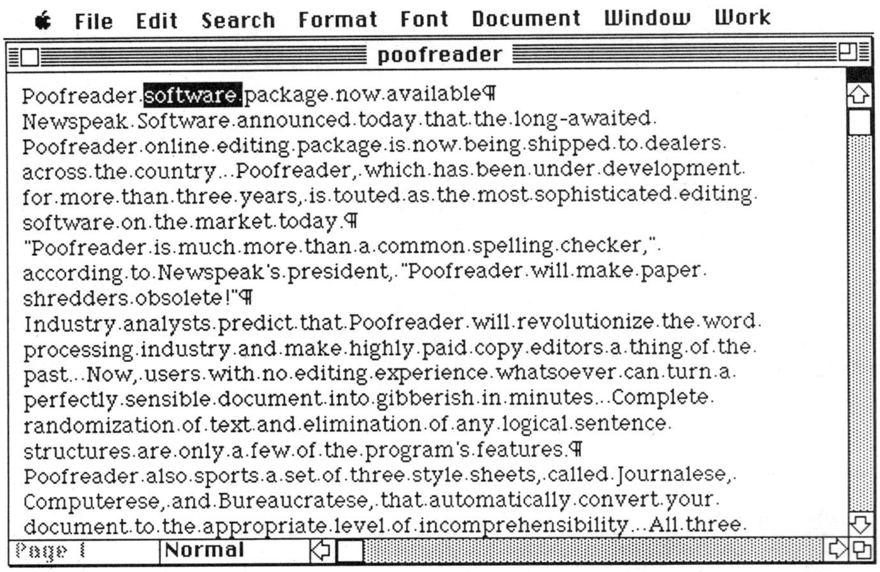

To select an entire word, double-click anywhere on that word.

If you double-click on a word that is followed by a period, comma, or some other demarcation character, Word will not highlight the demarcation character or blank spaces after that word. For example, if you double-click on the word *country* in the fourth line of our sample document, Word will highlight only the characters *country*, not the period or two blank spaces that appear after that word. Instead, those trailing characters will be treated as a separate word. In fact, if you double-click just to the right of the word *country*, Word will highlight the period and blank spaces that mark the end of that word and sentence.

You can use a similar technique to select an entire sentence in Word. Just press the ⌘ key and click anywhere on the sentence that you want to select. Word will highlight the entire sentence, as well as any trailing blank characters that appear after the sentence. If a sentence happens to fall at the end of a paragraph, Word will not highlight the ¶ character. Like the period and blank spaces in word selection, the ¶ symbol is treated separately when you are selecting sentences.

The selection bar

To select an entire line or paragraph in Word, use the invisible selection bar on the left side of your document window. Though you cannot see this selection bar, you will know you are there when your I-beam pointer takes on the right arrow shape.

To select an entire line of text, just move the pointer to the left of the screen until it takes on the right arrow shape, then point to the line of text you want to select and click. For example, if we click in the selection bar to the left of the line that begins *across the country* in the first paragraph in our sample document, our screen will look like the one in Figure 4-7.

FIGURE 4-7

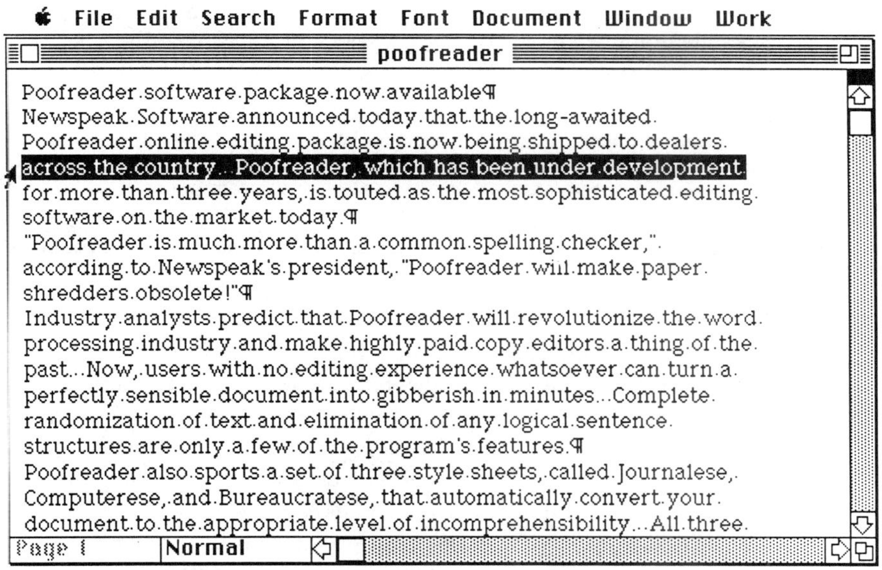

To select an entire line, click next to that line in the selection bar.

To select an entire paragraph, move your pointer to the selection bar and double-click anywhere to the left of the paragraph. Figure 4-8 on the next page shows the Word screen after we selected the entire second paragraph of the document. As you can see, the ¶ marker at the end of the paragraph is also highlighted. Notice the right arrow shape of the pointer as it lies in the selection bar in Figures 4-7 and 4-8.

Finally, to select the entire Word document, move the pointer to the selection bar and press the ⌘ key as you click. All of your text will appear highlighted in reverse video to indicate your selection. As you will learn in Chapter 6, this technique is particularly helpful when you need to make a global change to your document—changing the font or indentions for all of your text, for example.

FIGURE 4-8

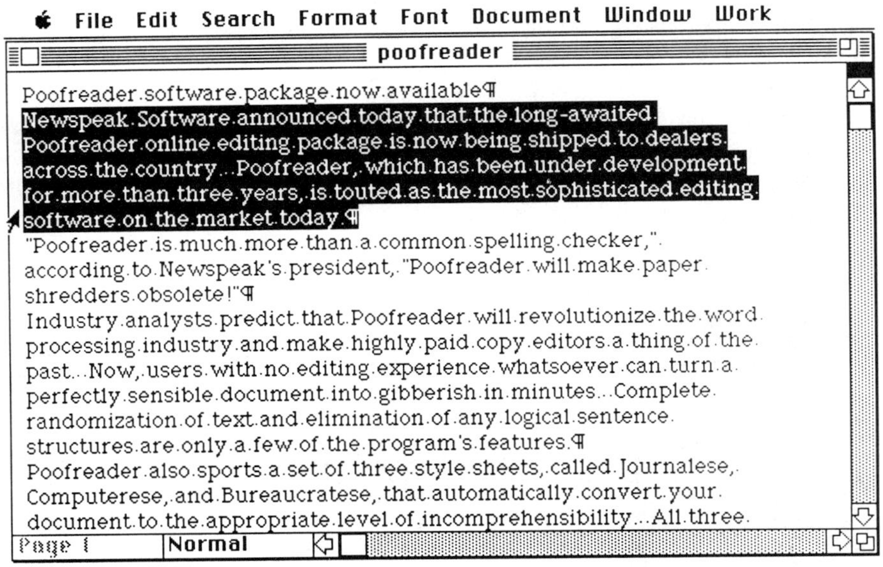

Double-click on the invisible selection bar to select a paragraph of text.

Making block selections

Another selection technique that you'll find particularly convenient when you're working with tabular data is the block selection. To make a block selection, press the Option key, then drag through the desired characters.

For example, in our sample document, if we press the Option key, click to the left of the word *package* in the first line of the document, then drag down and to the right, our selection will look like the one in Figure 4-9.

As you can see, we have selected a strip of text from the middle of the document, with no regard for word, sentence, or paragraph breaks. In fact, some of the characters in our selection are only partially highlighted. When you use the Option key to make a block selection, Word considers any character that is more than half highlighted to be part of the selection.

We'll look at this technique in more detail in Chapters 5 and 6 when we talk about formatting and editing tables.

FIGURE 4-9

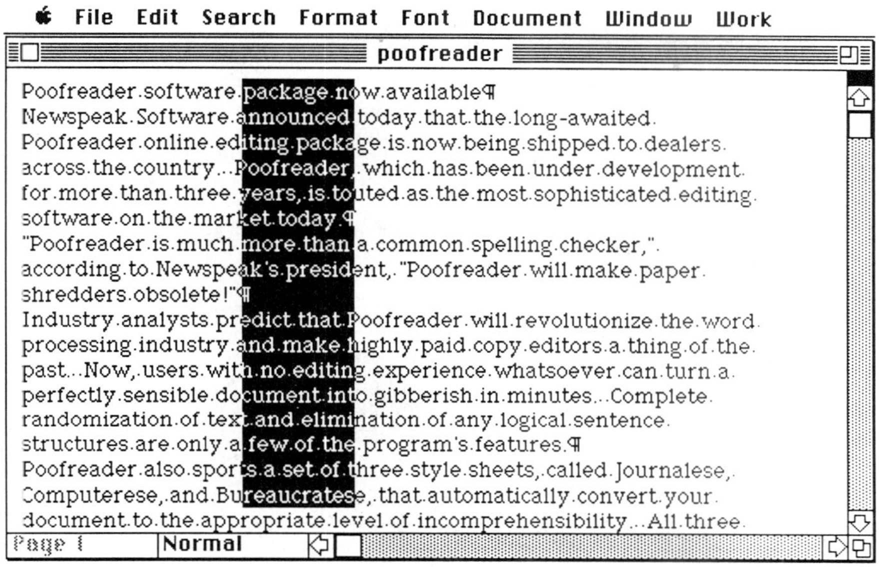

To make a block selection, press the Option key, then drag through the desired text.

Anchoring Your Selection

When you select text in Word, your insertion point marker serves as the pivot or anchor point for one end of the selection. Whether you drag or click above, below, or to the left or right of the insertion point marker, it always represents one edge of your selection. For example, if you click to the left of the word *much* in line 7 of our sample document, then drag down and to the right of the comma after the word *president*, your screen will look like the one in Figure 4-10 on the following page. However, if you now drag up and to the left of the word *the* in the previous line without releasing the mouse button, your screen will look like the one in Figure 4-11. As you can see, our initial anchor point now becomes the end-point of our selection. You can continue to change the size and shape of your selection by dragging around this anchor point, as long as you don't release the mouse button.

The easiest way to see the effect of the pivot point is to click in the middle of a line of text in your document and move your mouse in a broad circular motion. As you drag up, right, down, and left, the size and shape of your highlighted selection will change, but the insertion point will always mark one end of your selection.

FIGURE 4-10

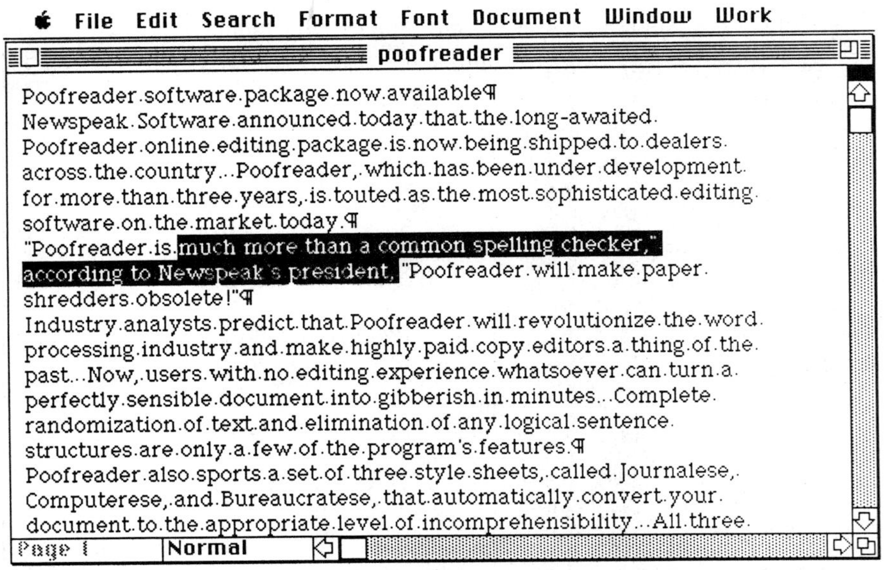

When you drag down or to the right, your insertion point marks the start of your selection.

FIGURE 4-11

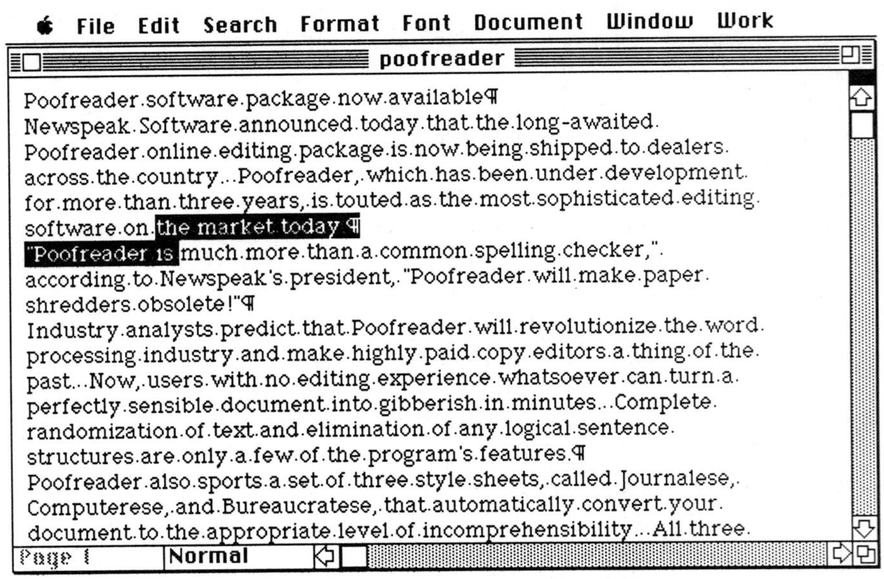

When you drag up or to the left, your insertion point marks the end of your selection.

Selection Modes

Interestingly, when you use one of the mouse selection techniques described above, Word will "remember" that technique as you drag through additional text. For example, suppose you have double-clicked on a word to select it. In effect, you have entered the "word selection mode." If you drag to the right or left, Word will highlight the next word that your pointer touches. Even if you drag up or down through several lines, Word will continue to highlight entire words.

Similarly, if you press the ⌘ key and double-click on a sentence to select it, you can select adjacent sentences by dragging up, down, left, or right. The selection mode that you started with will remain in effect until you release the mouse button.

Mouseless Selection Techniques

As we mentioned earlier, you can select an entire Word document by pressing the ⌘ key and clicking in the selection bar. You can achieve the same effect without using your mouse by pressing Option-⌘-m.

If you use a Mac Plus with a numeric keypad, another special selection feature lets you extend your selection from the current insertion point to a specified character in your document. For example, suppose you want to select all of the text beginning with the phrase *Poofreader, which has been under development* through the period that ends the sentence. Just click in front of the character *P* in *Poofreader*, then press the minus key (-) on the numeric keypad. You'll see the prompt *Extend to* in the status box at the bottom-left of your screen. Just type the character to which you want to extend your selection—in this case, you'll press the period key on your standard keyboard (not the decimal point on the numeric keypad). Word will highlight everything between the insertion point marker and the next occurrence of that character, as shown in Figure 4-12 on the next page.

When you are using the minus key to extend your selection from the insertion point to a specified character, Word will continue to display the *Extend to* prompt at the bottom of your screen until you issue a command or click anywhere on your screen. Thus, after typing the first character to which you want to extend your selection, you can type another character if you wish to extend your selection beyond the current highlighted text to the next occurrence of a given character. For example, in the sample screen shown in Figure 4-12, if we type the character *g*, Word will extend our selection from the original insertion point—to the left of the word *Poofreader*—through the end of the word *spelling* in the seventh line.

FIGURE 4-12

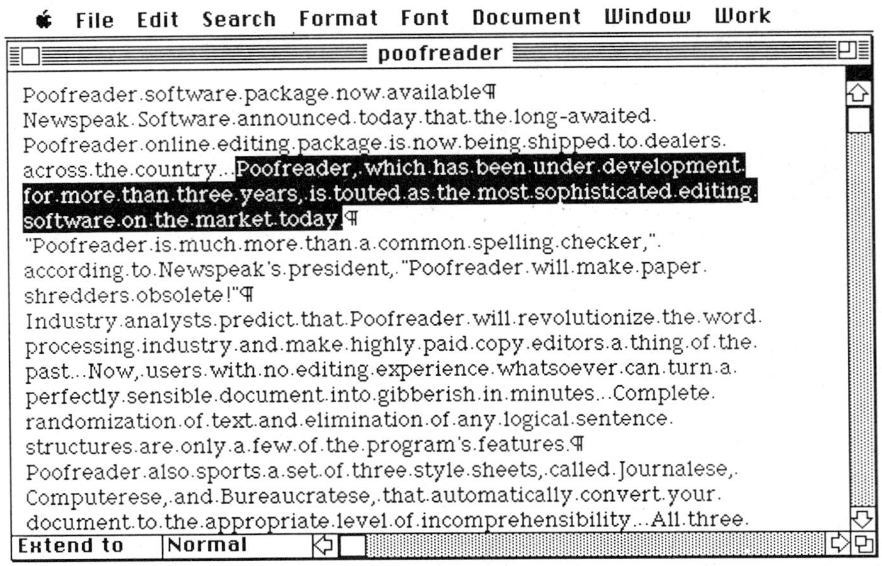

You can also select a block of text by clicking at the beginning of the block, pressing the minus key on the numeric keypad, and typing the character to which you want to extend your selection.

NAVIGATION

As we hinted earlier, when you were typing the sample text in Figure 4-1, the text at the beginning of your document becomes lost from view after you fill up the screen. Obviously, if you have created a document that is more than 18 or 20 lines long, you won't be able to see all of that document on the small Macintosh screen. The amount that you can view at one time depends, of course, on the size of the window and the size of the type that you are using.

Word offers several techniques for navigation through your document, some of which require the use of your mouse and some of which can be performed directly from the keyboard. We'll start with the standard mouse techniques, then we'll show you some keyboard navigational devices.

Navigating with the Mouse

The primary means of viewing all of the text in your document is a technique called scrolling. As you learned in Chapter 2, the gray bars to the right and at the bottom of your document windows are called scroll bars. (Recall that the horizontal scroll bar at the bottom of each window shows up only when you've activated the Full Menu setting.) The white boxes within the scroll bars are called scroll boxes, and the white arrows at either end of each scroll bar are called scroll arrows.

To move through your document a line at a time (without necessarily selecting any text), you can use the scroll arrows that appear above and below the vertical scroll bar.

For example, in the previous screen samples, the first 18 lines of our document are in view. If we click on the scroll arrow below the vertical scroll bar, we'll see lines 2 through 19. Line 1 will move out of view, as shown in Figure 4-13.

FIGURE 4-13

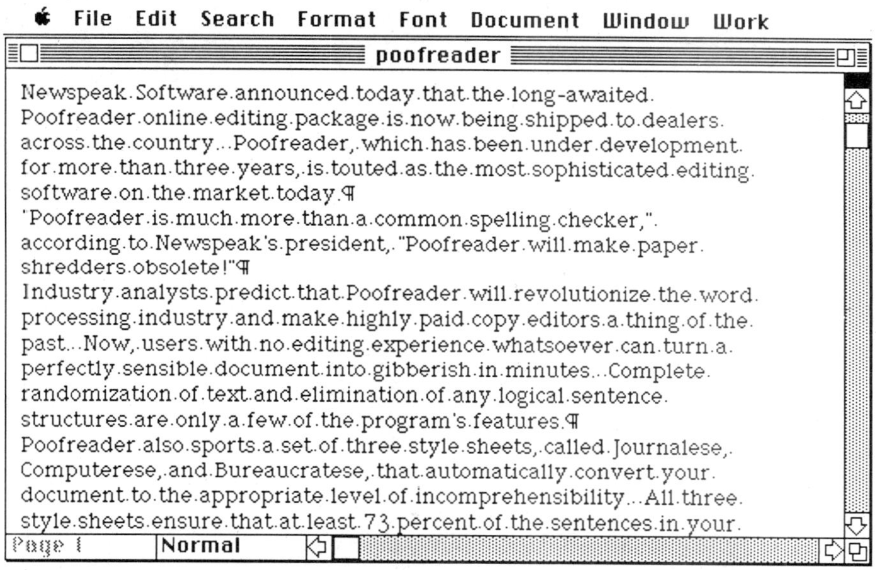

Use the scroll arrows at either end of the vertical scroll bar to move through your document one line at a time.

Moving through your document one line at a time is satisfactory for fine-tuning your view through the document window, but you'd soon find this method tedious in a long document. To move through your document a full screen at a time, click in the gray area of the scroll bar above or below the scroll box. Word will scroll the next screenful into view.

For example, if we click below the scroll box in the vertical scroll bar while lines 1 through 18 of our sample document are in view, our screen will look like the one in Figure 4-14 on the next page. As you can see, lines 17 through 31 are now in view. Notice that two lines from the bottom of the previous screen remain in view at the top of the second screen to help you get your bearings.

Of course, the distance that you scroll depends on the size of the document window. For example, if we reduce our document to half-screen size, as shown in Figure 4-15, only the first eight lines of our document will be in view. If we now click in the gray area of the scroll bar, Word will bring lines 7 through 14 into view. In Figure 4-16 on page 79, the last two lines from the bottom of the previous screen now appear at the top of the document window.

FIGURE 4-14

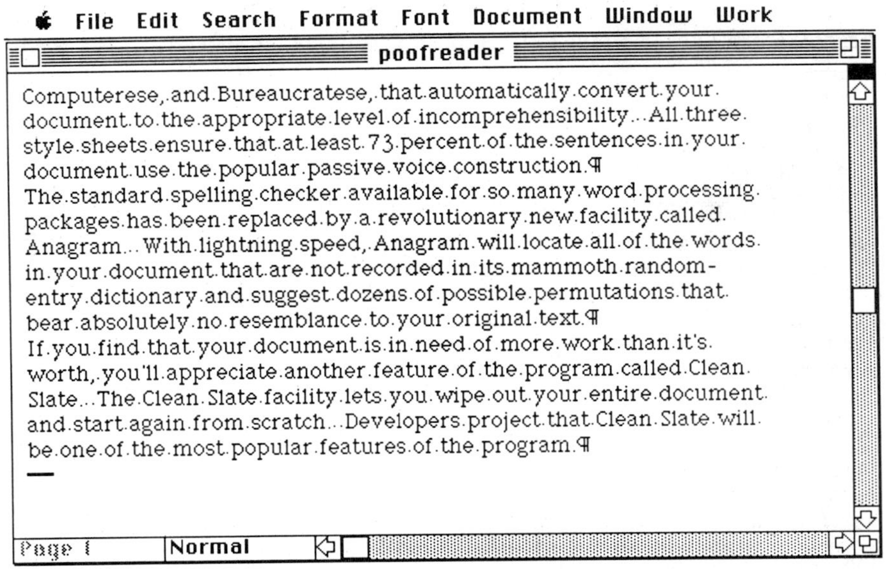

To move a new screenful of data into view, click in the gray area of the scroll bar.

FIGURE 4-15

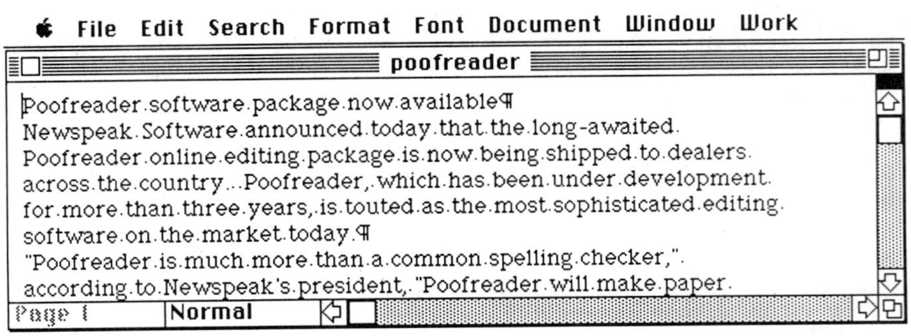

We have reduced our document window to half-sceen size to show the effects of window size on scrolling.

FIGURE 4-16

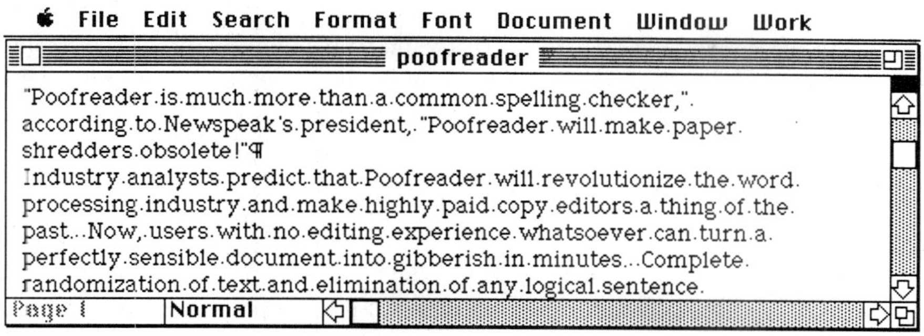

Word brings lines 7 through 14 into view when we click in the gray area of the scroll bar.

You can also drag the white scroll box to the desired position in the scroll bar to quickly scroll large distances through your document. The distance you travel by dragging the white scroll box depends on the length of your document. The scroll bar is relative to the length of your document. Thus, in a very short document like the one that holds our sample Poofreader text, dragging the scroll box to the middle of the scroll bar will advance you to the third or fourth paragraph of the document. However, if you drag to the middle of the vertical scroll bar in a 50-page document, you'd be scrolling through 25 pages of text. As you might have guessed, if you drag the scroll box to the top of the scroll bar, you'll see the first screen of your document; if you drag the scroll box to the bottom of the scroll bar, you'll see the last screenful of information.

Though it's difficult to fine-tune your navigation by dragging the scroll box, you'll soon get a feel for the relative distances you are traveling. Unlike previous versions of the program, Word 3 displays the page number in the status box at the bottom-left corner of your screen. You can watch the status message change as you drag the scroll box and zero in on the page you want to view. Generally, in a long document, you'll want to drag the scroll box to the approximate location that you want to view, then click in the scroll bar or on the scroll arrows to fine-tune your position.

Using the horizontal scroll bar

If you are working with a document that is too wide to be displayed on one screen—for example, if you are printing a document with wide margins or if you are viewing your text through a partial-screen window—you can use the scroll arrows at either end of the horizontal scroll bar to move right and left through your document. As you might guess, horizontal scrolling is much like vertical scrolling. You use the scroll arrows to move short distances through your document; you click in the scroll bar to move a new screenful of information into view; and you drag the scroll box to reposition the window manually.

Starting with the scroll arrows, let's look at a few examples. We have narrowed our sample document window in Figure 4-17 so that only the first four inches of the document are visible. To see the remaining text on the right side of the document, we can click on the right scroll arrow. As you can see in Figure 4-18, Word scrolls the document window about a half inch to the right. If we now click on the left scroll arrow, our screen will look like the one in Figure 4-17 again.

FIGURE 4-17

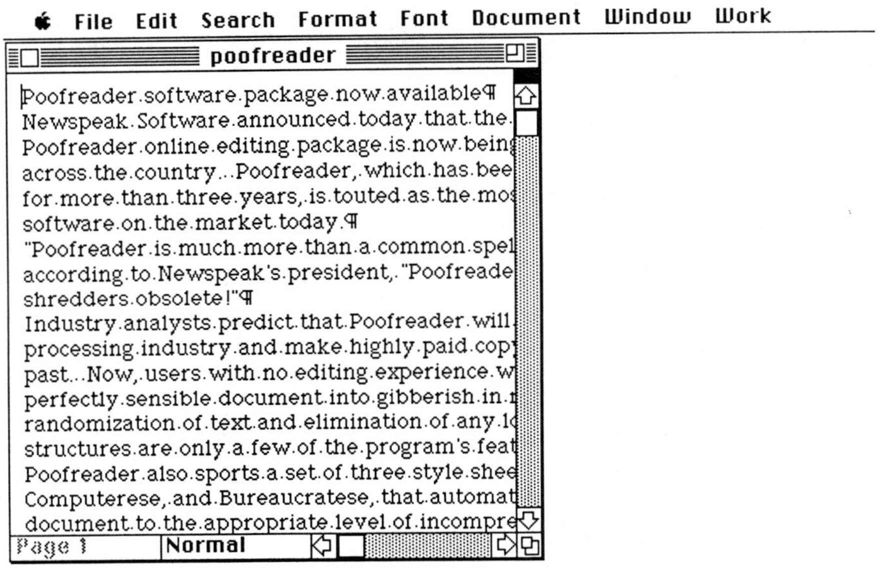

We have narrowed our document window to illustrate Word's horizontal scrolling features.

When you click in the gray area of the scroll bar to the left or right of the scroll box, Word will move the document window a full screen to the left or right. Again, the distance that you travel depends on the size of the document window. For example, in Figure 4-17, if you click to the right of the scroll box, Word will bring the next four inches of the document into view, as shown in Figure 4-19. If you now click to the left of the scroll box, your screen will again look like the one in Figure 4-17.

FIGURE 4-18

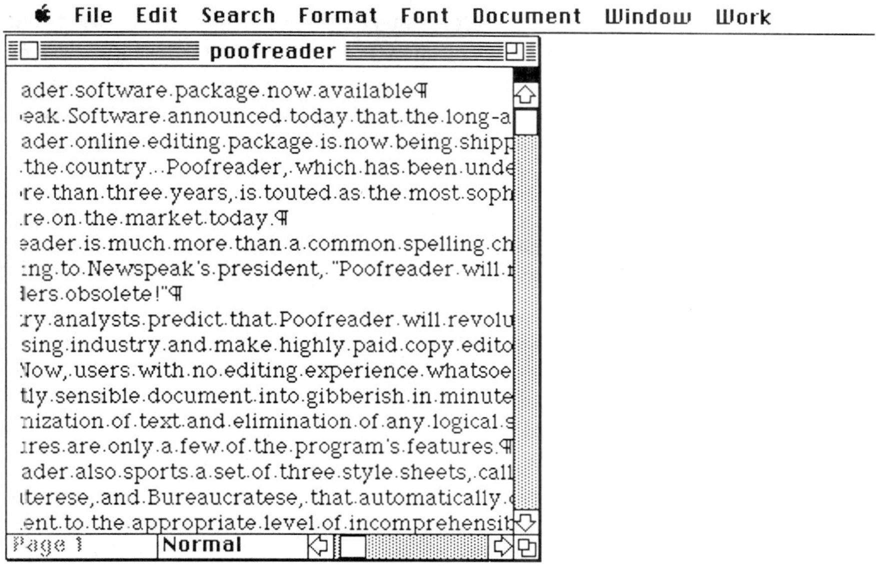

When you click on a scroll arrow, the next half inch of the document scrolls into view.

FIGURE 4-19

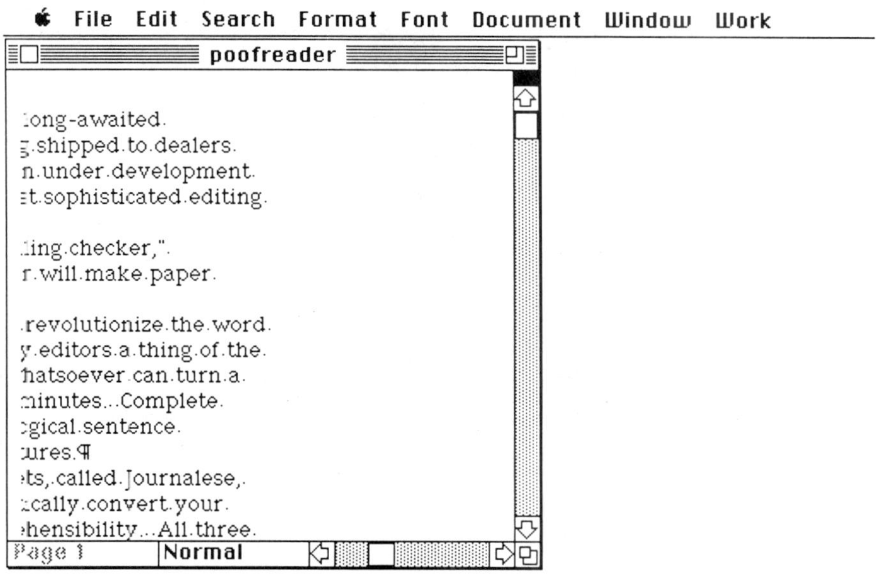

Click in the gray area of the scroll bar to bring a new screenful of information into view.

Unlike the vertical scroll bar, the distance that you travel when you drag the white scroll box in the horizontal scroll bar is constant. Although only about 6 $^{3}/_{4}$ inches of your document are visible in a full-screen window, Word actually allows you to create columns as wide as 21 $^{3}/_{4}$ inches. Thus, if you drag the scroll box to the extreme right side of the scroll bar, you'll travel 21 $^{3}/_{4}$ inches; if you drag the scroll box to the middle of the horizontal scoll bar, you'll travel a little over ten inches.

Scrolling as you select text

Often you'll want to select a block of text that is too large to display on one screen. In this event, you'll need to combine the selection technique described earlier in this chapter with the navigational techniques we've just discussed.

For example, suppose lines 1 through 18 of your document are in view and you want to select the block of text that begins with *Poofreader also sports* and ends with *most popular features of the program.* Though the last part of this text block is not currently visible on the screen, you can select it by clicking to the left of the word *Poofreader* in line 17 and dragging downward. As you drag the pointer past the horizontal scroll bar at the bottom of the screen, the rest of your text will scroll into view a line at a time. The text that was displayed at the top of the window will scroll out of view, as shown in Figure 4-20.

FIGURE 4-20

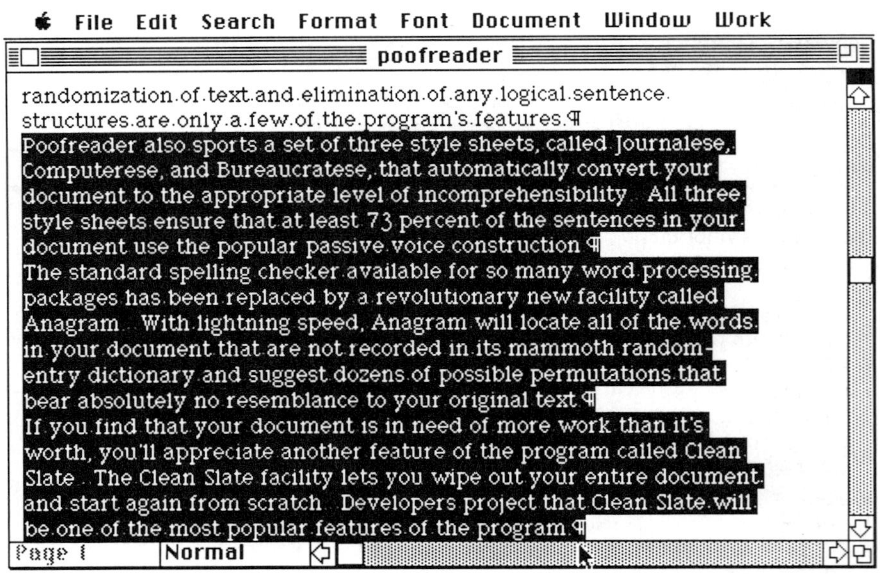

If you drag past the bottom of the document window, Word will scroll succeeding lines of text into view.

Similarly, if you drag toward the top of the screen, Word will scroll the document window upward as your mouse pointer comes in contact with the title bar at the top of the document window. The text will be highlighted automatically as you drag.

Unfortunately, you can't drag to the left or right edge of the document window to scroll horizontally as you select text. Though Word will select text that is not in view on the screen, it will not scroll the document window so that you can see your selection. You'll have to go on blind faith, or use the scroll bar, once you've made your selection to ensure that you have highlighted all of the needed text.

However, you can use the scroll bars in conjunction with the click/Shift-click technique described on page 70 to see all of the text you are selecting. Just click at the beginning of your selection, scroll to the end of the block you want to highlight, then press the Shift key and click at the end of the block.

Mouseless Navigational Techniques

In addition to the horizontal and vertical scroll bars, you can use the keyboard to move through your Word text. Keep in mind that when you use the scroll bars to move through your document, your insertion point does not move with you. You must still click in the text area of your screen to move your insertion point marker.

When you use most of the keyboard techniques described below, however, your insertion point marker will travel with you as you navigate through your document window.

The Go To... command

In addition to the scroll bars, you can use the Go To... command on Word's Search menu to go to the top of a specific page in your document. To access the Go To dialog box quickly, just press ⌘-g.

You'll see a dialog box like the one in Figure 4-21. Notice that the value in the Page Number edit bar is already highlighted. All you need to do is type the number of the page that you want to view in the Page Number edit bar and click OK or press Return or Enter. Word will display the first line of the specified page at the top of your document window and place the insertion point marker at the beginning of that line.

The page numbers, which appear at the bottom-left corner of your screen, relate to the way the document will appear when it is printed. (More on page numbering in Chapter 7.)

FIGURE 4-21

Use the Go To... command to move quickly to a specified page in your document.

Moving the insertion point back to its previous location

Often when you are editing a document, you'll find yourself skipping from one spot to another to move text or to make minor changes. Word 3 offers a new navigational feature to help streamline this process: You can quickly return to your last insertion point by pressing Option-⌘-z. If you have a numeric keypad, you can save keystrokes by pressing the 0 (zero) key to move back to your previous cursor location.

This technique is also convenient for toggling between two remote areas of your document when you need to compare two sets of text. For example, suppose you have just finished editing a table that appears on the first page of your document, then you move to the end of your document to transfer some of the data from that table into your text. You need to move back to the table to pick up some more information. Just press Option-⌘-z or 0 on the numeric keypad to move between the two areas quickly.

Word can remember as many as three insertion point locations in addition to your current location. For example, suppose you have made editing changes in the four locations marked in the sample screen in Figure 4-22. After making your change at point 4, if you press Option-⌘-z or 0 on the numeric keypad, Word will move you back to point 3. Pressing Option-⌘-z or 0 again will take you to point 2, then to point 1. If you press Option-⌘-z or 0 a fourth time, Word will cycle back to point 4 again.

FIGURE 4-22

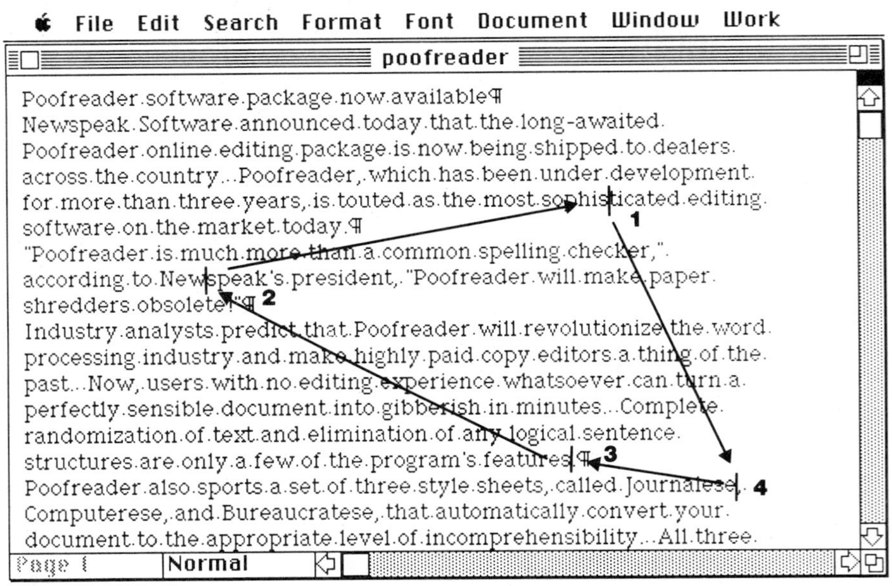

Word will remember your last three insertion point locations.

Using the arrow keys

If you have the expanded Mac Plus keyboard, you'll find that the ⬆, ⬇, ⬅, and ➡ arrow keys are tremendously convenient for moving short distances in your document. As you might expect, the ⬆ and ⬇ keys let you move the insertion point marker up or down one line at a time. Generally, when you use the ⬆ and ⬇ keys, your insertion point marker will move in a straight line. However, because line lengths vary and characters occupy different amounts of space, you may notice that your insertion point marker jumps around a bit as you press the ⬆ and ⬇ keys.

For example, Figure 4-23 shows the path of the insertion point marker as we press the ⬇ key to move through our sample document. As you can see, the marker moves slightly to the right and left as we travel downwards through the document, staying in line as much as possible with our original insertion point between the characters *n* and *o* in line 1. Also, notice that the insertion point jumps to the left when we reach line 9 since that line does not extend as far as our insertion point. When we reach line 10, however, the marker moves back toward the middle of the screen.

FIGURE 4-23

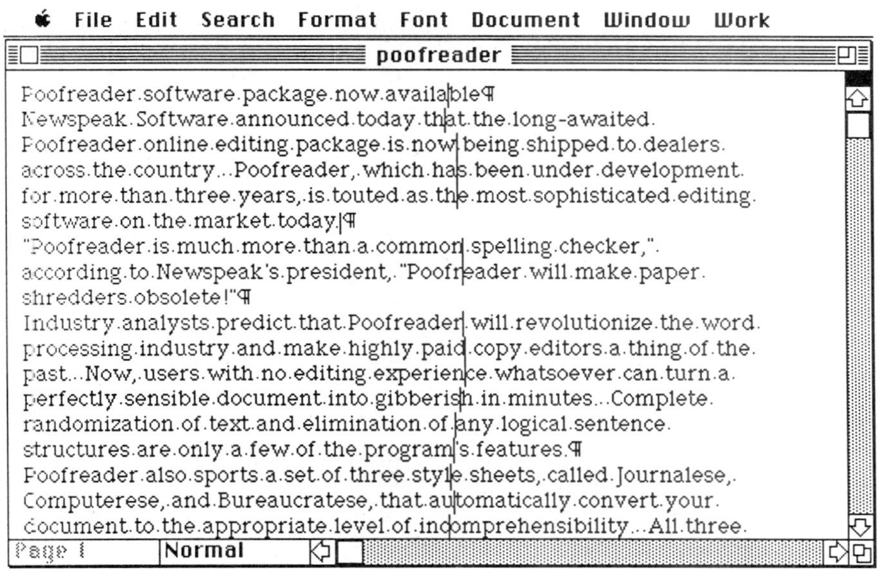

When you press the ⬆ and ⬇ keys, the insertion point marker will follow a fairly straight path through your document.

If you press the ⬆ key or the ⬇ key while the insertion point marker is at the top or bottom of the document window, Word will scroll additional text into view automatically.

When you press the ← and → arrow keys, the insertion point marker moves one space to the left or right. When you press ← at the beginning of a line, the insertion point marker will move to the end of the previous line. Similarly, when you press → at the end of a line, the marker jumps to the beginning of the next line.

For example, suppose your insertion point marker is between the characters *o* and *r* of the word *for* in line 5 of our sample document. If you press the ← key twice, the insertion point marker will appear at the very beginning of the line, just to the left of the character *f*. If you press ← again, the insertion point marker will jump to the end of the previous line, just to the right of the word *development*. (Oddly enough, Word will skip the blank space at the end of the fourth line.)

Particularly when you are working with very small font sizes or text that is formatted in italics, it can be difficult to click in the exact location you need. The ← and → keys are very convenient for fine-tuning your selection once you've clicked in the general area you want to work in.

To move through your document a little more quickly, you can press the ⌘ key as you press the ↑, ↓, ←, and → keys. If your insertion point marker is currently in the middle of a paragraph, the ⌘-↑ combination lets you jump to the beginning of that paragraph. If your insertion point marker is already at the beginning of a paragraph, ⌘-↑ takes you to the beginning of the previous paragraph. Similarly, the ⌘-↓ combination takes you to the beginning of the next paragraph.

For example, suppose your insertion point marker is currently in the middle of the word *common* in the third paragraph of our sample document. If you press ⌘-↑, the insertion point will move to the left of the " character at the beginning of the paragraph. Pressing ⌘-↑ again will land you just to the left of the character *N* at the beginning of the second paragraph. If you press ⌘-↓ while the insertion point marker is in the middle of the word *common* in paragraph 3, you'll land just to the left of the character *I* at the beginning of the fourth paragraph.

You can also jump from one word to the next by pressing ⌘ as you press the ← and→ keys. The ⌘-← key combination lets you move one word to the left while the ⌘-→ key combination lets you move one word to the right. In either case, the insertion point marker will land just to the left of the next word, between the first character in that word and any preceding blank spaces or demarcation characters.

For example, suppose your insertion point marker is currently just to the left of the word *today* in the second line of our sample document. If you press ⌘-←, your insertion point will appear just to the left of the word *announced*. Similarly, if you press ⌘-→ while the insertion point marker is just to the left of the word *today* in line 2, your insertion point marker will move just to the left of the word *that*.

If your insertion point marker is in the middle of a word when you press ⌘-←, Word will jump to the beginning of that word. If you press ⌘-→ while the insertion point marker is in the middle of a word, Word will move to the beginning of the next word to the right. Similarly, if you click just to the right of a word (between the last letter of the word and any trailing blank spaces) before pressing ⌘-→, Word will move past any blank spaces or other demarcation characters to the beginning of the next word.

Navigating with the numeric keypad

If you have a numeric keypad, you can simulate the action of the ↑, ↓, ←, and → arrow keys with the 8, 2, 4, and 6 keys. You'll find these navigational keys easier to remember if you visualize the 8, 2, 4, and 6 keys as a diamond shape, radiating from the 5 key at the center of the keypad.

You can also use the ⌘ key in conjunction with the 8, 2, 4, and 6 keys on your keypad to move up and down a paragraph at a time and left and right a word at a time. The highlighted keys in Figure 4-24 work exactly like the arrow keys described above.

FIGURE 4-24

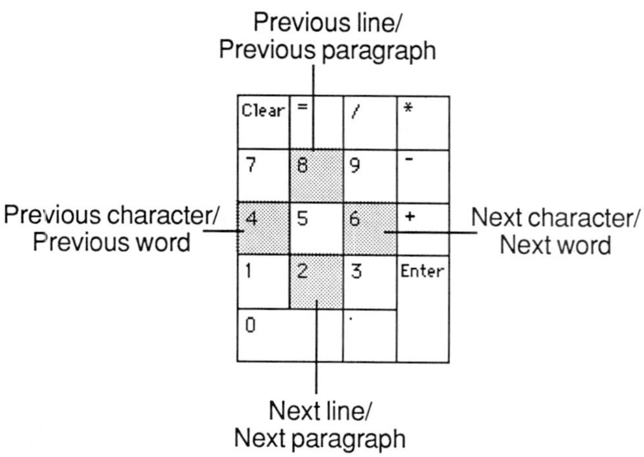

The 8, 2, 4, and 6 keys let you move the insertion point marker up, down, left, and right.

In addition to the 8, 2, 4, and 6 keys, you can use the 7, 9, 1, 3, and 5 keys on your numeric keypad to move through your Word document.

Press the 7 key on your numeric keypad to move to the beginning of the current line, and the 1 key to move to the end of the current line. To continue with our sample document, if the insertion point marker is currently in the middle of the word *package* in line 3 when you press the 7 key, Word will move just to the left of the letter *P* at the beginning of that line. If you press 1 on the numeric keypad, Word will move to the right of the letter *s* at the end of that line. (Oddly, Word does not move to the right of the blank space at the end of the line as you might expect. Thus, if you want to insert a new word at this point, you'll need to press the Spacebar before you begin typing new text.)

If your insertion point marker is already at the beginning of a line when you press the 7 key, Word will move up to the beginning of the previous line. As you might have guessed, if the insertion point marker is already at the end of a line when you press 1, Word will move to the end of the next line.

You can also use the ⌘ key in conjunction with the 1 and 7 keys to move through your document a sentence at a time. Press ⌘-1 to move forward to the beginning of the next sentence and ⌘-7 to move back to the beginning of the previous sentence. If your insertion point marker is in the middle of a sentence when you press ⌘-7, Word will move to the beginning of that sentence. However, if your insertion point marker is already at the beginning of a sentence when you press ⌘-7, Word will skip that sentence and move to the beginning of the previous sentence.

For example, if your insertion point marker is in the middle of the word *touted* in line 5 of our sample document and you press the ⌘-7 key combination, the insertion point marker will appear just in front of the letter *P* at the beginning of that sentence. If you press ⌘-7 again at this point, your insertion point marker will appear just to the left of the letter *N* in the sentence that begins *Newspeak Software announced....*

Similarly, if your insertion point marker is in the middle of the word *online* in line 3 of our sample document and you press ⌘-1, the insertion point marker will appear just in front of the letter *P* at the beginning of the next sentence, which begins with the word *Poofreader*. If you press ⌘-1 again at this point, your insertion point marker will appear just to the left of the ¶ character at the end of the paragraph. If you press ⌘-1 a third time, you'll land to the left of the " character at the beginning of the next paragraph.

The 9 and 3 keys let you move through your document a screen at a time, just as if you had clicked in the vertical scroll bar on the right side of your screen. To move up one screen, press 9 on the keypad; to move down one screen, press 3. One difference between using the numeric keypad rather than the vertical scroll bar is that your insertion point marker moves when you use the keypad to move through your document. When you press the 9 key, your insertion point marker will appear at the top-left corner of the screen. When you press the 3 key, your insertion point marker will appear at the bottom right corner of the screen.

You can also use the ⌘ key in conjunction with the 9 and 3 keys to move the insertion point marker to the beginning or end of your document. Regardless of your current location, ⌘-9 will place the insertion point marker at the very first character space in your document, and ⌘-3 will place the insertion point marker at the very last character space in your document.

Finally, to move the insertion point marker to the top-left corner of your Word screen, press ⌘-5. Figure 4-25 summerizes the finctions of the 7, 9, 1, 3, and 5 keys.

FIGURE 4-25

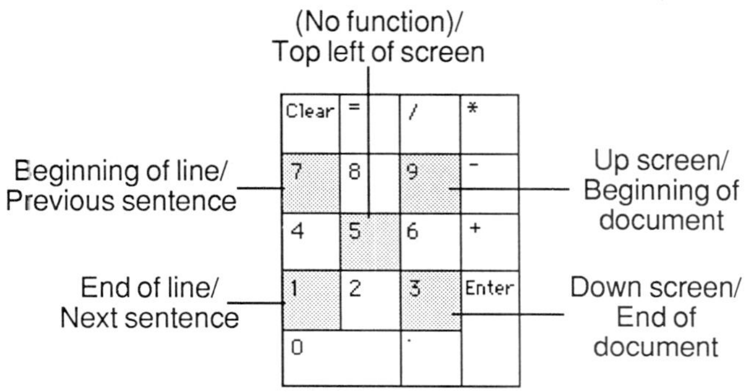

You can also use the 7, 9, 1, 3, and 5 keys for navigation in Word.

By the way, you can also use your numeric keypad to enter numbers into your document; however, the default "mode" for the keypad is navigational. In order to enter numbers, you must press the Clear key before you begin typing. An *N* will appear in the upper-right corner of your screen to indicate that you are in the "numbers" mode. Before you can use the numeric keypad for navigation again, you must press the Clear key again to remove the *N* from your screen.

Navigating with the standard Macintosh keyboard

If you don't have a Mac Plus keyboard or a numeric keypad, don't despair. You can still use many of the navigational techniques described above on your standard Mac keyboard. Though the key combinations for the standard Mac keyboard are not quite as easy to remember, with a little practice you can still use the keyboard to move quickly through your Word documents.

Like the 8, 2, 4, and 6 keys on the numeric keypad, the *o,* comma (,), *k,* and *l* keys let you move up, down, left, and right through your document. Notice that these four keys form a diamond shape on the keyboard, indicating the direction in which they move the insertion point when pressed in conjunction with the Option and ⌘ keys.

For example, to move the insertion point marker up one line, you can press Option-⌘-o. To move down one line, press Option-⌘-,. In the same way, to move the insertion point marker forward one character space to the right, you can press Option-⌘-l. To move back one character space to the left, you can press Option-⌘-k.

To move through your document a word at a time on a standard Macintosh keyboard, use the semicolon (;) and *j* keys in conjunction with the Option and ⌘ keys. To move forward to the beginning of the next word, press Option-⌘-;. To move back to the beginning of the previous word, press Option-⌘-j.

Finally, you can use the *y* and *b* keys in conjunction with the Option and ⌘ keys to move from the beginning of one paragraph to another. Press Option-⌘-y to move to the beginning of the paragraph that currently contains the insertion point marker. If your insertion point marker is already at the beginning of a paragraph, Word will move to the beginning of the previous paragraph. Press Option-⌘-b to move forward to the beginning of the next paragraph in your document.

Figure 4-26 summarizes the special navigation functions available on your standard Macintosh keyboard.

FIGURE 4-26

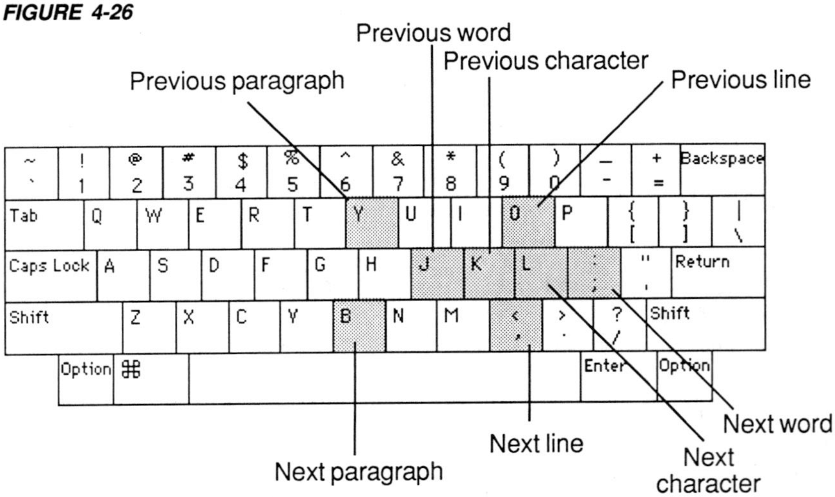

Use these character keys in conjunction with the Option and ⌘ keys to navigate with a standard Mac keyboard.

If you have the dexterity, you can add the single quote key (') to the above key combinations to perform some additional keyboard navigation. For example, you can press Option-⌘-'-; to move to the beginning of the next sentence and Option-⌘-'-j to move to the beginning of the previous sentence.

If your insertion point marker is in the middle of a line of text, you can use Option-⌘-'-k to move to the beginning of a line, while Option-⌘-'-l moves you to the end of a line. If your insertion point marker is already at the beginning of a line, Option-⌘-'-k moves to the beginning of the next line. Similarly, if your insertion point marker is already at the end of a line, Option-⌘-'-l moves to the end of the next line.

To move to the top-left corner of your Word screen, press Option-⌘-'-o. To move to the bottom of the Word screen, press Option-⌘-'-,.

Finally, the *p* and period (.) keys let you toggle between the first and last character spaces in your document. You can press Option-⌘-'-p to move to the beginning of your document or Option-⌘-'-. to move to the end of your document.

Figure 4-27 shows a summary of these Option-⌘-' techniques.

FIGURE 4-27

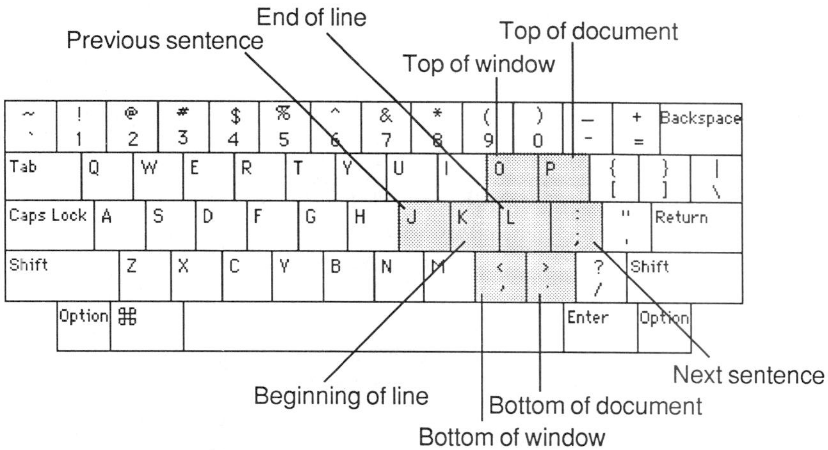

You can also use the Option, ⌘, and ' keys in conjunction with these character keys to move through your Word document.

Though these key combinations are pretty complex, it may give you some comfort to know that you need only repeat the last two keys in the Option-⌘-' combinations described above to repeat an action. If you continue to depress the Option and ⌘ keys with your left hand and then press the ' key with your right hand, you'll see the notation *More* in the status box at the bottom of your screen. This message indicates that you can continue moving through your document by pressing the *'* key, along with the *;* and the *j*, *k*, *l*, *o*, or comma (,) keys. (Obviously, there is no need to use this technique wth the . or *p* keys since these Option-⌘-' key combinations take you to the beginning and end of your document.)

For example, if you have pressed Option-⌘-'-; to move to the beginning of the next sentence in your document, you can continue holding the Option and ⌘ keys with your left hand, as you repeat the '-; combination with your right hand, to jump to the beginning of the next sentence.

Selecting text with the Shift key

If you haven't overdosed yet on all the selection and navigation shortcuts that we've explored in this chapter, here's one more technique to try: Press the Shift key as you use the various navigational devices described above to select text as you move around in your Word document.

For example, you already know that you can press ⌘-7 to move to the beginning of the sentence in your document. If you press Shift-⌘-7, Word will highlight everything from the current insertion point marker to the beginning of the current sentence. If you press Shift-⌘-7 again while this partial sentence is highlighted, Word will extend your selection through the beginning of the next sentence.

Similarly, you can press Shift-⌘-➡ to select words of text as you scroll through your document or Shift-⌘-⬇ to select entire paragraphs. In short, all of the navigational shortcuts that we have discussed in this section double as selection shortcuts when you add the Shift key to the original key combination.

BASIC EDITING TECHNIQUES

The simplest way to edit text in your Word document is to insert new characters, delete existing characters, or overwrite the characters you want to change. These three techniques are among Word's most basic—and most important—editing features. Though we'll be talking much more about editing in Chapter 6, we'll introduce these three basic editing techniques now because they relate closely to the selection and navigation techniques that we've explored over the last several pages.

As we mentioned earlier, the WordWrap feature lets Word reflow your text whenever you make editing or formatting changes—that is why we cautioned you against entering carriage returns at the end of lines of text. As we walk through the insertion, deletion, and overwriting techniques in the next few pages, notice the way that Word reflows your text to adjust for your changes. As you'll see, WordWrap is one of the features that make electronic word processing so popular. This vital feature makes editing text virtually effortless.

Inserting New Text

Inserting text in your Word document is as easy as typing. To insert a block of text into an existing document, all you have to do is move the insertion point marker to the spot where you want to insert the text and click. When your blinking insertion bar appears to mark the insertion spot, just begin typing. Make sure that you have not highlighted any characters before you begin typing, or Word will overwrite those characters.

For example, suppose you want to change the phrase *according to Newspeak's president,...* in line 8 of our sample document to read *according to Newspeak's president, who asked that his name be withheld for security reasons.* Begin by clicking just to the right of the comma and space after the word *president*, and type the rest of the new phrase.

As you can see in Figure 4-28, when you type the new characters, Word will push the remaining characters on the line to the right to make room for your insertion. Thanks to the WordWrap feature, Word will push the words at the end of the line to the beginning of the next line as you go, reflowing your existing text all the way through to the end of the document, if necessary, to make room for your insertion.

FIGURE 4-28

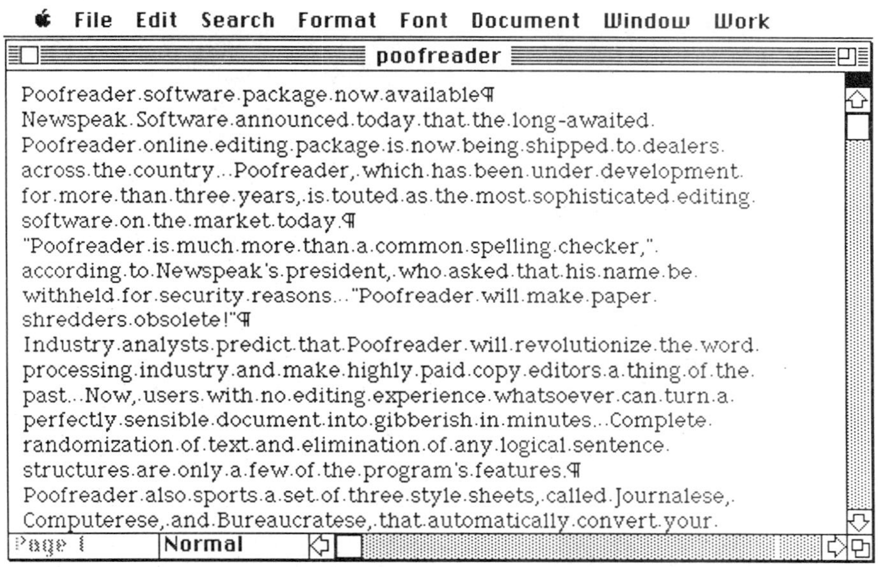

As you insert new text, Word will reflow your text to make room for your changes.

Inserting a ¶ marker

If you find it distracting to watch Word reflow the remaining text in a paragraph as you insert text, try pressing Option-⌘-Return to begin a new paragraph before you begin typing. Word will insert a new ¶ marker (which will be visible only if the Show ¶ command is in effect) and move the text to the right of the insertion point marker into a new paragraph.

Of course, you can press the Return key at any time to insert a new ¶ marker and break the current paragraph into two smaller paragraphs. When you simply press Return, however, your insertion point marker moves down to the beginning of the next paragraph. When you use the Option-⌘-Return technique, your insertion point marker will remain in place so that you can continue to insert text in the current paragraph.

If you want to recombine the two paragraphs after inserting your text, just press Option-⌘-f to delete the ¶ marker. Option-⌘-f lets you delete the character immediately to the right of the insertion point. This brings us to our next topic: deleting text in Word.

Deleting Text

As we hinted at the beginning of this chapter, the easiest way to delete individual characters in your text is to click to the right of the character(s) that you want to delete and press the Backspace key. Word will delete the characters immediately to the left of the insertion point marker one at a time, pulling them characters to the right of the insertion point marker one character space to the left as you go.

To delete several characters at once, you can highlight the unwanted block and then press the Backspace key to delete the entire selection.

Suppose you want to delete the word *whatsoever* in line 13 of our sample document in Figure 4-28. Begin by double-clicking on the word *whatsoever*, then press the Backspace key to erase the highlighted block. As you can see in Figure 4-29, Word will delete the selected word and automatically pull the remaining characters in your document up and to the left to fill in the gap.

FIGURE 4-29

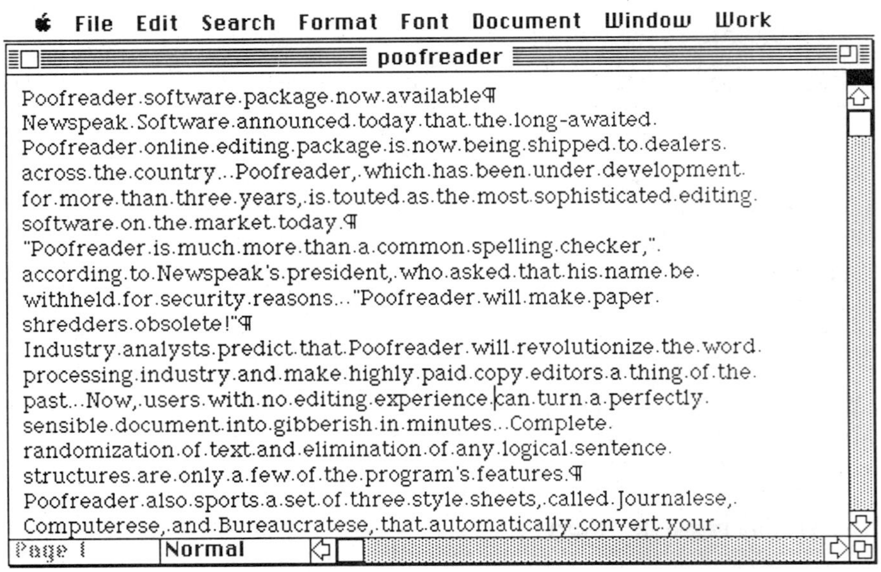

When you delete a block of text, Word will reflow your document to fill the gap.

If you press the Backspace key while your insertion point marker is at the beginning of a line, Word will move the insertion point to the end of the previous line and delete the last character in that line. Similarly, if you press Backspace while the insertion point marker is at the beginning of a paragraph, Word will delete the ¶ marker at the end of the previous paragraph and reflow your text to combine the two paragraphs.

If you hear a beep when you try to press Backspace at the beginning of a paragraph, Word is probably trying to tell you that it cannot combine the two paragraphs because they carry different formatting characteristics. If you're determined to combine the two paragraphs, anyway, you'll have to select the ¶ marker at the end of the first paragraph and press Backspace. The combined paragraph will take on the formatting characteristics of the second paragraph. We'll talk more about this topic in the next chapter.

Deletion shortcuts

Word also offers some special keyboard shortcuts for deleting text. For example, rather than using the Backspace key to delete the characters to the left of the insertion bar one at a time, you can press ⌘-Option-Backspace to delete the entire word to the left of the insertion bar. If you want to delete the space to the right of the word as well, click to the right of that space before you press ⌘-Option-Backspace. If you want to leave that space intact (for instance, so that you can insert another word or phrase in that spot), click to the left of the blank space, just after the word to be deleted.

For example, to change the phrase *...users with no editing experience whatsoever can...* to read *...users with no editing experience can...*, you could click to the right of the blank space after the word *whatsoever* and press ⌘-Option-Backspace. Word will delete the word *whatsoever* and the blank space after it.

If you click in the middle of a word and press ⌘-Option-Backspace, Word will delete all of the characters to the left of the insertion bar up to but not including the blank space that divides the current word from the previous word.

For example, suppose you want to change the phrase *level of incomprehensibility* to *level of comprehensibility* in the second paragraph of our sample document. You can click between the letters *n* and *c* in the word *incomprehensibility* and press ⌘-Option-Backspace to delete the characters *in*. The blank character to the right of the word *of* will remain intact.

Overwriting Text

Often when you delete a block of text in Word, you'll need to insert some new text to take the place of the text you deleted. Rather than erasing a block of text and then inserting new characters, you can overwrite existing characters by dragging through the characters that you want to replace and then—rather than pressing the Backspace key—typing your new text. Word will automatically delete the existing characters and replace them with the new characters that you type. You can think of this overwriting technique as a combination deletion/insertion process.

For example, suppose you want to replace the phrase *is now being shipped to dealers* in line 3 with the new phrase *has made its debut on dealer shelves.* Just drag through the characters *is now being shipped to dealers* and type the replacement text. As you can see in Figure 4-30, Word replaces the old characters with the new ones and reflows the remaining text in our document.

FIGURE 4-30

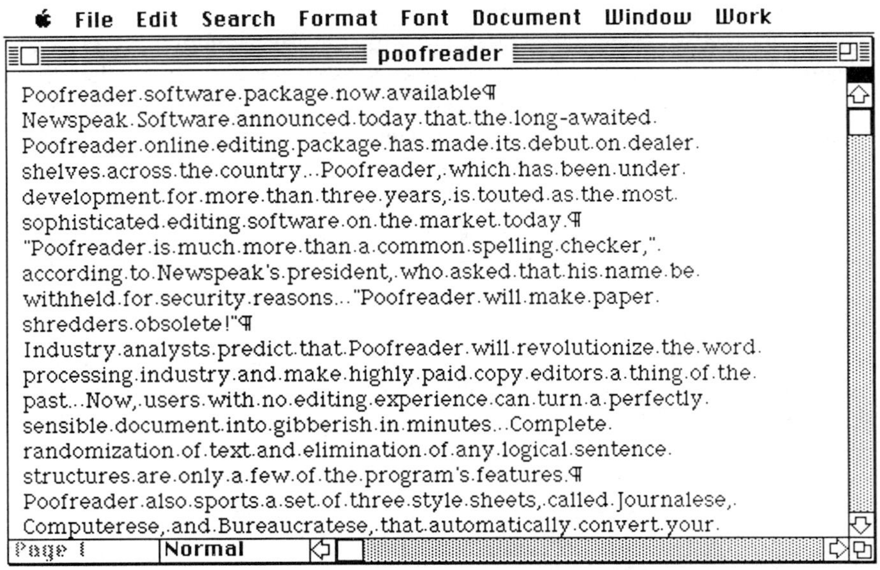

To overwrite text, just select the characters that you want to delete and type your replacement text.

Interestingly, Word will not allow you to overwrite a ¶ marker by selecting it and typing. Instead, you must select the ¶ marker, press the Backspace key, and then type your new text. When you press Backspace, Word will combine the current paragraph with the paragraph below, as described in our discussion of deleting text above. As you might have guessed, this idiosyncrasy occurs because Word tries to prevent you from inadvertently changing the format of the current paragraph by picking up the formats assigned to the next paragraph. Again, we'll talk more about the ¶ marker and its function in Chapter 5.

Selection modes and editing

As you know, when you double-click on a word to select it, Word automatically highlights any trailing blank spaces that fall after that word. Naturally, if you press the Backspace key to delete that word, those trailing blank spaces will be deleted as well. However, if you double-click on a word and then overwrite it by typing new characters, Word will leave any trailing blank spaces intact. Basically, the program assumes that you are replacing one (or more) words with another word and saves you a few keystrokes by leaving the blank spaces in place for you.

This technique works even if you have selected several words. As long as you entered the word selection mode by double-clicking on a word and then dragging through additional words, Word will apply this treatment. The last set of blank spaces will be deleted if you press Backspace but will be left intact if you overwrite the selected text.

If you double-click in the selection bar to highlight an entire paragraph, Word will use a similar technique to decide whether the ¶ marker at the end of the paragraph should stay or go. As you might have guessed, if you press Backspace to delete the paragraph, the ¶ marker will disappear as well. However, if you overwrite the paragraph, the ¶ marker will remain in place.

Again, as long as you entered the paragraph selection mode by double-clicking in the selection bar to select the paragraph, Word will apply this technique, no matter how many paragraphs you have selected. The ¶ symbol that marks the end of the last paragraph in your selection will remain intact if you type new text and will be deleted if you press Backspace.

If you plan to insert new text but want to delete the ¶ marker or blank spaces that appear after your selection, you can drag through the block you want to overwrite rather than double-clicking. Alternatively, you can double-click on the word or paragraph, press Backspace, then type your new text.

Interestingly, Word does not apply this technique when you select entire sentences. Although the program will highlight the punctuation mark and trailing spaces that appear after a sentence when you use the ⌘-click technique to select it, Word will always delete those characters when you delete or overwrite the selection.

CANCELLING AND REPEATING ACTIONS

When you insert, delete, or overwrite text in your document, Word remembers the last set of keystrokes that you performed. One reason for this is that you can often elect to undo an editing change by selecting the Undo command from the Edit menu. Another is so that you can repeat a command or a series of keystrokes automatically. First, let's explore the workings of the Undo command, then we'll show you how to repeat a command or a series of keystrokes in Word.

The Undo Command

The Undo command is one of the most important commands on the Edit menu because it gives you a second chance when you make a mistake. As you'll undoubtedly learn at some time in your relationship with Word, Undo can be a real lifesaver when you find that you have inadvertently altered a critical passage in your document.

Undo is a context-sensitive command; that is, it changes to reflect your last action. If you've inserted new text or overwritten some existing text, you'll see the command Undo Typing at the top of the Edit menu. If you have used the Backspace key to delete some characters, you'll see the command Undo Cut.

In fact, you can even undo an Undo command. When you issue the Undo command, Word changes that command to read *Redo*. Thus, if you delete a block of text then select Undo Cut, you can select Redo Cut to delete the text again. You should keep in mind, however, that the Undo command remains in effect only until you issue another command or begin typing new text. As soon as you perform another action, Word will change the Undo command to reflect your new activity.

In addition to undoing the manual editing procedures that we have discussed in this chapter, you can also undo many of Word's other commands. If a command or action cannot be undone, you'll see the notation *Can't Undo* in dimmed characters at the top of your Edit menu.

None of the commands on the menu, File menu, or Window menu can be reversed with the Undo command. Table 4-2 summarizes those actions on the other Word menus that can be undone and those that are "undoable."

We'll be talking more about all of these commands later. For now, just make a mental note about which actions in Word are easily remedied and which ones are not. Some commands—like Page Setup, which we'll discuss in Chapter 7—can easily be "undone" by reissuing the command and selecting the correct options. However, if you use the Delete... command to erase a file or accidentally overwrite a file with the Save As... command, you won't be able to reverse that action. This is the reason you should use extreme caution when handling files.

Repeating an Action

As we mentioned in our discussion of the Undo command, Word remembers the last action that you performed so that it can undo that action for you. Another reason that Word remembers your last action is so that it can repeat a command or a series of keystrokes for you automatically. To repeat an action, all you need to do is press ⌘-a.

For example, if you insert a series of characters at one spot in your document, and then decide that you need to insert the same series of characters in another location, you can click in the second location and press ⌘-a to "replay" your keystrokes. Similarly, if you select a block of text and press Backspace to delete it or type to overwrite it, you can select another block and press ⌘-a to repeat the same action.

Though you can use ⌘-a to repeat just about any command or series of keystrokes, one of the most common uses for this shortcut is to "replay" complex formatting instructions that you want to apply in more than one area of your document.

TABLE 4-2

Menu	Command	Can Undo
Edit	Undo/Redo	•
	Cut	•
	Copy	•
	Paste	•
	Insert Graphics	•
	Glossary…	• Insert option only
	Hide ¶/Show ¶	
	Short Menus/Full Menus	
	Preferences…	
Search	Find…	
	Change…	• Last change only
	Go To…	
Format	Show Ruler/Hide Ruler	
	Character…	•
	Paragraph…	•
	Section…	•
	Styles…	• Apply option only
	Define Styles…	• Apply option only
	(Character Format Options)	•
Font	(Font Names)	•
	(Font Sizes)	•
Document	Open Header…	
	Open Footer…	
	Footnote...	•
	Repaginate	
	Outlining	
	Spelling…	
	Hyphenate…	
	Index…	•
	Table of Contents…	•
	Calculate	
	Renumber…	•
	Sort	•

You can use the Undo/Redo command to reverse those actions marked by a • character in the table above.

FORMATTING 5

Word's formatting capabilities are among the most sophisticated and easy to use that we've seen in any word processing program. As we mentioned earlier, one reason that formatting in Word is so easy is that you see on screen exactly what your printed document will look like. In addition to Word's extensive on-screen formatting capabilities, you can also use special markup characters and formulas to format your text and to create sophisticated special effects.

On Word's Format and Font menus, you'll find lots of options to help you lay out and design your document. Another important formatting feature is the ruler, which you'll use to control tabs, line and paragraph spacing, and margin settings in your Word documents.

You can format your Word document on three levels: character, paragraph, and section. Character formatting involves choosing the font, style, and size of your text, as well as letter positioning and spacing. Paragraph formatting involves margins, tabs, line and paragraph spacing, and paragraph borders. Section formatting is used primarily to control factors that affect the entire document, like header and footer positioning, page number formats, and multicolumn layout settings. Since these formatting options take effect only when you print your document, we'll look at the Section... command in more detail in Chapters 7 and 8.

CHARACTER FORMATTING

When you format characters in your Word document, you need to make a number of decisions about how those characters will look: the font you want to use, the size of the characters, special emphasis like boldfacing, italics, and underlining, the amount of space between characters, and the position of those characters in relation to each other. In this section, we'll show you how to control all of these factors.

The Language of Type

As we've said before, Word's default character format is New York, 12-point Plain. However, we've never really explained in any detail what this designation means. Before we launch into the many character formatting options available to you in Word, let's review a few typographical terms. We'll explore briefly the concepts of fonts, point size, serifs, and letter and line spacing.

Fonts

Let's start with the concept of fonts. In typographer's terms, a font is defined as a collection of type of one size and "face." The term "face" refers to style elements like bold, italic, and so forth. Thus, 18-point Helvetica type and 12-point Helvetica type are considered different fonts. Similarly, 18-point Helvetica bold type is considered a different font than 18-point Helvetica italic type. Though all of these faces are part of the same type family, each is defined as a very distinct font.

In Macintosh terminology, however, different type sizes and styles do not constitute different fonts. Instead, each family of type, with all its associated formatting options, is considered part of the same font. Thus 18-point Helvetica, 12-point Helvetica, 18-point Helvetica bold, and 18-point Helvetica italic are looked upon simply as formatting variations of the same font.

Type sizes

You may also have wondered what the numeric type size specifications on your Font menu and in the Character dialog box actually represent. It's not too hard to figure out that 18-point type is larger than 10-point, but what do these point sizes really mean?

In typography, a point is a printer's measurement of the height of a letter. A point is $^1/_{12}$ of a pica. If that doesn't help much, then you should also know that a pica is $^1/_6$ of an inch. Thus, there are 72 points to an inch. (One point equals $^1/_{12}$ times $^1/_6$, or $^1/_{72}$ of an inch.) In other words, if you select a block of text and tell Word to display it in 72-point type, the characters you have selected will be one inch high. Similarly, if you specify 36 points, your type will be half an inch high; if you specify 18 points, your type will be a quarter of an inch high, and so forth.

Of course, not every letter in the alphabet is of the same height. The letter *h* is almost twice as high as the letter *e*. So how do point sizes relate to the height of any given character in your text? Let's back up a step and introduce three new terms: ascender, descender, and x-height. As Figure 5-1 illustrates, the x-height represents the height of the "body" of the letter. Ascenders and descenders extend above and below the x-height of the letter.

In typography, the height of a character is determined by the distance from the bottom of the lowest descender to the top of the highest ascender. Thus, any individual letter in your document is not necessarily going to be the same height because not every character has ascenders or descenders. Even when you specify 36 points for your type, the face of any given letter might be only 30 points high. The remaining height is dedicated to the ascending and descending strokes, like the ascending vertical bars in the letters *h* and *k* and the descending strokes in the letters *g* and *q*.

FIGURE 5-1

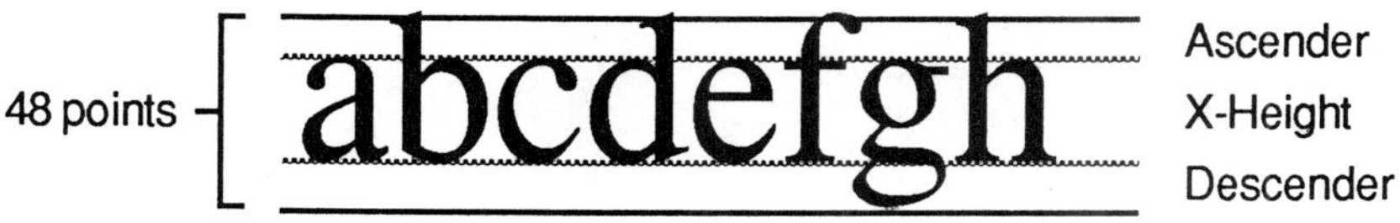

Type size is measured from the top of the ascender to the bottom of the descender.

The x-height of corresponding letters of the same type size may also vary significantly. (The x-height is equal to the distance between the mean line and the base line, the two gray lines that appear above and below the bodies of the characters in Figure 5-1.) For example, Table 5-1 shows the letters *h* and *g* in several different type styles. All of the characters in this table appear in 18-point Plain style. As you can see, however, even though the overall height of the letters is the same, the x-height of the letters varies significantly, depending on the emphasis given to ascenders and descenders.

TABLE 5-1

Times	Helvetica	Chicago	Venice	Geneva
hg	hg	hg	hg	hg
New York	**Boston**	**Courier**	**Dover**	**Dover PS**
hg	hg	hg	hg	hg

The x-height of fonts of the same type size may vary.

Serifs

One of your major design decisions in formatting any document is whether or not to use serif type. Serifs are the short crosslines that appear at the ends of the main strokes of a letter. As you might have guessed, type faces that use these crosslines are called serif fonts; those that do not are called sans serif fonts.

In Table 5-1, Times, New York, Boston, Venice, Courier, Dover, and Dover PS are serif types; Helvetica, Chicago, and Geneva are sans serif. Figure 5-2 shows a close-up of the letter *k* in the Times font with the serifs circled.

FIGURE 5-2

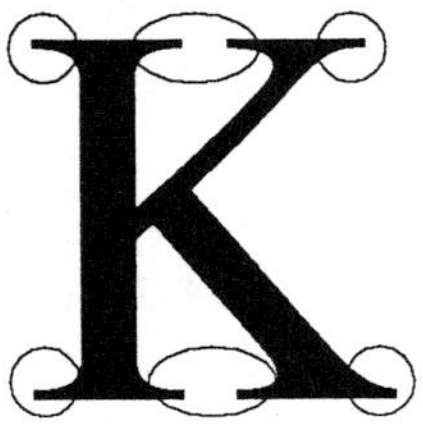

Serifs are the short crosslines at the ends of the main strokes of a letter.

Generally, you'll find that either serif or sans serif type works just fine for display type, such as headings. Studies have shown, however, that serif type is more readable in the body of your document because the serifs help the reader to easily distinguish characters and words. They also add "horizontal stability," establishing a flow from left to right across a line of text.

Letter spacing

Before you select a type face, you should also know whether that font is proportional or nonproportional—that is, whether the width of the character spaces varies. In proportional fonts (also called variable-pitch fonts), the amount of horizontal space assigned to a letter varies according to the width of that letter. In nonproportional fonts (also called fixed-pitch fonts), every letter is assigned the same amount of space. Typewriters and daisy-wheel printers generally use nonproportional spacing. Thus, even though the letters *i* and *l* are much narrower than the letters *m* and *w*, all four characters would occupy the same amount of space in a nonproportional font.

As Table 5-2 shows, the Times, Chicago, Helvetica, Venice, New York, Boston, Dover PS, and Geneva fonts are proportional, while the Courier and Dover fonts are nonproportional. Generally, we think you'll find that a proportional font lends a more finished appearance to your document. The two nonproportional fonts listed here are included primarily for users with daisy-wheel printers (more on this in Chapter 7).

In addition to offering both proportional and nonproportional font options, Word lets you manually control the amount of space that appears between letters in your document. As you'll see later, you can use this letter spacing technique to open up crowded lines of text or to help balance two or more blocks of text.

Line spacing

Line spacing, also referred to as leading, is similar to letter spacing except that it applies to the vertical spacing between lines of type rather than the horizontal spacing between individual letters within a line. Word gives you a number of spacing options to control the positioning of individual characters within a line of text as well as the spacing between lines of text.

TABLE 5-2

Proportional

Times	Helvetica	Chicago	Venice
iwiw	iwiw	iwiw	iwiw
wiwi	wiwi	wiwi	wiwi
New York	**Boston**	**Dover PS**	**Geneva**
iwiw	iwiw	iwiw	iwiw
wiwi	wiwi	wiwi	wiwi

Nonproportional

Courier	Dover
iwiw	iwiw
wiwi	wiwi

Word offers both proportional and nonproportional font options.

Unless you specify otherwise, Word automatically adds one point of leading between the lines of text in your document. This buffer space prevents the descenders in one line from overlapping the ascenders in the next line. Thus, if you measure from base line to base line, a 12-point line of text is actually 13 points high, an 18-point line is 19 points high, and so forth. Figure 5-3 on the following page illustrates this concept.

If you are using two or more type sizes on the same line, Word will use the appropriate line spacing for the largest characters. For example, as you can see in Figure 5-4, if you use a range of point sizes from 12 to 24, the distance from base line to base line will be 25 points—high enough to allow for one extra point of leading above the 24-point characters.

FIGURE 5-3

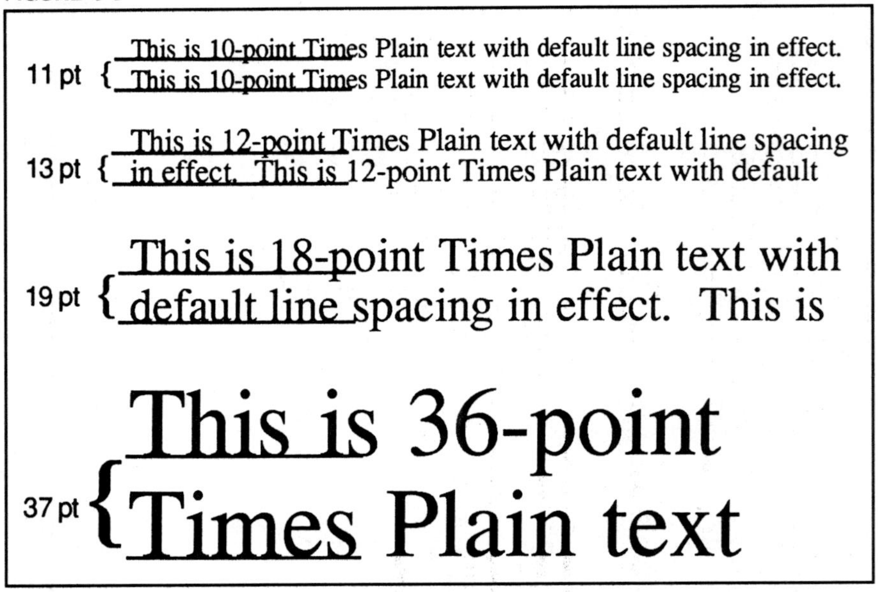

Word adds one extra point of leading between lines of text.

FIGURE 5-4

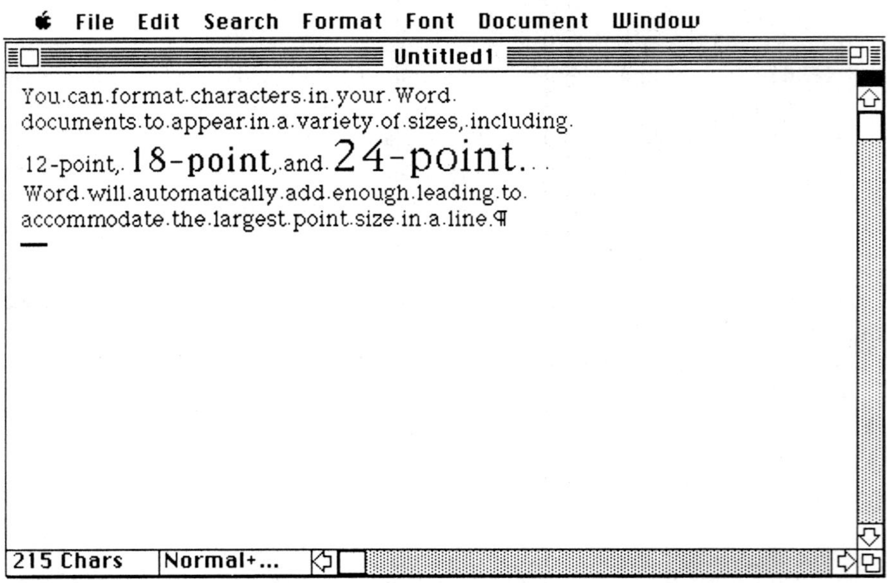

Word will use the appropriate spacing for the largest character on a line.

Using the Format and Font Menus

Now that we've defined some of the basic elements of typography, let's apply these theories to the Word document that we created in Chapter 4. The simplest way to format characters in your Word document is to select a font, size, or style from the Font or Format menu. As you'll soon see, you can also use the Character... command to assign additional character formatting options.

We listed the font and size options that are initially available on your Word disk in Table 1-1 on page 16 of Chapter 1. However, if you have used the Font/DA mover to install additional fonts or to remove some fonts from your System file, your Font menu and Character dialog options may look a bit different from ours.

When you're formatting existing text, remember that your character formatting selections will apply only to the text that is highlighted in your document when you issue a Format or Font menu command. Thus, you must use the techniques described in Chapter 4 to select the block of text you want to format. (This is not necessarily the case if you use style sheets to format your document, as you'll see in Chapter 9.)

Now, any text that you type in your Word document will take on the characteristics of the text immediately preceding it. If you click in the middle of a line of text that is formatted in 18-point type, any new characters that you type will be 18 points high as well. If you want to change formats in midstream, Word also lets you assign character formats to text before you enter it. To "predefine" your character formats, just place the insertion point marker at the point where you want to begin typing the formatted text, and select the options you want before you begin typing.

We'll start with the sample document that we created in Chapter 4 to illustrate a few of Word's character formatting features. Figure 5-5 on the next page shows part of that news release, which currently appears in the default New York, 12-point, Plain type.

Now, suppose we decide to display the first line of our sample document (the title) in 18-point, Geneva, bold type. We'll begin by clicking in the selection bar on the left side of the screen to select the entire line, then we'll select the font name Geneva from the Font menu. At this point, our document looks like the one in Figure 5-6. (We have deselected the text to show the results of our formatting; however, you'll want to keep the line highlighted until you have selected all of your format settings.)

FIGURE 5-5

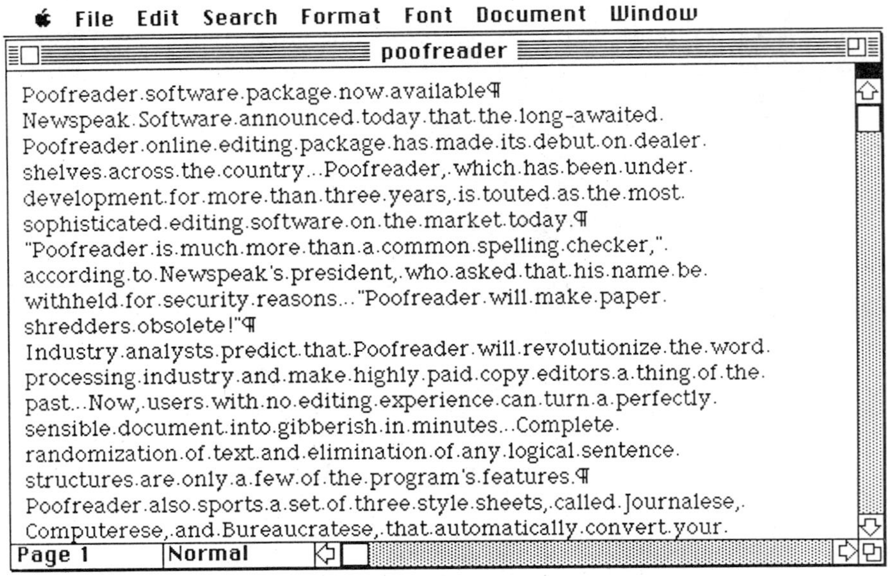

Our sample document initially appears in Word's default 12-point, New York, Plain type.

FIGURE 5-6

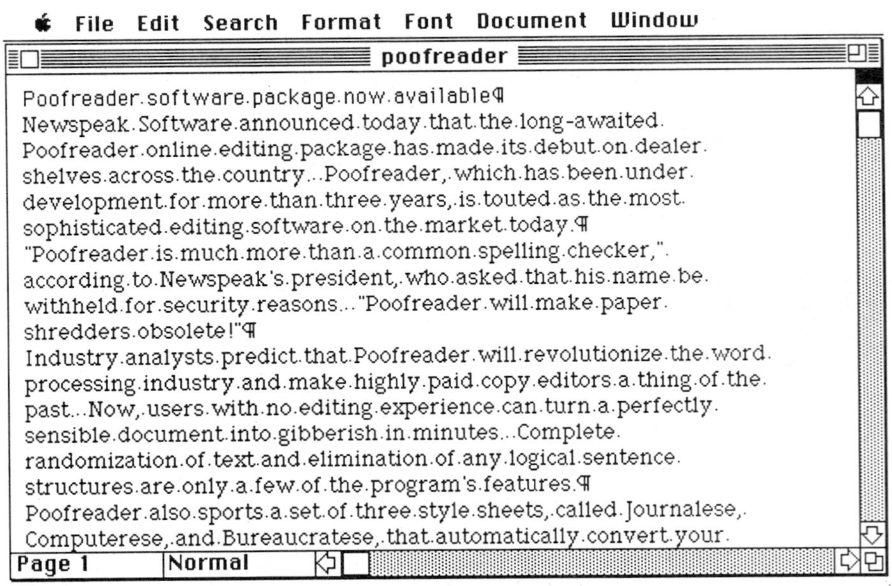

The heading now appears in 12-point, Geneva, Plain type.

Next, to change the size of the selected characters, we'll point to the Font menu again and select 18 Point from the bottom half of the menu. Figure 5-7 shows the results.

FIGURE 5-7

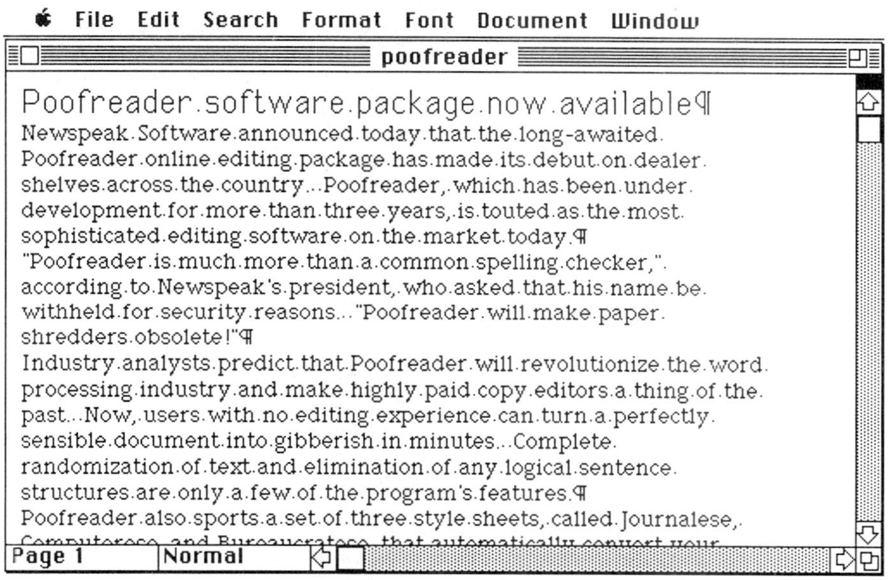

The heading now appears in 18-point, Geneva, Plain type.

Finally, to assign the bold format to the selected characters, pull down the Format menu and select the Bold option. Figure 5-8 on the following page shows the results.

Now, let's format the body text for our sample document to appear in 12-point, Times, Plain type. Begin by double-clicking in the selection bar to select the second paragraph, then drag downward to select the remaining paragraphs. Since the text is already in 12-point Plain type, all we'll need to do is select the Times option from the Font menu. Figure 5-9 shows the results.

Notice that all of our line breaks have changed because we have selected a different type face. Word has automatically "reflowed" the text for us to fill the specified margins.

It's as easy as that! You can take care of most of your character formatting needs in Word with a few simple selections from the Font and Format menus.

FIGURE 5-8

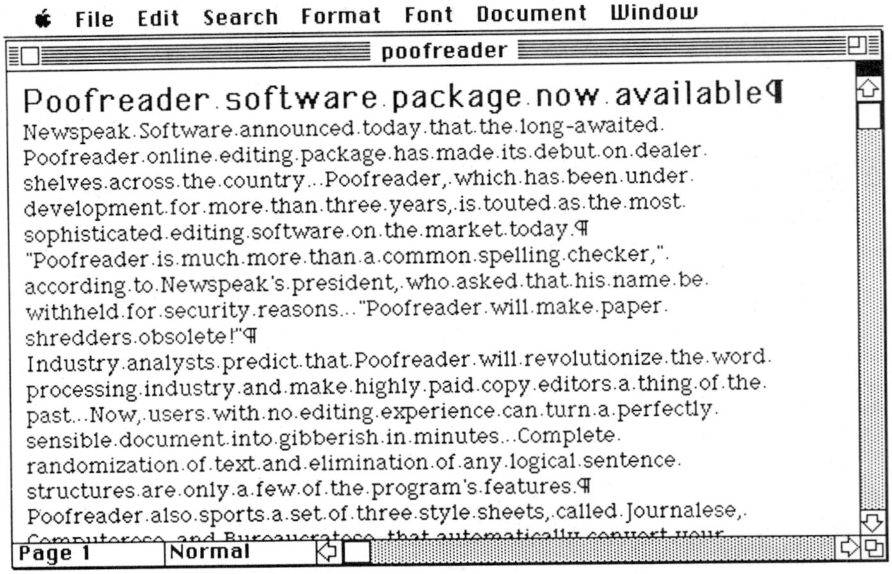

The heading now appears in 18-point, Geneva, Bold type.

FIGURE 5-9

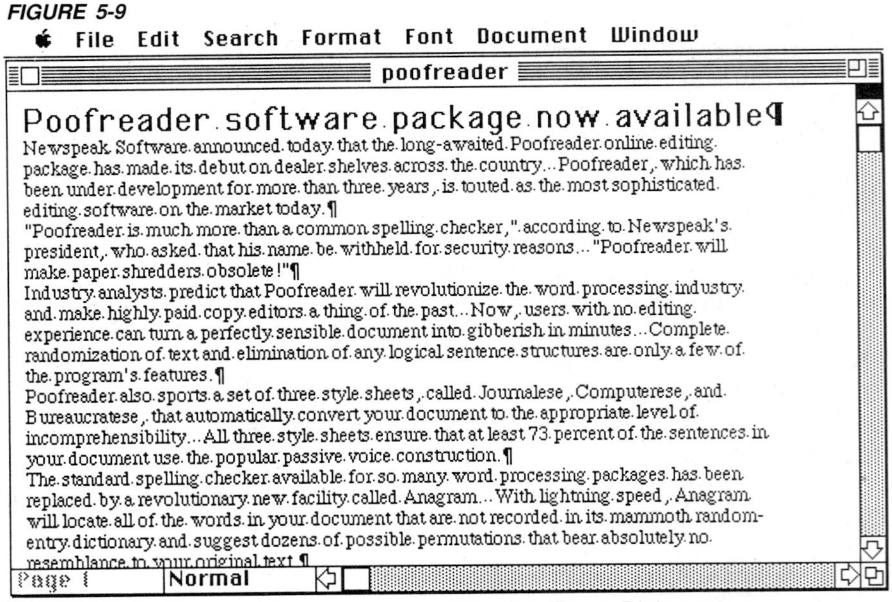

The body of our document now appears in 12-point, Times, Plain type.

Word's suggested type sizes

Click on the first line of text in the sample document again and take a look at the Font menu shown in Figure 5-10. (Your menu may look a bit different, depending on the fonts that you have installed on your System file and the printer drivers that you have selected.) As you can see, check marks appear to the left of the Geneva and 18 Point commands, indicating the formats that we have applied to the selected text. Now, look at the available sizes that appear at the bottom of the menu.

As you can see in Figure 5-10, all of the size options on the Font menu are outlined. The outlined options represent Word's suggested sizes for that font. That is not to say that you cannot use another type size—only that these sizes have been installed in your System file.

Since the range of point sizes that have been installed for each font on your System file varies, you'll find that the outlined size options on the Font menus vary according to the font you have selected. For example, if you select Chicago from the Font menu, you'll see the size options shown in Figure 5-11.

FIGURE 5-10

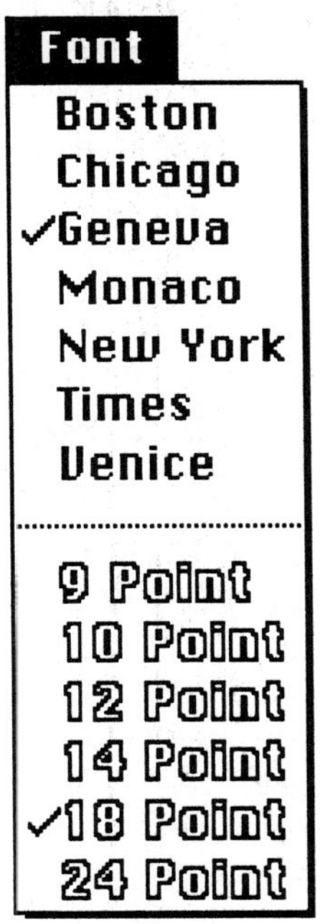

Word displays checkmarks to the left of the selected formats.

FIGURE 5-11

Word's suggested type sizes vary according to the font you have selected.

When you choose a point size that is not outlined on the Font menu (or if you specify a custom size, which we'll discuss in a moment), Word will extrapolate the size you need from information it has about existing sizes in the System file. Though these scaled fonts may not look too great on your screen, they generally look just fine when they are printed. If you use an ImageWriter printer, you may notice a few jagged edges or some "muddy" characters here and there when the document is printed, but if you use a LaserWriter, you'll find that most any type size between 2 and 127 points looks just fine.

Revising a format

You can change the font or size for a block of text simply by selecting a new font or size from the Font menu. The check marks to the left of the original option will appear next to the newly selected option.

The options on the Format menu work a bit differently, however. Since you can assign more than one format to the same selection (bold and italic, for example), you must toggle most of the Format menu options on and off by selecting them again. For example, if you select a block of text and then select Bold from the Format menu, Word will display a check mark next to the Bold option. If you select Bold again with the same text selected, the check mark will disappear, and the text will no longer appear in bold format.

The Plain Text option is the only Format option that will automatically be deselected when you choose another format. If you have used previous versions of Word, you know that the Plain Text option is used to instruct the program to remove any special formatting, like bold or italic, from the selected text. We should warn you that the function of this command has changed slightly in Word 3. Because of the addition of style sheets, the Plain Text option now tells Word to revert to the formats originally defined for the specified style. That is, if you've used a named style to format text in your document, and you've changed the format of that text manually, you can use the Plain Text command to revert to the formats you originally assigned with the Styles… command.

For example, if you were to select the first paragraph of the sample document shown in Figure 5-8 and select the Plain Text option, you might expect Word to remove the Bold setting from that line and display the headline as it appears in Figure 5-7. Since Word's default style for all of your text is 12-point, New York, Plain Text, however, if you were to issue the Plain Text command, the selected block would look just as it did in Figure 5-5—before we added any special formatting. (If this reasoning doesn't make a lot of sense at this point, everything will become clear when we talk about style sheets in Chapter 9. For now, just keep in mind that you should use the Plain Text command carefully; it may alter the selected text more than you had planned.)

The Character… Command

While the font, style, and size options available on the Font and Format menus are fine for most applications, you may occasionally need to do more sophisticated character formatting. The Character… command, which appears on the Format menu when you have Full Menus in effect, lets you do just that.

When you select Character… from the Format menu, you'll see a dialog box like the one in Figure 5-12. (By the way, you can quickly access the Character dialog box by pressing ⌘-d.) Notice that our current character formats are already reflected in the dialog box.

FIGURE 5-12

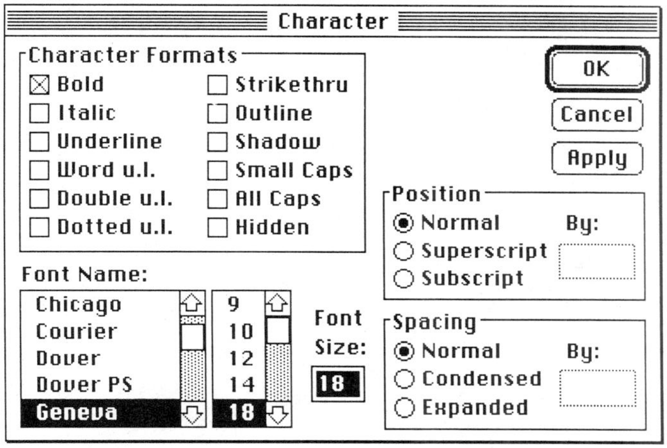

If you use Full Menus, you can use the Character dialog box to format your text.

As you can see, the Character dialog box offers quite a few more options than the Font and Format menus. In addition to the Bold, Italic, Underline, Outline, and Shadow options that appear on the Format menu, the Character dialog box offers three additional underline options: Word u.l., Double u.l., and Dotted u.l., as well as the Strikethru, Small Caps, All Caps, and Hidden options. You can select almost any combination of these type styles to format the selected text in your document. Just click in the check boxes to select the character formats you want. (Notice that there is no Plain Text option in the Character dialog box. To revert to "plain" text, you'll need to deselect all of the character format options.)

Figure 5-13 on the following page illustrates several combinations of character format options. All of the characters in this table appear in 14-point Times type.

FIGURE 5-13

Plain
Bold
Italic
Bold Italic
Plain Underline
Word Underline
Double Underline
Dotted Underline
~~Strikethru~~
Outline
Bold Outline
Shadow
Bold Shadow
Outline Shadow
Bold Outline Shadow
Bold Outline Shadow Italic
Bold Outline Shadow Underline
SMALL CAPS
BOLD SMALL CAPS
ALL CAPS
BOLD ALL CAPS
BOLD OUTLINE SHADOW SMALL CAPS
BOLD OUTLINE SHADOW ALL CAPS

You can combine style options to create different typographical effects in Word.

A few of the character format options are mutually exclusive, however. Obviously, you can't use both All Caps and Small Caps for the same block of text. Similarly, you can select only one of the four underline options.

The All Caps and Small Caps options

The All Caps and Small Caps options are interesting in that they appear to change the case of the characters that you have entered into your document. When you use All Caps, Word will display all of the selected text in upper-case letters. However, the underlying characters will still be in the case that you originally typed. For example, if you type the word *microsoft* in all lower-case letters, Word will display that word as *MICROSOFT* after you apply the All Caps format.

Even more interesting is that when you use the Small Caps option, Word displays all of your text in capital letters, but it also reduces the size of any characters that were originally entered in lower case. For example, if you format the word *WordWrap* in small caps, Word will display that word as *WordWrap*. As you can see, the appearance of the two *W* characters has not changed. However, the letters *o*, *r*, *d*, *r*, *a*, and *p* now appear in the next smaller type size in capital letters. Again, the underlying characters have not changed. If you remove the Small Caps format, your text will revert to its original form.

Both options are convenient for quickly changing the case of letters without retyping. However, Word will still consider these characters to be lower case. (As you'll see in the next chapter, the distinction between upper- and lower-case letters becomes significant when you use Word's Find..., Change..., Spelling..., and Hyphenation... commands.)

We mentioned a moment ago that Word will use the next smaller point size to display lower-case letters when you use the Small Caps option. This does not necessarily mean that Word uses the next standard option in the Font Size list for that font, however. When you use Small Caps, Word will use the sequence of point sizes shown in Figure 5-14 to format your lower-case letters.

FIGURE 5-14

7 9 10 12 14 18 24 36 48 60 72

Word uses this sequence of point sizes to scale your letters when you use the Small Caps option.

For example, if you use Small Caps to format 18-point characters, Word will display the lower-case letters in 14-point type. If you use Small Caps to format 24-point characters, Word will display the lower-case letters in 18-point type, as shown in Figure 5-15. If the size of the selected text falls between these sizes, however, Word will use the next smaller size to format the lower-case letters in the selection.

FIGURE 5-15

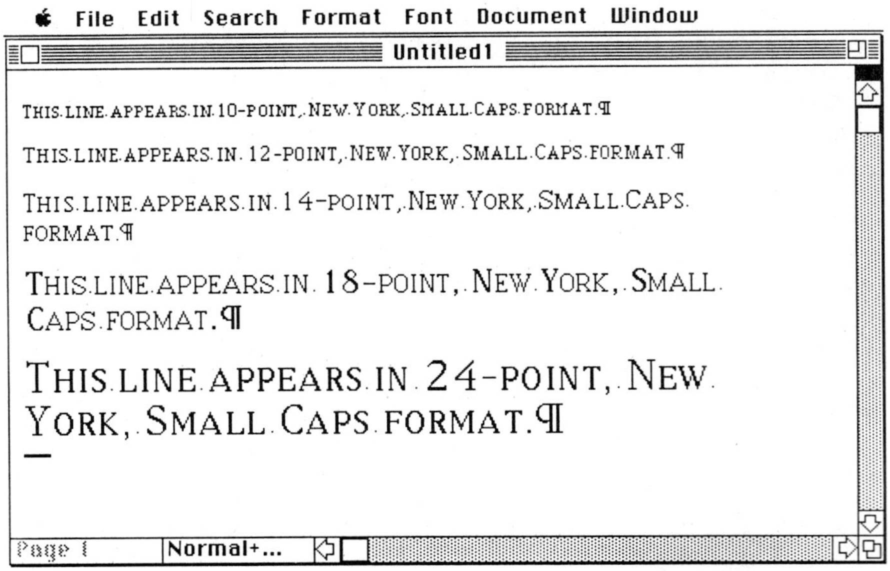

When you use Small Caps, Word will display the lower-case letters in the next smallest size.

Because of the way that Word increments point sizes, the Small Caps option is more effective in larger point sizes than in smaller point sizes. For example, if you use Small Caps for 10-point text, the lower-case letters will appear in 9-point. This 1-point difference in character sizes may make it difficult to distinguish between the All Caps and Small Caps formats.

The Hidden format

One character format that we didn't address in Figure 5-13 was the Hidden format. The Hidden format is a new feature that lets you suppress the display of characters in your document. Though it is used primarily for flagging special items, like PostScript commands and index notations, hidden text is great for entering notes and questions into your text that can be hidden from view when not needed.

You can also use the Hidden format when you need to vary the content of a document. For example, in Figure 5-16 we added a new paragraph to our sample news release that refers to a complimentary review copy of the Poofreader software. We plan to send these complimentary copies only to selected persons on our mailing list. One way to vary the content of the document for different readers is to hide the optional paragraph when we don't need it.

FIGURE 5-16

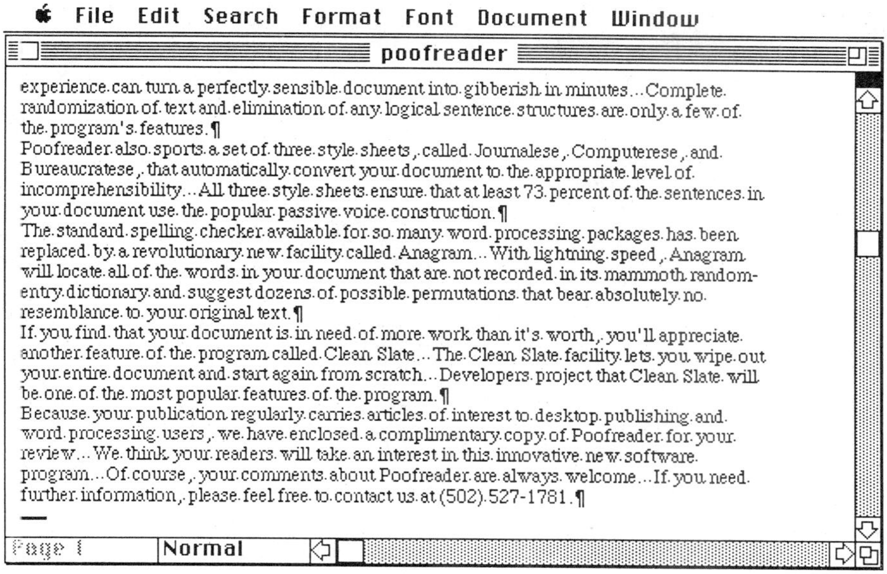

The last paragraph in the document is optional.

As you can see in Figure 5-17 on the next page, when you assign the Hidden format to text in your document, Word will display a gray underline to indicate that the text is hidden. (Unfortunately, this underline is identical to the underline that Word displays when you assign the Dotted u.l. format to your text. If you're using both formats, be careful not to confuse the two.)

When you assign the Hidden format to text, you can opt to suppress the display of that text on your screen and/or in your printed documents. As you'll see in Chapter 16, you'll also use the Hidden format to identify linked text and graphics when you use the QuickSwitch facility. We'll show you how to hide text in your printed documents when we talk about the Print... command in Chapter 7.

To suppress the display of Hidden text in your document window, just select Preferences... from the Edit menu. (Full Menus must be in effect before you can select the Preferences... command.) In the Preferences dialog box shown in Figure 5-18, click on the Show Hidden Text option to deselect it.

FIGURE 5-17

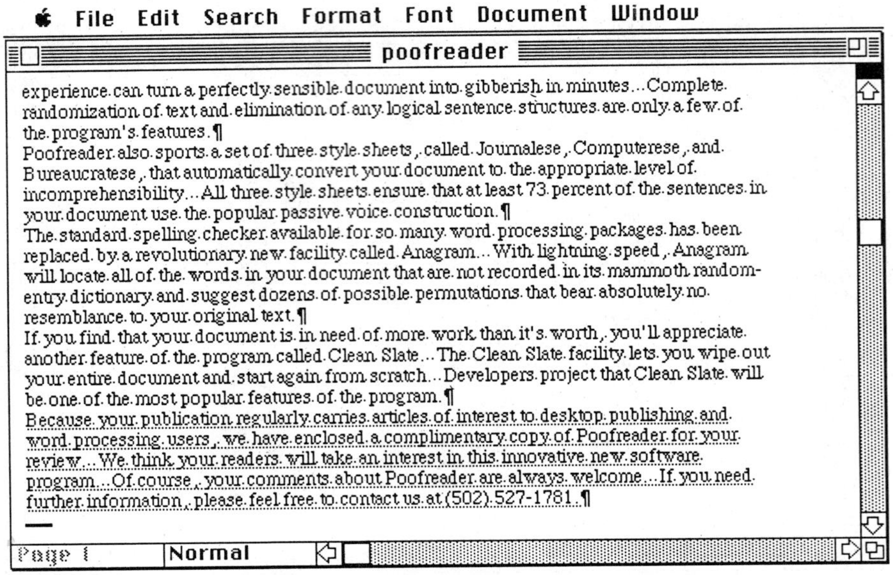

You can use the Hidden format to suppress the display of a block of text.

FIGURE 5-18

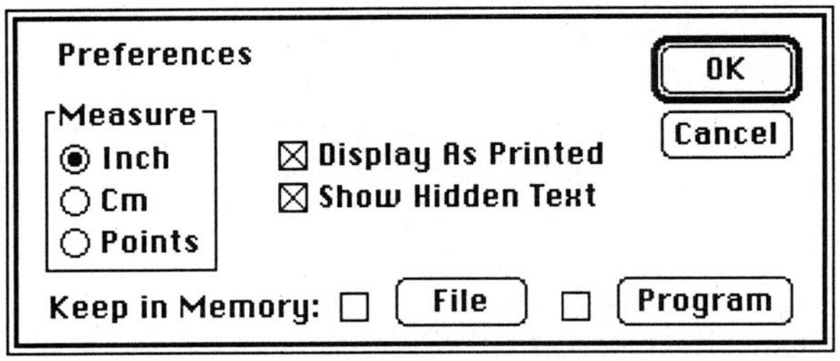

To suppress the display of Hidden text, click on the Show Hidden Text option to deselect it.

When you turn off the Show Hidden Text setting, any text that has been assigned the Hidden format will disappear from your screen, but it will remain in your document "behind the scenes." You can display the hidden text again at any time by reissuing the Preferences... command and reselecting the Show Hidden Text setting.

Specifying a font size

To select a size setting for your text, you can either select one of the standard size options from the Font Size list box just to the right of the Font Name list box, or you can specify a custom size in the Font Size edit bar. For example, if you choose the Chicago font from the Font Name list box, Word will display only one size option, 12-point. Though this is the only standard size installed on the System file for this font, you can type your own custom size value in the Font Size edit bar. (As you might have guessed, the Font Size list box contains the point size options that appear outlined on the Font menu when you have selected a font.)

For example, if you want to use 18-point Chicago type rather than the default 12, you can just type the value 18 in the Font Size edit bar. Notice that the entry currently in the edit bar is already highlighted so that you can just overtype the existing entry without dragging through the edit bar. Your Font Size value can be any whole number from 2 through 127. Word will not accept decimal values like 10.5 in the Font Size edit bar.

The Position options

You can also format your text to appear in Subscript or Superscript style by selecting one of those position options from the Position box on the right side of the Character dialog box. Of course, the Normal option is the default in Word. The Subscript and Superscript options are used most commonly for mathematical notations like exponents and fractions. However, you may also be able to find some more creative applications for these options.

To understand the function of the Subscript and Superscript options, you need to visualize all of the text in your document as sitting on a base line. This base line appears in the graphics that we used to illustrate type sizes and leading in Figures 5-1 and 5-3. The Superscript and Subscript options tell Word to shift the selected characters above or below this base line. For example, the sample text in Figure 5-19 contains two mathematical notations that are very difficult to read because there is no way to distinguish the base and exponent values from the rest of the text.

FIGURE 5-19

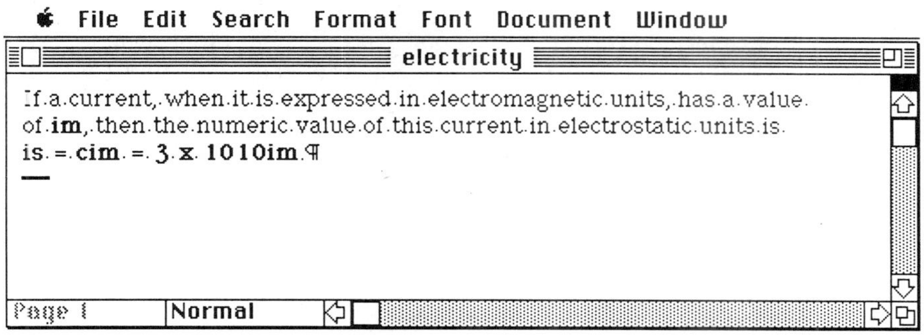

The mathematical notations in bold type are difficult to read because there are no base or exponential notations.

To correct this problem, we could select the desired characters one at a time, issue the Character... command, and click on the Subscript or Superscript options to format the formulas. Figure 5-20 shows our sample line of text, formatted in Word's default 2-point Subscript and 3-point Superscript.

FIGURE 5-20

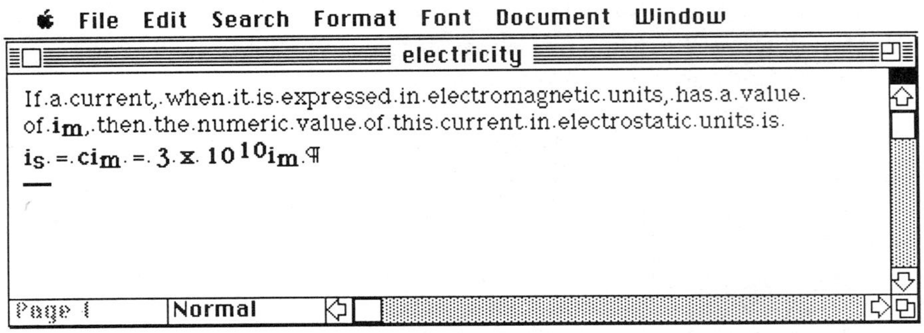

We used the Subscript and Superscript settings to format the mathematical notations.

When you click the Superscript option in the Character dialog box, Word will automatically display the default value *3 pt* in the By edit bar. Similarly, the default Subscript setting in the Character dialog box is *2 pt*. You can change this By value to control the distance between the base line of the superscript or subscript character and the base line of the rest of the text on the line. Word will accept any value between 0 and 63.5; however, it will generally round your By setting to the nearest half point.

Keep in mind that Word may have to adjust your line spacing to prevent the subscript and superscript characters from overlapping succeeding or preceding lines of text. Adding a 3-point superscript to a line of text will have the same effect as using a type size three points larger than the rest of the text on the line. If you find the change in line-spacing unattractive, you may be able to avoid this problem by reducing the size of the subscript or superscript characters. For example, notice the gap between the second and third lines of the sample text in Figure 5-20. If we change the size of the subscript and superscript characters from 12-point to 9-point, however, we can close up the line spacing again, as shown in Figure 5-21.

FIGURE 5-21

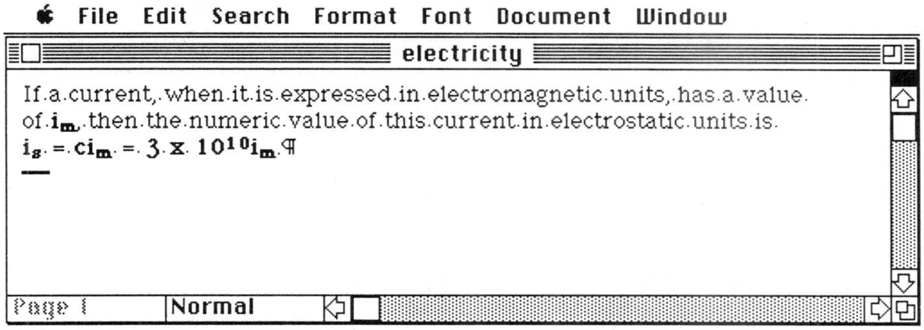

To eliminate the extra line spacing, you can reduce the size of the subscript or superscript characters.

Others uses for subscript and superscript characters

Though the Subscript and Superscript options are used most often for mathematical and scientific notation, a little imaginative use of these options can lead to interesting effects. For example, Figure 5-22 shows a logo designed with the Subscript and Superscript options. We created the Rollercoaster effect by formatting the text in 18-point, Times, Outline type, then selecting each character in turn and assigning different Subscript or Superscript settings.

FIGURE 5-22

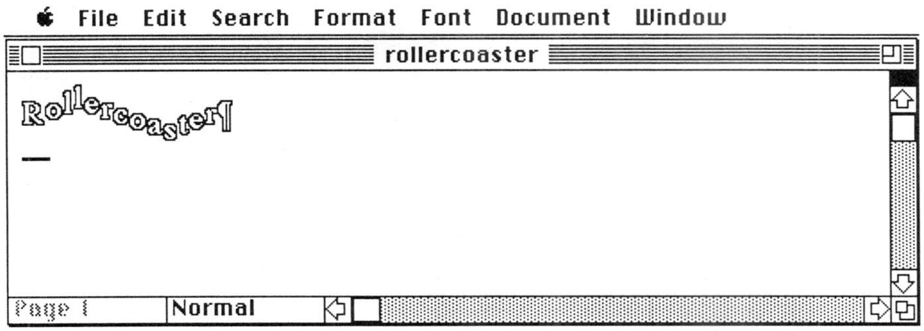

You can use the Subscript and Superscript options for more than scientific and mathematical notation.

Controlling character spacing

Unlike previous versions of the program, Word 3 also lets you control the spacing between characters in your document with three new Spacing options: Normal, Condensed, and Expanded. The Normal Spacing option is the default.

When you select the Expanded or Condensed options, Word will activate the By edit bar. The default setting for both the Expanded format is 3 points, and the default setting for the Condensed format is 1.5 points. However, you can type your own spacing setting in the By edit bar. When you are using the

Condensed option, Word will accept any value from 0 to 1.8 points. When you are using the Expanded option, you can use a By setting from 0 to 14 points. When you specify decimal values, Word may round your By setting slightly.

Figure 5-23 illustrates the relationship between the Normal, Condensed, and Expanded formats, respectively. All three lines of text are set in 18-point, Times, Bold type.

FIGURE 5-23

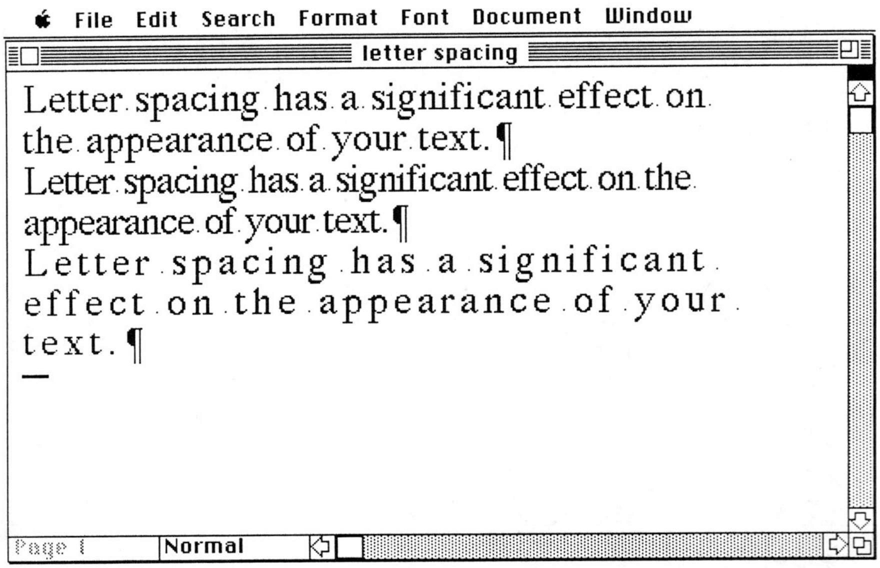

The Normal, Condensed, and Expanded Spacing options control the letter spacing between characters in your text.

Letter spacing can often be used creatively for special display type. For example, to create the logo shown in Figure 5-24, we formatted both lines of text to appear in 14-point Times type. We used the All Caps option to format the first line, then we used the 14-point Expanded Spacing setting to widen the character spaces in the first line.

FIGURE 5-24

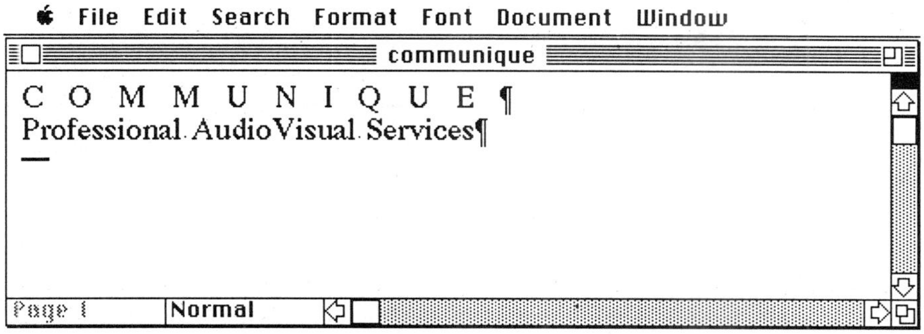

You can use Word's Spacing options to balance lines of text.

Character Formatting Shortcuts

In addition to the Font and Format menus and Character dialog box, Word gives you a number of keyboard shortcuts for formatting characters. All of these shortcuts let you combine the Shift and ⌘ keys with character keys to select character formatting options quickly.

For example, to increase or decrease the size of your text, you can press Shift-⌘-> or Shift-⌘-<. The effects of the Shift-⌘-> and Shift-⌘-< key combinations will depend on the current type size that you are using. If you are currently using 10-point type and you press Shift-⌘->, you'll get 12-point type. If you are currently using 18-point type and you press Shift-⌘->, you'll get 24-point. Figure 5-14 on page 117 shows the series of point sizes that Word will use in response to your Shift-⌘-> and Shift-⌘-< keystrokes. If you are currently between sizes, Word will increase or decrease the point size to the next nearest size. That is, if you are using 16-point type and you press Shift-⌘->, you'll get 18-point type.

Table 5-3 on the next page contains a summary of the Shift-⌘ keyboard shortcuts that you can use to format characters in Word.

As with the Format and Font menu commands, if you have highlighted text when you use one of these Shift-⌘ key combinations, Word will assign that format to the selected text. Alternatively, if you want to begin typing in a new format, you can place your insertion point marker at the desired location and use one of the key sequences to specify your new format. When you begin typing, Word will apply that format to all subsequent text until you select another insertion point or change formats again.

You can toggle many of these formatting options on or off by repeating the same keystrokes. For example, suppose you have selected a block of text and pressed Shift-⌘-] to assign the Word Underline format to it. Then you decide (too late to use the Undo command) that you did not want to underline that text after all. Just reselect the text block, if necessary, and press Shift-⌘-] a second time to remove the underline formatting from the selected block.

TABLE 5-3

Format	Shift-⌘- Key	Toggle	Full Menus Only
All Caps	k	•	
Bold	b	•	
Change Font	e (plus font name)		•
Decrease Size	<		
Dotted Underline	\	•	•
Double Underline	[	•	•
Hidden	x	•	•
Increase Size	>		
Italic	i	•	
Outline	d	•	
Plain	Spacebar		
Shadow	w	•	
Small Caps	h	•	•
Strikethru	/	•	•
Subscript 2 point	-		
Superscript 3 points	+		
Underline	u	•	
Word Underline	]	•	•

Use these keys along with the Shift and ⌘ keys to format characters in Word.

Similarly, if you are in the process of typing a sentence and you need to underline the next several words, you can press Shift-⌘-u to begin underlining with the next character, then press Shift-⌘-u again when you have finished typing the text you want to underline. The next characters that you type will appear in Plain Text format (or whatever format you were using before you invoked underlining).

Though some of the formatting options shown in Table 5-3 cannot be toggled on and off, you can still turn them on and off as you are typing by pressing Shift-⌘-Spacebar. For example, if you need to apply the Superscript option as you are typing, you can press Shift-⌘-+, type the characters that you want to appear in Superscript, then press Shift-⌘-Spacebar to revert to the Plain Text style. Of course, this technique will work only if you are not currently using any other special character formats, like bold or italic text, because Word will remove these formats too when you press Shift-⌘-Spacebar.

The change font shortcut is a bit different than the other Shift-⌘ shortcuts because you must type the name of the font you want to use after you press Shift-⌘-e. For example, suppose you are currently using the New York font and you decide that you want to switch to Geneva. You can select the text that you want to reformat, or click in the spot where you want to begin using the Geneva type, and press Shift-⌘-e to signal a font change. Word will display the prompt *Font* in the status box at the lower-left corner of your screen, as shown in Figure 5-25. Just type the name of the font that you want to use (the characters that you type will appear in the status box) and press Return or Enter. Figure 5-26 shows the results.

FIGURE 5-25

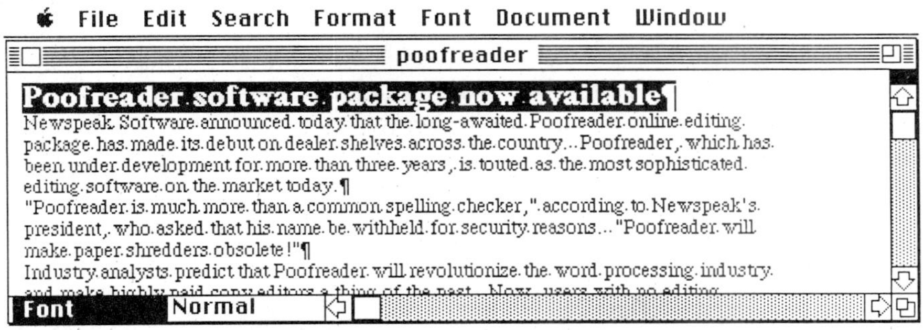

When you press Shift-⌘-e to signal a font change, Word will prompt you for a font name.

FIGURE 5-26

The selected text appears in the new font.

If you decide not to change fonts, press the ⌘ and period keys (⌘-.) to cancel the change, or click anywhere in the document window. Also, you can generally abbreviate the font name that you type in response to Word's Font prompt. As long as you type enough characters to uniquely identify the font you want to use, the shortcut will work. For example, since we have only one font installed on our System file that begins with the letter *g*, a *g* will suffice to invoke the Geneva font. To distinguish between the Chicago and Courier fonts, however, you must type at least two characters—*ch* or *co*. (By the way, you must type the full font names for Dover and Dover PS. Since those two names are so similar, Word cannot distinguish between the two unless you enter all of the characters.)

PARAGRAPH FORMATTING

All of the formatting features that we have discussed so far can be applied to any size selection in your document—from a single character to an entire file. Word's paragraph formatting commands work a bit differently. Whether you select a single character or an entire paragraph, your commands will apply to the entire paragraph. In fact, to format a single paragraph, all you have to do is click anywhere on that paragraph. To format two or more paragraphs simultaneously, you can use any of the selection techniques described in Chapter 4 to highlight any portion of the paragraphs you want to work with.

Word's paragraph formatting options cover a lot of territory, ranging from line spacing and alignment to indentions and borders. You can also specify tab settings on the ruler, but we'll save that important topic for a little later in the chapter. Let's start by reviewing the default paragraph formats, then we'll take a tour of Word 3's new and improved ruler formatting capabilities.

The Defaults

Word's default paragraph settings are flush left, single-spaced, with no left or right indents. The term flush left refers to how the text is aligned—with an even left and "ragged" right margin. As you'll see in a moment, you can also format paragraphs to appear with centered, flush-right, or justified alignment.

Single-spacing refers to the amount of leading between lines of text. As we explained earlier, Word automatically adds 1 point of leading between lines of text to create buffers between the ascenders and descenders of adjacent lines. You can increase or decrease this line spacing to suit your needs.

To explain indents, we need first to explore briefly how your document margins are defined. We'll go into all of these factors in much more detail in Chapter 7. For now, you just need to get a general understanding of how Word defines your overall page settings.

Unless you specify otherwise, Word assumes that you are using letter-size paper (8 $^1/_2$ by 11 inches) with 1 $^1/_4$ inch left and right margins. These settings, which are controlled by the Page Setup... command, allow for a 6-inch-wide column of text (8 $^1/_2$ - 1 $^1/_4$ - 1 $^1/_4$ = 6).

The measurements that you see on your ruler relate to these Page Setup settings, not to the actual position of your text on the printed page. That is, if you are using Word's default left and right margins, the zero point on your ruler, which represents the left edge of your text, actually corresponds to the 1 $^1/_4$ inch mark on the printed page. The 6 inch mark on your ruler, which represents the right edge of your text, corresponds to the 7 $^1/_4$ inch mark on the printed page.

If you find this relationship confusing, you're probably not alone. Just remember that your ruler settings refer to the position of text *within* the margins that you specify in the Page Setup dialog box. If you change your Page Setup options, Word will change the width of your text blocks. Figure 5-27 illustrates this concept.

FIGURE 5-27

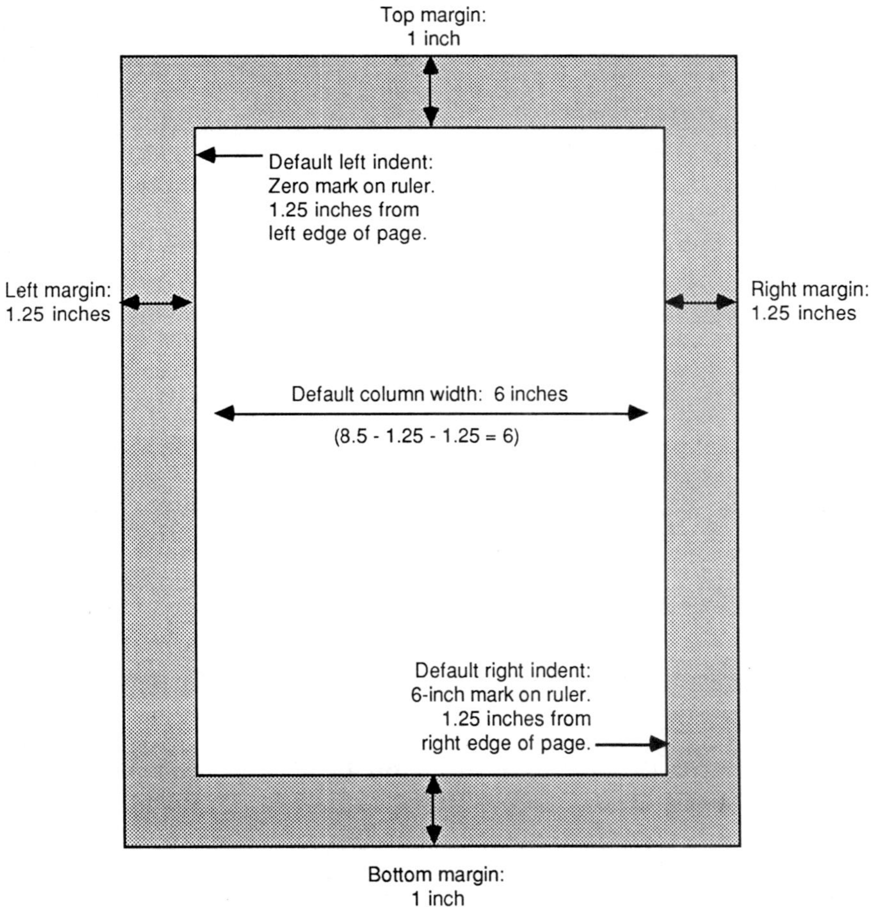

Your ruler settings are relative to your Page Setup dialog box margin settings.

Getting back to indents—while the Page Setup... command controls the overall width of your text, the ruler indent markers let you increase or decrease the width of selected text. For example, if you need to set a quotation off from the rest of your text, you might shift the left and right indent markers to narrow that paragraph. You can also indent the first line of text in a paragraph.

(A note of warning: You may be tempted to change your overall margin settings by moving the indent markers on your ruler. We strongly urge you to resist this temptation. If you later make any changes to your Page Setup dialog box, you'll undoubtedly find that all of your margin settings are scrambled. Thus, if you need to use a column width other than the default six inches, use the Page Setup… command, described in detail in Chapter 7.)

The Ruler

Most of your common paragraph formats can be applied directly from the ruler. To display the ruler on your screen, just select Show Ruler from the Format menu or press ⌘-r. Show Ruler is a toggle command that changes to read Hide Ruler when the ruler display is turned on. To remove the ruler from your screen, just select Hide Ruler or press ⌘-r again.

As you can see from the tick marks that appear along the ruler line, Word divides the ruler into $^1/_8$ inch increments. You can click between these tick marks to position text at $^1/_{16}$ inch increments. As you'll see in a few pages, if you need more precise control, you can also use the Paragraph… command to specify your ruler settings.

Unlike previous versions of the program, Word 3 lets you control factors like alignment and line spacing directly from the ruler. The ruler settings that are available vary, depending on whether you are using Short or Full Menus. Figures 5-28 and 5-29 show the various ruler icons available in Word 3.

FIGURE 5-28

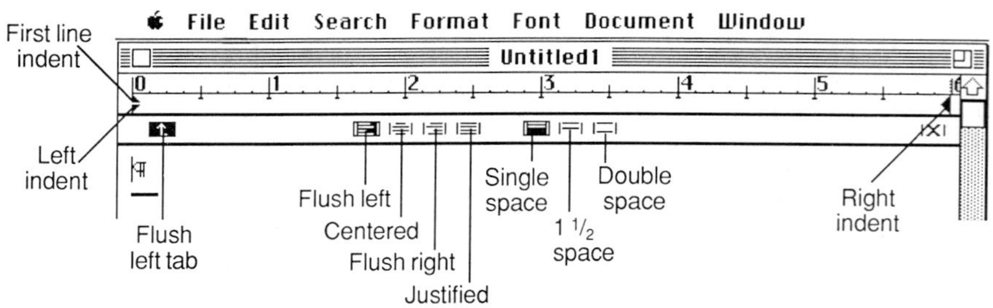

When the Short Menus command is in effect, Word displays these ruler icons.

FIGURE 5-29

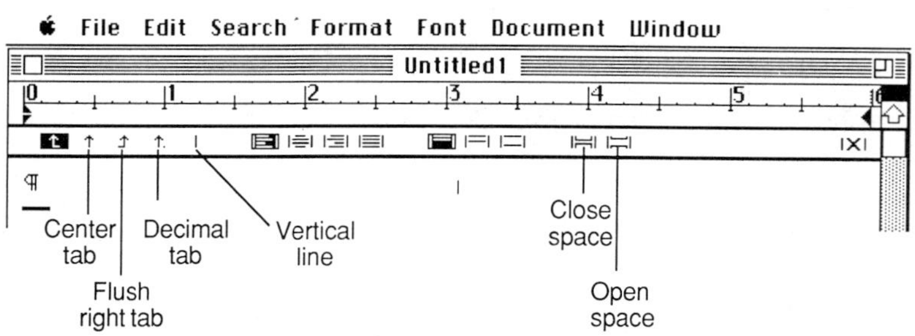

When the Full Menus command is in effect, Word displays additional ruler icons.

Notice the vertical gray line that appears at the 6 inch mark on your ruler. This line represents the default right edge of your text. If you change your left or right margin settings in the Page Setup dialog box, this gray line will move to reflect the current position of the right margin. The zero point on the ruler always represents your left margin, regardless of your Page Setup settings.

Indents

To change the width of a paragraph, just click anywhere on that paragraph and drag the left and right indent markers. For example, the third paragraph in the sample document in Figure 5-30 is a quotation from James Joyce's <u>Dubliners</u>. To set this quotation apart from the rest of the text, begin by clicking on or selecting some portion of the paragraph, then point to the left indent marker (the bottom of the two indent markers on the left side of the ruler) and drag it to the $^1/_2$ inch mark. The first-line indent marker will move with the left indent marker, as shown in Figure 5-31.

FIGURE 5-30

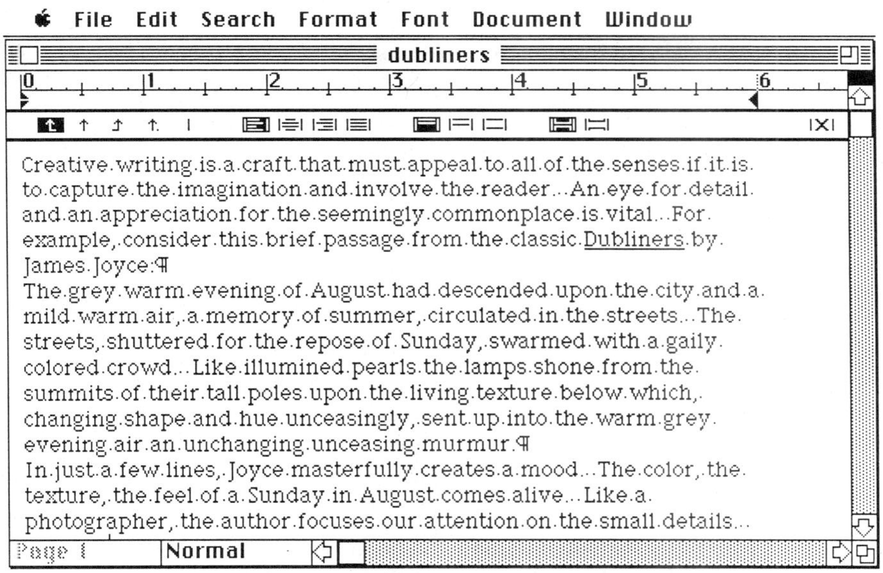

The second paragraph in this sample document is a quotation.

Next, to indent the right edge of the paragraph, point to the right indent marker and drag it to the 5 $^1/_2$ inch mark. Figure 5-32 shows the results.

FIGURE 5-31

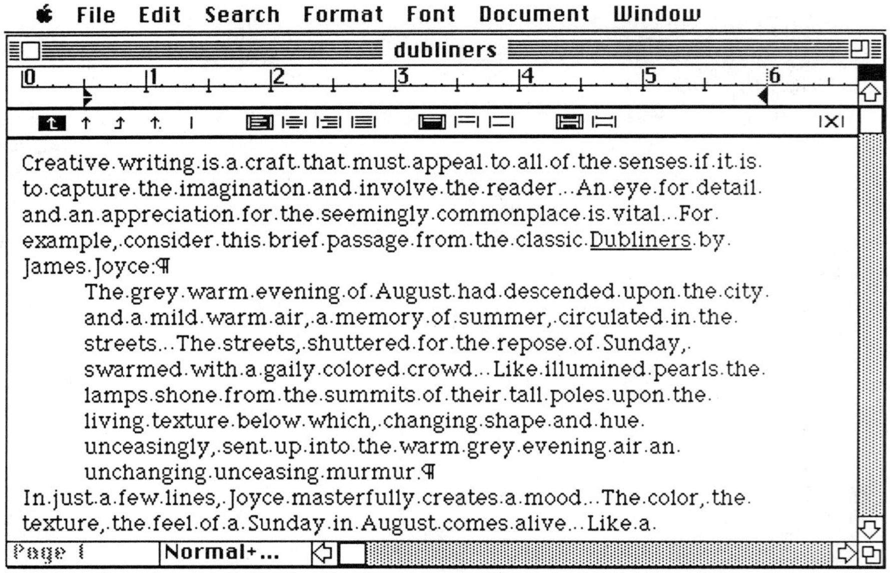

To indent the left edge of the selected paragraph, drag the left indent marker to the right.

FIGURE 5-32

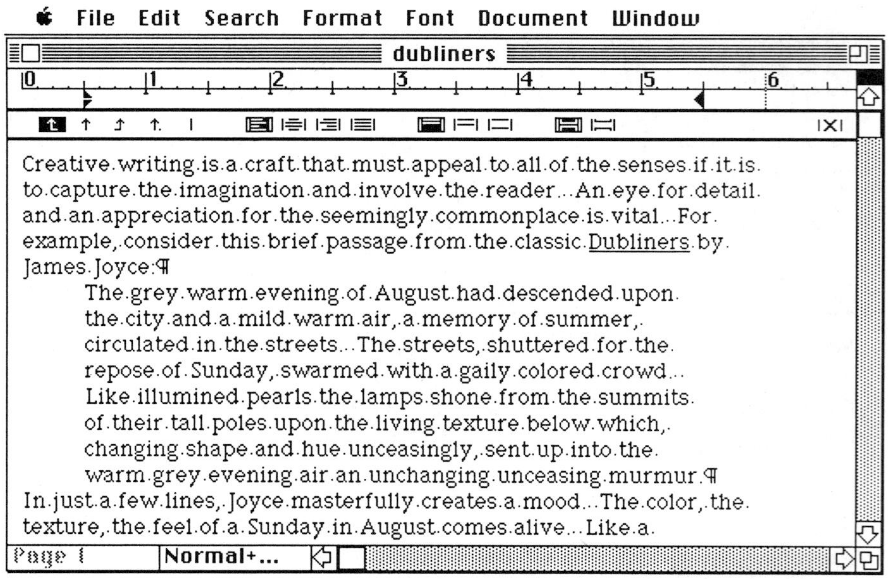

To indent the right edge of the selected paragraph, drag the right indent marker to the left.

Again, keep in mind that your paragraph indentions are relative to the margin settings that you have specified in the Page Setup dialog box. In our sample document, the quotation will appear $1\,{}^{3}/_{4}$ inches from the left and right edges of the page.

Indenting the first line in a paragraph

Often, you'll want to indent only the first line of the paragraphs in your documents to make it easier to distinguish paragraph breaks. That's why the left indent icon is split into two parts—the top half of the icon, called the first-line indent marker, lets you format the first line of the paragraph independently of the rest. To change your first line indention setting, just drag the top marker.

For example, Figure 5-33 shows our sample document with a ${}^{1}/_{2}$ inch first-line indention added to each paragraph. As you can see on the ruler, the first-line indent marker for the first and third paragraphs now appears at the ${}^{1}/_{2}$ inch mark, while the left indent marker remains at zero. In the quotation paragraph, the left indent marker is at the ${}^{1}/_{2}$ inch point and the first-line indent marker is at 1 inch.

FIGURE 5-33

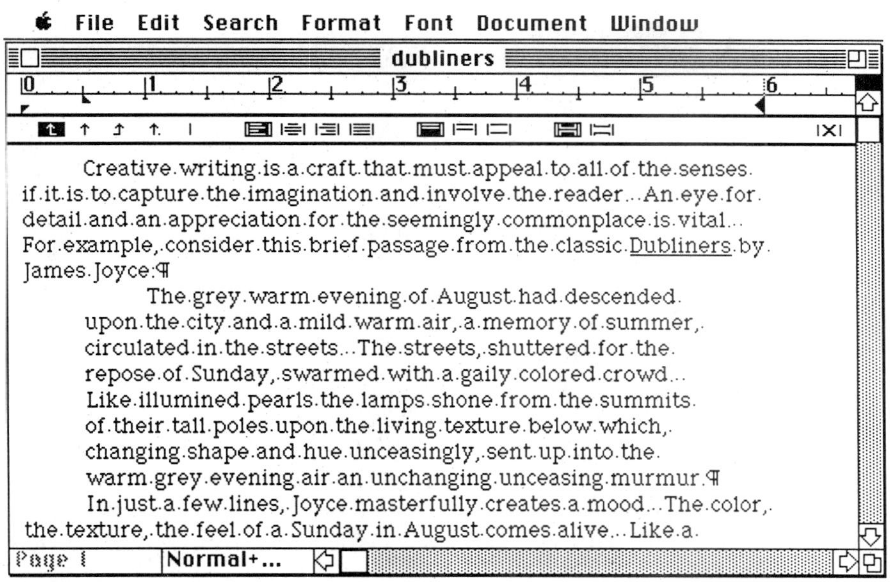

We have indented the first line of each paragraph.

Once you split the first-line indent and left indent markers, you can still move both icons simultaneously by dragging the left indent marker. The distance between the two icons will remain unchanged. For example, if we decide to shift the quotation in our sample document an additional ${}^{1}/_{2}$ inch to the right, we can point to the left indent marker and drag it to the 1 inch mark on the ruler. As you can see in Figure 5-34 on the following page, the first-line indent marker is now set at $1\,{}^{1}/_{2}$ inches.

FIGURE 5-34

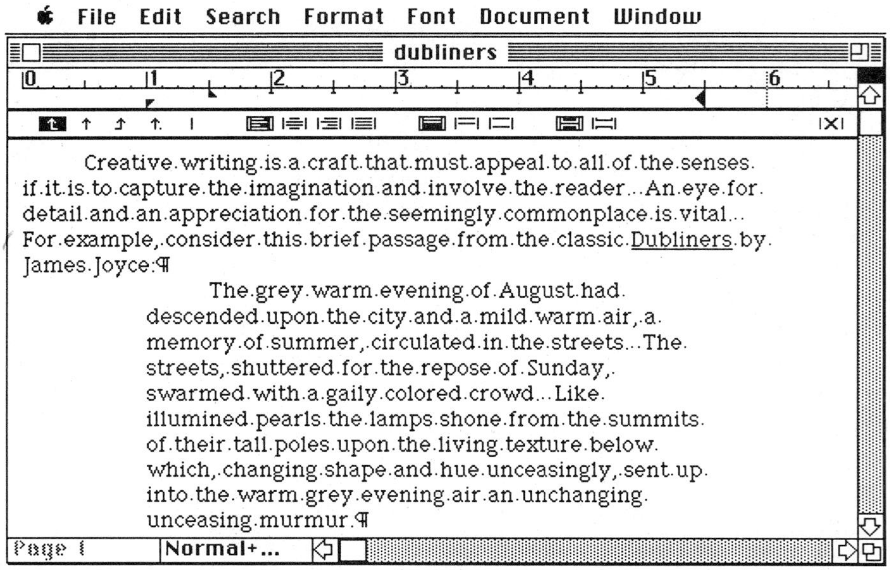

When you drag the left indent marker, the first-line indent marker will move too.

If you want to move the left indent marker without changing the first-line indent, just press the Shift key as you drag the marker. Word will "release" the left indent marker so that you can move it independently.

Hanging indentions

When you present numbered or bulleted lists in a Word document, you'll probably want to format your text so that the numbers, bullets, or other symbols are set apart from the text. Generally, you'll want the numbers or symbols to appear to the left of the left indention. This effect is called hanging indention or outjustified text.

For example, consider the sample document shown in Figure 5-35. This numbered list is difficult to read because the numbers that mark each step blend into the body of the text. To fix this problem, just select the appropriate paragraphs press the Shift key, and drag the left indent marker to the right. Figure 5-36 shows the results.

When you use this technique, you may find that the first few characters in each list paragraph are slightly out of alignment with the remaining text. To ensure that the first line in each list paragraph is justified with the remaining lines of text, you may want to insert some tabs in your text. Begin by selecting the blank spaces that currently separate the numbers from the text in each list

FIGURE 5-35

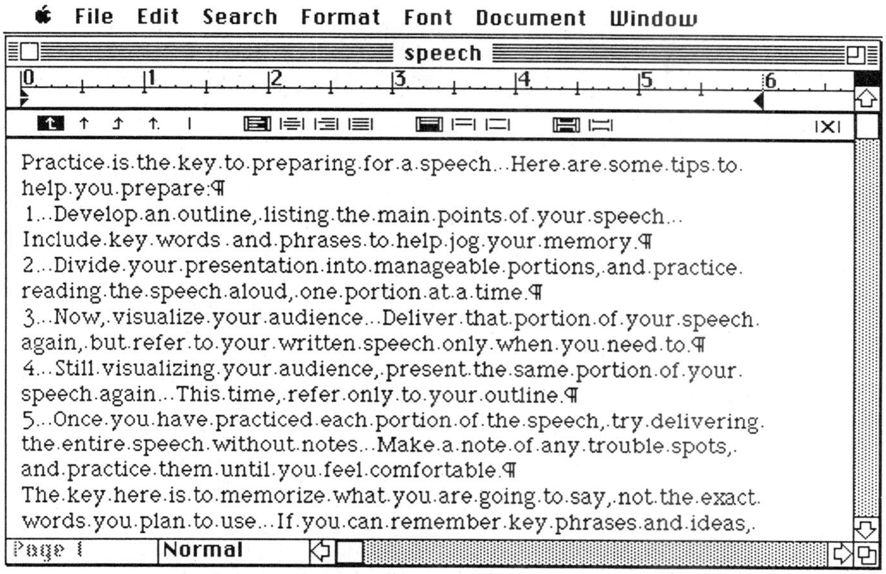

This list is difficult to read because the numbers blend in with the body text.

FIGURE 5-36

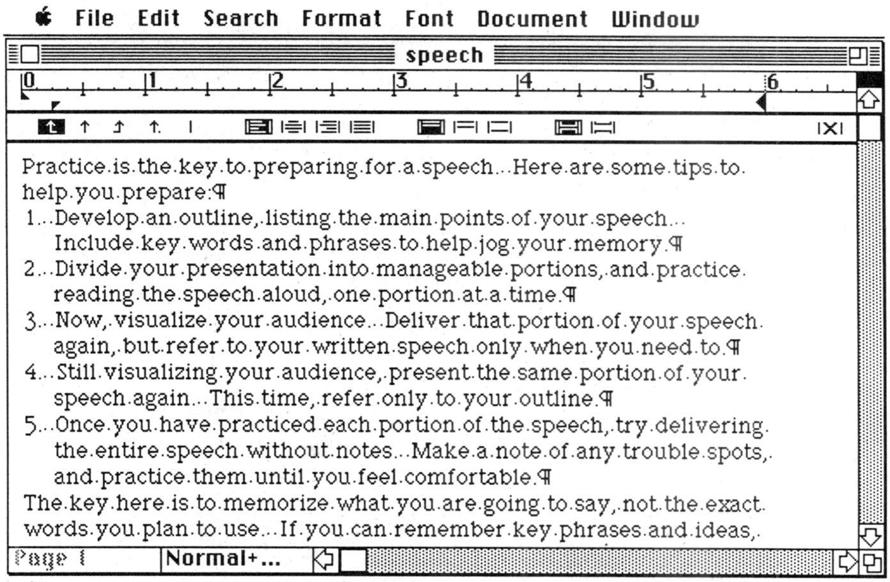

To create a hanging indention, press the Shift key and drag the left indent marker to the right.

paragraph, then press the Tab key to replace these blank spaces with a ➡ symbol. Word will automatically push the text to the right of the tab mark into alignment with the left indent marker. Figure 5-37 shows the results. (We'll be talking about tabs in much more detail in a few pages.)

FIGURE 5-37

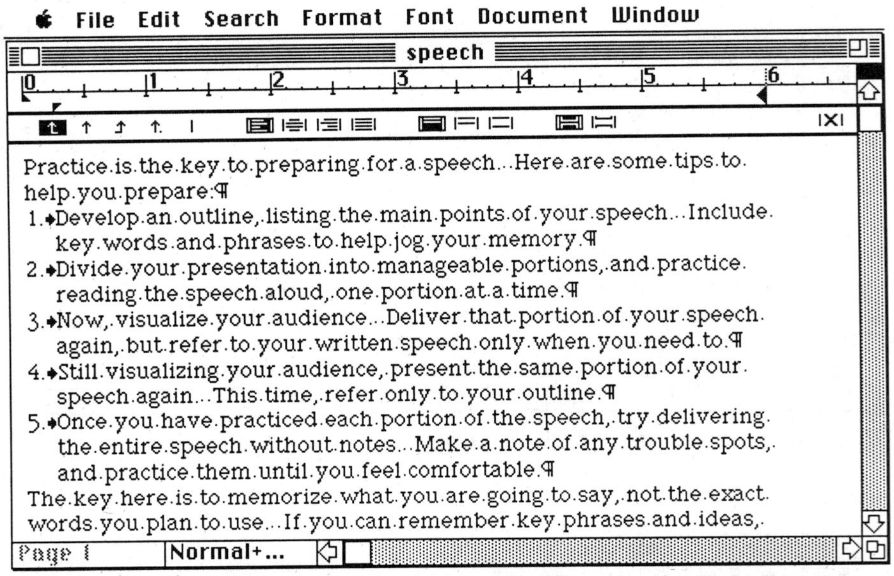

Use a tab to ensure that the first line of text is aligned with the remaining text in each paragraph.

Placing text in the margins

Generally, you'll use the left, right, and first-line indent markers to decrease the width of selected paragraphs, as illustrated in the examples above. However, Word also lets you place text in the margin areas of your printed page. As we've mentioned before, your ruler extends far beyond the 6 $^{3}/_{4}$ inches or so that are visible in a standard document window—from -11 to 22, as a matter of fact.

For example, suppose you want to include a headline in your document that is wider than your body text. To extend the headline into the right margin, all you need to do is click on that headline text, then drag the right indent marker past the default (6-inch, in this case) margin, as shown in Figure 5-38.

To print in the left margin of the page, you need to drag the left and first-line indent markers to the left of the zero point on the ruler. To move past the zero point, you need to press the Shift key as you drag the markers. Word will scroll the document window to bring the negative ruler values into view, as shown in Figure 5-39. This technique, called a negative indention, is similar to the hanging indention shown in Figure 5-37.

FIGURE 5-38

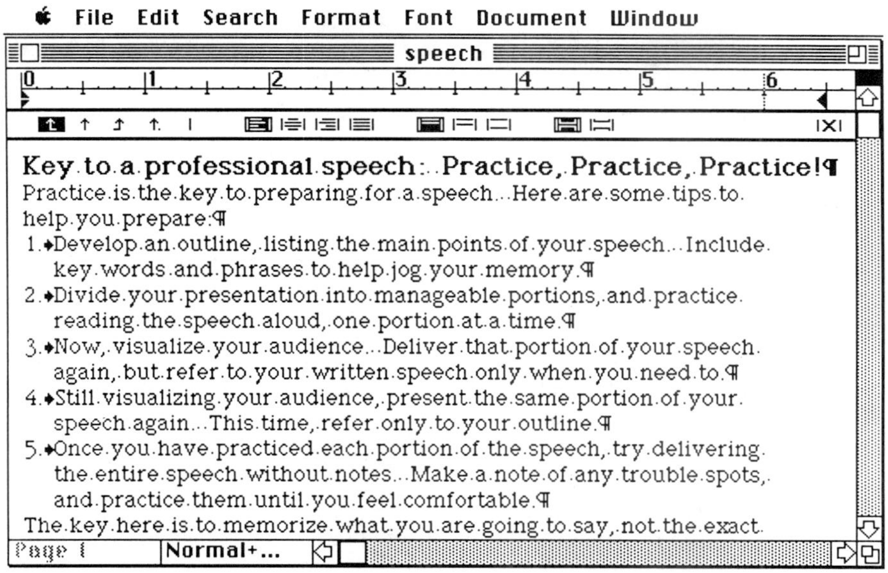

To print in the right margin, just drag the right indent marker to the right.

FIGURE 5-39

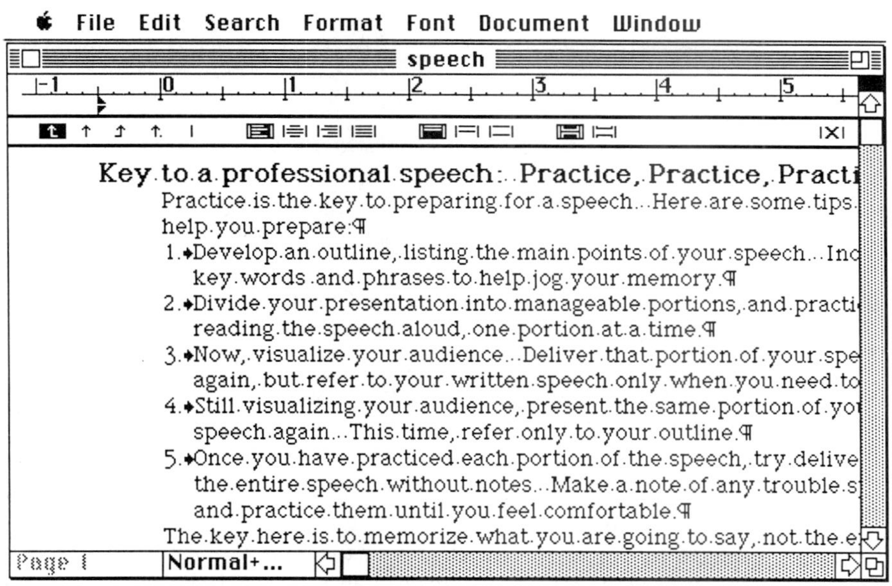

To create a negative indention, press the Shift key as you drag the left indent and first-line indent markers to the left.

Another common use for negative indents is to place special symbols in the margin of a page to highlight selected paragraphs. For example, in Figure 5-40, we used a $^1/_2$-inch negative first-line indent to display the words *Save 33%* to the left of the first paragraph. Notice that the left indent marker remains at the zero point so that the remainder of the paragraph is aligned with the rest of the text in the document.

FIGURE 5-40

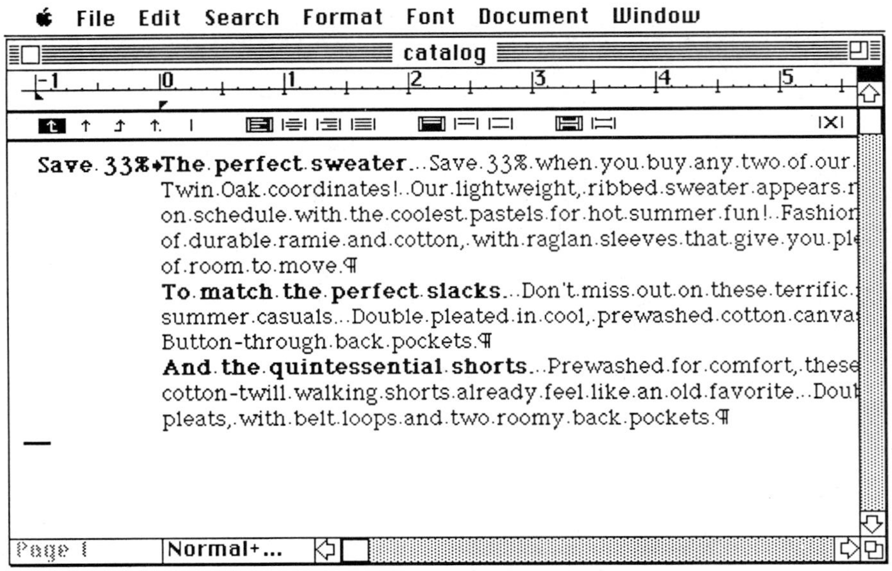

You can use negative indents to highlight key paragraphs.

When you drag a ruler icon to the left of the zero point, you may not be able to see the text in this area on your screen the next time you scroll the document window to the right. (In addition, when you close a file and then reopen it, Word will automatically position the window so that the zero point appears at the left edge of the window.) If you try to click in the horizontal scroll bar to bring the margin text into view, Word will beep stubbornly and refuse to scroll past the zero point. To scroll to the left of the zero point, you need to press the Shift key as you click on the left scroll arrow.

Alignment

As you know, Word automatically aligns all of the text in your document evenly with the left indent marker. The length of each line of text varies, creating a ragged right margin. To change this default alignment, all you need to do is click on or highlight the paragraph(s) that you want to format and click on one of the alignment icons on the ruler.

The effects of the various alignment icons are fairly self-evident: The Centered alignment icon instructs Word to center the selected text between the left and right indent markers. The Flush-Right icon aligns the text with the right indent marker, creating a ragged left margin. The Justified alignment icon aligns both edges of the text evenly with the left and right indent markers. Word may increase or decrease the width of the blank spaces in your text to keep the left and right edges of your text in line.

Let's use the title page in Figure 5-41 to illustrate Word's alignment features. At first glance, the various elements of the page are difficult to distinguish because all of the text is aligned to the left side of the page. Now, notice the difference when we change the alignment of the various blocks of text in Figure 5-42.

FIGURE 5-41

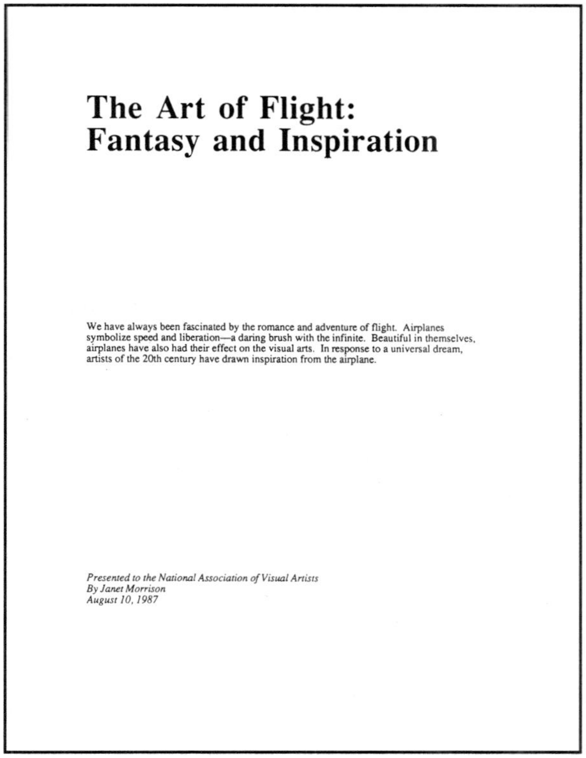

The Art of Flight:
Fantasy and Inspiration

We have always been fascinated by the romance and adventure of flight. Airplanes symbolize speed and liberation—a daring brush with the infinite. Beautiful in themselves, airplanes have also had their effect on the visual arts. In response to a universal dream, artists of the 20th century have drawn inspiration from the airplane.

Presented to the National Association of Visual Artists
By Janet Morrison
August 10, 1987

Currently, all of the text in this sample document is left aligned.

FIGURE 5-42

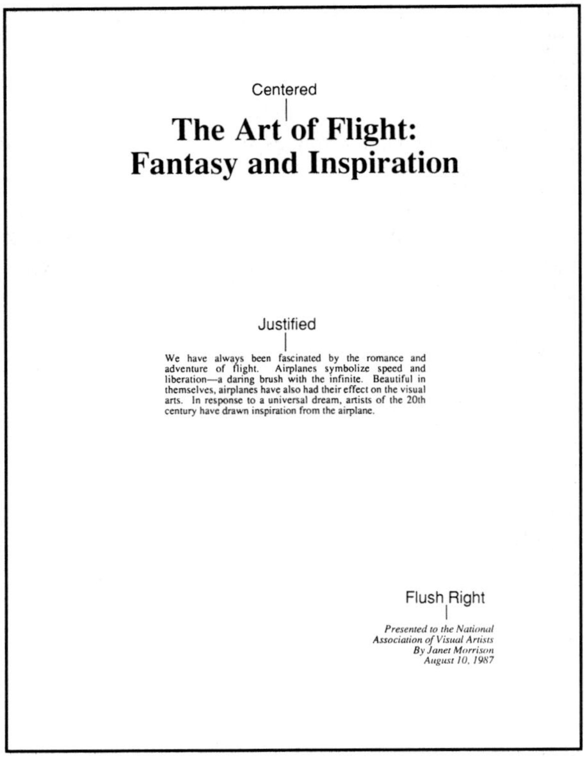

You can dress up your page designs by varying the alignment of paragraphs.

To format the first two lines of the sample page, we simply selected the title lines and clicked the Centered alignment icon on the ruler. Next, to format the summary paragraph in the center of the page, we clicked on that text, then placed the left indent and right indent markers at the 1 inch and 5 inch marks, respectively. Then we selected the Justified alignment icon from the ruler. To format the last four lines of text, we selected the Right alignment icon.

By the way, when you use centered and flush-right alignment formats, you'll generally want to keep the left indent and first-line indent settings equal. Since the left edge of centered and right-aligned paragraphs is normally "freeform," a first-line indention may throw the first line of the paragraph out of balance with the remaining text.

Line spacing

The line spacing options on your ruler let you create single-spaced, 1 $^1/_2$-spaced, and double-spaced lines of text. The 1 $^1/_2$-space and double-space formats are convenient for creating manuscript pages because they give you some extra room on the printed page for writing notes and corrections.

To apply the single-space, 1 $^1/_2$-space and double-space line settings, just click on or select the text you want to format and then click on the appropriate ruler icon.

With the exception of the title page shown in Figure 5-42, all of the sample documents you've seen thus far have used the single-space setting. When you use 1 $^1/_2$-line spacing, Word sets your line spacing to 18 points. If you are using 12-point type, this means that there will be 6 points of leading or white space between each line rather than the default 1 point. Similarly, when you use double spacing, Word sets your line spacing to 24 points. If you are using 12-point type, this means 12 points of leading. Figures 5-43 and 5-44 show the effects of the 1 $^1/_2$-space and double-space options.

FIGURE 5-43

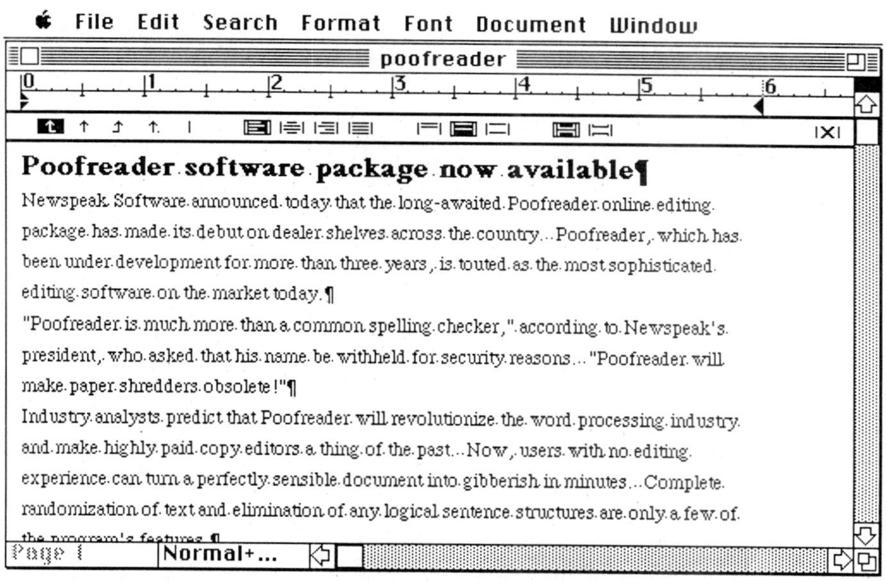

The 1 $^1/_2$-space setting places 6 points of leading between lines.

FIGURE 5-44

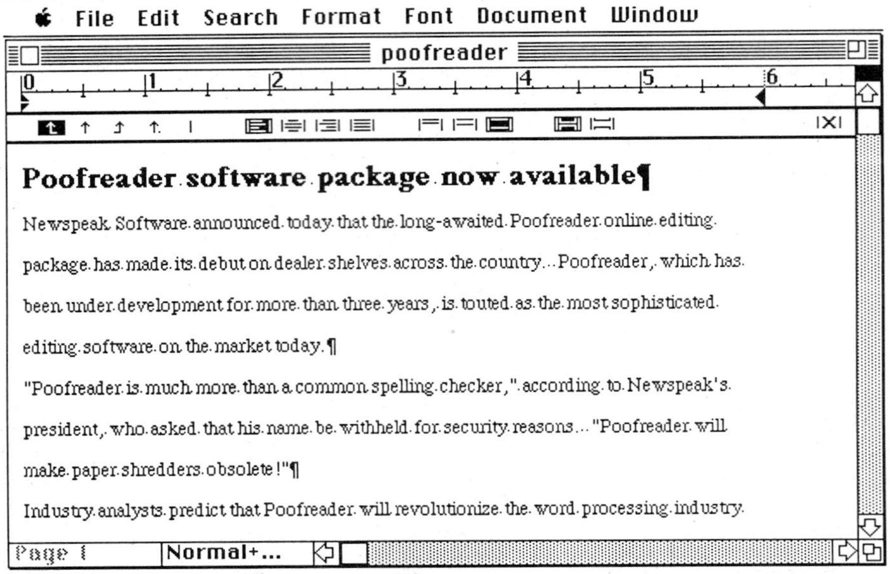

The double space setting places 12 points of leading between lines.

Though these line spacing settings are fine for small type sizes like 10 or 12 point, unfortunately, Word does not increase the leading between lines of larger text. For example, the sample text in Figure 5-45 shows 36-point type formatted with single, 1 $^1/_2$, and double spacing. As you can see, there is no difference in the leading between the sample paragraphs. Because the 18-point and 24-point line spacing settings are smaller than the line spacing that would normally be applied to this text, Word ignores your 1 $^1/_2$ and double-space settings. In fact, if Word were to use these line spacing settings, the lines of text would overlap! We'll show you how to overcome this problem in a few pages when we talk about the Paragraph dialog box.

Paragraph spacing

Paragraph spacing is similar to line spacing except that your changes apply only to the first line of the selected paragraph. Word offers two standard paragraph spacing options: open and closed. When you use closed paragraph spacing, Word uses the standard 1 point of leading between paragraphs of text. When you use the open setting, you get 12 points of white space before the first line of text in the selected paragraphs.

To apply the open and closed paragraph settings, just click on or select the text you want to format, then click on the appropriate ruler icon.

With the exception of the title page shown in Figure 5-42, all of the sample documents you've seen thus far have used the closed setting. Figure 5-46 shows the effects of the open setting.

FIGURE 5-45

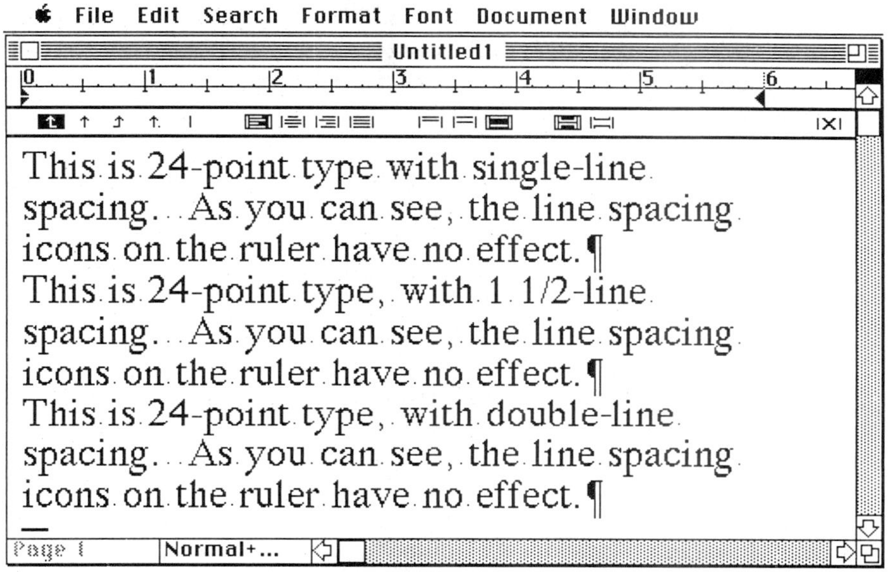

If you use 1 $^{1}/_{2}$-spacing or double spacing with large type, Word will ignore your settings.

FIGURE 5-46

You can use the open setting to add 12 points of white space above paragraphs.

Reverting to normal

If you have added a number of paragraph formatting changes to a block of text and then decide that you want to revert to Word's default settings, you can simply click on the Normal Paragraph icon on the right side of the ruler. Word will automatically remove all special paragraph settings and display the selected text in the default single-spaced, flush-left, no-indent format.

A paragraph spacing tip

Many users insert extra blank paragraphs in order to insert space manually between paragraphs. For example, when you reach the end of one paragraph and are ready to begin a new one, you may press the Return key twice to insert a blank space between the two paragraphs. This technique is inferior to using the Open space icon in a couple of important ways. First of all, when you use the Open space icon to add space between paragraphs, Word will omit that extra space if the new paragraph happens to fall at the beginning of a page. If you have manually inserted a blank paragraph, however, that extra space will appear regardless of the position of the text on the page. This means that your text will not be properly aligned at the top of the page, leaving unsightly gaps in your document.

Also, if you decide to increase or decrease the amount of space between paragraphs, you can simply select all of the paragraphs at once and change the Space Before and/or the Space After settings in your Paragraph dialog box to reformat all of the text at once. (You can also use style sheets to make this type of formatting change, as you'll learn in Chapter 9.) If you have inserted blank paragraphs in your document, however, you'll have to manually change the amount of space between each paragraph.

The Paragraph… Command

If you need to change several paragraph formatting specifications, you may prefer to use the Paragraph… command on the Format menu instead of the ruler icons to format your text. In addition, the Paragraph dialog box gives you some options that are not available on the ruler.

Like the Character… command, the Paragraph… command is available only when the Full Menus setting is in effect. You can access the Paragraph dialog box quickly by pressing ⌘-m. When you open the Paragraph dialog box, Word will also display the ruler, if it is not already in view. As with the Character dialog box, when you open the Paragraph dialog box, any settings that you have already applied to the paragraph will appear selected.

For example, if we click on the second paragraph in Figure 5-46 and choose Paragraph… from the Format menu, we'll see a dialog box like the one in Figure 5-47. As you can see, Word displays the value *12 pt* in the Before edit bar, indicating that we have applied the open setting to this paragraph.

FIGURE 5-47

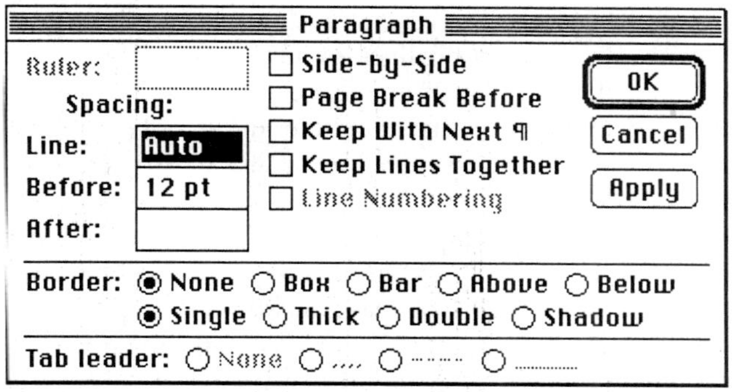

When you open the Paragraph dialog box, Word displays your current paragraph settings.

The Ruler option

The Ruler option at the top-left corner of the Paragraph dialog box appears dimmed when you initially open the dialog box. However, if you click on a ruler icon, this option will change to black. The text of the option will also change when you click on a ruler icon to indicate the type of formatting change you are making. For example, as you can see in Figure 5-48, if we drag the first-line indent marker to the right while the dialog box is open, Word will change the Ruler option to read *First* and will display the position of the first-line indent marker in the edit bar.

FIGURE 5-48

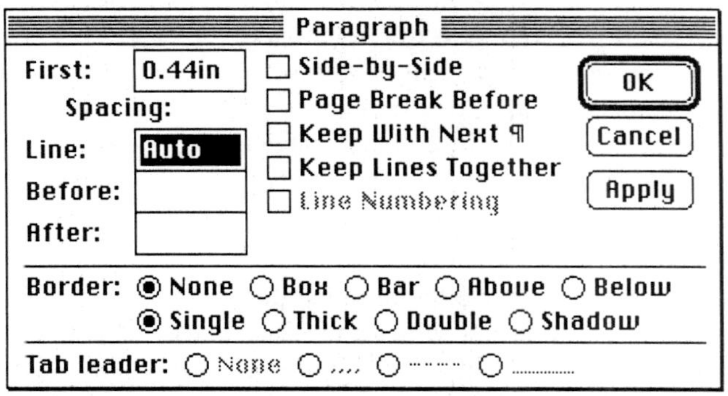

Word will display your ruler setting in the Ruler edit bar.

You may wonder why you should bother to open the Paragraph dialog box in order to make changes that you can specify on the ruler. As we mentioned earlier, you can specify ruler settings with up to $^1/_{16}$ of an inch of accuracy. The Ruler edit bar, however, lets you make much more exacting specifications than you can make on the ruler. Therefore, you can apply your general paragraph formats on the ruler, then change the entry in the Ruler edit bar to make a more precise setting.

The Line option

The Line edit bar in the Paragraph dialog box is similar to the single, 1 $^1/_2$, and double-spacing icons on the ruler. You can use this edit bar to specify the exact amount of leading you want between lines of text. The default Line setting is Auto, which means that Word will automatically adjust the spacing between lines to accommodate the text size you are using. To override automatic line spacing, just type a value in the Line edit bar. To return to automatic spacing, you can type Auto or 0.

When you use the Line option, you need to add to your spacing setting the point size you have applied to the selected text. For example, if you are using 12-point type and you want 12 points of white space between each line of text, you need to specify a Line setting of 24 points. (As we mentioned earlier, this is the setting that Word uses when you click on the Double-space icon on the ruler.) If you are using 36-point type and you want 12 points of leading, you need to use a line setting of 48 points. We recommend that you select your type sizes before you specify your Line settings in Word. The program will not automatically adjust your line spacing if you later decide to change the size of your text.

The Before and After options

The Before edit bar is similar to the Open and Close paragraph spacing icons on your ruler. You can use this option to add white space above the first line of the paragraph. Unlike the Line option, the value that you type in the Before edit bar is not relative to the size of type that you are using. If you want to add 12 points of leading above a paragraph, simply type 12 in the Before edit bar.

The After edit bar works just like the Before edit bar, except that it adds white space below a paragraph. Thus, if you want to add 12 points of leading after a paragraph of text, you'll type 12 in the After edit bar.

Often, you'll use the Before and After edit bars to set headlines apart from the rest of the text in your document. For example, in the sample document shown in Figure 5-49, the headline text between the first and third paragraphs is a bit difficult to distinguish from the rest of the document. Now, watch what happens when we add 12 points of leading before and 6 points of leading after this headline in Figure 5-50.

Notice that we used more space above the headline than below. Generally, you'll want to follow this practice when you format headlines in your own documents to help link the headlines and associated body text. The space before separates the headline from the preceding body copy, while the smaller space below helps to draw the reader's eye down to the subsequent body text.

FIGURE 5-49

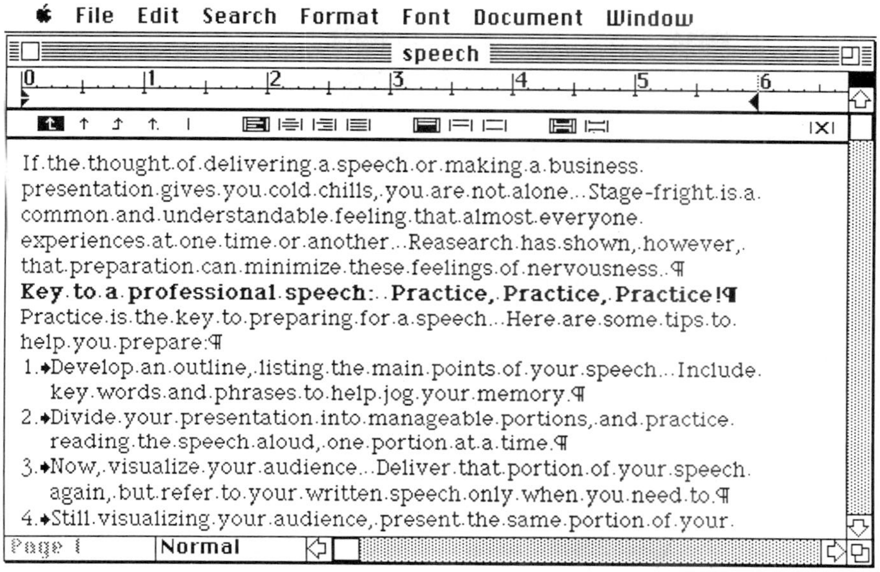

The headline in the second paragraph is not easily distinguishable from the body text in this document.

FIGURE 5-50

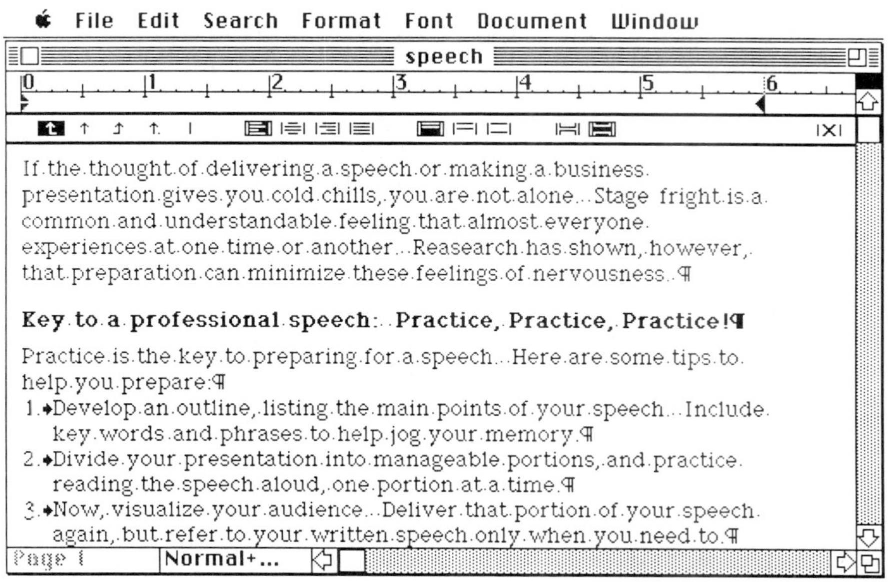

Extra space before and after makes the headline easier to see.

Overlapping lines of text

Normally, Word will not let you overlap lines of text. If you specify a Line, Before, or After setting that is less than or equal to the size of the type in the paragraph that you have selected, Word will ignore your settings and use its default 1-point leading. If you want to force the program to eliminate the leading between lines or even to overlap lines of text, you can type a negative spacing setting in the Paragraph dialog box. For example, to create the sample logo in Figure 5-51, we used 24-point Times text with a Line setting of -11.

FIGURE 5-51

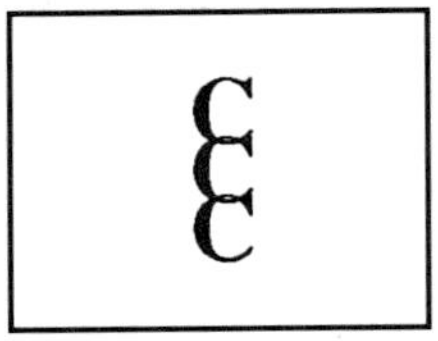

To overlap lines of text, just type a negative spacing value in the Paragraph dialog box.

When you use negative line or paragraph spacing, some of your text may be truncated on the screen. All of the characters will appear in their entirety when you print the document, however.

Using borders

One of Word 3's most exciting new features is the ability to format a paragraph with a border. Word gives you five Border options: None, Box, Bar, Above, and Below. (Obviously, None is the default.) In addition, you can choose from among four line types: Single, Thick, Double, or Shadow.

To add border lines to a paragraph, just click on or drag through the text you want to format, issue the Paragraph... command, and choose the desired Border type and line type. Figure 5-52 shows the available Border combinations.

As you can see, the Bar Border setting places a vertical line to the left of the selected paragraph. If you are using the Facing Pages option to print your document, Word will place this vertical bar to the left of paragraphs that appear on even-numbered pages and to the right of paragraphs that appear on odd-numbered pages. (We'll talk more about the Facing Pages option in Chapter 7.)

The Above and Below settings tell Word to extend a horizontal line from the paragraph's left indent mark (or first-line indent mark, if you are using a hanging indent) to the right-indent mark. The Box option places a border on all four sides of the selected paragraph.

For example, to create the title block for the page shown in Figure 5-52, we set our first-line and left indent markers to the 2 inch mark and our right indent marker to the 4 $^{1}/_{2}$ inch mark.

FIGURE 5-52

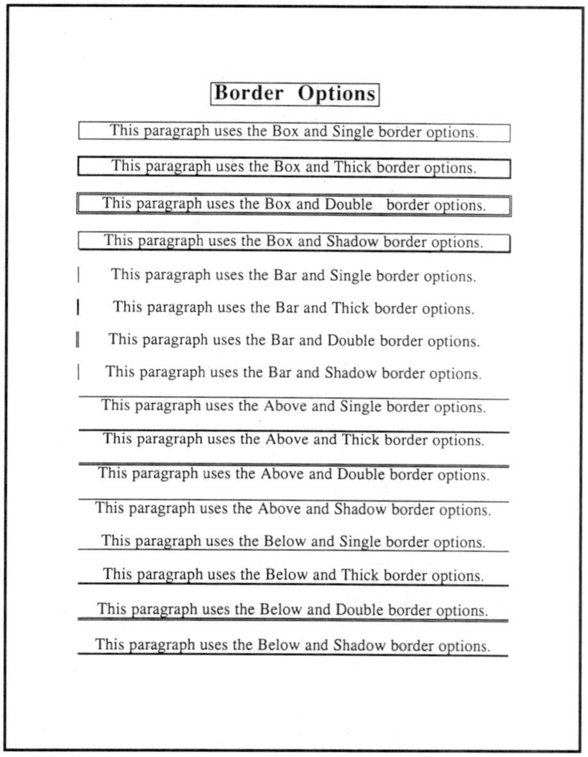

Use the Paragraph dialog box Border options to add borders to paragraphs in your Word documents.

Other Paragraph formatting options

There are several more Paragraph dialog box options that we have not discussed yet—namely Side-by-Side, Page Break Before, Keep Lines Together, Keep With Next Paragraph, and Tab Leaders. We'll get to Tab Leaders in a few pages. We'll save our discussion of the Side-by-Side option for Chapter 8, when we look at multicolumn document design. The remaining paragraph formatting options relate to the way your printed document is paginated—we'll discuss these settings when we talk about printing in Chapter 7.

Paragraph Formatting Shortcuts

As with character formatting, there are a number of keyboard shortcuts that you can use to speed up your paragraph formatting in Word. These keyboard shortcuts also use the Shift and ⌘ keys. For example, you can press Shift-⌘-c to center a paragraph or Shift-⌘-j to justify a paragraph. You can also press Shift-⌘-p to remove any special paragraph formatting and revert to the default paragraph formats for your document.

Table 5-4 offers a summary of Shift-⌘ key techniques for paragraph formatting.

TABLE 5-4

Format	Shift-⌘-Key	Incremental
Centered	c	
Double space	y	
First-line indent	f	
Flush Left	l	
Flush Right	r	
Hanging indent	t	•
Justified	j	
Nest paragraph	n	•
Open Space	o	
Plain	p	
Unnest paragraph	m	•
Side-by-side	g	

You can use these keys along with the Shift and ⌘ keys to format paragraphs in Word.

The plain, double space, open space, centered, justified, flush right, and flush left shortcuts need little additional explanation. They are equivalent to clicking the icons on your ruler. Similarly, the Side-by-Side shortcut is equivalent to selecting the Side-by-Side option from the Paragraph dialog box. (More about Side-by-Side formatting in Chapter 8.) The nest, unnest, and hanging indent shortcuts require a little more explanation, however.

The nest shortcut (Shift-⌘-n) lets you move the left indent marker for the selected paragraph $^1/_2$ inch to the right of the existing margin setting. As you might have guessed, the unnest shortcut (Shift-⌘-m) lets you move the left indent marker back $^1/_2$ inch to the left again. For example, suppose you are typing the sample document that we used in Figure 5-31. When you are ready to enter the quotation in the second paragraph, you can press Return to begin a new paragraph, then press Shift-⌘-n to indent that paragraph $^1/_2$ inch. After typing the paragraph, you can press Return again to begin the third paragraph, then press Shift-⌘-m to move the left margin back to its original location at the 0 inch mark. (Unfortunately, there is no keyboard shortcut that lets you move to the left and right indent markers simultaneously.)

The first-line indent shortcut (Shift-⌘-f) is similar to the nest shortcuts, except that it indents only the first line of the selected paragraph $^1/_2$ inch from the existing left margin position on the ruler. Thus, if your left indent and left-margin markers are currently set to 0, pressing Shift-⌘-f will indent the first line of that paragraph to $^1/_2$ inch. If both markers are set to 1 inch, Shift-⌘-f will indent the first line of the paragraph to 1 $^1/_2$ inches.

The Shift-⌘-f technique is not incremental—that is, you can't repeat the keyboard shortcut to increase the amount of first-line indention. In addition, even if your first-line indent marker is already positioned to the left or right of the left-margin marker, Word will create a $^1/_2$ inch first-line indent for you. In other words, if your left-margin marker is at 0 and your first-line indent marker is at 1 $^1/_2$ inches, Shift-⌘-f will still move the first-line indent marker to the $^1/_2$ inch point.

The hanging indent shortcut (Shift-⌘-t) lets you move the first-line indent marker $^1/_2$ inch to the left rather than to the right. Hanging indentions are commonly used for numbered or bulleted lists like those we showed you in Figure 5-36 on page 135. When you press Shift-⌘-t, Word will move the first-line indent marker $^1/_2$ inch to the left and leave the left indent marker set to 0.

We noted in Table 5-4 that the hanging indent, nest, and unnest shortcuts are incremental. That is, if you repeat that Shift-⌘ key shortcut, Word will continue to change the current margin specification by $^1/_2$ inch. However, the effects of repeating one of these shortcuts are not always what you would expect.

For example, if you repeat the hanging indent shortcut (Shift-⌘-t), Word will not increase the distance between the first-line indent marker and the left-margin marker by moving the left-margin marker an additional $^1/_2$ inch to the right. Instead, it will move both markers an additional $^1/_2$ inch to the right, maintaining a $^1/_2$ inch between the two markers.

If you repeat the nesting shortcut (Shift-⌘-n), Word will continue to move both the first-line indent and left-margin markers $^1/_2$ inch to the right, even if that means moving the first-line indent and left-margin markers to the right of the right-margin marker. Similarly, the unnest shortcut (Shift-⌘-m) will allow you to move the first-line indent and left-margin markers to the left of the zero point marker on your ruler.

By the way, you can use the unnest shortcut to move the first-line indent and left-margin markers for hanging indentions back to the left, as well. The unnest shortcut also removes any first-line indention you may have assigned to the selected paragraph, even if you moved the first-line indent marker manually. If this is not what you had intended, you may need to press Shift-⌘-t or Shift-⌘-f again or drag the first-line indent marker back into its proper position.

WORKING WITH TABS

Working with tabs in Word is a two-step process: You specify your tab settings on the ruler and then use the Tab key to position the text in your document. If you do not specify any tab setting on the ruler, Word will use the default format settings: left-aligned tabs every $^1/_2$ inch. When you use a negative first-line indention on your ruler, like the one shown in Figure 5-39, Word also places a tab stop at your left indent marker.

When you use Full Menus, Word offers three tab formats in addition to flush-left tabs: flush right, centered, and decimal. The chart in Figure 5-53 shows examples of each tab type.

FIGURE 5-53

	Centered	Right	Decimal	Left
Name	**Sun**	**Height**	**Price**	**Description**
Ageratum	•••	6"	$1.25	Long-lasting blue or white blooms
Alyssum	•••	3"	.75	Great for rock gardens or borders
Aster	•••	6" to 18"	$1.25	Blue, pink, or crimson blooms
Begonia	••	10" to 15"	$1.75	Easy to grow; blooms all summer
Caladium	•	8" to 20"	$1.99	Prefers humid climate and indirect sun
Calendula	••	12" to 15"	$1.99	Bright orange or yellow blooms
Candytuft	••	8"	.75	Hardy pink, white, or lavender blooms
Celosia	•••	7" to 18"	$1.00	Feathery bright plumes
Cineraria	••	8" to 12"	$1.99	Blooms form colorful nosegays
Coleus	•	6" to 15"	$1.00	Beautiful multicolored leaves
Dahlia	••	12" to 20"	$2.25	Compact hardy growth; bright blooms
Fuchsia	•	12" to 20"	$2.75	Needs pampering, but well worth it!
Geranium	••	10" to 12"	$1.25	Long-time favorite for window boxes
Impatiens	••	12" to 20"	$1.00	Easy-care; blooms all summer
Marigold	•••	18" to 20"	$1.25	Sturdy, bright blooms in lots of colors
Nasturtium	•••	12" to 18"	$1.25	Cascades of sky-blue blooms
Pansy	••	7"	$1.75	Charming, delicate blooms; easy-care
Petunia	•••	8" to 14"	$1.00	A window-box champion!
Phlox	••	7"	.75	Compact blooms; great ground cover
Portulaca	•••	6"	$1.75	Roselike blooms; thrives in heat and sun
Snapdragon	•••	12" to 20"	$1.75	Adds color and texture to any garden
Verbena	••	10"	$1.50	Brilliant colors; needs good drainage
Vinca	••	3" to 10"	.75	Fast-spreading hardy ground cover
Zinnia	•••	10" to 18"	$1.75	A hardy sun-loving favorite

Word offers four tab options.

Though they require a little planning, tables like the one in Figure 5-53 are not difficult to create. Perhaps the easiest way to learn to use tabs is to work with a sample document. Let's walk through the process for creating the table in Figure 5-53.

Creating a table

Your first step is to decide how many columns you need and how much space you should allow for each column. The space required by each column depends on the size of the type you are using and the length of the entries in each column. You may find it helpful to type your header line for the chart and one or two sample lines to "get your bearings." Don't worry about the proper ruler settings for now; just enter some sample text, pressing the Tab key at the end of each column to move to the next column. When you press the Tab key, your insertion point marker will automatically jump to the next default tab stop.

Next, assign any desired character and paragraph formats to your sample lines so that you can get a feel for the amount of space required for each column. Figure 5-54 shows the first two lines of our sample table at this point. As you can see, our columns are not yet properly aligned because the entries in each line vary in length. Word simply pushes each entry to the next $^1/_2$ inch tab stop.

FIGURE 5-54

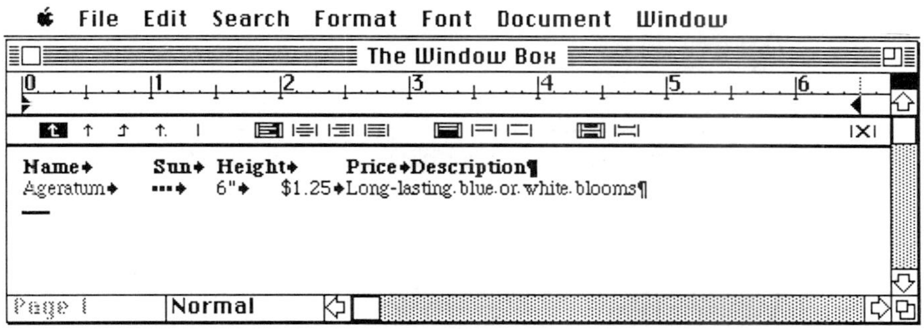

You may want to enter and format some sample text to determine the appropriate tab stops for your charts and tables.

Next, you need to decide how you want to align and position the text in each column. When you're working with currency values, you'll probably want to use decimal tabs to align the decimal points in each entry, as shown in the fourth column of our sample table. Left-aligned tabs generally work best for long text entries, like those in the fifth column of our table, because they help guide the reader's eye from one line to the next.

Adding tab stops

To set your tab positions and alignment, click on the tab icon that represents the alignment you want to use, then, with that icon selected, click in the desired position on the ruler. When you insert a tab stop on your ruler, Word will remove all of the default $^1/_2$ inch tab stops to the left of your new tab setting. However, the default $^1/_2$ inch tab stops to the right of your tab mark will remain in effect. (If you want to remove a tab that you've added, just drag the icon up or down away from the ruler.)

Try to allow enough room between each column to accommodate the longest entry in that column. For example, in the first column of our sample table, the word *Snapdragon* is our longest entry, extending almost to the 1 inch mark. So, we decided to center our second column at the 1 $^1/_4$ inch mark. Then, to position columns three, four, and five, we used a right-aligned tab at the 2 $^1/_2$ inch mark, a decimal tab at the 3 $^1/_8$ inch mark, and a left-aligned tab at the 3 $^3/_4$ inch mark. Figure 5-55 shows the results.

FIGURE 5-55

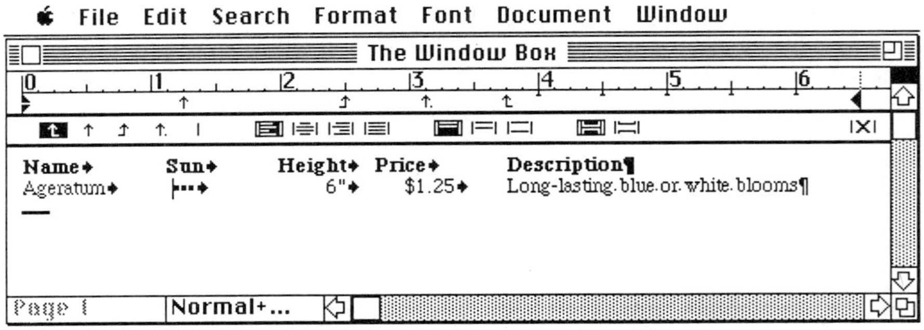

To select your tab positions and alignment, click on a tab icon, then click at the desired position on the ruler.

If you use decimal tabs, you may have to make some adjustments to your header line. As you can see in the Price column of Figure 5-55, our heading is not properly aligned with the subsequent currency values. When Word cannot locate a decimal point in a string of characters, it aligns the last line in the character string with your decimal points—flush right with the decimal tab stop.

To overcome this problem, we selected the first line of text and deleted the decimal tab at the 3 $^{1}/_{8}$ inch mark. (Remember, to delete a tab, just point to the tab icon and drag it off the ruler.) Then we added a right-aligned tab at the 3 $^{3}/_{4}$ inch mark to reposition the heading.

FIGURE 5-56

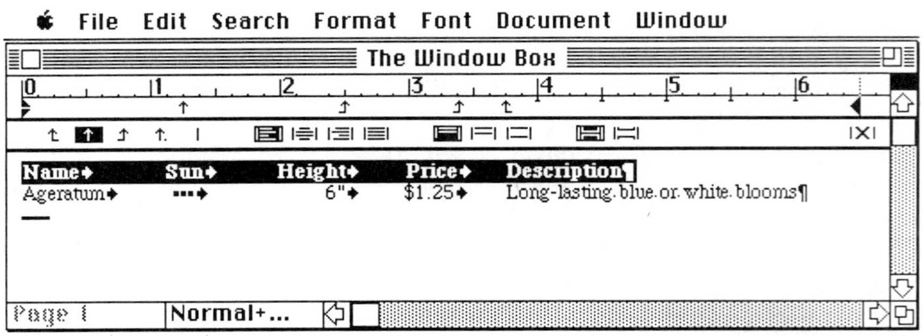

You may need to reposition the header that appears above your decimal tabs.

Once you have defined the width and alignment for each column in your table, you're ready to enter the remainder of your text. Keep in mind that your ruler settings will carry over from one line to the next. So, once you have set up your tab formats, click just to the left of the ¶ marker at the end of the last line in your table, then press the Return key to begin a new line.

If you need to adjust your tab settings later, just highlight all of the paragraphs in the table and drag the tab markers to a new positions on the ruler. Again, if you need to change tab formats, just drag the old tab marker off the ruler, then select the tab format you want to use, and click on the ruler again to specify your new tab position.

Formatting columns of text

One of Word's most convenient new features is the block selection capability, which allows you to select individual columns in a table to format or edit. For example, suppose we decide that the names in the first column of our sample table should appear in bold type.

To format only the first column, we can press the Option key, click in front of the first character that we want to format, then drag through the remainder of the text, as shown in Figure 5-57. Then, select Bold from the Format menu. As you can see in Figure 5-58, Word now displays the names in bold type.

FIGURE 5-57

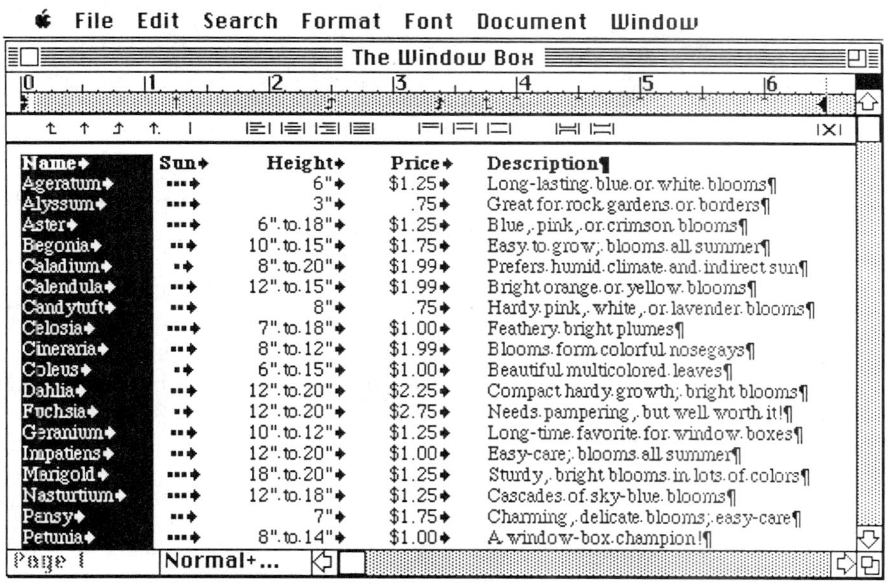

Name	Sun	Height	Price	Description
Ageratum	•••	6"	$1.25	Long-lasting blue or white blooms
Alyssum	•••	3"	.75	Great for rock gardens or borders
Aster	•••	6" to 18"	$1.25	Blue, pink, or crimson blooms
Begonia	••	10" to 15"	$1.75	Easy to grow; blooms all summer
Caladium	•	8" to 20"	$1.99	Prefers humid climate and indirect sun
Calendula	••	12" to 15"	$1.99	Bright orange or yellow blooms
Candytuft	••	8"	.75	Hardy pink, white, or lavender blooms
Celosia	•••	7" to 18"	$1.00	Feathery bright plumes
Cineraria	••	8" to 12"	$1.99	Blooms form colorful nosegays
Coleus	•	6" to 15"	$1.00	Beautiful multicolored leaves
Dahlia	••	12" to 20"	$2.25	Compact hardy growth; bright blooms
Fuchsia	•	12" to 20"	$2.75	Needs pampering, but well worth it!
Geranium	••	10" to 12"	$1.25	Long-time favorite for window boxes
Impatiens	••	12" to 20"	$1.00	Easy-care; blooms all summer
Marigold	•••	18" to 20"	$1.25	Sturdy, bright blooms in lots of colors
Nasturtium	•••	12" to 18"	$1.25	Cascades of sky-blue blooms
Pansy	••	7"	$1.75	Charming, delicate blooms; easy-care
Petunia	•••	8" to 14"	$1.00	A window-box champion!

To select a block of text, press the Option key, then drag through the column(s) you want to work with.

FIGURE 5-58

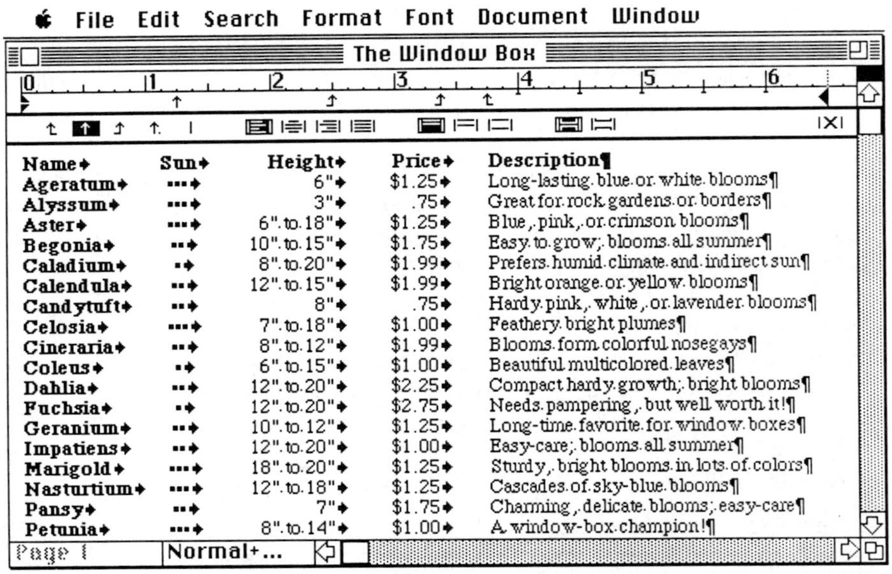

Name	Sun	Height	Price	Description
Ageratum	•••	6"	$1.25	Long-lasting blue or white blooms
Alyssum	•••	3"	.75	Great for rock gardens or borders
Aster	•••	6" to 18"	$1.25	Blue, pink, or crimson blooms
Begonia	••	10" to 15"	$1.75	Easy to grow; blooms all summer
Caladium	•	8" to 20"	$1.99	Prefers humid climate and indirect sun
Calendula	••	12" to 15"	$1.99	Bright orange or yellow blooms
Candytuft	••	8"	.75	Hardy pink, white, or lavender blooms
Celosia	•••	7" to 18"	$1.00	Feathery bright plumes
Cineraria	••	8" to 12"	$1.99	Blooms form colorful nosegays
Coleus	•	6" to 15"	$1.00	Beautiful multicolored leaves
Dahlia	••	12" to 20"	$2.25	Compact hardy growth; bright blooms
Fuchsia	•	12" to 20"	$2.75	Needs pampering, but well worth it!
Geranium	••	10" to 12"	$1.25	Long-time favorite for window boxes
Impatiens	••	12" to 20"	$1.00	Easy-care; blooms all summer
Marigold	•••	18" to 20"	$1.25	Sturdy, bright blooms in lots of colors
Nasturtium	•••	12" to 18"	$1.25	Cascades of sky-blue blooms
Pansy	••	7"	$1.75	Charming, delicate blooms; easy-care
Petunia	•••	8" to 14"	$1.00	A window-box champion!

Your character format selections will apply only to the highlighted columns.

As you'll see in Chapter 6, you can also use this block selection technique to copy or move columns of data in a table.

Using Vertical Lines and Borders

Just to the right of the tab icons on your ruler is a vertical line icon. As the name suggests, you can use this icon to insert vertical rules in your document. You apply the vertical rule format much as you do the tab format—just select the paragraphs you want to work with, click on the vertical rule icon, then click at the desired ruler position. These rules do not affect your tab positions.

For example, we added vertical lines at the 1, 1 5/8, 2 3/4, and 3 5/8 inch marks to separate the columns in our sample table. As you can see, Figure 5-59 shows the results.

You can also combine the Border options in the Paragraph dialog box with the vertical line option to create grids in your document. For instance, to format the table shown in Figure 5-60, we highlighted the entire table and added vertical rules, then we issued the Paragraph... command and selected the Box and Single Border options.

FIGURE 5-59

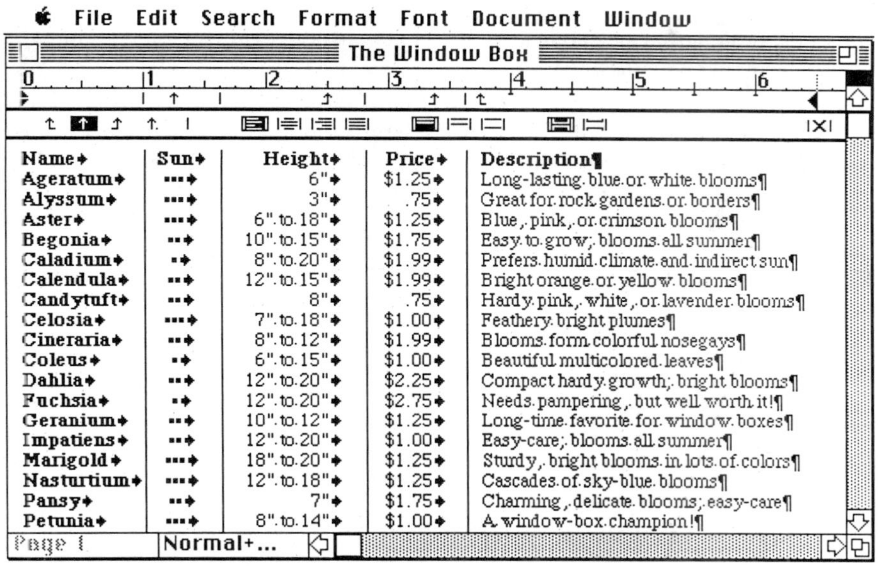

Name	Sun	Height	Price	Description
Ageratum	•••	6"	$1.25	Long-lasting blue or white blooms
Alyssum	•••	3"	.75	Great for rock gardens or borders
Aster	•••	6" to 18"	$1.25	Blue, pink, or crimson blooms
Begonia	••	10" to 15"	$1.75	Easy to grow; blooms all summer
Caladium	•	8" to 20"	$1.99	Prefers humid climate and indirect sun
Calendula	••	12" to 15"	$1.99	Bright orange or yellow blooms
Candytuft	••	8"	.75	Hardy pink, white, or lavender blooms
Celosia	•••	7" to 18"	$1.00	Feathery bright plumes
Cineraria	••	8" to 12"	$1.99	Blooms form colorful nosegays
Coleus	•	6" to 15"	$1.00	Beautiful multicolored leaves
Dahlia	••	12" to 20"	$2.25	Compact hardy growth; bright blooms
Fuchsia	•	12" to 20"	$2.75	Needs pampering, but well worth it!
Geranium	••	10" to 12"	$1.25	Long-time favorite for window boxes
Impatiens	••	12" to 20"	$1.00	Easy-care; blooms all summer
Marigold	•••	18" to 20"	$1.25	Sturdy, bright blooms in lots of colors
Nasturtium	•••	12" to 18"	$1.25	Cascades of sky-blue blooms
Pansy	••	7"	$1.75	Charming, delicate blooms; easy-care
Petunia	•••	8" to 14"	$1.00	A window-box champion!

To add vertical rules to your tables, just click on the vertical ruler icon, then click on the ruler to position your vertical rules.

FIGURE 5-60

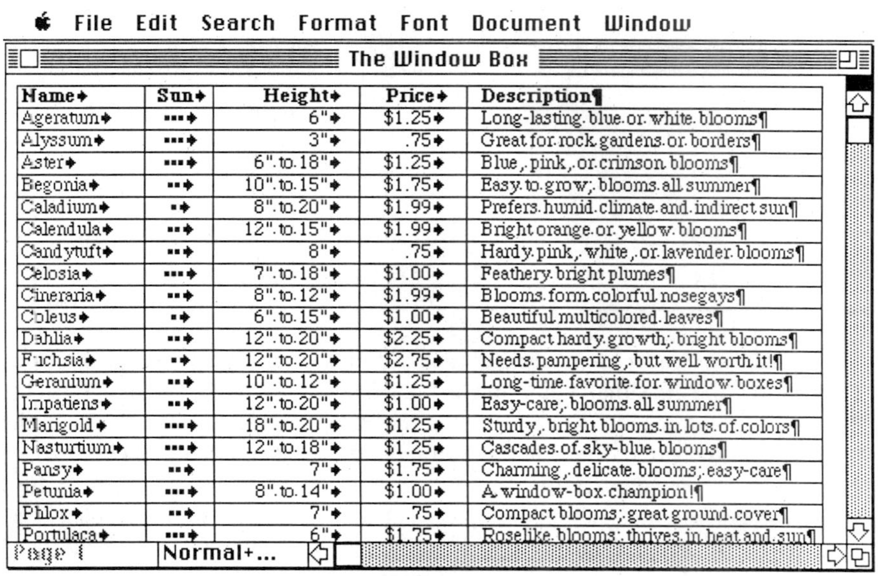

Name	Sun	Height	Price	Description
Ageratum	•••	6"	$1.25	Long-lasting blue or white blooms
Alyssum	•••	3"	.75	Great for rock gardens or borders
Aster	•••	6" to 18"	$1.25	Blue, pink, or crimson blooms
Begonia	••	10" to 15"	$1.75	Easy to grow; blooms all summer
Caladium	•	8" to 20"	$1.99	Prefers humid climate and indirect sun
Calendula	••	12" to 15"	$1.99	Bright orange or yellow blooms
Candytuft	••	8"	.75	Hardy pink, white, or lavender blooms
Celosia	•••	7" to 18"	$1.00	Feathery bright plumes
Cineraria	••	8" to 12"	$1.99	Blooms form colorful nosegays
Coleus	•	6" to 15"	$1.00	Beautiful multicolored leaves
Dahlia	••	12" to 20"	$2.25	Compact hardy growth; bright blooms
Fuchsia	•	12" to 20"	$2.75	Needs pampering, but well worth it!
Geranium	••	10" to 12"	$1.25	Long-time favorite for window boxes
Impatiens	••	12" to 20"	$1.00	Easy-care; blooms all summer
Marigold	•••	18" to 20"	$1.25	Sturdy, bright blooms in lots of colors
Nasturtium	•••	12" to 18"	$1.25	Cascades of sky-blue blooms
Pansy	••	7"	$1.75	Charming, delicate blooms; easy-care
Petunia	•••	8" to 14"	$1.00	A window-box champion!
Phlox	••	7"	.75	Compact blooms; great ground cover
Portulaca	•••	6"	$1.75	Roselike blooms; thrives in heat and sun

To create a grid, add a Box Border setting to your vertical rule settings.

Tab Leader Characters

If the Full menus command is in effect, you can use the Tab Leader options in the Paragraph dialog box to fill the space between columns with periods, hyphens, or underlines. Tab leaders help to connect items in a table, guiding the reader from one column to the next.

For example, the sample table of contents page in Figure 5-61 uses period characters to help guide the reader's eye from the chapter names in the first column to the page numbers in the second column. We also used underline characters to help separate the different sections of the table.

FIGURE 5-61

Contents

Section 1	______________________________
Chapter 1	Worksheet Basics..3
Chapter 2	Formatting the Worksheet........................25
Chapter 3	Editing the Worksheet..............................76
Chapter 4	Working with Windows..........................103
Section 2	______________________________
Chapter 5	Built-in Functions...................................137
Chapter 6	Date and Time...165
Chapter 7	Other Worksheet Topics..........................200
Chapter 8	Printing the Worksheet............................254
Section 3	______________________________
Chapter 9	Basic Graphics Techniques......................311
Chapter 10	Chart Formatting.....................................349
Chapter 11	Advanced Charting Features....................398
Section 4	______________________________
Chapter 12	Database Management.............................444
Chapter 13	Working with a Database........................490
Chapter 14	Sorting the Database...............................501
Section 5	______________________________
Chapter 15	Macro Basics...555
Chapter 16	Command-Equivalent Functions...............599
Chapter 17	User-Defined Functions...........................639

Period characters help connect columns in a table of contents.

To add tab leader characters to your document, set your tab stops as usual. Then select the line that you want to add leader characters to and issue the Paragraph... command. After you open the Paragraph dialog box, click on the tab mark on the ruler whose leader settings you want to change. (This will be the tab mark that appears to the right of the column that you want to fill.) Word will activate the Tab leader options at the bottom of the dialog box. Just click on the leader option that you want to use, then click OK. (By the way, you can also add your tab stop markers from within the Paragraph dialog box if you prefer to set your tab positions and format them simultaneously.)

To format our sample table of contents, we highlighted all of the section and chapter name lines, then we placed a left-aligned tab at the 1 $^1/_2$ inch mark and a right-aligned tab at the 6 inch mark. (This last tab mark overlaps the right indent marker, ensuring that our page numbers are flush with the right margin of the page.) Next, we issued the Paragraph... command, clicked on the tab mark that appears at the 6 inch mark, and selected the dotted line Tab Leader option in the Paragraph dialog box. Figure 5-62 shows the sample document as it appears in the document window.

FIGURE 5-62

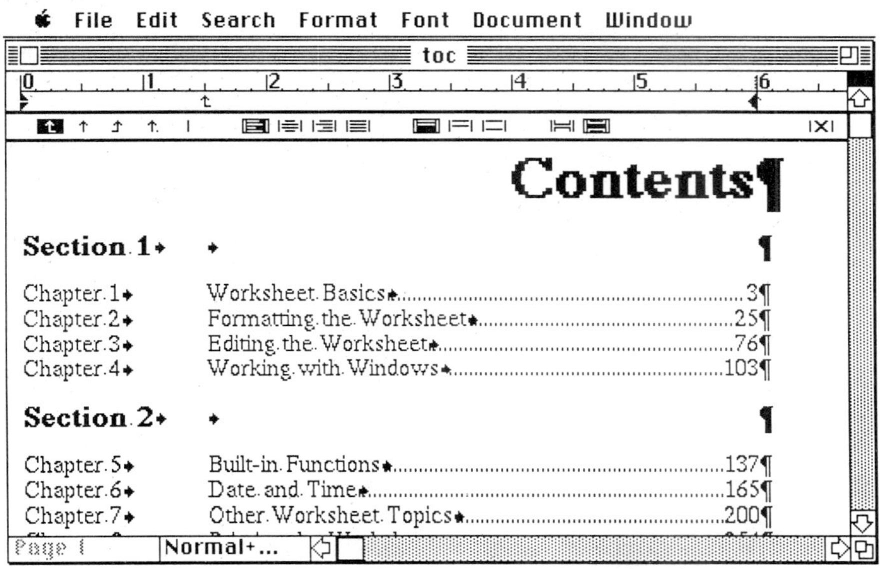

We used a dot leader to fill in the blank space between the chapter names and page numbers.

Notice that we have placed two tab markers after the section names in our text, even though no text appears to the right of these names. These empty tabular columns allow us to add leader characters to these lines as well. To create our underline tab leaders, we selected the *Section 1* line, issued another Paragraph... command, clicked on the right-aligned tab at the 6 inch mark, and selected the underline Tab Leader option. To format the remaining section name lines, we used the ⌘-a shortcut described on page 100.

A tab tip

When you're creating a long table of text, you may want to use end-of-line markers (↵) rather than paragraph markers (¶) to begin new lines of text. By using the Shift and Return keys to begin a new line of text, you can define your table as a single paragraph. Remember, when you specify paragraph formats, you do not need to highlight the entire paragraph. All you have to do is click anywhere on a paragraph to change its ruler settings, alignment, Paragraph dialog box settings, and so forth.

Thus, if you use the ↵ marker to set up your tables, you can simply click anywhere on a table to change its settings, rather than highlighting each line of the table. If you're using any special formats for the first line of your table—extra line spacing or different tab settings, for example—you'll want to place that heading in a separate paragraph.

For example, in the sample document shown in Figure 5-58, you might split the table into two parts: the heading paragraph and the body of the table. As you'll remember, the heading paragraph carries slightly different settings because we adjusted the position of the fourth column to align it with the decimal values below. All of the lines in the body of the table carry identical formats, however. We can enter these lines by pressing Shift-Return to begin the next line after typing the text for the fifth column.

There are a few drawbacks to this technique. First, if you need to change paragraph settings for a few lines of text—a border to highlight your totals line or extra spacing to set apart a new group of data, for example—you'll have to use ¶ markers to set apart those lines of text. Second, you won't be able to use Word's Sort or Renumber... commands (discussed in Chapter 15) to rearrange data in your table or to number each line of text.

Changing the Default Tab Stops

If the Full Menus command is in effect, you can use the Page Setup... command to change the default $^1/_2$ inch tab stop increments on your ruler. When you issue the Page Setup command, you'll see a dialog box like the one in Figure 5-63. In the Default Tab Stops edit bar, type the tab increment that you want to use. For example, if you want to place tab stops at every $^1/_4$ inch, type .25. This new default setting will apply to all of the text in the active document window. Unless you click the Set Default button, the default tab increments for your other Word documents will not change. (We'll take a much more in-depth look at the Page Setup dialog box in Chapter 7.)

FORMATTING NOTES

As we've mentioned before, the ¶ marker that you use to separate paragraphs of text in your Word documents also serves as a storage bin for your formatting selections. When you press Return or Enter to begin a new paragraph, all of your paragraph formats carry over to the next paragraph. Thus, Word will automatically remember any special indentions, borders, line spacing, tabs, or other formats that you used in the first paragraph and apply those formats to successive paragraphs. In addition, the character formats that you have assigned to the last character to the left of the ¶ marker are carried over from one paragraph to the next.

FIGURE 5-63

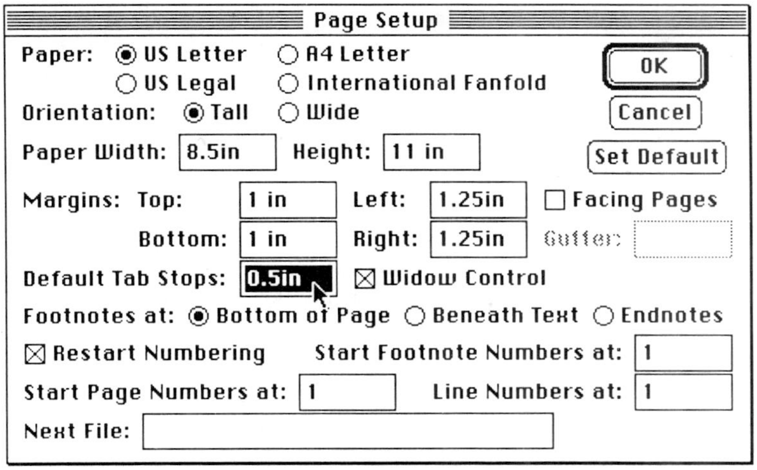

You can edit the Default Tab Stops setting in the Page Setup dialog box to change your default tab increments.

If you click to the left of the first character in a paragraph and press the Backspace key, Word will delete the ¶ marker at the end of the previous paragraph and reflow your document to combine the two paragraphs. If you hear a beep when you try this technique, Word is trying to warn you that you are trying to combine two paragraphs that have been assigned different formats.

If you want to combine the paragraphs anyway, select the ¶ marker at the end of the first paragraph and press the Backspace key. Word will combine the two paragraphs, using the format specifications for the second paragraph to format the combined text. In other words, Word will use the formats that are stored "within" the remaining ¶ marker at the end of the combined paragraph.

The Apply Button

You may have noticed the Apply button in the Character and Paragraph dialog boxes shown throughout this chapter. Apply is a new feature that lets you implement your formatting selections without closing the dialog box. Once you click Apply, you can see the effects of your formatting specifications and make adjustments as necessary.

Also, notice the stripes across the title bar of the Character and Paragraph dialog boxes. These stripes indicate that you can move the dialog box around on your screen to see the underlying text. You'll find this capability convenient when you use the Apply button to see the effects of your formatting selections.

To move a dialog box window, point to the title bar and drag, just as you would if you were moving a document window. If need be, you can even drag the dialog box partially off the screen so that you can see most of the underlying document window. A portion of the dialog box will always be accessible so that you can drag it back into view if you need to select new options.

Mixed Selections

When you open the Character and Paragraph dialog boxes, any formats that you have already assigned to the selected text will be reflected in the dialog box. For example, we selected the first line of text in our sample document in Figure 5-9 before we opened the dialog box shown in Figure 5-12. As you can see, the Geneva, 18-point, and Bold settings are all selected.

If the block of text that you have selected contains different formats, however, the dialog box might look a little different. For example, if we drag through the first two paragraphs in our sample document in Figure 5-62 before selecting Character... from the Format menu, the dialog box will look like the one in Figure 5-64. Notice that the Bold check box option is dimmed. Similarly, no Font Name, Font Size, Position, or Spacing options appear.

FIGURE 5-64

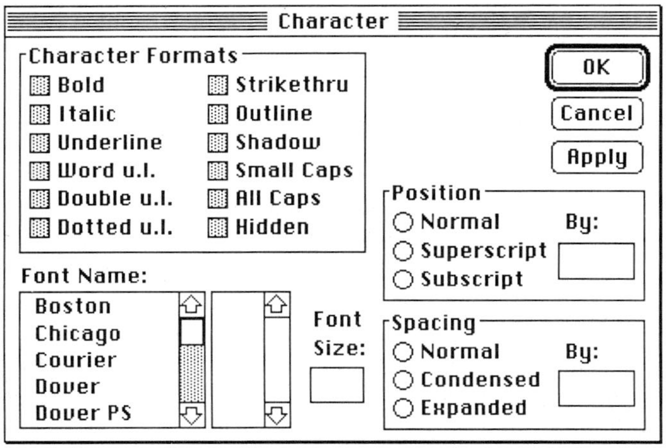

When you select a block of text that has different formats, no options will be selected in the Character dialog box.

If you select new options, those options will affect all of the selected text. However, unless you specifically instruct it to do so, Word will not change any of the previously selected options. For example, if you select the Chicago and 14 Point options while the first two paragraphs in the document are selected, Word will apply those selections to both paragraphs, regardless of their existing font or size specifications.

Character formats work a little differently from font and size options since you can apply more than one formatting option at a time. When an option is dimmed in the Character Formats box, you can click once on that option to apply it to all of the selected text. An x will appear in the box to show your selection. If you click twice in a gray check box, the box will be empty and that formatting option will be removed from all of the selected text. If you leave the box dimmed, Word will retain the existing character formats and add any additional formats that you select.

If you drag through two or more paragraphs that have different formats, your ruler will also appear dimmed, as shown in Figure 5-57 on page 155. Similarly, the check boxes in your Paragraph dialog box will be dimmed, and all of the edit bars will be blank.

FORMATTING WITH SPECIAL CHARACTERS

Thus far, we have shown you how you can use formatting techniques to control the appearance of characters in your document. In some cases, however, the characters that you enter actually affect your document formats.

Word treats the special markup characters in your document a bit differently from the standard typewriter characters. As we hinted in Chapter 4, these characters (which are shown in Table 4-1) affect the way Word defines words and sentences. In addition, they affect the way the WordWrap facility handles line breaks in your documents.

Spaces

A nonbreaking space is a space that Word treats like a character. If you place a nonbreaking space (or several nonbreaking spaces) between two words, then Word will not split those words at the end of a line. As far as Word can tell, the two words and the nonbreaking space are a single unit.

To create a nonbreaking space, just type Option-Spacebar or ⌘-Spacebar. If Show ¶ is in effect, each nonbreaking space will appear as a ⍽ on your screen. Of course, these special markers will not appear in your printed document; instead, Word will print a blank space.

Nonbreaking spaces can be useful when you want to keep two or more words together on the same line. For example, when you enter a date like *February 23, 1988*, in a document, it is a good idea to enter nonbreaking spaces between *February* and *23* and before the year *1988*. You also might use nonbreaking spaces between the different portions of a multipart number, such as a social security number, between a person's first name and middle initial, and between the different words that comprise a single proper noun, such as New York.

One important characteristic of a nonbreaking space is that it always has a specific width. You may have noticed that the width of a regular space may vary in a justified paragraph as Word increases or decreases the space between words to keep the left and right margins aligned. A nonbreaking space, on the other hand, is always about the width of a lower-case *n*. (Word adjusts the width of nonbreaking spaces according to the point size you have selected for your text and any character formatting you may have assigned. For instance, a nonbreaking space that appears in the middle of a line of bold text will be slightly larger than a nonbreaking space that falls in the middle of plain text.)

You can use nonbreaking spaces to exercise some control over the awkward spacing that sometimes appears between words in a justified paragraph. Although the best way to solve this problem is to hyphenate one or more words, you also can control the problem to some extent by using nonbreaking spaces instead of regular spaces. To replace a regular space with a nonbreaking space, just select the regular space and then type Option-Spacebar or ⌘-Spacebar. Keep in mind that when you replace a regular space with a nonbreaking space, Word will "make up the difference" by increasing the width of any other regular spaces on the same line.

Hyphens

In addition to a regular hyphen, Word 3 offers an optional hyphen and a nonbreaking hyphen. For the most part, Word treats a regular hyphen, which you enter by pressing the - key, like any other character in your document. If the word that is hyphenated happens to fall at the end of a line, however, Word will split that word between two lines. All of the characters to the left of the hyphen and the hyphen itself will appear on the first line, and the characters to the right of the hyphen will wrap to the beginning of the next line.

There may be occasions when you don't want to split a hyphenated word between two lines, however. Similarly, there may be words that you would not normally hyphenate that you need to split in order to balance lines of text. Word offers two special characters to help you handle these situations: optional and nonbreaking hyphens.

Optional hyphens

As the name implies, an optional hyphen appears only when the hyphenated word is broken at the end of a line. When you use Word's Hyphenate... command to insert hyphens automatically, Word will insert only optional hyphens. (The Hyphenate... command is discussed in detail in Chapter 6.) If you want to create an optional hyphen manually, press the ⌘ key as you type the hyphen. An optional hyphen appears on the screen as ⌐ when the Show ¶ feature is activated. When you choose Hide ¶, an optional hyphen will not appear at all, unless it occurs at a line break. If an optional hyphen occurs at a line break, it will look exactly like a regular hyphen and will appear on the screen whether or not the Show ¶ feature is activated.

We recommend that you use an optional hyphen whenever you hyphenate a word to break it at the end of a line. That way, if you later revise your document so that the word does *not* fall at the end of a line, Word will not hyphenate the word in the middle of a line.

Nonbreaking hyphens

The second kind of special hyphen in Word is the nonbreaking hyphen. A nonbreaking hyphen is similar to a nonbreaking space. If you hyphenate a word, such as great-grandfather, and that word occurs at the end of a line, Word may break the word at the hyphen. If you don't want a word to break at the hyphen, then you should use a nonbreaking hyphen. For example, suppose you are writing about the software program Lotus 1-2-3. To prevent Word from breaking 1-2-3 at the end of a line, you should always use nonbreaking hyphens between the *1* and *2* and between the *2* and *3*. To create a nonbreaking hyphen, press the ⌘ key as you type a ~. Nonbreaking hyphens are always visible on your screen, though they are marked by the ≂ symbol when Show ¶ is activated and they look like regular hyphens when you choose Hide ¶. Of course, when Word prints a nonbreaking hyphen, it looks just like a regular hyphen.

Other hyphens

You can use the hyphen key to create dashes as well as hyphens. A dash (or "long hyphen") is often used to introduce a pause in a sentence or to set apart an explanatory phrase. Word offers both a long dash and a short dash. If you want to create a long dash (—), type Shift-Option-Hyphen. If you want to create a short dash (–), type Option-Hyphen. Word will treat the — and – characters just as it does a normal hyphen.

Line Breaks

As you know, the WordWrap automatically determines how many words can fit on a line of text. If you want to force a word to the beginning of the next line, however, you can override WordWrap by pressing the Shift and Return keys. If Show ¶ is in effect, Word will display a nonprinting ↵ character in your document.

The ↵ character lets you control line breaks without starting a new paragraph. This is particularly convenient when you are using indented paragraphs because the new line will start at the left margin, rather than being indented to the first-line indent marker as it would be if you were to press the Return key to begin a new paragraph.

Other Characters

All of the text that we have entered into our sample documents thus far has been in standard keyboard characters that you can enter onto your screen by typing a letter or number, or by pressing the Shift key and typing a letter or number. Some additional characters are also available through the ⌘ and Option keys. These characters vary according to the font you're using at any given time. For example, if you are working with the default New York font, the Shift-Option-~ key combination will yield a [robot symbol] character. In the Times font, however, the same key combination would result in a Ÿ character.

You can use the Key Caps desk accessory, described on page 13, to see the various characters available in each font.

Another important character is the ellipsis(…), which you can enter into your document by pressing the Option key as you type a semicolon (Option-;). Though the ellipsis looks like three period characters, Word treats it as a single character. Thus, the spacing between the periods will not be affected when you justify text.

The Symbol font

Word's Symbol font is full of special characters and symbols that you'll find convenient for entering scientific and mathematical text. To make it easier to use the Symbol font, Microsoft has provided a handy Option-⌘-key shortcut to let you enter single symbol characters into your text as you are typing. Rather than stopping to issue the Character… command to change fonts, just press Option-⌘-q, then type the Symbol font character that you want to use. When you type your next character, Word will automatically revert to the font that you were using before you invoked the Symbol font.

For example, suppose you want to enter the phrase

A = (A - B)∪ (A ∩ B)

into a Word document. The ∪ and ∩ symbols can be obtained by choosing the Symbol font and pressing Shift-Option-\ and Option-\ respectively. So, to enter this phrase, you would type *A = (A - B)*, then you would press Shift-⌘-q to invoke the Symbol font. To enter the ∪ symbol, you would press Shift-Option-\, then you would proceed to type the characters *(A,* press Shift-⌘-q again, and press Option-\ to enter the ∩ symbol. Finally, you would type the letter *B* and the closing parenthesis to finish your formula.

Other techniques

In addition to the many special characters available directly from the keyboard, Word allows you to create sophisticated special effects by entering character formulas into your document. We'll talk more about this topic in Chapter 15.

EDITING 6

You have a number of tools at your disposal for editing text in Word. In Chapter 4, we covered Word's most basic editing functions: inserting, deleting, and overwriting text. In this chapter, we'll introduce you to Word's scissor and glue functions—the Cut, Copy, and Paste commands.

Next, we'll explore some of Word's more sophisticated editing features, like finding and changing, spell-checking, and automatic hyphenation. We'll also show you how the Clipboard and Scrapbook facilities are designed to aid your editing tasks.

As with formatting, generally, your first task in editing a document is to select the text you want to work with. We suggest that you refer to the selection and navigation techniques presented in Chapter 4 as you practice the editing concepts presented here. By learning to select text blocks quickly and accurately, you will speed your editing time significantly.

COPYING AND MOVING TEXT

Word's Cut, Copy, and Paste commands are the scissors and glue that make editing your text much faster than working with hard copy documents. With just a few keystrokes or mouse clicks, you can easily reorganize your document or repeat a block of text—and simultaneously reflow the entire document to adjust for your changes. You can also copy items from one Word document to another or even from one Macintosh program to another. We'll cover copying and moving text within Word in this chapter. In Chapter 16, we'll show you how to share information with other Macintosh programs.

Moving and copying text in Word is a two-step process: First you select the text that you want to copy or move, then you select the spot where you want to paste that text. Word also offers a few keyboard shortcuts that let you copy character or paragraph formats only and select text to paste at the current insertion point. Let's start with the more straightforward Copy, Cut, and Paste commands, then we'll take a look at these handy keyboard shortcuts.

Copying Text

Rather than typing the same block of text over and over again, you can use Word's Copy and Paste commands to copy a selected block and repeat it in one or more locations throughout your document. As you might expect, the Copy command can be a great time-saver when you need to duplicate a word, a paragraph, or even an entire document in another location.

To copy a block of text, begin by highlighting the characters that you want to copy, then select the Copy command from the Edit menu. Now, point to the location where you want the copy block to appear and click. When you select Paste from the Edit menu, a copy of the text you selected will appear to the left of the insertion point and the insertion point marker will move to the end of the pasted block. The original block of text will remain unchanged.

For example, suppose you want to insert the word *revitalization* in front of the word *efforts* in the twelfth line of the sample document in Figure 6-1. Rather than retyping the word, you could double-click on the word *revitalization* in the sixth line of the document (to select the word and the trailing blank space after it), issue the Copy command, then click in front of the word *efforts* in the twelfth line and issue the Paste command. As you can see in Figure 6-2, a duplicate of the copied word will appear in front of the word *efforts*.

FIGURE 6-1

We need to insert the word revitalization *in the twelfth line of this sample document.*

FIGURE 6-2

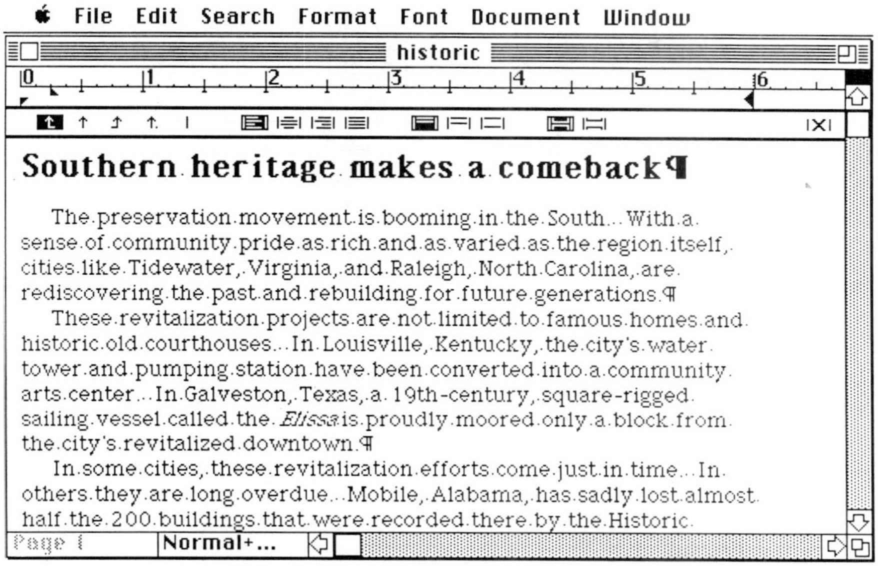

When you issue the Paste command, Word will insert the copy block to the right of the insertion point.

When you indicate your paste position with the insertion point marker, Word will insert your copy block to the right of the insertion point marker. When the paste is completed, your insertion point marker will move to the end of the pasted text. If you are pasting a large block of text, Word will automatically scroll the end of the pasted block into view for you.

By the way, you can save yourself a few mouse clicks by pressing ⌘-c to copy the selected block of text and then—after you have selected a new insertion point—pressing ⌘-v to paste it into another location.

Replacing as you paste

If you want to paste your copy block over an existing block of text, all you have to do is select the text you want to overwrite before you issue the Paste command. Returning to the sample document shown in Figure 6-2, suppose we want to change the word *revitalization* that we pasted into line 12 to read *preservation* instead. All we need to do is double-click on the word *preservation* from the second line and press ⌘-c. Then we can double-click on the word *revitalization* in the twelfth line and press ⌘-v. As you can see in Figure 6-3 on the next page, Word overwrites the selected text with the pasted text.

FIGURE 6-3

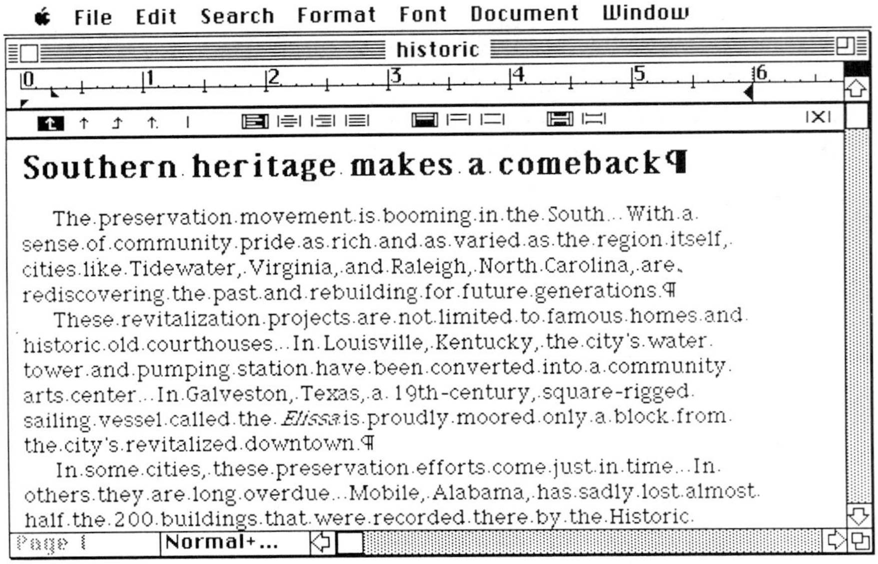

If you select a block of text before you paste, Word will overwrite that text.

Moving Text

Moving text in Word is much like copying, except that the original selection is removed from its current location and pasted in another location. To move a block of text, begin by selecting the characters that you want to move, then select Cut from the Edit menu. Now, place the insertion point marker at the spot where you want the text to appear, and select Paste from the Edit menu.

To illustrate, let's move the sentence that begins *In Louisville* in Figure 6-3 to follow the sentence that begins *In Galveston*. Begin by pressing the ⌘ key and clicking on the sentence that begins *In Louisville*. Select the Cut command from the Edit menu, then click just to the right of the sentence that begins *In Galveston* and issue the Paste command. You'll need to press the Spacebar twice to insert the proper number of blank spaces between the two sentences. Figure 6-4 shows the results.

Again, when you paste a block of text, Word will insert the text to the right of the insertion point and then move the insertion point marker to the end of the pasted block. As you would expect, Word reflows the area from which you cut the text as well as the area in which you pasted the text.

You can speed up the move process by pressing ⌘-x to cut a selection and ⌘-v to paste it into another location.

FIGURE 6-4

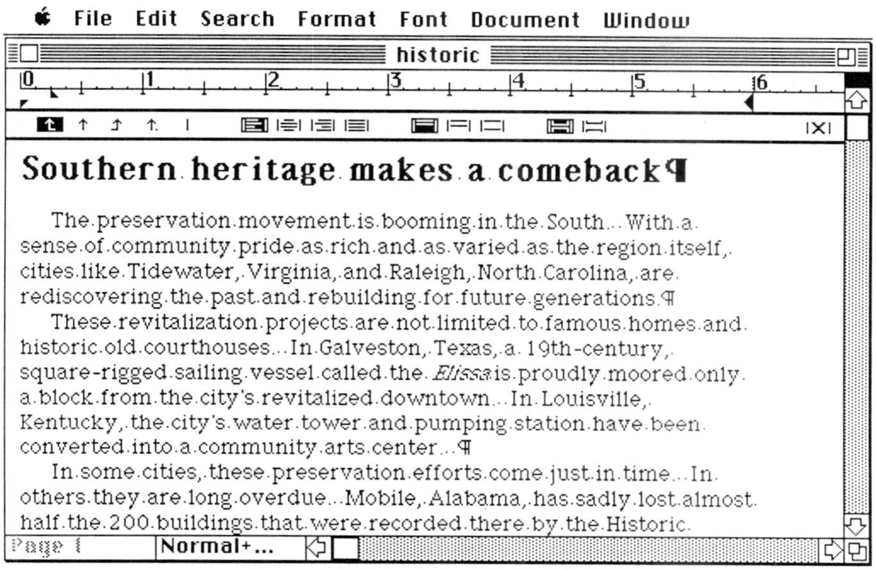

Use the Cut and Paste commands to move a block of text.

Replacing as you paste

As with the Copy and Paste procedure, if you make a selection before you issue the Paste command, Word will delete the selected block and paste the cut selection in its place.

For instance, suppose that you want to move the sentence *The preservation movement is booming in the South.* in the second line of Figure 6-4 to the first line in the document. Since you want this sentence to serve as your headline, suppose you also want to replace the existing headline with the selected phrase as you paste.

Begin by pressing the ⌘ key and clicking on the first sentence in the second paragraph, then press ⌘-x. Next, highlight the phrase that begins *Southern heritage* in the first line and press ⌘-v. Figure 6-5 on the following page shows the result.

As you can see, Word did indeed replace the headline with the selected sentence. However, we lost the character formatting for the headline in the process. Notice that the ¶ marker at the end of the first line still reflects our original headline formats (since we did not overwrite the ¶ marker), but the pasted text appears in 12-point, New York, plain format. This brings us to our next topic: copying and moving formats.

FIGURE 6-5

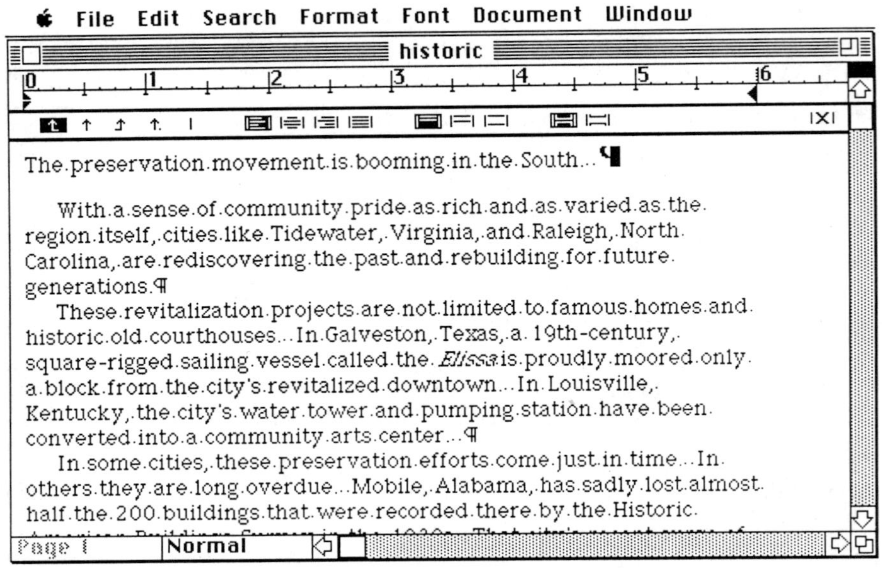

You can also use the Paste command to overwrite a block.

Copying and moving formats

When you copy or cut a block of text and paste it into another location, Word will generally retain the original character formats that you assigned to that text as it pastes the characters in the new location. When you copy or move an entire paragraph, Word will also retain the paragraph formats of the copied selection when you paste. If you copy or move only a portion of a paragraph, however—that is, if the ¶ marker is not included in your selection—Word will use the paragraph formats that you have assigned to the surrounding text in the paste area.

You may need to revise the character and paragraph formats of the pasted text to match the formats of the surrounding text. Often you can use Word's Format From and Format To shortcuts to speed up this process. We'll show you those techniques in a few pages.

The effects of your Paste command may vary slightly if you are using Word's style sheet facility to format your document. We'll talk about the effects of editing text that is formatted with style sheets in Chapter 9.

Pasting to other Word documents

There may be occasions when you want to use the same block of text in two or more Word documents. Rather than retyping this text, you can copy the original block to your other documents. For example, Figure 6-6 shows two document windows open on the Word DeskTop. Suppose you want to repeat the paragraph that is displayed in the top document window (sales report1) in the second document (sales report2).

First click in the sales report1 document window to activate it if it isn't already active, then double-click in the invisible selection bar next to the paragraph you want to copy. Now, issue the Copy command and click in the sales report2 window to activate it. Point to the spot where you want to paste the paragraph (or make a selection if you want to overwrite some existing text in the second window) and issue the Paste command. We decided to insert the copied paragraph in front of the paragraph that begins *As for our*, so we clicked just in front of the word *As* before issuing our Paste command. As you can see in Figure 6-7 on the next page, a copy of the paragraph from sales report1 now appears in the sales report2 window.

FIGURE 6-6

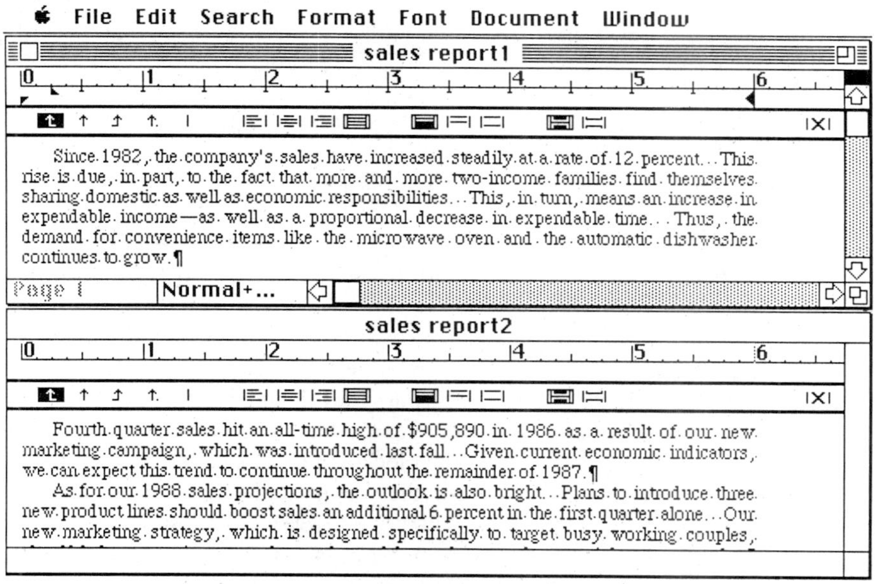

We want to copy the paragraph in the top document window into the bottom document window.

By the way, you can use Word's File menu and Window menu commands to open new documents, retrieve existing files, or activate an open document window before you paste. Word will remember your copy block until you issue another Copy or Cut command or until you quit from the program.

The Clipboard and Scrapbook

When you issue the Cut or Copy command, Word places the text you have selected on the Clipboard. The Clipboard is a temporary holding area where Word stores your cut and copy blocks until they are needed.

Though the Clipboard can accommodate any size text block—ranging from one character to an entire document (memory permitting)—it is very important

FIGURE 6-7

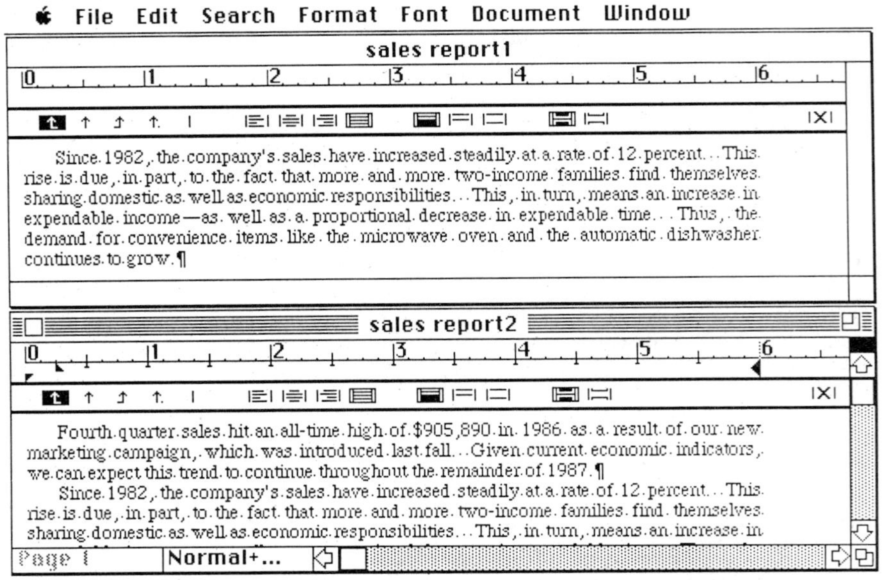

A copy of the paragraph now appears in the second document window as well.

to understand that the Clipboard can hold only one selection at a time. If you issue the Cut or Copy command, and then issue another Cut or Copy command before you paste the first selection back into your document, that selection will be lost. Of course, if you are only copying the text, you have lost nothing but time. You must go back and reselect the block and issue a new Copy command. If you have issued the Cut command and then cut or copied another block of text before pasting the first block, however, that first block will be lost.

You can paste a cut or copied selection as many times as you like, as long as you don't overwrite the contents of the Clipboard by issuing another Copy or Cut command. Word will remember the current contents of your Clipboard, even if you issue other commands or edit your document before you paste. As we mentioned before, you can even open and edit new documents without losing the contents of your Clipboard.

If you are ever in doubt about the last selection that you have cut or copied, you can select the Show Clipboard command from the Window menu to see the contents of the Clipboard. Figure 6-8 shows the contents of the Clipboard after we copied the paragraph in Figure 6-6.

FIGURE 6-8

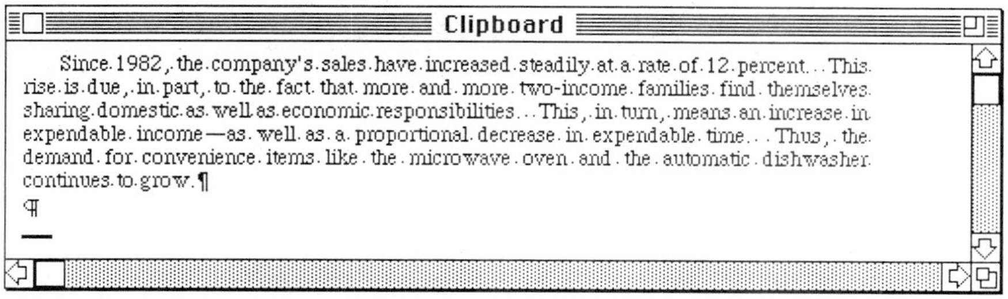

The Clipboard window reflects the last selection that you cut or copied.

While the Clipboard saves only one piece of data at a time, the Scrapbook can hold as many items as you have room for on your startup disk. As a matter of fact, the Scrapbook is a great place to store commonly used text, graphics, and other data. As you'll learn in Chapter 16, you can even use the Scrapbook to transfer information from one application to another. (You can also save commonly used data in a glossary file, as explained in Chapter 10, but you won't be able to transfer that data to other programs.)

If you have issued a Cut or Copy command and want to save that piece of text for later use, you can place it in your Scrapbook. Then, you can freely cut and copy other blocks of text without fear of losing the first block. To place a selection in the Scrapbook, select the text you want to cut or copy, then select Scrapbook from the menu.

If you have copied a selection to the Scrapbook before, the last selection that you pasted will appear in the Scrapbook window. Otherwise, you'll see the phrase *Empty Scrapbook* in this window, as shown in Figure 6-9 on the next page. When you select Paste to enter your selection into the Scrapbook, your window will look like the one in Figure 6-10.

Notice that a set of status messages now appears at the bottom of the Scrapbook window. The notation on the left indicates that the entry you are viewing is 1 of 1 item in the Scrapbook. When you add another item, that item will be labeled 1 of 2, and the previous item will become 2 of 2. You can enter as many items into the Scrapbook as you have room for on your startup disk. Your most recent selections will always appear at the beginning of the list. As soon as you add a second item to the Scrapbook, the scroll bar in the lower portion of the window will be activated so that you will be able to move from one item to another.

In the bottom-right portion of the Scrapbook window, you'll see the notation TEXT, indicating that the selection you pasted was a text block. As you'll see in Chapter 16, you can also use the Scrapbook to hold graphics.

FIGURE 6-9

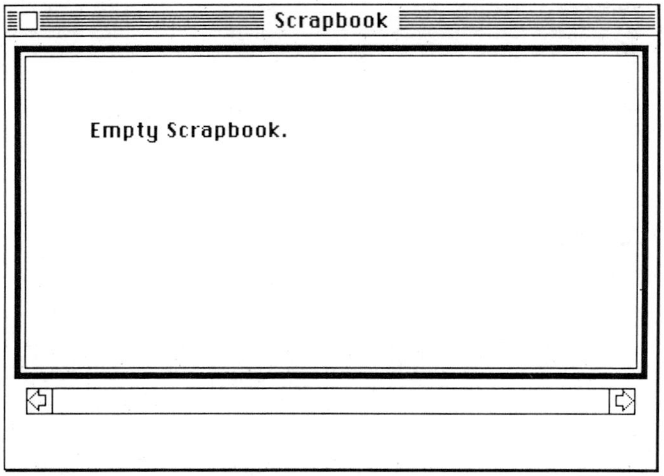

The Scrapbook window appears when you select Scrapbook from the menu.

FIGURE 6-10

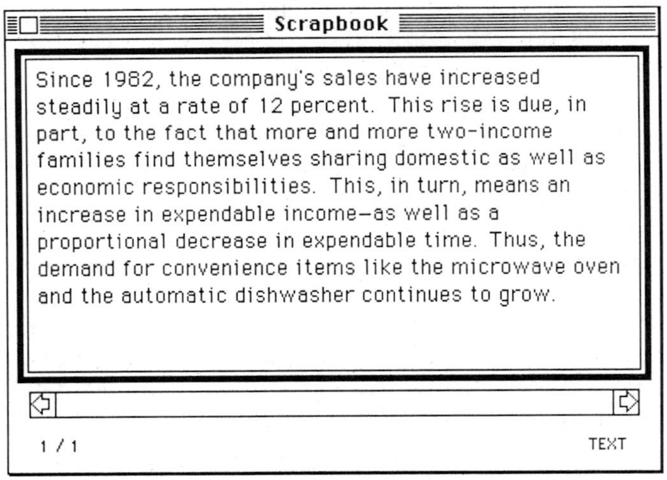

Your pasted block will appear in the Scrapbook window.

To close the Scrapbook window and resume working on the Word DeskTop, just click the close box at the upper-left corner of the Scrapbook window. If you like, you can leave the Scrapbook window open and click in one of your document windows to begin working again in Word. The Scrapbook will remain open and accessible until you quit from Word.

To retrieve a selection from the Scrapbook, select Scrapbook from the menu again (or click on the Scrapbook window if it is already open), then scroll to the selection that you want to use. Now, issue another Copy or Cut command to place the selection on the Clipboard. If you issue the Cut command, the selection will be permanently removed from the Scrapbook, and the remaining selections will be renumbered to reflect this change. If you use the Copy command, however, your selection will remain in the Scrapbook, available for reuse later.

Don't worry if you can't see your entire selection in the Scrapbook window. Though there is room to display only about 11 lines of text in this window, you'll be able to retrieve the entire selection by issuing the Copy or Cut command later. If you have assigned special formats to the selection that you pasted in the Scrapbook (more on this in Chapter 16), those formats will be retained, even though they are not reflected in the Scrapbook window. In fact, the contents of the Scrapbook window will always appear in 12-point, Geneva, plain font, even though Word's default font is 12-point, New York, plain.

Unfortunately, there is one drawback to using the Scrapbook to store text: When you paste text from the Scrapbook into your document, any special character or paragraph formatting that you assigned to that text will be lost. When you issue the Paste command, the pasted text will appear in Word's default *Normal* style. (See Chapter 9 for more on the *Normal* style.)

Creating multiple Scrapbooks

The content of your Scrapbook remains on disk even after you quit from Word and reboot your Mac. In fact, you can even copy your Scrapbook from one startup disk to another and rename the file so that you can keep multiple Scrapbooks. To copy your Scrapbook to another disk, just open the System folder on your startup disk and drag the Scrapbook icon to the System folder of the second disk. If the second disk already contains a Scrapbook file, you'll see the message *Replace items with the same name?* If you want to overwrite the existing Scrapbook file on the target disk, click OK. Otherwise, rename the Scrapbook file on the target disk before you begin the copy procedure.

When you select the Scrapbook command from the menu, Word will always open the file with the name Scrapbook. However, if no file called Scrapbook is present on your startup disk, Word will present a new empty Scrapbook window.

To maintain multiple Scrapbooks, you must rename all of your Scrapbook files at the Finder level. For example, you might use names like *Graphics Scrap*, *Sales Scrap*, and so forth to identify your various Scrapbook files. When you need to reuse a Scrapbook, just assign the name *Scrapbook* to that document at the Finder level before you load the Word program.

Keyboard Shortcuts

In addition to the ⌘-c, ⌘-x, and ⌘-v shortcuts that you can use to copy, cut, and paste text in Word, you have three additional keyboard shortcuts at your disposal. These Option-⌘-key shortcuts let you quickly copy and move text and copy formats from one location to another. You can use these shortcuts only when the Full Menus setting is in effect.

Copy from and Copy to

Rather than using separate Copy and Paste commands to duplicate a block of text, you can use Word's Option-⌘-c shortcut to reduce this process to one step. The effect of the Option-⌘-c shortcut depends on your selection when you issue the command. If you have selected a block of text, that highlighted text will become your copy block. Word will ask you where you want to paste the selection. If you have not selected any text before pressing Option-⌘-c, Word assumes that you want to paste text at the current insertion point location and asks you to select a copy block.

For example, suppose you are typing the sample document shown in Figure 6-11 and you want to include the company name *Consolidated Industrial Manufacturing Company* at the insertion point. (Your insertion point marker is at the very end of the document right now, just to the left of the last ¶ symbol.) Rather than typing this long name, you can copy it from the paragraph above.

FIGURE 6-11

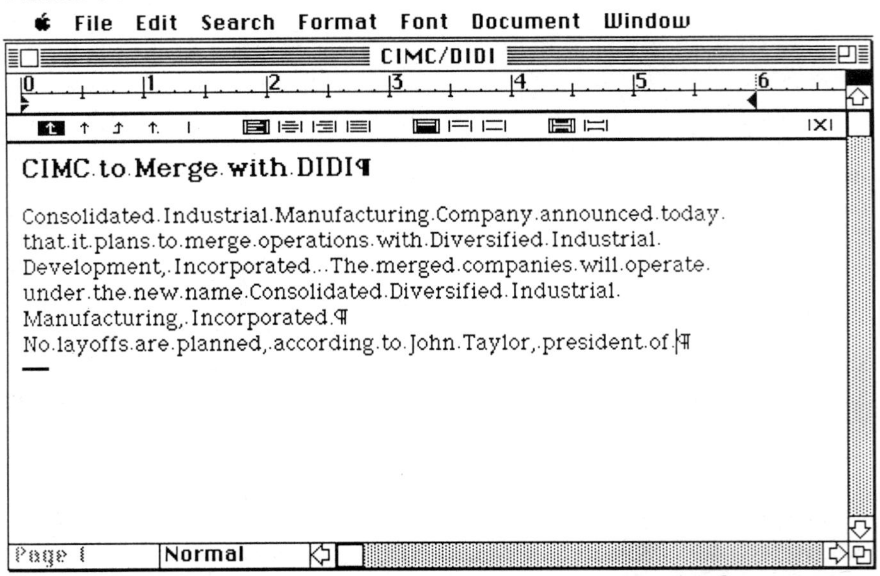

You want to repeat the phrase Consolidated Industrial Manufacturing Company *at the current insertion point.*

To use the Copy from technique, begin by pressing Option-⌘-c. You will see the prompt *Copy from* in the status box at the lower-left corner of your screen. Just drag through the phrase *Consolidated Industrial Manufacturing Company* in the first paragraph—Word will display a gray underline beneath the selected copy block, as shown in Figure 6-12. When you press the Return or Enter key to lock in your copy selection, your document will look like the one in Figure 6-13 on page 178. Notice that your insertion point marker automatically jumps to the end of the pasted block so that you can resume typing without interruption.

FIGURE 6-12

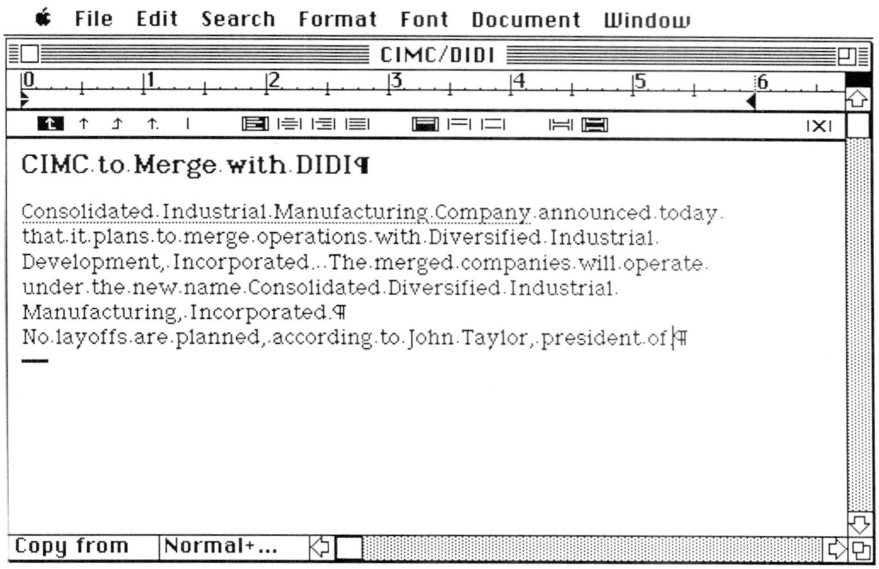

Word will display the prompt Copy from *in the status box and will underline your copy selection.*

Now, suppose you discover that John Taylor is actually president of the Diversified Industrial Development Corporation, not Consolidated Industrial Manufacturing Company. You decide to go back and copy the name *Diversified Industrial Development Corporation* from the first paragraph line. You can use a similar Option-⌘-c technique to copy and paste that block in one step.

FIGURE 6-13

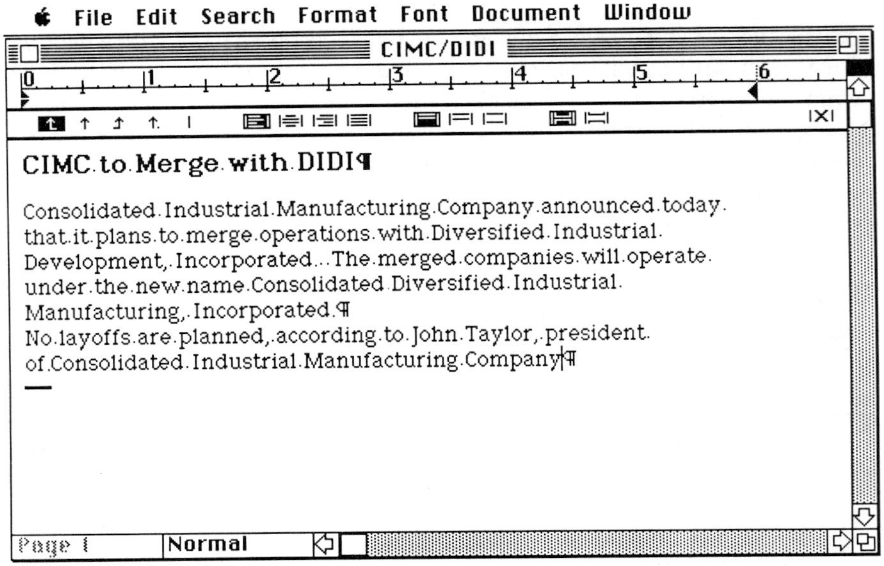

When you press Return or Enter, the selected block will be copied at the insertion point.

Begin by highlighting the phrase *Diversified Industrial Development Corporation*, then press Option-⌘-c. You'll see the prompt *Copy to* in the status box at the lower-left corner of your screen. Now, select the spot where you want to place a copy of the selected text. If you simply click on a new insertion point, Word will display a flashing vertical gray bar at the paste location. If you drag through some text in your document, Word will display a dotted line under your selection to indicate that those characters will be overwritten when you press Return or Enter to lock in your paste selection. Since we want to overwrite the words *Consolidated Industrial Manufacturing Company* in the second paragraph, we'll drag through that company name, as shown in Figure 6-14. When we press Return or Enter, our document will look like the one in Figure 6-15.

FIGURE 6-14

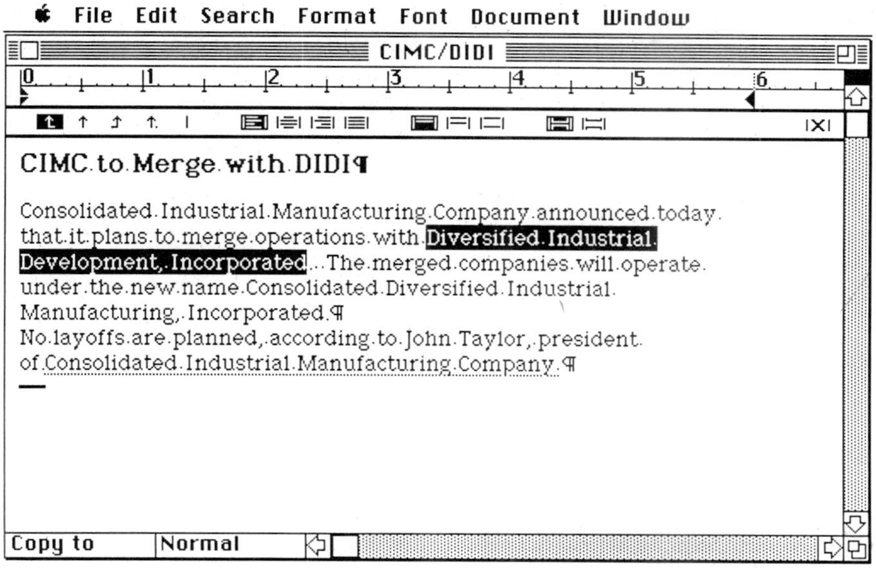

Word will display the prompt Copy to *in the status box and indicate your paste selection with a gray underline.*

FIGURE 6-15

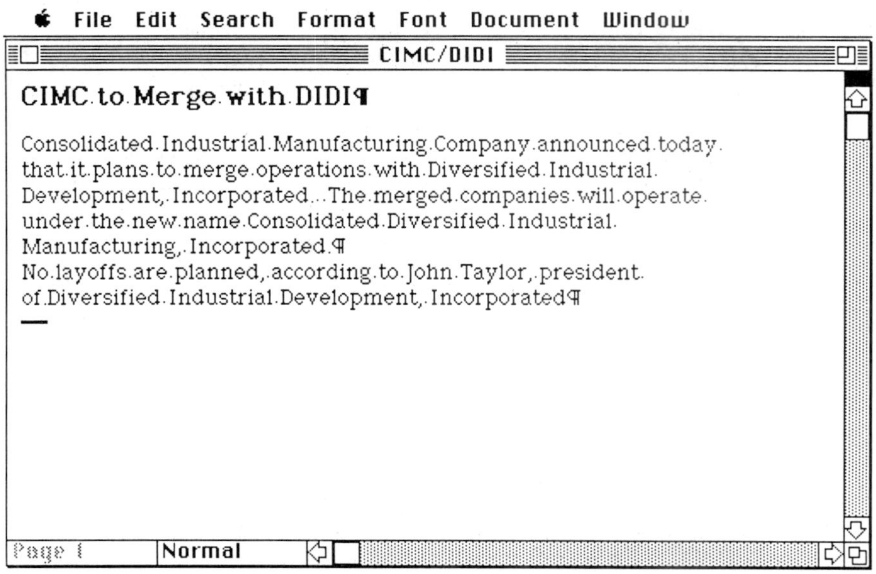

When you press Return or Enter, the copy block will overwrite the underlined text.

Incidentally, you can use this Option-⌘-c shortcut to copy text from one document to another as well as within an active document window. You can click on an open document window to activate it, and you can drag and resize any open window, if needed, to bring another window into view. When you activate another window, the *Copy* to or *Copy from* message will appear in that window's status box.

However, you cannot use the File or Window menus to open or activate another file. Both the source file and destination file must be open before you can use the Option-⌘-c shortcut.

To cancel the copy procedure, just press the ⌘ and period keys (⌘-.).

Move from and Move to

You can use a similar keyboard shortcut—Option-⌘-x—to quickly move text in your document from one location to another. This keyboard shortcut works just like the Option-⌘-c shortcut described above: If you have selected a block of text when you press Option-⌘-x, you'll see the message *Move to* in the status box at the bottom-left corner of your screen. Just click on a new insertion point to specify a paste location for the selected text. Word will delete the selected text from its current location and place it in the new location that you have specified. If you drag through a block of text rather than clicking an insertion point when you are choosing your paste location, Word will display a dotted line under that text and overwrite it when you press Return or Enter.

If you do not select any text before pressing Option-⌘-x, Word assumes that you want to move a block of text to the current insertion point and will display the message *Move from.* Just drag through the text you want to move and press Return or Enter.

For example, suppose you want to move the sentence that begins *The merged companies will operate* in the first paragraph of the sample document in Figure 6-15 to the end of the second paragraph. Assuming that your insertion point is already at the end of the second paragraph, all you need to do is press Option-⌘-x. When you see the message *Move from,* press the ⌘ key and click anywhere on the sentence that begins *The merged companies will operate* to select that entire sentence. Figure 6-16 shows the document window at this point. When you press Return or Enter, your document window will look like the one in Figure 6-17.

Again, you can drag, resize, or activate document windows while you're performing a Move From or Move To operation, but you cannot use the File or Window menu commands to access another window. To cancel the move procedure, just press the ⌘ and period keys (⌘-.)

FIGURE 6-16

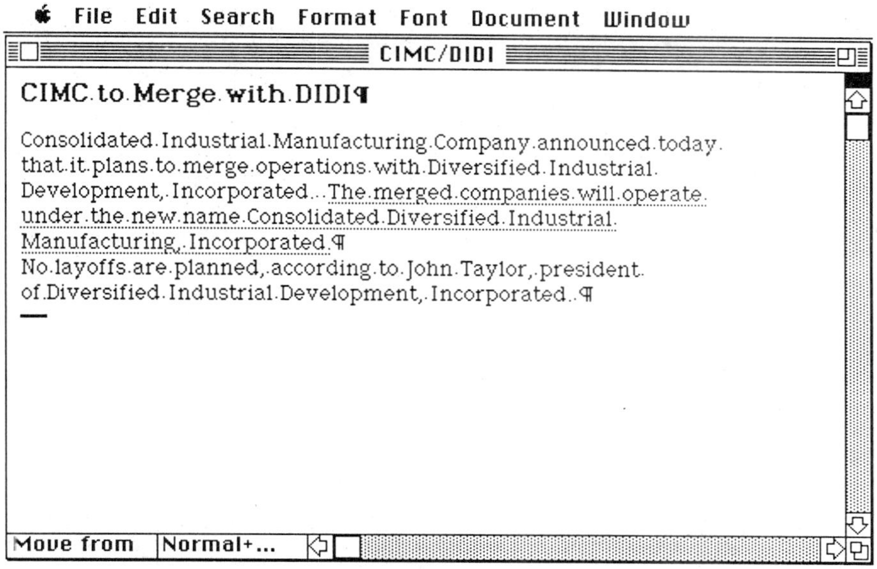

To move a block of text to the current insertion point, press Option-⌘-x, then mark the text that you want to move.

FIGURE 6-17

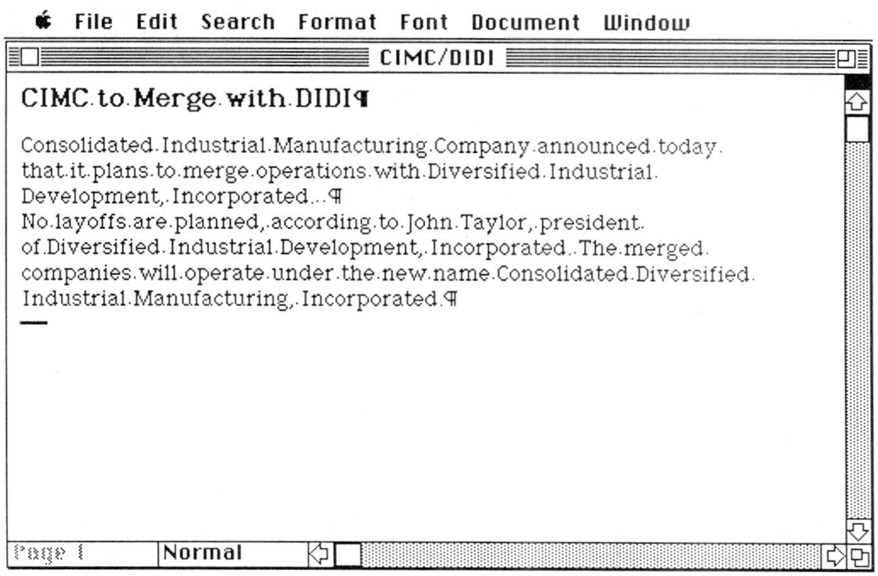

When you press Return or Enter, Word will move the selected text from its current location to the insertion point.

Format from and Format to

Word 3 also allows you to copy the paragraph and character formats from one block of text to another by pressing Option-⌘-v. Again, the effects of this shortcut depend on whether you've selected any text before pressing Option-⌘-v. If you have selected a block of text, Word assumes that you want to copy the formats of the current selection to another part of your document; if you have not selected any text, Word assumes that you want to copy the formats of another text block to your insertion point marker. (As we explain in Chapter 5, if you select new character formats while the insertion point marker is blinking, your new formats will apply to the next characters that you type.)

Suppose you want to format the heading that occupies the third paragraph of the sample document shown in Figure 6-18 to appear in the same format as the heading at the top of the screen. Rather than reformatting the text manually, you can select one or more characters from the first headline, which is already formatted, and press Option-⌘-v. Word will display the prompt *Format to* in the status box at the lower-left corner of your screen. Now, drag through the characters that you want to format. As you can see in Figure 6-19, Word displays a dotted line under your *Format to* selection. When you press Return or Enter to confirm your selection, your document will look like the one in Figure 6-20. As you can see, Word has changed the character formats of the selection, without changing its content.

FIGURE 6-18

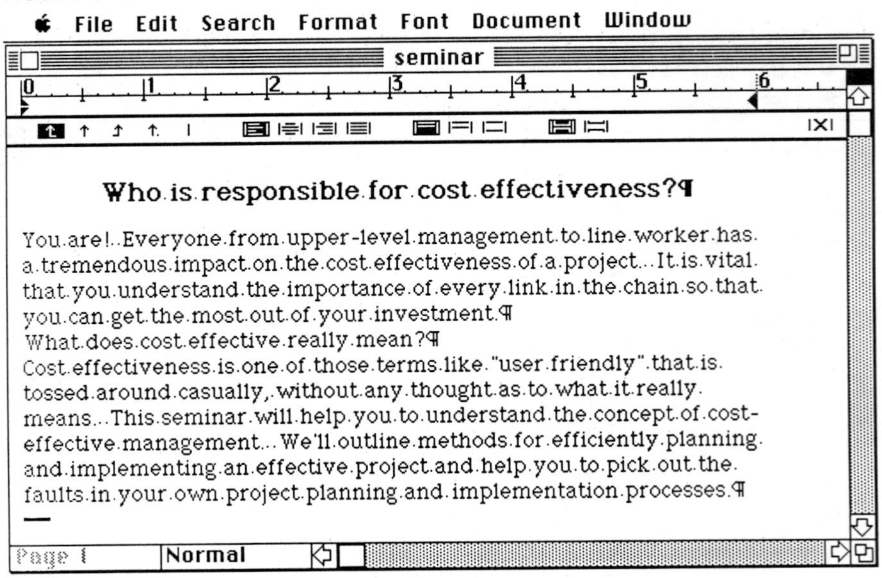

We want to copy the character formats from line 1 to line 6.

FIGURE 6-19

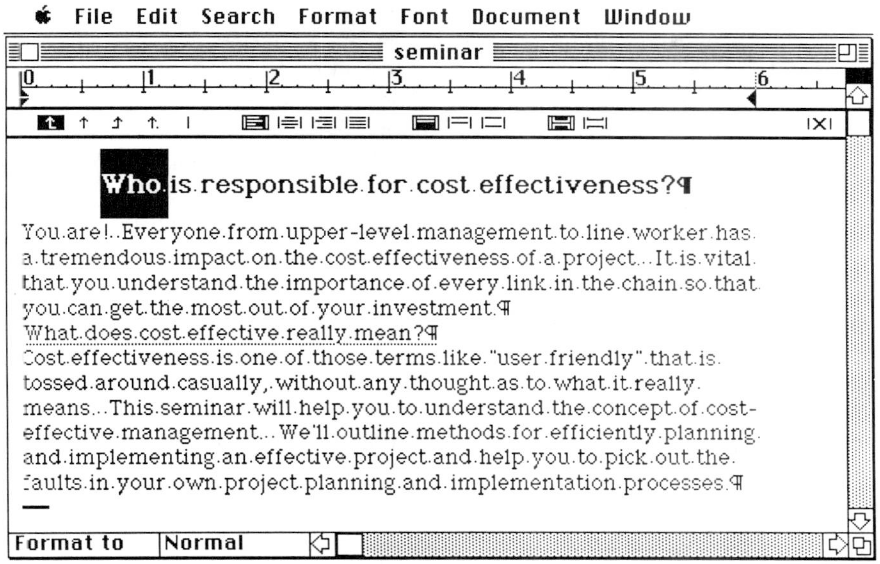

When you press Option-⌘-v, Word will prompt you to select the text block to which you want to copy your formats and then will display a gray line under the Format to *selection.*

FIGURE 6-20

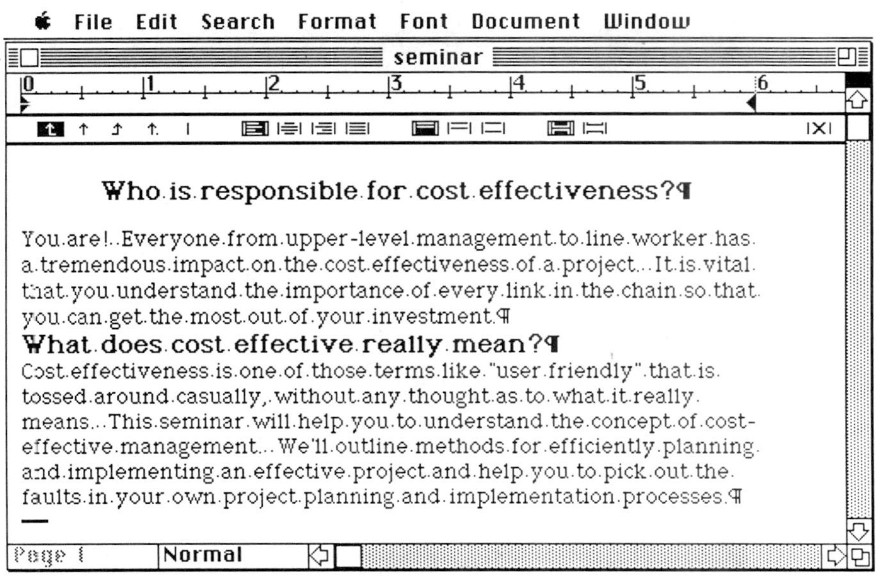

The second heading now carries the same character formats as the first.

Notice that Word has copied the character formats from line 1 to line 6, but not the paragraph formats. Line 1 has centered alignment with spacing above and below the paragraph, while line 6 displays flush-left alignment and no paragraph spacing above and below. If you want to copy paragraph formats, you need to double-click in the selection bar to select your entire source paragraph, then press Option-⌘-v and double-click in the selection bar to select your target paragraph. When you use this technique, Word will transfer paragraph formats only—not character formats.

Of course, if you want to copy both character and paragraph formats, you can always perform the Option-⌘-v operation twice—once with the desired characters selected and once with entire paragraphs selected. For example, suppose we decide to copy the paragraph formats from the first paragraph in Figure 6-20 to the third paragraph. We would double-click in the selection bar next to the first paragraph in line 1 of Figure 6-20, then press Option-⌘-v. Then, we'd double-click next to the third paragraph, as shown in Figure 6-21, and press Enter. As you can see in Figure 6-22, our paragraph formats have now been transferred as well.

FIGURE 6-21

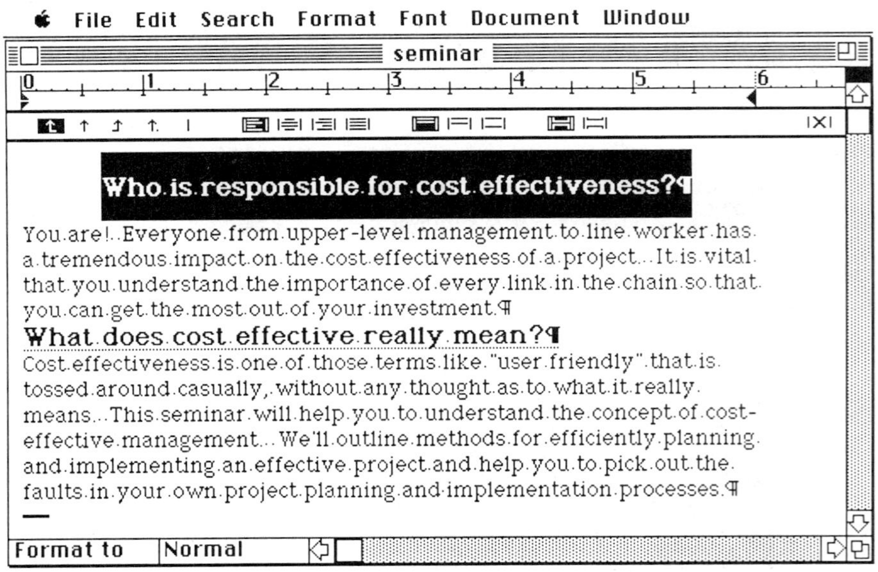

To copy paragraph formats, perform the Option-⌘-v procedure with entire paragraphs selected.

FIGURE 6-22

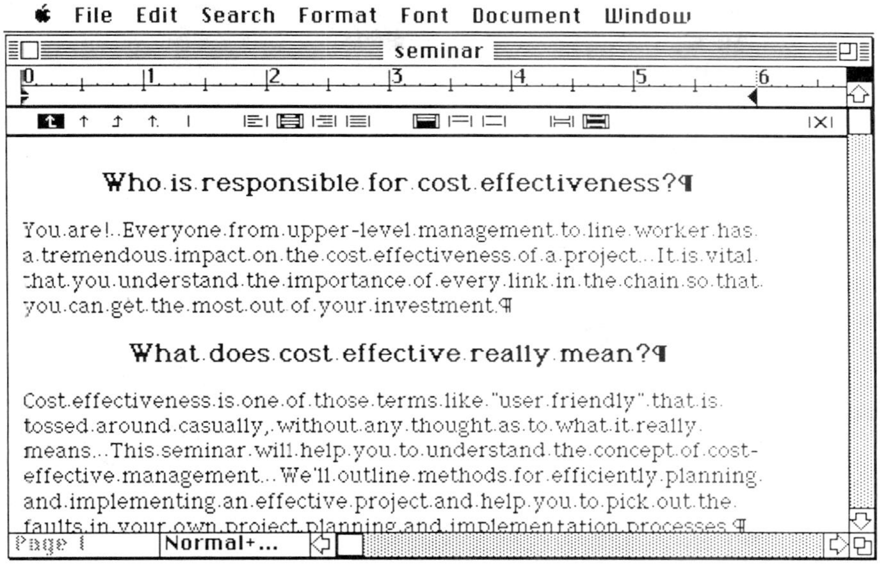

The target paragraph now carries the same character and paragraph formats as the source paragraph.

If you want to change character formats of text as you type, just press Option-⌘-v without making a selection. Word will display the prompt *Format from* in the status box at the lower-left corner of your screen. Now, click on or drag through a character or block of text in your document that carries the character formats you want to use, and press Return or Enter. Any new text that you type at the current insertion point will appear in the selected format.

As with the Copy and Move shortcuts, you can drag, resize, or activate document windows while you're formatting, but you cannot use the File or Window menu commands to access another window. To cancel the Format from or Format to procedure, just press the ⌘ and period keys (⌘-.).

Option-⌘-key shortcuts and the Clipboard

When you use the Option-⌘-c and Option-⌘-x techniques to copy and move text, Word does not place a copy of your text on the Clipboard. This is not necessary because the original selection remains highlighted and is not removed from your document. Similarly, when you press Option-⌘-v to transfer formats from one location to another, nothing takes place on the Clipboard. If you have previously issued a Cut or Copy command to place a block of text on your Clipboard, that text will remain undisturbed while you carry out the Option-⌘-key maneuver.

Thus, Option-⌘-key shortcuts not only streamline the copy and move procedures, they let you perform intermediate moves and copies without losing your last Clipboard selection. This capability is quite handy when you find that you need to rearrange some data before you paste a selection in your document.

THE FIND... AND CHANGE... COMMANDS

Like most word processors, Word 3 allows you to search through a document to find occurrences of a particular word or character sequence. Similarly, Word lets you find and change a series of characters—or search and replace, as many word processing programs call it. In other words, you can ask Word to find every occurrence of a given character sequence and replace it with a different sequence of characters. When we use the term "character sequence," we are talking about any string of characters. It can be as small as a single letter or as long as several sentences. However, the sequence you are searching for cannot exceed 255 characters. Typically, your character sequence will be only one or a few words.

Finding and changing can be two of the most useful capabilities in any word-processing program. Word 3 takes these capabilities a little further than most other word processors, letting you change formats as well as characters. In this section, we'll explain how to use the Find... and Change... commands on Word's Search menu. We'll also show you a few special ways to apply these features and warn you about certain traps that can arise when you use the Find... and Change... commands.

Finding Text

To find a character sequence, just choose the Find... command from the Search menu. Word will display the dialog box shown in Figure 6-23. When this dialog box first appears, you'll see a blinking pointer in the Find What edit bar. Type the characters that you want to search for—this is called your find text—then click the Start Search button to tell Word to begin its search.

FIGURE 6-23

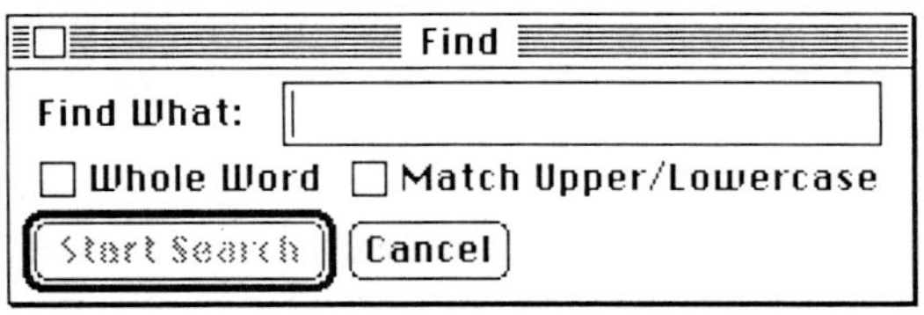

To search for a character sequence, enter your find text in the Find dialog box.

Though there is room in the Find What edit bar to display only about 25 characters, your find string can be as long as 255 characters. The characters on the left side of the edit bar will scroll out of view as you type, but you can view and change any hidden characters by dragging to the left or right to scroll the hidden portion of the find text into view.

In performing a search, Word begins at the current location of the pointer in your document and scans forward to the end of the document. When it finds the first occurrence of your find text, Word highlights that occurrence on your screen and temporarily halts the Find procedure. To continue the search, just click the Find Next button in the dialog box. (The Find Next button replaces the Start Search button once the Find procedure is underway.) Figure 6-24 shows how your screen might appear when Word finds an occurrence of the word *silver*.

FIGURE 6-24

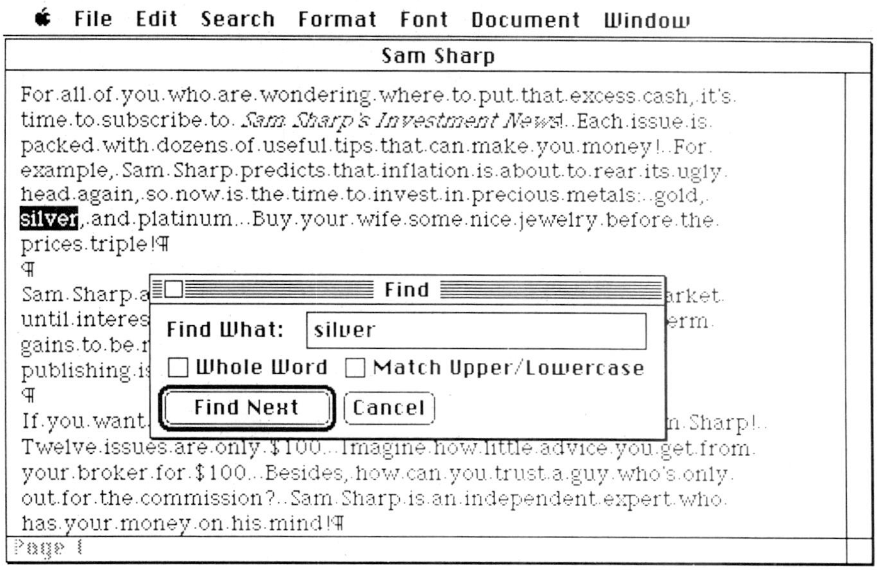

When Word locates an occurrence of the find text, it will highlight that occurrence in your document.

As Word scans through your document looking for your find text, it will scroll the document on your screen as necessary to bring the next occurrence of the find text into view.

When you want to stop searching, click the Cancel button or click the close box on the Find dialog box. Word will save the find text in the dialog box. In fact, this text will remain in the Find dialog box until you replace it or remove it or until you quit from Word. In fact, you can even open another file or activate another document window to search for the same text string in two or more documents. However, the next time you issue the Find... command, you will notice that the contents of the Find What edit bar are highlighted; therefore, any characters that you type will replace the current contents of the Find What edit bar.

Once you have closed the Find dialog box, you can use a shortcut to go to the next occurrence of the find text. Just press Option-⌘-a instead of choosing the Find... command. As we'll discuss in a few pages, this shortcut is particularly helpful when you want to edit your document as you search for the find text.

When Word has searched through the end of the document, you'll see the Continue Search alert box shown in Figure 6-25. This does not necessarily mean that the search is complete; it just tells you that Word has reached the end of your document. If you want Word to continue the search by cycling back to the beginning of the document, click Yes in the Continue Search alert box. Word will then go to the beginning of your document and continue scanning for your find text. If you want to halt the search procedure, click No in the Continue Search alert box. The Find dialog box will remain open, so you can type a new find text string if you like, or you can click Cancel to stop the search procedure altogether.

FIGURE 6-25

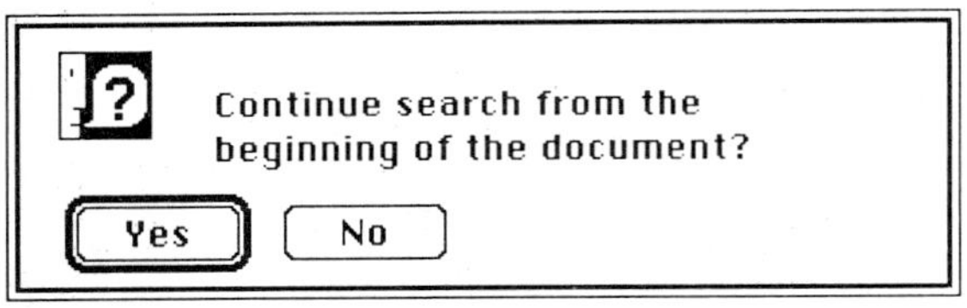

To search from the top of your document, click Yes in the Continue Search alert box.

If you click Yes in the Continue Search alert box, Word will find each occurrence of your find text, starting at the beginning of your document. When Word reaches the end of the document for the second time, however, you'll see an alert box with the message, *End of document reached.* When you click OK in this alert box, the Find dialog box will remain open, so you can enter some new find text or halt the Find procedure by clicking the Cancel button. By the way, if your insertion point marker is positioned at the beginning of your document when you issue the Find... command, Word will display the *End of document reached* message after one complete pass through the document. You won't see the Continue Search alert box at all.

If Word displays the *End of document reached* message without highlighting any occurrences of the find text, this tells you that no occurrences of the find text can be located. If you're puzzled by this, you might try retyping the find text. Keep in mind that Word looks for exact matches to your find text. (Case does not matter unless you click the Match Upper/Lowercase option, which we'll talk about in a few pages.) Therefore, if you've entered extra blank spaces or typed a single character incorrectly in the Find What edit bar, Word won't be able to locate the find text in your document.

As you are using the Find... command, Word will not tell you when it has searched through the entire document. That is, when Word has scanned the document from the original insertion point location to the end of the document, then scanned from the beginning of the document back to the insertion point location, it will not automatically end the Find procedure. You must watch the text on your screen, and then cancel the Find procedure when you've searched the entire document, unless you want to search part or all of your document again. Thus if you want to search your entire document, you may find it easier to move to the beginning of the document before you issue the Find... command. That way, you'll know that you have searched through the entire document when you see the *End of document reached.* message.

Navigating with the Find... command

The Find... command offers a very quick way to jump from one part of your document to another as you make revisions. For example, suppose you want to edit a section of your document that appears under the heading named *Part II.* To move quickly to this section of your document without scrolling, you can issue the Find... command and type *Part II* as your find text. When you click Start Search, Word will scroll your document on the screen to bring the *Part II* heading into view. You can then close the Find dialog box and perform any needed revisions.

You may even want to insert hidden "bookmarks" into your text to help you find key sections quickly. Use short, easy-to-remember symbols or codes to mark selected areas. For example, if there is a paragraph in your document that you want to remember to verify later, you might enter the characters ***check*** just in front of that paragraph, then highlight those characters and use the Character... command to assign the Hidden format to them. When you are ready to return to that paragraph, just issue the Find... command and type ***check*** as your find text.

As long as you display the hidden text on your screen, Word will be able to locate that text when you issue the Find... command. If you use the Preferences... command to suppress the display of Hidden text, however, Word will not be able to locate your bookmark. (As you'll see in Chapter 7, you can instruct Word to omit this hidden text when the document is printed.)

Find options

The Find dialog box offers two options, Whole Word and Match Upper/Lowercase. The Whole Word option is used primarily when your find text is a short word such as *the* or *for*. If you do not select the Whole Word option, Word will search for any character sequence that matches your find text, even if it occurs in the middle of another word. For example, if you type *for* in the Find What edit bar, Word will highlight occurrences in such words as *forecast* and *platform*. To avoid this, just click the Whole Word option before you click the Start Search button.

The Whole Word option also can be useful in cases where you want to find only the singular or present tense of a word. For instance, suppose that you enter the word *book* as your find text. By selecting the Whole Word option before you begin searching, you will avoid finding the plural form of the word *books* or the past tense *booked*. Although there will be times when you want to find different forms of a word, in general we recommend that you select the Whole Word option before you start your search. Of course, you can always activate this option in the middle of a search, if you want; just click the check box in the Find dialog box before you click the Find Next button.

The Match Upper/Lowercase option works exactly as you might expect. If you do not activate this option, then Word will ignore case as it searches for occurrences of your find text. For example, if you enter *Microsoft* as your find text and do not click the Match Upper/Lowercase option, Word will highlight occurrences such as *microsoft*, *MicroSoft*, and *MICROSOFT*. However, if you do select the Match Upper/Lowercase option, Word will find only those occurrences where the capitalization exactly matches the capitalization of your find text. All other occurrences will be ignored.

The Match Upper/Lowercase option can be helpful when you need to search for a proper noun that has the same spelling as a common noun. For example, suppose you want to search a document for all references to the software program *Word*. However, you do not want to find other occurrences of the word *word*. Enter *Word* as your find text and then click the Match Upper/Lowercase option before you start the search. (You may also want to activate the Whole Word option.) Of course, there's one possible disadvantage to using the Match Upper/Lowercase option. If you have accidentally used the improper case in some instances—for example, if you've entered the name of the software program as *word* instead of *Word*—your Find procedure will not highlight these occurrences. Keep in mind that you may at times want to perform a search without the Match Upper/Lowercase option activated so you can check for the correct case of a certain word.

Using wildcards

One very helpful feature of Word's Find... command is the ability to use the question mark character (?) as a wildcard. You can use a ? in place of any single character in your find text. For example, if you enter *ba?e* as your find text, Word will highlight occurrences of *bale*, *base*, *bane*, *bake*, and any other words that begin with *ba* followed by a single character and an *e*.

Wildcards come in handy for a variety of situations. For example, suppose you are working on a document in which you have not been consistent in spelling the name *Anderson*. In some cases, you have entered *Anderson*, with an *o*, and in other cases, you've entered *Andersen*, with an *e*. You can find all occurrences of the name by using the Find... command and entering *Anders?n* as your find text. Of course, you will probably want to change some of the occurrences so that the spelling will be consistent throughout the document. We'll show you how to do that when we discuss the Change... command.

Since Word considers a question mark in your find text to be a wildcard, you may be wondering how you can search for a question mark in a document. Fortunately, there is a way to do this. Just enter *^?* (a carat followed by a question mark) as your find text. This tells Word that, instead of using the ? as a wildcard, you want to find all occurrences of a literal question mark. Of course, you can combine *^?* with other characters as you are entering the find text. For example, suppose you want to find all occurrences of the question, *Is this correct?* in your document. You can do this by entering *Is this correct^?* or perhaps just *correct^?* as your find text.

Finding hidden text

When you assign the Hidden format to text in your document, Word will not be able to locate occurrences of your find text if it is hidden from view. If you want Word to locate occurrences of your find text within a hidden text block, you must activate the Show Hidden Text option in the Preferences dialog box before you begin your search.

Finding formats

Word also lets you find character and paragraph formats. Here's how it works. Select the character sequence or paragraph that has the formatting that you want to find. (To select a paragraph, double-click in the invisible selection bar at the left edge of that paragraph.) Then press Option-⌘-r. Word will find the next character or paragraph whose formatting is the same as your selection and highlight it on your screen.

You cannot use the Option-⌘-r technique to search for *both* a paragraph format and a character format. If the text that you select before pressing Option-⌘-r includes a ¶ symbol marking the end of a paragraph, Word will assume that you want to find the next block of text with the same paragraph formats as your selected text. If your selection does not include a ¶ symbol, Word will assume that you're looking for text with the same character formats.

One terrific application for this feature is moving quickly between subheadings in a large document. For example, suppose that you have formatted the second-level subheadings in a document with 12-point, Helvetica, bold type. You can select one subheading and then press Option-⌘-r to move directly to the next subheading that has 12-point, Helvetica, bold formatting.

This technique can find only one format at a time. For example, suppose you have a heading that includes some 12-point bold text and some 12-point, bold, italic text. If you select the entire heading and press Option-⌘-r, Word will find the next character in your document that has either 12-point bold formatting or 12-point, bold, italic formatting. How does Word decide which format to search for? Word looks at the format of the last character in the text you selected and uses that as its guide. So, for example, if the last character in the heading has 12-point, bold, italic formatting, Word will search for the next character in the document with that same formatting.

Finding markup characters

Another useful feature of Word's Find... command is its ability to search for special markup characters in a document, such as end-of-paragraph markers, nonbreaking spaces, and optional hyphens. To find a special character, you must insert a carat symbol (^) in your find text. Table 6-1 on the next page summarizes the markers that you can search for, and the character combination for each.

TABLE 6-1

Find Text	Finds all occurrences of
^p	Paragraph mark (¶)
^t	Tab mark (➡)
^n	End-of line mark (↵)
^s	Nonbreaking space (˜)
^-	Optional hyphen (¬)
^d	Section mark (:::::::)
^w	White space

You can use these codes to locate special markers.

Word can find markup characters in your text even when they are not visible on the screen. For example, if you've chosen the Hide ¶ command from the Edit menu, the ¶ symbols at the end of every paragraph will not be visible on your screen (nor will other special markers, such as the dots that mark blank spaces and the arrows that mark tab spaces). However, if you use a code like ^p in your find text, Word will highlight the space following each paragraph instead of the ¶ marker. Similarly, Word can find tab markers, optional hyphens, and end-of-line markers, even when they are not displayed on the screen.

The last item in the table, *^w*, needs a little explaining. When you specify *^w* as your find text, Word will find the blank space that appears between any two characters in your document. This will include the single spaces that occur between words as well as whole line spaces. The amount of white space that Word highlights on the screen will vary, depending on the situation. For example, suppose that you have two blank lines between two paragraphs in your document, and the second paragraph begins with a one-half-inch tab. As you can see in Figure 6-26, when you search for white space in this document, Word will highlight the ¶ at the end of the first paragraph, as well as the two blank lines between paragraphs and the space created by the tab.

As you might guess, your find text can include any combination of these special markup characters and other text. For example, to find every instance of a paragraph that begins with the word *For,* you can choose the Find... command and enter *^pFor* as your find text. Word will highlight the paragraph symbol at the end of the previous paragraph as well as the word *For* at the beginning of the next paragraph.

FIGURE 6-26

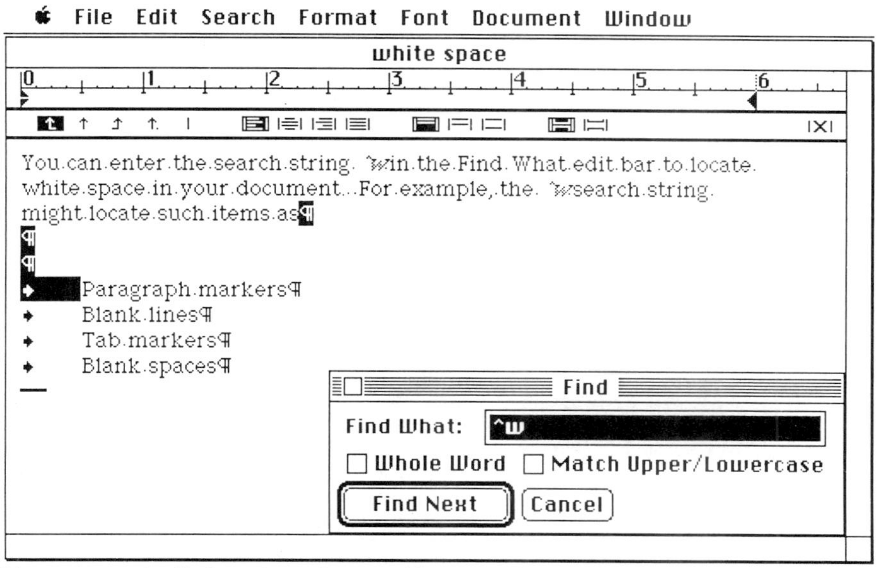

You can use the find text ^w to locate white space in your document.

In addition to the special markers listed in Table 6-1, you can search for any character by entering a carat followed by the three-digit decimal ASCII code for that character as your find text. For example, if you enter *^97* (or *^097*) as your find text, Word will find every occurrence of the letter *a*. Interestingly, even though 97 is the ASCII code for a lower-case *a* and 65 is the ASCII code for an upper-case *A*, Word will find every *a*, regardless of case, unless you activate the Match Upper/Lowercase option.

Editing as you find

Word will not let you edit text while the Find dialog box is active. However, if you want to make changes to your document as you are finding, you can switch between your document window and the Find dialog box. After Word locates an occurrence of your find text, just click anywhere on the document window to activate it. The Find dialog box will then move behind your document window, although it still will be open on your DeskTop. While the document window is active, you have complete access to all of Word's menu commands and you can type any characters from the keyboard.

After you've made your editing changes, you'll probably want to locate the next occurrence of your find text and make additional changes. To locate the next occurrence of the find text, reactivate the Find dialog box and click the Find Next option. There are a couple of different ways to reactivate the dialog box. First, you can resize your document window so that it no longer overlays the dialog box, then click anywhere on the dialog box. Second, you can type ⌘-f, which will cause the active dialog box to overlay your document window once again. If you plan to do a lot of finding and editing, you may want to go ahead and resize your document window and drag the Find dialog box so that at least part of the Find dialog box will be visible when your document window is active, as shown in Figure 6-27. This way, you can quickly switch between the dialog box and your document by clicking on one or the other.

FIGURE 6-27

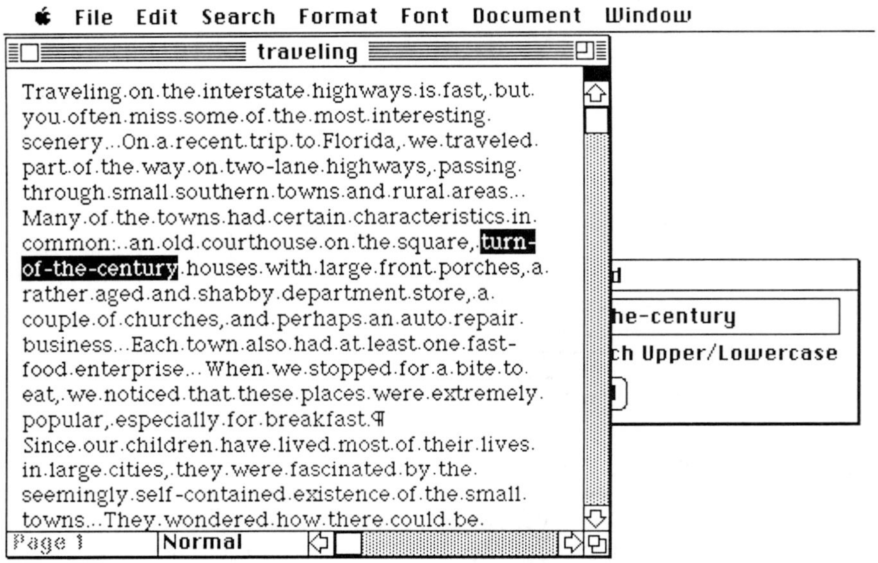

You can create nonoverlapping windows to view the Find dialog box and document window simultaneously.

Shortcuts

Instead of reactivating the Find dialog box and clicking Find Next, you can locate the next occurrence of your find text by simply typing Option-⌘-a. You can use Option-⌘-a even when the Find dialog box is not open. Recall that when you close the Find dialog box, Word does not discard the contents of the Find What edit bar. So, when you type Option-⌘-a, Word will be able to locate the next occurrence of the find text even if the Find dialog box is closed.

There's another shortcut you can take advantage of when you are editing as you find. After you make a change to one occurrence of your find text and then you search for the next occurrence, you can make the same editing change to that next occurrence by simply typing ⌘-a. For example, suppose that you want to boldface your company name everywhere it appears in a document. You could begin by selecting the Find... command from the Edit menu and entering the company name in the Find What edit bar. Then click Start Search in the Find dialog box. When Word highlights the first occurrence of the company name, click anywhere on your document window, then choose Bold from the Format menu. (Since Word will have selected the company name in the text, there's no need for you to drag through the name before you choose the Bold command.) After boldfacing the first occurrence, press Option-⌘-a to go to the next occurrence of the company name. Then press ⌘-a to boldface this occurrence as well. You can continue this procedure until you have boldfaced every occurrence of your company name in the document.

If you do not want to boldface every occurrence, you can skip some of the occurrences without losing the shortcut advantage. Just press Option-⌘-a to skip from one occurrence to another, and press ⌘-a only when you reach an occurrence that you want to change. Keep in mind that Word remembers and repeats only your most recent editing change. So use this ⌘-a technique only when you haven't made any other intermediate editing changes to your document.

You must also be careful with certain kinds of changes that you do not erase your original find text when you use the ⌘-a technique to edit that text. For example, suppose that you want to change the word *system* from its singular form to the plural form *systems*. You begin by finding the first occurrence of the word *system*, then you click on the space at the end of the word and type an *s*. Next, press Option-⌘-a to find the next occurrence. When you find this occurrence, be sure that you click on the space at the end of the word before you press ⌘-a to repeat the editing change. Otherwise, Word will erase the highlighted occurrence of the word *system* and replace it with a single *s*.

Because of the limitations that you encounter when you use the ⌘-a shortcut, you will probably want to use the Change... command when you need to make a significant number of editing changes to your document. Let's look at the Change... command in detail.

Changing Text

The Change... command on Word's Search menu is closely related to the Find... command. Instead of just finding every occurrence of a character sequence, however, the Change... command lets you find each occurrence of a character sequence and replace it with a different character sequence. If you've used other word processors, you may know this feature as search and replace.

When you choose the Change... command from the Search menu, you will see the dialog box shown in Figure 6-28. Notice that this dialog box is very similar to the Find dialog box shown in Figure 6-23.

FIGURE 6-28

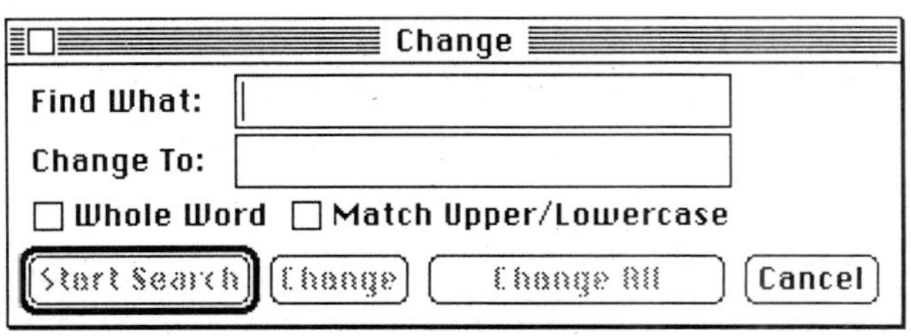

The Change dialog box is similar to the Find dialog box.

Enter the text that you want to find and change in the Find What edit bar. (As in the Find dialog box, you will see a blinking pointer in the Find What edit bar when you first open the Change dialog box. If you have used the Find or Change command in a previous search or replace procedure, the Find What edit bar will reflect the last find text that you entered.) After entering your find text, press the Tab key to move the pointer to the Change To edit bar (or click anywhere on that edit bar), and enter the text with which you want to replace your find text. Your replacement text can contain from zero to 255 characters, though only about 25 characters will be visible in the edit bar.

If you want to change every occurrence of the find text in your document, click the Change All button. Beginning at the pointer location and moving to the end of the document, Word will automatically replace every occurrence of your find text with the replacement text you specified. As the replacement text is pasted into your document, it will assume the same format as the find text that it replaces. (If you leave the Change To edit bar blank, Word will delete every occurrence of the find text when you click the Change All button.)

For example, suppose you want to replace every occurrence of the word *year* with the word *period* in the sample document shown in Figure 6-29. Your insertion point marker is currently at the beginning of the third paragraph. Begin by issuing the Change... command, then enter *year* as your find text and *period* as your replacement text. When you click Change All in the Change dialog box, your document will look like the one in Figure 6-30.

FIGURE 6-29

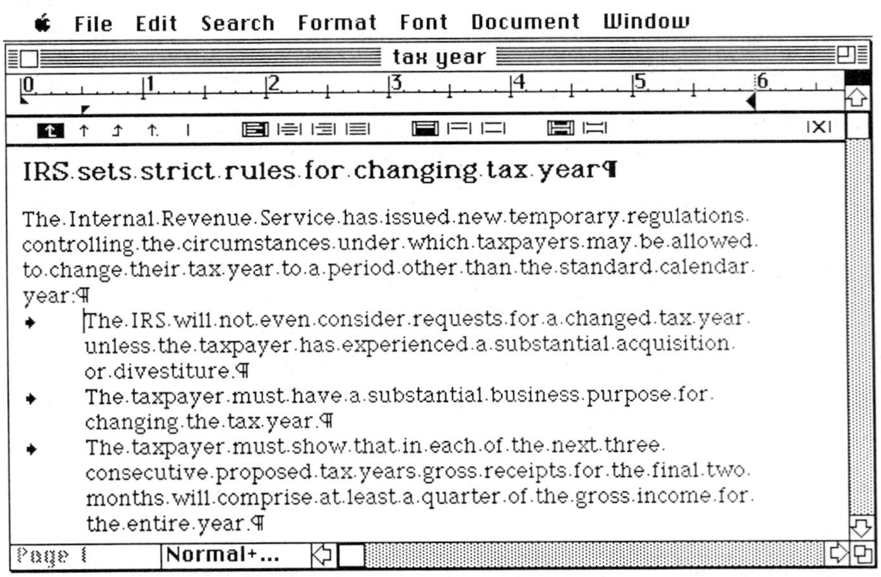

We want to replace the word year *with the word* period *in this sample document.*

FIGURE 6-30

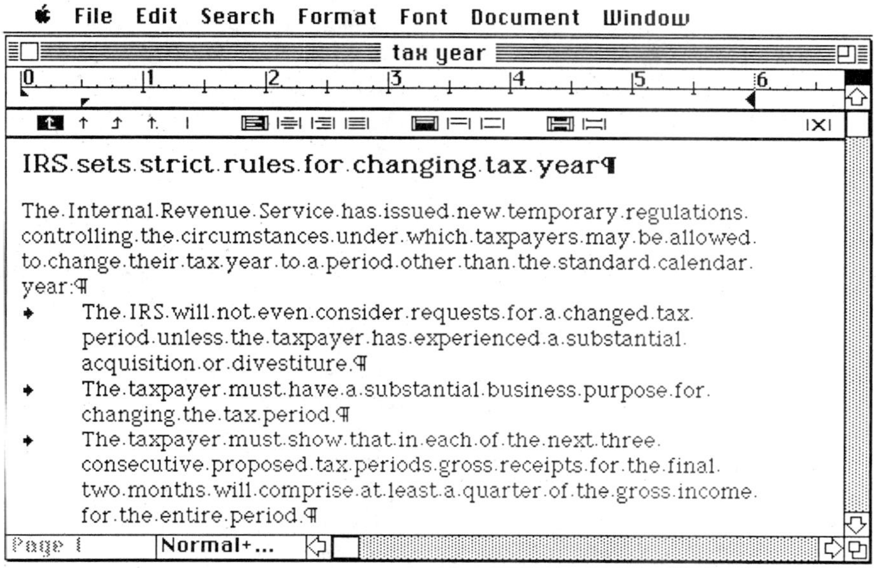

Word replaced text from the current insertion point to the end of the document.

Notice that all ocurrences of the word *year* in the last three paragraphs have been changed. However, Word has not changed the text in the first two paragraphs. When you start a search and replace procedure from the middle of your document, clicking the Change All button will cause Word to replace every occurrence of the find text from the insertion point location through the end of your document. Then it will show you the alert box depicted in Figure 6-25. (This dialog box will not appear if the insertion point marker was at the very first character space in the document when you issued the Change... command.) If you want to continue the Change procedure starting from the beginning of the document, click Yes. If you want to halt the Change procedure at this point, click No. If you click No, Word will display the number of changes made in the status box at the bottom-left corner of your screen and reactivate the Change dialog box. At this point, you can click the close box or the Cancel button to close the Change dialog box, or you can enter new find text or new replacement text to perform another Change operation.

If you choose to continue the Change procedure from the beginning of your document, Word will change all occurrences of the find text from the beginning of the document through to the original insertion point location. When it has completed all of the changes, you'll see a message in the status box in the lower-left corner of your screen telling you how many changes were made.

Selective changing

In many cases, you will not want to indiscriminately replace every occurrence of one character sequence with another character sequence. Word allows you to perform selective changes in two different ways. First, you can examine each occurrence of the find text as you go and decide whether or not you want to change it. Second, you can change every occurrence of the find text within only a selected portion of your document.

Examining each occurrence of the find text

If you want to examine each occurrence of your find text as you go and decide whether or not to change it, click the Start Search button in the Change dialog box. Beginning with the current insertion point location, Word will highlight the next occurrence of your find text on the screen. If you want to change this occurrence, click the Change button. If you want to skip this occurrence and examine the next occurrence of the find text, click the No Change option. (No Change replaces the Start Search button once the Change procedure is underway.)

In either case, Word will follow your instructions and then highlight the next occurrence of the find text on your screen. Again, you can choose either Change or No Change. As in a Find procedure, Word will scroll your document on the screen to bring new occurrences of the find text into view. Occasionally, you may need to drag the Change dialog box out of the way so that you can see the highlighted find text.

One advantage of examining each occurrence of the find text as you go is that you can alter the contents of the Change To edit bar. This is useful in those instances where you want to use a different tense or form in the replacement text. For example, suppose you are changing the word *walk* to *run*. As you're going through the document, you run across a past tense occurrence of the find text, *walked*. If Word were performing the Change procedure automatically, this occurrence would become *runed*. However, when you come across an occurrence like this, you can alter the contents of the Change To edit bar to *ran* before you click the Change button. (Another way to solve this type of problem is to click the Whole Word option, which we'll discuss in a minute.)

Instead of altering the replacement text in the Change dialog box, you may want to make changes directly to the document. Just click anywhere on your document to activate it, then you can type characters from the keyboard or access any of Word's menu commands. As in a Find procedure, if you click on your document window during a Change procedure, Word does not close the Change dialog box. Instead, it moves the dialog box behind your document window on the DeskTop. To reactivate the Change dialog box, you can either resize your document window and click anywhere on the dialog box, or you can type ⌘-h, which will bring the dialog box back on top of your document window and activate it.

As you're finding and changing individual occurrences of your find text, Word will display the *Continue search from the beginning of the document?* message shown in Figure 6-25 when it reaches the end of your document. You can stop the Change procedure at this point, or you can continue your selective changing, starting at the beginning of the document. If you choose to cycle back to the beginning of your document and continue the Change procedure, Word will continue to look for the find text until it reaches the end of your document. Then you'll see the message *End of document reached.*

Changing all occurrences of the find text in a selected area

If you select a portion of your document before you choose the Change... command, then you can change all occurrences of the find text within just that selection. Continuing with the sample document that we used in Figure 6-29 on page 198, suppose you want to change the word *year* to *period* only within the second paragraph of your document. Begin by selecting that paragraph, then issue the Change... command. When the Change dialog box appears, you'll see that the Change All button now reads Change Selection.

To perform the Change procedure, just enter your find text (*year*) and your replacement text (*period*), then click the Change Selection button. Word will automatically change every occurrence of the find text within the paragraph you selected. Again, the number of changes will be reflected in the status box at the lower-left corner of your screen.

When you want to change one character sequence to another within a selected portion of your document, be sure that you do not click the Start Search button when you begin the Change procedure. If you do this, the text that you selected before you issued the Change... command will no longer be selected. Instead, only the first occurrence of the find text will be selected. When you click Change Selection, Word will change only the currently highlighted occurrence of the find text, not every occurrence in the portion of the document that you originally selected.

Change options

You've probably noticed that the Change dialog box offers the same two options that appear in the Find dialog box: Whole Word and Match Upper/Lowercase. The Whole Word option works exactly like the Whole Word option in the Find dialog box. When you activate this option, Word will change only whole-word matches to your find text. Again, this option is likely to be important when your find text is a single short word. For example, suppose that you want to replace every occurrence of the word *top* with the word *bottom.* If you do not activate the Whole Word option, Word will replace the characters *top* in such words as *topic* and *stop.* Your document may end up with some nonsensical "words" such as *bottomic* and *sbottom.*

The Whole Word option also can come in handy when the word you are changing appears in more than one tense or form throughout your document. For example, suppose you want to change every occurrence of the word *boy* to *child.* If your document happens to contain the plural form of *boy—boys*—and you do not select the Whole Word option, Word will change *boys* to *childs*. To avoid this kind of problem, you can use the Whole Word option to perform separate Change procedures for each form of the word.

The Match Upper/Lowercase option works a little differently in a Change procedure than it does in a Find procedure. You may recall that when you activate this option in the Find dialog box, Word will search only for occurrences of the find text where the capitalization exactly matches the capitalization of the find text. This rule still applies when you issue the Change command. However, the Match Upper-Lowercase option also affects your replacement text. If you do not activate this option during a Change procedure, and you enter your Change To text in lower-case letters, Word will use the existing capitalization of each occurrence of the find text to determine the capitalization of the replacement text.

For example, suppose you want to replace the word *May* with the word *April* throughout the sample document shown in Figure 6-31. If you enter your find and replacement text in all lower-case letters and do not activate the Match Upper/Lowercase option, Word will find all occurrences of *may*, ignoring case, and replace them with the word *april*, as shown in Figure 6-32.

FIGURE 6-31

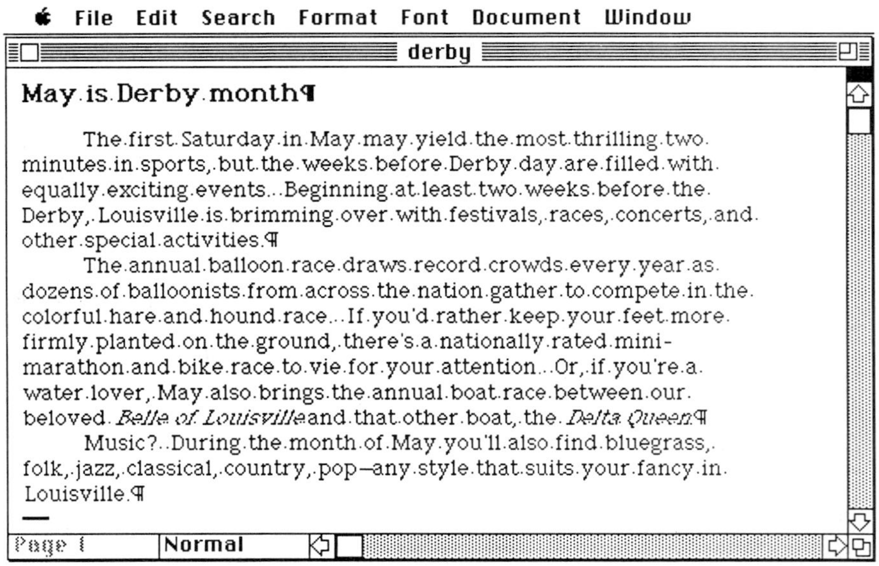

We want to change the word May *to* April *in this sample document.*

FIGURE 6-32

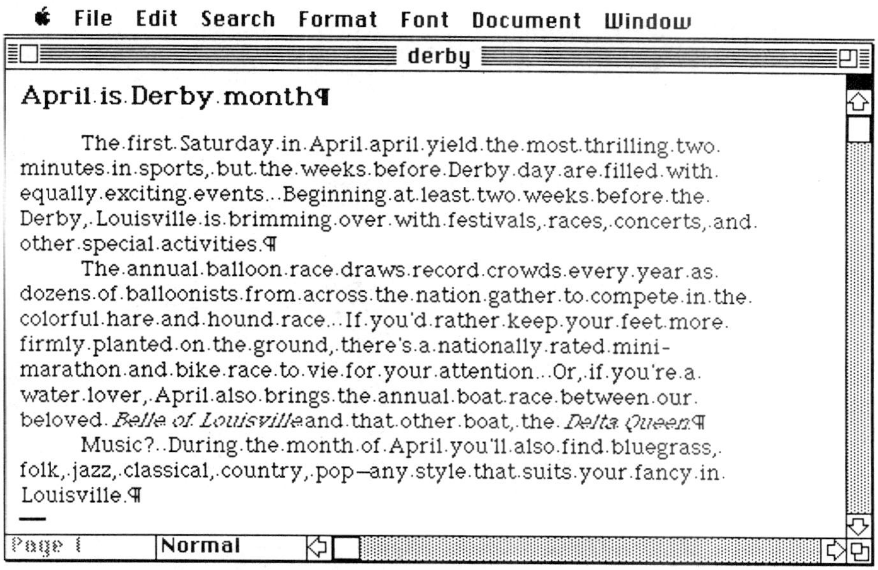

If you enter your find and replacement text in all lower-case letters and do not activate the Match Upper/Lowercase option, Word will use the existing capitalization to change all occurrences of the find text.

Notice that in every instance where the word *may* appeared capitalized, Word also capitalized the replacement text, *april*. However, if you capitalize the first letter of the Change To text, *April*, Word will capitalize all instances of the replacement text when it executes the Change... command, as you can see in Figure 6-33 on the next page.

Notice that the second occurrence of the word *may* in the second line of our document was changed to *april* in Figures 6-32 and 6-33, even though we intended to change only the month names with our search and replace procedure. We could get around this problem by using the Match Upper/Lowercase option.

If you activate the Match Upper/Lowercase option, Word will find only those occurrences of the find text whose capitalization exactly matches the capitalization of the find text in the Find dialog box. In addition, Word will always paste in your replacement text exactly as you have entered it in the Change To edit bar, rather than adapting the replacement text to fit the style of each occurrence of the find text. Figure 6-34 shows the effect of the Change... command on our sample document when we used the Match Upper/ Lowercase option to change *May* to *April*. Notice that the second occurrence of the word *may* in the second paragraph remains unchanged in this example.

FIGURE 6-33

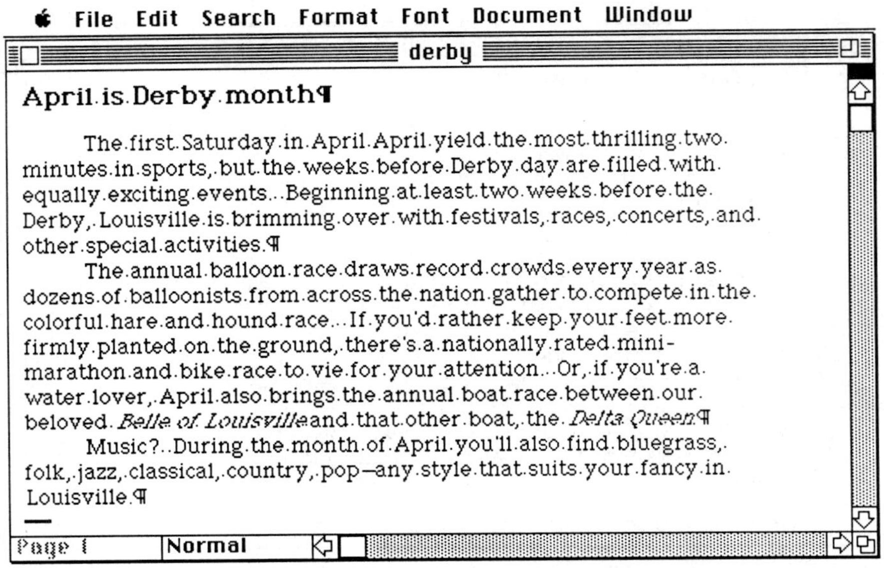

If you capitalize your entry in the Change To edit bar, Word will capitalize all instances of the replacement text.

FIGURE 6-34

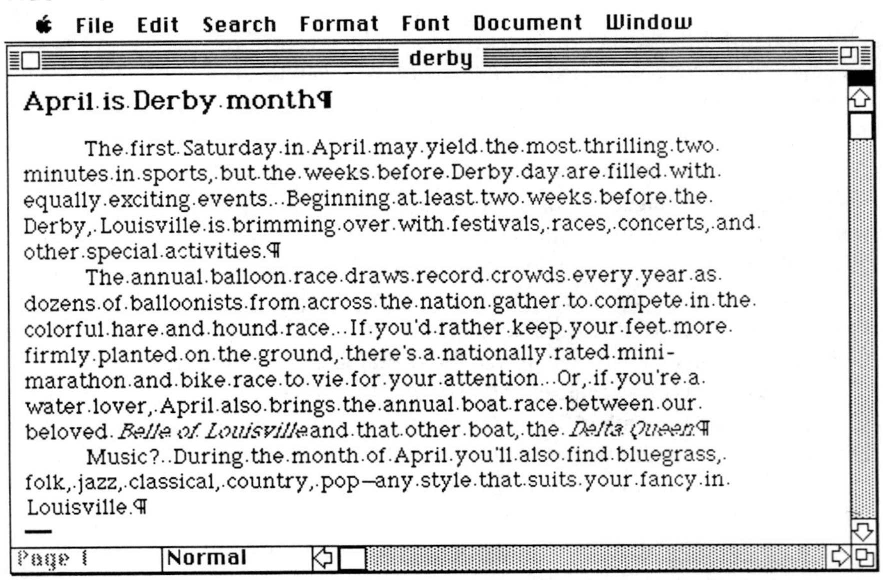

When you use the Match Upper/Lowercase option, Word will change only those words that exactly match the find text.

Using wildcards

The ? wildcard is available in a Change... procedure just as it is in a Find... procedure. However, you can use a wildcard only in your find text. If you include a ? as part of your replacement text, Word will interpret it as a literal question mark. Sometimes the ? wildcard can enable you to perform only one Change... procedure where you otherwise might need two. For example, suppose that you want to replace every occurrence of *software* and *hardware* with the words *computer supplies.* After you choose the Change… command, enter *????ware* as your find text, then enter *computer supplies* as your replacement text. Word will look for all words that begin with any four characters followed by *ware* and replace those words with *computer supplies.*

Changing hidden text

The Change… command will affect hidden text only if you have chosen to display that text on your screen. If you use the Preferences… command to suppress the display of any text that carries the Hidden character format, Word will ignore that text when it performs the search and replace procedure. Thus, if you want to change hidden text, we recommend that you activate the Show Hidden Text option before you begin a Change... procedure.

Changing text and formats

When you enter replacement text in the Change dialog box, there is no way to format that text. Word formats your replacement text to match the format of each occurrence of the find text that it replaces. This is exactly what you want in most cases. For example, suppose you are replacing a word that appears both in the body of your document and in several headings and subheadings. You probably want the replacement text to assume the same format as the surrounding text. Fortunately, Word handles all of this automatically.

Suppose, however, you want your replacement text to be pasted into your document in a special format. Word 3 allows you to change formats as well as text by storing your replacement text on the Clipboard. Here's how it works. First, type the text that you want to use as your replacement text (either in your current document or in another document that is open on your DeskTop). Then select that text and use either the Cut or Copy command from the Edit menu to place it on the Clipboard. Next, issue the Change… command and type your find text in the dialog box. Instead of entering your replacement text in the Change To edit bar, enter ^c. The ^c code instructs Word to use the contents of the Clipboard as replacement text during the Change... procedure. Now you can choose either Change All (or Change Selection), or you can click the Start Search button to examine each occurrence of the find text.

Why might you want to enter replacement text from the Clipboard? There are two primary reasons. First, when you store your replacement text on the Clipboard, you are not bound by the 255-character limitation that applies in the dialog box. Second, when your replacement text is on the Clipboard, it will come into your document in exactly the same format that appears on the Clipboard. Therefore, you can include special style characteristics (different fonts, point sizes, character formats, and so forth) in your replacement text. As you might imagine, this capability can come in pretty handy.

Let's use the ^c technique to replace the word *Excellence* with the full title *Excellence: The Microsoft Excel User's Journal* in the sample document that is shown in Figure 6-35. We want this title to appear in bold italic character format as well.

We'll begin by selecting the first occurrence of the word *Excellence* in line *3* and changing it to *Excellence: The Microsoft Excel User's Journal*, then we'll assign the bold and italic character formats to the title. Now, with the new text still highlighted, we'll issue the Copy command to place a copy of the formatted replacement text on our Clipboard. Then, we'll issue the Change... command, type *Excellence* in the Find What edit bar and ^c in the Change To edit bar. When we click Change All, our sample document will look like the one in Figure 6-36.

FIGURE 6-35

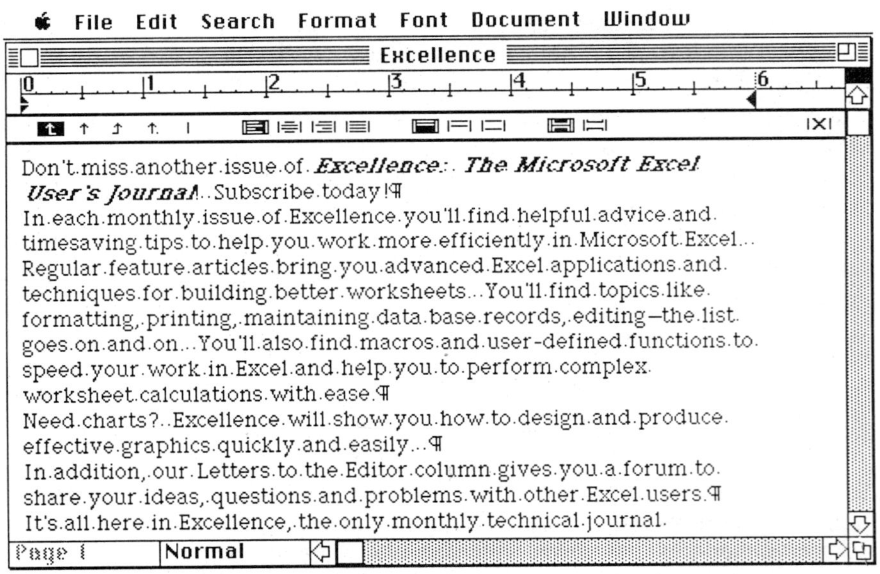

We want to change Excellence *to* Excellence: The Microsoft Excel User's Journal, *then we want to format the replacement text to appear in bold italic type.*

FIGURE 6-36

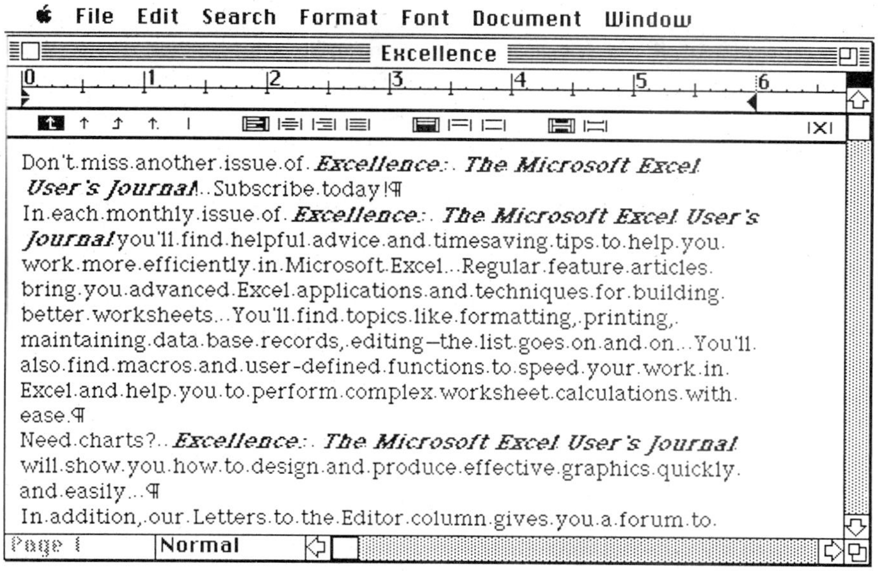

If we copy the replacement text to the Clipboard, Word will apply our character formats when we issue the Change... command.

Although Word allows you to use special formatting in your replacement text, and allows you to search for a particular format using the Option-⌘-r technique, there's no way to search for one format and replace it with another. For example, suppose you have formatted certain words throughout your document using 12-point, bold, italic type. You would like to find every word that has this formatting and change it to 14-point italic with no boldfacing. If you select any character sequence that has 12-point, bold, italic formatting, you can find another occurrence of a character with that same formatting by pressing Option-⌘-r. However, if you change the formatting of the first occurrence from 12-point, bold, italic to 14-point italic, then you cannot use Option-⌘-r to find the next occurrence of 12-point, bold, italic text. In other words, once you have changed from the old format to the new format, the old format will no longer appear on your screen, so you cannot select it and use Option-⌘-r to find the next occurrence.

Using special markers in replacement text

On page 194, we explain how you can search for special markers in a document. For example, if you want to search for every paragraph break (¶), you can enter *^p* as your find text. Table 6-1 summarizes the codes you must use when you want to search for special markers throughout a document. Each of these codes, with the exception of *^w*, can also be included in your replacement text. For example, suppose you want to replace every normal hyphen in your document with an optional hyphen. (As we explain in Chapter 5, a normal hyphen always appears in your document, whereas an optional hyphen appears only when that hyphen occurs at the end of a line.) Choose the Change... command from the Search menu and type a single hyphen as your find text. Then enter ^- as your replacement text. As with any other change, you can choose the Change All option or click Start Search to search for and replace each occurrence individually.

Your change text also can consist of a ^ followed by the three-digit decimal ASCII code for a character. For example, if you enter *^65* as your change text, Word will paste an upper-case *A* in your document as the replacement for each occurrence of the find text. If you enter *^97*, Word will paste a lower-case *a* in your document if the selected occurrence of the find text is lower case, or an upper-case *A* if the selected occurrence is upper case.

CHECKING SPELLING

Your Word 3 package includes a utilities disk with a Main Dictionary file of more than 80,000 words. Word uses this dictionary to identify misspelled words in a document. In addition to the Main Dictionary, you also can develop your own custom dictionaries to check for and correct misspelled words. Typically, a user-created dictionary will contain proper nouns, technical terms, and other words that are not found in the Main Dictionary. Before you use any dictionary to spell-check a document, there are a few minor housekeeping details that you need to take care of, so we'll address these first.

Diskette Considerations

In order to avoid disk switching when you're spell-checking a document, you will need to copy the Main Dictionary file from your utilities disk onto another disk. Since the Main Dictionary file occupies around 161K of disk space, you may need to do a little reorganizing of your files in order to copy the dictionary onto another disk. If you're using a Mac Plus with two double-sided (800K) disk drives, then you should, if possible, copy the Main Dictionary and any user dictionaries onto the disk that contains the document file that you want to spell-check. As usual, this disk will reside in your external drive, while the disk containing the System folder and the Word program file will reside in your internal drive.

If your Macintosh has one double-sided (800K) internal drive and one single-sided (400K) external drive, you should try to fit the Main Dictionary file, any user dictionary files, and the document that you want to spell-check onto one single-sided disk. Again, this will mean that the System folder and the Word program file will reside in the internal 800K disk drive, while the Main Dictionary file and the document file will reside on the disk in the external drive.

If you are using a 512K Macintosh with two single-sided (400K) disk drives or if your Macintosh has only one 800K drive, then you must put up with some disk-switching in order to use Word's spell-checking feature. With one 800K drive, you will need to copy the Main Dictionary file onto the same disk as your document. Then you can use the Spelling... command by switching between this disk and the Word program disk. If you have two 400K drives, you can minimize the amount of disk-switching by leaving the disk that contains the Word program and your document file in the external drive, and switching between the system disk and the utilities disk (or whatever disk contains the Main Dictionary) in the internal drive. In other words, you want Word to be able to read your document file from one drive and the Main Dictionary file from the other drive. Any user dictionary files that you want to access can be on either your Word program disk or on the same disk as the Main Dictionary.

Whether you use a 512K Mac or a Mac Plus, you may be able to avoid some of the disk-management hassles that are associated with spell-checking by taking advantage of the Keep in Memory setting in the Preferences dialog box. Chapter 17 covers this setting and the other Preferences options.

Although copying files and disk-switching are somewhat inconvenient, they're not major obstacles to using the Spelling... command if you've organized your files properly, so we would encourage all Macintosh users, no matter what their configuration, to take advantage of Word's spelling capability.

Spell-checking with the Main Dictionary

Before we get into the subject of custom dictionaries, let's examine how you go about spell-checking a document using just the Main Dictionary. To check the spelling in a document, choose the Spelling... command from the Document menu or press ⌘-l. Word will then go to disk and open the Main Dictionary file. If Word cannot find the Main Dictionary file on one of the currently active disks, it will ask you to locate the file. Use the Eject button to replace one of your active disks with the utilities disk or another disk that contains the Main Dictionary file. Click on the name Main Dictionary, as shown in Figure 6-37, and click the Open button. As soon as Word opens the Main Dictionary file, you will see the dialog box shown in Figure 6-38.

FIGURE 6-37

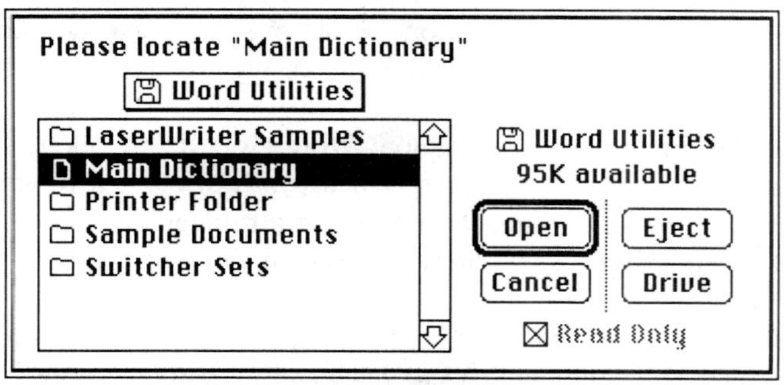

Word will ask you to locate the Main Dictionary file if it is not available on your startup disk.

FIGURE 6-38

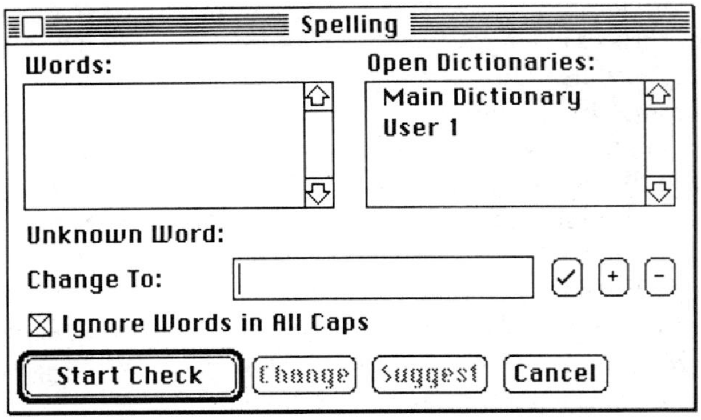

The Spelling dialog box appears once Word has loaded your Main Dictionary file.

A quick tour of the Spelling dialog box

We will be exploring the various elements in the Spelling dialog box as we go along, but for now, let's get a quick overview of each item. At the upper-right corner of the dialog box, you see the Open Dictionaries list box. This box will always show the Main Dictionary, plus any user dictionaries that you have opened. Word always opens the User 1 dictionary automatically and displays its name in this list box when you first issue the Spelling... command.

Next to the Open Dictionaries list box is the Words list box. This box displays Word's suggested correction text and entries from your user dictionaries. Below the two list boxes is the Unknown Word line. During a spelling check, when Word finds a term that it cannot recognize, it displays that term in this area of the dialog box.

You'll use the Change To edit bar to correct misspelled words and to add new words to user dictionaries. Next to the Change To edit bar are three buttons—a check, a plus, and a minus. You can use the check to see if a word that you type in the Change To edit bar is in one of the open dictionaries. As you'll see in a few pages, you'll use the plus and minus buttons to add words to and delete words from your user dictionaries.

The next item in the dialog box is the Ignore Words in All Caps option. This option does exactly what you might expect. When you've selected it, Word will not check the spelling of any word that appears in all upper-case letters. This option is handy when you are spell-checking a document that contains a number of special codes or acronyms.

Finally, the Spelling dialog box includes four buttons: Start Check (which also appears as No Change and Continue Check), Change, Suggest, and Cancel. As you're spell-checking a document, the purpose of each of these is pretty clear.

Finding and correcting misspelled words

After you've opened the Spelling dialog box, the first thing that Word checks is the spelling of the word on which the insertion point is positioned (or the word immediately to the left of the insertion point). Assuming that this word is spelled correctly, you can start scanning forward through the rest of the document by clicking the Start Check button. At first, it may appear as if nothing is happening. However, if you watch the status box at the lower-left corner of your screen, you'll see a percentage—such as 14%—where the page number usually appears. This indicates the portion of the document that Word has already scanned. (For example, 40% means that Word has searched for misspelled words in 40% of that portion of the document between the insertion point and the end of the document.) When Word finds a word that it does not recognize—that is, a word that is not in the Main Dictionary—it will highlight that word in your document and then display it in the dialog box, as shown in Figure 6-39.

FIGURE 6-39

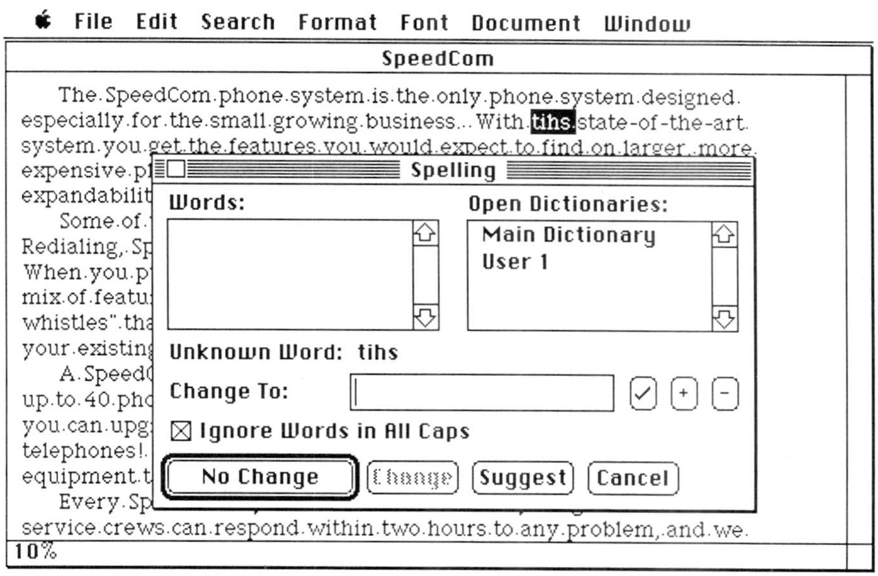

When Word finds a term that it cannot recognize, it highlights that word in your document and displays it in the Spelling dialog box.

When Word finds an unknown word and displays it in the dialog box, you have several options. If you want to leave the word as it is, just click the No Change button. (Notice that No Change replaces Start Check in the dialog box.) Word will then continue scanning the document until it finds another word that it does not recognize.

By the way, after you've clicked No Change once for an unknown word, Word will not display subsequent occurrences of that term in the Unknown Word line of the dialog box. However, Word will continue to highlight any additional occurrences in your document window as it scans the text. In fact, Word will remember the term for the duration of the Word session. If you issue the Spelling... command again (even in another document), Word will not pause and display the term in the Unknown Word line of the Spelling dialog box.

Making manual corrections

If you want to change the unknown word, there are several different approaches you can take. First, you can simply type a new word in the Change To edit bar and then click the Change button. Word will replace the misspelled word in your document with the word you type in the Change To edit bar and automatically continue checking for more unrecognized words. Instead of typing a new word from scratch, you can click on the unknown word that's displayed in the dialog box to display it in the Change To edit bar. Once it is in the edit bar, you can edit the unknown word and then click Change to correct the error and continue with the spelling check.

Sometimes, the typographical error in your document may be the result of an unintentional blank space or other error that cannot be corrected directly in the Change To edit bar. If that is the case, you can click on the document window and type your change manually. The Spelling dialog box will remain open, but it will move behind the document window. Once you have made your change, you can click on the Spelling dialog box again to continue your spelling check.

For example, in Figure 6-40, the Spelling dialog box displays the unknown character string *lence*. If you take a look at the document window, you will see that the correct word is really *Excellence*, but because there is a blank space in the middle of the word, Word treats it as two words. In order to correct this spelling error, you will need to click on the document window and erase the blank space manually.

Using the Suggest button

Another way to change a misspelled word is to click the Suggest button. Word will display a list of similar words in the Words list box. For example, after Word finds the misspelled word *tihs*, if you click the Suggest button, you'll see the list of words shown in Figure 6-41.

Notice that the first word in the list of suggested words also appears in the Change To edit bar. If you want to substitute this word for the misspelled word in your document, just click the Change button. Word will make the substitution and continue checking your document. If you want to use a different word in the list as your replacement, just click on that word before you click Change.

For example, suppose that when you see the dialog box displayed in Figure 6-41, you realize that you want to use the word *this* instead of the suggestion in the edit bar, *ties*. You can simply click *this* in the Words list box to display that word in the Change To edit bar. If you then click the Change button, Word will substitute the word *this* in the Change To edit bar for the unrecognized word in your document and then continue scanning for other possible misspellings.

FIGURE 6-40

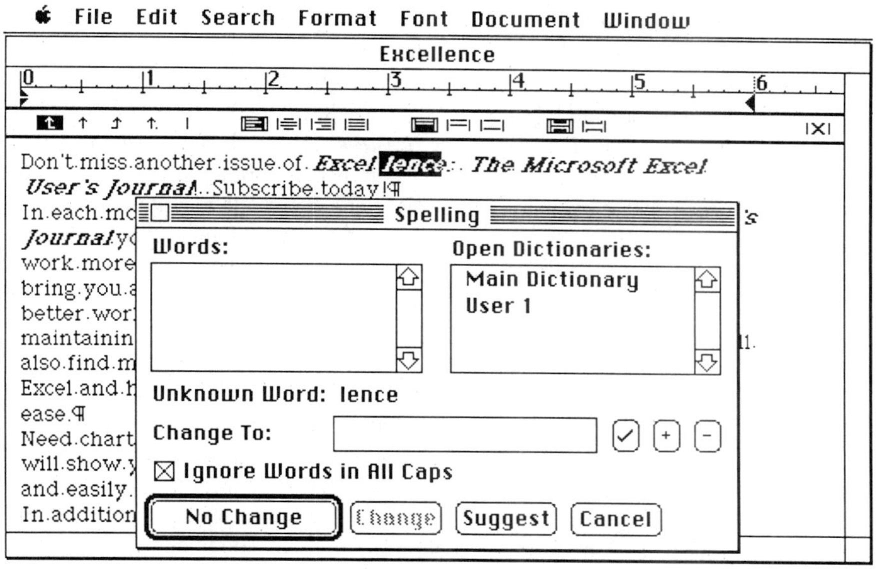

You may have to correct some spelling errors manually.

FIGURE 6-41

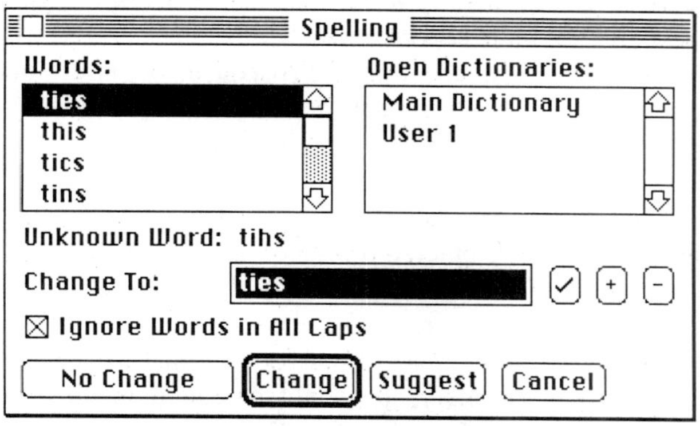

You can use the Suggest button to see a list of suggested alternatives for a misspelled word.

By the way, if the unknown word in your document begins with an uppercase letter, then the suggested list of alternatives in the Words list box will also appear in this form. For example, suppose that your document contains a reference to a book called *Business Statistics*, and you have misspelled the word

Business. When Word flags this misspelling and you click the Suggest button, you'll see a list of alternatives that all begin with a capital *B*. Similarly, if a misspelled word appears in your document in all upper-case letters, then the suggested alternatives will also appear in all upper-case letters. (Keep in mind that unless you deactivate the *Ignore Words in All Caps* option, Word will skip over any misspelled words that appear in all upper-case letters.)

Occasionally, Word will be totally perplexed by the unknown word and will not be able to make an intelligent guess about alternatives. In that case, you'll see an alert box that says *Unable to suggest alternative.* In this case, you must type the correct word in the Change To edit bar. Another problem with the Suggest feature is that it occasionally gives you a list of alternatives that are not even close to the correct answer. This is most likely to happen when the first letter of a word is incorrect. For example, when we misspelled the word *during* as *suring*, Word suggested alternatives that all began with the letter *s* or *c*, such as *surfing*, *curing*, and *surging*.

Using the Change To edit bar

As we mentioned above, you can use the Change To edit bar to enter an alternative for a misspelled word or to correct a misspelled word. By using the Change To edit bar creatively, you can make even more significant changes to a document without having to get into your document window and halt the spelling check. Going back to the example in Figures 6-39 and 6-41, suppose that you've misspelled the word *this* as *tihs* in your document. After Word catches the misspelling and suggests *this* as a possible alternative, you realize that, instead of the word *this*, you want to use the word *these*. All you have to do is edit *this* in the Change To edit bar to be *these*, and then click the Change button. Word will then substitute *these* for the misspelled word in your document and continue scanning for more unrecognized words.

When you're editing the contents of the Change To edit bar, you are not limited to typing a single word. Although the edit bar can display only about 19 characters, you can type many more characters than this. You can even type a sentence or more, if you wish.

Normally, Word will not alert you if the text that you type in the Change To edit bar is misspelled. Once you've entered a correction in the Change To edit bar, however, you can check the spelling of your correction text against the entries in all open dictionaries. To do this, click the check symbol next to the edit bar before you click the Change button. Word will look for that word in the open dictionaries. If the word that you typed cannot be found in an open dictionary, then Word will place a copy of that word in the Unknown Word line in the dialog box. If Word *does* find the word that you typed in a dictionary, then the Unknown Word area will be blank. You can assume that the word is spelled correctly and click the Change button to correct your document. Unfortunately, you can check only single-word entries in the edit bar. If you've typed more than one word, then Word will automatically see the contents of the edit bar as "unknown."

Repeated misspellings

If you have made the same spelling error more than once in your document, Word will remember the last editing change you made and suggest that same solution the next time it runs into the error.

For example, suppose you commonly transpose the letters *a* and *h* in the word *that*. The first time Word highlights the character sequence *taht*, you click on the word in the Unknown Word line of the Spelling dialog box, change the typographical error to *that* in the Change To edit bar, and click the Change button. The next time Word highlights the character sequence *taht*, it will automatically enter the word *that* in the Change To edit bar. All you have to do is click the Change button to accept Word's suggestion.

Notes

It's interesting to note that, in addition to misspelled words, the Spelling... command will find words that appear to have unusual patterns of upper- and lower-case letters. For example, Word will flag such occurrences as BOok, boOk, and BooK. These occurrences will be flagged whether or not the *Ignore Words in All Caps* option is activated.

If your document contains a hyphenated word, such as well-dressed, then Word will check each part of that word separately. For example, if you've entered *well-dressd*, then Word will flag only the *dressd* portion as an unknown word. Word can recognize any combination of hyphenated words as long as all the component words are in the Main Dictionary and are spelled correctly within your document.

Word also can recognize most words that are created by adding common prefixes and suffixes to other words. However, the program is not totally foolproof in this regard; it's possible that an illogical combination of a word plus a prefix or suffix will *not* be flagged during a spelling check.

If you have assigned the Hidden character format to text in your document, Word will check the spelling of that text as long as it is displayed in the document window. If you use the Preferences... command to suppress the display of your hidden text, however, Word will not check the spelling of any hidden words.

Halting the spelling check

When Word has checked every word through the end of your document, you'll see an alert box that asks, *Continue checking from beginning?* If you click OK, Word will go back to the beginning of the document and continue checking for misspelled words. When Word reaches the end a second time, you'll see the *End of document reached* message. If you click Cancel, Word will halt the spelling check and remove the Spelling dialog box from your screen.

You also can cancel the spelling check at any other time. If you press the ⌘ and period keys (⌘-.) while Word is scanning your document, Word will stop scanning, but the Spelling dialog box will remain open. If Word is not scanning your document, you can cancel the spelling check by clicking the Cancel button, by clicking in the close box to close the Spelling dialog box, or by typing ⌘-period.

If you click anywhere on your document window while the Spelling dialog box is open, Word will activate the document window but will not close the Spelling dialog box. To reactivate the Spelling dialog box, just click anywhere on that box, choose Spelling... from the Document menu, or type ⌘-l.

Spell-checking a selected portion of a document

Word makes it easy for you to check for spelling errors in only a selected portion of a document. All you have to do is drag through the part of the document that you want to check to select it and then issue the Spelling... command. When you choose Spelling... from the Document menu, Word will check the first word in the selection and then pause until you click the Start Check button. After you click this button, Word will proceed to scan only the text you have selected and flag any unrecognized words. After scanning the entire selection, you'll see the alert box shown in Figure 6-42. When you click OK to close this box, Word will also close the Spelling dialog box automatically.

FIGURE 6-42

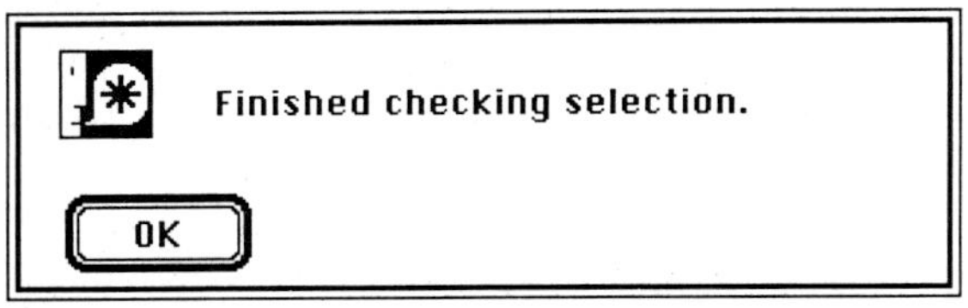

After checking the selected text, Word presents this alert message.

Spell-checking a single word

To check the spelling of a single word, just select that word and issue the Spelling... command. Instead of selecting just the word you want to check, you can select that word and any following text. It's important, however, that the word you want to check be the very first thing in your selection. After you make your selection and choose Spelling... from the Document menu, Word will check the word against the entries in all open dictionaries. If Word cannot recognize the word you have selected, then that word will appear in the Unknown Word area of the spelling dialog box. You can then correct the word using the methods we described above, or you can click the No Change button to leave the word as is. After you've corrected the word or clicked No Change, Word will display the alert box shown in Figure 6-42. (If you've selected more than one word, you won't see this alert box until Word has checked your entire selection.) When you click OK in the alert box, Word will close the Spelling dialog box and terminate the spell-check.

Instead of selecting the word whose spelling you want to check, you can click anywhere on that word (including just before or just after that word) and then issue the Spelling... command. Again, if Word does not recognize the word on which you've positioned the insertion point marker, then that word will appear in the Unknown Word line of the Spelling dialog box. You can then correct the word, or you can click the No Change button. In either case, Word will proceed to scan forward through your document for other unrecognized words. If you don't want Word to do any further scanning, close the Spelling dialog box and change the word manually, if it needs to be corrected. If the word already is correct, just close the dialog box without clicking No Change.

You can also use the Spelling... command to check the spelling of text in your header, footer, and footnote windows. We'll talk about headers and footers in Chapter 7 and footnotes in Chapter 13.

The UK Dictionary

Microsoft has also added a UK Dictionary to the utilities disk for users in the United Kingdom. If you live in or commonly correspond with users in the United Kingdom, you may want to use this dictionary file instead of the default Main Dictionary file. However, you cannot access the UK Dictionary file from within the Spelling dialog box because the program recognizes only the name *Main Dictionary* when it is searching for your main dictionary file. Thus, if you prefer to use the UK version rather than the US version of the Main Dictionary, you'll need to change the name of both files before you load the Word program.

Assuming that you want to keep your original Main (US) Dictionary on hand, begin by changing the name of that dictionary to US Dictionary, then change the name of the UK Dictionary to Main Dictionary. When you open the Spelling dialog box for the first time during a Word session, the UK dictionary will be loaded automatically.

User Dictionaries

In order to use Word's Spelling... command efficiently, you will almost certainly want to create at least one user dictionary or custom dictionary that you can use in conjunction with the Main Dictionary. Chances are, your documents will contain one or more frequently used words that are not in the Main Dictionary file. It can be annoying and time consuming for the program to flag these words as "unknown" when they are perfectly legitimate terms. You can get around this problem by adding these terms to a user dictionary and then opening that dictionary file each time you perform a spelling check. Since Word automatically checks your document against *all* open dictionaries, it will be able to recognize any specialized terms that you have stored in a user dictionary. Of course, if your document contains a specialized term that is misspelled, Word will flag it during a spelling check. You will then be able to consult your user-created dictionary to obtain the correct spelling for that term.

There are a couple of different ways to add new terms to a custom dictionary. First, you can add them during a spell-checking procedure—whenever Word finds a legitimate word that is not in its Main Dictionary, you can simply add it to a user dictionary. Second, you can type terms directly into the Spelling dialog box. We will discuss both of these methods as we explain how to create a custom dictionary.

In addition to adding words to a user dictionary, you can revise and delete earlier entries. You also can copy terms from one user dictionary to another. Of course, any changes like this must be saved to disk if they are to be permanent.

Although Word offers a great deal of flexibility with user dictionaries, it does not allow you to make changes to the Main Dictionary. That file is protected so you can neither add nor delete terms, nor can you revise an existing word in the Main Dictionary.

Creating a custom dictionary

Creating a custom dictionary involves three steps: opening an empty user dictionary, adding terms to that dictionary, and then saving it to disk. When you issue the Spelling... command for the first time during a Word session, Word automatically opens a dictionary called User 1 (in addition to opening the Main Dictionary). Unless you've added terms to this dictionary and saved it to disk, the User 1 dictionary will be empty. You also can open other empty user dictionaries and add terms to them.

Opening a new user dictionary file

As you know, Word automatically opens the User 1 dictionary whenever you issue the Spelling command for the first time during a Word session. To start a new user dictionary, just choose New from the File menu while the Spelling dialog box is open. Word will automatically open another user dictionary called User *x*, where *x* is a sequential number. For example, the first time you choose New from the File menu, Word will open a dictionary called User 2 (since User 1 is already open). The second time you choose New, Word will open the User 3 dictionary, and so forth. Of course, each of these dictionaries is initially blank, much like a new Word document file.

You can have up to four user dictionaries open at once, RAM permitting. As you are adding new terms to your dictionaries, you may want to have two or more open at once so that you can place different kinds of terms in different dictionaries.

Adding new terms during a spelling check

As you are spell-checking a document, Word may occasionally flag a word that it does not recognize, which in fact is a legitimate word. The most likely candidates are proper nouns, such as company names, technical jargon, and other specialized terms. When Word displays an unrecognized word in the Spelling dialog box, you can add it to a user dictionary by clicking on the unknown word to display it in the Change To edit bar, then clicking the plus button in the dialog box. Unless you have selected another dictionary name from the Open Dictionaries list box, Word will then add the term to the first user dictionary in the list of open dictionaries (probably User 1).

Now that you have "legitimized" the term, Word will remove it from the Unknown Word area of the dialog box amd display it in the Words list box. If this term is the first one to be added to the dictionary, then it will be the only entry in the Words list box. For example, Figure 6-43 shows the Spelling dialog box after we have added the word *Microsoft* to the User 1 dictionary.

FIGURE 6-43

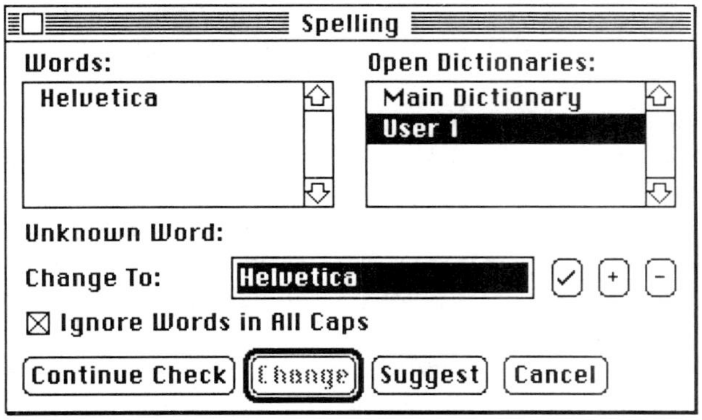

You can add new terms to the User 1 dictionary.

If you want to add the term to a dictionary other than the first user dictionary on the list, just click on the name of that dictionary in the Open Dictionaries list box before you click the plus symbol. When you add a word to a dictionary, that word will remain displayed in the Change To edit bar until you click the Continue Check button or close the dialog box. If you want to add the term to more than one dictionary, just click on the name of the dictionary where you want to place the term and click the plus button again.

Adding new terms by typing

You do not have to wait until Word flags an unrecognized word before you add that word to a user dictionary. Another way to add a term is to open the Spelling dialog box, type that term in the Change To edit bar, click the name of the dictionary in which you want to place the term, and then click the plus symbol. For example, suppose that you are about to spell-check a legal document that contains numerous references to a person named Schaeffer. You can add this name to the User 1 dictionary before you begin checking your document. First choose Spelling... from the Document menu. Then, with the Spelling dialog box open, type *Schaeffer* in the Change To edit bar and click the plus symbol. Word will automatically add this word to the User 1 dictionary (or whatever user dictionary is first in the list of open dictionaries).

Again, after you've added a word to a dictionary, that word will remain in the Change To edit bar. To add it to another user dictionary, just click on the name of that dictionary in the Open Dictionaries list box, and then click the plus button again.

Capitalization

When you add a new term to a user dictionary, you need to keep in mind how Word deals with capitalization during a spelling check. If the term you add to a dictionary is in all lower-case letters, then Word will be able to recognize any occurrence of that word in a document, no matter what case is used. If you use one or more upper-case letters in the term that you add to a dictionary, then

Word will be able to recognize only occurrences that have the same letters in upper-case. For example, suppose you add the name MacArthur to a user dictionary. In performing a spelling check, Word will flag any occurrence of this name where either the *M* or the *A* is not capitalized. Thus, Macarthur, macarthur, and macArthur would all be unrecognized words.

Because of the way Word handles capitalization, you should be sure that you add any nonproper words in all lower-case letters. For example, the word *repaginate* is not in the Main Dictionary. If you add this word to a user dictionary, be sure that you enter it in all lower-case letters. If you don't—for example, if you enter it with an upper-case *r*—Word will flag all occurrences of that word where the *r* is not capitalized.

Capitalization also affects the way Word displays dictionary terms in the Words list box. At the top of a list of user dictionary terms, you'll see all of the words that begin with an upper-case letter, arranged alphabetically. Following these, you'll see a list of all other words, also arranged alphabetically.

Editing a user dictionary

Fortunately, Word's user dictionaries are very flexible. Not only can you add new terms to a dictionary, you also can revise existing terms, delete terms, and even copy terms from one user dictionary to another. If there's a dictionary that you use during most of your spelling checks, you will probably need to make frequent changes to that file in order to adapt it to different situations.

Revising a dictionary term

To revise a term in a user dictionary, open the Spelling dialog box, then open the dictionary file that contains the term that you want to revise. When you click on the name of that dictionary file in the Open Dictionaries list box, its contents will appear in the Words list box. Click on the word that you want to revise to display it in the Change To edit bar. You can then edit the term in any way you wish. Once you have completed your revisions, click the plus symbol to add the edited term to your dictionary. When Word places the edited term in the user dictionary, it will *not* automatically delete the original term on which the edited term is based. If you want to remove the original term from the dictionary, you must use the minus button to delete it.

Deleting a dictionary term

To delete a term, click on the name of the dictionary that contains the term you want to delete. Then click the term you want to delete in the Words list box. When that word appears in the Change To edit bar, click the minus symbol. This will remove the word from the dictionary, but the word will still appear in the Change To edit bar. If you want, you can edit the term and add the edited version to the dictionary that contained the original term. Or you can select another dictionary and add the term to that dictionary.

Moving a term from one dictionary to another

If you have two or more user dictionaries open, you can easily move a term from one to another. All you have to do is click on the name of the dictionary that contains the term you want to move, then select that term in the Words list box. Word will then place the word you selected in the Change To edit bar. Next, click on the name of the dictionary to which you want to copy that word, and click the plus symbol. The word will now be in both the original dictionary and the dictionary to which you copied it. If you want, you can now delete the term from the original dictionary.

Managing dictionary files

As we mentioned earlier, once you have added terms to a user dictionary, you will need to save that dictionary to disk in order to be able to use those terms again. After a dictionary has been saved, it can be recalled for use with any document. The dictionary on disk is an independent file; it is not in any way "attached" to the particular document that was open when the dictionary was created. For this reason, Word will *not* automatically open a dictionary file whenever you use the document in which that file was first created. The only dictionary files that Word opens automatically are Main Dictionary and User 1. Moreover, Word will not let you open *any* user dictionary until the Main Dictionary has been opened. When you issue the Spelling... command for the first time in a Word session, you must first open the Main Dictionary. Then you can open user dictionaries as you need them.

You can close user dictionary files when you no longer need them. To close a dictionary, just click on the name of the dictionary you want to close in the Open Dictionaries portion of the Spelling dialog box and select Close from the File menu.

Word does not allow you to have more than four user dictionaries open at one time, so you may need to close one dictionary in order to open another. Moreover, you may be able to speed up a spell-checking procedure by closing any extraneous dictionary files. In fact, we recommend that you create one "general" user dictionary file that contains frequently used terms, and open only this file whenever you spell-check a document.

In addition, you can create a handful of "specialty" dictionaries, each of which contains terms that are used in a particular kind of document. You would then open one of these specialty dictionaries only when you need to spell-check the kind of document for which it was created.

As you might expect, Word won't let you close the Main Dictionary file. Once that file has been opened, it will remain open until you quit from Word.

Saving a user dictionary

Saving a user dictionary works much like saving any other type of file. To save a user dictionary for the first time, click on that dictionary name in the Spelling dialog box and then—while the dialog box is still open—choose Save or Save As... from the File menu. Word suggests the name User *x* in the Save Current Dictionary As edit bar. Word also displays in dim video the names of other files on the current disk (if any) in the list box.

You can either save the dictionary under the suggested User *x* name or you can type a new name in the edit bar. Once you decide on a name for the dictionary, just click the Save button to save the dictionary to the current disk. Of course, you can use the Drive and/or Eject buttons if you want to save the file on a different disk. After a file has been saved once, you can save it again under the same name by simply opening the Spelling dialog box, clicking on the name of the dictionary you want to save, and then choosing Save from the File menu.

In general, we recommend that you type a new name when you save a dictionary file rather than using the suggested User *x* name. Here's why: Suppose you save a dictionary under the name *User 2* and then quit from Word. The next time you load Word, you decide to create another user dictionary. When you choose New from the File menu, Word will automatically add the name *User 2* to the list of Open Dictionaries in the Spelling dialog box. However, this User 2 dictionary is not the same as the User 2 dictionary that you saved to disk in the earlier Word session. Like all new dictionaries, it will be blank. Suppose you then decide to open the User 2 dictionary that's stored on disk. When you do this, your Open Dictionaries list box will display *two* User 2 dictionaries! Obviously, this could lead to some confusion.

Another reason for saving user dictionaries under a name other than User *x* is to help you remember which dictionaries in the Open Dictionaries list have been saved to disk and which have not. When you save a dictionary under a different name, Word replaces the original User *x* name in the Open Dictionaries list box with the name of the file on disk.

There is one possible exception to this rule of avoiding User *x* names for dictionary files. If you've created a dictionary of terms that you will need to use in virtually every document that you spell-check, then it would be a good idea to save that dictionary under the name User 1. Because Word always opens the dictionary for you automatically, you won't have to use an Open... command to access that dictionary. (Of course, the User 1 dictionary must be on one of the active disks when you first issue the Spelling... command in order for this technique to work properly. If Word does not find User 1 on one of your current disks, it will create a new, blank User 1 file.)

By the way, if you make changes to a user dictionary and do not save those changes to disk, Word will alert you to this fact when you choose Quit from the File menu. You'll see an alert box with a message like, *Save changes to dictionary User 2?* If you click Yes, Word will save the terms in that dictionary under whatever name is displayed in the Open Dictionaries list box. If you click No, Word will quit to the Finder level without saving the dictionary, and if you click Cancel, Word will return to your document and not quit to the Finder level.

If there are two or more dictionaries with unsaved changes when you issue the Quit command, Word will display this alert box for each dictionary. In each case, you can click Yes, No, or Cancel.

Opening and closing a user dictionary

After a user dictionary has been saved to disk, you can open it by choosing Open... from the File menu after you issue the Spelling... command. Word will then search the current disk for dictionary files and display a list of those files (along with other files) in the Open dialog box.

Select the file you want to open by double-clicking its name in the list box. Of course, you can use the Drive or Eject buttons to access a dictionary file on a different disk. As soon as you open a dictionary file, its name will appear in the Open Dictionaries list in the Spelling dialog box.

To close a dictionary, just click on its name in the list of Open Dictionaries and then choose Close from the File menu. Word will then delete the name from the list of Open Dictionaries in the Spelling dialog box. If you have made changes to the dictionary that have not been saved to disk, then Word will alert you with a dialog box that asks, *Save changes to Dictionary?* If you want to save those changes before you close the dictionary file, click Yes. If you click No, Word will close the dictionary without saving the changes. There's also a Cancel option, which allows you to back out of the Close procedure altogether.

By the way, Word will not allow you to close the Main Dictionary file. As we mentioned earlier, once you issue the Spelling... command and open the Main Dictionary, it will remain open until you quit from Word.

Deleting a user dictionary file

You can delete a dictionary file from within Word just as you would delete any other file. When you choose Delete... from the File menu, Word will display a list of all the files on the current disk, including dictionary files. Just click on the name of the dictionary file that you want to delete, and then click the Delete button (or double-click the file name). Next, click Yes in the dialog box to complete the deletion.

By the way, as with document files, Word will not allow you to delete a dictionary that is currently open. Before you can delete a dictionary that you have opened during a spell-check session, you must click on the dictionary name in the Spelling dialog box and choose Close from the File menu.

Using custom dictionaries

In most instances, using a dictionary that you've created is no different from using the Main Dictionary. Once a dictionary file is open, Word will automatically refer to the terms in that dictionary as it spell-checks a document. However, you cannot use the Suggest feature with a user dictionary. Whenever you click the Suggest button, Word looks only in the Main Dictionary for alternatives to the unknown word.

Of course, you can still access an alternative word from a user dictionary. To do this, click on the name of that dictionary in the Open Dictionaries list box. Word will then display the entries in that dictionary in the Words list box, as shown in Figure 6-44.

FIGURE 6-44

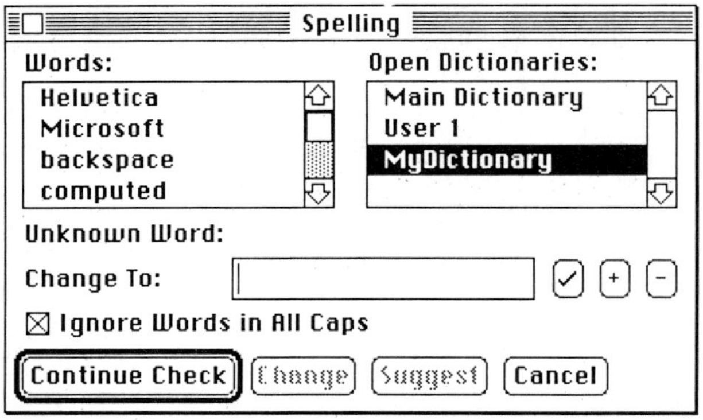

To see the entries in a user dictionary, click on the dictionary name in the Open Dictionaries list box.

If the dictionary contains more words than can be displayed in the Words list box, you can click the scroll arrows to bring additional words into view. When you find the word that you want to use as a replacement for the misspelled word, just click on it to place it in the Change To edit bar. You can then click the Change button to make the replacement in your document.

One interesting thing you can do with user dictionaries is create temporary entries—that is, entries that you use for only one Word session. All you have to do is add the terms to a user dictionary without saving that dictionary. The words will remain in the user dictionary until you close the dictionary file or quit from Word. For example, suppose that you're writing a letter that describes your hometown of Plano, Texas. You can add the word *Plano* to the User 1 dictionary (or to any other user dictionary) and then spell-check the letter. If you don't think you'll need to use the Plano entry again, then you can quit without saving the dictionary. Of course, you can also save the dictionary after you've added a word and then delete the word later, when you're sure you won't need it.

A Final Note

As a final note, we must remind you that Word's ability to find misspelled words does not necessarily mean that you'll discover every wrong word in a document. The program has no way of recognizing incorrect tense or form or improper usage of a word. Always supplement your spelling checks with a thorough human read-through.

HYPHENATION

Like many other word processing programs, Word 3 offers a hyphenation feature. Word will not automatically hyphenate words as you are entering text. However, you can use the Hyphenate... command on the Document menu to hyphenate text that you've already created. Of course, the benefit of using hyphenation is that it allows you to create better-looking documents. Hyphenation is particularly helpful when you are using justified paragraphs and/or narrow columns of text. By hyphenating selected words, you can avoid the unsightly extra spaces that Word occasionally inserts to achieve a justified right margin. If you are using left-aligned paragraphs instead of justified paragraphs, hyphenation can help you to create more uniform lines of text.

Word's Hyphenate... command allows you to hyphenate an entire document or only a selected portion of a document. You also can check each possible hyphenation as you go or have Word perform all the hyphenation automatically. We'll talk about the different hyphenation options as we explain how to use the Hyphenate... command.

One major advantage of Word's hyphenation feature is that it inserts optional hyphens instead of "real" hyphens. An optional hyphen appears in your printed document only if the word that you have hyphenated occurs at a line break. If you edit or reformat your text so that the hyphenated word gets shifted to the middle of a line, then Word will not print the optional hyphen.

The optional hyphen is one of two special hyphens offered by Word 3. Word also offers a nonbreaking hyphen, which can be created by typing ⌘-~. This will appear on your screen as ÷. By the way, you can create an optional hyphen manually by typing the ⌘ key followed by a hyphen (⌘--). When Show ¶ is activated, each optional hyphen will appear on your screen as ⌐. In Chapter 5, we explain special hyphens in more detail. For now, however, you just need to be aware of how an optional hyphen differs from a regular hyphen.

Before we explain how to use Word's Hyphenate... command, we need to go over a few details related to managing your disks during a hyphenation procedure. As you might expect, the issue of how you arrange your disk files is more critical for 512K Mac users than for Mac Plus and Mac SE users.

Diskette Considerations

Word's Hyphenate... command calls up a special algorithm that is stored in the Word Hyphenation file, which is on the utilities disk in your Word 3 package. (If you're using the 400K version of Word, the Hyphenation file will be delivered on your Word program disk.) When you first issue the Hyphenate... command during a Word session, the program will look for this file on one of the current disks. If the file cannot be found on one of the current disks, Word will display the dialog box shown in Figure 6-45. When you see this dialog box, eject one of your current disks and insert the utilities disk or another disk that contains a copy of the Word Hyphenation file. Then click on the file name *Word Hyphenation* and click the Open button.

FIGURE 6-45

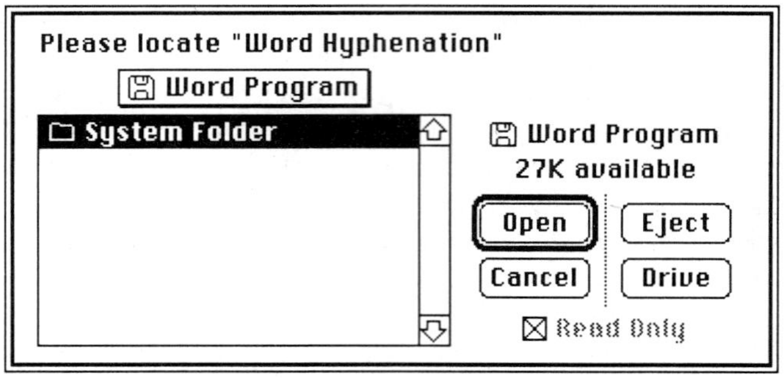

Word will ask you to locate the Word Hyphenation file if it is not on your startup disk.

If you're using a Mac Plus, Word will probably be able to load the hyphenation instructions into RAM and won't need to keep checking the Word Hyphenation file on disk each time you issue the Hyphenate... command. Therefore, you probably will be able to read the Word Hyphenation file from the utilities disk one time and then reinsert whatever disk was current when you first issued the Hyphenate... command. If you find that, as you're using the Hyphenate... command, Word does need to check the Word Hyphenation file on disk occasionally, you can speed things up by copying this file onto the disk that contains your document file (or onto your Word program disk). That way, you won't have to repeatedly eject one of your current disks and insert the utilities disk to read the Word Hyphenation file.

If you're using a 512K Macintosh, then the Hyphenate... command is going to be somewhat inconvenient. Word will not be able to store the hyphenation instructions in RAM, so nearly every time you issue the Hyphenate... command, Word will read the Word Hyphenation file on disk. This is time consuming and annoying, even if the Word Hyphenation file is stored on one of your current disks. If the Word Hyphenation file is *not* stored on one of your current disks, then you will need to do some disk-switching each time you want to use the Hyphenate... command.

To minimize the hassle of using the hyphenation feature on a 512K Mac, we have three recommendations. First, if at all possible, make sure that the Word Hyphenation program is stored on one of the disks that will be current when you issue the Hyphenate... command. If your internal disk drive is a double-sided (800K) drive, then you should be able to copy the Word Hyphenation file onto the disk that contains your System files and the Word program file. The Word Hyphenation file consumes only about 24K of disk space. However , if you have two single-sided drives, then things are going to get pretty crowded. You can try to copy the Word Hyphenation file onto the disk that contains your Word program file and your document file. As usual, this disk will reside in your external drive. If you can't fit the Word

Hyphenation file onto the disk that contains the Word program file, then you may be able to copy it onto the disk that contains your System files. The amount of space available on this disk will be determined partly by the number and kind of printer drivers that you have installed.

If you can't fit the Word Hyphenation file onto either one of the disks that will be current when you use the Hyphenate... command, then you must be prepared to put up with some disk-switching each time you issue the command. This leads into our second suggestion for 512K Macintosh users: If you have to switch disks, you should eject the disk that does *not* contain your document file, and insert the disk containing the Word hyphenation file. For example, if your document file is stored on your Word program disk, you should eject the startup disk from the internal drive and insert the utilities disk (or whatever disk contains the Word Hyphenation file).

Our third suggestion for 512K Mac users is that you perform all of your hyphenation at once. Rather than hyphenating one section of your document at a time, wait until you have completed the document, and then hyphenate the entire thing. That way, Word will need to read the hyphenation instructions from disk only once.

Using the Hyphenate... Command

To hyphenate a document, choose Hyphenate... from the Document menu. After Word reads the hyphenation instructions from disk, you'll see the Hyphenate dialog box shown in Figure 6-46.

FIGURE 6-46

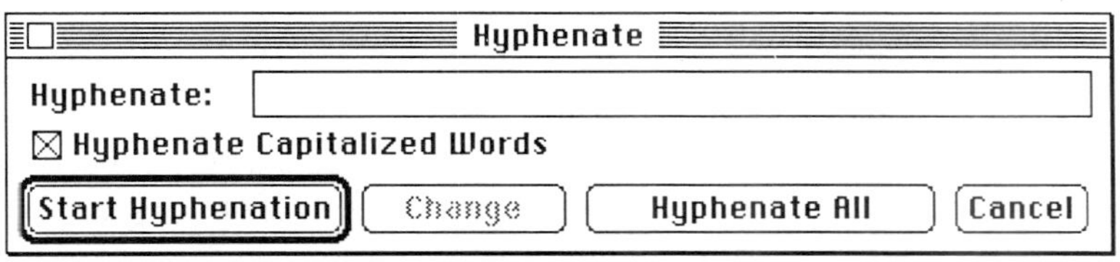

The Hyphenate dialog box appears once the Word Hyphenation file has been loaded.

At this point, you have two choices. First, you can use automatic hyphenation. Just click the Hyphenate All button, which will cause Word to scan through the entire document and automatically hyphenate words at line breaks, where possible. Instead of clicking Hyphenate All, you can click Start Hyphenation. Word will then pause each time it finds a word to hyphenate and display that word in the Hyphenate edit bar. Word will highlight the place where it plans to hyphenate the word. You will then have the choice of accepting the suggested word break. The Word reference manual refers to this pause-and-check procedure as "confirming hyphenation."

Whether you use automatic or confirming hyphenation, you have the choice of ignoring or hyphenating capitalized words. As you can see in Figure 6-46, the Hyphenate Capitalized Words option is selected when you first open the Hyphenate dialog box. If you do not want to hyphenate words that begin with an upper-case letter, click this option to deselect it.

Automatic hyphenation

If you click the Hyphenate All button, Word will automatically decide which words to break between lines and how to break each word. This automatic hyphenation occurs very rapidly and affects all the text between the insertion point and the end of the document. When Word reaches the end of the document, you will see the alert box shown in Figure 6-47. If you click OK, Word will cycle back to the beginning of the document and automatically hyphenate words at line breaks until it reaches the end of the document. Word will then display the message *End of document reached.* If you click Cancel in the continue Hyphenation alert box, Word will stop the hyphenation procedure and automatically close the Hyphenate... dialog box.

FIGURE 6-47

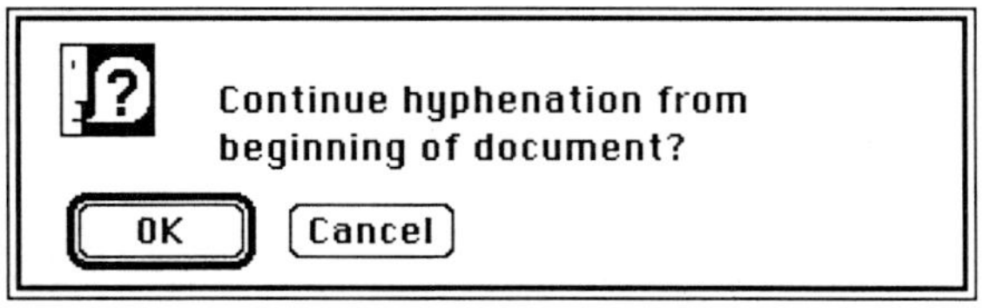

You'll see this alert box when Word has hyphenated through the end of your document.

You can cancel the automatic hyphenation procedure by pressing the ⌘ key as you type a period (⌘-.). You also can undo hyphenation after the procedure is completed. We will explain a couple of methods for undoing hyphenation at the end of this chapter.

Problems with automatic hyphenation

In general, we recommend that you avoid automatic hyphenation since it can lead to some problems. First, Word may hyphenate words at the end of two or more consecutive lines in your document. This is not good form since it makes the document more difficult to read. Second, Word may hyphenate words that already are hyphenated. For example, if your document contains the word *long-suffering*, Word may hyphenate the *suffering* portion at the end of a line. A final reason for avoiding automatic hyphenation is that Word's syllable breaks are not always correct. For example, in one of our documents, Word hyphenated the word *dictionary* between *dictio* and *nary*, rather than between *diction* and *ary*. If you use confirming hyphenation instead of automatic hyphenation, you can avoid these kinds of problems during the hyphenation procedure.

Confirming hyphenation

Instead of clicking the Hyphenate All button, you can click Start Hyphenation in the Hyphenate dialog box. Starting at the insertion point, Word will look through your document for the first possible word to hyphenate and display that word in the Hyphenate edit bar. Word also will highlight the suggested word break in your document. For example, Figure 6-48 shows what the Hyphenate dialog box will look like when Word has found a word to hyphenate.

FIGURE 6-48

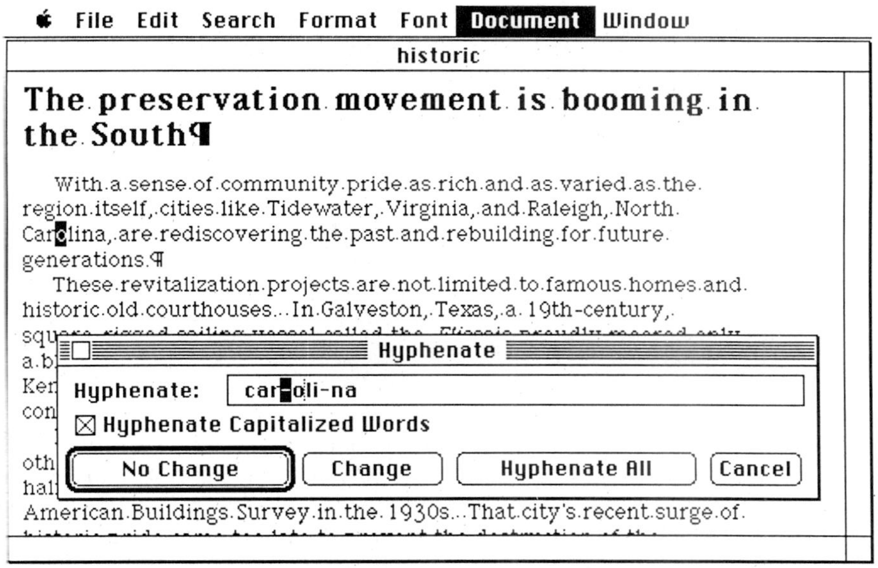

Word will suggest a word break when it locates a "candidate" for hyphenation.

Notice that Word displays the different syllable breaks in the word shown in the Hyphenate edit bar. As you can see, Word highlights in the edit bar the place where it plans to make the word break. Of course, this corresponds to the word break that's highlighted in the document. If you want to accept Word's suggested hyphenation, just click the Change button in the dialog box. If you do not want to break this word at all, click the No Change button. (No Change replaces the Start Hyphenation button.) Word will then look for the next word to hyphenate and display it in the edit bar.

If you want to hyphenate the word in the edit bar, but you want the word break to occur at a location other than that suggested by Word, you can simply click on the place where you want the hyphen to occur. For example, in Figure 6-48, Word suggests that the word *carolina* be broken between *car* and *olina.* Suppose you want to break the word between the *caro* and *lina.* Just click at the spot where you want to insert your hyphen. Word will highlight that syllable break in the edit bar. Click the Change button to implement the word break.

By the way, you can hyphenate the word between any two letters—you do not have to break it between syllables. If you click somewhere other than a syllable break in the edit bar, Word will display a vertical bar at that place rather than highlighting the break. This flexibility in placing word breaks is very helpful in those few situations where the syllable breaks that Word displays in the edit bar are incorrect.

You might notice a dotted vertical line that appears on the word in the edit bar. This line is a guideline for the approximate number of characters in the word that will fit on the current line. In general, if you try to hyphenate the word to the right of the dotted line, there will not be enough room on the previous line of text to hold the first part of the hyphenated word. Word will still insert the optional hyphen in your document, however, without breaking the word. For instance, in the dialog box shown in Figure 6-48, if you clicked between *carol* and *ina*, Word probably would not be able to break the word. However, it still would place an optional hyphen in your document at the location you specified.

After Word has scanned through to the end of your document looking for possible word breaks, you'll see the alert box shown in Figure 6-47. If you want to cycle back to the beginning of the document and look for more word breaks, click OK. If you want to stop the hyphenation procedure, click Cancel. Word will then close the Hyphenate dialog box automatically.

One last note about confirming hyphenation: Although you have considerable flexibility in hyphenating words, you cannot edit your document while the Hyphenate dialog box is open. You may recall that as you are performing some dialog box procedures, such as Finding and Changing, Word allows you to click on your document window and edit text without closing the dialog box. With the Hyphenate command, however, you must close the dialog box before you can access your document text.

Hyphenating a selected part of a document

If you select a portion of your document before you issue the Hyphenate... command, Word will perform the hyphenation procedure only on that selection. Your selection can be as small as a single word, though you probably will want to select at least a paragraph or more. Again, you will have the choice of using either automatic or confirming hyphenation. If you select a block of text in your document and then issue the Hyphenate... command, you'll see a Hyphenate Selection button in the Hyphenate dialog box instead of the Hyphenate All button. If you click Hyphenate Selection, Word will automatically break words at the end of lines and insert hyphens, as necessary, throughout the selected text. When Word has completed hyphenating the selection, you'll see the alert box in Figure 6-49. When you click OK, Word will automatically close the Hyphenate dialog box.

FIGURE 6-49

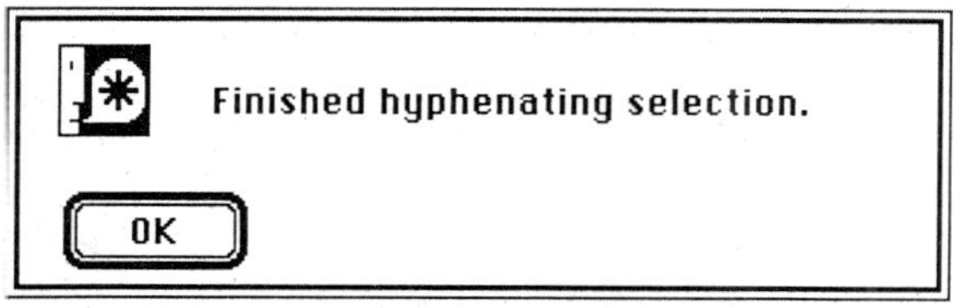

You'll see this alert box after Word has hyphenated a selection of text.

If you click Start Hyphenation instead of Hyphenate Selection, Word will pause and display each suggested word break. Again, you can choose No Change or you can break a word at a place other than the spot that Word suggests. When Word has scanned the entire selection, you'll see the alert box in Figure 6-49.

Editing after You Hyphenate

If you make substantial changes to a document after you've used the Hyphenate... command, you will probably change the location of a number of hyphenated words. Some hyphenated words will end up in the middle of lines. Moreover, a number of words that need to be hyphenated will not be. Of course, you can solve the second problem by simply issuing the Hyphenate... command again. Before you issue the Hyphenate... command, however, you may want to get rid of the hyphens that are now in the middle of lines of text. We explain in the next section how you can use the Change... command to search for and delete unnecessary hyphens. Keep in mind that, if you don't get rid of these hyphens, they will *not* affect the appearance of your printed document since Word does not print optional hyphens unless they appear at line breaks.

We recommend that you delete any unnecessary optional hyphens before you rehyphenate your document. That way, you can get rid of some of the clutter on your screen, which makes your document more difficult to read. For example, the document shown in Figure 6-50 on the next page has been through several hyphenation procedures. Though none of the midline hyphens will appear in the printed document, they make it difficult to read and edit the text on the screen.

Undoing Hyphenation

After you have hyphenated a document or a selected portion of a document, you have the option of using the Undo command to delete all of the hyphens that were just added. As with other Undo commands, you must select Undo Hyphenation from the Edit menu immediately after you complete the hyphenation procedure. As soon as you do something else—typing a few characters, changing formats, etc.—the Undo Hyphenation command will no longer be available.

FIGURE 6-50

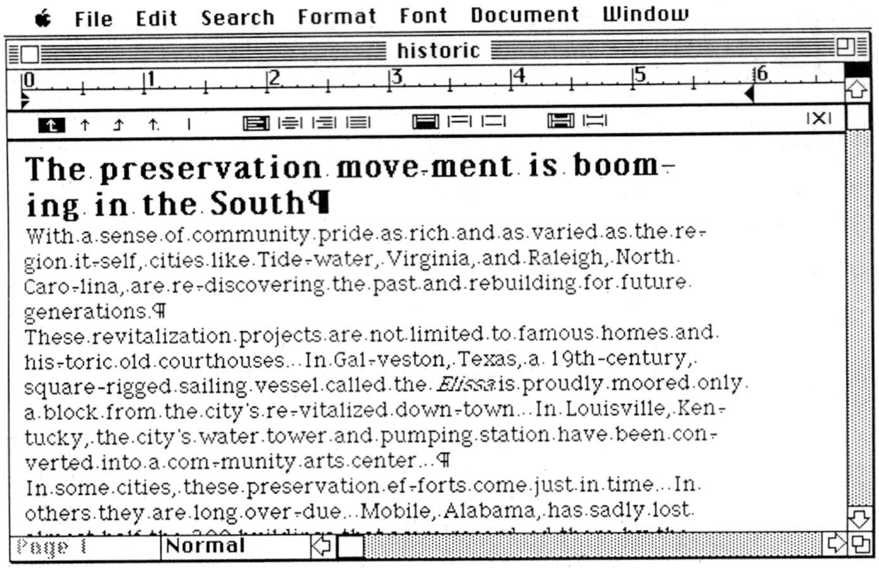

To eliminate clutter, you'll probably want to delete unnecessary optional hyphens from your document.

Fortunately, there's another way to undo hyphenation. By using the Change… command, you can delete all the hyphens that were added during a hyphenation procedure. (Actually, you use the Change... procedure to find every optional hyphen in your document and replace it with nothing.) Just choose Change… from the Search menu and enter a carat followed by a hyphen (^-) in the Find What edit bar. Leave the Change To edit bar blank. Then click Change All if you want to delete every optional hyphen in your document. If you want to delete only some of the hyphens, click Start Search instead of Change All. Word will then pause at each optional hyphen and give you the choice of deleting it or not. For more information on using the Change… command, see pages 197 through 208.

PRINTING AND PAGE LAYOUT 7

Printing and page design are the most complex topics you'll have to address in learning to use Word 3 effectively. The appearance of your printed document depends on a number of related factors. The character and paragraph formats that you learned about in Chapter 5 are the most obvious factors. The font, size, and style of your text and the indentions, tabs, line spacing, and paragraph spacing you select all affect the way your printed document will look. Just as important, however, are the settings that you select when you use the Print..., Page Setup..., Page Preview..., Section..., Open Header... and Open Footer... commands, which we'll be discussing in this chapter. Obviously, the printer you decide to use also determines the quality and overall appearance of your finished document.

Many of these design factors are preset for you and never have to be changed unless you want to create a special page layout or print a particularly complex document. For example, Word's default print settings are generally adequate for a quick memo or letter. Often, you'll find that you can just select the Print... command from the File menu—with no special arrangements beforehand.

When you do need to change the appearance of your printed document, however, it's important that you understand the relationship between the various formatting and page layout settings available in Word. Let's start by discussing how to install and select a printer, then we'll explore the many printing and layout options at your disposal.

Once we've covered the various components that affect the appearance of your printed document, we'll move on to Chapter 8, where we'll present some additional design tips for creating document layouts and show you how to set up multicolumn documents.

INSTALLING AND SELECTING A PRINTER

If you use an Apple ImageWriter printer, you won't need to follow any special installation procedures before printing your document. The ImageWriter is the default printer for the Macintosh, and an ImageWriter printer driver has already been installed on your Word startup disk. All you'll need to do is define the printer for your Macintosh before you print for the first time. If you use an Apple LaserWriter or some other printer, however, you must first install the printer driver on your startup disk and then define the printer you want to use.

Installing a New Printer

In addition to the ImageWriter, which is already located on your startup disk, Microsoft has provided you with driver files for LaserWriter, Brother, Diablo630, NEC7710, and AppleDaisy printers. You'll also see two printer drivers called SerialPrinter and Typewriter. These printer drivers are stored on your utilities disk in the folder named Printer Folder. (If you have purchased the 400K version of the Word software, no LaserWriter driver is provided in your Printer Folder. However, if you have a LaserWriter, you should already have the driver files for that printer.)

To install a printer other than the ImageWriter, insert your startup disk in your internal drive and your utilities disk in the external drive. Double-click on the Printer Folder icon to access the printer drivers stored on that disk. (If you have no LaserWriter driver on your utilities disk, insert any disk that contains those driver files in your external drive.) Now, click on the icon that represents the printer you want to use, and drag that driver file to your startup disk. You'll probably want to place the driver file inside your System folder.

Making room on your startup disk

If you see the alert message *There isn't enough room on the disk to duplicate or copy the selected items,* you'll have to free up some space on your startup disk before you can install the new printer driver. Start by clicking on the icon for the printer driver you want to use, and select Get Info from the File menu to see how much room the new printer driver will require. For example, if you click on the LaserWriter driver and select Get Info, you'll see a window like the one in Figure 7-1. As you can see, the LaserWriter driver file requires a hefty 37K of disk space. In addition, if you want to use the LaserWriter, you'll need to add another file, called Laser Prep, to your startup disk. As its name suggests, the Laser Prep file helps to prepare your document for printing on the LaserWriter. This file requires an additional 24K of disk space.

Once you've determined how much disk space you need, take a look at the files on your startup disk and decide which ones you can do without. For example, if you don't plan to use the ImageWriter printer, you can drag the icon for the ImageWriter into the trash and select the Empty Trash command from the Special menu to free another 31K on your startup disk. (You'll probably want to copy the ImageWriter driver to your utilities disk first so that you have a copy of the driver set available should you ever need it.)

FIGURE 7-1

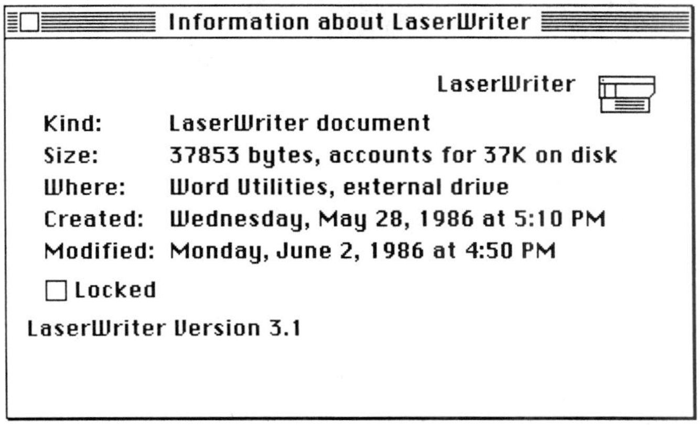

Use the Get Info command to determine how much space your printer driver requires.

If you still don't have enough space to install the desired printer driver, you may need to use the Font/DA Mover to clear out some fonts and desk accessories. (Your Macintosh owner's guide explains this process in detail.) Of course, if there are any data files or seldom-used application files on your startup disk, you also can move those files to another disk.

If you commonly use more than one printer and you can't make enough room on your startup disk for all the printer drivers you need, consider making several copies of your startup disk and installing one printer driver on each disk. Make sure you load the Word program with the startup disk that contains the printer driver you plan to use during that session.

Selecting a Printer

The first time you use any printer—including the default ImageWriter—you need to use the Chooser desk accessory on the menu to select that printer. You can issue the Chooser command from the Finder level, or you can issue it anytime after you load the Word program. Before you select Chooser, however, make sure that your Macintosh is connected to the printer that you plan to use.

When you issue the Chooser command, you'll see a dialog box like the one in Figure 7-2 on the next page. Of course, the contents of the dialog box will vary, depending on the number and type of printer drivers you have installed.

If you use an ImageWriter printer, begin by clicking on the ImageWriter icon in the Chooser dialog box. In a few seconds, you'll see an additional set of icons on the right side of the dialog box, as shown in Figure 7-3. These icons represent your communication and printer ports. Just click on the icon that represents the port you want to use. (Generally, you'll attach your ImageWriter to the printer port.)

FIGURE 7-2

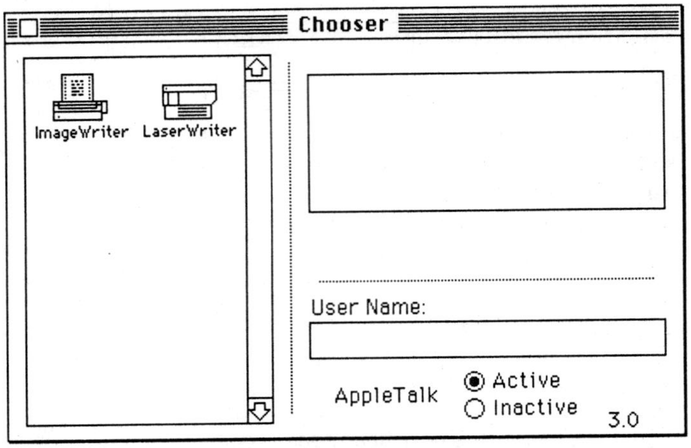

Use the Chooser dialog box to select the printer you want to use.

FIGURE 7-3

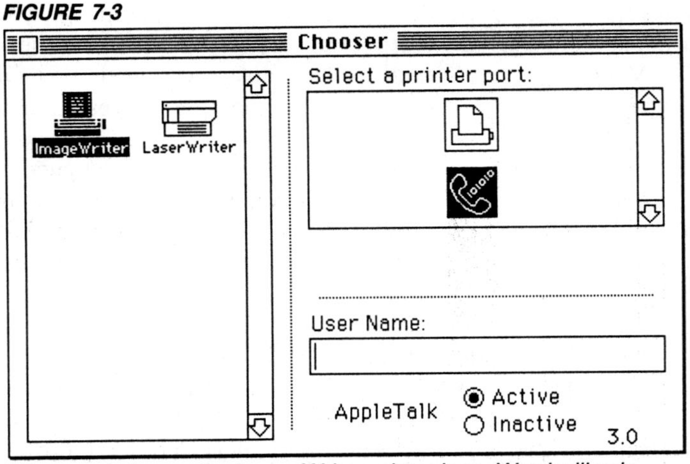

When you choose the ImageWriter printer icon, Word will ask which port you plan to use.

If you click on the LaserWriter icon in the Chooser dialog box, you'll see one or more printer names on the right side of the dialog box, as shown in Figure 7-4. Only the names of those printers that are connected to your Macintosh will appear. If you don't see any names, recheck your printer cable connections to make sure that you are making contact with the printer. Next, click on the name of the printer you want to use.

FIGURE 7-4

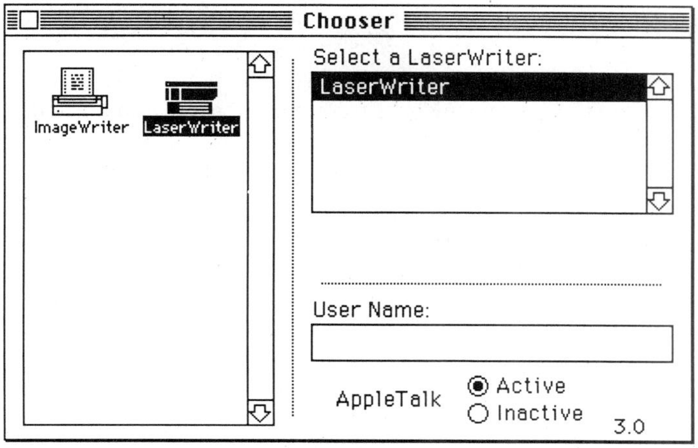

When you choose the LaserWriter printer icon, you'll see a list of available printers.

Next, type your name or initials in the User Name edit bar. This edit bar appears primarily for users who are connected to an AppleTalk network. When more than one Macintosh is connected to the same printer, the Mac presents a status box that identifies the user who is currently printing. (By the way, you'll need to type your name only once; the Mac will remember the text that you type in the User Name edit bar.)

If you are using a LaserWriter, or if you are part of a network of printer users, you'll also need to click the Active option to indicate that you are hooked into the AppleTalk network. (You can also choose the Connected option from the Control Panel dialog box. If you select the Active option in the Chooser dialog box, the program will automatically activate the Connected option in the Control Panel dialog box as well.)

That's all there is to it! If you use only one printer, you won't have to use the Chooser command again. If you use more than one printer, however, you'll need to reissue the Chooser command and select the printer and AppleTalk settings you want to use each time you change printers.

As long as the printer driver file for the printer that you want to use is located on the startup disk that you use to load Word, you can change printers at any time during a session—either from the Finder level or from within Word.

Other printers

It is not within the scope of this book to discuss all of the possible hardware configurations for printing from the Macintosh. Your Macintosh owner's guide and printer owner's guide discuss all of these combinations in much more detail. If you have trouble with any of the steps outlined above, refer to those manuals or contact you local hardware dealer.

If you use a printer other than the ImageWriter or LaserWriter, please see your owner's manual for special instructions on installing that printer on your startup disk. You may need to perform some special setup operations before you can use a printer other than the ImageWriter or LaserWriter. Similarly, if you use a hard disk, see your owner's manual for more information on installing printer drivers.

THE PRINT... COMMAND

Once you've installed and selected your printer, you can use the Print... command to produce a hard copy of your document. When you issue the Print... command, Word will always print the document that is currently active on the DeskTop. Any other documents that happen to be open on the DeskTop will not be printed unless you activate those document windows individually and issue a separate Print... command for each.

The contents of the Print dialog box will vary, depending on the type of printer you are using and your choice of Short or Full Menus. If you use an ImageWriter and the Short Menus setting is in effect, you'll see a dialog box like the one in Figure 7-5. If you use an ImageWriter and the Full Menus setting is in effect, your Print dialog box will look like the one in Figure 7-6. Notice that Word adds a Print Hidden Text option when you have selected the Full Menus setting.

FIGURE 7-5

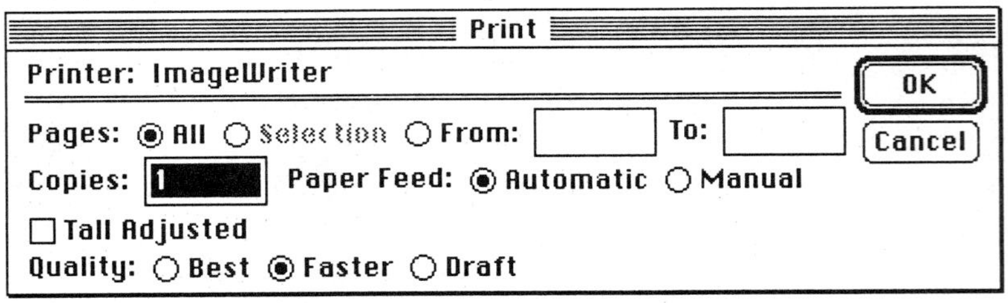

This Print dialog box appears if you're using an ImageWriter printer and Short Menus.

FIGURE 7-6

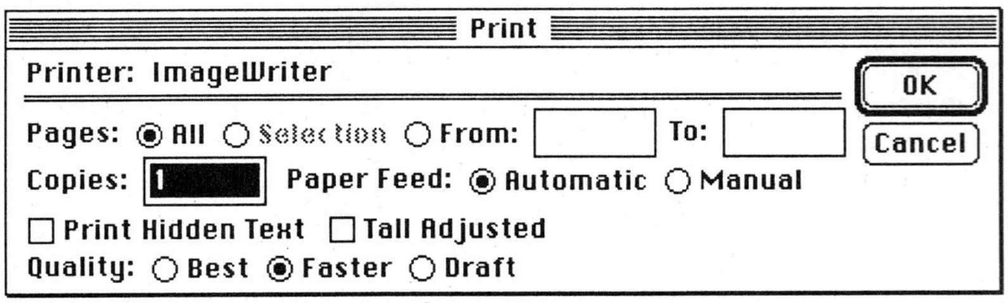

This Print dialog box appears if you're using an ImageWriter printer and Full Menus.

Similarly, if you use a LaserWriter and the Short Menus setting is in effect, you'll see a dialog box like the one in Figure 7-7. If you use a LaserWriter and the Full Menus setting is in effect, your Print dialog box will look like the one in Figure 7-8. Again, notice that Word adds a Print Hidden Text option when you have selected the Full Menus setting.

FIGURE 7-7

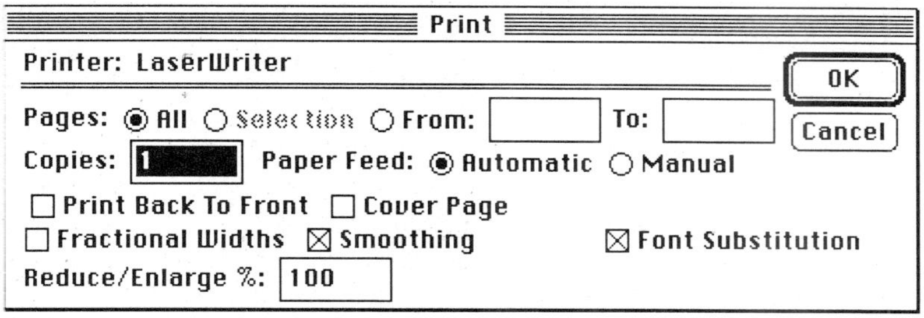

This Print dialog box appears if you're using a LaserWriter printer and Short Menus.

FIGURE 7-8

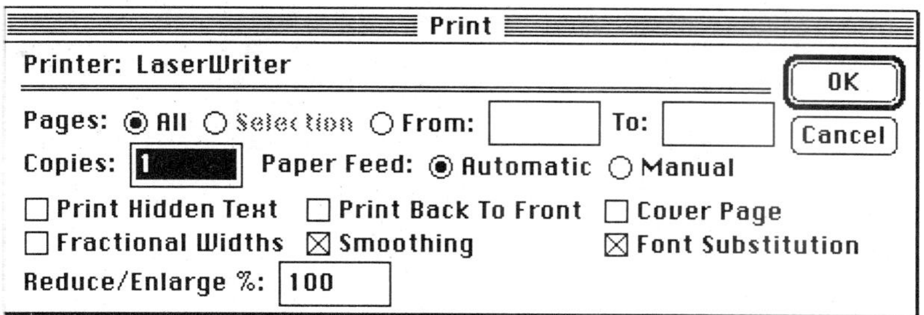

This Print dialog box appears if you're using a LaserWriter printer and Full Menus.

When you select your Print dialog box options, Word will remember all of the dialog box options you have selected except for the Pages and Copies settings. These two settings will always revert to All and 1, respectively, the next time you open the dialog box. The other Print dialog box options, however, will remain in effect from one Print... command to the next, and, in some cases, even from one Word session to the next. (In Chapter 17, we explain which Print settings are document-specific and which settings will be carried over from one Word session to the next.) Let's look first at the dialog box options that are common to both printers, then we'll discuss the printer-specific options.

Specifying a Print Range

The Pages options in the Print dialog box are fairly self-explanatory. To print the entire document, just leave the default All setting selected. If you want to print only part of the document, use the Selection or From and To options.

The Selection option tells Word to print only that part of your document that is highlighted on the screen. This option, which will remain dimmed unless you select a block of text in your document before you issue the Print... command, provides a quick way to print only a few lines or paragraphs of text. Just select the text that you want to print, then select Print... from the File menu, and click the Selection option.

When you print a selection, Word will print the highlighted text, beginning at the top-left corner of the page, even if the text you have selected would normally appear in the middle of a page. If you have added any page numbers, headers, or footers to your document (we'll talk more about these items in a few pages), they will not appear when you use the Selection option.

For example, to reprint the third paragraph in the sample page shown in Figure 7-9, you would double-click in the selection bar on the left side of the screen to select that paragraph, then choose the Selection option in the Print dialog box. As you can see in Figure 7-10, Word reprints the selected paragraph, beginning at the top-left corner of the page. Notice that the header and footer that we saw in Figure 7-9 no longer appear.

FIGURE 7-9

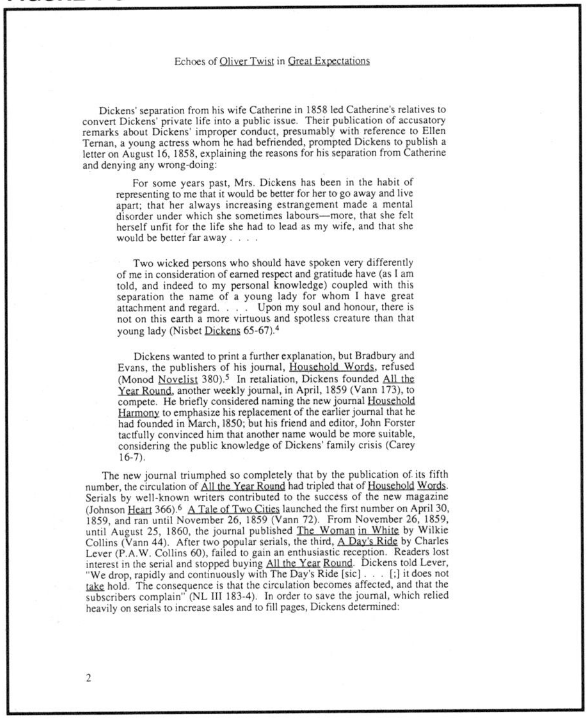

Echoes of Oliver Twist in Great Expectations

Dickens' separation from his wife Catherine in 1858 led Catherine's relatives to convert Dickens' private life into a public issue. Their publication of accusatory remarks about Dickens' improper conduct, presumably with reference to Ellen Ternan, a young actress whom he had befriended, prompted Dickens to publish a letter on August 16, 1858, explaining the reasons for his separation from Catherine and denying any wrong-doing:

> For some years past, Mrs. Dickens has been in the habit of representing to me that it would be better for her to go away and live apart; that her always increasing estrangement made a mental disorder under which she sometimes labours—more, that she felt herself unfit for the life she had to lead as my wife, and that she would be better far away . . . .
>
> Two wicked persons who should have spoken very differently of me in consideration of earned respect and gratitude have (as I am told, and indeed to my personal knowledge) coupled with this separation the name of a young lady for whom I have great attachment and regard. . . . Upon my soul and honour, there is not on this earth a more virtuous and spotless creature than that young lady (Nisbet Dickens 65-67).[4]
>
> Dickens wanted to print a further explanation, but Bradbury and Evans, the publishers of his journal, Household Words, refused (Monod Novelist 380).[5] In retaliation, Dickens founded All the Year Round, another weekly journal, in April, 1859 (Vann 173), to compete. He briefly considered naming the new journal Household Harmony to emphasize his replacement of the earlier journal that he had founded in March, 1850; but his friend and editor, John Forster tactfully convinced him that another name would be more suitable, considering the public knowledge of Dickens' family crisis (Carey 16-7).

The new journal triumphed so completely that by the publication of its fifth number, the circulation of All the Year Round had tripled that of Household Words. Serials by well-known writers contributed to the success of the new magazine (Johnson Heart 366).[6] A Tale of Two Cities launched the first number on April 30, 1859, and ran until November 26, 1859 (Vann 72). From November 26, 1859, until August 25, 1860, the journal published The Woman in White by Wilkie Collins (Vann 44). After two popular serials, the third, A Day's Ride by Charles Lever (P.A.W. Collins 60), failed to gain an enthusiastic reception. Readers lost interest in the serial and stopped buying All the Year Round. Dickens told Lever, "We drop, rapidly and continuously with The Day's Ride [sic] . . . [;] it does not take hold. The consequence is that the circulation becomes affected, and that the subscribers complain" (NL III 183-4). In order to save the journal, which relied heavily on serials to increase sales and to fill pages, Dickens determined:

2

We want to reprint the third paragraph from this sample page.

FIGURE 7-10

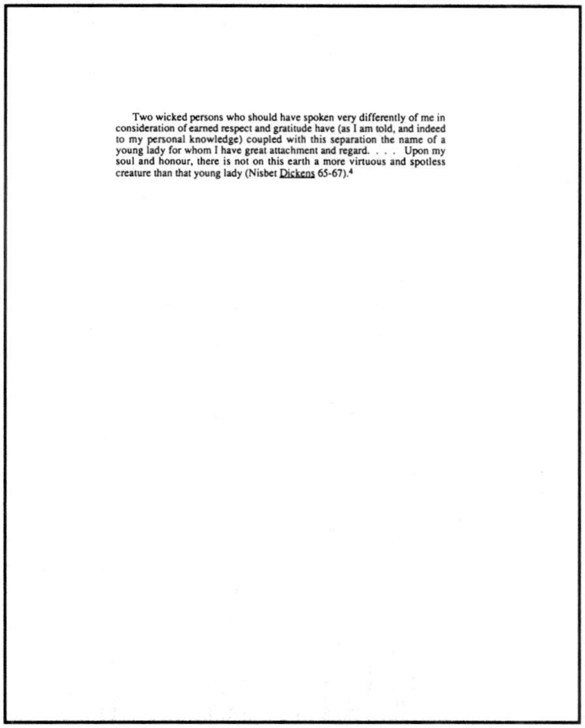

Two wicked persons who should have spoken very differently of me in consideration of earned respect and gratitude have (as I am told, and indeed to my personal knowledge) coupled with this separation the name of a young lady for whom I have great attachment and regard. . . . Upon my soul and honour, there is not on this earth a more virtuous and spotless creature than that young lady (Nisbet Dickens 65-67).[4]

When you use the Selection option, Word prints only the selected text.

If you need to print several consecutive pages from a document, you'll probably want to use the From and To settings rather than dragging through the text you want to print. To do so, just specify the range of pages you want to print in the From and To edit bars.

If you click on the radio button that appears in front of the From edit bar, Word will display the value 1 in the From edit bar and the value 9999 in the To edit bar. Chances are, this is not the page range you'll be printing, so you'll want to edit one or both of these entries to specify a new page range. If you type a value in the From or To edit bar without clicking the radio button, Word will automatically select the From/To radio button for you, but it will not enter the default values 1 and 9999 in the From and To edit bars. We find it easier to type our From and To values, rather than editing Word's default entries.

For example, suppose you want to print pages 5 through 11 of a 25-page document. After you issue the Print... command, just click on the From edit bar, and type the value 5. Then press the Tab key, or click in the To edit bar, and type the value 11.

If you make an entry in the To edit bar but leave the From edit bar blank, Word assumes that you want to begin printing with the first page of the document and print through to the end of the specified To page. Similarly, if you make an entry in the From edit bar but leave the To edit bar blank, Word assumes that you want to start printing at the beginning of the specified From page and print through to the end of the document.

For example, to print pages 1 through 10 of your 25-page document, you can leave the From edit bar blank and simply type the value 10 in the To edit bar. To print from page 10 through the end of the document, you can leave the To edit bar blank and type the value 10 in the From edit bar. To print only one page of a document, enter the same number in the From and To edit bars. For example, if you want to print the third page of a document, enter a 3 in both the From and To edit bars.

As you've seen, specifying a page range is generally as simple as typing the starting and ending page numbers in the Print dialog box. Specifying a page range can get a little complicated, however, if you are using different numbering schemes for different sections of your document. We'll talk more about numbering schemes when we look at the Section… command.

Copies

If you want to print more than one copy of your document at a time, just type the number of copies you want in the Copies edit bar. If the document you are printing is longer than one page, Word will begin by printing all of the copies of page 1, followed by all of the copies of page 2, then all of the copies of page 3, and so on, until you have the number of copies you specified. This method of printing multiple copies is faster than printing one complete document and then repeating the process for each new copy. That's because the LaserWriter can set up each page only once for printing. But there is one drawback to doing it this way: When your pages come out of the printer, you must collate them.

(By the way, if you use Word 3.0 instead of Word 3.01, the Copies option works differently. Instead of printing all of the copies for each page at once, Word 3.0 prints a full set of pages, then prints another full set, repeating this process until it has printed the number of copies you specified. You get complete document sets this way, but printing takes longer.)

Printing Hidden Text

If you have assigned the Hidden format to text in your document, you can opt to print this text along with the rest of your document or to hide it in the printed version. The appearance of hidden text in your printed document is completely independent of the appearance of hidden text on your screen. In other words, if you select the Print Hidden Text option, which is available only when the Full Menus setting is in effect, Word will print any text that has been assigned the Hidden format, even if it is not currently visible on your screen. On the other hand, if you use the Show Hidden Text option in the Preferences dialog box to display your hidden text on the screen, Word will not print any text that has been assigned the Hidden format if you deselect the Print Hidden Text option in the Print dialog box.

For example, we assigned the Hidden format to the third paragraph text of the sample document shown in Figure 7-11. If we select the Print Hidden Text option, Word will print this paragraph as usual, as shown in Figure 7-12 on the following page.

FIGURE 7-11

We have assigned the Hidden format to the third paragraph in this sample document.

If we deselect the Print Hidden Text option in the Print dialog box, however, Word will omit any text that has been assigned the Hidden format, even though it still appears on the screen, as shown in Figure 7-13. Notice that Word prints the second and fourth paragraphs sequentially, with no blank space in between, as if the hidden text did not even exist.

FIGURE 7-12

iii

Acknowledgments

I must first thank my husband Jim and my son Alex who helped me through many graduate school projects, most especially this one. I also thank faithful friends for their encouragement: Dr. Judith Jennings, Dr. William Cogar, Mrs. James Montgomery, Mrs. Claggett Offutt, Mr. and Mrs. William Lamp'l, Mrs. Jackson M. Andrews III, Ms. Marjorie Maddox, Ms. Violet White, Mrs. David Wright, and Dr. Philip Cochran.

Dr. William F. Axton has directed my thesis cheerfully and generously. To him I owe the inspiration for my thesis, a result of his Dickens course, and its completion. I am grateful to Drs. Leon V. Driskell and Samuel C. Fulkerson for serving on my committee and for sharing their suggestions and time with me. I also thank Drs. E. R. Hagemann, Mary Ellen Rickey, and Mary Rosner for challenging and teaching me.

A Graduate Teaching Assistantship from the English Department helped me complete my course work; and the Ekstrom Library, particularly the Interlibrary Loan Department and Special Collections, provided materials that I needed. My employer, Mr. Douglas Cobb, allowed me to use office equipment and to adjust my work schedule according to the demands of my thesis. I thank all of these people and organizations for making my thesis possible, and I thank my grandparents, the late Mr. and Mrs. Frank Weber, for introducing me to Dickens.

If we select the Print Hidden Text option, Word will include the hidden text in our printed document.

FIGURE 7-13

iii

Acknowledgments

I must first thank my husband Jim and my son Alex who helped me through many graduate school projects, most especially this one. I also thank faithful friends for their encouragement: Dr. Judith Jennings, Dr. William Cogar, Mrs. James Montgomery, Mrs. Claggett Offutt, Mr. and Mrs. William Lamp'l, Mrs. Jackson M. Andrews III, Ms. Marjorie Maddox, Ms. Violet White, Mrs. David Wright, and Dr. Philip Cochran.

A Graduate Teaching Assistantship from the English Department helped me complete my course work; and the Ekstrom Library, particularly the Interlibrary Loan Department and Special Collections, provided materials that I needed. My employer, Mr. Douglas Cobb, allowed me to use office equipment and to adjust my work schedule according to the demands of my thesis. I thank all of these people and organizations for making my thesis possible, and I thank my grandparents, the late Mr. and Mrs. Frank Weber, for introducing me to Dickens.

If we deselect the Print Hidden text option, Word will not include the Hidden text in our printed document.

Hiding markup characters

When you use hidden text in your document, make sure that you also hide any special markup characters that surround that text. Otherwise, your printed document will contain extra blank lines or blank spaces.

For example, if you choose to assign the Hidden format to an entire paragraph, make sure you assign the Hidden format to the ¶ marker at the end of that paragraph as well. If you want to hide an entire sentence, make sure you hide the blank space that separates that sentence from the next. Finally, if you want to hide a word, make sure you hide the blank space or other demarcation character that appears after that word.

Suppose we assign the Hidden character format to all of the text in paragraph 3 of Figure 7-11 but not to the ¶ marker at the end of that paragraph. If we choose to omit this hidden text when we print this sample page, our document will look like the one in Figure 7-14. Notice that a blank line appears between the second and third paragraphs.

FIGURE 7-14

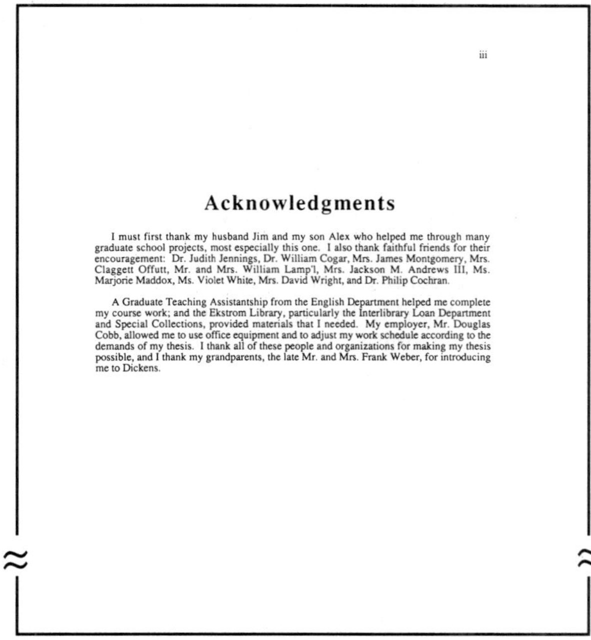

iii

Acknowledgments

I must first thank my husband Jim and my son Alex who helped me through many graduate school projects, most especially this one. I also thank faithful friends for their encouragement: Dr. Judith Jennings, Dr. William Cogar, Mrs. James Montgomery, Mrs. Claggett Offutt, Mr. and Mrs. William Lamp'l, Mrs. Jackson M. Andrews III, Ms. Marjorie Maddox, Ms. Violet White, Mrs. David Wright, and Dr. Philip Cochran.

A Graduate Teaching Assistantship from the English Department helped me complete my course work; and the Ekstrom Library, particularly the Interlibrary Loan Department and Special Collections, provided materials that I needed. My employer, Mr. Douglas Cobb, allowed me to use office equipment and to adjust my work schedule according to the demands of my thesis. I thank all of these people and organizations for making my thesis possible, and I thank my grandparents, the late Mr. and Mrs. Frank Weber, for introducing me to Dickens.

If you do not assign the Hidden format to the ¶ marker, you'll see a blank line in your printed document.

Paper Feed Options

If you are using special paper stock—like letterhead, envelopes, or odd-sized paper stock—that you need to feed through your printer manually, you'll want to select the Manual option in the Print dialog box before you print.

On the ImageWriter, you'll probably use the Manual option whenever you need to print on sheet-fed paper, rather than the standard continuous form paper. (Continuous form paper is designed to advance through the printer automatically with the help of the tractor feed assembly.) If you're using a LaserWriter, which uses sheet-fed paper only, you can insert your paper sheet by sheet into the manual feed slot at the back of the machine. Word will print on this paper instead of the paper that is stored in your paper tray.

Before you use any special paper stock, we recommend that you see your printer owner's manual for more information about acceptable paper sizes and weights for your printer.

LaserWriter Options

In addition to the options discussed above, the Print dialog box that appears when you are using the LaserWriter offers six other printing options: Font Substitution, Smoothing, Back to Front, Reduce/Enlarge %, Quality, and Cover Page. Let's take a look at each of these options.

Font Substitution

As you may know, the Helvetica, Times, Symbol, and Courier fonts are designed specifically for the LaserWriter printer, while the remaining fonts on your startup disk are designed for the ImageWriter. If you have installed other fonts on your startup disk, you should also know whether they are designed for the ImageWriter or the LaserWriter printer.

Though you can use any of the fonts that are installed on your startup disk, regardless of the printer you have selected, ImageWriter fonts, such as Geneva and New York, do not give the finished appearance of Helvetica and Times when you use them on the LaserWriter.

The Font Substitution option in the Print dialog box tells Word to convert the fonts you have used in your document to an appropriate LaserWriter font. For example, if you have used Word's default New York type to format your document text, and you use the Font Substitution option when you print that document on the LaserWriter, then your printed text will be converted to the Times font.

Table 7-1 shows the fonts that Word will use if the Font Substitution option is selected.

TABLE 7-1

If your document contains	The LaserWriter will print
Boston	Boston
Dover PS	Dover PS
Dover	Dover
Geneva	Helvetica
Monaco	Courier
New York	Times
Venice	Venice

Word will substitute the fonts that are appropriate for your printer when you select the Font Substitution option.

As you can see, Word offers no substitutes for the Boston, Dover PS, Dover, or Venice fonts. If you use these fonts in your document, the LaserWriter will attempt to reproduce the characters for that font.

You'll find that printing with Font Substitution takes much longer than usual. In addition, Font Substitution may produce unsightly gaps between letters and words in your printed document. Though this decrease in quality may be acceptable if you are preparing a mockup or "proof copy" of a document that will be typeset or reprinted later, you generally won't find Font Substitution acceptable for a finished document.

For example, the sample text shown in Figure 7-15 was entered into the document in 12-point Geneva type. When we used the Font Substitution option to print this paragraph, Word converted the Geneva font to Helvetica. Though the quality of the characters is fine, the spacing between words is uneven and gives a slightly gappy appearance.

FIGURE 7-15

This paragraph is formatted in 12-point Geneva type. We have used the Font Substitution option in the Print dialog box to substitute the Helvetica font for the Geneva font that appears on the screen.

When you use Font Substitution, you may notice some unsightly gaps in your printed document.

If you turn the Font Substitution option off, Word will use the fonts you have selected for your document without converting them. Though you can print any font on the LaserWriter, you may find that the quality of the non-LaserWriter fonts is not acceptable. In addition, you'll find that it takes much longer to print text that is formatted with ImageWriter fonts.

For example, the text shown in Figure 7-16 was also formatted in 12-point Geneva type. However, when we printed this paragraph, we turned the Font Substitution option off. As you can see, Word prints the text in the specified Geneva font, but the quality of the characters is rather ragged and uneven.

FIGURE 7-16

> This paragraph is formatted in 12-point Geneva type. We have turned off the Font Substitution option in the Print dialog box so that Word will print the Geneva font as it appears on the screen.

When you turn Font Substitution off, Word will attempt to build the characters in the specified fonts.

All in all, your best bet is to use fonts that are designed for your printer. If you use a LaserWriter Plus, you already have access to a number of fonts in addition to those that come with the Word package. If the range of available fonts does not suit your needs, ask your software dealer about the many fonts packages that are available for the Macintosh. If you purchase a fonts package, however, make sure that it is designed specifically for your printer.

By the way, you can also use fonts designed for the LaserWriter when you are printing on the ImageWriter. Generally, the Times, Helvetica, and Courier fonts can be reproduced quite effectively on the ImageWriter.

Smoothing

The Smoothing option helps to smooth out the rough edges when you print ImageWriter fonts or nonstandard font sizes on the LaserWriter. For example, suppose you have used the Venice font—which is designed for the ImageWriter—to format some characters in your Word document. Figures 7-17 and 7-18 show the difference in print quality when you use the Smoothing option to print this font on the LaserWriter.

FIGURE 7-17

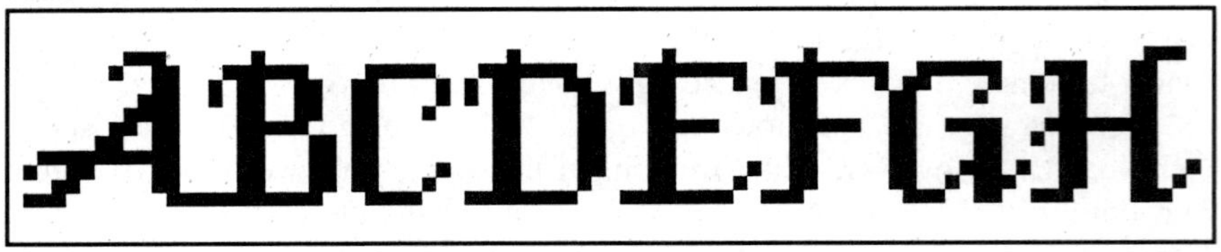

These characters were printed without Smoothing.

FIGURE 7-18

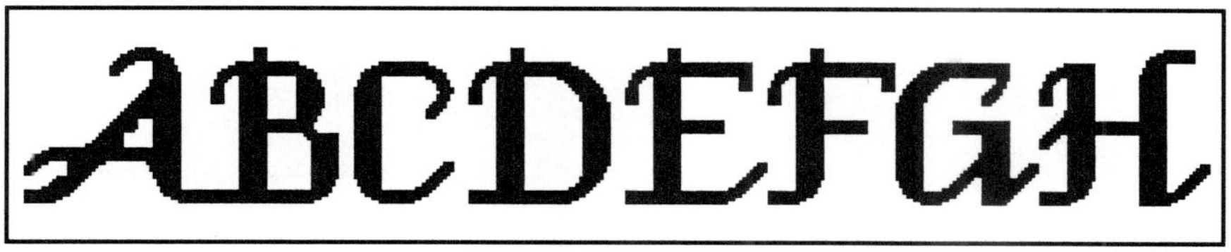

These characters were printed with Smoothing.

The smoothing option may also help to give your printed graphics a more finished appearance. (We'll talk more about graphics in Chapter 16.)

Printing back to front

The Print Back To Front option is particularly convenient when you are printing long documents or when you are printing multiple copies of a document. Back To Front tells Word to print the pages of your document in reverse order so that the pages will be in the correct order when you retrieve them from the printer. For example, if you print a ten-page document on the LaserWriter without activating the Print Back To Front option, Word will print the pages in order from 1 to 10, as you might expect. However, when you retrieve the printed document from the paper tray, you'll have to reverse the order of the pages since page 10 will be on top of page 9, page 9 will be on top of page 8, and so forth.

To get around this problem, choose the Print Back To Front option. Word will then print the pages in reverse order—from 10 to 1—so that they will be in the correct order when you retrieve the printed document from the paper tray.

Printing a cover page

The Cover Page option is handy when you need to document the date and time that you printed a document or when several users share the same printer. When you select the Cover Page option, Word prints out a sheet like the one shown in Figure 7-19 to identify your document.

As you can see, the cover page sheet lists the user's name (the name or initials you type in the Name edit bar of the Chooser dialog box), the application from which the document was printed, the document name, the date and time at which the document was printed, and the name of the printer.

Though it may seem contradictory, the cover page is the last page to be printed. That is, Word will print your entire document (or the specified portion) before it prints your cover page. That way, the cover page will appear on top of your printed document in the paper tray to separate it from any documents that might follow.

FIGURE 7-19

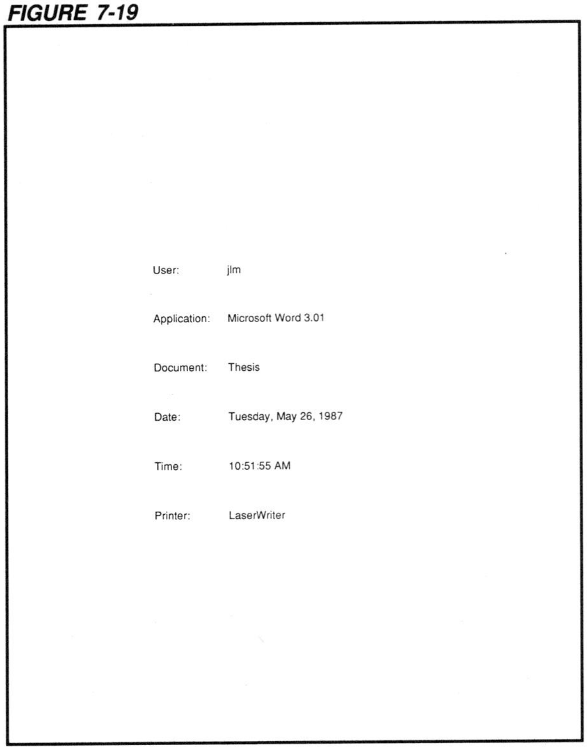

User: jlm

Application: Microsoft Word 3.01

Document: Thesis

Date: Tuesday, May 26, 1987

Time: 10:51:55 AM

Printer: LaserWriter

When you choose the Cover Page option, Word prints out a sheet like this one.

Fractional Widths

The Fractional Widths option in the LaserWriter Print dialog box is new to Word 3.01. (If you're using Word 3.0, you'll see two Quality settings—Best and Faster—instead of the Fractional Widths option.) Activating the Fractional Widths option allows the LaserWriter to achieve more accurate character placement in your printed document. You'll also notice a difference in the placement of characters on your screen. Instead of calculating character widths to determine their placement, your Macintosh is able to use information stored in ROM to establish the exact widths of characters. As a result, the Fractional Widths option will give you better-looking text and allow you to print faster.

In order to use this option, you must have a Macintosh Plus (or later version of the Mac) or a 512K Macintosh installed with new ROM chips. Unfortunately, the Fractional Widths option is not compatible with justified paragraph alignment. If your document contains justified paragraphs, then you must be sure that this option is not activated before you print. In addition, the Fractional Widths option applies only to LaserWriter fonts. ImageWriter fonts, such as New York, will not be affected when you activate this option.

Reducing and enlarging the page image

Word allows you to reduce and enlarge the page image when you print documents on the LaserWriter. Just type the reduction or enlargement percentage you want to use in the Reduce/Enlarge % edit bar. You can specify any reduction or enlargement setting between 25% and 400%—that is, from one quarter to four times the original image size—but you must type a whole number in the Reduce/Enlarge % edit bar.

Keep in mind that the Reduce/Enlarge % setting does not allow you to fit more data on a page. Instead, it reduces or enlarges the entire page image. For example, Figure 7-20 shows a printed page that was printed 100%. Figure 7-21 on the next page shows the same page with a Reduce/Enlarge % setting of 50%.

FIGURE 7-20

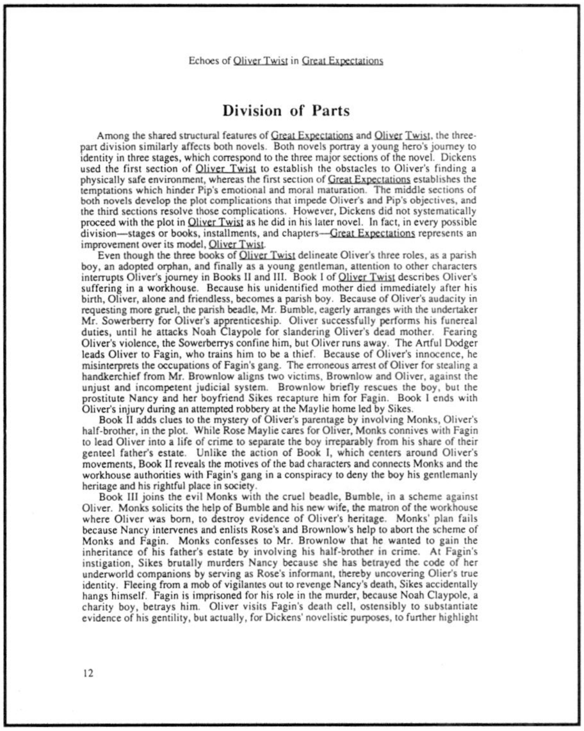

Echoes of Oliver Twist in Great Expectations

Division of Parts

Among the shared structural features of Great Expectations and Oliver Twist, the three-part division similarly affects both novels. Both novels portray a young hero's journey to identity in three stages, which correspond to the three major sections of the novel. Dickens used the first section of Oliver Twist to establish the obstacles to Oliver's finding a physically safe environment, whereas the first section of Great Expectations establishes the temptations which hinder Pip's emotional and moral maturation. The middle sections of both novels develop the plot complications that impede Oliver's and Pip's objectives, and the third sections resolve those complications. However, Dickens did not systematically proceed with the plot in Oliver Twist as he did in his later novel. In fact, in every possible division—stages or books, installments, and chapters—Great Expectations represents an improvement over its model, Oliver Twist.

Even though the three books of Oliver Twist delineate Oliver's three roles, as a parish boy, an adopted orphan, and finally as a young gentleman, attention to other characters interrupts Oliver's journey in Books II and III. Book I of Oliver Twist describes Oliver's suffering in a workhouse. Because his unidentified mother died immediately after his birth, Oliver, alone and friendless, becomes a parish boy. Because of Oliver's audacity in requesting more gruel, the parish beadle, Mr. Bumble, eagerly arranges with the undertaker Mr. Sowerberry for Oliver's apprenticeship. Oliver successfully performs his funereal duties, until he attacks Noah Claypole for slandering Oliver's dead mother. Fearing Oliver's violence, the Sowerberrys confine him, but Oliver runs away. The Artful Dodger leads Oliver to Fagin, who trains him to be a thief. Because of Oliver's innocence, he misinterprets the occupations of Fagin's gang. The erroneous arrest of Oliver for stealing a handkerchief from Mr. Brownlow aligns two victims, Brownlow and Oliver, against the unjust and incompetent judicial system. Brownlow briefly rescues the boy, but the prostitute Nancy and her boyfriend Sikes recapture him for Fagin. Book I ends with Oliver's injury during an attempted robbery at the Maylie home led by Sikes.

Book II adds clues to the mystery of Oliver's parentage by involving Monks, Oliver's half-brother, in the plot. While Rose Maylie cares for Oliver, Monks connives with Fagin to lead Oliver into a life of crime to separate the boy irreparably from his share of their genteel father's estate. Unlike the action of Book I, which centers around Oliver's movements, Book II reveals the motives of the bad characters and connects Monks and the workhouse authorities with Fagin's gang in a conspiracy to deny the boy his gentlemanly heritage and his rightful place in society.

Book III joins the evil Monks with the cruel beadle, Bumble, in a scheme against Oliver. Monks solicits the help of Bumble and his new wife, the matron of the workhouse where Oliver was born, to destroy evidence of Oliver's heritage. Monks' plan fails because Nancy intervenes and enlists Rose's and Brownlow's help to abort the scheme of Monks and Fagin. Monks confesses to Mr. Brownlow that he wanted to gain the inheritance of his father's estate by involving his half-brother in crime. At Fagin's instigation, Sikes brutally murders Nancy because she has betrayed the code of her underworld companions by serving as Rose's informant, thereby uncovering Olier's true identity. Fleeing from a mob of vigilantes out to revenge Nancy's death, Sikes accidentally hangs himself. Fagin is imprisoned for his role in the murder, because Noah Claypole, a charity boy, betrays him. Oliver visits Fagin's death cell, ostensibly to substantiate evidence of his gentility, but actually, for Dickens' novelistic purposes, to further highlight

12

This page was printed with no reduction or enlargement.

FIGURE 7-21

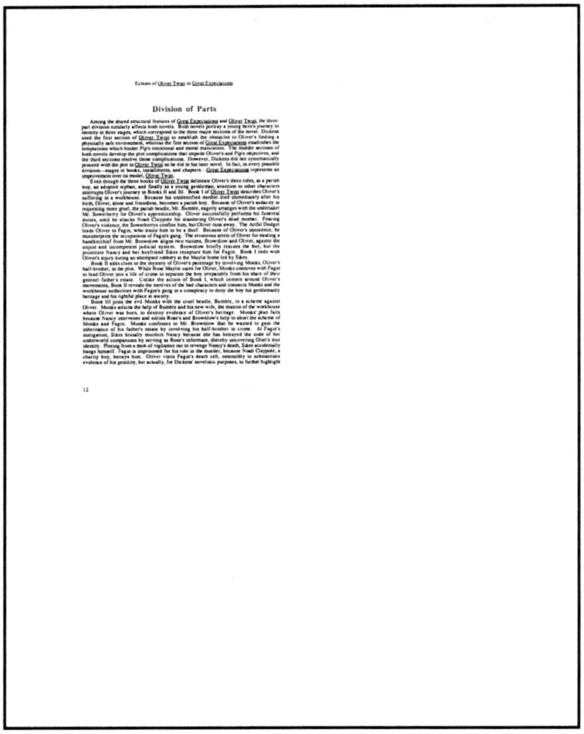

This page was reduced by 50 percent.

To enlarge a page image, just type a value greater than 100 in the Reduce/Enlarge % edit bar. If you enlarge a printed image, some of your data may be truncated on the printed page. For example, Figure 7-22 shows our sample page enlarged to 150 percent of its original size.

Though you generally won't be able to fit an entire page image on a standard sheet of paper when you enlarge a document image, you may on occasion want to enlarge only a portion of a page—a graphic or a key phrase that you want to extract from the body of the document, for example. If this is the case, just select the item that you want to enlarge before you issue the Print... command, then use the Selection and Reduce/Enlarge % options to "blow up" that particular item.

FIGURE 7-22

Echoes of Oliver Twist in Great Expectation:

Division of Parts

Among the shared structural features of Great Expectations and C
part division similarly affects both novels. Both novels portray a yc
identity in three stages, which correspond to the three major sections
used the first section of Oliver Twist to establish the obstacles
physically safe environment, whereas the first section of Great Expec
temptations which hinder Pip's emotional and moral maturation. T
both novels develop the plot complications that impede Oliver's anc
the third sections resolve those complications. However, Dickens c
proceed with the plot in Oliver Twist as he did in his later novel. In
division—stages or books, installments, and chapters—Great Expe
improvement over its model, Oliver Twist.
Even though the three books of Oliver Twist delineate Oliver's t
boy, an adopted orphan, and finally as a young gentleman, attentic
interrupts Oliver's journey in Books II and III. Book I of Oliver Tw
suffering in a workhouse. Because his unidentified mother died i
birth, Oliver, alone and friendless, becomes a parish boy. Because c
requesting more gruel, the parish beadle, Mr. Bumble, eagerly arrang
Mr. Sowerberry for Oliver's apprenticeship. Oliver successfully p
duties, until he attacks Noah Claypole for slandering Oliver's de
Oliver's violence, the Sowerberrys confine him, but Oliver runs awa
leads Oliver to Fagin, who trains him to be a thief. Because of C
misinterprets the occupations of Fagin's gang. The erroneous arrest c
handkerchief from Mr. Brownlow aligns two victims, Brownlow ai
unjust and incompetent judicial system. Brownlow briefly resc
prostitute Nancy and her boyfriend Sikes recapture him for Fagi
Oliver's injury during an attempted robbery at the Maylie home led by
Book II adds clues to the mystery of Oliver's parentage by invol
half-brother, in the plot. While Rose Maylie cares for Oliver, Monk
to lead Oliver into a life of crime to separate the boy irreparably fi
genteel father's estate. Unlike the action of Book I, which cer
movements, Book II reveals the motives of the bad characters and co
workhouse authorities with Fagin's gang in a conspiracy to deny the
heritage and his rightful place in society.
Book III ioins the evil Monks with the cruel beadle. Bumble.

This text on page was enlarged to 150 percent of its original size.

ImageWriter Options

If you use the ImageWriter, you'll find two additional options in the Print dialog box: Tall Adjusted and Quality. You generally don't need to worry about the Tall Adjusted option unless you have included graphics in your Word document. When you print graphics, the Tall Adjusted setting helps keep your text and graphic in proportion. We'll talk more about graphics and the Tall Adjusted setting in Chapter 16.

Quality

On the ImageWriter, you have three Quality settings: Best, Faster, and Draft. For proofreading and for informal use, we recommend that you use the Faster or Draft option. The Best option, though it produces much higher quality results, requires quite a bit more time to print.

When you use the Draft option, Word will print your document very quickly, but it will ignore almost all of your character formatting. In the middle quality range is the Faster option. The Faster option does recognize your character and paragraph formats, but you trade some quality for the faster speed.

Figures 7-23, 7-24, and 7-25 show the differences between the Best, Faster, and Draft Quality options. All three text samples are formatted in 12-point New York, with the first line plain, the second line bold, and the third line italic. As you can see, Word ignores our font and character formatting (except for boldfacing) when we use the Draft option.

FIGURE 7-23

This text was printed with the Best Quality option selected.

This text was printed with the Best Quality option selected.

This text was printed with the Best Quality option selected.

The Best option produces high quality results but causes slower printing.

FIGURE 7-24

This text was printed with the Faster Quality option selected.

This text was printed with the Faster Quality option selected.

This text was printed with the Faster Quality option selected.

The Faster option retains all your character formats and allows you to print fairly quickly.

FIGURE 7-25

This text was printed with the Draft Quality option selected.

This text was printed with the Draft Quality option selected.

This text was printed with the Draft Quality option selected.

Use the Draft option when you want to print quickly and do not need special formatting.

Printing from the Finder Level

As you already know, when you issue the Print... command from within Word, only the active document will be printed. If you need to print several documents, you may be able to save some time by printing them from the Finder level. Here, you can select several documents to print at the same time by dragging across all of the files you want to work with or by pressing the Shift key and clicking on each document icon in turn. Once you have highlighted all of the files that you want to print, select the Print command from the File menu.

The Print dialog box will appear only once when you use this Finder level printing technique. Word will print one copy of each document, using the same Print dialog box settings for each. The documents will be printed in the order that they appear on the DeskTop—from top to bottom and from right to left.

Though this technique is fine when you need to print several unrelated documents, you may need more precise control when you are printing several files that make up a single document. For example, if you need to print the documents in a specified order or to number the pages sequentially from one document to another, you'll probably want to take advantage of the Next File option in the Page Setup dialog box instead. We'll talk about the Next File option in Chapter 8. First, let's introduce the Page Setup dialog box.

THE PAGE SETUP... COMMAND

While the Print dialog box contains options that you are likely to change from one printing to the next—like page ranges and number of copies—the Page Setup... command lets you define more "global" settings for the way your printed document should look. The Page Setup... command controls factors like margin settings, page size, and orientation. Chances are, once you have specified your Page Setup dialog box settings, you won't need to change them again unless you decide to change your document design.

The contents of the Page Setup dialog box vary, depending on whether you're using Full Menus or Short Menus. Figures 7-26 and 7-27 show both versions of the dialog box. As you might expect, the dialog box that appears when you are using Full Menus contains several more options.

FIGURE 7-26

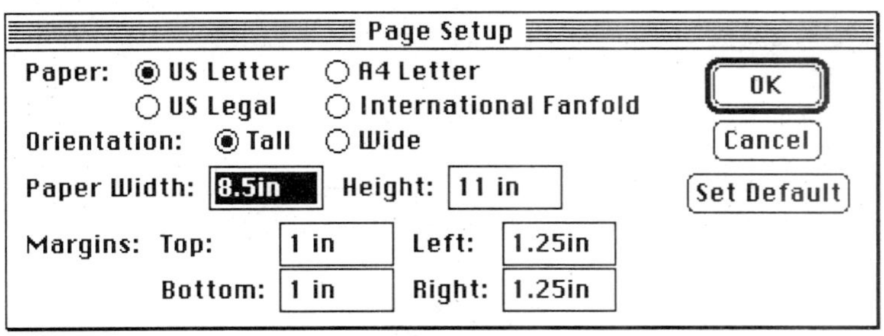

This Page Setup dialog box appears if you're using Short Menus.

FIGURE 7-27

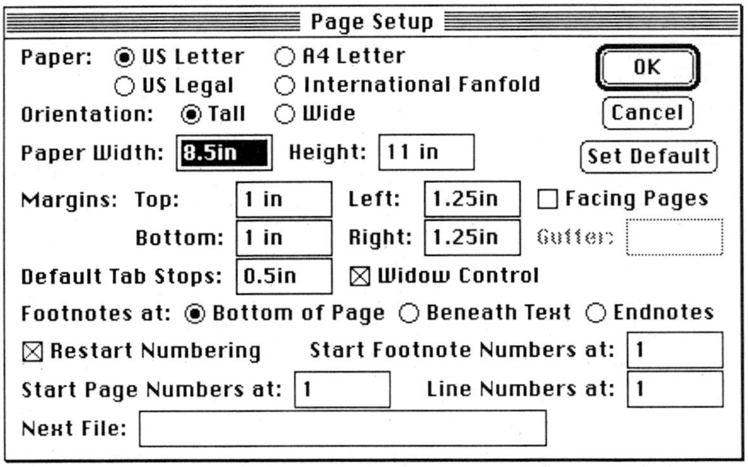

This Page Setup dialog box appears if you're using Full Menus.

The Page Setup options that you select are saved to disk with your document. Any changes that you make in the Page Setup dialog box will apply only to the document that is active when you issue the Page Setup… command. If you create a new document, Word will revert to the default Page Setup settings. If you open an existing document, the Page Setup specifications that you originally applied to that document will be unchanged.

There is only one exception to this rule: If you click the Set Default button in the Page Setup dialog box, any new documents that you create will initially carry the Page Setup settings that were specified in the dialog box at the time you clicked the Set Default button. Of course, you can change the dialog box settings again at any time to tailor them to your needs. For more on changing Word's default settings, see Chapter 17.

Paper Size and Orientation

One of the first steps in defining your page layout for Word should be to define the parameters of your printed page. The first four lines of the Page Setup dialog box control these parameters. You'll use the Paper, Orientation, Paper Width, and Height options to define the type of paper you are using and how you want your text to be oriented on the page.

Word offers four standard paper options: US Letter, US Legal, A4 Letter, and International Fanfold. For business correspondence and reports, you'll probably use the default US Letter option most often. Table 7-2 describes each of Word's standard Paper options.

TABLE 7-2

Option	Size (width x height)
US Letter	8 1/2 x 11
US Legal	8 1/2 x 14
A4 Letter	8 1/4 x 11 2/3
International Fanfold	8 1/4 x 12

Word offers four standard Paper options.

Paper Width and Height options

When you select one of the standard Paper options from the Page Setup dialog box, Word automatically enters the size of the page in the Paper Width and Height edit bars. As you can see in Figures 7-26 and 7-27, when the US Letter option is in effect, Word uses the default values 8.5 and 11 in the Paper Width and Height edit bars. However, if you click on the International Fanfold option, Word will automatically change the Paper Width setting to 8.25 and the Height setting to 12.

In addition to the four standard Paper options, Word allows you to specify your own page sizes in the Paper Width and Height edit bars. For example, if you are using sheets of paper that measure 7 x 9 inches, just type the value *7* in the Paper Width edit bar and the value *9* in the Height edit bar.

If you are printing on standard-size paper stock, but you plan to have your document reproduced on paper of a different size, you'll probably want to use the Paper Width and Height settings to define the size of your finished document. For example, suppose you are setting up a form that you plan to have reproduced on a 3 x 5 inch index card. Chances are, you will not be able to use a paper stock of this size with your printer since it is too small to feed through the rollers properly. However, you can still enter the values 5 and 3 in the Paper Width and Height edit bars to define the size of your finished document. As you'll see in a moment, by entering your *finished* document size rather than the actual size of the paper stock you plan to print on, you can eliminate some of the guesswork from defining your document layout.

Orientation

The Orientation option in the Page Setup dialog box allows you to specify whether you want your document to be printed vertically or horizontally. If you plan to print your text across the width of the page, you should use the default Tall option. If you plan to print your text across the length of the page, you should select the Wide option.

You may have seen the Tall and Wide settings referred to as Portrait and Landscape orientation, respectively. These terms evolved because portrait-style paintings and photographs are generally taller than they are wide, while landscapes are generally wider than they are tall. These "visual" terms may help you to remember that the Tall option refers to documents that are printed with the lines of text going across the short side of the page while the Wide option refers to documents that are printed with the lines of text going across the long side of the page—as though you had rotated the paper ninety degrees. The effects of the Tall and Wide Orientation options are illustrated in Figures 7-28 and 7-29.

FIGURE 7-28

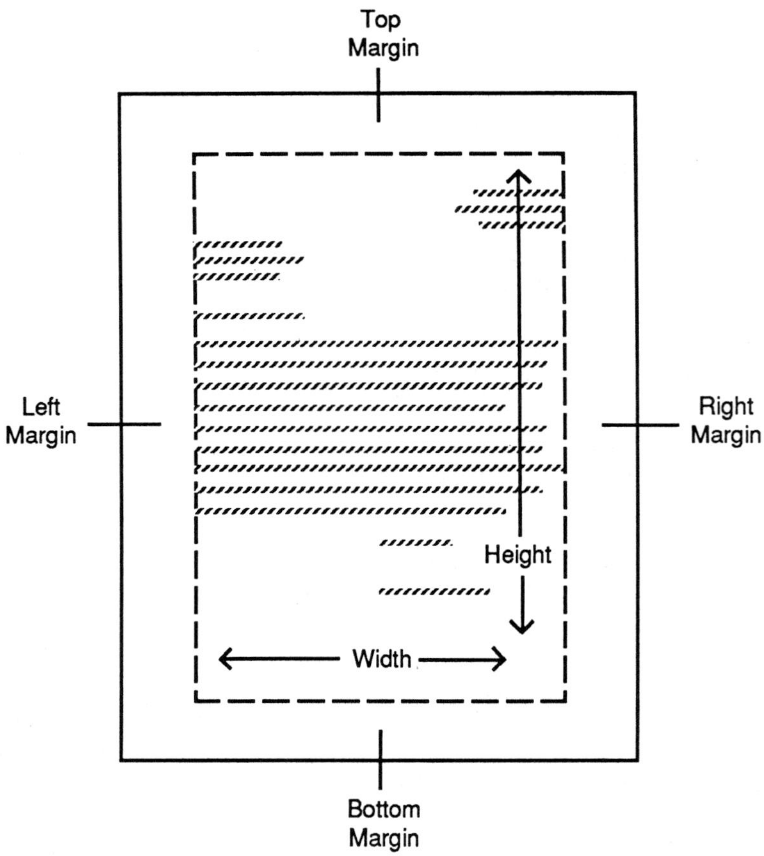

When you choose the Tall option, Word prints across the width of the page.

FIGURE 7-29

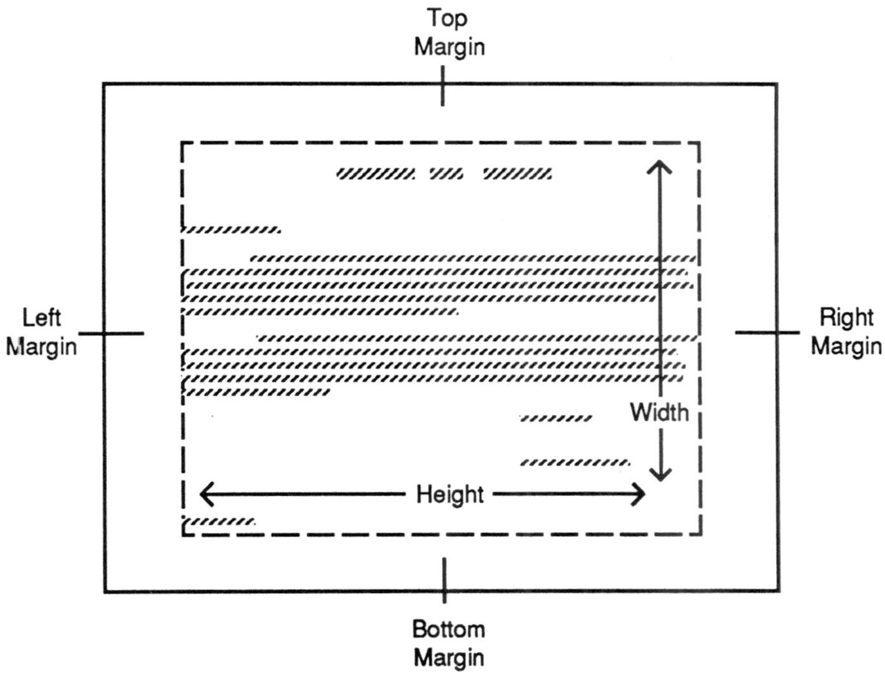

When you choose the Wide option, Word prints across the length of the page.

When you select the Wide option, Word does not change the Paper Width and Height settings to reflect your page orientation. However, your left, right, top, and bottom margins do change "orientation." For example, if you select the Wide and US Letter options, Word still considers your page to be 8 $^1/_2$ inches wide and 11 inches high. However, your Left and Right margin settings will refer to the 11 inch side of the page and your top and bottom margins will refer to the 8 $^1/_2$ inch side of the page. Though this may seem a bit confusing, just remember that you are changing only the *orientation* of your printed text, not the actual size parameters of the page.

Margins

You can use the Top, Bottom, Left, and Right margin settings to control the positioning of text on your printed page. The Left and Right margin settings determine the amount of space between your text and the left and right edges of the paper. The Top and Bottom options determine the amount of space between your text and the top and bottom edges of the paper.

No matter what paper size or orientation you specify, the default Top and Bottom margin settings are 1 inch each, while the default Left and Right margin settings are 1 $^1/_4$ inches each. Of course, you can change these settings at any time to increase or decrease the amount of space between your printed text and the edges of the paper.

Defining Your Text Area

When you change your Paper, Paper Width, Height, Orientation, and Margin settings, keep in mind that you are also changing the height and width of your text area. For example, when you use the default US Letter Paper option and the Tall Orientation with 1 inch top and bottom margins, the remaining text area is 9 inches high.

To determine the height of your text area, you can use the formula

Total page height - top margin - bottom margin = height of text area

For example, if you increase your Top and Bottom margin settings to 2 inches each, the remaining text area is only 7 inches high, as revealed by the formula

$$11 - 2 - 2 = 7$$

Even though Word does not change the values in the Paper Width and Height edit bars, if you decide to use the Wide Orientation option, you must also account for the effects on the height of your text area. Again, assuming that you are using US Letter-size paper and Top and Bottom margin settings of 2 inches each, you can use the formula

$$8\,^1/_2 - 2 - 2 = 4\,^1/_2$$

to determine that the height of your text area has been reduced to 4 $^1/_2$ inches.

When you change the Left and Right margin settings, of course, you also change the width of the available text area. In fact, your Left and Right margin settings, in conjunction with your Paper and Orientation selections, have a direct effect on your document ruler. Let's take a look at this relationship.

How orientation, paper size, and margins affect your ruler settings

The settings you select in the Page Setup dialog box have a significant effect on your ruler settings in the document window. Word uses the Orientation, Page, and Margin settings that you specify in the Page Setup dialog box to determine the width of your text area, as well as the default right indent for your document. In short, the overall width of your body text is determined by the Page Setup dialog box.

As you've already seen in most of the sample documents that we've created throughout this book, the default column width in Word is 6 inches. That is, when you are using the default Page Setup dialog box settings shown in Figures 7-26 and 7-27, you have 6 inches of horizontal space left on the page for your text. The default column width for your document is marked by a dotted vertical line on the ruler. This vertical line will move to indicate your new column width each time you change one of your Orientation, Paper, or Margin settings.

For example, the sample document shown in Figure 7-30 was created with Word's default Page Setup dialog box settings. As you can see, the dotted vertical line at the 6 inch mark indicates that our text area is 6 inches wide. To format the quotation shown in the middle of the screen, we placed our left-indent marker at the $^1/_2$ inch mark and our right-indent marker at the 5 $^1/_2$ inch mark. We did not change the position of the left-indent marker for the remaining body text, but we did drag the first-line indent marker to the $^1/_4$ inch mark to indent the first line of each paragraph.

FIGURE 7-30

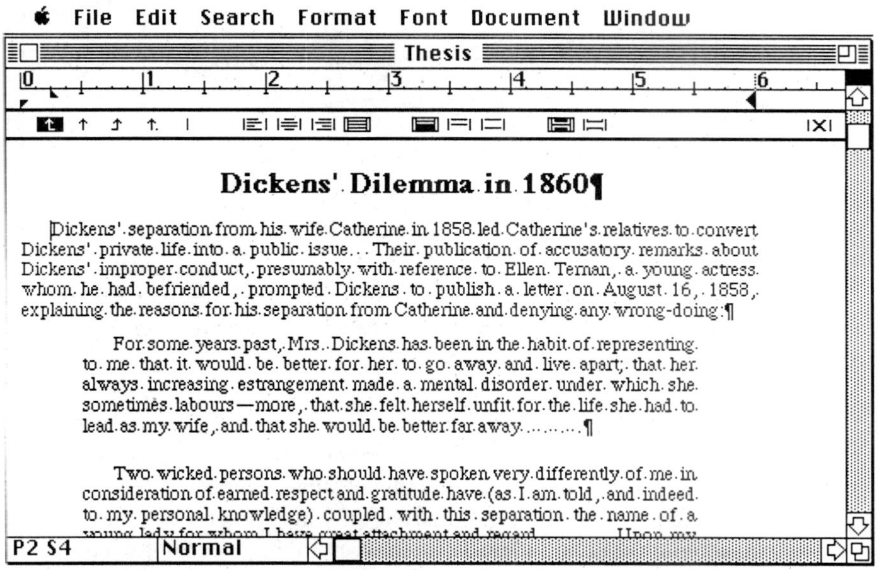

When we use Word's default Page Setup dialog box settings, our text area is 6 inches wide.

If we use the Wide orientation option to format this sample document (we'll keep the default US Letter Paper setting and the 1 $^1/_4$ inch Left and Right margin settings, for now), Word will display a vertical line at the 8 $^1/_2$ inch mark on our ruler. Our right indent marker will shift 2 $^1/_2$ inches to the right as well, as shown in Figure 7-31.

FIGURE 7-31

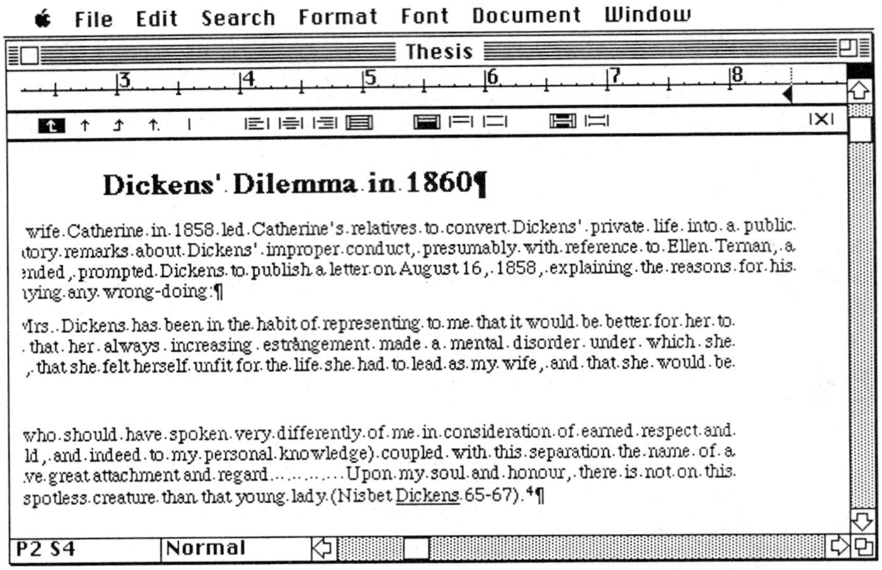

When we choose the Wide Orientation option, the width of our text area increases by 2 1/2 inches.

Our left indent and first-line indent positions did not change in Figure 7-31. Although they are not visible on the screen right now, they remain at the zero mark because the zero point on the ruler always marks the left edge of the text area. Though the position of the left margin on your printed page may change, your left indent and first-line indents stay constant in the document window—no matter how you manipulate your Paper, Orientation, or Margin settings.

If you need to manipulate the width of your text to fit a specific need, you can use this formula to determine the proper Page Setup dialog box settings for your document:

Total page width - left margin - right margin = width of text area

Keep in mind that the total page width for your document depends both on the paper size and the orientation that you select. In other words, if you are using the Tall option to print on a letter-size sheet of paper, your page width will be 8 1/2 inches. If you are using the Wide option, however, your page width will be 11 inches.

For example, when you use the default Page Setup dialog box settings shown in Figures 7-26 and 7-27, your text will be 6 inches wide, as this formula shows:

$$8\ ^1/_2 - 1\ ^1/_4 - 1\ ^1/_4 = 6$$

However, when you select the Wide option, your calculations change to

$$11 - 1\ ^1/_4 - 1\ ^1/_4 = 8\ ^1/_2$$

Though the same rules hold true, this formula gets a little more complicated when you are creating multicolumn documents. We'll talk more about multicolumn formatting in Chapter 8.

We strongly recommend that you use the Page Setup dialog box to determine the overall width of your text, rather than dragging the left and right indent markers on the ruler. The left and right indent markers are designed to handle special circumstances—indenting a quotation or adding margin notes to your document, for example. If you use the indent markers on your ruler to change your overall column widths, you may find yourself in trouble if you later need to alter your Page Setup dialog box settings.

If you're still unclear as to the effects of the Page Setup dialog box on your ruler settings, we suggest that you review the illustration that appears on page 129 in Chapter 5. We'll also talk more about using the Page Setup dialog box to create a document design in Chapter 8.

Facing Pages

The Facing Pages option lets you set up your document for double-sided printing. When you use this option, Word does not actually print on both sides of your paper. Instead, it adjusts the left and right orientation of certain page elements to allow for odd and even page formats.

When you click the Facing Pages option, a number of changes take place. First of all, the Gutter option in the Page Setup dialog box becomes active. Second, if you've used the Bar Border option in the Paragraph dialog box, Word will change the position of your borders on odd pages.

When you choose the Facing Pages option, Word also adds the commands Open Even Header…, Open Even Footer…, Open Odd Header…, and Open Odd Footer… to your Document menu. And, if you're using page numbers, Word will change the position of those numbers on your odd pages. We will discuss headers, footers, and page numbers later in this chapter. First, let's look at the Gutter option and the effects of the Facing Pages option on paragraph borders.

Gutters

Often, when you print facing pages, you'll want to include some extra margin space to allow for three-hole punching or binding. This binding allowance, or gutter, appears on the left side of odd pages and on the right side of even pages.

To include extra binding space in your document, just type a value in the Gutter edit bar in the Page Setup dialog box. Normally, the Gutter setting is dimmed. When you choose the Facing Pages option, however, Word will activate the Gutter edit bar.

For example, consider the sample pages shown in Figure 7-32. Though we used the Facing Pages option to print these pages, we have not yet added any extra gutter space. Suppose we decide to include a 1/2 inch gutter binding allowance to make room for three-hole punching. We can just click in the Gutter edit bar and type .5. Figure 7-33 shows the effect on our printed pages. Notice that an extra 1/2 inch of margin space now appears on the binding edge of both printed pages.

FIGURE 7-32

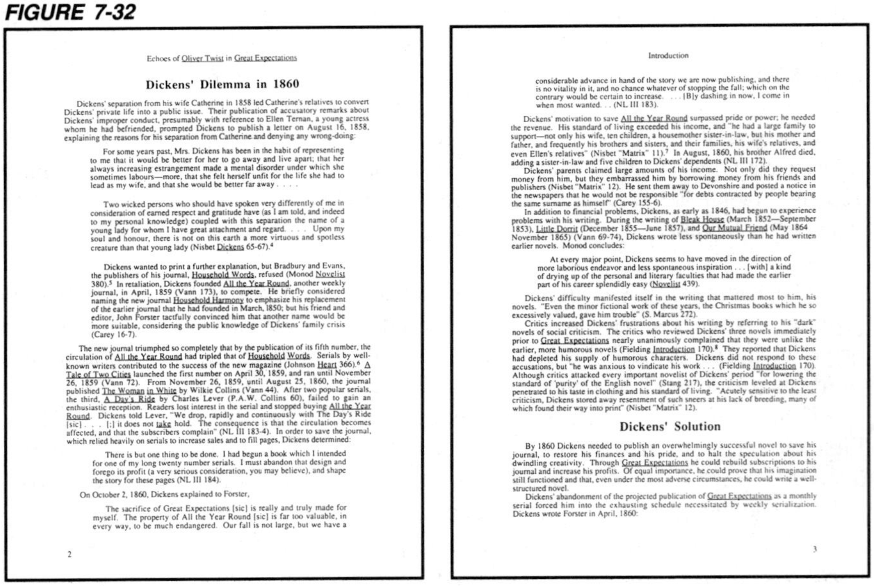

Echoes of Oliver Twist in Great Expectations

Dickens' Dilemma in 1860

Dickens' separation from his wife Catherine in 1858 led Catherine's relatives to convert Dickens' private life into a public issue. Their publication of accusatory remarks about Dickens' improper conduct, presumably with reference to Ellen Ternan, a young actress whom he had befriended, prompted Dickens to publish a letter on August 16, 1858, explaining the reasons for his separation from Catherine and denying any wrong-doing:

> For some years past, Mrs. Dickens has been in the habit of representing to me that it would be better for her to go away and live apart; that her always increasing estrangement made a mental disorder under which she sometimes labours—more, that she felt herself unfit for the life she had to lead as my wife, and that she would be better far away . . . .
>
> Two wicked persons who should have spoken very differently of me in consideration of earned respect and gratitude have (as I am told, and indeed to my personal knowledge) coupled with this separation the name of a young lady for whom I have great attachment and regard. . . . Upon my soul and honour, there is not on this earth a more virtuous and spotless creature than that young lady (Nisbet Dickens 65-67).[4]
>
> Dickens wanted to print a further explanation, but Bradbury and Evans, the publishers of his journal, Household Words, refused (Monod Novelist 380).[5] In retaliation, Dickens founded All the Year Round, another weekly journal, in April, 1859 (Vann 173), to compete. He briefly considered naming the new journal Household Harmony to emphasize his replacement of the earlier journal that he had founded in March, 1850; but his friend and editor, John Forster tactfully convinced him that another name would be more suitable, considering the public knowledge of Dickens' family crisis (Carey 16-7).

The new journal triumphed so completely that by the publication of its fifth number, the circulation of All the Year Round had tripled that of Household Words. Serials by well-known writers contributed to the success of the new magazine (Johnson Heart 366).[6] A Tale of Two Cities launched the first number on April 30, 1859, and ran until November 26, 1859 (Vann 72). From November 26, 1859, until August 25, 1860, the journal published The Woman in White by Wilkie Collins (Vann 44). After two popular serials, the third, A Day's Ride by Charles Lever (P.A.W. Collins 60), failed to gain an enthusiastic reception. Readers lost interest in the serial and stopped buying All the Year Round. Dickens told Lever, "We drop, rapidly and continuously with The Day's Ride [sic] . . . [;] it does not take hold. The consequence is that the circulation becomes affected, and that the subscribers complain" (NL III 183-4). In order to save the journal, which relied heavily on serials to increase sales and to fill pages, Dickens determined:

> There is but one thing to be done. I had begun a book which I intended for one of my long twenty number serials. I must abandon that design and forego its profit (a very serious consideration, you may believe), and shape the story for these pages (NL III 184).

On October 2, 1860, Dickens explained to Forster,

> The sacrifice of Great Expectations [sic] is really and truly made for myself. The property of All the Year Round [sic] is far too valuable, in every way, to be much endangered. Our fall is not large, but we have a

2

Introduction

> considerable advance in hand of the story we are now publishing, and there is no vitality in it, and no chance whatever of stopping the fall; which on the contrary would be certain to increase. . . . [B]y dashing in now, I come in when most wanted. . . (NL III 183).

Dickens' motivation to save All the Year Round surpassed pride or power; he needed the revenue. His standard of living exceeded his income, and "he had a large family to support—not only his wife, ten children, a housemother sister-in-law, but his mother and father, and frequently his brothers and sisters, and their families, his wife's relatives, and even Ellen's relatives" (Nisbet "Matrix" 11).[7] In August, 1860, his brother Alfred died, adding a sister-in-law and five children to Dickens' dependents (NL III 172).

Dickens' parents claimed large amounts of his income. Not only did they request money from him, but they embarrassed him by borrowing money from his friends and publishers (Nisbet "Matrix" 12). He sent them away to Devonshire and posted a notice in the newspapers that he would not be responsible "for debts contracted by people bearing the same surname as himself" (Carey 155-6).

In addition to financial problems, Dickens, as early as 1846, had begun to experience problems with his writing. During the writing of Bleak House (March 1852—September 1853), Little Dorrit (December 1855—June 1857), and Our Mutual Friend (May 1864 November 1865) (Vann 69-74), Dickens wrote less spontaneously than he had written earlier novels. Monod concludes:

> At every major point, Dickens seems to have moved in the direction of more laborious endeavor and less spontaneous inspiration . . . [with] a kind of drying up of the personal and literary faculties that had made the earlier part of his career splendidly easy (Novelist 439).

Dickens' difficulty manifested itself in the writing that mattered most to him, his novels. "Even the minor fictional work of these years, the Christmas books which he so excessively valued, gave him trouble" (S. Marcus 272).

Critics increased Dickens' frustrations about his writing by referring to his "dark" novels of social criticism. The critics who reviewed Dickens' three novels immediately prior to Great Expectations nearly unanimously complained that they were unlike the earlier, more humorous novels (Fielding Introduction 170).[8] They reported that Dickens had depleted his supply of humorous characters. Dickens did not respond to these accusations, but "he was anxious to vindicate his work . . . (Fielding Introduction 170). Although critics attacked every important novelist of Dickens' period "for lowering the standard of 'purity' of the English novel" (Stang 217), the criticism leveled at Dickens penetrated to his taste in clothing and his standard of living. "Acutely sensitive to the least criticism, Dickens stored away resentment of such sneers at his lack of breeding, many of which found their way into print" (Nisbet "Matrix" 12).

Dickens' Solution

By 1860 Dickens needed to publish an overwhelmingly successful novel to save his journal, to restore his finances and his pride, and to halt the speculation about his dwindling creativity. Through Great Expectations he could rebuild subscriptions to his journal and increase his profits. Of equal importance, he could prove that his imagination still functioned and that, even under the most adverse circumstances, he could write a well-structured novel.

Dickens' abandonment of the projected publication of Great Expectations as a monthly serial forced him into the exhausting schedule necessitated by weekly serialization. Dickens wrote Forster in April, 1860:

3

These sample pages were printed with no extra gutter allowance.

FIGURE 7-33

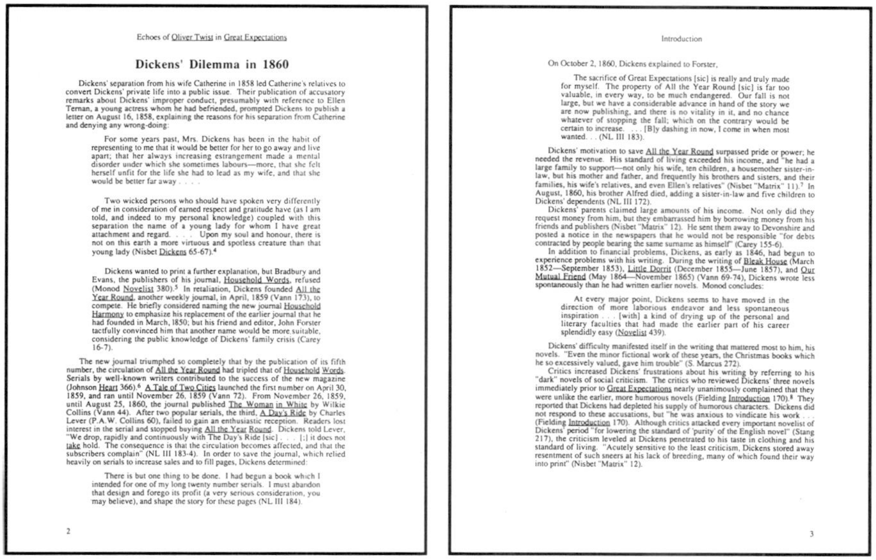

Echoes of Oliver Twist in Great Expectations

Dickens' Dilemma in 1860

Dickens' separation from his wife Catherine in 1858 led Catherine's relatives to convert Dickens' private life into a public issue. Their publication of accusatory remarks about Dickens' improper conduct, presumably with reference to Ellen Ternan, a young actress whom he had befriended, prompted Dickens to publish a letter on August 16, 1858, explaining the reasons for his separation from Catherine and denying any wrong-doing:

For some years past, Mrs. Dickens has been in the habit of representing to me that it would be better for her to go away and live apart; that her always increasing estrangement made a mental disorder under which she sometimes labours—more, that she felt herself unfit for the life she had to lead as my wife, and that she would be better far away . . . .

Two wicked persons who should have spoken very differently of me in consideration of earned respect and gratitude have (as I am told, and indeed to my personal knowledge) coupled with this separation the name of a young lady for whom I have great attachment and regard. . . . Upon my soul and honour, there is not on this earth a more virtuous and spotless creature than that young lady (Nisbet Dickens 65-67).[4]

Dickens wanted to print a further explanation, but Bradbury and Evans, the publishers of his journal, Household Words, refused (Monod Novelist 380).[5] In retaliation, Dickens founded All the Year Round, another weekly journal, in April, 1859 (Vann 173), to compete. He briefly considered naming the new journal Household Harmony to emphasize his replacement of the earlier journal that he had founded in March, 1850; but his friend and editor, John Forster tactfully convinced him that another name would be more suitable, considering the public knowledge of Dickens' family crisis (Carey 16-7).

The new journal triumphed so completely that by the publication of its fifth number, the circulation of All the Year Round had tripled that of Household Words. Serials by well-known writers contributed to the success of the new magazine (Johnson Heart 366).[6] A Tale of Two Cities launched the first number on April 30, 1859, and ran until November 26, 1859 (Vann 72). From November 26, 1859, until August 25, 1860, the journal published The Woman in White by Wilkie Collins (Vann 44). After two popular serials, the third, A Day's Ride by Charles Lever (P.A.W. Collins 60), failed to gain an enthusiastic reception. Readers lost interest in the serial and stopped buying All the Year Round. Dickens told Lever, "We drop, rapidly and continuously with The Day's Ride [sic] . . . [;] it does not take hold. The consequence is that the circulation becomes affected, and that the subscribers complain" (NL III 183-4). In order to save the journal, which relied heavily on serials to increase sales and to fill pages, Dickens determined:

There is but one thing to be done. I had begun a book which I intended for one of my long twenty number serials. I must abandon that design and forego its profit (a very serious consideration, you may believe), and shape the story for these pages (NL III 184).

2

Introduction

On October 2, 1860, Dickens explained to Forster,

The sacrifice of Great Expectations [sic] is really and truly made for myself. The property of All the Year Round [sic] is far too valuable, in every way, to be much endangered. Our fall is not large, but we have a considerable advance in hand of the story we are now publishing, and there is no vitality in it, and no chance whatever of stopping the fall; which on the contrary would be certain to increase. . . . [B]y dashing in now, I come in when most wanted. . . (NL III 183).

Dickens' motivation to save All the Year Round surpassed pride or power; he needed the revenue. His standard of living exceeded his income, and "he had a large family to support—not only his wife, ten children, a housemother sister-in-law, but his mother and father, and frequently his brothers and sisters, and their families, his wife's relatives, and even Ellen's relatives" (Nisbet "Matrix" 11).[7] In August, 1860, his brother Alfred died, adding a sister-in-law and five children to Dickens' dependents (NL III 172).

Dickens' parents claimed large amounts of his income. Not only did they request money from him, but they embarrassed him by borrowing money from his friends and publishers (Nisbet "Matrix" 12). He sent them away to Devonshire and posted a notice in the newspapers that he would not be responsible "for debts contracted by people bearing the same surname as himself" (Carey 155-6).

In addition to financial problems, Dickens, as early as 1846, had begun to experience problems with his writing. During the writing of Bleak House (March 1852—September 1853), Little Dorrit (December 1855—June 1857), and Our Mutual Friend (May 1864—November 1865) (Vann 69-74), Dickens wrote less spontaneously than he had written earlier novels. Monod concludes:

At every major point, Dickens seems to have moved in the direction of more laborious endeavor and less spontaneous inspiration . . . [with] a kind of drying up of the personal and literary faculties that had made the earlier part of his career splendidly easy (Novelist 439).

Dickens' difficulty manifested itself in the writing that mattered most to him, his novels. "Even the minor fictional work of these years, the Christmas books which he so excessively valued, gave him trouble" (S. Marcus 272).

Critics increased Dickens' frustrations about his writing by referring to his "dark" novels of social criticism. The critics who reviewed Dickens' three novels immediately prior to Great Expectations nearly unanimously complained that they were unlike the earlier, more humorous novels (Fielding Introduction 170).[8] They reported that Dickens had depleted his supply of humorous characters. Dickens did not respond to these accusations, but "he was anxious to vindicate his work . . . (Fielding Introduction 170). Although critics attacked every important novelist of Dickens' period "for lowering the standard of 'purity' of the English novel" (Stang 217), the criticism leveled at Dickens penetrated to his taste in clothing and his standard of living. "Acutely sensitive to the least criticism, Dickens stored away resentment of such sneers at his lack of breeding, many of which found their way into print" (Nisbet "Matrix" 12).

3

We added a $^1/_2$ inch gutter to these pages.

As you might have guessed, the Gutter option also has an effect on your ruler settings. In the sample pages shown in Figures 7-32 and 7-33, the right edge of our text was set to 6 inches before we specified our Gutter setting. After adding the $^1/_2$ inch gutter, the right edge moved to the 5 $^1/_2$ inch mark. Similarly, the indented quotation, which did carry a right indent of 5 $^1/_2$ inches, is now indented to the 5 inch mark. In short, Word has automatically narrowed the width of our print area by $^1/_2$ inch throughout the document to account for our Gutter setting.

Facing pages and borders

If you have ever used the Bar Border option in the Paragraph dialog box to highlight key paragraphs (updates and revisions for example), you know that Word typically places a bar in the left margin. When you use the Facing Pages option, however, Word places the bar in the left margin for even pages and in the right margin for odd pages. In other words, the bar always appears in the outside margin of the page.

For example, in the sample pages shown in Figure 7-34, we used the Bar Border option to highlight several paragraphs. Because we used the Facing Pages option to format this document, our borders appear in the left margin on page 4 and in the right margin on page 5.

FIGURE 7-34

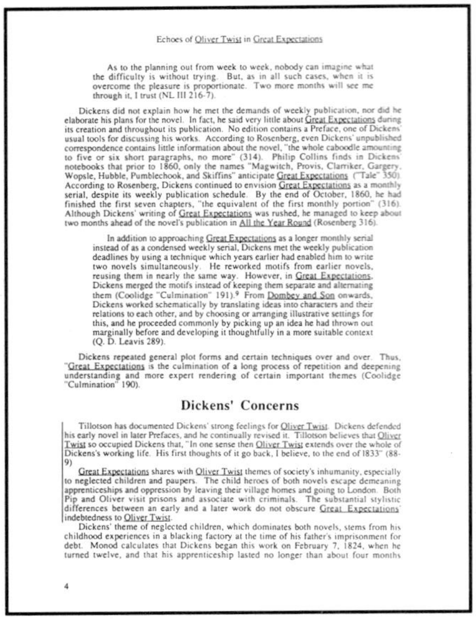

Echoes of Oliver Twist in Great Expectations

> As to the planning out from week to week, nobody can imagine what the difficulty is without trying. But, as in all such cases, when it is overcome the pleasure is proportionate. Two more months will see me through it, I trust (NL III 216-7).

Dickens did not explain how he met the demands of weekly publication, nor did he elaborate his plans for the novel. In fact, he said very little about Great Expectations during its creation and throughout its publication. No edition contains a Preface, one of Dickens' usual tools for discussing his works. According to Rosenberg, even Dickens' unpublished correspondence contains little information about the novel, "the whole caboodle amounting to five or six short paragraphs, no more" (314). Philip Collins finds in Dickens' notebooks that prior to 1860, only the names "Magwitch, Provis, Clarriker, Gargery, Wopsle, Hubble, Pumblechook, and Skiffins" anticipate Great Expectations ("Tale" 350). According to Rosenberg, Dickens continued to envision Great Expectations as a monthly serial, despite its weekly publication schedule. By the end of October, 1860, he had finished the first seven chapters, "the equivalent of the first monthly portion" (316). Although Dickens' writing of Great Expectations was rushed, he managed to keep about two months ahead of the novel's publication in All the Year Round (Rosenberg 316).

> In addition to approaching Great Expectations as a longer monthly serial instead of as a condensed weekly serial, Dickens met the weekly publication deadlines by using a technique which years earlier had enabled him to write two novels simultaneously. He reworked motifs from earlier novels, reusing them in nearly the same way. However, in Great Expectations, Dickens merged the motifs instead of keeping them separate and alternating them (Coolidge "Culmination" 191).[9] From Dombey and Son onwards, Dickens worked schematically by translating ideas into characters and their relations to each other, and by choosing or arranging illustrative settings for this, and he proceeded commonly by picking up an idea he had thrown out marginally before and developing it thoughtfully in a more suitable context (Q. D. Leavis 289).

Dickens repeated general plot forms and certain techniques over and over. Thus, "Great Expectations is the culmination of a long process of repetition and deepening understanding and more expert rendering of certain important themes (Coolidge "Culmination" 190).

Dickens' Concerns

Tillotson has documented Dickens' strong feelings for Oliver Twist. Dickens defended his early novel in later Prefaces, and he continually revised it. Tillotson believes that Oliver Twist so occupied Dickens that, "In one sense then Oliver Twist extends over the whole of Dickens's working life. His first thoughts of it go back, I believe, to the end of 1833" (88-9)

Great Expectations shares with Oliver Twist themes of society's inhumanity, especially to neglected children and paupers. The child heroes of both novels escape demeaning apprenticeships and oppression by leaving their village homes and going to London. Both Pip and Oliver visit prisons and associate with criminals. The substantial stylistic differences between an early and a later work do not obscure Great Expectations' indebtedness to Oliver Twist.

Dickens' theme of neglected children, which dominates both novels, stems from his childhood experiences in a blacking factory at the time of his father's imprisonment for debt. Monod calculates that Dickens began this work on February 7, 1824, when he turned twelve, and that his apprenticeship lasted no longer than about four months

4

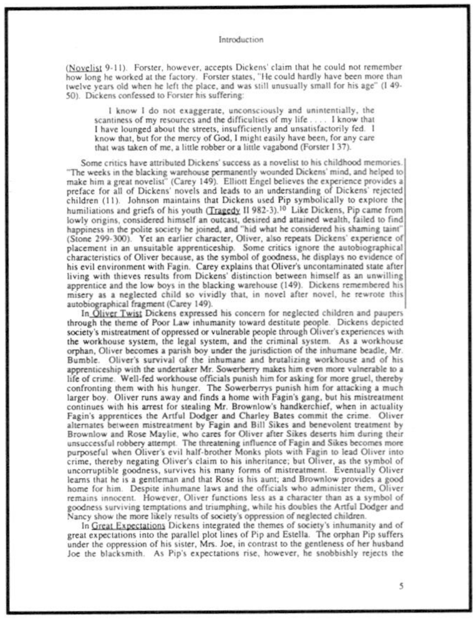

Introduction

(Novelist 9-11). Forster, however, accepts Dickens' claim that he could not remember how long he worked at the factory. Forster states, "He could hardly have been more than twelve years old when he left the place, and was still unusually small for his age" (I 49-50). Dickens confessed to Forster his suffering:

> I know I do not exaggerate, unconsciously and unintentionally, the scantiness of my resources and the difficulties of my life . . . . I know that I have lounged about the streets, insufficiently and unsatisfactorily fed. I know that, but for the mercy of God, I might easily have been, for any care that was taken of me, a little robber or a little vagabond (Forster I 37).

Some critics have attributed Dickens' success as a novelist to his childhood memories. "The weeks in the blacking warehouse permanently wounded Dickens' mind, and helped to make him a great novelist" (Carey 149). Elliott Engel believes the experience provides a preface for all of Dickens' novels and leads to an understanding of Dickens' rejected children (11). Johnson maintains that Dickens used Pip symbolically to explore the humiliations and griefs of his youth (Tragedy II 982-3).[10] Like Dickens, Pip came from lowly origins, considered himself an outcast, desired and attained wealth, failed to find happiness in the polite society he joined, and "hid what he considered his shaming taint" (Stone 299-300). Yet an earlier character, Oliver, also repeats Dickens' experience of placement in an unsuitable apprenticeship. Some critics ignore the autobiographical characteristics of Oliver because, as the symbol of goodness, he displays no evidence of his evil environment with Fagin. Carey explains that Oliver's uncontaminated state after living with thieves results from Dickens' distinction between himself as an unwilling apprentice and the low boys in the blacking warehouse (149). Dickens remembered his misery as a neglected child so vividly that, in novel after novel, he rewrote this autobiographical fragment (Carey 149).

In Oliver Twist Dickens expressed his concern for neglected children and paupers through the theme of Poor Law inhumanity toward destitute people. Dickens depicted society's mistreatment of oppressed or vulnerable people through Oliver's experiences with the workhouse system, the legal system, and the criminal system. As a workhouse orphan, Oliver becomes a parish boy under the jurisdiction of the inhumane beadle, Mr. Bumble. Oliver's survival of the inhumane and brutalizing workhouse and of his apprenticeship with the undertaker Mr. Sowerberry makes him even more vulnerable to a life of crime. Well-fed workhouse officials punish him for asking for more gruel, thereby confronting them with his hunger. The Sowerberrys punish him for attacking a much larger boy. Oliver runs away and finds a home with Fagin's gang, but his mistreatment continues with his arrest for stealing Mr. Brownlow's handkerchief, when in actuality Fagin's apprentices the Artful Dodger and Charley Bates commit the crime. Oliver alternates between mistreatment by Fagin and Bill Sikes and benevolent treatment by Brownlow and Rose Maylie, who cares for Oliver after Sikes deserts him during their unsuccessful robbery attempt. The threatening influence of Fagin and Sikes becomes more purposeful when Oliver's evil half-brother Monks plots with Fagin to lead Oliver into crime, thereby negating Oliver's claim to his inheritance; but Oliver, as the symbol of uncorruptible goodness, survives his many forms of mistreatment. Eventually Oliver learns that he is a gentleman and that Rose is his aunt; and Brownlow provides a good home for him. Despite inhumane laws and the officials who administer them, Oliver remains innocent. However, Oliver functions less as a character than as a symbol of goodness surviving temptations and triumphing, while his doubles the Artful Dodger and Nancy show the more likely results of society's oppression of neglected children.

In Great Expectations Dickens integrated the themes of society's inhumanity and of great expectations into the parallel plot lines of Pip and Estella. The orphan Pip suffers under the oppression of his sister, Mrs. Joe, in contrast to the gentleness of her husband Joe the blacksmith. As Pip's expectations rise, however, he snobbishly rejects the

5

When you select Facing Pages, the Bar border appears in the left margin of odd pages and in the right margin of even pages.

Widow Control

Though the jargon is none too complimentary, the term *widow* refers to those straggling single lines of text that are left stranded at the top or bottom of a printed page. For example, consider pages 14 and 15 of our sample document, shown in Figure 7-35. Notice that the last line of the paragraph that begins at the bottom of page 14 appears alone at the top of page 15. In addition, a widow from a paragraph that begins on page 13 appears at the top of page 14.

Generally, it is considered good style to ensure that no fewer than two lines of a paragraph appear on a page. That is, the first or last line of a paragraph should never stand alone. If there is not room for at least two lines of a paragraph at the bottom of the page, then you should "push" the entire paragraph to the beginning of the next page. By the same token, if there is room at the bottom of a page for all but the last line of a paragraph—meaning that the last line of the paragraph would stand alone at the top of the next page, as shown in Figure 7-35—then you should "pull" a line from the bottom of the first page to the top of the second page.

The Widow Control option in the Page Setup dialog box does exactly this. It ensures that no single line of text from a paragraph (unless, of course, it is a single-line paragraph) should stand alone on a page. If you use this option, Word will adjust the printed pages shown in Figure 7-35 to look like those in Figure 7-36. Notice that two lines from the paragraph that begins at the bottom of page 14 now appear at the top of page 15. An extra line from the bottom of page 13 has also been pushed forward to the top of page 14.

FIGURE 7-35

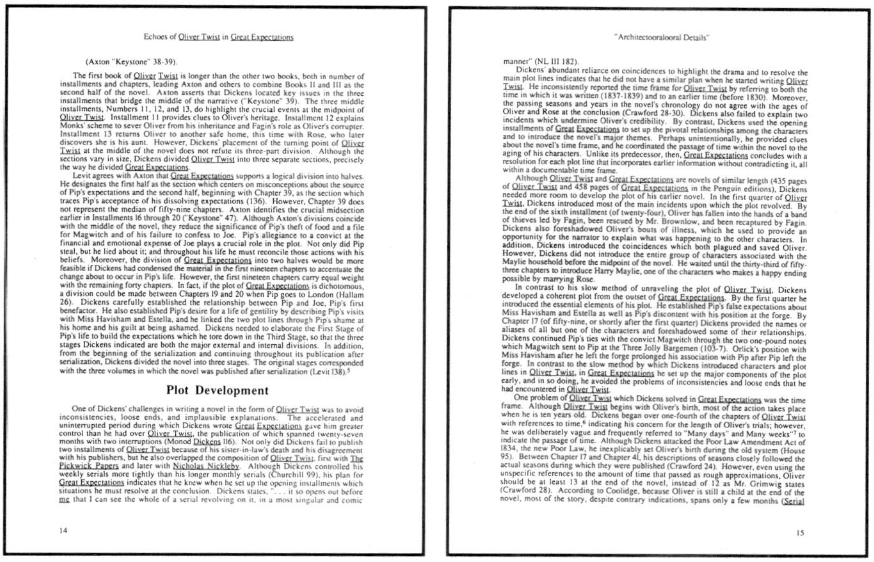

Echoes of Oliver Twist in Great Expectations

(Axton "Keystone" 38-39).

The first book of Oliver Twist is longer than the other two books, both in number of installments and chapters, leading Axton and others to combine Books II and III as the second half of the novel. Axton asserts that Dickens located key issues in the three installments that bridge the middle of the narrative ("Keystone" 39). The three middle installments, Numbers 11, 12, and 13, do highlight the crucial events at the midpoint of Oliver Twist. Installment 11 provides clues to Oliver's heritage. Installment 12 explains Monks' scheme to sever Oliver from his inheritance and Fagin's role as Oliver's corrupter. Installment 13 returns Oliver to another safe home, this time with Rose, who later discovers she is his aunt. However, Dickens' placement of the turning point of Oliver Twist at the middle of the novel does not refute its three-part division. Although the sections vary in size, Dickens divided Oliver Twist into three separate sections, precisely the way he divided Great Expectations.

Levit agrees with Axton that Great Expectations supports a logical division into halves. He designates the first half as the section which centers on misconceptions about the source of Pip's expectations and the second half, beginning with Chapter 39, as the section which traces Pip's acceptance of his dissolving expectations (136). However, Chapter 39 does not represent the median of fifty-nine chapters. Axton identifies the crucial midsection earlier in Installments 16 through 20 ("Keystone" 47). Although Axton's divisions coincide with the middle of the novel, they reduce the significance of Pip's theft of food and a file for Magwitch and of his failure to confess to Joe. Pip's allegiance to a convict at the financial and emotional expense of Joe plays a crucial role in the plot. Not only did Pip steal, but he lied about it; and throughout his life he must reconcile those actions with his beliefs. Moreover, the division of Great Expectations into two halves would be more feasible if Dickens had condensed the material in the first nineteen chapters to accentuate the change about to occur in Pip's life. However, the first nineteen chapters carry equal weight with the remaining forty chapters. In fact, if the plot of Great Expectations is dichotomous, a division could be made between Chapters 19 and 20 when Pip goes to London (Hallam 26). Dickens carefully established the relationship between Pip and Joe, Pip's first benefactor. He also established Pip's desire for a life of gentility by describing Pip's visits with Miss Havisham and Estella, and he linked the two plot lines through Pip's shame at his home and his guilt at being ashamed. Dickens needed to elaborate the First Stage of Pip's life to build the expectations which he tore down in the Third Stage, so that the three stages Dickens indicated are both the major external and internal divisions. In addition, from the beginning of the serialization and continuing throughout its publication after serialization, Dickens divided the novel into three stages. The original stages corresponded with the three volumes in which the novel was published after serialization (Levit 138).[5]

Plot Development

One of Dickens' challenges in writing a novel in the form of Oliver Twist was to avoid inconsistencies, loose ends, and implausible explanations. The accelerated and uninterrupted period during which Dickens wrote Great Expectations gave him greater control than he had over Oliver Twist, the publication of which spanned twenty-seven months with two interruptions (Monod Dickens 116). Not only did Dickens fail to publish two installments of Oliver Twist because of his sister-in-law's death and his disagreement with his publishers, but he also overlapped the composition of Oliver Twist, first with The Pickwick Papers and later with Nicholas Nickleby. Although Dickens controlled his weekly serials more tightly than his longer monthly serials (Churchill 99), his plan for Great Expectations indicates that he knew when he set up the opening installments which situations he must resolve at the conclusion. Dickens states, ". . . it so opens out before me that I can see the whole of a serial revolving on it, in a most singular and comic

14

"Architectooralooral Details"

manner" (NL III 182).

Dickens' abundant reliance on coincidences to highlight the drama and to resolve the main plot lines indicates that he did not have a similar plan when he started writing Oliver Twist. He inconsistently reported the time frame for Oliver Twist by referring to both the time in which it was written (1837-1839) and to an earlier time (before 1830). Moreover, the passing seasons and years in the novel's chronology do not agree with the ages of Oliver and Rose at the conclusion (Crawford 28-30). Dickens also failed to explain two incidents which undermine Oliver's credibility. By contrast, Dickens used the opening installments of Great Expectations to set up the pivotal relationships among the characters and to introduce the novel's major themes. Perhaps unintentionally, he provided clues about the novel's time frame, and he coordinated the passage of time within the novel to the aging of his characters. Unlike its predecessor, then, Great Expectations concludes with a resolution for each plot line that incorporates earlier information without contradicting it, all within a documentable time frame.

Although Oliver Twist and Great Expectations are novels of similar length (435 pages of Oliver Twist and 458 pages of Great Expectations in the Penguin editions), Dickens needed more room to develop the plot of his earlier novel. In the first quarter of Oliver Twist, Dickens introduced most of the main incidents upon which the plot revolved. By the end of the sixth installment (of twenty-four), Oliver has fallen into the hands of a band of thieves led by Fagin, been rescued by Mr. Brownlow, and been recaptured by Fagin. Dickens also foreshadowed Oliver's bouts of illness, which he used to provide an opportunity for the narrator to explain what was happening to the other characters. In addition, Dickens introduced the coincidences which both plagued and saved Oliver. However, Dickens did not introduce the entire group of characters associated with the Maylie household before the midpoint of the novel. He waited until the thirty-third of fifty-three chapters to introduce Harry Maylie, one of the characters who makes a happy ending possible by marrying Rose.

In contrast to his slow method of unraveling the plot of Oliver Twist, Dickens developed a coherent plot from the outset of Great Expectations. By the first quarter he introduced the essential elements of his plot. He established Pip's false expectations about Miss Havisham and Estella as well as Pip's discontent with his position at the forge. By Chapter 17 (of fifty-nine, or shortly after the first quarter) Dickens provided the names or aliases of all but one of the characters and foreshadowed some of their relationships. Dickens continued Pip's ties with the convict Magwitch through the two one-pound notes which Magwitch sent to Pip at the Three Jolly Bargemen (103-7). Orlick's position with Miss Havisham after he left the forge prolonged his association with Pip after Pip left the forge. In contrast to the slow method by which Dickens introduced characters and plot lines in Oliver Twist, in Great Expectations he set up the major components of the plot early, and in so doing, he avoided the problems of inconsistencies and loose ends that he had encountered in Oliver Twist.

One problem of Oliver Twist which Dickens solved in Great Expectations was the time frame. Although Oliver Twist begins with Oliver's birth, most of the action takes place when he is ten years old. Dickens began over one-fourth of the chapters of Oliver Twist with references to time,[6] indicating his concern for the length of Oliver's trials; however, he was deliberately vague and frequently referred to "Many days" and Many weeks"[7] to indicate the passage of time. Although Dickens attacked the Poor Law Amendment Act of 1834, the new Poor Law, he inexplicably set Oliver's birth during the old system (House 95). Between Chapter 17 and Chapter 41, his descriptions of seasons closely followed the actual seasons during which they were published (Crawford 24). However, even using the unspecific references to the amount of time that passed as rough approximations, Oliver should be at least 13 at the end of the novel, instead of 12 as Mr. Grimwig states (Crawford 28). According to Coolidge, because Oliver is still a child at the end of the novel, most of the story, despite contrary indications, spans only a few months (Serial

15

The last line of text from the paragraph that begins at the bottom of page 14 appears alone at the top of page 15.

FIGURE 7-36

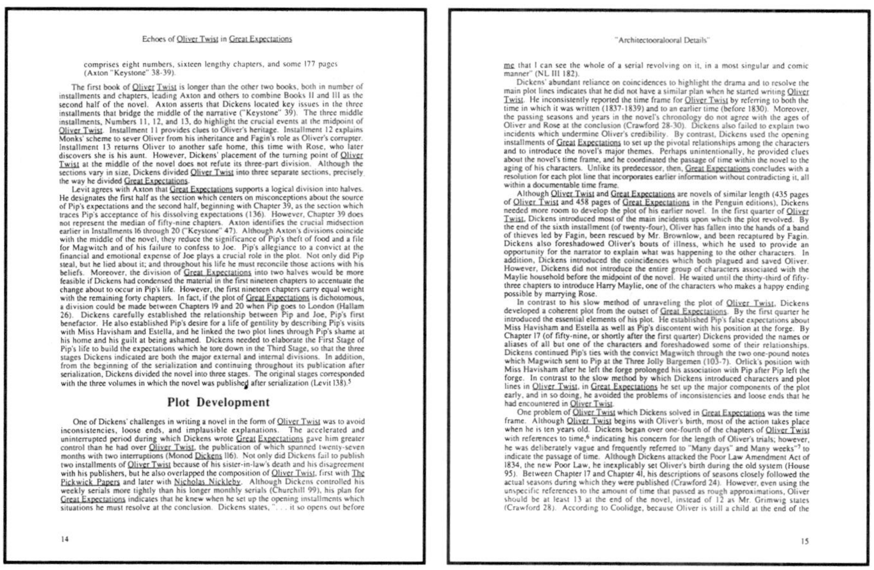

Echoes of Oliver Twist in Great Expectations

comprises eight numbers, sixteen lengthy chapters, and some 177 pages (Axton "Keystone" 38-39).

The first book of Oliver Twist is longer than the other two books, both in number of installments and chapters, leading Axton and others to combine Books II and III as the second half of the novel. Axton asserts that Dickens located key issues in the three installments that bridge the middle of the narrative ("Keystone" 39). The three middle installments, Numbers 11, 12, and 13, do highlight the crucial events at the midpoint of Oliver Twist. Installment 11 provides clues to Oliver's heritage. Installment 12 explains Monks' scheme to sever Oliver from his inheritance and Fagin's role as Oliver's corrupter. Installment 13 returns Oliver to another safe home, this time with Rose, who later discovers she is his aunt. However, Dickens' placement of the turning point of Oliver Twist at the middle of the novel does not refute its three-part division. Although the sections vary in size, Dickens divided Oliver Twist into three separate sections, precisely the way he divided Great Expectations.

Levit agrees with Axton that Great Expectations supports a logical division into halves. He designates the first half as the section which centers on misconceptions about the source of Pip's expectations and the second half, beginning with Chapter 39, as the section which traces Pip's acceptance of his dissolving expectations (136). However, Chapter 39 does not represent the median of fifty-nine chapters. Axton identifies the crucial midsection earlier in Installments 16 through 20 ("Keystone" 47). Although Axton's divisions coincide with the middle of the novel, they reduce the significance of Pip's theft of food and a file for Magwitch and of his failure to confess to Joe. Pip's allegiance to a convict at the financial and emotional expense of Joe plays a crucial role in the plot. Not only did Pip steal, but he lied about it; and throughout his life he must reconcile those actions with his beliefs. Moreover, the division of Great Expectations into two halves would be more feasible if Dickens had condensed the material in the first nineteen chapters to accentuate the change about to occur in Pip's life. However, the first nineteen chapters carry equal weight with the remaining forty chapters. In fact, if the plot of Great Expectations is dichotomous, a division could be made between Chapters 19 and 20 when Pip goes to London (Hallam 26). Dickens carefully established the relationship between Pip and Joe, Pip's first benefactor. He also established Pip's desire for a life of gentility by describing Pip's visits with Miss Havisham and Estella, and he linked the two plot lines through Pip's shame at his home and his guilt at being ashamed. Dickens needed to elaborate the First Stage of Pip's life to build the expectations which he tore down in the Third Stage, so that the three stages Dickens indicated are both the major external and internal divisions. In addition, from the beginning of the serialization and continuing throughout its publication after serialization, Dickens divided the novel into three stages. The original stages corresponded with the three volumes in which the novel was published after serialization (Levit 138).[5]

Plot Development

One of Dickens' challenges in writing a novel in the form of Oliver Twist was to avoid inconsistencies, loose ends, and implausible explanations. The accelerated and uninterrupted period during which Dickens wrote Great Expectations gave him greater control than he had over Oliver Twist, the publication of which spanned twenty-seven months with two interruptions (Monod Dickens 116). Not only did Dickens fail to publish two installments of Oliver Twist because of his sister-in-law's death and his disagreement with his publishers, but he also overlapped the composition of Oliver Twist, first with The Pickwick Papers and later with Nicholas Nickleby. Although Dickens controlled his weekly serials more tightly than his longer monthly serials (Churchill 99), his plan for Great Expectations indicates that he knew when he set up the opening installments which situations he must resolve at the conclusion. Dickens states, ". . . it so opens out before

14

"Architectooralooral Details"

me that I can see the whole of a serial revolving on it, in a most singular and comic manner" (NL III 182).

Dickens' abundant reliance on coincidences to highlight the drama and to resolve the main plot lines indicates that he did not have a similar plan when he started writing Oliver Twist. He inconsistently reported the time frame for Oliver Twist by referring to both the time in which it was written (1837-1839) and to an earlier time (before 1830). Moreover, the passing seasons and years in the novel's chronology do not agree with the ages of Oliver and Rose at the conclusion (Crawford 28-30). Dickens also failed to explain two incidents which undermine Oliver's credibility. By contrast, Dickens used the opening installments of Great Expectations to set up the pivotal relationships among the characters and to introduce the novel's major themes. Perhaps unintentionally, he provided clues about the novel's time frame, and he coordinated the passage of time within the novel to the aging of his characters. Unlike its predecessor, then, Great Expectations concludes with a resolution for each plot line that incorporates earlier information without contradicting it, all within a documentable time frame.

Although Oliver Twist and Great Expectations are novels of similar length (435 pages of Oliver Twist and 458 pages of Great Expectations in the Penguin editions), Dickens needed more room to develop the plot of his earlier novel. In the first quarter of Oliver Twist, Dickens introduced most of the main incidents upon which the plot revolved. By the end of the sixth installment (of twenty-four), Oliver has fallen into the hands of a band of thieves led by Fagin, been rescued by Mr. Brownlow, and been recaptured by Fagin. Dickens also foreshadowed Oliver's bouts of illness, which he used to provide an opportunity for the narrator to explain what was happening to the other characters. In addition, Dickens introduced the coincidences which both plagued and saved Oliver. However, Dickens did not introduce the entire group of characters associated with the Maylie household before the midpoint of the novel. He waited until the thirty-third of fifty-three chapters to introduce Harry Maylie, one of the characters who makes a happy ending possible by marrying Rose.

In contrast to his slow method of unraveling the plot of Oliver Twist, Dickens developed a coherent plot from the outset of Great Expectations. By the first quarter he introduced the essential elements of his plot. He established Pip's false expectations about Miss Havisham and Estella as well as Pip's discontent with his position at the forge. By Chapter 17 (of fifty-nine, or shortly after the first quarter) Dickens provided the names or aliases of all but one of the characters and foreshadowed some of their relationships. Dickens continued Pip's ties with the convict Magwitch through the two one-pound notes which Magwitch sent to Pip at the Three Jolly Bargemen (103-7). Orlick's position with Miss Havisham after he left the forge prolonged his association with Pip after Pip left the forge. In contrast to the slow method by which Dickens introduced characters and plot lines in Oliver Twist, in Great Expectations he set up the major components of the plot early, and in so doing, he avoided the problems of inconsistencies and loose ends that he had encountered in Oliver Twist.

One problem of Oliver Twist which Dickens solved in Great Expectations was the time frame. Although Oliver Twist begins with Oliver's birth, most of the action takes place when he is ten years old. Dickens began over one-fourth of the chapters of Oliver Twist with references to time,[6] indicating his concern for the length of Oliver's trials; however, he was deliberately vague and frequently referred to "Many days" and Many weeks"[7] to indicate the passage of time. Although Dickens attacked the Poor Law Amendment Act of 1834, the new Poor Law, he inexplicably set Oliver's birth during the old system (House 95). Between Chapter 17 and Chapter 41, his descriptions of seasons closely followed the actual seasons during which they were published (Crawford 24). However, even using the unspecific references to the amount of time that passed as rough approximations, Oliver should be at least 13 at the end of the novel, instead of 12 as Mr. Grimwig states (Crawford 28). According to Coolidge, because Oliver is still a child at the end of the

15

When you use the Widow Control option, Word ensures that the first and last lines of text from a paragraph do not stand alone at the bottom or top of a page.

We'll talk more about page breaks and show you some additional techniques for keeping lines of text together on a page in the section called "Pagination" later in this chapter.

Other Page Setup Dialog Box Options

The Page Setup dialog box contains several more settings that have less impact on your overall page appearance than the settings we've introduced so far. We'll discuss some of these other settings in detail in later chapters when we address such topics as footnotes and line numbering. For now, however, let's take a quick look at the last few options in the Page Setup dialog box.

Tabs

As we mentioned in Chapter 5, Word automatically places default tab stops every $^1/_2$ inch along your ruler. These default tab stops appear on your ruler as small tick marks below the main ruler line. If you want to change the default tab positions, you can type a new value in the Default Tab Stops edit bar.

Changing the default tab stops will have no effect on any custom tabs that you may have added to your document. However, if you've used Word's default tab stops to format paragraphs in your document, those paragraphs will be reformatted when you change the value in the Default Tab Stops edit bar. For example, Figure 7-37 shows some tabular text aligned to Word's default $^1/_2$ inch tab stops. If we type the value *1* in the Default Tab Stops edit bar, Word will reformat our text, as shown in Figure 7-38. As you can see, the columns in our table are now spaced 1 inch apart, and the tick marks for the default tab stops now appear every inch along the ruler instead of every $^1/_2$ inch.

FIGURE 7-37

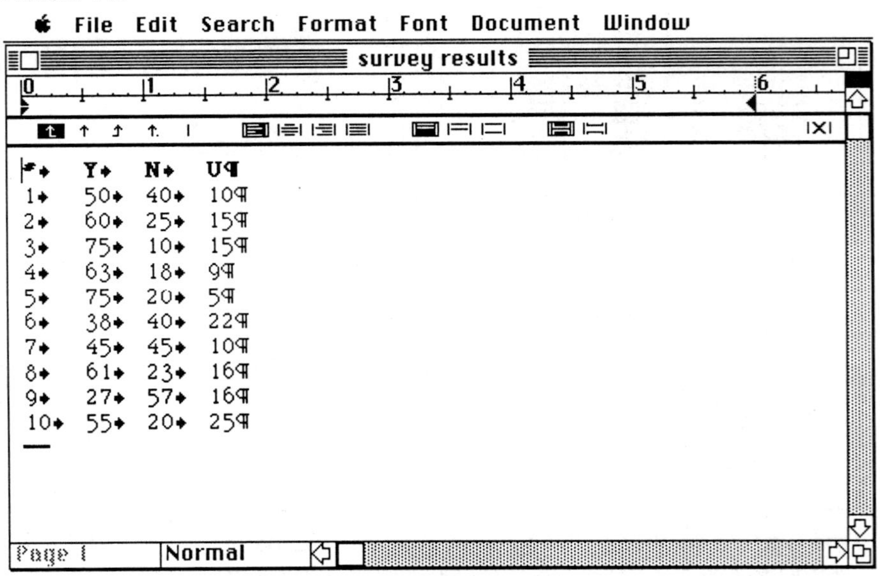

The text is aligned using Word's default $^1/_2$ inch tab stops.

FIGURE 7-38

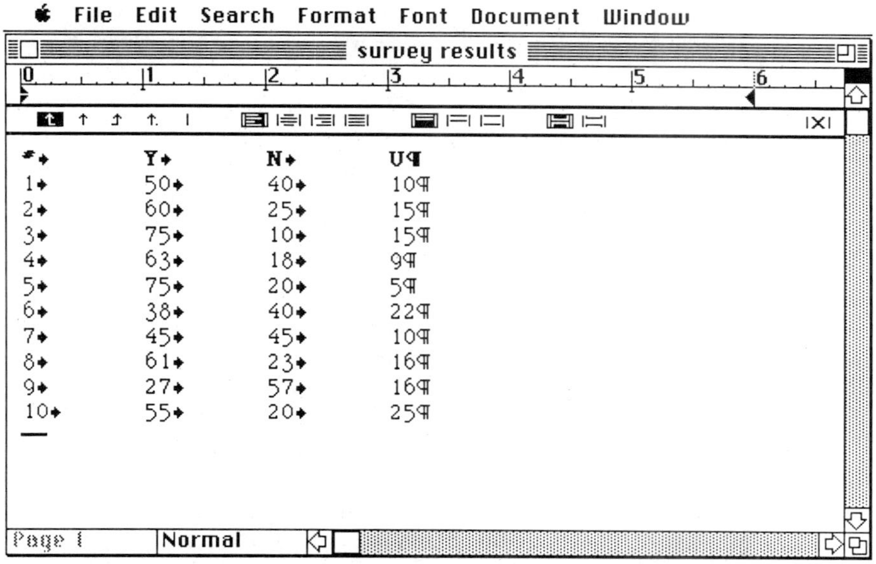

If we change the Default Tab Stops setting to 1 inch, Word will reformat our text.

Footnotes

Word offers a special facility that allows you to add footnotes to your document. When you use footnotes, you may opt to print them either at the bottom of each page or at the end of each section. You can also group all of your footnotes together at the end of the document. In addition, Word lets you control the way that foonotes are numbered. We'll show you how to use the Footnotes settings in the Page Setup dialog box when we discuss footnotes in Chapter 13.

Next File

On occasion, you may want to string together two or more document files to print consecutively. The Next File option in the Page Setup dialog box lets you do this by "linking" one document to the next. We'll talk more about the Next File option when we discuss techniques for working with long documents at the end of Chapter 8.

Page and line numbers

When you use the Next File option to string together two or more documents for printing, you'll probably want to ensure that the printed pages are numbered consecutively. You can use the Start Page Numbers at edit bar in the Page Setup dialog box to manually set a starting page number for each document in your series. We'll talk more about numbering pages in linked documents in Chapter 8.

As you will learn in Chapter 15, Word also allows you to number each line in your printed document for easy reference. When you link two or more documents for printing, and you decide to number the lines in your documents, you will probably want to ensure that the lines are numbered consecutively from one file to the next. You can use the Line Numbers at option in the Page Setup dialog box to set a starting line number for each document in your series.

THE SECTION... COMMAND

Like the Page Setup... command, which controls many page design factors, Word's Section... command contains a number of options that have global effects on your document. The Section... command, which appears under the Format menu when you're using the Full Menus setting, lets you control factors like page and line numbering, header and footer positioning, footnote positioning, and multicolumn layouts.

Before we can discuss these topics, we need to describe how you go about creating document sections. Then we'll look at page numbering and headers and footers in detail. We'll save multicolumn formatting for Chapter 8. For more on footnotes and line numbering, see Chapters 13 and 15, respectively.

Creating a New Section

To create a new section in your Word document, just click on the spot where you want the new section to begin and press the ⌘ and Enter keys. For example, consider the sample document shown in Figure 7-39. Suppose you want to start a new section, beginning with the heading *Chapter 1*. Just click in front of the character *C* at the beginning of that paragraph and press ⌘-Enter. Figure 7-40 shows the results.

FIGURE 7-39

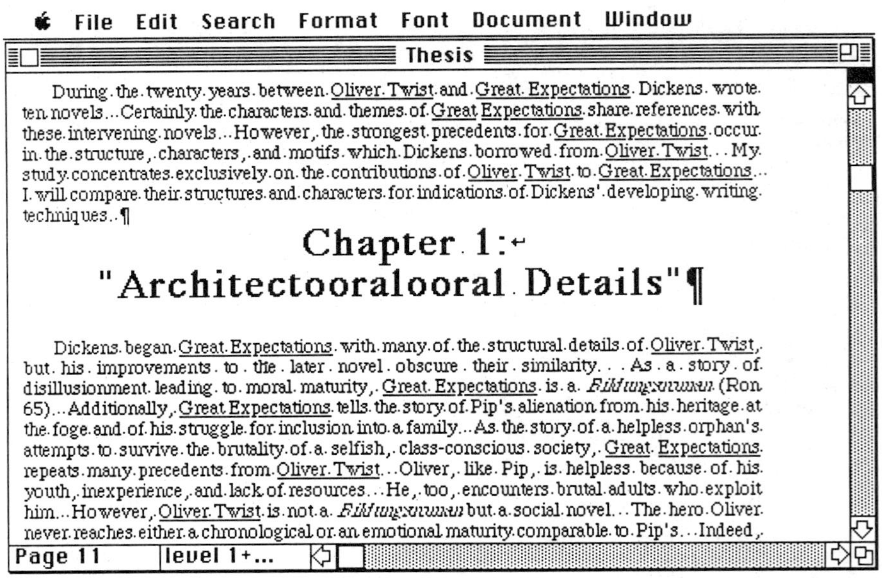

We want to start a new section beginning with the heading Chapter 1.

FIGURE 7-40

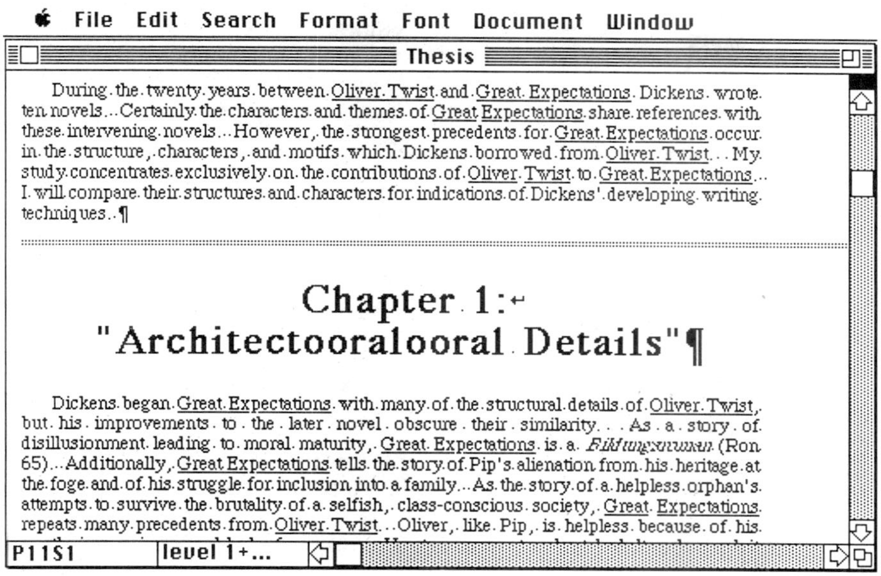

Our document is now divided into two sections.

Notice the double dotted line that appears to mark our section break. Also, notice that the page number status box at the bottom-left corner of the screen changes to display both the section and page numbers.

When you select the Section… command from the Format menu, you'll see a dialog box like the one in Figure 7-41 on the following page. As you can see, the dialog box is divided into six parts: Section Start, Page Number, Line Numbers, Header/Footer, Footnotes, and Columns. You can vary each of these settings for each section in your document.

If you do not insert any section breaks in your document, Word will treat your entire document as one section and will apply your Section dialog box settings to the entire file. When you use the ⌘ and Enter keys to begin a new section, Word will initially assign the same formats to that section as you specified for the previous section. To change the settings for a single section, just click anywhere in the section you want to work with before you select the Section… command. If you click on a section break line, your dialog box settings will apply to the section immediately above the section break.

You can also apply a Section dialog box setting to two or more adjacent sections by selecting some text in sections. As long as some portion of a section is highlighted, your Section dialog box settings will apply to that entire section. For example, to make a change to both of the sections created in Figure 7-40, all you have to do is select any part of the paragraphs that appear immediately above and below the section marker.

FIGURE 7-41

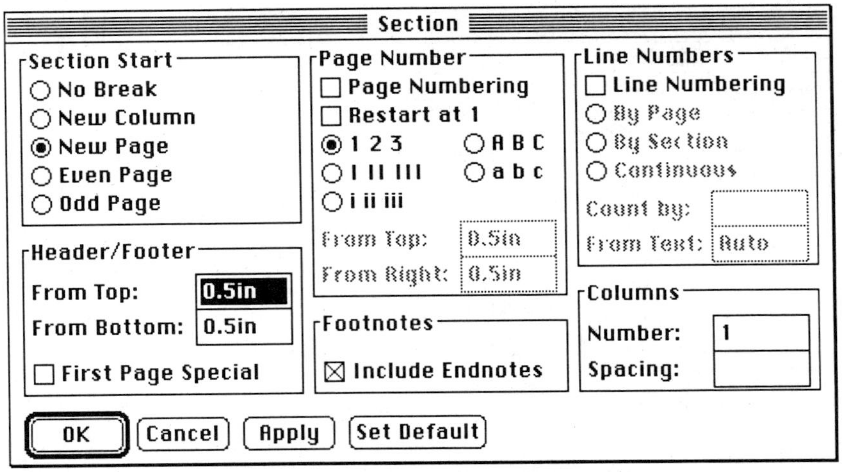

You'll see this dialog box when you issue the Section... command.

Finally, if you want to apply a Section dialog box setting to all of the sections in your document, press the ⌘ key and click in the selection bar on the left side of your screen to select the entire document before you issue the Section... command.

If you have selected two or more sections that carry different Section settings, the Section dialog box will look like the one in Figure 7-42. Notice that no options in this dialog box are selected. In addition, the check boxes are gray. Any selection you make at this point will apply to all of the selected sections. If you click on a check box option, Word will display an X in that check box to indicate that it is selected. Click on the check box a second time to deselect it. Your changes will apply to all of the selected sections.

Starting a Section

Word's Section Start options let you specify how you want each section in your document to start—that is, whether you want the first paragraph in a section to appear at the top of the next column or page or whether you want to start the section on an odd or even page.

The default Section Start setting is New Page. When the New Page setting is in effect, Word will move the paragraph immediately after the section break to the top of the next page when you print the document. For example, in the sample document shown in Figure 7-40, Word will insert a page break to ensure that the heading *Chapter 1* appears at the top of a page in the printed document. As a result, part of the previous page may be left blank.

FIGURE 7-42

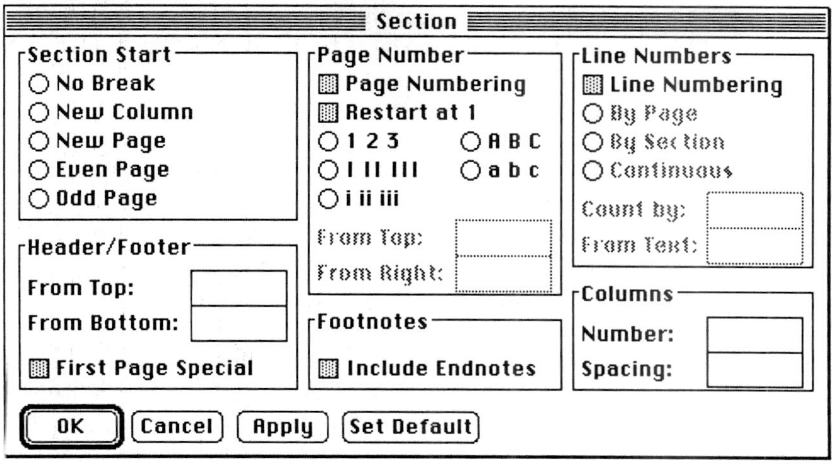

If you select two or more sections that carry different Section settings, no options will be selected in the dialog box.

If you are using the Facing Pages option in the Page Setup dialog box, you may want to use the Even Page or Odd Page option to begin new sections. For example, in books, it is common practice to begin each chapter on an odd page. If you are creating a technical publication that contains diagrams and descriptions, you may want to ensure that all of your descriptions appear on even pages while all of your diagrams appear on odd pages.

When you use the Even Page or Odd Page option, Word may insert a blank page in your printed document to "force" the first paragraph in a section to the top of the next even or odd page. For example, if one section ends on page 9, and you have used the Odd Page option to format the next section, Word will insert a blank page 10 in order to begin the next section on page 11.

If you choose the No Break option, Word will not change the position of the first paragraph after the section break. Most often you'll use the No Break option when you want to start a new column layout in the middle of a page. Similarly, the New Column option, of course, applies only if you are working in a multicolumn document. We'll talk more about this multicolumn formatting in Chapter 8.

PAGINATION

You've already learned of two ways that you can manipulate page breaks in your Word documents: with the Widow Control option in the Page Setup dialog box, and with the Section Start options in the Section dialog box. However, we haven't yet addressed how Word treats these page breaks in your document window. Since the on-screen version of your document appears as a continuous stream of text, how can you tell where page breaks will occur or on what page a given paragraph will appear?

As you've no doubt guessed by now, the status box at the bottom-left corner of your document window tells you where the text in your document window will appear when you print your document. Let's see how this status box works, then we'll show you some additional techniques for controlling page breaks in your printed documents.

The Repaginate Command

Whenever you add, delete, edit, or format text in your document, Word dims the entries in the page number status box to indicate that the displayed page number is not current. To see where your current page breaks occur, you need to select the Repaginate command from the Document menu. You'll see the page numbers flash through the status box at the bottom of your screen as Word recalculates your page breaks. When the page numbers at the bottom of your screen appear in black again, you'll know that you are seeing the current page numbers as they will appear in your printed document. You'll also see a single dotted line across the document window to flag the exact location of each page break in your printed document.

For example, in the sample screen shown in Figure 7-43, the page number at the bottom-left corner of the screen is dimmed. However, when we issue the Repaginate command, our screen will look like the one in Figure 7-44. Notice that the page number at the bottom of the screen now appears in black, and a dotted line appears between the third and fourth paragraphs to indicate that a page break occurs at this spot.

FIGURE 7-43

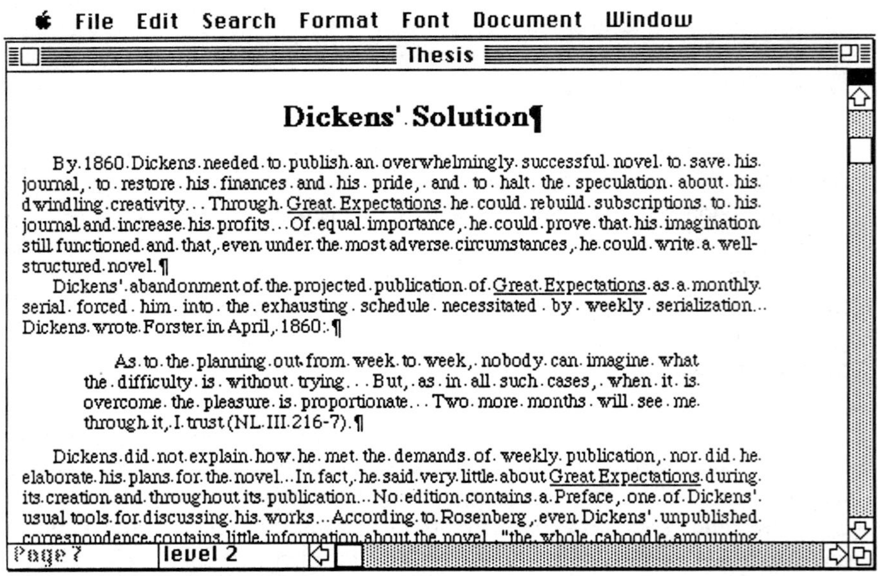

The dimmed entry indicates that the contents of our page number status box are not current.

FIGURE 7-44

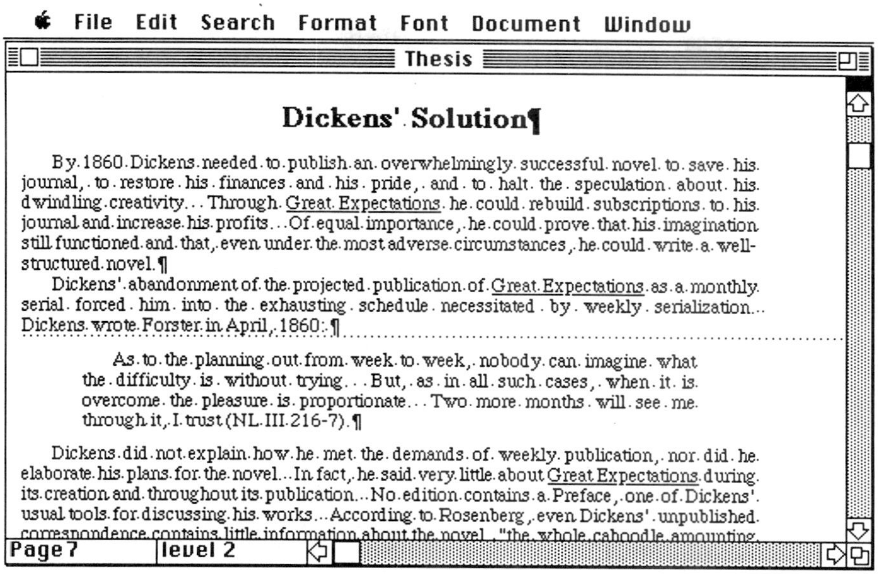

When we repaginate the document, Word will update our page numbers.

The numbers in the page number status box reflect the page on which the first line at the top of your screen will be printed. The entry in this status box will change each time one of the dotted lines that marks a page break scrolls past the top edge of the window. For example, if we scroll the eleventh line in Figure 7-44 to the top of the screen, Word will display the page number 8 in the page number status box, as shown in Figure 7-45 on the following page.

Repagination notes

To save time, when you use the Repaginate command to update the page breaks in your document, Word updates only those paragraphs that have changed since you last repaginated the document. As a result, you may notice a few idiosyncrasies when you print your document—overlapping lines of text and duplicated text, for example. These problems generally occur when you change printers or when your document contains a font that is not installed on your current System file. To overcome the problem, try pressing the Shift key as you choose Repaginate from the Document menu. The Shift key tells Word to repaginate the entire document, rather than just those paragraphs that you have revised. (By the way, you must press the Shift key before you point to the Document menu. Otherwise, Word will not repaginate all of the text in your document.)

FIGURE 7-45

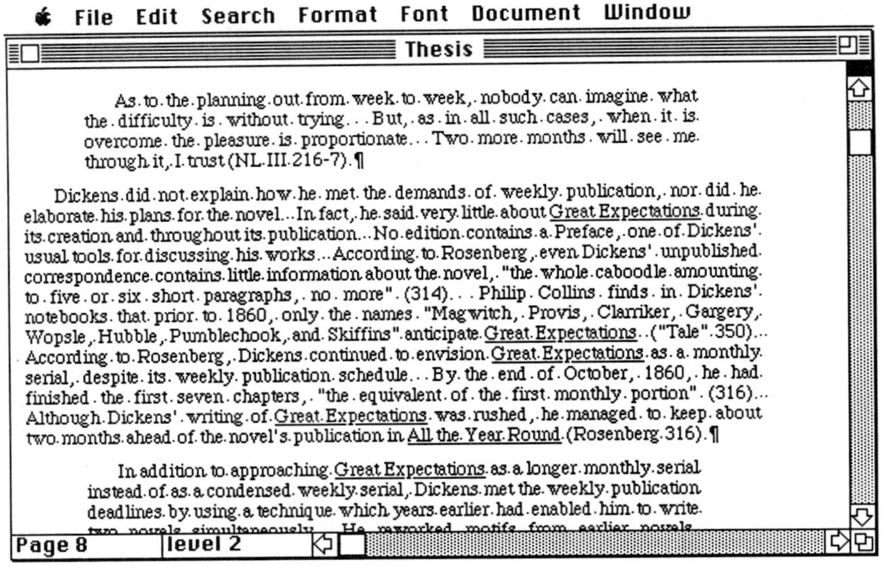

The entry in the page number status box changes each time a page break marker scrolls past the top edge of the document window.

You can press ⌘-j to issue the Repaginate command from the keyboard. However, you cannot press Shift-⌘-j to repaginate your entire document. Oddly enough, Word will not recognize your Repaginate command at all if you press Shift-⌘-j.

If your document is very long or you've made a number of changes that will affect pagination, you may find that it takes several seconds or even minutes to repaginate. For example, if you change printers or edit your margin settings in the Page Setup dialog box, Word will have to update every paragraph in your document to calculate the proper pagination. If you want to stop repagination, just press the ⌘ and period keys (⌘-.). The repagination process will halt, but any page breaks that have already been recalculated will still be accurate.

By the way, you don't have to issue the Repaginate command before you print your document. Word automatically repaginates your document whenever you issue the Print... command. (The Print Merge..., Page Preview..., Index..., and Table of Contents... commands also cause your document to be repaginated automatically.)

Manual Page Breaks

In addition to using the Section Start options in the Section dialog box to control page breaks, you can "force" page breaks in your printed document in two ways: by inserting a manual page break marker and by using the Page Break Before option in the Paragraph dialog box.

To insert a manual page break marker in your document, just click at the spot where you want the new page to begin, and press the Shift and Enter keys. Word will insert a manual page break marker after the current insertion point. Like the automatic page breaks that appear when you repaginate your document, your manual page breaks will be represented by a single dotted line. You can distinguish between the two page break markers by the density of the line; manual page break markers are slightly heavier. As we mentioned earlier, section markers appear as double dotted lines to help distinguish them from the two page break markers. Figure 7-46 compares the three marker types.

FIGURE 7-46

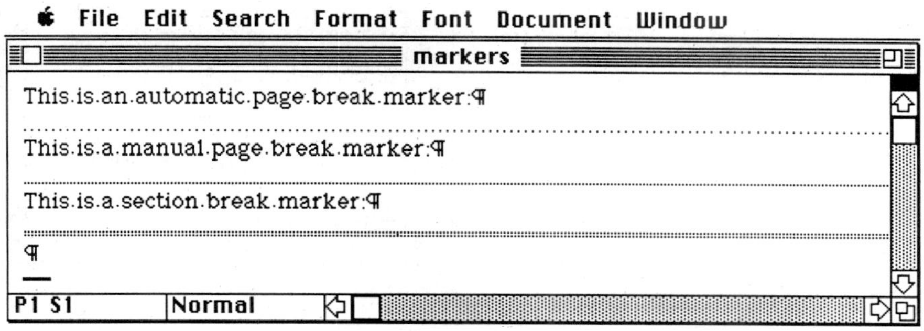

Manual page break markers are heavier than automatic page break markers.

Keep in mind that Word's automatic page break markers will change position each time you repaginate your document. Any manual page breaks that you have inserted, however, will always occur at the spot where you inserted them. For this reason, we suggest that you use manual page breaks sparingly. Otherwise, if you reformat or edit your document, these page breaks could cause unwanted gaps and awkward breaks in your printed document.

For example, in the sample document shown in Figure 7-47 on the next page, our table is split between two pages—the heading appears at the bottom of page 2, but the body of the table jumps to page 3. Since we want to make sure that the entire table appears together on one page, we'll insert a manual page break in front of the table heading and repaginate the document, as shown in Figure 7-48.

When we repaginate the document, Word removes the automatic page break marker shown in Figure 7-47. When we print the document, the table heading will appear at the top of page 3, along with the body of the table.

FIGURE 7-47

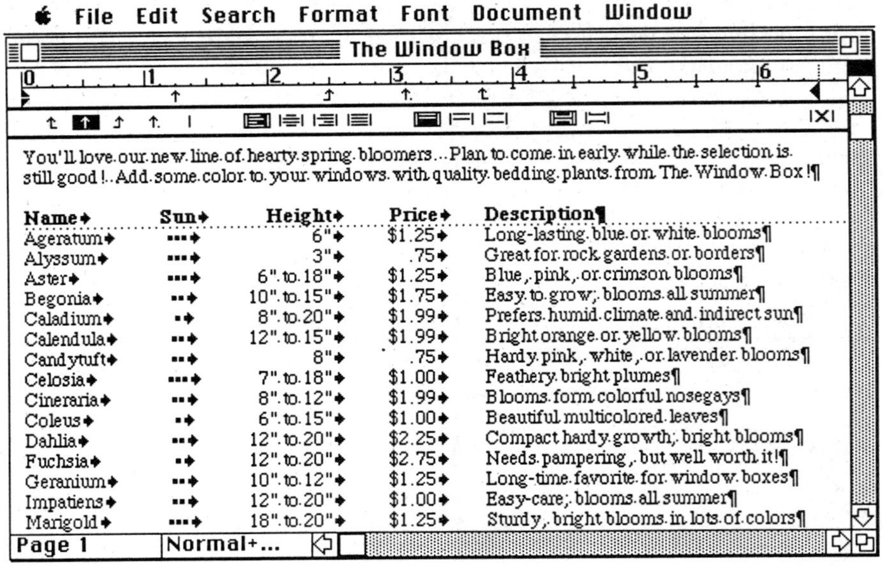

Our sample table is split between two pages.

FIGURE 7-48

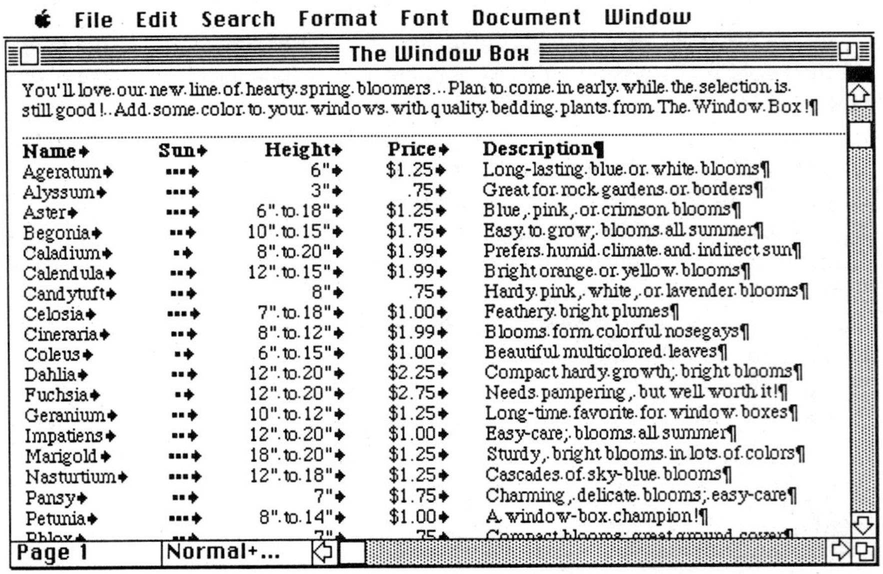

We inserted a manual page break to force the table to the top of the next page.

Now, suppose that we edit our document so that the paragraph immediately above the table occupies an additional two lines. As you can see in Figure 7-49, when we repaginate the document, two consecutive page breaks will occur above the table—one automatic and one manual. As a result, when we print the document, Word will print an extra blank page between the end of the paragraph and the beginning of the table.

FIGURE 7-49

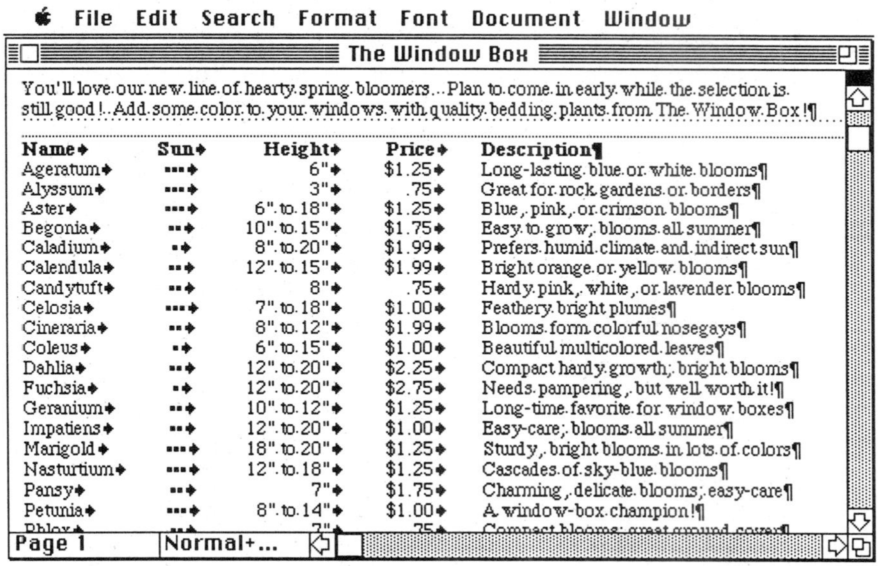

You'll love our new line of hearty spring bloomers... Plan to come in early while the selection is still good! Add some color to your windows with quality bedding plants from The Window Box!

Name	Sun	Height	Price	Description
Ageratum	•••	6"	$1.25	Long-lasting blue or white blooms
Alyssum	•••	3"	.75	Great for rock gardens or borders
Aster	•••	6" to 18"	$1.25	Blue, pink, or crimson blooms
Begonia	••	10" to 15"	$1.75	Easy to grow; blooms all summer
Caladium	•	8" to 20"	$1.99	Prefers humid climate and indirect sun
Calendula	••	12" to 15"	$1.99	Bright orange or yellow blooms
Candytuft	••	8"	.75	Hardy pink, white, or lavender blooms
Celosia	•••	7" to 18"	$1.00	Feathery bright plumes
Cineraria	••	8" to 12"	$1.99	Blooms form colorful nosegays
Coleus	•	6" to 15"	$1.00	Beautiful multicolored leaves
Dahlia	••	12" to 20"	$2.25	Compact hardy growth; bright blooms
Fuchsia	•	12" to 20"	$2.75	Needs pampering, but well worth it!
Geranium	••	10" to 12"	$1.25	Long-time favorite for window boxes
Impatiens	••	12" to 20"	$1.00	Easy-care; blooms all summer
Marigold	•••	18" to 20"	$1.25	Sturdy, bright blooms in lots of colors
Nasturtium	•••	12" to 18"	$1.25	Cascades of sky-blue blooms
Pansy	••	7"	$1.75	Charming, delicate blooms; easy-care
Petunia	•••	8" to 14"	$1.00	A window-box champion!

Our sample document now contains an extra page break, which will create an unwanted blank page in our printed document.

In short, we recommend that you use manual page breaks only when you are *sure* that you always want to start a new page at the indicated spot. If you simply want to prevent two or more blocks of text from being split between two pages, use one of Word's optional page break options, described below.

The Page Break Before option

The Page Break Before option in the Paragraph dialog box tells Word that you want the selected paragraph to appear at the top of a page. This option has exactly the same effects, and the same drawbacks, as inserting a manual page break above a paragraph.

When you assign the Page Break Before setting to a paragraph, you won't see any immediate effect on your document. No special marker will appear to flag your manual page break. The next time you repaginate the document, however, you'll see a page break marker above each paragraph that carries the Page Break Before setting. This page break will look just like the automatic page break marker that you saw earlier. However it will remain in place until you reissue the Paragraph... command and deselect the Page Break Before option, even if you insert or delete text in your document.

The Page Break Before option has one major advantage over the Shift-Enter technique described above: Your manual page break is permanently "attached" to the selected paragraph, just like any other paragraph format. If you use the Cut or Copy and Paste commands to copy or move the paragraph to another location in your document, the Page Break Before format will automatically move with the paragraph. You don't have to worry about copying or moving the manual page break marker as well.

Like the New Page option in the Section dialog box, you'll find the Page Break Before option convenient for formatting major headings in your document. For example, suppose you want to ensure that all of the chapter titles in your document begin at the top of a new page.. If your document is comprised of only one section, you won't be able to use the New Page option in the Section dialog box to create these page breaks. You can, however, use the Page Break Before option to format each of your chapter title paragraphs. You'll find this technique quite convenient when you are using style sheets to define your text formats, as described in Chapter 9.

Keeping text together

We explained earlier in this chapter how you can prevent widows in your documents by using the Widow Control option in the Page Setup dialog box. You'll also find two options in the Paragraph dialog box that help you control awkward page breaks: Keep With Next ¶ and Keep Lines Together. The Keep With Next ¶ option prevents breaks between paragraphs, while the Keep Lines Together option prevents breaks within paragraphs. We refer to these settings as optional page break options since they go into effect only as needed, much like the optional hyphens you learned about in Chapter 6.

When you want two adjacent paragraphs to be printed on the same page, just assign the Keep With Next ¶ setting to the first paragraph. For example, in the sample table that we showed you in Figure 7-47, you could assign the Keep With Next ¶ format to the table heading to ensure that it is not separated from the body of the table.

Keep in mind that the Keep With Next ¶ setting does not guarantee that all of the lines in each paragraph will remain on the same page. If you have selected the Widow Control option in the Page Setup dialog box, Word will make certain that at least two lines from each paragraph appear together on a page. If you have deselected the Widow Control option, Word will ensure that at least one line from each paragraph will appear on the same page.

For example, suppose you want part of the first paragraph shown in Figure 7-50 to appear on the same page as the quotation that follows. If you assign the Keep With Next ¶ setting to the introductory paragraph and then repaginate the document, your screen will look like the one in Figure 7-51. Notice that the last two lines of the introductory paragraph now appear just below the page break line. When you print this document, these two lines, along with the quotation paragraph, will appear at the top of page 21. (Because the Widow Control option is activated in the Page Setup dialog box, Word placed two lines of the introductory paragraph—instead of just one line—at the top of the new page.) By the way, when you assign the Keep With Next ¶ setting to a paragraph, Word will not change your page breaks until you repaginate.

If you want both paragraphs to appear together on the same page in their entirety, you must assign the Keep Lines Together setting to both paragraphs as well. The Keep Lines Together option ensures that all of the lines of a paragraph are printed on the same page. If Word does not have room for an entire paragraph at the bottom of one page, it will push the entire paragraph forward to the beginning of the next page.

FIGURE 7-50

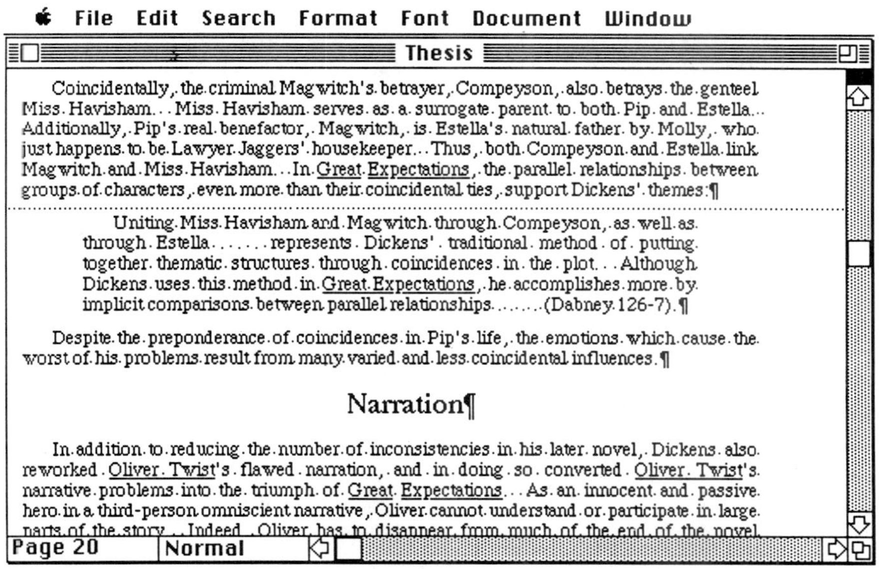

We want to keep the introductory paragraph and quotation together on the same page.

FIGURE 7-51

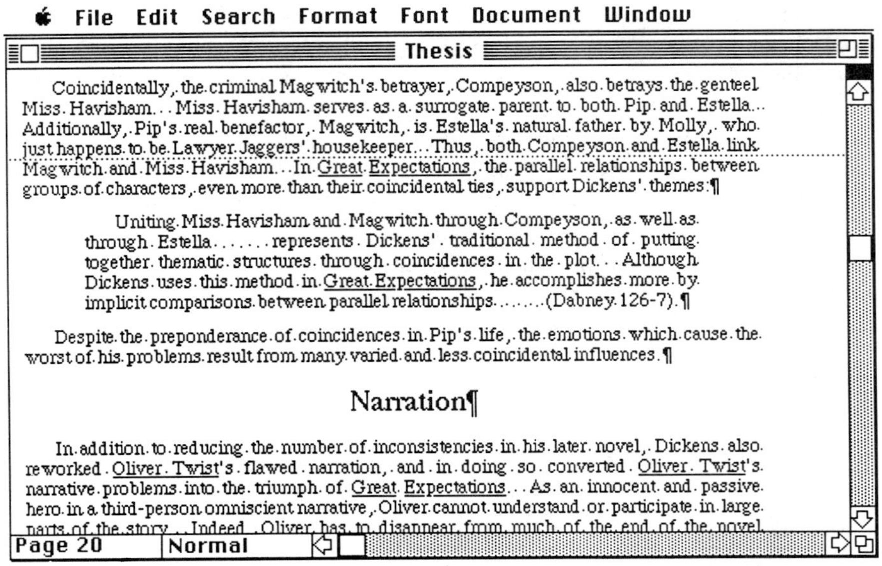

If we assign the Keep With Next ¶ setting to the introductory paragraph, Word will ensure that at least two lines from that paragraph appear on the same page as the quotation.

For example, if we assign the Keep Lines Together setting to the introductory paragraph shown in Figure 7-51, our repaginated document will look like the one in Figure 7-52. Notice that the introductory paragraph now begins at the top of page 21.

Generally, you'll apply the Keep With Next ¶ setting to single paragraphs in your document to ensure that they are not separated from the paragraph immediately below. However, if you want to ensure that three or more paragraphs appear together on the same page, just assign the Keep With Next ¶ setting to all but the last paragraph in the series.

If you apply the Keep With Next ¶ and/or Keep Lines Together settings to a block of text that is too long to fit on one page, Word will keep as much of the block together as it can. However, the program may have to allow some text to flow over to the next page if it cannot make room on the current page for all of your text.

FIGURE 7-52

If we assign the Keep Lines Together setting to the introductory paragraph, Word will push the entire paragraph forward to the top of page 21.

Adding Page Numbers to Your Printed Document

Unless you specifically instruct it to do so, Word will not automatically add page numbers to each page of your printed document. There are two ways to add these page numbers: with the Page Numbering option in the Section dialog box or with headers and footers. Let's talk first about Word's Page Number settings, then we'll take a look at headers and footers.

To add page numbers to your printed document, just issue the Section... command and select the Page Numbering option in the Page Number portion of the dialog box. When you select the Page Numbering option, the dimmed From Right and From Top edit bars will become active. Initially, your page numbers will appear in the top-right corner of each page—$^1/_2$ inch from the top and right edges of the paper—as shown in Figure 7-53 on the next page.

However, you can edit the contents of the From Right and From Top edit bars to position your page numbers anywhere you like. For example, if you want your page numbers to appear $^1/_2$ inch from the bottom of the page, you might change your From Top setting to 8; if you want your page numbers to appear in the center of the page, you might enter a From Right setting of 4.25.

FIGURE 7-53

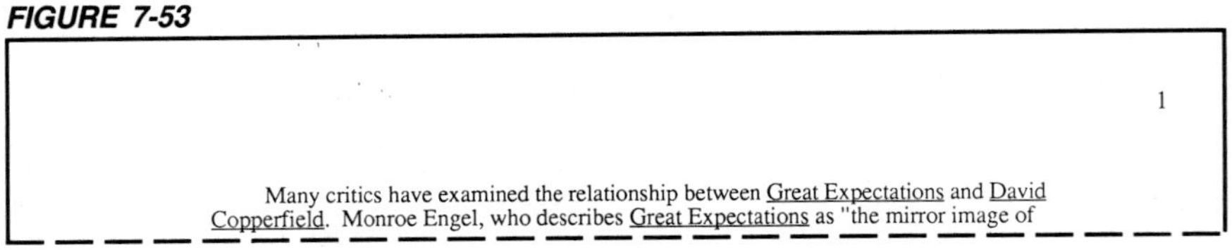

When you choose the Page Numbering option, Word will add a page number in the top-right corner of your printed page.

If you have selected the Facing Pages option in the Page Setup dialog box, Word will interpret your From Right setting as a From Left setting when it prints even numbered pages. In other words, the position of your page numbers will be reversed on even pages because Word assumes that you always want your page numbers to appear on the outside edge of the page.

For example, Figure 7-54 shows a pair of facing pages that have been numbered using Word's default From Right and From Top settings. Notice that the page number on the odd page appears in its usual position, but the page number on the even page appears $^1/_2$ inch from the left edge of the paper.

FIGURE 7-54

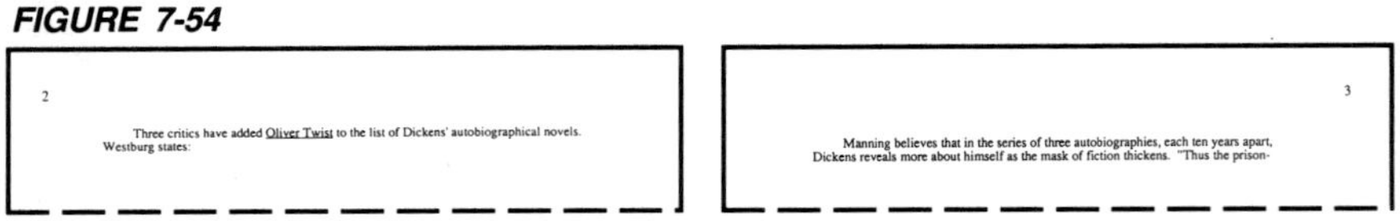

When you use the Facing Pages option, Word positions even page numbers relative to the left side of the page.

Keep in mind that your Page Number settings will apply only to the current section. If you have created more than one document section, you'll probably want to apply the Page Numbering option to each section. As you'll see in a moment, you can use different numbering schemes for each section if you like.

Numbering schemes

Now that we've discussed different techniques for controlling page breaks and adding page numbers to your Word documents, let's take a look at the various schemes that you can use to number the pages in your printed document. You'll find five numbering schemes in the Page Number portion in the Section dialog box, as shown in Table 7-3.

TABLE 7-3

Number style	Appears as
Arabic	1 2 3 4 5 6
Upper-case Roman	I II III IV V VI
Lower-case Roman	i ii iii iv v vi
Upper-case alphabetic	A B C D E F
Lower-case alphabetic	a b c d e f

Word offers five numbering schemes.

You can apply different numbering schemes to each section in your document by clicking anywhere in the section you want to work with, issuing the Section... command, and selecting a numbering option. You can also use the Restart at 1 option in any section to restart your page numbers from the beginning of the selected sequence (1, I, i, A, or a).

If you change numbering schemes in one of your document sections, you'll almost certainly want to apply the Restart at 1 option to that section. For example, suppose you have used the lower-case Roman setting (i, ii, iii, iv…) to number the table of contents and other front matter for your document. This section occupies ten pages, which are numbered i to x. Then, when you reach the first chapter of the document, you apply the Arabic numbering option (1, 2, 3…). If you don't choose the Restart at 1 option for this new section, your page numbers will start at 11 rather than at 1.

If you use one of the alphabetic numbering schemes in a section that is more then 26 pages long, Word will use the characters AA, BB, CC, and so forth, for pages 27 though 52. Pages 53 through 78 will be numbered AAA, BBB, CCC, and so forth.

By the way, Word always displays your page numbers in the same formats as your document's *Normal* style. New York, 12-point, plain format. To change the character format of your page numbers, you can use the style sheet, described in Chapter 9.

Specifying a page range for printing

As we mentioned earlier in this chapter, specifying page numbers can get a little tricky when your document contains several sections with different numbering schemes.

For example, suppose you have created a document that uses a numbering scheme like the one shown in Table 7-4. You want to print page B from the fifth section of the document, the appendix. How can you go about specifying a page range without adding up all of your pages to determine the actual page value for page B in the appendix? Chances are, you won't know the correct number for the page you want to print. Fortunately, when Word repaginates a multisection document, it provides you with both the section number and the page number for each page. For example, the first page in the Introduction would be numbered *Pi S1* in the page number status box at the bottom of your screen. The first page in Chapter 1 would be labeled *P1 S2*. Since we did not restart numbering with page 1 in Chapters 2 and 3, the first pages of these chapters would be labeled *P28 S3* and *P60 S4*, respectively. Finally, the first page in the appendix would be labeled *PA S5*.

TABLE 7-4

Section	Name	Numbered	Actual Page Count
1	Introduction	i to xi	1 to 11
2	Chapter 1	1 to 27	12 to 38
3	Chapter 2	28 to 59	39 to 70
4	Chapter 3	60 to 93	71 to 104
5	Appendix	A to L	105 to 116

This table shows a complex numbering scheme for a multisection document.

When you specify a page range in the Page Setup dialog box, you can enter page values like P23 S2 and P2 S5 in the From and To edit bars. (You can drop the *P* if you like and simply enter 23 S2 or 2 S5, and you don't have to type the space between the page number and the section number.)

Unfortunately, you must use Arabic numbers in the From and To edit bars. If one of your document sections uses alphabetic or Roman numerals, you'll have to translate those page number values for Word. In other words, to print page B from Section 5 of your document, you have to enter the value P2 S5 in the From and To edit bars. If you try to type PB S2 or B S2, Word will beep and refuse to accept your entry.

The Go To... command

The same numbering rules apply in Word's Go To... dialog box. When you want to go to a specific page in a multisection document, you can select the GoTo... command from the Search menu and enter a value like P2 S5 in the Page Number edit bar. However, you cannot enter alphabetic or Roman characters like Pi S1 or PA S5.

By the way, keep in mind that Word does not automatically repaginate your document when you issue the Go To... command. If you want to be sure that you are going to the correct page, remember to issue the Repaginate command before you issue the Go To... command.

HEADERS AND FOOTERS

You see headers and footers in just about every book, magazine, and other publication you read. Generally, headers and footers serve as guideposts for the reader, carrying information such as page numbers and the name of the publication. Longer publications sometimes have variable headers and footers that reflect the names of sections and chapters as well. On dated materials, like periodicals or technical materials that are subject to frequent updates, information such as the date of publication and volume and issue numbers commonly appear in the header or footer.

Word offers the most flexible system we've seen for creating, formatting, and editing headers and footers. In Word, headers and footers can carry any character and paragraph formats you choose and can be as short as a single character or as long as several paragraphs. You can also vary the appearance and content of headers and footers for odd and even pages and even control the appearance of headers and footers on the first page of a document or section.

In this section, we'll show you how to add headers and footers to your document and how to use the Section... and Page Setup... commands to integrate headers and footers into your page layout. In the next section of this chapter, you'll also see how you can use the Page Preview screen to quickly reposition headers and footers.

As their names imply, headers generally appear at the top of each page in your document while footers appear at the bottom. However, Word allows you to control the positioning of headers and footers so that you can place them anywhere on the printed page.

One difference between Word 3 and previous versions of the program is that the headers and footers that you create do not actually appear in your document window. Instead, they are tucked out of sight in separate windows that are stored along with your document when you save it to disk. Let's get started by creating a sample header, then we'll look at some of the handy tools that Word offers for tailoring headers and footers to fit your publication needs.

The steps that you follow to create, format, and position footers are almost identical to those you follow to create, format, and position headers. If you know how to work with headers, you will be able to work with footers as well. Therefore, in this section, we will illustrate Word's header and footer techniques with examples that focus mainly on headers. However, we'll address any minor differences relating to footers as they arise.

A Brief Tour

To add a header or footer to your document, begin by selecting the Open Header... or Open Footer... command from the Document menu. A small window will appear at the bottom of your screen. If you're using the Short Menus setting, your header window will look like the one in Figure 7-55. If you are using Full Menus, your header window will look like the one in Figure 7-56. Notice that Word adds a Same as Previous button to the header window when you're using the Full Menus setting.

FIGURE 7-55

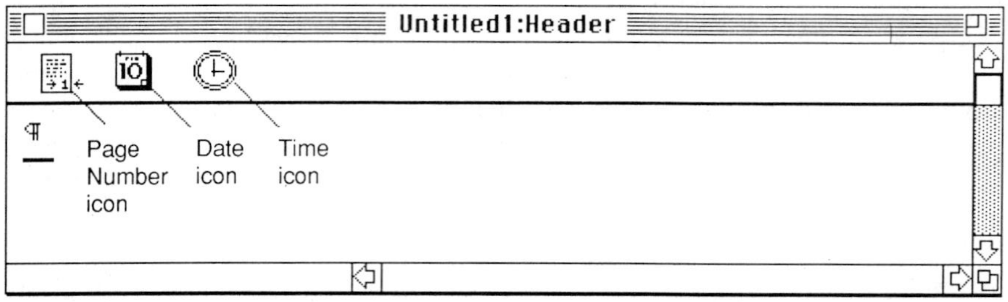

If you're using Short Menus, your header window will look like this.

FIGURE 7-56

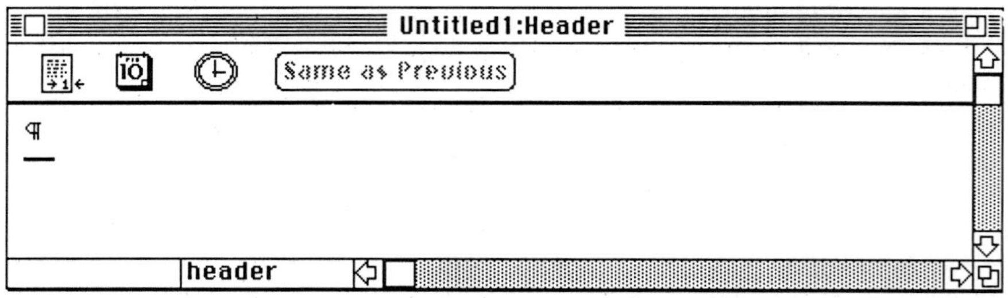

If you're using Full Menus, Word will add a Same as Previous button to your header window.

Also, notice that your insertion point marker initially appears at the first character space in this empty window, much as it does in a new document window. The horizontal bar that currently appears just below the insertion point serves as an end mark—just like the one you see in your document window.

In most ways, this header window functions just like a standard document window. It has a title bar, a close box and zoom box, scroll bars, and a size box. You can use the Show ¶ and Show Ruler commands in this window, just as you do in a standard document window. A pair of status boxes even appears at the bottom of the window. Though you won't see page numbers in the status box in the left corner of the window, you can use this area to make glossary entries (described in Chapter 10) and to perform other actions, just as you do in your document window.

The title bar in this window displays the name of the document to which the header is attached, as well as the word *Header*, to help you identify the contents of the window. (Obviously, in a footer window you'll see the word *Footer*.) If your document is divided into sections, you'll also see notations like *(S1)* and *(S2)* that tell you which section's header you're working with. As you'll see when we talk about odd, even, and first page headers, Word also tells you what type of header you are working with.

At the top of the header window, you'll find three new icons and a new button option. As you'll see in a few moments, you can use the page number, date, and time icons to add dynamic page numbers, dates, and times to your headers and footers. The Same as Previous button, which appears only when the Full Menus setting is in effect, does not come into play unless you have created variable headers or footers. We'll talk more about this option in a few pages.

A new footer window looks exactly like the header windows we've shown, except for two minor details. As we've mentioned, the word *Footer* appears in the window's title bar. In addition, you'll see the name *footer* in the style status box in the lower-left corner of the window. (As we explain in Chapter 9, Word automatically creates the styles named *header* and *footer*, which you can use to format your header and footer text.)

Creating a Header

First let's type some data into our empty header window and see how we go about formatting that information. Let's suppose we are creating a project proposal called *Managing Computer Documentation Projects*, and we want the name of the report to appear at the top of each page. We'll begin by typing the phrase *Managing Computer Documentation Projects* in the empty header window, as shown in Figure 7-57.

FIGURE 7-57

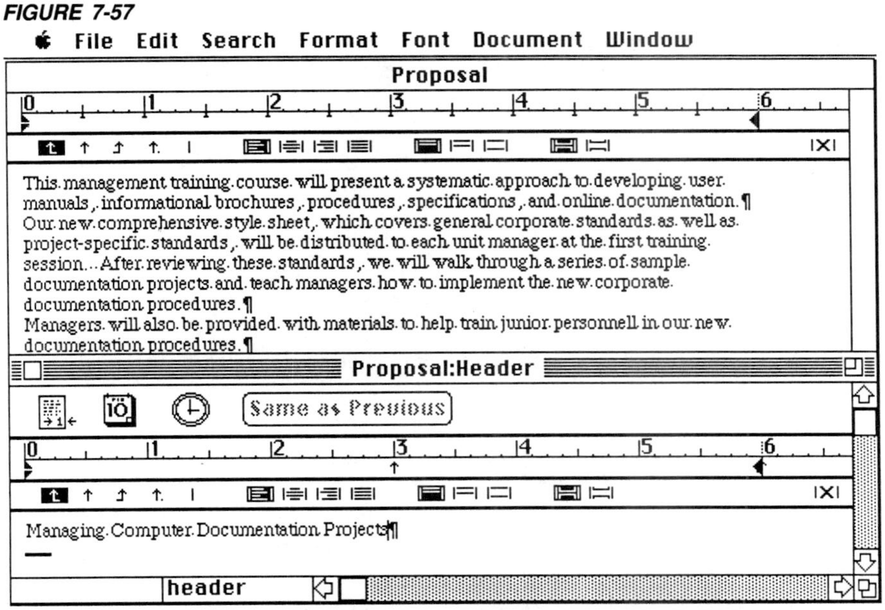

To add a header to your document, just type the text you want to use in the header window.

Notice that the text of the header initially appears in Word's default style: 12-point, New York, plain. If you use the Show Ruler command to turn on the ruler display in the header window, as we have done in Figure 7-57, you'll also see that the header's paragraph formats are initially flush left, with a centered tab at 3 inches and a right-aligned tab at 6 inches. At this point, our right indent marker falls at the 6 inch mark since we are using Word's default Page Setup dialog box specifications. Of course, your ruler settings in the header window will vary according to the Page Setup options you specify, just as they do in your document window. (See page 260 in this chapter for more on the relationship between margins settings and the ruler.) If you are using style sheets, which we'll discuss in Chapter 9, your header will initially appear in the style that you have defined as *Normal* to match the text you are using in the body of your document. However, as we'll demonstrate in a moment, you can change the format of the header at any time.

Though we'll certainly want to do some more work on this sample header, let's pause here for a moment to see what happens when we print the document. To save our new header text, all we need to do is click the close box in the header window title bar. Word will remove the header window from the screen and reactivate the document window.

As you can see in Figure 7-58, when we print the sample document, our header appears $^{1}/_{2}$ inch from the top of the page. The body of our document begins $^{1}/_{2}$ inch below the header, 1 inch from the top of the page. Notice also that the header begins 1 $^{1}/_{4}$ inches from the left side of the page, in alignment with our body text.

FIGURE 7-58

Managing Computer Documentation Projects

This management training course will present a systematic approach to developing user manuals, informational brochures, procedures, specifications, and online documentation.

The header initially appears $^{1}/_{2}$ inch from the top of the page, left-aligned with your body text.

Formatting and Positioning the Header Text

Now, suppose we want to reformat our header text to appear in 12-point, Helvetica, bold type, centered in the middle of the page. All we need to do is select the text and format it, just as we would in a document window. We'll begin by clicking in the invisible selection bar on the left side of the header window to select the entire line, then we'll issue the Character... command and select the Helvetica and Bold settings from the Character dialog box. Next, we'll click on the centered alignment icon on the header window ruler. Figure 7-59 shows the results.

FIGURE 7-59

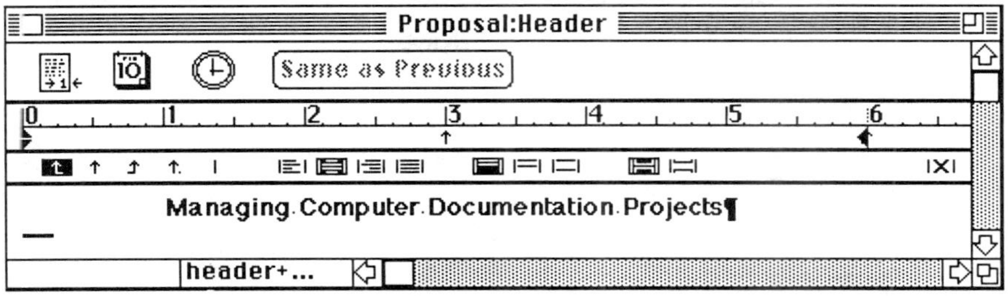

We have formatted our header to appear in 12-point, Helvetica, bold type with centered alignment.

As you can see in Figure 7-60, when we print our sample document with this header in place, Word will center our formatted header text between the left and right page margins.

FIGURE 7-60

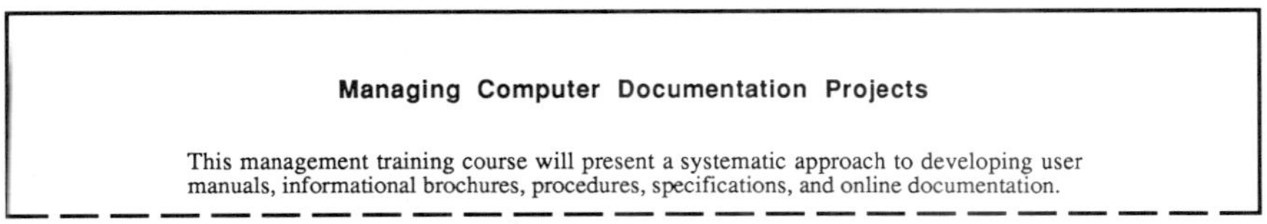

Managing Computer Documentation Projects

This management training course will present a systematic approach to developing user manuals, informational brochures, procedures, specifications, and online documentation.

Our formatted header text is centered between our page margins.

Similarly, if you want to align your header text to the right side of the page, just click on the right alignment icon. If you're creating a multiline header, you may want to use the justified setting to align the left and right margins of your header text. Borders can also jazz up your headers and help separate them from your body text.

Placing headers in the left and right margins

There may be occasions when you want your header text to appear in your document margins rather than aligned with your main document text. For example, in the sample page shown in Figure 7-61, our header consists of the document title and the current date, and we've placed this header in the left margin of the page. (We'll show you how to add a date to a header in a few pages.) To create this header, we used a left indent of -1 inch, as shown in the header window in Figure 7-62.

FIGURE 7-61

6/12/87
Update

This update replaces all previous procedures, policies, and instructions for operation of the CSHS Automated Security Control System. Please remove pages 1-23 through 1-36 from your CSHS user manual and replace them with these updated pages.

You can place headers and footers in the left and right margins.

FIGURE 7-62

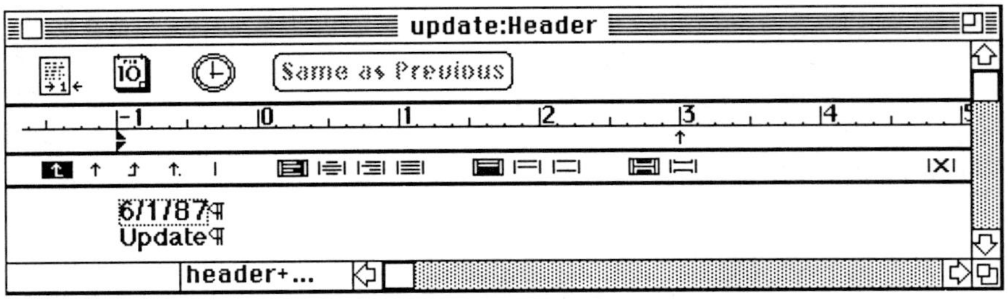

We used a negative left indent to format this header.

To create the negative indent, you must press the Shift key before dragging the first-line and left indent markers to the left of the zero point on the ruler. Similarly, if you want to place your header in the right margin of the printed page, just drag the right indent marker to the right, then move the first-line and left indent markers past the dotted line that marks your right margin. Keep in mind that the horizontal scroll bar is active only when the Full Menus setting is in effect. Therefore, before you can drag your indent markers to the left of the zero point or to the right of the 6 $^3/_4$ inch mark, you must select Full Menus from the Edit menu. (For more on changing a paragraph's left and right indents, see Chapter 5.)

Multiline headers

Notice that the sample header in Figure 7-62 is two lines long. As we hinted earlier, your header (or footer) can contain as many lines of text as you like. For example, you might want to create your company's letterhead in the header window, as shown in Figure 7-63. Figure 7-64 shows the resulting printed header.

Notice that Word automatically expands the top margin of our document to make room for our long header. The first line of text in our document, which normally starts 1 inch from the top of the page, now appears about 1 $^3/_4$ inches from the top of the page. If we take a look at our Page Setup box for this document, however, we'll see that Word has not changed our default Top margin setting of 1 inch. You'll see a similar situation when you create a multiline footer. Word will automatically expand the bottom margin of your document to accommodate the footer text. However, your Bottom Margin setting in the Page Setup dialog box will not change.

Notice that Word does not add any extra white space between the header and the first line of text. If you want to insert extra space between the header and the first line of text in your document, you'll need to manually change your Top margin setting in the Page Setup dialog box. This brings us to the next topic: controlling the vertical positioning of your headers.

FIGURE 7-63

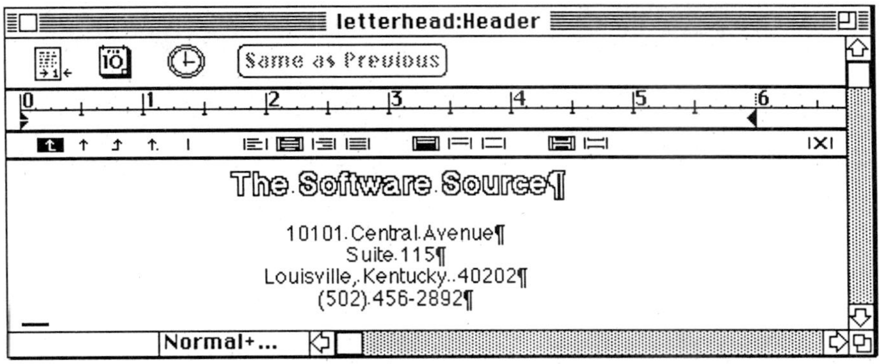

Your header can contain more than one line of text.

FIGURE 7-64

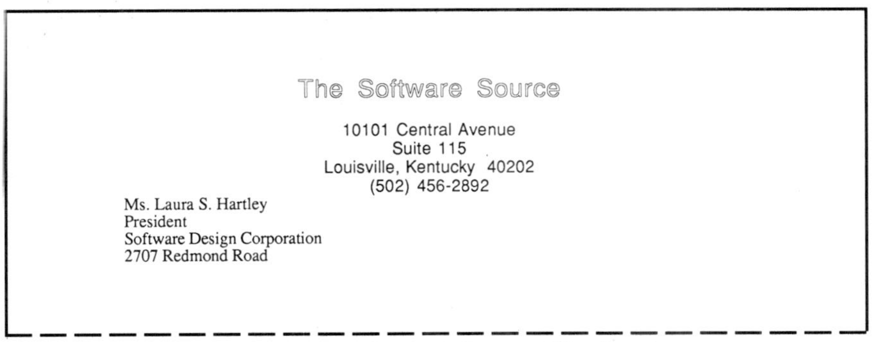

Word expands the top margin to make room for a multiline header.

Vertical positioning

As you've seen, you can use the ruler in the header window to alter the horizontal positioning and alignment of your header. However, we haven't shown yet how you can move the header vertically on the page. The distance between the top of the page and the first line of your header is controlled by the From Top setting in the Header/Footer portion of the Section dialog box. As you already know, the distance between the top of the page and the first line of regular text on the page is controlled by the Top margin setting in the Page Setup dialog box. Similarly, the distance between the bottom of the page and the last line of your footer is controlled by the From Bottom setting in the Section dialog box, and the distance between the bottom of the page and the last line of regular text on the page is controlled by the Bottom margin setting.

The default From Top setting in the Section dialog box is $^{1}/_{2}$ inch, while the default Top margin setting in the Page Setup dialog box is 1 inch. This leaves $^{1}/_{2}$ inch between the header and the first line of text in your document. However, as you saw in Figure 7-64, if your header takes up more than one line, Word will expand the top margin to make room for the header.

Suppose we decide to add some extra space between the top of the page and the first line of our header in the sample page shown in Figure 7-64. All we have to do is issue the Section... command and type a new value—1.5, for example—in the From Top edit bar. Figure 7-65 shows the results.

FIGURE 7-65

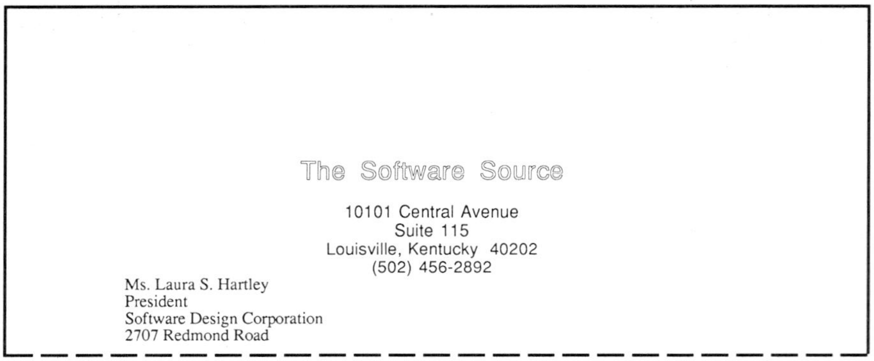
The Software Source

10101 Central Avenue
Suite 115
Louisville, Kentucky 40202
(502) 456-2892

Ms. Laura S. Hartley
President
Software Design Corporation
2707 Redmond Road

You can use the From Top setting in the Section dialog box to add extra white space above your header.

As you can see, Word adds an extra inch between the top of the page and the first line of our header. Word also moves the first line of text in our sample document down an inch to make room for our expanded header space.

Now, suppose we want to add some extra white space between the last line of the header and the first line of text on our sample page. All we need to do is issue the Page Setup... command and enter a new value in the Top edit bar. Since our header occupies a total of about 2 $^{3}/_{4}$ inches, we might set our top margin to 3 $^{1}/_{4}$ inches (you would type 3.25 in the Top edit bar) to add an additional $^{1}/_{2}$ inch between the bottom of the header and the top of the text area.

Using the Before and After settings

In addition to changing the From Top and From Bottom settings in the Section dialog box, you can alter the distance between your header and footer text and the edge of the page by using the Before and After settings in the Paragraph dialog box. For example, to open up more space between your header and the top of the page, select the first paragraph of header text, then choose Paragraph... from the Format menu. In the Paragraph dialog box, enter a number—such as 12—in the Before edit bar, then click OK. Word will automatically allow 12 points of space above your header text—in addition to the amount of space specified in the From Top edit bar of the Section dialog box. As usual, Word will also expand the top margin to make room for the additional space that you've inserted in the header.

Similarly, you can add more space between a header or footer and the body text of a document by using the Before and After settings. For example, suppose you would like to insert another $^1/_4$ inch of space between your footer and the last line of document text on each page. Begin by selecting the first paragraph of your footer text, then open the Paragraph dialog box. Type an 18 in the Before edit bar, then click OK. Word will add 18 points of space ($^1/_4$ inch) above the footer text and expand the bottom margin to accommodate the extra space. (For more on the Before and After settings in the Paragraph dialog box, see Chapter 5.)

Placing headers in the text area

Though it is convenient that Word automatically adjusts your top margin to make room for long headers, you may occasionally want to override this automatic adjustment to enter your header below the top margin of the page. In other words, you may want to place your header in your text area. For example, consider the sample header that we created in Figure 7-61. We assigned a negative 1-inch left indent to this header so that we could print it in the left margin of the page.

Now, suppose we want both the header and the first line of text to begin 1 inch from the top of the page. As you learned in the previous examples, if you simply expand the amount of space that you allot to the header, Word will move your first line of text down to accommodate your larger header area. To override Word's automatic top margin adjustment, we'll begin by issuing the Section... command and typing a 1 in the From Top edit bar to place the header 1 inch from the top of the page.

Now, to ensure that our header appears even with the first line of text in this sample document, we need to issue the Page Setup... command and specify a Top margin setting of -1 inch. By typing -1 in the Top edit bar of the Page Setup dialog box, we're not telling Word that we want to create a negative margin—the minus sign simply indicates that we want to make our 1-inch margin setting absolute. This absolute margin setting prevents Word from adjusting the top margin to accommodate the header.

Figure 7-66 shows the resulting printed page. Notice that our header and body text are now evenly aligned 1 inch from the top of the page. (By the way, we also expanded our Left margin setting in the Page Setup dialog box to 1.75 to make room for our header in the left margin.)

FIGURE 7-66

6/10/87
Update

This update replaces all previous procedures, policies, and instructions for operation of the CSHS Automated Security Control System. Please remove pages 1-23 through 1-36 from your CSHS user manual and replace them with these updated pages.

Both the header and text now appear 1 inch from the top of the page.

Formatting headers and footers with the style sheet

As we have shown, it's very easy to select and format text in a header window; the process is no different from selecting and formatting text in your main document window. However, as you'll learn in Chapter 9, you also can format your header text by altering the definition of the style named *header* on your style sheet. (Word automatically adds this style to the style sheet whenever you create a header.) Similarly, you can format the text in a footer window by using either manual formatting techniques or by altering the *footer* style on the style sheet. If you've used different headers and footers for different sections of a document (we'll show you how to do this in a few pages), the *header* and *footer* styles will apply to all sections. In other words, Word does not create a separate style to format the header and footer of each new section. In some cases, you can use this to your advantage. When your document contains variable headers and/or footers, you can format all of them consistently simply by changing the *header* or *footer* style instructions. In situations where you want to use a different format for the headers and footers of each section, however, you're probably better off using manual formatting techniques.

Adding Dates, Times, and Page Numbers

As you've probably guessed by now, the icons at the top of the header window let you insert the current page number, date, and time into your header text. (These icons are also available in the footer window.) All three of these elements are dynamic; that is, Word updates the date and time whenever you open the header window or print your document so that they remain current. (By the way, you can use the Alarm Clock desk accessory to adjust the date and time settings.) The page number that appears in the header window reflects the number of the page that is currently being displayed in your document window. Of course, when you print the document, the page number entry will change for each page in the document.

To insert a dynamic date, time, or page number entry into your header text, just click at the spot where you want the date or time to appear, then click on the appropriate icon at the top of the header window. For example, Figure 7-67 shows a sample header in which we've entered the date, time, and page number.

FIGURE 7-67

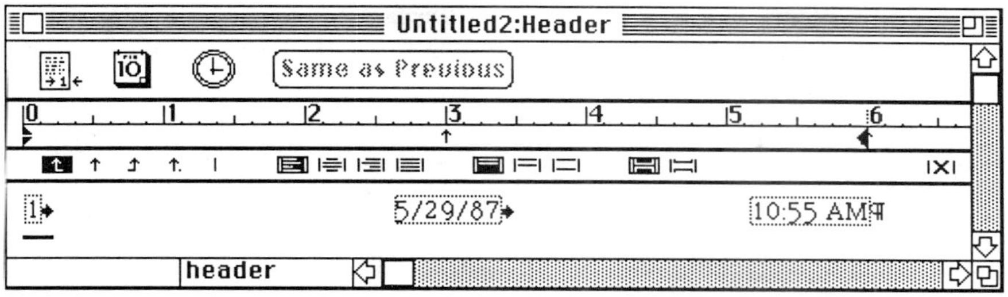

You can enter dynamic dates, times, and page numbers into your header.

When the Show ¶ setting is in effect, as in Figure 7-67, Word displays a dotted border around the date, time, and page number to indicate that they are dynamic entries. Of course, these borders do not appear when you print the document, nor will they appear if you choose Hide ¶.

Word treats each date, time, and page number entry as a single character. As a result, any character formats you assign to these entries will apply to the entire entry. To select one of these entries, just double-click anywhere on that item.

Though you can assign any character formats to your date, time, and page number entries, you cannot change the content of those entries—the date will always appear in the form M/D/YY, and the time will always appear in the form H:M AM/PM. However, as we'll explain next, you can use the Section... command to change the form of your page number entries.

Working with page numbers

When you add a dynamic page number entry to your header text, Word uses the numbering scheme that you selected in the Section dialog box to format those numbers. Table 7-3 on page 285 shows the available numbering schemes. For example, the sample header shown in Figure 7-67 appears in Word's default Arabic format. However, you can change the style of this entry by selecting one of the Roman or alphabetic numbering schemes from the Section dialog box.

By the way, we explained earlier in this chapter how you can use the Page Numbering option in the Section dialog box to add page numbers to each page of your printed document. When you add a dynamic page number entry to your document's header or footer, Word will deselect the Page Numbering option and place the page number in the header or footer only. If you later decide to remove the page number entry from your header or footer, Word will not automatically reselect the Page Numbering option for you. You must reissue the Section... command and select Page Numbering again if you want to use that option.

Sectional Headers

You can vary the headers and footers in your document by dividing your document into sections. Most often, these section breaks will correspond to major document divisions, like chapters. However, you can change headers and footers at any time by adding a section break to your document.

When you divide a document into sections, each section will initially carry identical headers, footers, and Section dialog box settings. As a result, if you make a change to the header and footer in the first section of the document, your changes will apply to all of the headers and footers throughout the document.

To vary the text or format of a particular section's header or footer, just click anywhere in the section you want to work with and then select Open Header... or Open Footer... from the Document menu. Word will display the section number in the header or footer window title bar to let you know which section your changes will apply to. By the same token, if you want to change the position or numbering scheme for a particular header or footer, just click in the section you want to work with, issue the Section... command, and make your changes in the dialog box.

When you reformat or edit the contents of a header or footer window, your changes will be applied to all successive headers or footers in your document. Any headers or footers that occur before the current section, however, will be unaffected. In addition, once you edit a header or footer, you break the link between it and any previous header or footer windows.

For example, suppose you have created a document that is divided into four sections. You enter the text *Chapter 1* in the header window for the first section. If you then open the header windows for the second, third, and fourth sections of your document, you'll see that they also contain the text *Chapter 1.* Now, suppose you click in the third section of your document and change the header text for that section to read *Chapter 3.* The headers for the third and fourth sections will now read *Chapter 3.* However, the headers for the first and second sections will still read *Chapter 1.* If you move back to the first section at this point and edit the header text for that section, your change will apply to the first and second sections only. The third and fourth sections will be unaffected by your changes.

We mentioned earlier that you can change the Section dialog box settings for two or more sections of your document by highlighting all or part of the sections you want to work with before issuing the Section... command. You can use this technique to change the From Top and From Bottom settings for the headers and footers in two or more sections. Unfortunately, this technique does not work for changes that you make to the text or formats of your headers and footers. If you select two or more sections of your document before issuing an Open Header... or Open Footer... command, your changes will apply only to the first section in your selection. If all of your headers and footers are currently identical, Word will carry your changes through to the other sections in your document as well. However, if you have created different headers or footers for different sections of your document, you cannot use this technique to make a global change to all of the headers and footers by selecting the entire document. You can, however, make global formatting changes to your headers and footers by altering the definition of the *header* and *footer* styles. (See Chapter 9 for more on style sheets.)

By the way, if you change the From Top or From Bottom setting in the Section dialog box without selecting any text, your changes will apply only to the headers and footers in the current section, even if the headers and footers in successive sections are linked to the current section. If you want your header and footer positions to be consistent from one section to the next, you must be sure to select your entire document berfore you change the From Top and From Bottom settings.

Odd and Even Headers

If you are working with a document that will be printed on facing pages, you'll probably want to change the orientation of your headers and footers on odd and even pages. For example, it is common style to place page numbers on the outside edge of the page—even page numbers on the left and odd page numbers on the right. In addition, you may want to change the content of your headers and footers on odd and even pages. For instance, in many books, you see the book title on even pages and the chapter title on odd pages.

Fortunately, Word allows you to create odd and even header and footer entries when you are using facing pages. When you select the Facing Pages option in the Page Setup dialog box, Word will replace the Open Header... and Open Footer... commands on your Document menu with four new commands: Open Even Header..., Open Odd Header..., Open Even Footer..., and Open Odd Footer.... (By the way, the Facing Pages option and the Odd and Even Header and Footer commands are available only when you use the Full Menus setting.)

Figures 7-68 and 7-69 show a pair of odd and even headers that we created for a book called *Fear and Loathing on the Remodeling Trail.* Notice that we placed our page number on the left side of the even header window and used a right-aligned tab at the 6 inch mark to align our book title with the right margin. In the odd header window, we placed our chapter title, "Dream Kitchen or Nightmare?", on the left and used a right-aligned tab at the 6 inch mark to align our odd page numbers with the right margin. Figure 7-70 on the next page shows how these headers will appear when the document is printed.

FIGURE 7-68

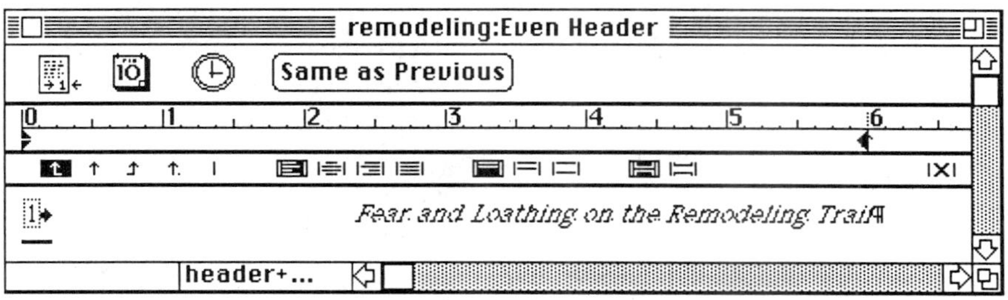

This header is designed for even pages.

FIGURE 7-69

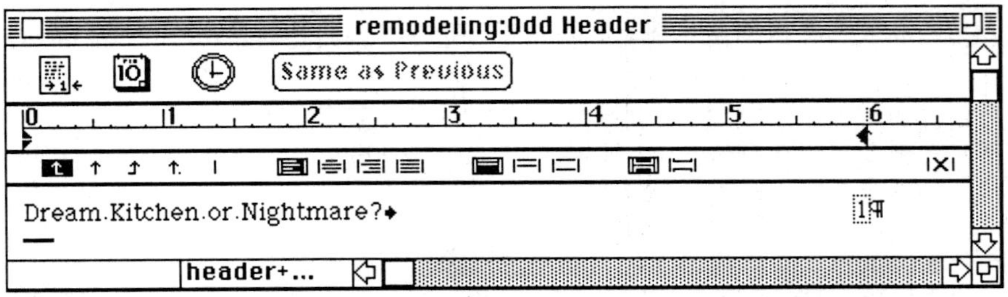

This header is designed for odd pages.

FIGURE 7-70

When we print the document, our page numbers are aligned to the outside edge of each page, while our book and chapter titles are aligned to the inside margins.

The First Page Special Option

Generally, the first page of a document or major section will contain special headings and formats to grab the reader's attention. For example, we use extra white space and larger headings for the first page in each chapter of this book. On the first page of a document or section, you may want to alter your headers and footers, or even eliminate them altogether. If you are designing a letterhead, like the one you saw in Figure 7-65, you may want to place the header on the first page only and eliminate it from successive pages.

If this is the case, just issue the Section... command and click the First Page Special option in the Header/Footer section of the dialog box. When you close the dialog box, Word will add a new pair of commands to your Document menu: Open First Header... and Open First Footer.... (Like the Odd and Even Header and Footer commands, the Open First Header... and Open First Footer... commands are available only when you use Full Menus.)

Initially, the first header and footer windows will contain the same header and footer information that you have specified for the rest of your document (or for the current section, if you have created a multisection document). If you are using the Facing Pages setting, your first header and first footer will be identical to your odd header and odd footer windows.

Of course, you can edit and format the contents of the first header and first footer windows completely independently from your other header and footer windows. If you want to eliminate the header or footer altogether, just delete the text in the first header or first footer window.

Linking

We mentioned earlier that all of the headers and footers in your document are initially identical. When you make a change to the first header or footer in a document, your changes apply to all of the headers and footers in following sections as well. However, once you edit a header or footer, you break the link between that header or footer and those that you created in earlier sections.

When you divide your document into several sections, each with different odd, even, and first-page headers and footers, the relationship between all of these headers and footers can get pretty complicated. Basically, the odd header for a section "sets the tone" for the other headers in that section. Similarly, the odd footer in a section will set the tone for the remaining footers in that section. For example, let's assume that you are working with a single-section document with no Facing Pages or First Page Special options. You issue the Open Header... command and enter the text *Chapter 1* in the header window. Now, if you issue the Page Setup... command and click the Facing Pages option, Word will use the text *Chapter 1* in both the odd and even header windows. If you issue the Section... command and choose the First Page Special option, Word will use the text *Chapter 1* in the new first-page header window as well.

Now, suppose that you decide to split your document into two sections. Initially, the odd, even, and first-page header windows in the second section will also contain the text *Chapter 1.* However, if you change the odd header for the second section to read *Chapter 2*, Word will change the even and first-page headers in that section to read *Chapter 2* as well. In other words, the even and first-page headers for each section are linked to the odd header for that section.

If you reopen the odd header window for Section 2 and click the Same as Previous button, however, Word will copy the odd header from the first section in your document and change your header to read *Chapter 1* again. If you have not made any changes to the even or first-page headers for the second section, Word will change those headers to read *Chapter 1* again as well. In short, the odd header for your second section is linked to the odd header for the first section. The remaining headers in the section are linked to the odd header for that section.

If at any time you choose the Short Menus command or deselect the First Page Special or Facing Pages options, Word will use the text in your odd header window for the entire section. However, if you reselect Full Menus or reapply the First Page Special or Facing Pages options, Word will remember the text and formats for those headers.

The Same as Previous Button

If you decide that you want a header or footer to contain the same text and formats as the header or footer in the previous section of your document, you can click on the Same as Previous button. Word will copy the header or footer text and formats from the previous section into the current window. If the contents of the open header or footer window are already identical to the previous section's header or footer, this button will be dimmed. However, if the current header or footer text differs from the header or footer for the previous section, this button will appear in black.

Oddly, when you use the Same as Previous button to copy a header or footer, you do not reestablish the link betwen the current header (or footer) and the previous header (or footer). As a result, if you change the contents of the first header or footer window, Word will not automatically update the second header or footer window to reflect those changes. You'll have to reopen the second header or footer window, and reselect the Same as Previous button.

Editing Headers and Footers

In general, you edit headers and footers as you edit any other text in your document. All of the techniques for selecting, inserting, deleting, and overwriting text that we discussed in Chapters 4 and 6 apply here as well. You can use the Cut, Copy, and Paste commands in the header and footer windows, just as you do in a document window, and you can move between your header, footer, and document windows to copy or move text from one to the other. In fact, you can even use Word's Find…, Change…, Spelling…, and Hyphenate… commands in your header and footer windows.

When you edit a header or footer window for one section of your document, keep in mind that your changes may also affect any subsequent "linked" headers or footers. As we explained above, the effects of your editing changes depend on which header or footer window you edit and whether you have broken the link between those headers and footers.

Copying and moving text in header and footer windows

When you are copying or moving text, you treat your header and footer windows just as you would treat any other document window. For example, suppose you have included the heading *Policies and Procedures* in your document, and you decide that you want to use this title in your document header. Rather than retyping the text, just highlight the heading in your document, and issue the Copy command. Next, select Open Header... from the Document menu, click at the spot where you want to add the heading, and issue the Paste command. It's as easy as that. After you've finished editing and formatting your header, just click the close box in the header window title bar to lock in your changes and close the window.

If you need to copy several items between your document and header or footer windows, keep in mind that the header and footer windows will remain open on your screen if you simply click on another window, rather than using the close box to remove the header or footer window from the DeskTop. You may want to temporarily resize and reposition the windows on your DeskTop to make it easier to access your header, footer, and document windows.

For example, Figure 7-71 shows our header and document windows open on the DeskTop at once. By resizing the document window, we have made it possible to move quickly from one window to the next. By the way, Word also adds the name of the open header and footer windows to the Window menu so that you can activate the window by selecting its name as well.

FIGURE 7-71

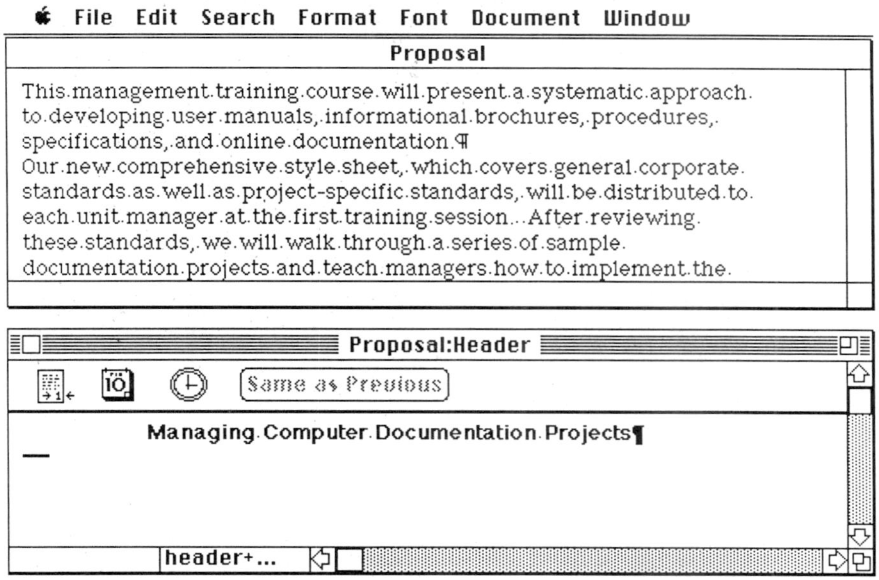

You can keep the document and header windows open on the DeskTop at the same time to help speed up your editing.

Unfortunately, you can open only one header or footer window at a time. For example, if you are using odd and even headers and you want to copy an item from the even header window to the odd header window, you must first open the even header window, select the text you want, and issue the Copy command. Then, you must open the odd header window, and issue the Paste command. Similarly, if you have created a multisection document and you want to copy a selection from one section header to another, you must issue separate Open Header... commands to access the header windows for each section.

For example, to copy an entry from your Header (S1) window to the Header (S3) window, you must click in the first section, open the header window, select the item you want to copy, and issue the Copy command. Then you must click in section three and issue a new Open Header... command before you can issue the Paste command.

Finding, changing, hyphenating, and spell-checking headers and footers

When you use Word's Find… and Change… commands to locate text or to replace one series of characters with another, Word finds and changes only the occurrences in the active window. This means that Word won't typically locate occurrences of your find text in a header or footer window, even if that window is open on the DeskTop when you issue the Find… or Change… command.

If you want to perfom a search or replace operation in a header or footer window, however, just activate that window before you issue the Find… or Change… command. If the window is already open on your DeskTop, click on the window to activate it. If the header or footer window you want to work with is not currently open, select one of the Open Header... or Open Footer... commands from the Document menu. Then, while the header or footer window is active, perform the search and replace procedure as you normally would in the document window. If you are using different odd, even, or first-page headers and footers, you'll have to open each header or footer window in turn and perform separate search and replace procedures. In a multisection document, you'll have to click in the appropriate section of your document, then use one of the header or footer commands to access the header or footer for that section.

Similarly, when you use the Spelling... or Hyphenate... commands in your document, Word will not automatically check your header and footer after it checks the main document. You must activate each of your header and footer windows before you can use the Spelling... and Hyphenate... commands in those windows. Once you activate the header or footer window that you want to check, you can proceed with your editing just as you would in a standard document window. (See Chapter 6 for more on the Find..., Change...., Hyphenate... and Spelling... commands.)

Deleting Headers and Footers

To delete a header or footer, open the header or footer window, select all the text in the window, then press the Backspace key to clear that text. (You also can choose Cut from the Edit menu to delete the text.) After you've deleted the text, just close the header or footer window.

THE PAGE PREVIEW... COMMAND

We've talked about a number of commands and settings that let you control the appearance of your printed document. However, it can sometimes be a bit confusing to figure out how all of these elements work together. A new feature of Word 3 lets you preview your document before you print. The new Page Preview... command, which shows you exactly what your printed pages will look like, can help you to avoid time-consuming (and possibly costly) bad print runs. In addition, you can quickly change many of your Page Setup, Section, and header and footer settings from the Page Preview screen.

When you issue the Page Preview... command, you'll see a window like the one in Figure 7-72. The icons on the left side of the Page Preview window let you zoom in on selected portions of the preview page, display single or facing pages, add page numbers to your document, change your top, bottom, left, and right margins, and reposition your headers and footers.

To close the Page Preview window, just click the close box in the window's title bar or select Page Preview... from the File menu again.

FIGURE 7-72

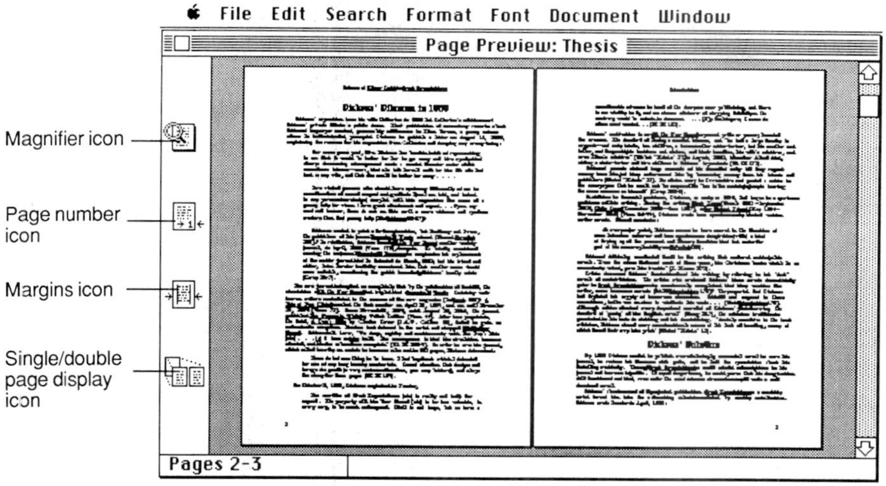

The Page Preview... command lets you preview and alter your page layout.

Navigating in the Page Preview Window

When you issue the Page Preview... command, Word will automatically repaginate your document and then display a preview of the page that is currently visible in your document screen. The number of the page or pages that are currently being previewed will appear at the bottom-left corner of the screen.

If you want to see another page while the preview screen is open, you can use the vertical scroll bar on the right side of the preview window to bring other pages into view. Click on the scroll arrows or in the gray area of the scroll bar to move through the document a page at a time, or drag the scroll box to move through several pages. When you drag the scroll box, you'll see the page numbers flash by in the page number status box. Just release the scroll box when you see the number for the page you want to preview.

Word will not let you edit your document or change its character and paragraph formatting while you are viewing it through the Page Preview window. However, if you notice an error or an item that you want to change while you are viewing a page in the preview window, you can quickly go to that spot in your document to make your change. When you close the preview window, Word will display the text that is currently visible on the preview screen in your document window. If, after making your editing or formatting change, you want to preview the results of your efforts, just issue the Page Preview... command again. As long as the text you want to view is visible in your document window, Word will display the page on which that text is located when you preview your printed document.

By the way, if you are using the Facing Pages option in the Page Setup dialog box and you have selected the single/double-page display icon, the odd pages will always appear on the right side of the preview screen, and the even pages will always appear on the left side of the preview screen. When you're viewing the beginning of a document, page 1 will appear on the left side of your screen, and the page opposite page 1 will be blank. When you use the vertical scroll bar to move through your preview page, Word will advance through the pages two at a time. Thus, you'll see page 1, then pages 2 and 3, then pages 3 and 4, and so forth.

Getting a Closer Look

Though the preview screen gives you an idea of the overall appearance of your printed page, it does not display any of the detail. Initially, Word shows you a two-page spread, which is handy when you are working with facing pages. However, you can get a closer look at a single page by clicking on the single/double page display icon. As you can see in Figure 7-73, when you click on this icon, Word will display only the first page of the two-page spread. Again, you can use the horizontal scroll bar to bring a new preview page into view. To display the two-page spread again, just click on the single/double page icon a second time.

FIGURE 7-73

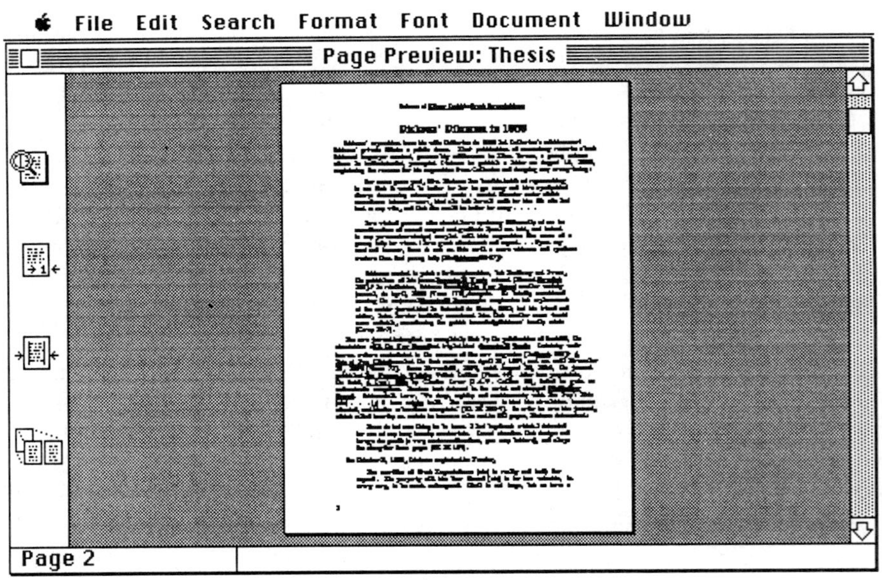

To preview a single page, click the single/double page display icon.

Magnifying Portions of the Page

For an even closer look, you can zero in on selected portions of a preview page by clicking on the magnifier icon on the left side of the preview window. When you click on this icon, your pointer will take on the magnifier shape. Use this pointer to click on the portion of the page you want to see. For example, if we click near the top center portion of the preview screen shown in Figure 7-73, Word will display the header that appears at the top of our printed page, as shown in Figure 7-74.

FIGURE 7-74

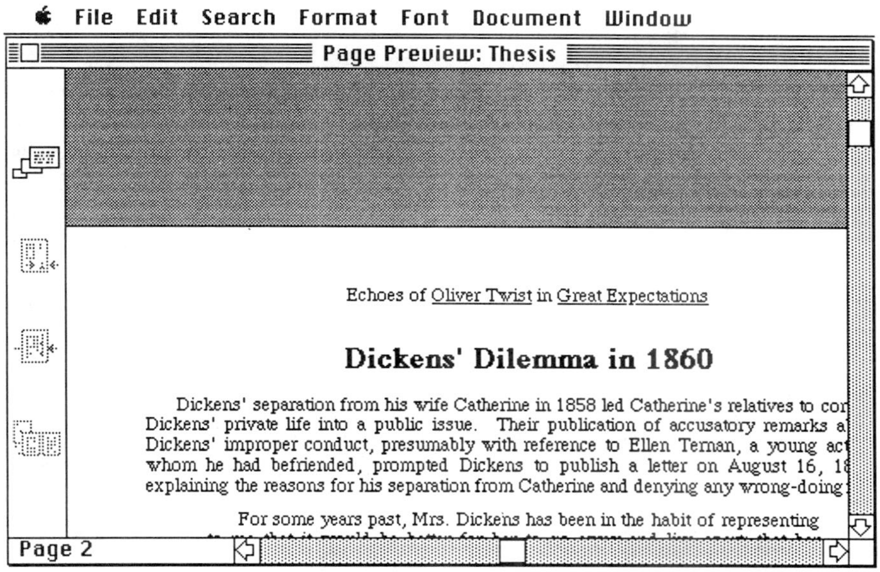

You can use the magnifying glass to enlarge selected portions of the preview page.

If you double-click on the magnifier icon, Word will automatically bring the top-left corner of the preview page into view. (Alternatively, you can double-click on a preview page at any time to toggle between the magnification and full-page views.) Notice in Figure 7-74 that the magnifier icon on the left side of the window changes to a page view icon once you're in the magnified view. To move back to the full-page preview again, just click this icon.

Once you have magnified a portion of the preview page, your pointer will change back to a standard arrow shape. In addition, Word will activate the horizontal scroll bar at the bottom of the preview window. You can use the horizontal and vertical scroll bars to bring different portions of the magnified preview page into view. You must click on the page view icon again before you can scroll new preview pages into view.

Page Size

All of the sample page preview screens we've see thus far have been standard letter size pages with Word's default Tall Orientation setting. If you use other page sizes or Orientation settings, however, Word will adjust the size and proportion of your preview pages to reflect your Page Setup dialog box specifications.

For example, the sample preview page in Figure 7-75 shows a letter size page that we set up to be printed with Wide orientation. The sample preview page shown in Figure 7-76, which is set up to be printed on index card stock, carries a Paper Width setting of 5 inches and a Height setting of 3 inches. Notice that Word adjusts the size of the preview page image to display as much detail as possible.

FIGURE 7-75

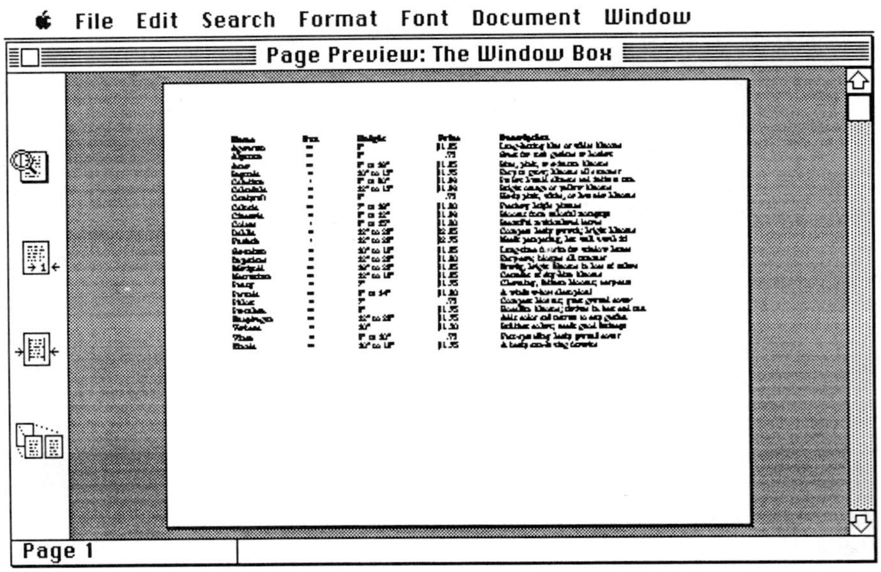

This document carries the Wide Orientation setting.

Gutters

If you are using the Facing Pages option and you have used the Gutter edit bar to add a binding allowance to your document, Word will display your gutter area in gray. For example, suppose you have created a document with a $^1/_2$ inch gutter allowance. As you can see in the sample preview screen shown in Figure 7-77, when you issue the Page Preview... command, Word displays a gray vertical stripe on the right side of page 2 and on the left side of page 3.

FIGURE 7-76

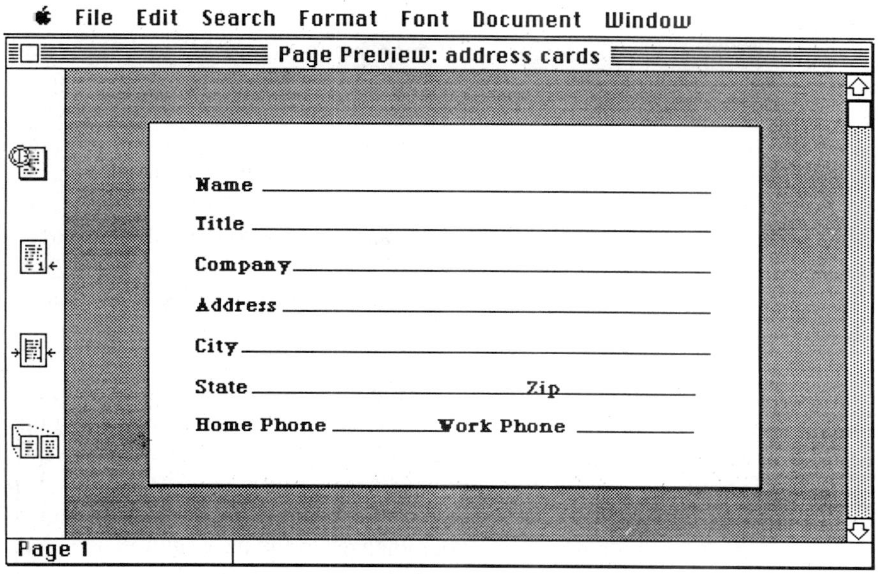

This document is set up to be printed on 3 x 5 inch index cards.

FIGURE 7-77

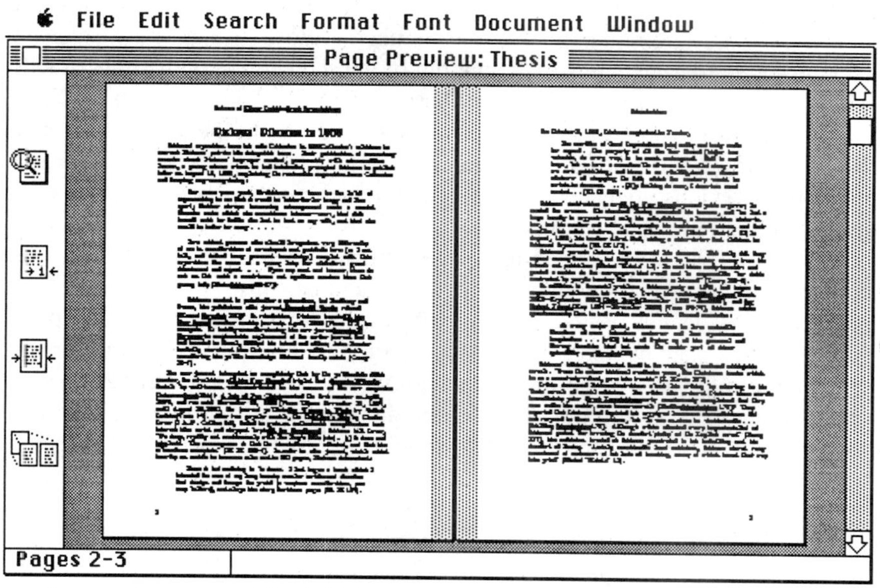

On the preview screen, Word displays your gutter area in gray.

Formatting from the Preview Window

As we hinted earlier, you can change many of your page layout specifications while the preview window is open on your DeskTop. For example, you can add and reposition page numbers, move your document margins, and reposition your headers and footers. We suspect that many users will find it easier to format their documents "visually" on the preview sceen, rather than using the Page Setup and Section dialog boxes.

By the way, you must be in the page view mode, rather than in the magnification view, in order to use the layout techniques described below. As you can see in Figure 7-74, the page number and margin icons are dimmed when your preview page is magnified. Also, if you have specified a Reduce/Enlarge % setting other than 100% in the Print dialog box, Word will not allow you to change your margin settings on the Page Preview screen.

Adding and positioning page numbers

You can use the page number icon on the page preview screen to add page numbers to your document and to reposition existing page numbers. Using this icon has exactly the same effects as clicking on the Page Numbering option in the Section dialog box and typing your page number positions in the From Top and From Right edit bars. As with the Page Numbering options, if you're working in a multisection document, your changes to the page number positions on the preview screen will apply to the current section only.

When you click on the page number icon, your pointer will take on the shape of the number 1. Just click at the spot where you want your page numbers to appear. To fine tune your page number position, you can drag the mouse as you're pointing to the page number. Word will display a pair of coordinates in the status box at the bottom of the screen to let you know exactly where the page number will appear. These coordinates correspond to the From Right and From Top entries that you would make in the Section dialog box. For example, in Figure 7-78, you can see the coordinates *(1.00, 4.50)* in the status box. This is equivalent to typing the value 1 in the From Right edit bar and 4.5 in the From Top edit bar.

If you have not yet added any page numbers to your document, you can double-click on the page number icon to automatically position your page number at the default position—$^{1}/_{2}$ inch from the top-right corner of the page. After adding a page number, you can reposition it by clicking on the number and dragging it to the desired position on the preview page. You also can reposition the page numbers at any time by clicking again on the page number icon and then clicking at a new spot on the preview page. Word will remove the page number from its current position and place it at the position you have selected.

If you are using the Facing Pages option in the Page Setup dialog box, Word will reverse the position of your page numbers on even pages. For example, if you place the page number *1* inch from the right edge of an odd page, as shown in Figure 7-78, that number will appear *1* inch from the left edge of your even pages.

FIGURE 7-78

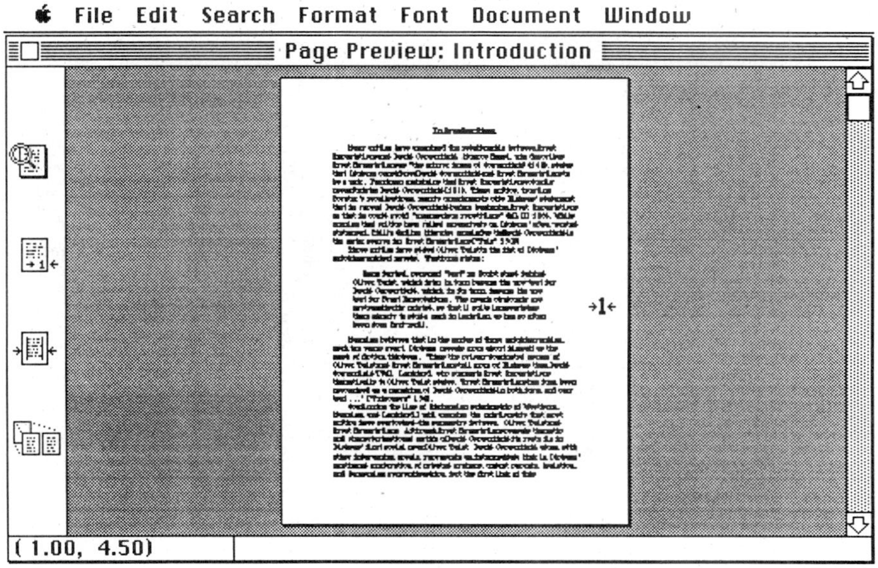

To add page numbers to your document, just click on the page number icon and click on the spot where you want your page numbers to appear.

Changing margins

Rather than typing Top, Bottom, Left, and Right margin settings in the Page Setup dialog box, you can specify your margin settings from the preview window. Begin by clicking on the margins icon on the left side of the preview screen. Then, if you are viewing two pages, click on the page you want to work with. When you click on the margins icon, Word will display dotted lines that represent your current margin positions, as well as your header and footer positions and page breaks, as shown in Figure 7-79 on the next page.

Notice the black squares or handles that appear at the edge of the top, bottom, left, and right margin markers in Figure 7-79. To change a margin setting, just point to one of these handles and drag it to the desired position. Word will display the margin setting in the status box at the bottom of your screen as you drag. This is the value that will appear in the Page Setup dialog box when you release the mouse button to lock in your change.

For example, suppose you want to increase the Left and Right margin settings for the sample document shown in Figure 7-79 to 1 3/4 inches each. Begin by clicking on the margins icon, then click on the handle at the bottom of the left margin line and drag it to the right. Release the mouse button when you see the value *1.75* in the status box at the bottom-left corner of the preview screen. To adjust the right margin, click on the handle at the bottom of the right margin line and drag it to the left. Again, release the mouse button when you see the value *1.75* in the status box.

FIGURE 7-79

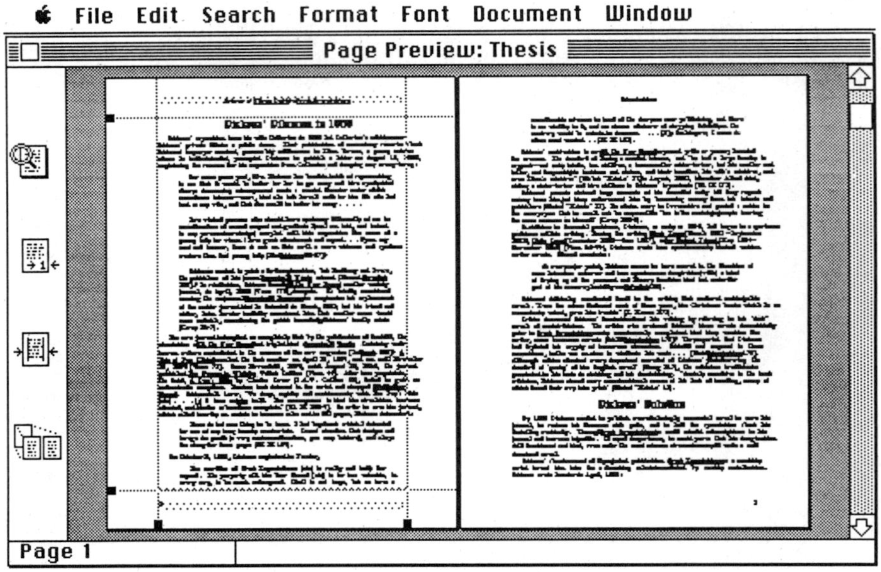

When you click the margins icon, Word will display dotted lines that represent your current page layout settings.

Once you've positioned your margins, click on another icon, double-click on the page, or click anywhere outside the page display portion of the screen to see the effects of your changes. Word will repaginate your document and put your new margin settings into effect, as shown in Figure 7-80. Keep in mind that your margin settings apply to your entire document, not just to the page or section that you are previewing.

Changing page breaks

You can also insert manual page breaks into your document from the preview screen by dragging the page break line that appears below the last line of text on the preview page. When you release the mouse button, Word will immediately repaginate the document. If you move the page break line up, any text that appears below that line will move to the top of the next page. If you drag the page break marker down, Word will pull text from the top of the next page back down to the bottom of the current page.

For example, suppose we want to move the last three lines at the bottom of page 2 in Figure 7-79 to the top of page 3. All we need to do is drag the page break marker up three lines, as shown in Figure 7-81. As you can see, Word will reflow the document and reposition the lines. When you return to your document window, you'll also see that Word has inserted a manual page break marker at this spot in your document.

FIGURE 7-80

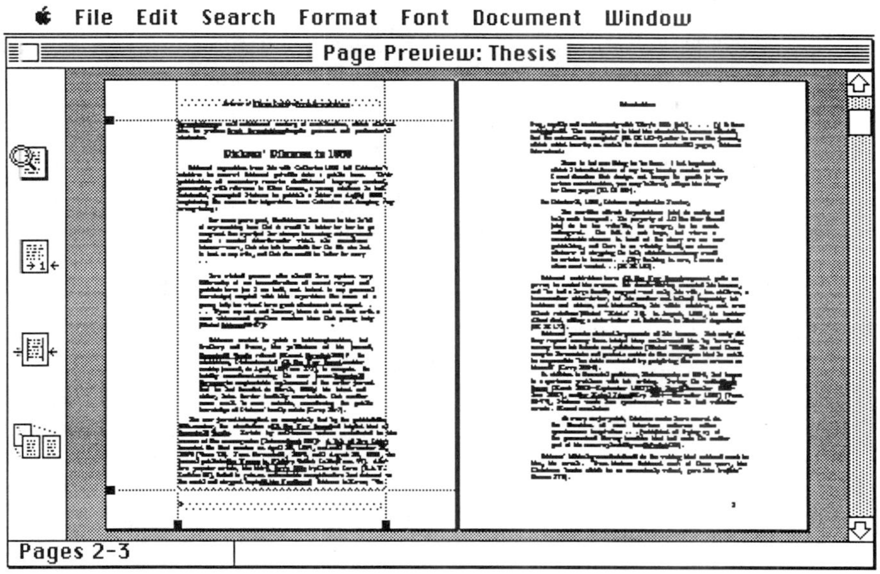

To adjust your page margins, just click on the margin handles and drag them to the desired position.

FIGURE 7-81

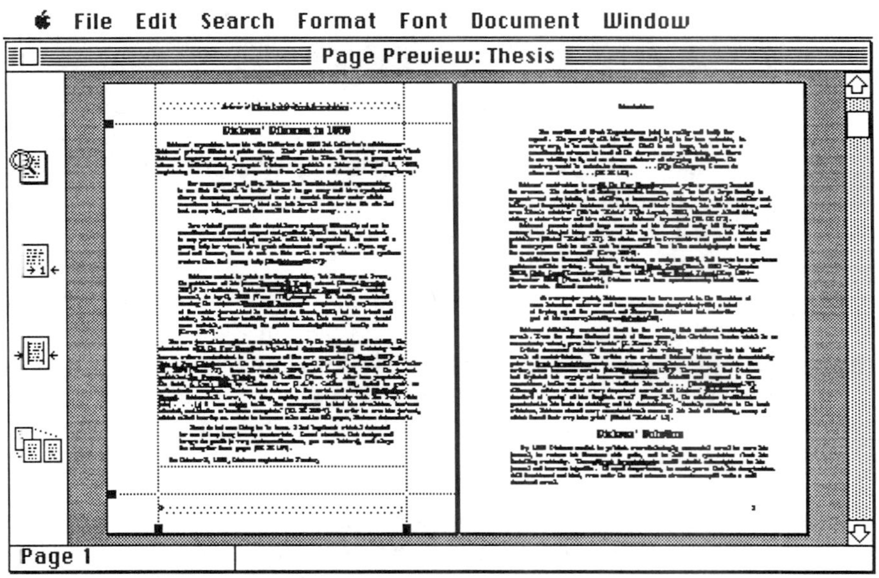

Word automatically inserts a manual page break in our document when you drag the page break marker.

By the way, the page break marker will often appear just above the line marking the bottom margin. This can make it difficult for you to distinguish the page break from the margin marker. However, you can move the page break line without affecting your bottom margin marker. In order to drag the page break marker, you must click between the left and right margins on the preview page. Since the bottom margin marker must be dragged by its handle—which appears on the left edge of the page—you'll be able to move the page break marker independently of the margin marker. Word will not let you use the page break marker to flow text past the bottom margin marker. However, if you have inserted a manual page break in your document and you decide that you want to remove it, you can do so by dragging the page break marker past the bottom margin marker on the preview screen. Word will reflow your document to fill the current page.

Repositioning headers and footers

When you click on the margins icon in the preview window, Word displays a dotted border around your headers and footers. To reposition your header or footer, just click anywhere within this border and drag the header or footer up or down to the desired position. This action is equivalent to changing the values in the From Top and From Bottom edit bars in the Section dialog box. As you drag the header or footer, Word will display the distance from the edge of the page in the status box at the lower-left corner of the preview screen.

If your headers and footers will require more space than is currently available in the top and bottom margin areas, you'll want to reposition your top and bottom margin markers before you move the headers and footers. Word will not allow you to drag a header or footer past your top or bottom margin marker.

For example, suppose you want the header shown in Figure 7-81 to appear 1 inch from the top of the page. Because our current Top margin setting is 1 inch from the top of the page, we'll need to drag the top margin marker down before we can move our header. So, we'll click on the handle on the right side of the top margin marker and drag it until we see *1.75* in the status box. Then we'll click on the header and drag it to the 1 inch position. Figure 7-82 shows the results.

If you want to drag a header or footer past the current top or bottom margin so that it will print in the text area, just press the Shift key as you drag the header and footer on the preview screen. This is equivalent to using a minus sign to type an absolute Top or Bottom margin setting in the Page Setup dialog box. (See page 295 for more on placing headers and footers in the text area.)

If you're working in a multisection document, your changes to the header and footer positions will apply to the current section only. If you want to change the header and footer positions in more than one section, you may find it easier to highlight some text in two or more sections in your document window and then use the Section... command to make your adjustments.

FIGURE 7-82

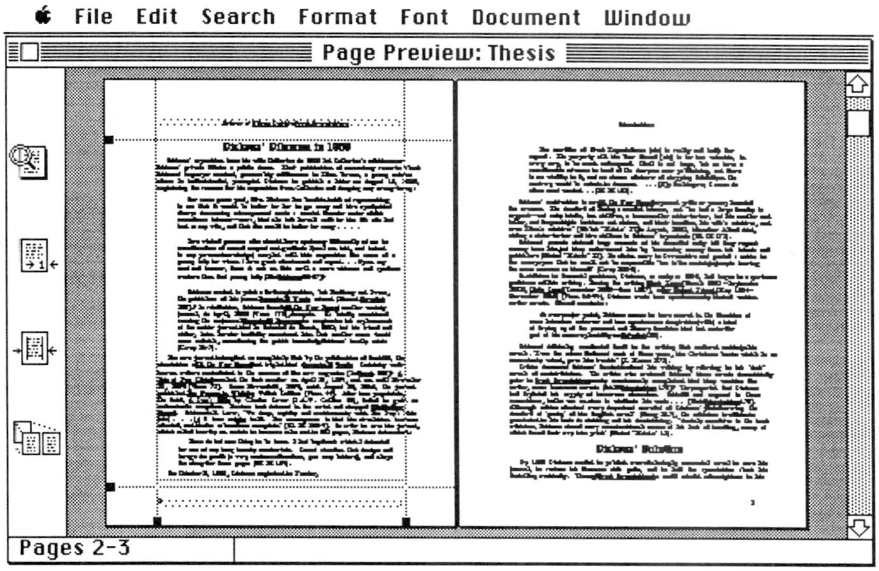

To reposition a header or footer, just drag it to the desired position on the page. You may want to move your margin markers before repositioning your header or footer.

Printing from the Preview Window

Though most of the commands on your Word menus are dimmed while the preview window is open, Word does allow you to issue the Print... command while you are previewing a document. When you issue the Print... command, Word will display the Print dialog box and will automatically enter the number of the page you are viewing in the From and To edit bars. You can change the From and To settings if you like, or click OK to print the current page. The preview window will remain open after the page has been printed.

DESIGNING COMPLEX DOCUMENTS 8

In Chapter 7, we discussed a number of factors that affect the appearance of your printed document, including your header, footer, Page Setup dialog box, and Section dialog box settings. Of course, the character and paragraph formats you select also have an important impact on the appearance of the printed document. In this chapter, we'd like to pull together all of this information and give you a better idea of how Word's various formatting and page design capabilities relate to each other.

We'll start with the concept of top-down document design, then we'll move on to some more complex design techniques. We'll show you two techniques for creating multicolumn page layouts, then we'll show you how you can link two or more documents with Word's Next File option.

TOP-DOWN DOCUMENT DESIGN

As you saw in Chapter 7, many of Word's formatting features are interrelated. For example, your page size, orientation, Left and Right margin settings, and gutters control the width of your text area—and, as a result, your document's ruler settings. In addition to page size and orientation, your Top and Bottom margin settings and your header and footer positions affect the depth of your text area. For these reasons, it makes sense to design your documents from the top down.

By top-down page design, we mean that you should move from the general to the specific. Decide first on the most general aspects of your page layout—your paper size, margins, and orientation, for example—then, you can fine-tune factors like paragraph and character formats. We think you'll find that this approach simplifies the page design process and eliminates a lot of backtracking. Figure 8-1 illustrates the general concept of top-down document design.

FIGURE 8-1

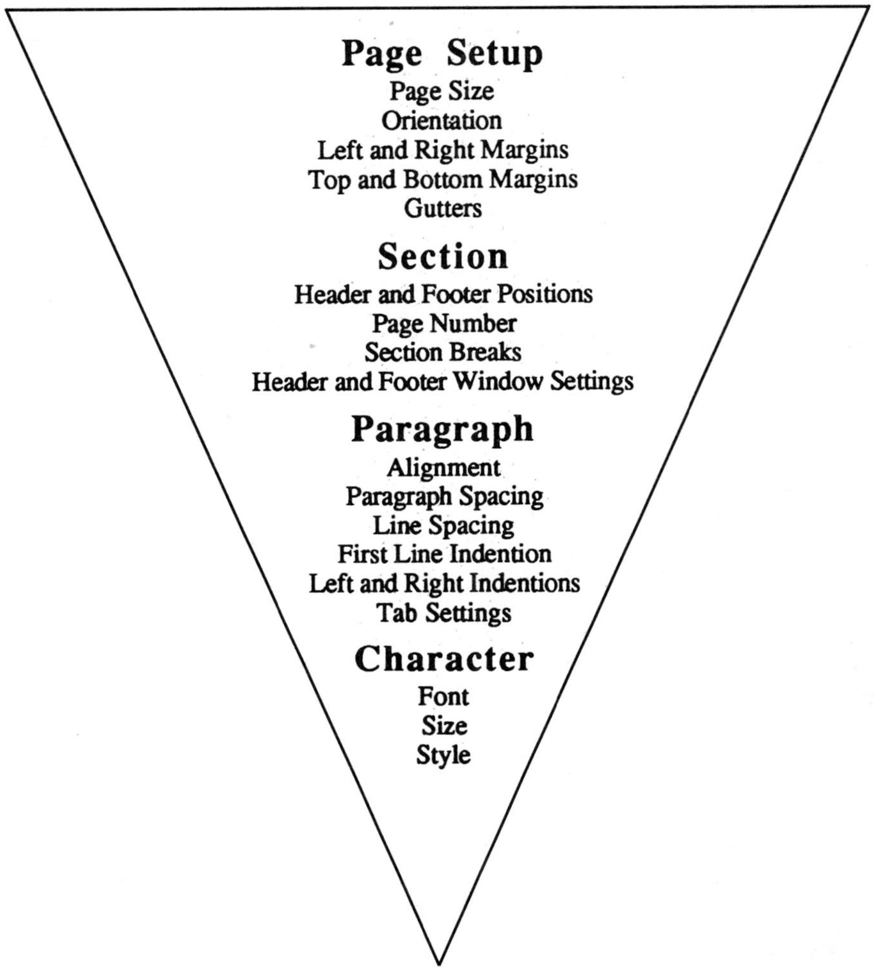

You can simplify the document design process by moving from the general to the specific.

Creating a Layout Sketch

One of the best ways to plan your page design is to jot down a layout sketch of what you want your printed page to look like. Once you have a clear picture in mind, you can translate your rough sketch into terms that Word can understand. Figure 8-2 shows a layout sketch of a document that uses Word's default Page Setup, Section, and Paragraph formats.

FIGURE 8-2

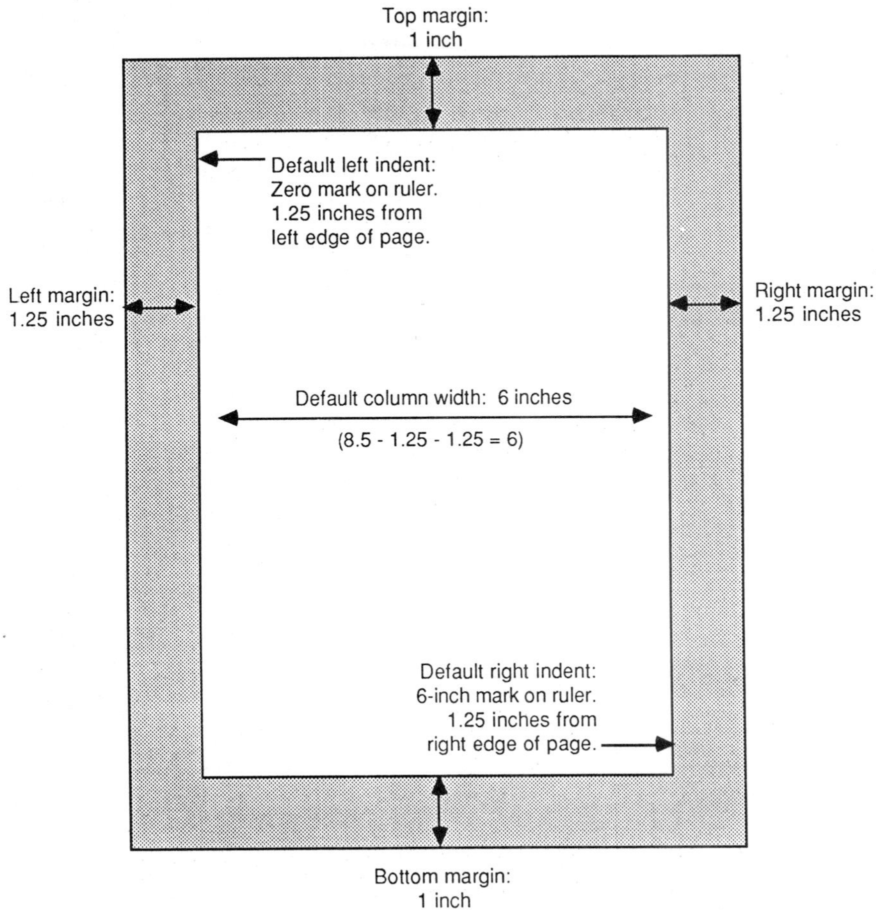

This layout sketch reflects Word's default page layout settings.

If you noticed that this layout sketch looks a lot like the Page Preview screen that you saw in Chapter 7, then you're already a step ahead of the game. In fact, Word's Page Preview... command offers a great way to experiment with different page design elements and get an immediate bird's-eye view of your design changes.

The amount of detail that you include in your page layout sketch will depend on your specific project needs. If you are developing a short document that does not need to conform to particular style specifications, then you may prefer to rough out your general ideas on paper and then experiment with different formatting techniques in Word until you arrive at a style that you like.

If you are creating a long document or a series of documents that you will be using time after time, then you should carefully define your style and design elements before you begin formatting in Word. Think about the kinds of information that you will include in your document and how you want to handle each element. Otherwise, you'll find yourself reformatting your entire document time and again in order to incorporate some unexpected element.

You may even want to experiment with two or three different document designs and try them out on some representative sample text before you begin formatting your actual document. In short, the better your advance preparation, the smoother the design process.

Defining your page parameters

Whether you're using the Page Preview screen or the Page Setup... command, your first step in defining the page layout should be to specify the page parameters. Before you can decide on factors like character and paragraph formats, you need to know exactly how much room you have to work with. Of course, as we explained in Chapter 7, your page size, orientation, and margin settings are the most important factors in determining the size of your text area. If you're planning on using facing pages, you will also need to consider how much gutter space you want to add to each page.

You also must consider how and where your headers and footers will be placed on the printed page. How much room will your headers and footers require? If you plan to use variable headers or footers, you should decide on how your sections will be divided. Will you be starting each section on a new page? If so, will you want to use special headers and footers on the first page of each section? How much margin space do you want to leave at the top and bottom of each page? All of these questions affect the depth of your print area.

Unfortunately, you can't always use the Page Preview... command to set up all of your initial page parameters. You must go to the Page Setup dialog box first to specify your page size, orientation, facing pages, and gutter options. These factors cannot be changed in the preview window. If you're using Word's default page size and orientation settings but you don't plan to use facing pages, you can go straight to the Page Preview... command.

Filling in the details

Once you've mapped out the parameters of your printed page, you're ready to start filling in the details. What size and style headings and subheadings will you use? How many levels of subheadings will you use? What font and size will work best for your body text? Do you want to add any extra white space above or below headings? Do you want to use open spacing or a first-line indention to help break up paragraphs in your body text? Do you want to indent the left and right margins on special paragraphs, such as those containing long quotations? How can you use borders to help set off elements of your layout?

Of course, the answers to these questions will vary widely for each document, depending on its audience, purpose, and content. A corporate policies and procedures manual, for instance, is likely to take on a very different format from an employee newsletter. By the same token, a display page that advertises a new product is likely to look quite different from a technical specifications sheet for that product.

You can save yourself a lot of time and ensure consistency throughout the document (or throughout a series of documents) by addressing these issues up front. As you'll learn in Chapter 9, once you've answered these questions, you can also speed up the formatting process significantly by creating a style sheet that contains all of your character and paragraph specifications.

An Example

Now that we've covered the generalities of top-down document design, let's put some of these ideas to work. Suppose you're designing a workbook to train new users of your company's computer system. Your first step will be to identify the various elements of the document so that you can determine the best way to present the information. Then you can create your layout sketch and put your ideas into action.

Let's suppose that the workbook consists of several sets of exercises and step-by-step solutions that explain how to complete a task. You plan to start each one-page exercise at the top of an odd-numbered page so that the reader can easily locate the beginning of each exercise. At the top of each new exercise page, you'll want to place a heading that identifies the topic to be covered. Then you plan to present an overview of the tasks that the user will perform and provide a series of references to the user manual that the trainees will be using on the job. Below this introductory information, you will list the specific tasks that the trainee must perform.

On the even page immediately following each exercise, you will present step-by-step solutions to the tasks that you presented on the previous page. For easy reference, these solution steps will be numbered as well, so that they correspond to the numbered tasks presented on the exercise page. The length of the solution text will vary, depending on the complexity of the exercise.

The document will be printed on a 7 x 9 inch paper stock and will use spiral wire binding. You'll want to place headers that list the name of the workbook at the top of each even page and headers that list the name of the exercise on odd pages. Because you're using special headings to flag the beginning of each new exercise, you'll probably want to omit the header from the top of the odd-numbered exercise pages. Page numbers will appear at the bottom of each page.

With all of this information in mind, you might develop a set of layout sketches, like the ones shown in Figures 8-3 and 8-4, to help develop your workbook design. The first sketch shows the general format for our exercise pages, which will always appear on odd pages. The second sketch shows the general design of the solution pages, which will begin on an even page but may carry over to the next odd page as well.

FIGURE 8-3

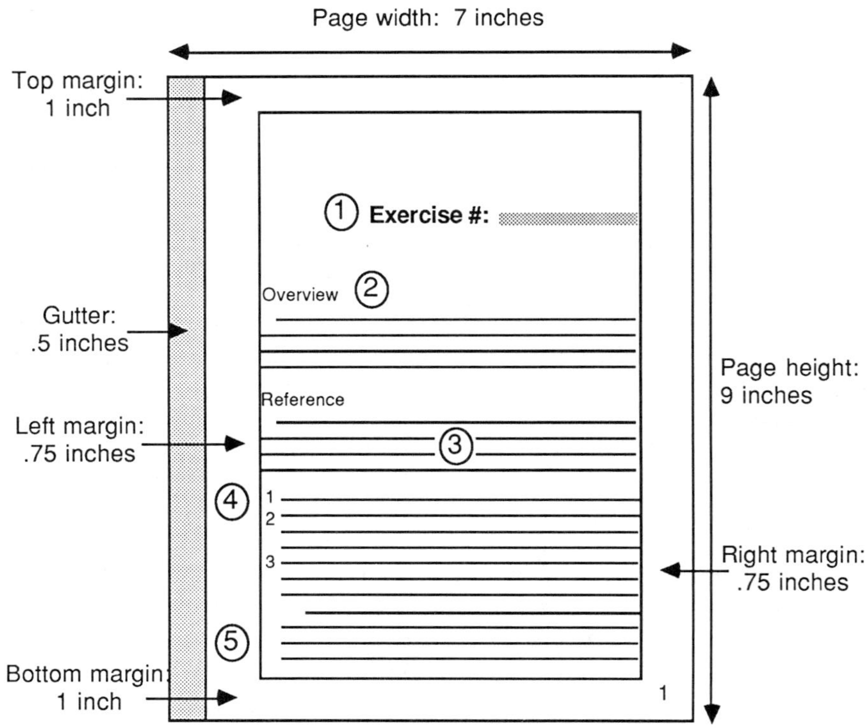

This layout sketch shows the general layout of the exercise pages.

Table 8-1 on page 324 shows the character and paragraph formats that we'll use to format the text for the document. The circled numbers in Figures 8-3 and 8-4 correspond to the numbers on the left side of the table.

Your first step in designing this workbook will be to issue the Page Setup... command and set up your page parameters. Since the 7 x 9 inch page size is not among Word's standard page sizes, you'll need to type the values *7* and *9* in the Paper Width and Height edit bars.

Let's leave the Top and Bottom margin settings as they are for now. Since your headers and page numbers will occupy only one line each, the standard 1 inch top and bottom margins should allow plenty of room. Since you're

FIGURE 8-4

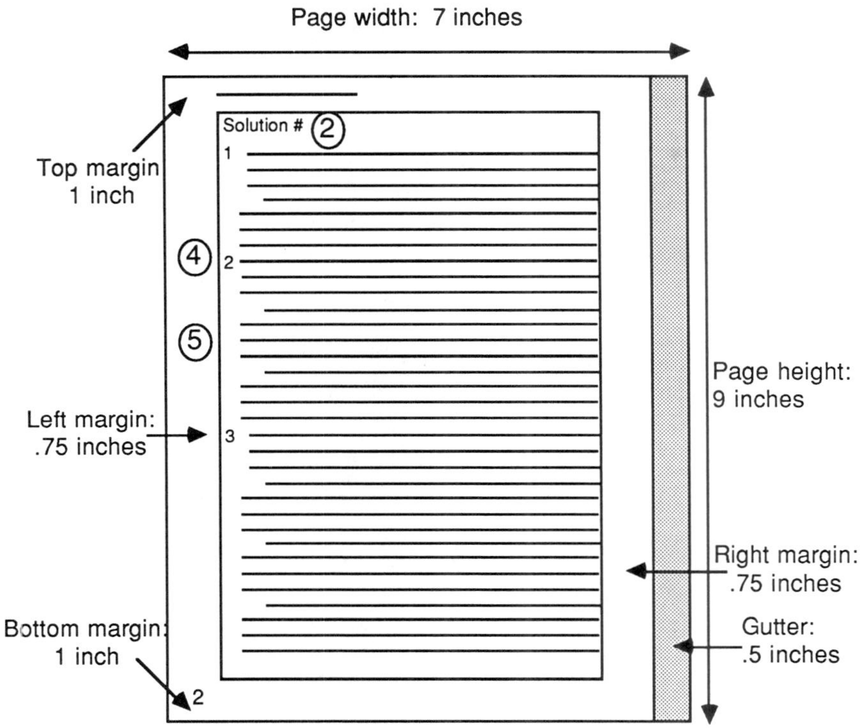

This layout sketch shows the general layout of the solution pages.

working with such a narrow page width, however, you may need to narrow your left and right margins a bit. Let's try entering *.75* in these two edit bars. Since the workbook will be spiral bound and printed on both sides of the paper, you'll need to click the Facing Pages option and type *.5* in the Gutter edit bar to allow an extra 1/2 inch for your spiral binding.

You can leave the Widow Control and Default Tab Stops options set at their defaults. Because the Next File, numbering, and footnote options in the bottom portion of the dialog box don't apply to this particular document, you can leave those options set to their defaults as well. At this point, your Page Setup dialog box will look like the one in Figure 8-5 on the next page.

TABLE 8-1

	Text Element	Character and Paragraph Formats
1	Exercise Title	18 Point, Helvetica, Bold Flush Right, 96 Point Space Before, 72 Point Space After
2	Secondary Titles	14 Point, Helvetica, Bold Flush Left, Open Space
3	Body Text	12 Point, Times, Plain Justified, Open Space, $^{1}/_{4}$ inch First-Line Indention
4	Numbered List Paragraphs	12 Point Times, Plain Justified, Open Space, $^{1}/_{4}$ inch Left Indention, 0 First-Line Indention
5	Secondary List Paragraphs	12 Point, Times, Plain Justified, Open Space, $^{1}/_{4}$ inch Left Indention, $^{1}/_{2}$ inch First-Line Indention

These are the character and paragraph formats that we will use in our sample workbook.

FIGURE 8-5

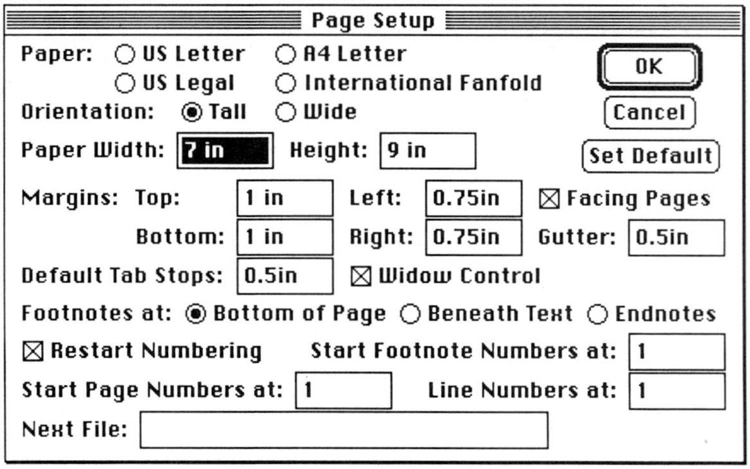

This Page Setup dialog box shows the settings for our sample workbook.

Now it's time for the Section… command. Since you want each exercise to begin on an odd page, and you have decided to omit the header from these pages, you'll need to place each exercise in its own section. Then you can use the Odd

Page option in the Section Start portion of the Section dialog box to instruct Word to skip to the top of the next odd page every time it reaches a section break. You'll also need to select the First Page Special option in the Header/Footer portion of the dialog box so that you can omit the header from the first page of each section. If you plan to place your headers and footers $^1/_2$ inch from the top and bottom of each page, you can leave the From Top and From Bottom settings at their defaults.

Since you plan to use the Arabic (1, 2, 3) numbering scheme for your page numbers, you can leave the default 1 2 3 numbering option in the Page Number section of the dialog box in effect as well. (We'll show you how to attach section numbers to these page numbers in a few moments.)

Since the line numbering, column, and footnote options don't apply to this document, you can ignore those parts of the dialog box. Figure 8-6 shows the Section dialog box settings for the workbook.

FIGURE 8-6

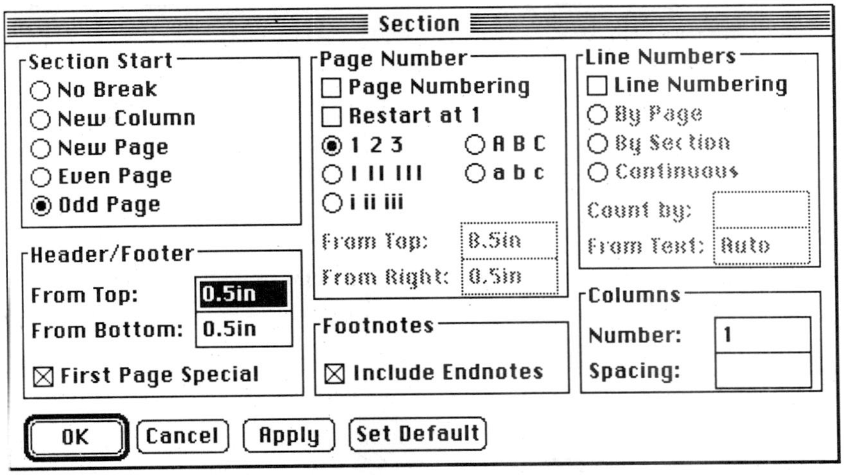

This Section dialog box shows the settings for the sample workbook project.

Next up: headers and footers. Since you've already selected the Facing Pages option from the Page Setup dialog box and the First Page Special option from the Section dialog box, you'll find six header and footer commands on your Document menu: Open First Header..., Open First Footer..., Open Even Header..., Open Even Footer..., Open Odd Header..., and Open Odd Footer.... At this point, all six header and footer windows will be empty. Begin by selecting the Open Odd Header... command and typing the name of your first exercise. (If you've already created the text for your workbook, you can copy this text from the document window.) For purposes of illustration, we'll use the name *Exercise 1.1: Getting Started.*

Now, to format your header, select that text, issue the Character... command, and select the 12 Point and Helvetica options. Next, issue the Paragraph... command, and select the Below and Double Border options. Choose the Show Ruler command from the Format menu to bring the header window ruler into view, then click on the right alignment icon. By using right alignment, you ensure that your exercise titles will appear on the outer edge of your odd pages. Figure 8-7 shows the resulting header window.

FIGURE 8-7

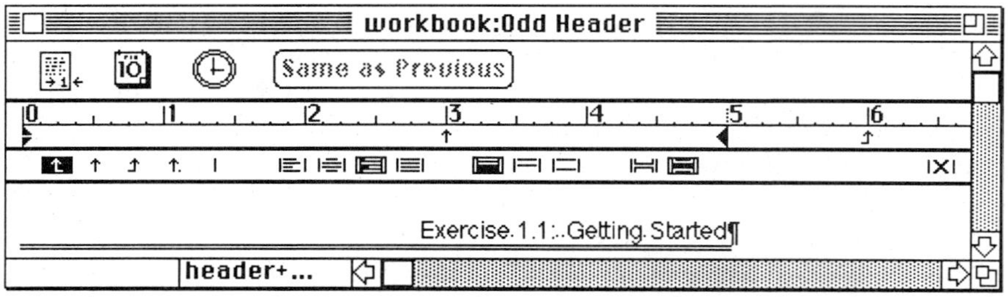

This header will appear on odd pages in the sample workbook.

When you issue the Open Even Header... command, you'll see a header identical to the one in Figure 8-7. Most of your character and paragraph formatting is already done for you. Just drag through the text that you entered for your odd header, and overwrite that text with the title of your book. (We'll use the name *Softsell Order Entry System Training Workbook.*) You'll also need to issue another Show Ruler command and click on the left alignment icon so that your book title will appear on the outer edge of your even pages. Figure 8-8 shows the header window for the workbook's even pages.

FIGURE 8-8

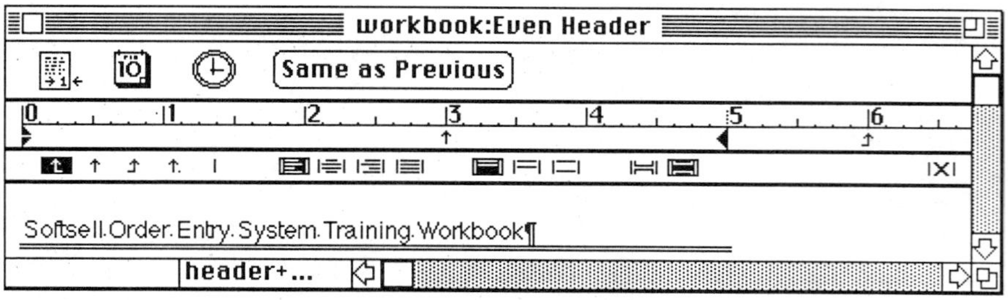

This header will appear on all even pages in the sample workbook.

Your last step in setting up your headers will be to issue the Open First Header... command and erase the contents of that window. After deleting the header text, you'll still see a border line in the empty header window. In order to erase this border line, you'll need to open the Paragraph dialog box and click the

None Border option. (Remember, we're planning to place a special heading at the beginning of each new exercise, so we don't need a header on that page to repeat the exercise name.)

To enter page numbers in your footer window, follow the same basic steps described above: Open the Odd Footer window; click on the page number icon to enter the page number; then select the page number, and format it to appear in 12-point Helvetica type. Next, issue the Show Ruler command and click on the right alignment icon to place the page number at the right margin. Now, open the Even Footer window and again issue the Show Ruler command. Click on the left alignment icon to move the page number in the even footer window to the left side of the page. Since the first-page footer already carries the same formats as those that will appear on your other odd pages, there is no need to alter that footer.

Now that you have specified all of your page parameters, you can get to work on the body of the workbook. Table 8-1 on page 324 shows the character and paragraph formats that we selected for the workbook text. We won't walk through all of the steps necessary to format the body of the sample workbook at this point. Instead, we'll refer you to Chapters 5 and 9. Chapter 5 covers all of Word's character and paragraph formatting options in detail. In Chapter 9, we'll discuss a number of ways you can speed up your character and paragraph formatting with style sheets.

Figures 8-9 and 8-10 show the results of our efforts. True to form, these sample pages look a lot like the layout sketches that we developed earlier. To carry these design elements through to the rest of your document, all you need to do is insert a section break at the beginning of each new exercise. Then place your insertion point marker in that section, issue the Open Odd Header... command, and type the name of the exercise in the Odd Header window. You won't have to edit any of your other headers or footers. Of course, you'll want to apply the same character and paragraph formats we established for the main body text in this first section throughout the rest of your document as well.

FIGURE 8-9

Exercise 1.1: Getting Started

Overview

Before you can access the new Softsell Order System, you must log into the system. Then you can choose the task you want to perform from the order entry menu. In this exercise, you'll learn to access SOS, enter your name and PIN code, and access the order entry menu.

Reference

Pages 3-22 and 3-24 of your <u>Softsell Order System User Reference Manual</u> explain how to log into the system and access the order entry menu.

1. Begin the log-in procedure by requesting access to the Softsell Order System.
2. Enter your name and personal identification number in response to the SOS prompts.
3. Once you've logged into the system, request access to the SOS order entry menu.

1

The first page of our printed document looks like this.

FIGURE 8-10

Softsell Order Entry System Training Workbook

Solution 1.1

1. When you begin, your computer screen will be empty except for a question mark prompt (?) and a blinking cursor. Type *SOS* at the prompt, then press the Return key to request access to the Softsell Order System.
2. When you enter the SOS request, you'll see a beautiful multicolor graphic display screen that contains the SOS logo. Below the logo you'll see your terminal identification number as well as the current date and time.

   Yet another blinking cursor will appear at the bottom of the screen, along with the prompt **_Please enter your first and last name_**. Type your first and last name—exactly as it appears on your employee ID card—at the prompt. If you make an error, you can use the Backspace key to erase the incorrect characters. You can also press the Clear button to start again. When you're finished, press the Return key to lock in your entry.

   Next, SOS will present the prompt **_Please enter your PIN_**. Type your 27-digit personal identification number at the prompt. The numbers you type will not appear on the screen. Instead, a series of asterisks will appear for each character you type. If you make an error, you can use the Backspace key to erase the incorrect characters. You can also press the Clear button to start again. When you're finished, press the Return key to lock in your entry.

   If you enter the incorrect PIN, you'll see the prompt **_Invalid number: Please try again_**. Follow the same steps described above to reenter your personal identification number. SOS will give you three chances to enter the correct number.

   If you blow it on the last try, you can expect a visit from Guido, the friendly SOS attack dog. Don't try to run. You'll only make him angry. No one has ever been able to outdistance Guido, so we'd advise you to memorize the 27-digit identification number and type your PIN very carefully. Though the company's very generous medical coverage plan does cover limb replacement, we think you'll find that the $5000 deductible makes repeated use of this feature less than practical.

2

Exercise 1.1: Getting Started

3. Assuming you've successfully logged into the system—and that all of your limbs are intact—you'll see the prompt **_So? What do you want now?_**. To access the SOS order entry menu, type *Let me in* at the prompt and press the Return key. If you don't get any response, try banging on the side of the terminal a few times to get its attention. If that doesn't work, call Guido at extension 5261. He'll fetch someone from the SOS Operations Division right away.

   When and if the *SOS* order entry menu appears, you're ready to stop wasting time and get to work. If you don't have any orders to enter at this point, get out the want ads and start looking for another job. This company spent $850,000 on SOS installation, and if it doesn't start paying off very soon, we're all going to be out of jobs.

3

The second and third pages of our printed document look like this.

MULTICOLUMN FORMATTING

Thus far, all of the page designs you've seen in this book have consisted of a single column of text that extends from the left to the right margin of the printed page. Of course, there are a lot of publications—newspapers and journals being the most obvious examples—that contain two or more columns.

Word offers two types of multicolumn formats: snaking and side-by-side. The text in snaking columns, as shown in Figure 8-11, automatically wraps or "snakes" from the bottom of one column to the top of the next. You use the Side-by-Side format, on the other hand, to place individual paragraphs side-by-side on the page. For example, in the sample page shown in Figure 8-12, we've used the Side-by-Side format to place headings alongside our body text.

FIGURE 8-11

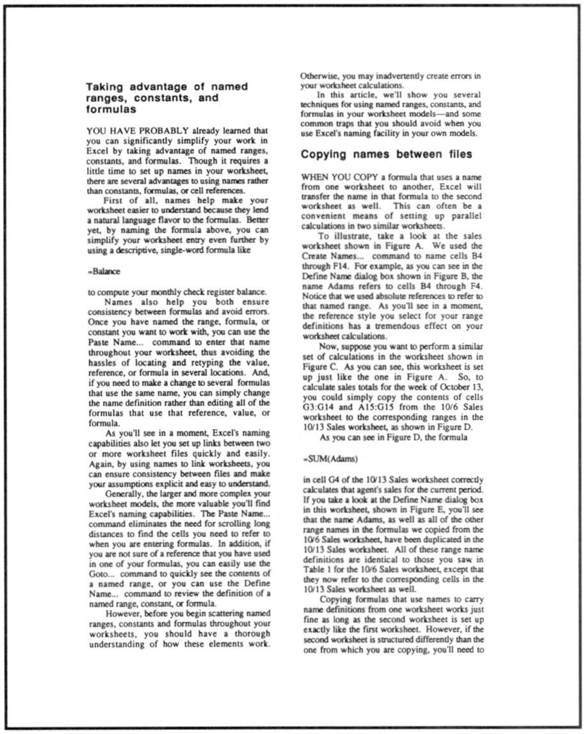

Taking advantage of named ranges, constants, and formulas

YOU HAVE PROBABLY already learned that you can significantly simplify your work in Excel by taking advantage of named ranges, constants, and formulas. Though it requires a little time to set up names in your worksheet, there are several advantages to using names rather than constants, formulas, or cell references.

First of all, names help make your worksheet easier to understand because they lend a natural language flavor to the formulas. Better yet, by naming the formula above, you can simplify your worksheet entry even further by using a descriptive, single-word formula like

=Balance

to compute your monthly check register balance.

Names also help you both ensure consistency between formulas and avoid errors. Once you have named the range, formula, or constant you want to work with, you can use the Paste Name... command to enter that name throughout your worksheet, thus avoiding the hassles of locating and retyping the value, reference, or formula in several locations. And, if you need to make a change to several formulas that use the same name, you can simply change the name definition rather than editing all of the formulas that use that reference, value, or formula.

As you'll see in a moment, Excel's naming capabilities also let you set up links between two or more worksheet files quickly and easily. Again, by using names to link worksheets, you can ensure consistency between files and make your assumptions explicit and easy to understand.

Generally, the larger and more complex your worksheet models, the more valuable you'll find Excel's naming capabilities. The Paste Name... command eliminates the need for scrolling long distances to find the cells you need to refer to when you are entering formulas. In addition, if you are not sure of a reference that you have used in one of your formulas, you can easily use the Goto... command to quickly see the contents of a named range, or you can use the Define Name... command to review the definition of a named range, constant, or formula.

However, before you begin scattering named ranges, constants and formulas throughout your worksheets, you should have a thorough understanding of how these elements work. Otherwise, you may inadvertently create errors in your worksheet calculations.

In this article, we'll show you several techniques for using named ranges, constants, and formulas in your worksheet models—and some common traps that you should avoid when you use Excel's naming facility in your own models.

Copying names between files

WHEN YOU COPY a formula that uses a name from one worksheet to another, Excel will transfer the name in that formula to the second worksheet as well. This can often be a convenient means of setting up parallel calculations in two similar worksheets.

To illustrate, take a look at the sales worksheet shown in Figure A. We used the Create Names... command to name cells B4 through F14. For example, as you can see in the Define Name dialog box shown in Figure B, the name Adams refers to cells B4 through F4. Notice that we used absolute references to refer to that named range. As you'll see in a moment, the reference style you select for your range definitions has a tremendous effect on your worksheet calculations.

Now, suppose you want to perform a similar set of calculations in the worksheet shown in Figure C. As you can see, this worksheet is set up just like the one in Figure A. So, to calculate sales totals for the week of October 13, you could simply copy the contents of cells G3:G14 and A15:G15 from the 10/6 Sales worksheet to the corresponding ranges in the 10/13 Sales worksheet, as shown in Figure D.

As you can see in Figure D, the formula

=SUM(Adams)

in cell G4 of the 10/13 Sales worksheet correctly calculates that agent's sales for the current period. If you take a look at the Define Name dialog box in this worksheet, shown in Figure E, you'll see that the name Adams, as well as all of the other range names in the formulas we copied from the 10/6 Sales worksheet, have been duplicated in the 10/13 Sales worksheet. All of these range name definitions are identical to those you saw in Table 1 for the 10/6 Sales worksheet, except that they now refer to the corresponding cells in the 10/13 Sales worksheet as well.

Copying formulas that use names to carry name definitions from one worksheet works just fine as long as the second worksheet is set up exactly like the first worksheet. However, if the second worksheet is structured differently than the one from which you are copying, you'll need to

The text in snaking columns wraps or "snakes" from the bottom of one column to the top of the next.

FIGURE 8-12

Are all mutual company dividends determined by the same method?	No. In most cases your dividends are determined on an annual basis by a complex formula that takes into account the mutual company's investment and claims experience, as well as its cost of doing business. However, methods of determining your dividend shares are likely to vary from one mutual company to the next. Before you decide on a mutual company, you should be familiar with the company's methods for determining dividends.
How does the cash value of my life insurance policy grow from one year to the next?	Your policy's value may increase in two ways: through increased cash value and through dividends. Increases in your accumulated cash value represent your policy's growing equity. Mutual companies also share their profits with their policyholders in the form of dividends. You have the option of receiving these dividend payments directly or applying them to your future policy premium payments.
How can I evaluate my insurance policy's real worth?	Three factors affect the value of your whole life policy: your premium rate, your policy's cash value, and the dividends that you receive. These amounts are interdependent. However, when you measure your policy's value, your actual accumulated cash value is the bottom line. The actual cash value of your policy depends on the guaranteed cash value specified for your policy, as well as those dividends that you use to increase the cash value.
Is a life insurance policy really a worthwhile financial investment?	Only if you really need life insurance coverage. The primary goal of any life insurance policy is to protect the financial security of the policy's beneficiary. However, your life insurance policy does provide an unbeatable combination of protection, savings, and growth. In addition to the steady growth in cash value, with a mutual life insurance policy, you also have the opportunity to participate in the profitability of your insurer through dividends.

By using the Side-by-Side format, you can align individual paragraphs in two or more columns.

Though neither of these multicolumn formats is difficult to master, we've been holding out on these two design features until now because both require that you understand the page design principles that we have discussed in this chapter and in Chapter 7. Now that we have a handle on the various factors that affect the appearance of your printed documents, let's take a look at Word's multicolumn formatting capabilities. We'll start with Word's snaking column layout style, then we'll take a look at the Side-by-Side format in a few pages.

Snaking Columns

Creating snaking columns—the kind you see commonly in newspapers and journals—is easy. Begin by choosing the Section... command from the Format menu. In the Columns portion of the Section dialog box, type the number of columns you want in the Number edit bar. In the Spacing edit bar, indicate the amount of gutter space that you want to appear between columns.

(The word *gutter* is used to refer to the space between columns of text as well as to the extra binding space that you use when you are printing facing pages. Throughout the remainder of this chapter, we'll use the term *column gutter* to refer to the space between columns and the term *page gutter* to refer to the extra left and right margin space that appears on facing pages.)

That's all there is to it—when you click OK to close the Section dialog box and return to your document, your text will appear in one narrow column on the screen. You won't be able to see both columns in your document window as they will appear on the printed page, but you can use the Page Preview... command to see the effects of your columnar formatting.

For example, to create the sample page shown in Figure 8-11, we started with Word's default Page Setup and Section dialog box settings. Then we issued the Section... command and specified a Number setting of 2 and a Spacing setting of .5. Figure 8-13 shows how this document appears on the screen.

FIGURE 8-13

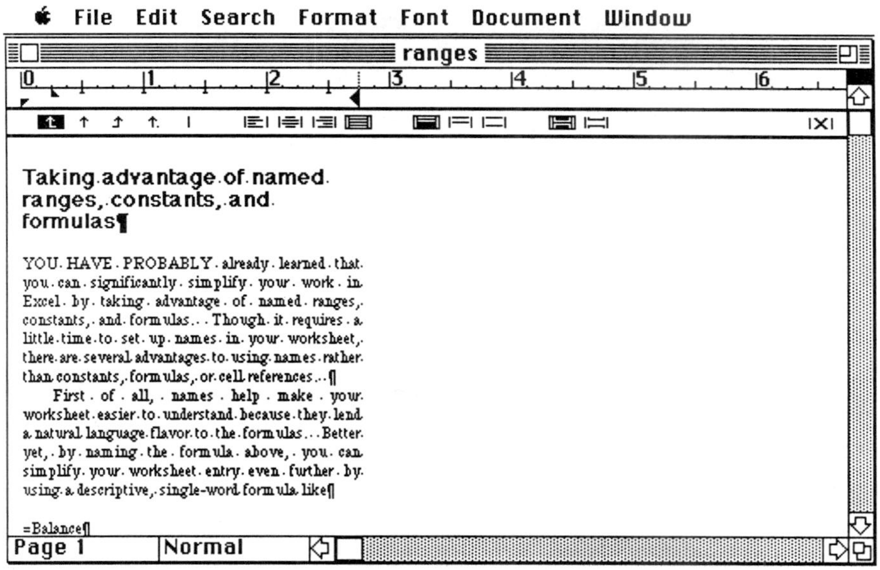

In our document window, the text appears in one long column.

Notice that the default right edge for our columnar text (indicated by the dotted vertical line on the ruler) now appears at the 2 $^3/_4$ inch mark instead of at the 6 inch mark. However, if you check the Page Setup dialog box, you'll see that Word has not changed the default Right margin setting of 1.25. When you use the snaking column format, the width of your columns depends on a number of factors, including the width of your text area, the number of columns to be placed on a page, and the distance between columns (the column gutter).

As you may remember from Chapter 7, to determine the width of your text area, you need to take into account your page size and orientation and your Left and Right margin settings. If you are using the Facing Pages option, you also need to consider the width of the page gutter that appears in the margin area of each odd and even page. Thus you can use a formula like this

Page width - left margin - right margin - page gutter = width of text area

to determine how much room you have to work with on the printed page. In addition to all of these factors, in order to determine the width of your columns in a multicolumn layout, you need to take into account the number of columns that will appear on the page as well as the gutter space between columns.

For example, in the sample document shown in Figures 8-11 and 8-13, our 6 inch text area is divided into two columns. This allows 3 inches for each column. Since we have decided to place an extra $^1/_2$ inch of gutter space between columns to separate them, we must subtract an equal amount from the width of each column to allow for this column gutter. Thus, the $^1/_2$ inch space between the columns in our sample document reduces the width of each of our columns by $^1/_4$ inch, leaving a total of 2 $^3/_4$ inches for the text.

To determine how wide your columns will be in any document, you can use the formula

$$\frac{\text{Width of text area - (Column gutter * (Number of columns - 1))}}{\text{Number of columns}} = \text{Column width}$$

Though this formula looks a little complicated, you'll find that it's really quite simple if you walk through it step-by-step. The *(Column Gutter * (Number of columns - 1))* portion of the formula computes the total amount of space between columns (or the total amount of space allotted to column gutters). You must subtract this number from the width of your text area before you can determine the amount of space available for text in each column.

Why do you need to subtract 1 from the number of columns in order to determine the total amount of gutter space? Your column gutters appear *between* columns, not to the left or right of each column. Thus, in a two-column page layout, you'll have one column gutter; in a three-column layout, you'll have two column gutters; and so forth. For example to determine the column widths for the sample page shown in Figure 8-11, you can use the formula

$$\frac{6 - (.5 * (2 - 1))}{2} = \frac{6 - .5}{2} = 2.75$$

If you are creating a three-column layout, on the other hand, you would use a formula like this:

$$\frac{6 - (.5 * (3 - 1))}{3} = \frac{6 - 1}{3} = 1.66$$

to determine the total column width. This formula allows room for two $^1/_2$ inch column gutters, rather than one. Thus, you must subtract a total of 1 inch from your text area before you can determine the width of each column.

To test out this formula, let's go back to the sample document window shown in Figure 8-11 and issue a new Section… command. If we specify a Number setting of 3 and leave the Spacing setting at .5, our document window will look like the one in Figure 8-14. Notice that Word has now narrowed our columns to about 1 $^{11}/_{16}$ inches (or approximately 1.66 inches). Figure 8-15 on the next page shows the resulting printed page.

FIGURE 8-14

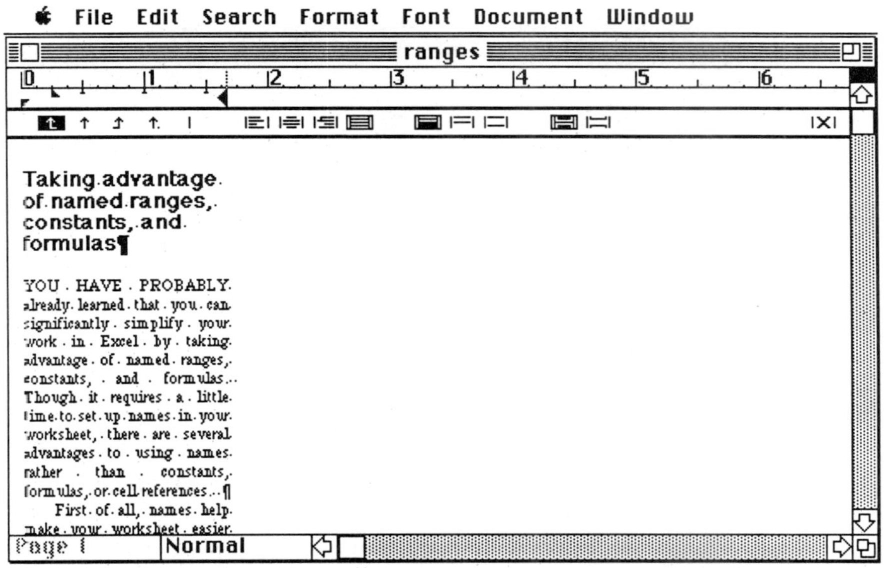

When we use a Number setting of 3 and a Spacing setting of .5, Word narrows our columns to 1 $^{11}/_{16}$ inches each.

If you find these formulas hard to grasp, perhaps you'll find it easier to visualize the effects of your column settings by creating a layout sketch of your multicolumn page. For example, Figure 8-16 on page 335 shows a layout sketch of the three-column page that we created in Figure 8-15.

Controlling column breaks

In Chapter 7, we presented several techniques for controlling page breaks in documents. Most of these same techniques can be applied in multicolumn documents to control column breaks as well as page breaks. For example, you can use the Widow Control option in the Page Setup dialog box to ensure that no single line from a paragraph will appear alone at the top or bottom of a column. You can also use the Keep Lines Together and Keep With Next ¶ options in the Paragraph dialog box to ensure that a paragraph is not split between two columns.

FIGURE 8-15

Taking advantage of named ranges, constants, and formulas

YOU HAVE PROBABLY already learned that you can significantly simplify your work in Excel by taking advantage of named ranges, constants, and formulas. Though it requires a little time to set up names in your worksheet, there are several advantages to using names rather than constants, formulas, or cell references.

First of all, names help make your worksheet easier to understand because they lend a natural language flavor to the formulas. Better yet, by naming the formula above, you can simplify your worksheet entry even further by using a descriptive, single-word formula like

=Balance

to compute your monthly check register balance.

Names also help you both ensure consistency between formulas and avoid errors. Once you have named the range, formula, or constant you want to work with, you can use the Paste Name... command to enter that name throughout your worksheet, thus avoiding the hassles of locating and retyping the value, reference, or formula in several locations. And, if you need to make a change to several formulas that use the same name, you can simply change the name definition rather than editing all of the formulas that use that reference, value, or formula.

As you'll see in a moment, Excel's naming capabilities also let you set up links between two or more worksheet files quickly and easily. Again, by using names to link worksheets, you can ensure consistency between files and make your assumptions explicit and easy to understand.

Generally, the larger and more complex your worksheet models, the more valuable you'll find Excel's naming capabilities. The Paste Name... command eliminates the need for scrolling long distances to find the cells you need to refer to when you are entering formulas. In addition, if you are not sure of a reference that you have used in one of your formulas, you can easily use the Goto... command to quickly see the contents of a named range, or you can use the Define Name... command to review the definition of a named range, constant, or formula.

However, before you begin scattering named ranges, constants and formulas throughout your worksheets, you should have a thorough understanding of how these elements work. Otherwise, you may inadvertently create errors in your worksheet calculations.

In this article, we'll show you several techniques for using named ranges, constants, and formulas in your worksheet models—and some common traps that you should avoid when you use Excel's naming facility in your own models.

Copying names between files

WHEN YOU COPY a formula that uses a name from one worksheet to another, Excel will transfer the name in that formula to the second worksheet as well. This can often be a convenient means of setting up parallel calculations in two similar worksheets.

To illustrate, take a look at the sales worksheet shown in Figure A. We used the Create Names... command to name cells B4 through F14. For example, as you can see in the Define Name dialog box shown in Figure B, the name Adams refers to cells B4 through F4. Notice that we used absolute references to refer to that named range. As you'll see in a moment, the reference style you select for your range definitions has a tremendous effect on your worksheet calculations.

Now, suppose you want to perform a similar set of calculations in the worksheet shown in Figure C. As you can see, this worksheet is set up just like the one in Figure A. So, to calculate sales totals for the week of October 13, you could simply copy the contents of cells G3:G14 and A15:G15 from the 10/6 Sales worksheet to the corresponding ranges in the 10/13 Sales worksheet, as shown in Figure D.

As you can see in Figure D, the formula

=SUM(Adams)

in cell G4 of the 10/13 Sales worksheet correctly calculates that agent's sales for the current period. If you take a look at the Define Name dialog box in this worksheet, shown in Figure E, you'll see that the name Adams, as well as all of the other range names in the formulas we copied from the 10/6 Sales worksheet, have been duplicated in the 10/13 Sales worksheet. All of these range name definitions are identical to those you saw in Table 1 for the 10/6 Sales worksheet,

This printed page shows the results of our three-column page layout.

Unfortunately, when you are working with snaking columns, there is no easy way to tell where the column breaks will occur in your document. When you repaginate a document that contains two or more columns, Word displays only your page breaks—not your column breaks—in your document window. The only way to see where your column breaks will fall is to print the document or to issue the Page Preview… command.

By the same token, Word does not make it easy for you to insert a column break in your document. If you use the Shift and Enter keys to force a manual page break in a multicolumn document, Word will force all of the text after the break to the top of the next page—not to the top of the next column. The only way to force a column break in your document is to create a new section (by pressing ⌘-Enter), click in the section where you want the new column to start, and then select the New Column option in the Section dialog box.

FIGURE 8-16

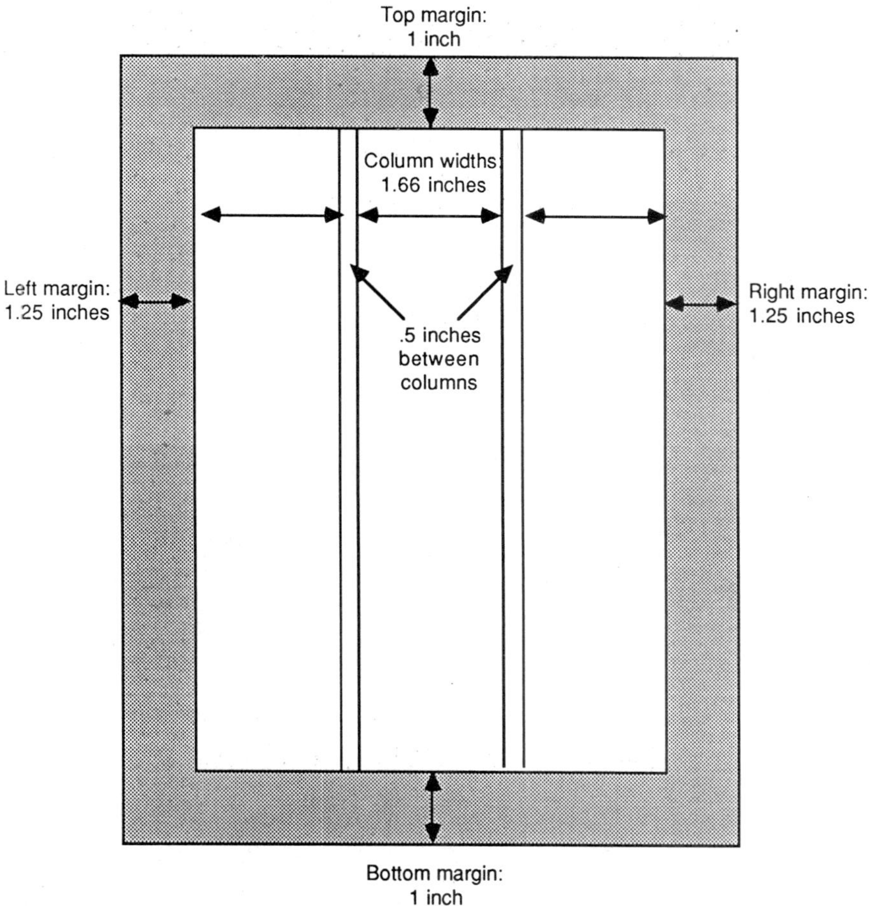

When you design a multicolumn layout, a layout sketch like this one may help you work out your column widths.

For example, in the sample document shown in Figure 8-15, suppose we want the headline in column 2 that reads *Copying names between files* to appear at the top of the third column in our sample document. In our document window, we'd have to click in front of the paragraph that contains this heading and press ⌘-Enter. Then, we'd click below the section break marker and issue the Section… command. Next, we'd choose the New Column option in the Section Start portion of the Section dialog box. Figure 8-17 shows the results.

FIGURE 8-17

Taking advantage of named ranges, constants, and formulas

YOU HAVE PROBABLY already learned that you can significantly simplify your work in Excel by taking advantage of named ranges, constants, and formulas. Though it requires a little time to set up names in your worksheet, there are several advantages to using names rather than constants, formulas, or cell references.

First of all, names help make your worksheet easier to understand because they lend a natural language flavor to the formulas. Better yet, by naming the formula above, you can simplify your worksheet entry even further by using a descriptive, single-word formula like

=Balance

to compute your monthly check register balance.

Names also help you both ensure consistency between formulas and avoid errors. Once you have named the range, formula, or constant you want to work with, you can use the Paste Name... command to enter that name throughout your worksheet, thus avoiding the hassles of locating and retyping the value, reference, or formula in several locations. And, if you need to make a change to several formulas that use the same name, you can simply change the name definition rather than editing all of the formulas that use that reference, value, or formula.

As you'll see in a moment, Excel's naming capabilities also let you set up links between two or more worksheet files quickly and easily. Again, by using names to link worksheets, you can ensure consistency between files and make your assumptions explicit and easy to understand.

Generally, the larger and more complex your worksheet models, the more valuable you'll find Excel's naming capabilities. The Paste Name... command eliminates the need for scrolling long distances to find the cells you need to refer to when you are entering formulas. In addition, if you are not sure of a reference that you have used in one of your formulas, you can easily use the Goto... command to quickly see the contents of a named range, or you can use the Define Name... command to review the definition of a named range, constant, or formula.

However, before you begin scattering named ranges, constants and formulas throughout your worksheets, you should have a thorough understanding of how these elements work. Otherwise, you may inadvertently create errors in your worksheet calculations.

In this article, we'll show you several techniques for using named ranges, constants, and formulas in your worksheet models—and some common traps that you should avoid when you use Excel's naming facility in your own models.

Copying names between files

WHEN YOU COPY a formula that uses a name from one worksheet to another, Excel will transfer the name in that formula to the second worksheet as well. This can often be a convenient means of setting up parallel calculations in two similar worksheets.

To illustrate, take a look at the sales worksheet shown in Figure A. We used the Create Names... command to name cells B4 through F14. For example, as you can see in the Define Name dialog box shown in Figure B, the name Adams refers to cells B4 through F4. Notice that we used absolute references to refer to that named range. As you'll see in a moment, the reference style you select for your range definitions has a tremendous effect on your worksheet calculations.

Now, suppose you want to perform a similar set of calculations in the worksheet shown in Figure C. As you can see, this worksheet is set up just like the one in Figure A. So, to calculate sales totals for the week of October 13, you could simply copy the contents of cells G3:G14 and A15:G15 from the 10/6 Sales worksheet to the corresponding ranges in the 10/13 Sales worksheet, as shown in Figure D.

As you can see in Figure D, the formula

=SUM(Adams)

in cell G4 of the 10/13 Sales worksheet correctly calculates that agent's sales for the current period. If you take a look at the Define Name dialog box in this worksheet, shown in Figure E, you'll see

In order to insert a column break in your document, you must create a new section and use the New Column option in the Section dialog box.

Combining single and multiple columns

Because snaking columns are controlled by the Section... command, you can change the number of columns that appear in your document on a section-by-section basis. If you want to use two or more column formats on the same page, then you should use the No Break Section Start option in the Section dialog box.

As you already know, when you use the No Break option in a single-column document, Word will print the first paragraph after the section break marker without inserting a page break. However, if your document contains one or more sections with multicolumn formatting, then Word will break columns at the section boundaries. This does not mean that the text in each new section will necessarily start at the top of a new column. However, Word will wrap the the columnar text within each section between the section boundaries. In other words, even when the No Break option is selected, Word will wrap the columnar text within each section separately from the text in other sections. Therefore, the location of your section breaks will determine the depth of the columns within each section. In this regard, the section break markers act somewhat like page break markers, even though no page break occurs in your printed document.

For example, consider the sample page shown in Figure 8-18. To create this page layout, we used the ⌘ and Enter keys to split our document into two separate sections. Then we highlighted the entire document (so that both sections were selected), issued the Section... command, and selected the No Break option in the Section Start portion of the dialog box. After closing the Section dialog box, we clicked in the second section of the document, reissued the Section... command, and entered Number and Spacing settings of 2 and .5, respectively.

FIGURE 8-18

Dean's Banquet

Dr. Robert R. Grayson, Dean of the School of Journalism, cordially invites you to attend a special banquet in honor of the graduating class of 1987. The following students will be recognized for their high scholastic achievement and dedication to the high standards of their profession:

Travis Adams
John Armstrong
Larry Arnold
Eric Baer
Amelia Bronson
Andrea Brown
Beverly Byers
William Chesterfield
Joanne Clark
Richard Downing
Diane Drummond
Theresa Evans
Donald Everett
Leigh Fielding
William Fredericks
John Hammond
Laura Hendricks
Richard Hunter
Ellen Johnson
Marjorie Jones
Lee Kent
Amy Morrison
Julia Myers
Oliver Neuman
Paul Nolte
Barbara Peters
Terry Pierce
Phyllis Prescott
Mary Richardson
Linda Robertson
Anna Samuels
Peter Smith
Scott Smythe
Paul Stark
Julian Taylor
Aaron Thompson
George Tyler
Zachary Vandecamp
Maureen Wallace
Steven Wells
Douglas Willard
Constance Wilson

We divided our document into two sections to create this page layout.

In this document, Word printed the text in the second section beginning just below the section break and extending to the bottom margin—this creates the first column. Then Word wrapped the text in this second section back to the top of the section—not to the top of the page—creating the second column.

The only problem with the result shown in Figure 8-18 is that the two columns are not balanced in length. To solve this problem, we might add another section just below the two-column section. Word will then wrap the two-column text between the section breaks, as shown in Figure 8-19. (As you can see, we have formatted this last section of the document to have only one column, and we've added some text in this section. However, if our only purpose in adding this third section is to force a column break in the two-column section, we could simply have entered a section break without typing any text.)

FIGURE 8-19

Dean's Banquet

Dr. Robert R. Grayson, Dean of the School of Journalism, cordially invites you to attend a special banquet in honor of the graduating class of 1987. The following students will be recognized for their high scholastic achievement and dedication to the high standards of their profession:

Travis Adams	Amy Morrison
John Armstrong	Julia Myers
Larry Arnold	Oliver Neuman
Eric Baer	Paul Nolte
Amelia Bronson	Barbara Peters
Andrea Brown	Terry Pierce
Beverly Byers	Phyllis Prescott
William Chesterfield	Mary Richardson
Joanne Clark	Linda Robertson
Richard Downing	Anna Samuels
Diane Drummond	Peter Smith
Theresa Evans	Scott Smythe
Donald Everett	Paul Stark
Leigh Fielding	Julian Taylor
William Fredericks	Aaron Thompson
John Hammond	George Tyler
Laura Hendricks	Zachary Vandecamp
Richard Hunter	Maureen Wallace
Ellen Johnson	Steven Wells
Marjorie Jones	Douglas Willard
Lee Kent	Constance Wilson

The banquet will begin at 7:30 p.m. on Saturday, June 6, in the Student Union Building Reception Hall. If you plan to attend, please return the enclosed reply card no later than May 31.

We divided our document into three separate sections to create this page layout.

Creating long headings

In a newspaper-style layout, you may want to create headings that stretch across two or more columns. To accomplish this, you might be tempted to simply drag the right indent marker for your heading to the right so that the heading extends across the width of the page. If you use this method, however, the text in your second column will overwrite your heading.

For example, notice the dotted vertical line that appears at the 2 3/4 inch mark on our ruler in Figure 8-13 on page 331. In response to our Columns settings, Word has set the default right edge for this text to 2 3/4 inches. Now, suppose that we decide to alter the heading of this document so that it stretches across both columns. To do this, we might click on the heading and then drag the right indent marker to the 6 inch mark, as shown in Figure 8-20.

FIGURE 8-20

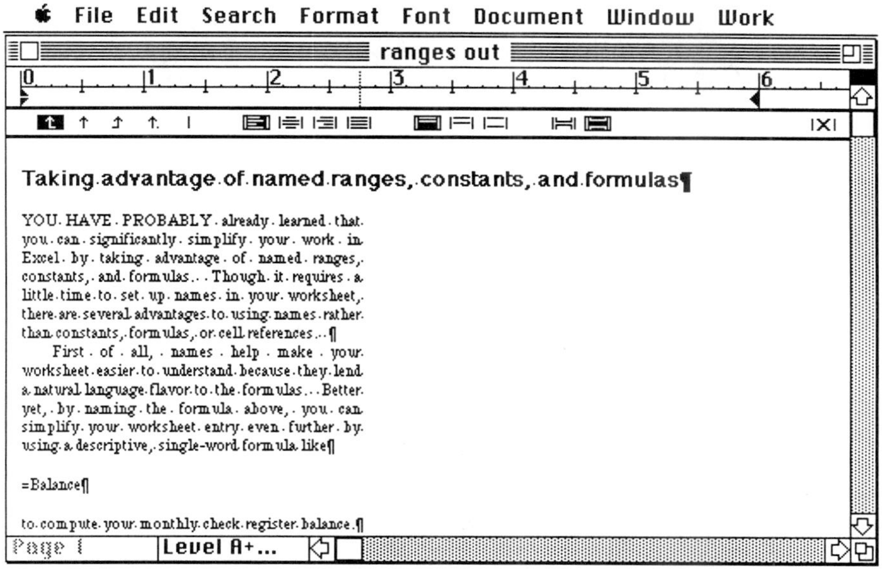

To format the heading for this document, we dragged the right indent marker to the 6 inch mark on the ruler.

Figure 8-21 on the following page shows what happens when we print this document. Though our heading does indeed extend across both columns, the text in the second column wraps back up to the top of the page and overwrites our wide heading.

To get around this problem, we can place our heading in a separate section. First we would click on the beginning of the first line after the heading and press ⌘-Enter to insert a section break. Then we would click anywhere in the first section (which contains the heading text), open the Section dialog box, and make sure that the Number setting in the Columns portion of the dialog box is 1. After closing the dialog box, we would click on the second section, choose the Section... command once more, and click the No Breaks option in the Section Start portion of the dialog box. Next, we would specify the number of columns (2) and the amount of space that we want to appear between columns (.5). As you can see in Figure 8-22 on page 341, when we print this document, the text in the second column starts on the same line as the text in the first column, rather than wrapping all the way back to the top of the page.

FIGURE 8-21

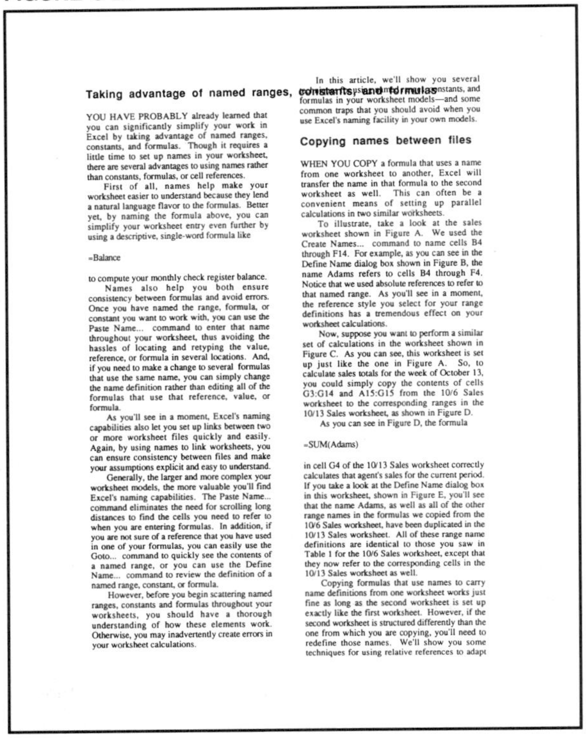

Taking advantage of named ranges, constants, and formulas

YOU HAVE PROBABLY already learned that you can significantly simplify your work in Excel by taking advantage of named ranges, constants, and formulas. Though it requires a little time to set up names in your worksheet, there are several advantages to using names rather than constants, formulas, or cell references.

First of all, names help make your worksheet easier to understand because they lend a natural language flavor to the formulas. Better yet, by naming the formula above, you can simplify your worksheet entry even further by using a descriptive, single-word formula like

=Balance

to compute your monthly check register balance.

Names also help you both ensure consistency between formulas and avoid errors. Once you have named the range, formula, or constant you want to work with, you can use the Paste Name... command to enter that name throughout your worksheet, thus avoiding the hassles of locating and retyping the value, reference, or formula in several locations. And, if you need to make a change to several formulas that use the same name, you can simply change the name definition rather than editing all of the formulas that use that reference, value, or formula.

As you'll see in a moment, Excel's naming capabilities also let you set up links between two or more worksheet files quickly and easily. Again, by using names to link worksheets, you can ensure consistency between files and make your assumptions explicit and easy to understand.

Generally, the larger and more complex your worksheet models, the more valuable you'll find Excel's naming capabilities. The Paste Name... command eliminates the need for scrolling long distances to find the cells you need to refer to when you are entering formulas. In addition, if you are not sure of a reference that you have used in one of your formulas, you can easily use the Goto... command to quickly see the contents of a named range, or you can use the Define Name... command to review the definition of a named range, constant, or formula.

However, before you begin scattering named ranges, constants and formulas throughout your worksheets, you should have a thorough understanding of how these elements work. Otherwise, you may inadvertently create errors in your worksheet calculations.

In this article, we'll show you several [illegible] constants, and formulas in your worksheet models—and some common traps that you should avoid when you use Excel's naming facility in your own models.

Copying names between files

WHEN YOU COPY a formula that uses a name from one worksheet to another, Excel will transfer the name in that formula to the second worksheet as well. This can often be a convenient means of setting up parallel calculations in two similar worksheets.

To illustrate, take a look at the sales worksheet shown in Figure A. We used the Create Names... command to name cells B4 through F14. For example, as you can see in the Define Name dialog box shown in Figure B, the name Adams refers to cells B4 through F4. Notice that we used absolute references to refer to that named range. As you'll see in a moment, the reference style you select for your range definitions has a tremendous effect on your worksheet calculations.

Now, suppose you want to perform a similar set of calculations in the worksheet shown in Figure C. As you can see, this worksheet is set up just like the one in Figure A. So, to calculate sales totals for the week of October 13, you could simply copy the contents of cells G3:G14 and A15:G15 from the 10/6 Sales worksheet to the corresponding ranges in the 10/13 Sales worksheet, as shown in Figure D.

As you can see in Figure D, the formula

=SUM(Adams)

in cell G4 of the 10/13 Sales worksheet correctly calculates that agent's sales for the current period. If you take a look at the Define Name dialog box in this worksheet, shown in Figure E, you'll see that the name Adams, as well as all of the other range names in the formulas we copied from the 10/6 Sales worksheet, have been duplicated in the 10/13 Sales worksheet. All of these range name definitions are identical to those you saw in Table 1 for the 10/6 Sales worksheet, except that they now refer to the corresponding cells in the 10/13 Sales worksheet as well.

Copying formulas that use names to carry name definitions from one worksheet works just fine as long as the second worksheet is set up exactly like the first worksheet. However, if the second worksheet is structured differently than the one from which you are copying, you'll need to redefine those names. We'll show you some techniques for using relative references to adapt

When we print the document, the text in column 2 overwrites our heading.

Side-by-Side Paragraphs

Newspaper-style "snaking" columns are fine when you want your copy to flow naturally from the bottom of one column to the top of the next. However, there may be times when you need to control the juxtaposition of individual paragraphs in each column. You can do this by assigning the Side-by-Side format to paragraphs. As far as we know, Word is the only word processing package that gives you this kind of control over the placement of your paragraphs. The Side-by-Side format is great for entering glossary-style text and for creating outjustified headings. You'll also find that the Side-by-Side format comes in handy for creating margin notes and for integrating text and graphics on a single page.

Though they are a little more complicated than snaking columns, side-by-side paragraphs can be an indispensable tool when snaking columns or other formatting techniques won't quite give you the result you want. For example, in the sample page that we showed you in Figure 8-12 on page 330, we used the Side-by-Side format to place the questions on the left side of the page next to selected paragraphs.

FIGURE 8-22

Taking advantage of named ranges, constants, and formulas

YOU HAVE PROBABLY already learned that you can significantly simplify your work in Excel by taking advantage of named ranges, constants, and formulas. Though it requires a little time to set up names in your worksheet, there are several advantages to using names rather than constants, formulas, or cell references.

First of all, names help make your worksheet easier to understand because they lend a natural language flavor to the formulas. Better yet, by naming the formula above, you can simplify your worksheet entry even further by using a descriptive, single-word formula like

=Balance

to compute your monthly check register balance.

Names also help you both ensure consistency between formulas and avoid errors. Once you have named the range, formula, or constant you want to work with, you can use the Paste Name... command to enter that name throughout your worksheet, thus avoiding the hassles of locating and retyping the value, reference, or formula in several locations. And, if you need to make a change to several formulas that use the same name, you can simply change the name definition rather than editing all of the formulas that use that reference, value, or formula.

As you'll see in a moment, Excel's naming capabilities also let you set up links between two or more worksheet files quickly and easily. Again, by using names to link worksheets, you can ensure consistency between files and make your assumptions explicit and easy to understand.

Generally, the larger and more complex your worksheet models, the more valuable you'll find Excel's naming capabilities. The Paste Name... command eliminates the need for scrolling long distances to find the cells you need to refer to when you are entering formulas. In addition, if you are not sure of a reference that you have used in one of your formulas, you can easily use the Goto... command to quickly see the contents of a named range, or you can use the Define Name... command to review the definition of a named range, constant, or formula.

However, before you begin scattering named ranges, constants and formulas throughout your worksheets, you should have a thorough understanding of how these elements work. Otherwise, you may inadvertently create errors in your worksheet calculations.

In this article, we'll show you several techniques for using named ranges, constants, and formulas in your worksheet models—and some common traps that you should avoid when you use Excel's naming facility in your own models.

Copying names between files

WHEN YOU COPY a formula that uses a name from one worksheet to another, Excel will transfer the name in that formula to the second worksheet as well. This can often be a convenient means of setting up parallel calculations in two similar worksheets.

To illustrate, take a look at the sales worksheet shown in Figure A. We used the Create Names... command to name cells B4 through F14. For example, as you can see in the Define Name dialog box shown in Figure B, the name Adams refers to cells B4 through F4. Notice that we used absolute references to refer to that named range. As you'll see in a moment, the reference style you select for your range definitions has a tremendous effect on your worksheet calculations.

Now, suppose you want to perform a similar set of calculations in the worksheet shown in Figure C. As you can see, this worksheet is set up just like the one in Figure A. So, to calculate sales totals for the week of October 13, you could simply copy the contents of cells G3:G14 and A15:G15 from the 10/6 Sales worksheet to the corresponding ranges in the 10/13 Sales worksheet, as shown in Figure D.

As you can see in Figure D, the formula

=SUM(Adams)

in cell G4 of the 10/13 Sales worksheet correctly calculates that agent's sales for the current period. If you take a look at the Define Name dialog box in this worksheet, shown in Figure E, you'll see that the name Adams, as well as all of the other range names in the formulas we copied from the 10/6 Sales worksheet, have been duplicated in the 10/13 Sales worksheet. All of these range name definitions are identical to those you saw in Table 1 for the 10/6 Sales worksheet, except that they now refer to the corresponding cells in the 10/13 Sales worksheet as well.

Copying formulas that use names to carry name definitions from one worksheet works just fine as long as the second worksheet is set up exactly like the first worksheet. However, if the

To avoid the overlap problem shown in Figure 8-21, we can place our long heading in a separate, single-column section.

Side-by-Side formatting requires two steps: First, you must issue the Paragraph... command and apply the Side-by-Side format to the paragraphs that you want to place beside each other on the printed page. Then, you must move the left and right indent markers on the ruler to position each paragraph. To determine where you should place your left and right indent markers, you need to decide how wide you want each column to be and how much space you want to appear between columns. In this respect, Side-by-Side formatting is not unlike the standard multicolumn formatting technique described above.

Let's walk through a quick example, then we will look at the rules for creating side-by-side layouts in more detail. To design the document shown in Figure 8-12, we began with the simple document shown in Figure 8-23. Currently, this document uses all of Word's standard Page Setup and Section dialog box settings.

FIGURE 8-23

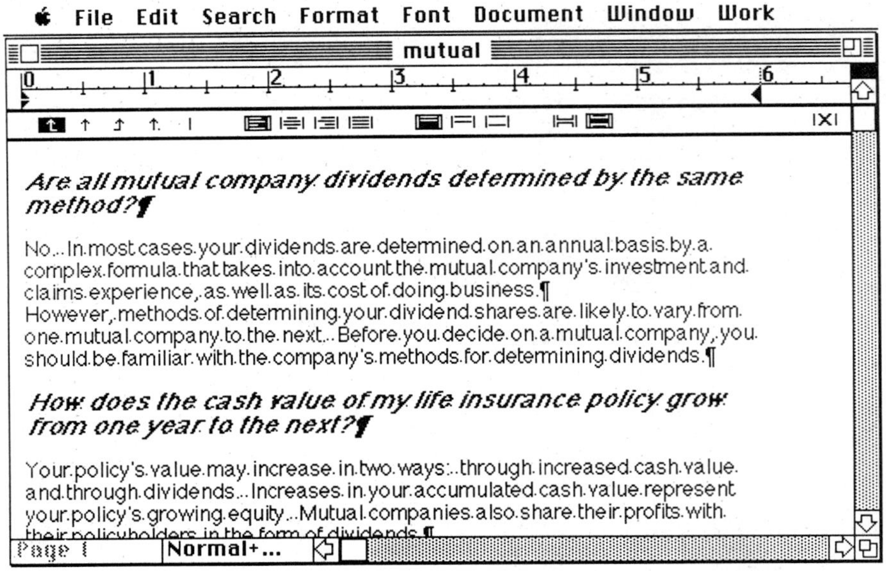

We'll use this sample document to illustrate Word's Side-by-Side formatting capabilities.

To change this document to a Side-by-Side format, we highlighted the first and second paragraphs, issued the Paragraph... command, and clicked the Side-by-Side option in the dialog box. Then we clicked on the first paragraph—our heading—and dragged the right indent marker to the 2 inch mark on the ruler. Next, we highlighted the second and third paragraphs and dragged the left and first-line indent markers to the 2 $^{1}/_{2}$ inch position. (We left the right indent marker at the default 6 inch position for these two paragraphs.) Then, we clicked on the third paragraph (the one that begins, *However, methods of determining*) and moved the first-line indent marker to the 2 $^{13}/_{16}$ inch point on the ruler. Figure 8-24 shows our screen at this point. Notice that the first two paragraphs don't actually appear side-by-side on the screen. Like the snaking column format, Side-by-Side formats are visible only when you print your document or when you view it on the Page Preview screen.

We used the same process to format the next three sets of side-by-side paragraphs. For example, we selected the fourth and fifth paragraphs, then opened the Paragraph dialog box and activated the Side-by-Side option for these paragraphs. Then we clicked on the fourth paragraph—our second heading—and dragged the right indent marker to the 2 inch position on the ruler. Next, we highlighted the two paragraphs that we want to place beside this second heading—the fifth and sixth paragraphs in our document—and again moved the left and first-line ident markers to the 2 $^{1}/_{2}$ inch position on the ruler. To create the first-line indent on the sixth paragraph, we clicked on that paragraph and then moved the first-line indent marker to the 2 $^{13}/_{16}$ inch mark on the ruler.

FIGURE 8-24

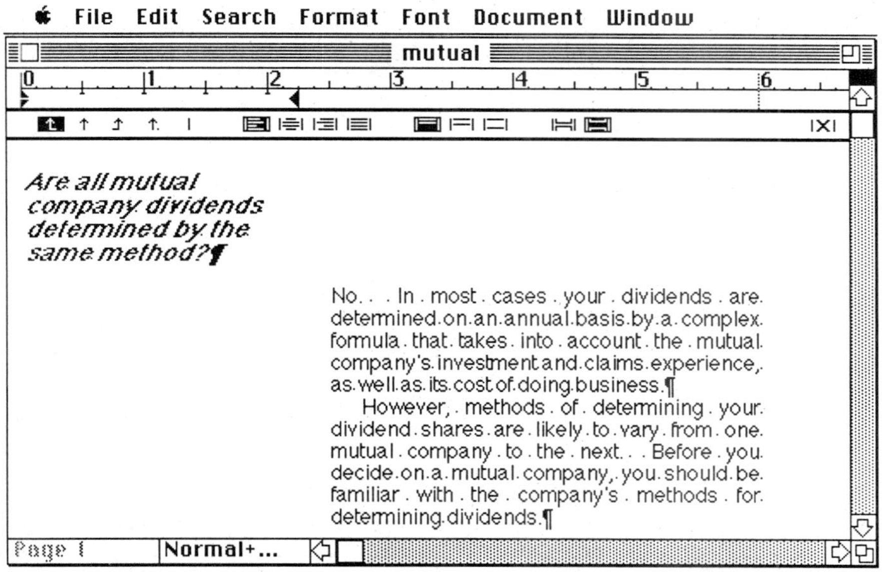

We have assigned the Side-by-Side format to these paragraphs and used the indent markers to divide the text into columns.

Page breaks

You may have noticed in our example that we did not assign the Side-by-Side format to every paragraph in our document. In fact, we assigned this format only to each of our bold headings and to the first paragraph next to each heading. We did not use the Side-by-Side format for our other paragraphs because this format can sometimes lead to problems in printing.

When you assign the Side-by-Side format to text, Word will attempt to keep all of the side-by-side text together on the same page. If necessary, the program will insert a page break to force all of the side-by-side paragraphs to the top of the next page in order to keep all of the text together.

For this reason, you should assign the Side-by-Side format only to those paragraphs that you actually want to appear beside one another. Even though you may indent the left and right margins for subsequent text so that it is aligned with your side-by-side paragraphs (as we did in our example), you should not assign the Side-by-Side format to these paragraphs. Otherwise, your printed document may contain awkward page breaks.

Line spacing

One of the tremendous advantages to side-by-side paragraphs is that you can use them to align text with different type sizes without creating awkward line-spacing problems. For example, in the document shown in Figure 8-12, the Side-by-Side format allowed us to place outjustified headings with 18-point bold type next to paragraphs with 12-point plain type. Naturally, the larger text in each of the headings requires greater line spacing than the 12-point text that appears in the paragraphs on the right side of the page. Nevertheless, Word is able to keep line spacing of the side-by-side paragraphs separate so that both the headings and the normal text paragraphs display proper leading.

Now, let's see what happens when you create a document with outjustified headings without the benefit of Side-by-Side formatting. Figure 8-25 shows a document in which we created outjustified headings by setting up a simple hanging indention. In this sample document, we combined our headings and body text in the same paragraph. Then we moved our left indent marker to the 3 inch mark and used a tab to separate the heading from the body text. (Because our first heading was two lines long, we also had to insert an extra paragraph to enter the second line of the heading next to the second line of our body text.) As you can see in Figure 8-25 and in the printed document shown in Figure 8-26, when we use this technique, our line spacing is uneven.

FIGURE 8-25

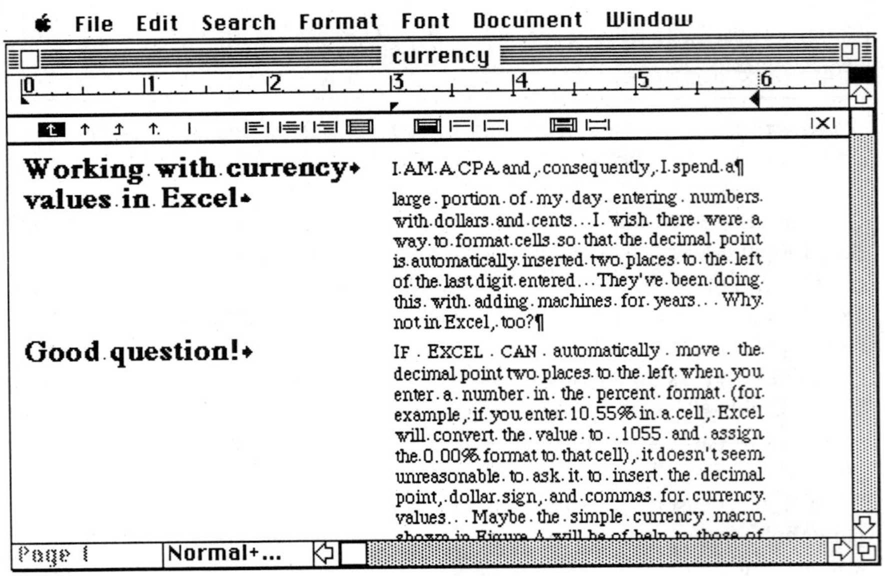

You can create outjustified headings with hanging indentions.

FIGURE 8-26

Working with currency values in Excel

I AM A CPA and, consequently, I spend a

large portion of my day entering numbers with dollars and cents. I wish there were a way to format cells so that the decimal point is automatically inserted two places to the left of the last digit entered. They've been doing this with adding machines for years. Why not in Excel, too?

Good question!

IF EXCEL CAN automatically move the decimal point two places to the left when you enter a number in the percent format (for example, if you enter 10.55% in a cell, Excel will convert the value to .1055 and assign the 0.00% format to that cell), it doesn't seem unreasonable to ask it to insert the decimal point, dollar sign, and commas for currency values. Maybe the simple currency macro shown in Figure A will be of help to those of you out there who work often with dollar and cent values.

You may remember a similar utility macro from the July issue of *Excellence*, in which Excel prompted the user for a numeric value and then transferred that entry to the worksheet in label form. That macro allowed the user to select only one value at a time, however.

We took a slightly different approach with this currency macro so that the user can enter labels, leave cells blank, or skip over existing entries without making a change. This interactive macro also allows you to select any size or shape range of cells for data entry, including discontinuous ranges.

When you use different font sizes in the same paragraph, your line spacing may be irregular.

By the way, when you use outjustified headings in side-by-side paragraphs, like the ones shown in Figure 8-12, you may want to add some line spacing above your headings to help break up the different portions of the document. If you decide to use this technique, be sure that you assign the same line spacing settings to all of your side-by-side paragraphs. Otherwise, the first line of your body text will not be properly aligned with your heading.

Aligning three or more paragraphs

If you want to place three or more paragraphs side-by-side, you must adjust both the left and right indents for your center columns. As with any complex page design, the best way to determine the proper settings for each set of side-by-side paragraphs is to create a sketch of your page layout. For example, suppose you want to create a page layout like the one shown in Figure 8-27.

FIGURE 8-27

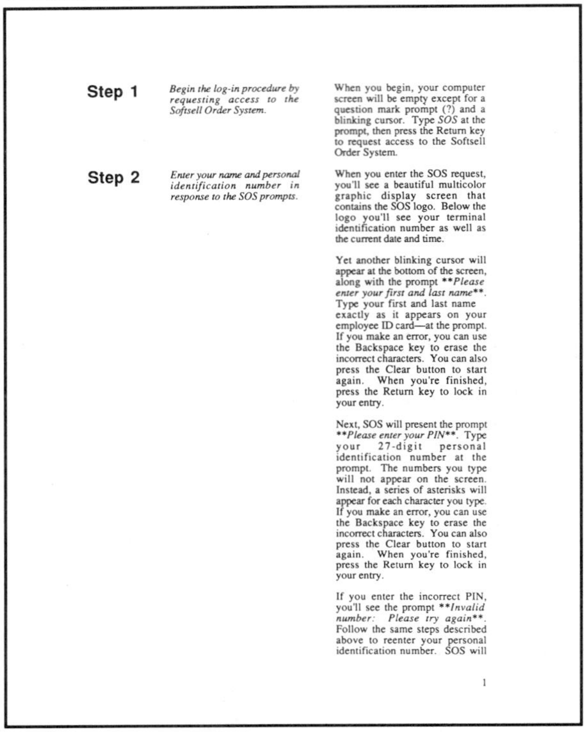

Step 1 *Begin the log-in procedure by requesting access to the Softsell Order System.* When you begin, your computer screen will be empty except for a question mark prompt (?) and a blinking cursor. Type *SOS* at the prompt, then press the Return key to request access to the Softsell Order System.

Step 2 *Enter your name and personal identification number in response to the SOS prompts.* When you enter the SOS request, you'll see a beautiful multicolor graphic display screen that contains the SOS logo. Below the logo you'll see your terminal identification number as well as the current date and time.

Yet another blinking cursor will appear at the bottom of the screen, along with the prompt ***Please enter your first and last name***. Type your first and last name exactly as it appears on your employee ID card—at the prompt. If you make an error, you can use the Backspace key to erase the incorrect characters. You can also press the Clear button to start again. When you're finished, press the Return key to lock in your entry.

Next, SOS will present the prompt ***Please enter your PIN***. Type your 27-digit personal identification number at the prompt. The numbers you type will not appear on the screen. Instead, a series of asterisks will appear for each character you type. If you make an error, you can use the Backspace key to erase the incorrect characters. You can also press the Clear button to start again. When you're finished, press the Return key to lock in your entry.

If you enter the incorrect PIN, you'll see the prompt ***Invalid number: Please try again***. Follow the same steps described above to reenter your personal identification number. SOS will

1

This document contains three side-by-side paragraphs.

To set up this page layout, you would first assign the Side-by-Side format to each of the paragraphs that you want to align across the page. Then, you would click on the first paragraph in the document and drag its right indent marker to the 1 inch point on the ruler. Next, you would click on the second paragraph and drag its left and first-line indent markers to the 1 $^1/_4$ inch point—this setting allows for $^1/_4$ inch between the right edge of the first paragraph and the left edge of the second. Now, with your insertion point marker still on the second side-by-side paragraph, drag the right indent marker to the 3 $^1/_4$ inch point. Finally, click on the third side-by-side paragraph and drag its left and first-line indent markers to the 3 $^1/_2$ inch point. Again, this allows $^1/_4$ inch between the right edge of the second paragraph and the left edge of the third. Figure 8-28 shows how your document window will look once you have formatted the first three paragraphs. Of course, you would follow the same steps to format the second set of side-by-side paragraphs, as well.

FIGURE 8-28

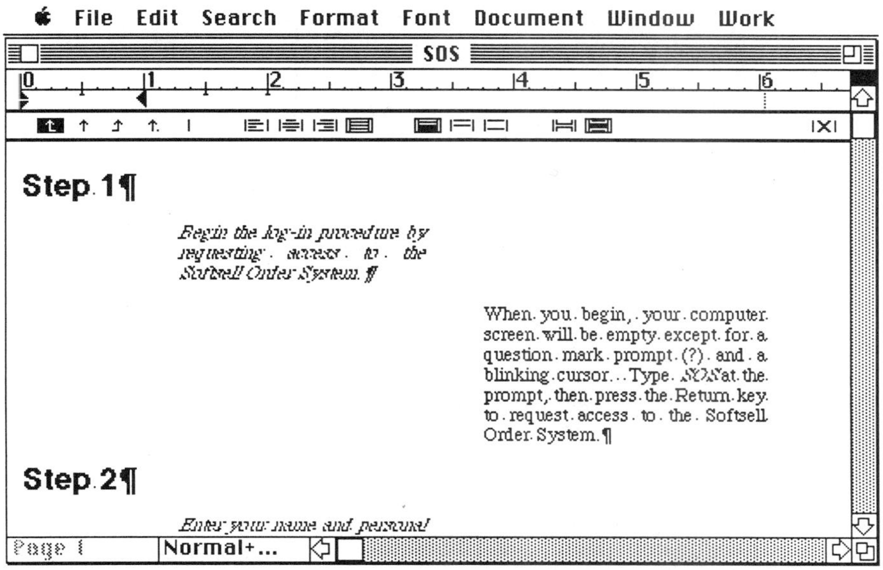

When you set up your first three side-by-side paragraphs, your document window will look like this.

Changing your column layout in the middle of a page

Because the Side-by-Side paragraph format is not a true multicolumn format—that is, you must manually place the text in the desired position on the page—you do not have to use section breaks to change your layout in the middle of a page. For example, suppose you want to create a page layout like the one in Figure 8-29 on the next page. You would assign the Side-by-Side format to the first two paragraphs to align them at the top of the page, then you would drag the right indent marker for the first paragraph to the 2 $^{1}/_{4}$ inch mark. Next, you would select the second and third paragraphs and drag the left indent marker to the 2 $^{1}/_{2}$ inch mark on your ruler. There is no need to create a new section or to alter the paragraph settings for the remainder of the text on the page; Word will automatically position this text below your last line of columnar text.

FIGURE 8-29

Are all mutual company dividends determined by the same method?	No. In most cases your dividends are determined on an annual basis by a complex formula that takes into account the mutual company's investment and claims experience, as well as its cost of doing business. However, methods of determining your dividend shares are likely to vary from one mutual company to the next. Before you decide on a mutual company, you should be familiar with the company's methods for determining dividends.

How does the cash value of my life insurance policy grow from one year to the next?

Your policy's value may increase in two ways: through increased cash value and through dividends. Increases in your accumulated cash value represent your policy's growing equity. Mutual companies also share their profits with their policyholders in the form of dividends.

You have the option of receiving these dividend payments directly or applying them to your future policy premium payments.

How can I evaluate my insurance policy's real worth?

Three factors affect the value of your whole life policy: your premium rate, your policy's cash value, and the dividends that you receive. These amounts are interdependent. However, when you measure your policy's value, your actual accumulated cash value is the bottom line.

The actual cash value of your policy depends on the guaranteed cash value specified for your policy, as well as those dividends that you use to increase the cash value.

Is a life insurance policy really a worthwhile financial investment?

Only if you really need life insurance coverage. The primary goal of any life insurance policy is to protect the financial security of the policy's beneficiary. However, your life insurance policy does provide an unbeatable combination of protection, savings, and growth.

In addition to the steady growth in cash value, with a mutual life insurance policy, you also have the opportunity to participate in the profitability of your insurer through dividends.

We used side-by-side paragraphs on the top portion of this page, then switched to a standard single-column layout in the bottom portion.

Using Side-by-Side formats within snaking columns

If you have used the Section... command to set up two or more snaking columns in your document, you can also use the Side-by-Side paragraph format within those columns. For example, to create the sample page shown in Figure 8-30, we used the Section... command to set up a two-column page layout with a $^1/_2$ inch gutter space between columns. As a result, Word automatically set our right indent marker to 2 $^3/_4$ inches.

Next, we assigned the Side-by-Side format to each paragraph. To format the Q and A headings, we shifted the right indent marker to the $^1/_2$ inch mark. Then we shifted the left indent marker for all the text paragraphs to the $^3/_4$ inch mark. Figure 8-31 shows how our formatted text appears in the document window.

FIGURE 8-30

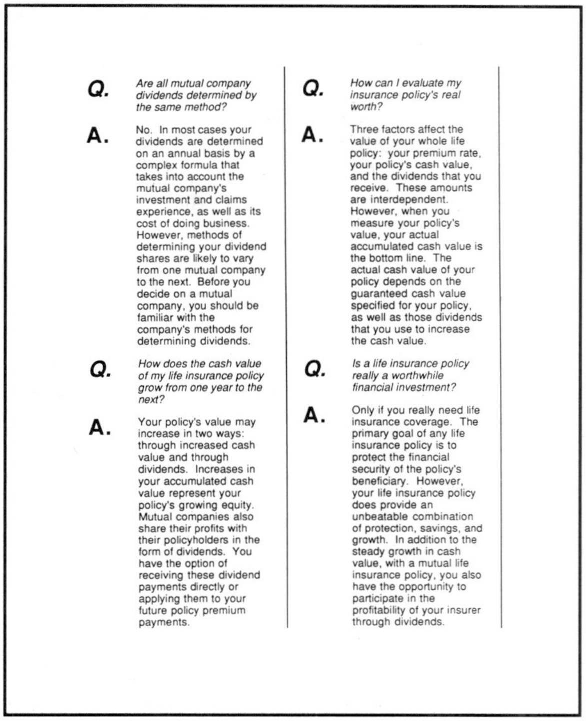

Q. *Are all mutual company dividends determined by the same method?*

A. No. In most cases your dividends are determined on an annual basis by a complex formula that takes into account the mutual company's investment and claims experience, as well as its cost of doing business. However, methods of determining your dividend shares are likely to vary from one mutual company to the next. Before you decide on a mutual company, you should be familiar with the company's methods for determining dividends.

Q. *How does the cash value of my life insurance policy grow from one year to the next?*

A. Your policy's value may increase in two ways: through increased cash value and through dividends. Increases in your accumulated cash value represent your policy's growing equity. Mutual companies also share their profits with their policyholders in the form of dividends. You have the option of receiving these dividend payments directly or applying them to your future policy premium payments.

Q. *How can I evaluate my insurance policy's real worth?*

A. Three factors affect the value of your whole life policy: your premium rate, your policy's cash value, and the dividends that you receive. These amounts are interdependent. However, when you measure your policy's value, your actual accumulated cash value is the bottom line. The actual cash value of your policy depends on the guaranteed cash value specified for your policy, as well as those dividends that you use to increase the cash value.

Q. *Is a life insurance policy really a worthwhile financial investment?*

A. Only if you really need life insurance coverage. The primary goal of any life insurance policy is to protect the financial security of the policy's beneficiary. However, your life insurance policy does provide an unbeatable combination of protection, savings, and growth. In addition to the steady growth in cash value, with a mutual life insurance policy, you also have the opportunity to participate in the profitability of your insurer through dividends.

In this sample document, we combined Word's Side-by-Side paragraph formats with the snaking column format.

FIGURE 8-31

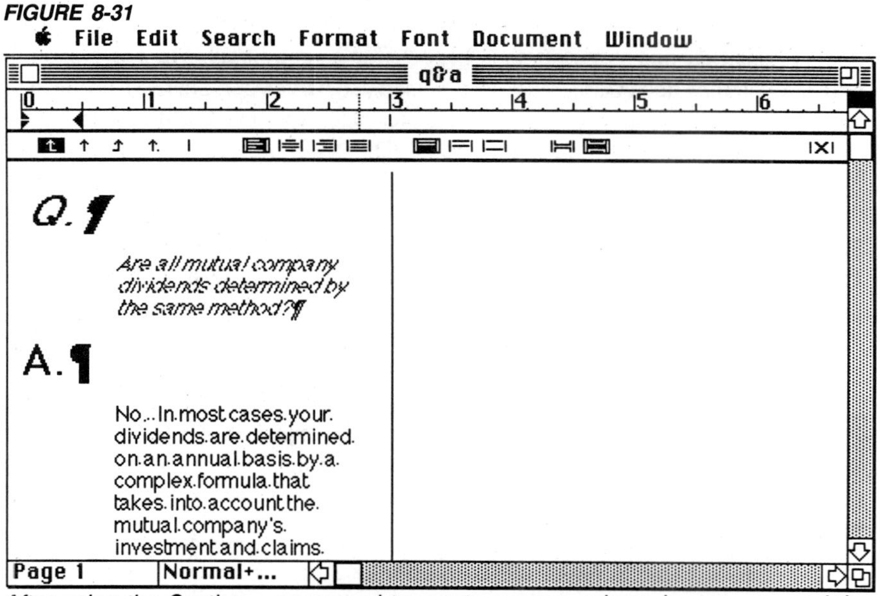

After using the Section... command to create our two-column layout, we used the Side-by-Side format to place the text in each column.

WORKING WITH LONG DOCUMENTS

Though your Word reference manual states that you can create documents as long as 250 pages (memory permitting), you'll probably find that files any longer than 50 pages increase processing time significantly and become difficult to handle. Of course, the practical size limit of any file depends on your Macintosh configuration and the complexity of the document.

If you have created a very long document that is divided into several sections, you may want to consider splitting that document into separate files and then linking the documents through the Page Setup dialog box. This technique is also helpful when you want the flexibility to mix and match various document files for printing.

For example, suppose you have created a 250-page document that consists of three chapters. Because you want to vary the headers and footers within each chapter and use multicolumn formatting on some pages, you've subdivided each chapter into several sections. As you might imagine, working with this document could get pretty complex. In addition, procedures like finding and changing, hyphenating, spell-checking, repaginating, and saving will slow down considerably when you're working with a document of this length.

The Next File option in the Page Setup dialog box makes it easy for you to break your complex documents down into smaller portions. With this option, you can split your document into smaller individual files and then pull all of the sections together when you print.

For example, suppose you've created a series of documents called Chapter 1, Chapter 2, and Chapter 3. Chapter 1 is 85 pages long, Chapter 2 is 97 pages long, and Chapter 3 is 68 pages long. To link these documents, begin by opening the Chapter 1 file and issuing the Page Setup... command. In the Page Setup dialog box, type the file name *Chapter 2* in the Next File edit bar. Now, open Chapter 2, and issue another Page Setup... command. In the Next File edit bar for that document, type the file name *Chapter 3*. There is no need to enter a Next File setting for the third chapter since it is the last document in the series. When you save the Chapter 1 and Chapter 2 files, Word will save your Next File settings to disk, along with your documents.

Now, whenever you print the file Chapter 1, Word will automatically print Chapter 2 and Chapter 3 as well. Chapters 2 and 3 do not have to be open when you issue the Print... command. Word will automatically retrieve from disk the information it needs to print those files. In fact, you can even print all three documents from the Finder level without loading the Word program. Just click on the icon for the Chapter 1 file, and issue the Print... command.

By the way, if you want to print Chapter 2 and Chapter 3 only, issue the Print... command from within Chapter 2, rather than Chapter 1. If you issue the Print... command while Chapter 2 is active on the Word DeskTop (or while the icon for Chapter 2 is selected at the Finder level), Word will start printing at the beginning of Chapter 2.

Page numbering

If you want the pages in your linked documents to be numbered sequentially when you issue the Print... command, you'll need to use the Start Page Numbers at option in the Page Setup dialog box to specify the starting page number for each document. To determine your starting page numbers, begin by opening the first file in the series and issuing the Repaginate command. Now, use the vertical scroll box on the right side of your document window to bring the last page of the document into view. Make a note of the page number in the status box at the lower-left corner of the screen. Continuing with our previous example, let's assume that the last page in Chapter 1 is page 85.

Next, open Chapter 2, issue the Page Setup... command, and type the value *86* in the Start Page Numbers at edit bar. When you close the Page Setup dialog box for Chapter 2, you'll see that Word displays *Page 86* in the page number status box at the bottom of your screen. Now, issue the Repaginate command. If Chapter 2 is 97 pages long, when you scroll to the last page in the document, you should see the page number reference *182*.

To number the pages in your third document, follow the same steps: Open the Chapter 3 file; issue the Page Setup... command; and type the starting page number *183* in the Start Page Numbers at edit bar. Again, if Chapter 3 is 68 pages long, when you repaginate this document, Word will number the pages from 183 to 250.

Line numbers and footnotes

If you are using line numbers or footnotes in your linked documents, you'll need to go through a similar process to set the starting values for these items. Use the Start Footnotes at and Line Numbers at edit bars to specify the beginning values you want to use for each document in the series. We'll talk more about these settings when we discuss footnotes in Chapter 13 and line numbers in Chapter 15.

Printing selected pages

When you link a series of documents for printing, you can use the From and To options in the Print dialog box to print any series of pages. If you have opted to number the pages in each document sequentially, just type the From and To values you want in the Print dialog box. For instance, in our previous example, suppose Chapter 1 in your series is 85 pages long and Chapter 2 is 97 pages long. Let's assume that you have opted to number the pages in these linked documents sequentially. If you issue the Print... command and enter a From setting of 80 and a To setting of 110, Word will print the last six pages of Chapter 1 and the first 25 pages of Chapter 2. The pages will be numbered 80 through 110, as you might expect.

If you have not used the Start Page Numbers at option to number each page in your document series sequentially, you may get some unexpected results when you use the From and To options to print linked documents. If the To option that you specify is less than the number of pages in the first document in the series, then Word will print the selected pages from that document only.

However, if your To setting is greater than the number of pages in the first document of the series, Word will begin printing again with the second document. If the second document contains fewer pages than you have specified in the To edit bar, then Word will continue printing with the third document, and so forth. In short, Word will keep printing until it finds a document that contains at least as many pages as you have specified in the To edit bar.

Again, suppose Chapters 1 and 2 in your linked series contain 85 and 97 pages, respectively, but you have not used sequential page numbering. When you issue the Print... command and type a From setting of 1 and a To setting of 90, Word will print pages 1 through 85 of Chapter 1 and pages 1 through 90 of Chapter 2.

Other Page Setup options

When you print linked documents, Word will remember most of the Page Setup dialog box options that you have selected for each file. For example, you can specify different Page, Paper Width, Height, Margins, Facing Pages and Gutter settings for each document. Generally, you'll probably want these settings to be consistent from one document to the next, but the ability to use different Page Setup options for each document may come in handy on occasion.

Oddly, Word will not remember your Orientation settings for each document. Instead, it applies the Orientation setting that you have specified for the first file in the series to all subsequent files. This idiosyncrasy is unfortunate since you might often find it handy to use the Next File option to incorporate a series of wide tables into a printed document.

By the way, if you are using headers, footers, or page numbers in your linked documents, keep in mind that you must create and format these items separately for each document in your linked series. Word will not automatically apply the headers and footers for your first document to any of the subsequent documents in your series. In addition, you must explicitly specify all of your Section dialog box settings for every document in the series—including activating the Page Numbering option, even if you plan to use the same Section settings for all of the documents.

3

SPECIAL SECTION THREE FEATURES

In Section Two, you learned all the basics you need to use Microsoft Word. By now, you should have mastered skills like creating, selecting, editing, formatting, and printing Word text. You should also have a handle on designing a page layout, creating and using document windows, and navigating in Word.

In this section, we'll go beyond these Word basics to look at a number of special features, like style sheets, the glossary, indexes, tables of contents, footnotes, form letters, and character formulas. You'll also learn how to customize your Word menus and control many default settings so that you can tailor the program to fit your needs. We'll show you how to share data with other programs — including PageMaker and Microsoft Excel — and describe how you can integrate graphics into your Word documents.

We urge you to explore these exciting, powerful features and take advantage of them. These are the added attractions that take Word 3 beyond simple word processing into the realm of desktop publishing.

STYLE SHEETS 9

WHAT IS A STYLE SHEET?

Style sheets are undoubtedly the most powerful new feature of Word 3. With style sheets, you can define the character and paragraph formats you want to use for various parts of your document and instruct Word to apply those formats automatically. As you can imagine, style sheets can save you a tremendous amount of time. They also help to ensure that your document is formatted consistently. As you'll learn in this chapter, you can even copy style sheets from one document to another to ensure that a group of files uses consistent formatting characteristics.

Each style sheet contains a collection of named styles. A named style is simply a set of instructions for formatting a paragraph. These instructions control the appearance of a paragraph by specifying both the character format options, such as font and point size, and the paragraph format options, such as indents and line spacing. (By the way, keep in mind that a paragraph in Word may be a block of text or a single line of text, such as a title.)

Typically, the instructions for a named style will control a combination of formatting features that you need to use in many paragraphs throughout a document. By recording these instructions on a style sheet, you won't need to repeat the same formatting process over and over again for similar paragraphs. Instead, you can simply apply a named style from the style sheet. In this way, a style sheet can greatly simplify and speed up the process of formatting a document.

For example, a style named *Figure Caption* might control all the formatting features that you need to apply to each figure caption in a document. Every time you create a figure caption, you can format it with one command, instead of issuing two or three commands and clicking on various ruler icons.

Style sheets also make it much easier and faster to modify a document's formatting. Once you have applied a named style in several places throughout a document, you can alter the format of every part of the document that uses this style in only one step. All you have to do is change the instructions for that named style on the style sheet. Word will then automatically reformat the appropriate parts of your document, using the new instructions.

Although style sheets are pretty complex, this is a topic that's well worth mastering. Using style sheets can greatly cut down on the time and tedium involved in creating and formatting documents, particularly lengthy documents. Once you begin to use style sheets, we think you'll find that they are one of the most important tools available in Word.

We'll begin our discussion of style sheets by covering a few basic concepts. Then we will walk through a brief example that illustrates some important style sheet techniques. After presenting this example, we'll examine each style sheet concept and technique in detail. You don't necessarily need to read this entire chapter from start to finish in order to use style sheets. If you feel that you have a sufficient grasp of a particular area, or if we're telling you more than you want to know, just skip on to the sections that interest you most.

STYLE SHEET BASICS

Whenever you start a new document, Word automatically creates a new style sheet for that document. This style sheet is called the default style sheet. Initially, the default style sheet will contain only one style, which is called *Normal*. You can modify the default style sheet to include other styles, if you want. (We will explain how to do this in the section at the end of this chapter called "Changing Defaults.")

Each document's style sheet is permanently linked to that document. However, you can change a document's style sheet in a number of different ways. You can add new styles, modify styles, delete styles, and even borrow styles from other documents. When you save a document, the style sheet—including any changes you've made—will be saved automatically.

It's important to note that every document uses a different style sheet. If you have more than one document open on your DeskTop, then each of those documents will have its own style sheet. Of course, several documents can use an identical collection of named styles. In fact, this is likely to be true if you've taken advantage of Word's ability to copy named styles from one document to another. (We'll explain how to do that later in this chapter.)

If you want to view the style sheet for a document, you can do so by choosing either Styles... or Define Styles... from the Format menu. Generally, you'll use the Styles... command to apply styles in your document and the Define Styles... command to edit your style sheet. However, you can apply styles from either dialog box. For example, when you begin a document, and *Normal* is the only style on the style sheet, the Styles... command will bring up the dialog box shown in Figure 9-1.

FIGURE 9-1

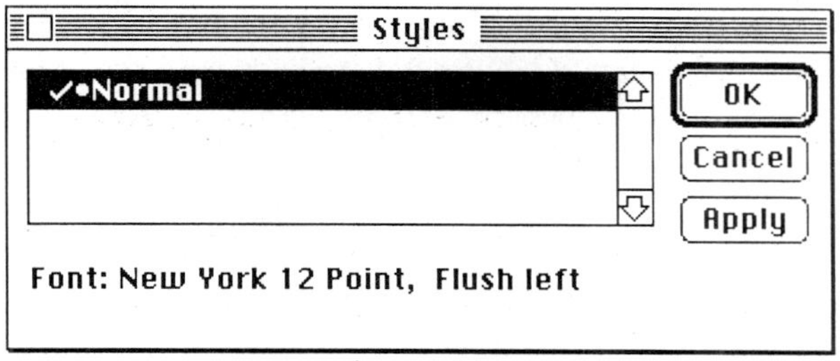

In a new document, Word's default style sheet will contain only the Normal *style.*

As you can see in Figure 9-1, the default *Normal* style specifies 12-point New York type with flush-left paragraph alignment. Text formatted with the *Normal* style will also have single spacing between lines and no indents. (As you may remember from Chapter 5, these are the default paragraph and character formats in Word.) If you want, you can change these default specifications for the *Normal* style, as we'll explain later.

The *Normal* style is what Word uses to format the main body text in a document. In fact, you can think of the *Normal* style as the default style for a document—any text that is not specifically assigned a different style will be formatted in the *Normal* style. Figure 9-2 shows how text that is formatted with the default *Normal* style will appear on your screen. Later in this chapter, we'll show how you can modify the appearance of this text by modifying the instructions for the *Normal* style.

FIGURE 9-2

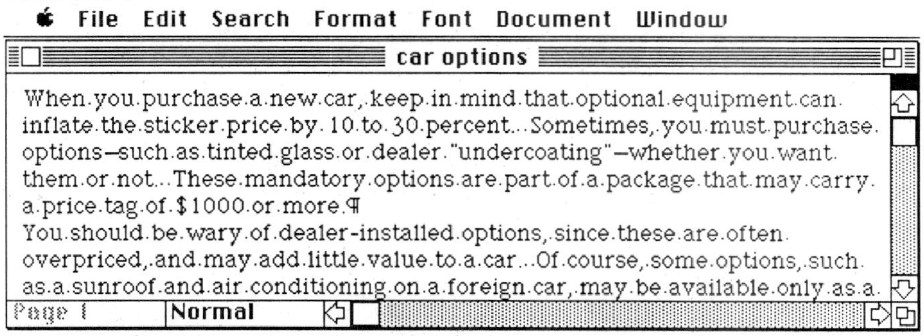

This screen shows how Word's default Normal *style will format text.*

Named Styles

As we mentioned in our introduction, every style sheet is made up of a collection of named styles. A style sheet might contain only one named style or as many as 255 styles. Each named style on a style sheet consists of a set of formatting instructions that control the appearance of a paragraph. We've already seen the instructions for the default *Normal* style and the effect of that style on the appearance of text. Those instructions are fairly simple and straightforward. In many cases, however, a style's instructions will be more complicated than those you see in Figure 9-1. For example, Figure 9-3 displays the instructions for a style named *list*, which we've added to the style sheet. In fact, the instructions for this style are so long, they cannot be displayed in their entirety in the dialog box.

FIGURE 9-3

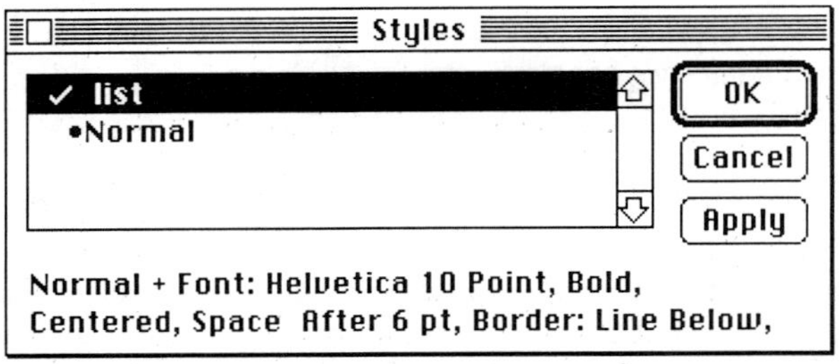

Style instructions can become fairly lengthy and complex.

You can use any named style on the style sheet to format any paragraph in a document, and you can apply a named style to as many paragraphs as you want. However, you cannot use a named style to format any part of a document that is less than a full paragraph. For example, you can use a named style to format several subheadings in a document, but you cannot use that style to format only one word in a subheading. (There are a few exceptions to this "full paragraph" rule. Word uses a named style to format page numbers and line numbers, when you choose to use them, and to format footnote references—the numbers or symbols that you use to call out footnotes in the body text of a document.)

Whether you choose to format your document using named styles or format your document text manually, every paragraph in a document will have a named style associated with it. Word displays the style name for the current paragraph in the style status box, which appears in the lower-left corner of the document window, next to the page number status box, as shown in Figure 9-4.

In most cases, unless you specifically choose another style, Word will assign the style named *Normal* to each paragraph in a document. This does not necessarily mean that each paragraph will manifest all of the formatting characteristics of the *Normal* style. The appearance of a paragraph can be controlled by *both* a named style and other formatting changes that you implement using menu commands and ruler icons. That's why you may see a plus sign after the style name on your screen—this tells you that the format of the current paragraph is determined by a named style *plus* other manual format changes that you have made.

FIGURE 9-4

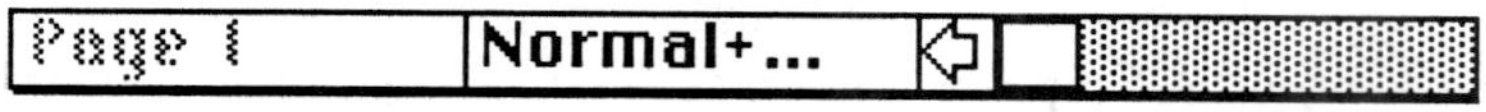

The Style Status box tells you which style has been used to format the current paragraph.

Although it's possible to format a paragraph using a combination of a named style and other formatting commands, you probably will find that, as you become familiar with style sheets, you will use named styles almost exclusively. With a named style, you can control every aspect of a paragraph's appearance. Table 9-1 summarizes the different characteristics that a named style can control.

TABLE 9-1

Left, Right, and First-line Indents
Tab Placement
Tab Type (Centered, Right Justified, Left Justified, Decimal)
Tab Leader
Paragraph Alignment (Flush Left, Centered, Flush Right, Justified)
Line Spacing within a Paragraph
Line Spacing above and below a Paragraph
Paragraph Border
Other Paragraph Formats (Side-by-Side, Keep With Next ¶, etc.)
Vertical Line Placement
Font
Point Size
Character Format (Bold, Italic, Underline, etc.)
Character Spacing (Normal, Condensed, Expanded)
Character Position (Superscript, Subscript, Normal)

You can control all of these formatting features with named styles.

In addition to the characteristics listed in Table 9-1, the instructions for a style can control which named style should be used next in a document. For example, suppose your style sheet includes the style named *level 2,* which controls the appearance of some of the subheadings in your document. The instructions for this style might also specify that the first paragraph after a *level 2* subheading should be formatted according to the *Normal* style. Thus, when you press Return after typing the *level 2* paragraph, Word will automatically start a new paragraph that is formatted in the *Normal* style. We will explain more about the Next Style and other style characteristics later in this chapter.

Viewing the instructions for a named style

If you want to view the instructions for a particular named style, choose either Styles... or Define Styles... from the Format menu and click on the name of the style whose instructions you want to see. (If the style sheet contains more than a few styles, you may need to scroll more names into view in order to click on the name of the style you're interested in.) Word will then display the instructions for the selected style in the dialog box on your screen. We've already seen, in Figures 9-1 and 9-3, how the Styles dialog box will display the instructions for a named style. Figure 9-5 shows the Define Styles dialog box, in which we've clicked on the style name *Normal*.

FIGURE 9-5

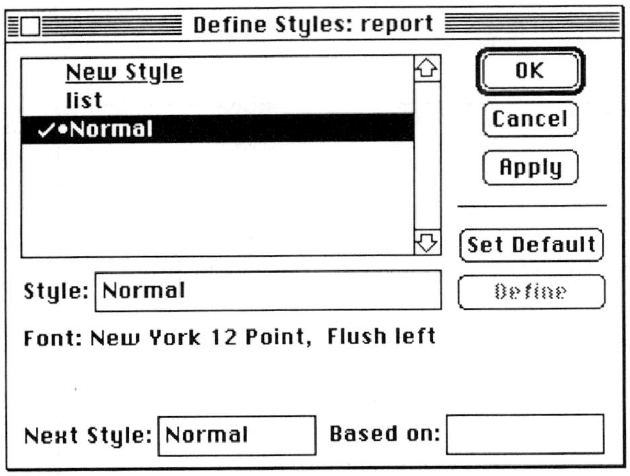

The Define Styles dialog box will display the formatting instructions for the style you select.

Although the instructions in the Define Styles dialog box are identical to the instructions that appear in the Styles dialog box, you might notice that the Define Styles dialog box gives a little more information about the selected style. Specifically, the Define Styles dialog box includes edit bars that list the Next Style and the Based on style. We'll be covering both the Next Style and the Based on style in detail later in this chapter.

Sometimes the formatting instructions for a style will be too long to be displayed in the dialog box. When this happens, you can examine the settings on the ruler and in the Character and Paragraph dialog boxes if you need to see all of the characteristics of the selected style.

By the way, if you compare the instructions for the *Normal* style in Figures 9-1 and 9-5 with the list of features in Table 9-1, you'll see that the instructions for the *Normal* style do not spell out every formatting characteristic. For example, the *Normal* style uses no indents, but this is not specifically stated in the instructions. Except for font, point size, and paragraph alignment, a style's instructions will make no mention of those formatting characteristics that are set to Word's defaults. (For additional information about Word's preset defaults, see Chapter 17.)

Another thing you should notice in Figures 9-1 and 9-5 is that a check mark appears next to the style name *Normal*. This check mark indicates that this is the style which has been applied to the current paragraph in your document (the paragraph on which the insertion point is positioned).

Linked styles

Often, the instructions for one named style will be based on the instructions for another style. In this case, the two styles are said to be linked to one another. The "dependent style" is the style whose instructions are based on another style, and the "Based on style" is the style on which the dependent style is based.

Many different styles can be linked to the same Based on style. For example, one style sheet might contain a dozen or more styles that are based on the style named *Normal*. When you view the instructions for a dependent style, you'll see that those instructions begin with the name of the Based on style. The remainder of the style's instructions will specify only those characteristics that are different from the instructions for the Based on style. For example, Figure 9-6 shows the instructions for a style named *Table*, which are *Normal + Centered*. These instructions are merely a shorthand way of saying, "Use all the style characteristics of the style named *Normal*, except use centered alignment instead of flush-left alignment."

FIGURE 9-6

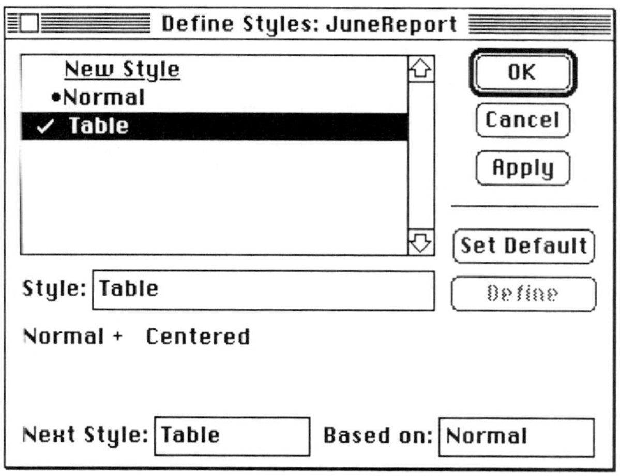

The instructions for a dependent style will specify the name of the Based on style and any characteristics that are different from the Based on style.

As you're setting up a style sheet, it's possible to create "chains" of linked styles. For example, you might have a style named *Style2*, which is based on a style named *Style1*. *Style1*, in turn, is based on the style named *Normal*. In this case, *Style2* is indirectly based on *Normal*. Thus, if you change the *Normal* style, *Style2* and *Style1* will change as well.

Throughout our discussion of styles, we will explain more about linked styles—how you can create a linked style, when you should use linked styles, and how to break the link between two styles. For now, however, you only need to be aware that they exist since the subject will crop up a number of times throughout our discussion of style sheets.

Automatic and custom styles

There's one final topic we need to cover in our discussion of style sheet basics, and that's the distinction between automatic and custom styles. Automatic styles are predefined styles, which are designed to format certain common elements of a document, such as subheadings, footnotes, headers, and footers. In fact, Word comes with a built-in "library" of 33 automatic styles.

The style named *Normal*, which Word always places on the default style sheet, is one of these 33 automatic styles. The other automatic styles do not appear on the default style sheet initially. However, Word will place them on a document's style sheet automatically as you add different elements to the document. For example, if you add a header to a document, Word will automatically format that header, using an automatic style called *header*. Word will also add the *header* style to that document's style sheet.

All of the automatic styles are based on the *Normal* style. Therefore, the formatting instructions for each of the automatic styles begin with *Normal* +. As we'll explain in a few pages, Word allows you to modify the instructions for any of its automatic styles.

In addition to automatic or predefined styles, a style sheet can contain custom styles that you create and name yourself. There are a couple of different ways to create a custom style for a style sheet, as we will explain later in this section. Before we talk about automatic styles, custom styles, and other style sheet concepts, however, let's walk through a quick example of creating, applying, and modifying styles.

AN EXAMPLE

Suppose you have begun a document by typing its title, as shown in Figure 9-7. As you can see, this text is formatted with Word's default *Normal* style. You would like to create a new style to format this title in 14-point, Helvetica, bold type.

Begin with the insertion point positioned anywhere on this title, and choose Define Styles... from the Format menu. In the Define Styles dialog box, make sure that New Style is selected, and enter the name *Title* in the Style edit bar. Then, without closing the Define Styles dialog box, issue the appropriate commands for formatting the title of the document. Choose Character... from the Format menu, and in the Character dialog box, select Helvetica from the Font Name list, then select 14 from the Font Size list box. Click the Bold format option, then click OK to close the Character dialog box. (The Define Styles dialog box will remain open.) Next, choose Paragraph... to open the Paragraph dialog box and display the ruler at the top of the screen. In the Paragraph dialog box, enter 12 in the After edit bar. Then, click the centered alignment icon on the ruler, and click OK in the Paragraph dialog box.

Next, in the Define Styles dialog box, click on the Next Style edit bar and enter the name *Normal.* When you've completed all of these steps, the dialog box should look like the one in Figure 9-8.

FIGURE 9-7

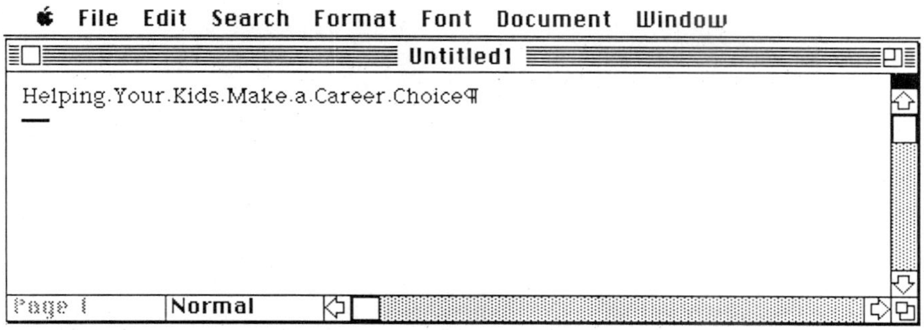

This screen shows the title for a new document.

FIGURE 9-8

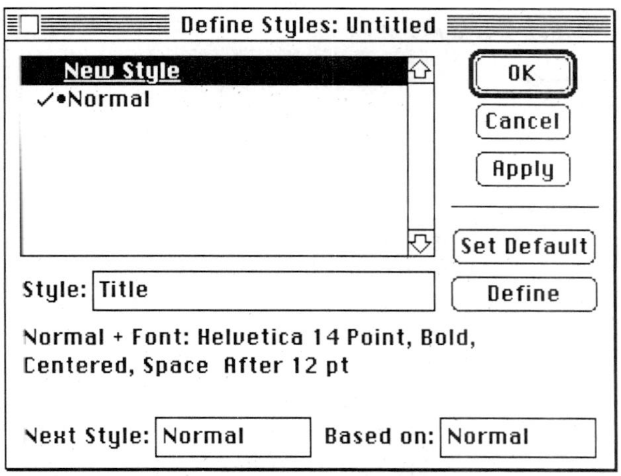

As you're defining a new style, Word will record your format selections in the Define Styles dialog box.

To apply the style to your document title and close the dialog box, click OK. Word will then automatically format the title according to the instructions for the new style that you just created.

If you place the insertion point at the end of the title and press Return, Word will start a new paragraph and format it using the *Normal* style. (Recall that we entered *Normal* in the Next Style edit bar of the Define Styles dialog box.) Figure 9-9 shows how your screen will look after you've formatted the title and entered a page or so of body text.

FIGURE 9-9

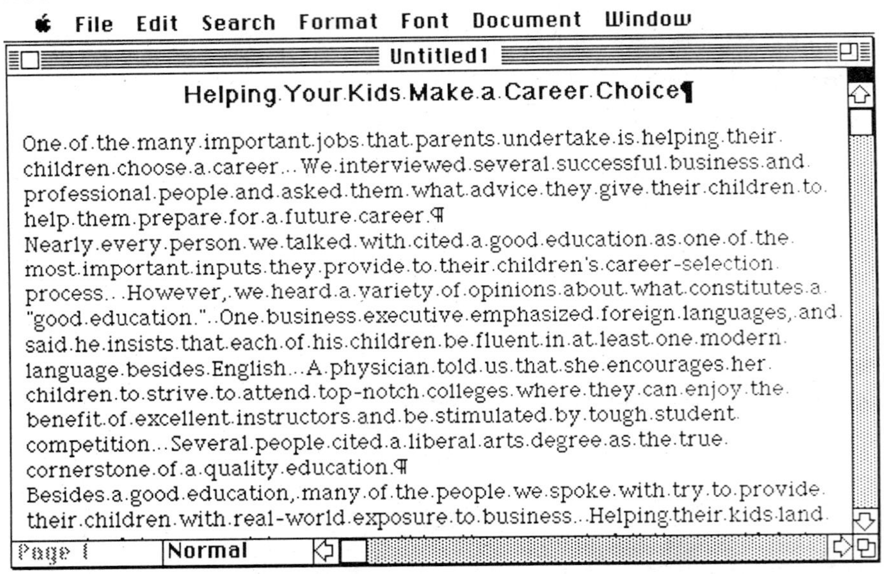

This screen shows the formatted document title and several lines of text formatted in the default Normal *style.*

Now, let us suppose you decide that you would prefer that the main body text in this document appear in 10-point New York type instead of 12-point New York. You also would like to indent the first line of each paragraph by $^1/_4$ inch. By changing the definition of the *Normal* style, you can automatically reformat all text that uses this style. Begin by opening the Define Styles dialog box, and then click on the style name *Normal* to select it. Next, choose 10 Point from the Font menu, then move the first-line indent marker to the $^1/_4$ inch mark on the ruler. To lock in the changes and close the dialog box, click OK. Figure 9-10 shows how your screen will appear at this point.

FIGURE 9-10

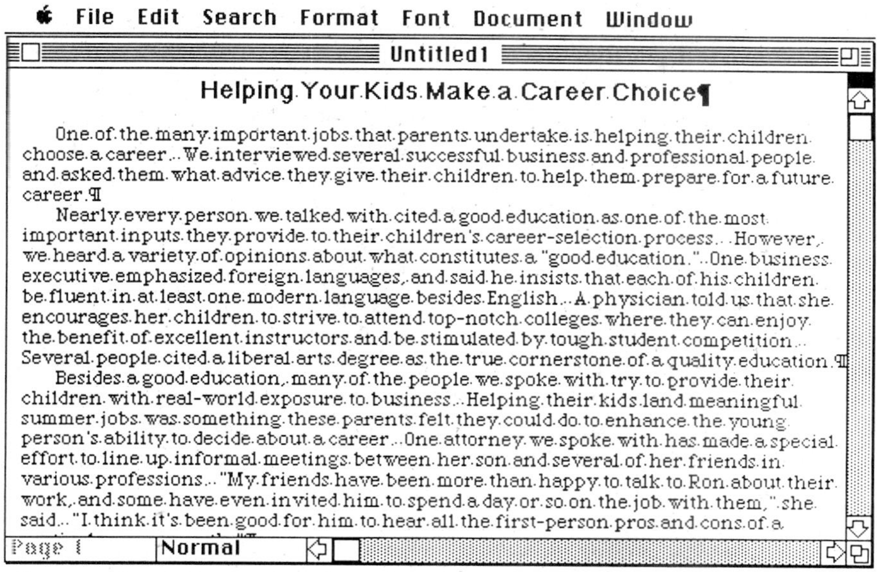

After you alter the instructions for the Normal *style, Word will automatically reformat the body text of the document.*

Notice that you did not need to select any text before you altered the *Normal* style. Word automatically applied the changes to all the text where this style had been used. Of course, in this example, the *Normal* style was used to format only a few paragraphs. You could easily have selected this text and reformatted it manually. If you were working with a longer document, however, you might have *Normal* text scattered among various other kinds of text with different formats—such as figure captions, subtitles, and so forth. When this is the case, changing the *Normal* style on the style sheet saves you the trouble of selecting and reformatting each individual section of body text.

Once you have defined one or more styles on a document's style sheet, you can apply a style to any paragraph in that document. To apply a style, you simply place the insertion point on the paragraph that you want to format, then choose Styles... or Define Styles... from the Format menu. In the dialog box, click on the name of the style that you want to apply, and click OK. Word will then automatically format the current paragraph and close the dialog box.

In the example we just described, you probably would not need to apply either of the styles on the style sheet since you've already formatted the title, and Word will continue to use *Normal* to format the remainder of the document. However, many, if not most, of the documents that you create in Word will require that you switch from one style to another as you create and format different sections of the document. Later in this chapter, we'll explain the techniques for applying styles in more detail. Before we talk about this and other style sheet techniques, however, let's take a look at the styles that Word creates for you—the automatic styles.

AUTOMATIC STYLES

As we explained in "Style Sheet Basics," automatic styles are predefined by Word. We use the term "automatic" to describe these styles because, in most cases, Word will place a predefined style on the style sheet automatically as it's needed. As you'll see in a minute, you also can add these styles manually, if you want.

The *Normal* Style

The *Normal* style is the predominant automatic style in Word. As we've already mentioned, whenever you start a new document in Word, the style sheet for that document will contain only one style—*Normal*. We've also seen in Figures 9-2 and 9-7 how text formatted with the default *Normal* style will appear on your screen. Because the *Normal* style is linked to most, if not all, of the other named styles in a document, it also controls, to some extent, the formatting of other elements in a document.

If you're like most users, the default *Normal* style will not be suitable for many of your documents. Therefore, you probably will want to modify the *Normal* style each time you start a new document. Of course, it's not imperative that you change the instructions for the *Normal* style on the style sheet. Instead, you can simply issue a few commands to alter the text on your screen in any way you want. However, as we will explain in a minute, there are certain advantages to modifying the *Normal* style on the style sheet, instead of manually formatting the text in your document.

We've already seen one example of what happens to a document when you modify the *Normal* style after you've entered some text. In many cases, however, you probably will want to modify the *Normal* style before you begin typing any document text. Suppose, for example, that you want to create a document whose main body text is 10-point Times type, with a $1/4$ inch indent on the first line of each paragraph, justified alignment, and double spacing. Before you type any characters in a new blank window, you can modify the *Normal* style to fit these characteristics. To do this, choose Define Styles... from the Format menu and click on the name *Normal* in the Define Styles dialog box. Then, without closing the Define Styles dialog box, choose Times, and then choose 10 Point from the Font menu. Next, choose Show Ruler from the Format menu (if the ruler is not already displayed on the screen). Move the first-line indent marker on the ruler to the $1/4$ inch position. Then, click the justified alignment icon and the double space icon. After you've completed these changes, the Define Styles dialog box will look like the one in Figure 9-11.

FIGURE 9-11

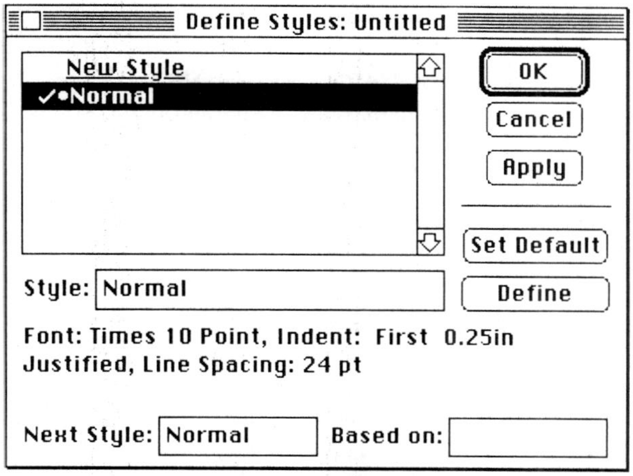

This dialog box shows the modified instructions for the Normal *style.*

Notice that Word has recorded all of the changes in the instructions for the *Normal* style. To complete the modification, click the Define button, or click OK or Apply. (After you create or modify style instructions, clicking Define will lock in your changes without closing the dialog box. If you click the Apply button, Word will lock in your changes and apply the style to the current paragraph without closing the Define Styles dialog box. Clicking OK will lock in the changes, apply the style to the current paragraph, and close the Define Styles dialog box.)

The procedure we have just described will change the *Normal* style for your current document only. In other words, the main body text of your document will be formatted with all of the characteristics you chose after you issued the Define Styles… command. However, if you start a new document in Word, the *Normal* style in that document will once again have the default style instructions (12-point New York type with single spacing, flush-left alignment, and no indents). Toward the end of this chapter, in the section entitled "Changing Defaults," we explain how you can modify the default *Normal* style.

Although we recommend that you change the *Normal* style before you type any text in a new document window, you can change the style at any time. As we demonstrated in our earlier example, if you have already typed some text using the "old" *Normal* style, then Word will automatically reformat that text according to any changes that you make to the style instructions.

Other Automatic Styles

As we mentioned above, Word offers 33 automatic styles that can be used to format certain elements found in many documents. Although these styles don't initially appear on the default style sheet, you can see a list of them by holding down the Shift key and choosing either Styles... or Define Styles... from the Format menu. (Word will not be able to display all of the automatic styles at one time, but you can scroll through the list of styles by clicking on the scroll bar next to the list box.) You'll notice that a bullet (•) appears next to the name of each automatic style. This symbol distinguishes the automatic styles from custom styles that you have created. Table 9-2 summarizes the name and purpose of each of Word's automatic styles.

TABLE 9-2

Style Name	Use to format
footer	Text in a footer window
footnote reference	The number or symbol that calls out a footnote in the document
footnote text	Text in a footnote window
header	Text in a header window
index 1, index 2,...index 7	Levels of entries in an index
level 1, level 2,...level 9	Levels of subheadings in a document
line number	Line numbers
Normal	All text that has not been assigned another style
page number	Page numbers
PostScript	PostScript commands that are embedded in document text
toc 1, toc 2,...toc 9	Levels in the table-of-contents text

Word's automatic styles are used to format specific elements of a document.

Adding an automatic style to a style sheet

We have mentioned briefly before how Word will place automatic styles on a document's style sheet when you add certain elements to that document. For example, if you add one or more footnotes to a document, Word will automatically place two styles on the style sheet. One style, named *footnote reference*, is used to format the number (or other symbol) that you place in the main body of your document to call out a footnote. The other style, called *footnote text*, is used to format the footnote itself.

All of the automatic styles are added to the style sheet in this way except the *PostScript* style and the styles named *level 1, level 2, level 3,* and so forth. The *PostScript* style must be added to the style sheet manually when you need to format PostScript commands that you have embedded in a document. (For more information on PostScript, refer to Chapter 15.) The various *level* styles, which are designed to format different levels of subheadings in a document, originate in an outline window.

Whenever you use Word's built-in Outliner to outline the subheadings in a document, Word will format these subheadings according to the automatic styles named *level 1*, *level 2*, and so forth. Word also will add these named styles to the style sheet. If you do not begin your document in an Outline window, Word will not automatically use the *level 1*, *level 2*, and so forth, styles to format your subheadings. That's because, without an outline, Word has no way of distinguishing a subheading from the rest of the document text. In Chapter 12, we will talk about the link between Word's Outliner and the automatic styles named *level 1*, *level 2*, and so forth.

If you want to use one of Word's automatic styles to format part of a document, you do not have to wait for Word to add that style name to the style sheet. Instead, you can add the style manually. To do this, hold down the Shift key, and choose Define Styles... from the Format menu. This will cause all of Word's automatic styles to appear in the list in the dialog box. Click on the name of the style that you want to add to the style sheet, then click OK or Apply. Apply will add the style to the style sheet and, at the same time, apply the style to the current paragraph. OK will perform both of these actions and close the Define Styles dialog box as well.

If you want to add an automatic style to the style sheet, but you don't want to apply that style to the current paragraph, you should click the Define button after you select the style. In order to make the Define button available (Word will initially display it in dim video), you must click on the Style edit bar where the style name is displayed. Then, after you've defined the style, you can close the Define Styles dialog box by clicking the Cancel button or by clicking the close box.

The Link between *Normal* and Other Automatic Styles

All of Word's automatic styles are based on the *Normal* style. This has two important consequences. First, the format specified by each of the automatic styles will, to some extent, be similar to the *Normal* style. For example, notice that the formatting instructions for the automatic style named *header* are displayed in the Define Styles dialog box that is shown in Figure 9-12 on the next page.

You can interpret these instructions as, "Use all the formatting characteristics of the *Normal* style and add two tab stops: one centered tab at the 3 inch ruler position and one flush-right tab at the 6 inch ruler position." If the *Normal* style specifies 12-point New York type (Word's initial default), then the text in a document's header also will be formatted with 12-point New York type.

Similarly, because the other automatic styles are based on *Normal*, other elements that you add to a document, such as a footer, page numbers, subheadings, and so forth, will use the New York font—or whatever font you've specified in the instructions for the *Normal* style.

FIGURE 9-12

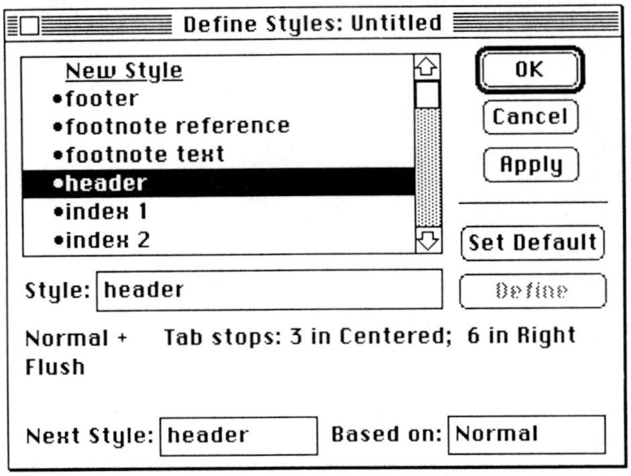

This dialog box shows the default formatting instructions for the automatic style named header.

Another consequence of the link between automatic styles and the *Normal* style is that any change that you make to the *Normal* style will affect each of the other automatic styles. For example, if you change the font for the *Normal* style from New York to Helvetica, then all of the other automatic styles will use the Helvetica font as well. Of course, the purpose of this is to help you maintain consistency of appearance among the different parts of a document.

We already have explained how you can modify the instructions for the *Normal* style, and in fact, we recommended that you do this each time you start a new document. This recommendation is especially important in light of the fact that all of the other automatic styles are based on the *Normal* style. By changing the *Normal* style first, you may be able to save yourself the trouble of changing each of the other automatic styles as well. On the other hand, if you do *not* modify the *Normal* style, but instead you manually format the main body text in your document, then you probably will need to adjust the formats of other document elements as well.

For example, suppose that you *don't* modify the instructions for the *Normal* style—you leave them with the default specifications of 12-point New York type with no indents. You then create a document and manually select and format the main body text in that document to appear in 10-point Helvetica type. Suppose you then decide to add a header to the document. Figure 9-13 shows how Word will format the text in the header window.

FIGURE 9-13

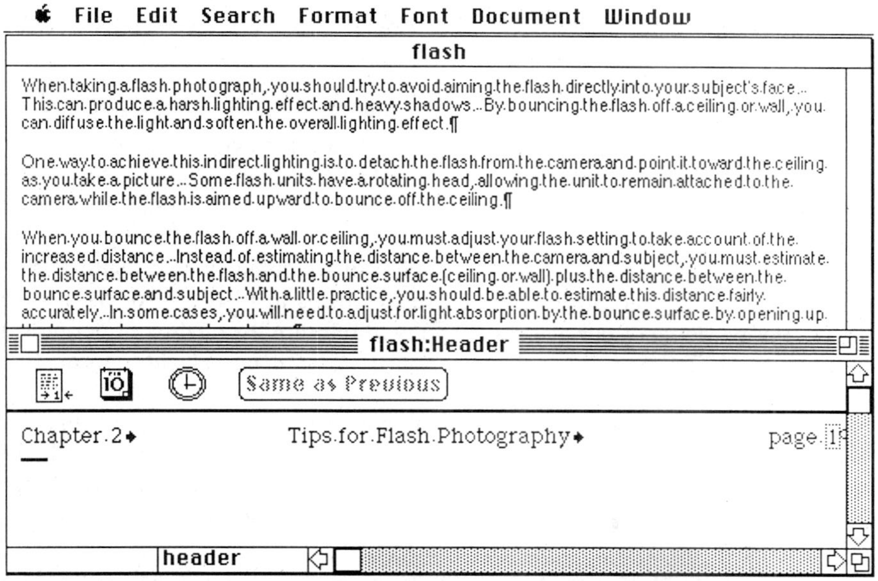

The appearance of text in a header window will reflect the formatting instructions of the Normal *style. Thus, the header won't necessarily match the format of the main body text of your document.*

Notice that the text of that header does not match the main body text of the document. Instead, it is formatted with 12-point New York type since its style is based on the *Normal* style. If you want the format of the header to be consistent with the rest of the document, you must either manually reformat the text in the header window or open the Define Styles dialog box and modify the instructions for the automatic style named *header*. The same thing will happen if you add a footer, page numbers, footnotes, or any other document element that is formatted according to one of Word's automatic styles. Each of these elements will come into your document in a format that is similar to the format for the *Normal* style but inconsistent with the main body text, which has been formatted manually.

To avoid the hassle of reformatting each document element or making extensive changes to the style sheet, one of your first steps in creating a document should be to modify the instructions for the *Normal* style. Then you won't need to worry about the various elements that you add to the document being inconsistent with the main body text of the document.

Although modifying the *Normal* style offers an excellent starting point for changing Word's other automatic styles, you can, of course, change each of these styles directly. You also can break the link between any automatic style and the *Normal* style. We will talk about the various techniques for modifying styles in a few pages. However, since style modification techniques apply to both custom styles and automatic styles, let's first consider how you can add custom styles to a style sheet.

CUSTOM STYLES

Adding a custom style to a style sheet involves two steps: entering a name for the style and defining the formatting instructions for that style. To create (or define) a new custom style, you issue the Define Styles... command, type a style name in the Style edit bar of the dialog box, and then select menu commands and click on ruler icons to specify the formatting characteristics that you want that style to have. As you're choosing commands and manipulating ruler icons, Word records your format selections as instructions for the named style. For purposes of our discussion, we will refer to this method of defining a new style as defining "by selection" since it involves selecting formatting options and ruler icons.

Another method for defining a new style is to define "by example." In other words, you can format a paragraph in your document to have all the characteristics that you want to use in a named style, then issue the Define Styles... command and assign a name to that collection of formatting characteristics.

The main difference between defining a style by selection and defining by example is that when you're defining by example, you issue all of the formatting commands *before* you open the Define Styles dialog box. One major advantage of defining a style by example is that you can see the effects of your formatting specifications before you "lock them in" in your style sheet. This is especially helpful when you are designing a new style that may require quite a bit of fine-tuning to achieve just the right appearance. Let's consider how you might use each of these methods to define a new style.

Defining by Selection

Suppose that you want to create a new style named *Figure Caption.* You want this style to specify 10-point, New York, bold type with centered alignment. The style instructions will also specify a 12-point line space above and a 12-point line space below the formatted text. To define this style by selection, you would first choose Define Styles... from the Format menu. Word will then display the Define Styles dialog box, as shown in Figure 9-14.

FIGURE 9-14

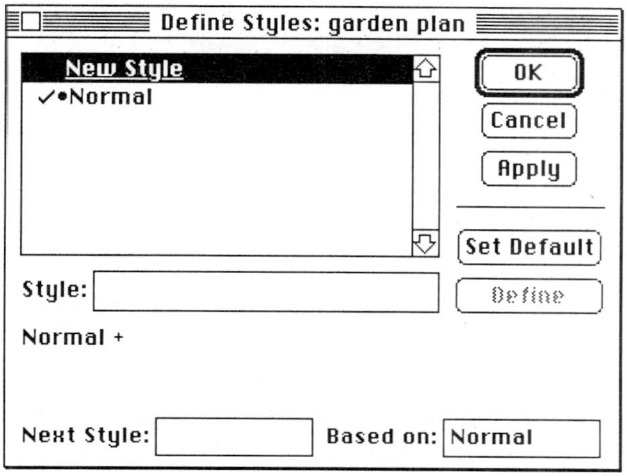

To create a new style, begin by opening the Define Styles dialog box.

There are two things that you should notice about this dialog box. First, you can see that Word automatically highlights New Style at the top of the list of styles in the dialog box. Each time you open the Define Styles dialog box, Word assumes that you want to add a new style to the style sheet.

Another thing to notice in this dialog box is that Word has begun the instructions for the new style with *Normal* +. Word also displays the style name *Normal* in the Based on edit bar in the lower-right corner of the dialog box. Whenever you define a new style, Word assumes that you want that style to be based on the style of the current paragraph (the paragraph where the insertion point is located when you issue the Define Styles... command). In our example, the insertion point was positioned on a paragraph that was formatted with the *Normal* style when we selected Define Styles.... Therefore, Word assumed that we wanted to create a new style that would be based on the *Normal* style.

In most cases, you will want to base each new style on an existing style, so we won't change this situation in our example. In a few pages, we will discuss the Based on style in more detail and explain how you can create a style that's *not* based on an existing style. For now, however, let's continue the process of defining the new style.

After you've opened the Define Styles dialog box, you need to enter a style name and then select the formatting features that you want that style to use. It makes no difference which you do first. In our example, you can begin by entering the style name *Figure Caption* in the Style edit bar. Then choose 10 Point from the Font menu, and choose Bold from the Format menu. Next, select Paragraph... from the Format menu. In the Paragraph dialog box, type a 12 in the Before edit bar and another 12 in the After edit bar. Then click on the ruler icon for centered paragraph alignment. Finally, click OK to close the Paragraph dialog box. At this point, the Define Styles dialog box should look like the one in Figure 9-15. Notice that Word has recorded all of our format selections in the style's instructions.

FIGURE 9-15

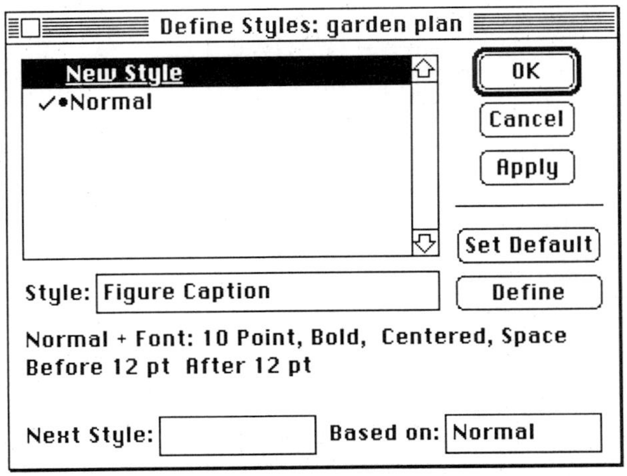

As you're creating a new style, Word will record your format selections in the instructions for that style.

The last step in defining the new style is to add it to the style sheet. You can do this by clicking the Define button. When you click Define, Word will place the style name *Figure Caption* in the list of styles, and the Define Styles dialog box will remain open. If you want to apply the style to the current paragraph at the same time that you define it, you should click either Apply or OK. OK will apply the style and automatically close the dialog box, whereas Apply will apply the style without closing the Define Styles dialog box.

Defining by Example

Now, let's consider how you might define this same style by example instead of by selection. Suppose that you have entered the text for a figure caption in a document, and you want to format that text. First, you would select the caption paragraph, then you would issue the appropriate formatting commands. For example, Figure 9-16 shows an unformatted figure caption that's been selected. To format this as a style example, you would choose 10 Point from the Font menu and choose Bold from the Format menu. Then you would select Paragraph... from the Format menu and enter 12 in the Before edit bar and type another 12 in the After edit bar. With the caption still selected, you would click on the centered alignment icon on the ruler. When you click OK to close the Paragraph dialog box, your figure caption will look like the one in Figure 9-17.

FIGURE 9-16

To define a new style by example, begin by entering and selecting the text that you want to format.

FIGURE 9-17

This screen shows the formatted text that will serve as the example for a new style.

Of course, in most cases, you won't be able to arrive at an acceptable format for a new style so quickly. Usually, the process of designing a format for a particular part of a document—such as a figure caption—is a matter of trial and error. That's why you might want to experiment with the format on your screen *before* you define it as a named style. In addition, this formatting by example technique can come in handy when you've manually formatted a paragraph and then decide that you want to use that format in other locations in your document. Rather than manually reformatting the other text, you can use the first paragraph as your example to define a new style. Then, you can just click on the paragraphs to which you want to apply this style and use the Apply button in the Styles dialog box to "copy" the format of your example paragraph to the other text.

To save your example format on the style sheet, choose Define Styles... from the Format menu while the insertion point marker is positioned anywhere on the formatted paragraph. As usual, Word will highlight New Style at the top of the list of styles in the dialog box. However, Word also will display the formatting instructions for the current paragraph in the dialog box, as shown in Figure 9-18. Notice that this dialog box looks identical to the one shown in Figure 9-15, except that the style name does not yet appear in the Style edit bar.

FIGURE 9-18

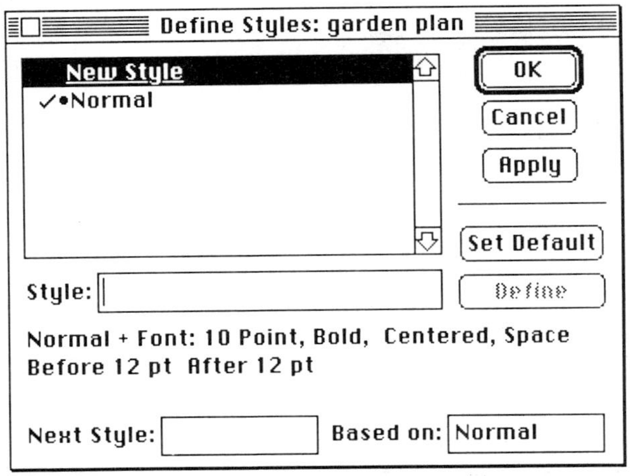

When the insertion point marker is positioned on formatted text, the Define Styles dialog box will display the formatting instructions for that text.

All you need to do at this point is enter the name *Figure Caption* in the Style edit bar and click either Define, OK, or Apply. Word will then add that style to the style sheet for the current document.

When you're defining a style by example, the instructions for the new style will probably be complete when you open the Define Styles dialog box. However, if you want, you can select additional commands and/or ruler icons after the dialog box is open. If you do this, Word will modify the initial style instructions according to your selections. (You might consider this technique to be a combination of defining by selection and defining by example.)

By the way, as you can see in Figure 9-18, the instructions for the new style begin with *Normal* + and the style name *Normal* appears in the Based on edit bar. When you define a new style by example—as when you define a style by selection—Word assumes that you want the new style to be based on the original style of the paragraph that you are using as the style example. As you'll see in a moment, you can edit the Based on style to change the links between styles.

The Apply and Define buttons

The Apply button in the Define Styles dialog box also gives you the flexibility to format by trial and error. For example, suppose you want to change the format of a heading in your document, but you are not sure exactly what you want the heading text to look like. Begin by placing the insertion point anywhere on the paragraph you want to format, and open the Define Styles dialog box. Enter a style name in the Style edit bar and define the instructions for that style. When you think that the style instructions are complete, click the Apply button. Word will then reformat the paragraph where the insertion point is positioned without closing the Define Styles dialog box. If you don't like the results of this new style's formatting, you can issue the appropriate commands to change the style instructions and click Apply again. Each time you click Apply, Word will reformat the text, incorporating any changes to the style instructions.

If the Define Styles dialog box blocks your view of the paragraph you're trying to format, just move the dialog box off your screen temporarily. When you drag the dialog box by its title bar, Word will allow you to hide almost the entire dialog box from view. About $^1/_4$ inch of the title bar will remain in view. To display the dialog box again, just drag it back to the middle of the screen.

The Define button lets you Define a style without necessarily changing the format of the paragraph where your insertion point marker is located. When you use the Define button to place a new style name in your style sheet or to change the instructions for an existing style, Word will record your changes and will apply them to any paragraphs that carry that style name. If your insertion point marker happens to be on a paragraph that carries another style, however, Word will not change the format of that paragraph unless you click the OK or Apply button. Thus, if you want to change a style definition without changing the format of the current paragraph, just click Define, then click the close box or the Cancel button in the Define Styles dialog box.

The Based on Style

We have already explained how one style can be based on or linked to another in the style sheet. You might recall that each of Word's automatic styles is based on the style named *Normal*. As we described, this link between *Normal* and the other automatic styles causes each of the automatic styles to reflect, to some degree, the characteristics of the *Normal* style. Moreover, any change that you make to the *Normal* style will affect the other automatic styles as well.

As we have just demonstrated, whenever you define a new custom style for a style sheet, Word assumes that you want that new style to be based on an existing style. In our examples, we created a new style that was based on *Normal*. However, each time you create a new style, that style won't necessarily be based on *Normal*. In fact, Word always assumes that you want each new style to be based on the style of the paragraph where the insertion point marker is located when you issue the Define Styles... command. This may be the

Normal style, or it may be another style. In any case, it's a good idea to think about which style you want to use as your Based on style before you begin to define a new style. That way, you may be able to save some time in defining the new style's formatting instructions.

For example, suppose that you want to create a new style named *Style1*, which has all the characteristics of the default *Normal* style except that the first line of each paragraph is indented by $^1/_2$ inch. Since this new style is so similar to *Normal*, it would make sense to use *Normal* as the Based on style. Therefore, before you begin defining *Style1*, you should be sure that the insertion point is positioned on a *Normal* paragraph. Then, when you choose Define Styles..., Word will automatically enter *Normal* in the Based on edit bar dialog box and will begin the instructions for the new style with *Normal* +. To complete the definition of *Style1*, you only need to drag the first-line indent marker to the $^1/_2$ inch position on the ruler, and then click Define. All of the other formatting characteristics of *Style1* will be "borrowed" from *Normal*, the Based on style.

Specifying a different Based on style

When you're defining a new style, you don't have to use the Based on style that Word suggests. Instead, you can enter a different style name in the Based on edit bar of the Define Styles dialog box. For example, suppose that you have created a style named *Sub1* to format the first-level subheadings in a document. This style specifies 14-point, Helvetica, bold type with a 6-point line space below the formatted text. Figure 9-19 shows the instructions for this style in the Define Styles dialog box.

FIGURE 9-19

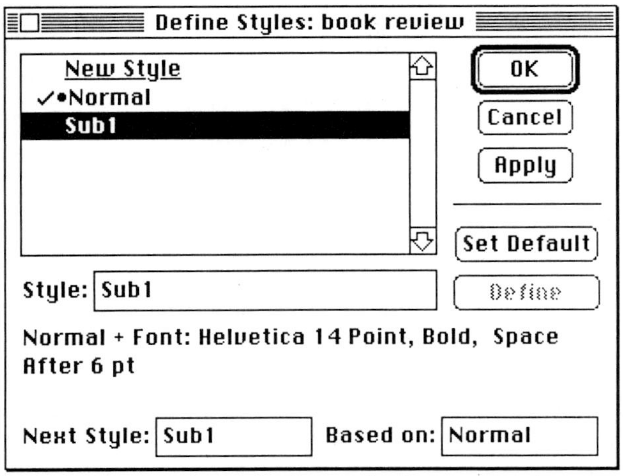

This dialog box shows the formatting instructions for a custom style named Sub1.

Let's suppose that you want to define another style, named *Sub2*, which will be identical to *Sub1*, except that it will specify 12-point font size. However, we'll assume that your insertion point is positioned on a paragraph that has been formatted with the default *Normal* style when you begin to define the *Sub2* style. When you issue the Define Styles... command, Word will assume that the new style should be based on *Normal*, as shown in the dialog box in Figure 9-20.

FIGURE 9-20

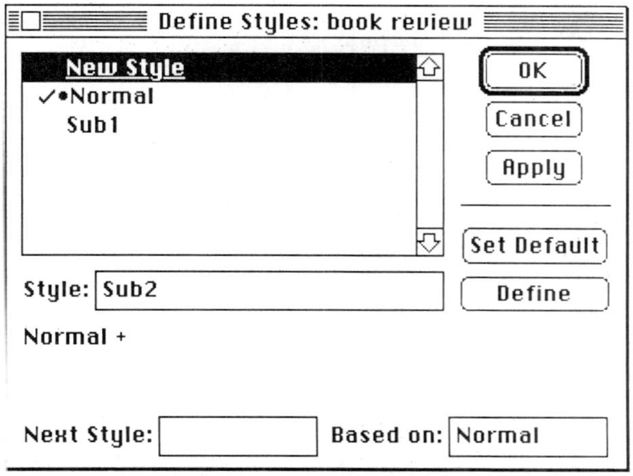

When you begin to define a new style, Word uses the style of the current paragraph as the Based on style for that new style.

To change the Based on style to *Sub1*, drag through the name *Normal* in the Based on edit bar to select it. Then, type the name of the style you want to use as the Based on style—in this case, *Sub1*. After you type a different name in the Based on edit bar, Word will not automatically use that name in the style's instructions. In other words, the instructions that appear just below the Style edit bar in the dialog box will still read *Normal* +. To incorporate the new Based on style in the instructions, you must click the Define button, or click anywhere on the Style edit bar. (You'll need to click the Style edit bar, anyway, if you haven't yet entered a name for the new style that you're defining.) Word will then change the instructions for the new style so that they begin with *Sub1* +.

Unfortunately, after you change the style name in the Based on edit bar from *Normal* to *Sub1*, Word still assumes that you want the format of the new style to match the format of the current paragraph. For example, Figure 9-21, shows the Define Styles dialog box after we changed the Based on style. As you can see, even though *Sub1* is the Based on style, Word has automatically altered the instructions for the new style so that they include all of the formatting characteristics of the current paragraph.

FIGURE 9-21

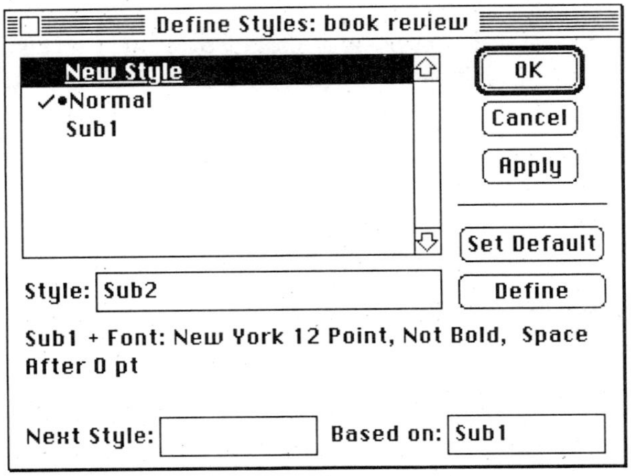

After you change the name of the Based on style, Word alters the formatting instructions of the new style that you're defining. These altered instructions will specify all of the characteristics of the style that has been used to format the current paragraph.

To correct this situation, you must issue the various formatting commands to define the *Sub2* style properly. Open the Character dialog box, and select Helvetica as your font, select 12 as your size, and then click the Bold option. After you close the Character dialog box, choose Paragraph... from the Format menu, enter 6 in the After edit bar, and click OK. When you click Define in the Define Styles dialog box, Word will change the instructions for the new *Sub2* style as shown in Figure 9-22.

Notice that the instructions for *Sub2* are now quite brief; they simply specify the Based on style, *Sub1*, and the single difference between *Sub2* and *Sub1*, point size. It would have been nice if we could have defined *Sub2* by entering *Sub1* as the name of our Based on style and then choosing 12 Point from the Font menu. Instead, we had to define *Sub2*'s formatting instructions as though we were starting from scratch.

This example illustrates how, even though Word allows you to specify a different Based on style as you're defining a new style, you can save yourself time and effort by positioning the insertion point marker on a paragraph that has been formatted with the style that you want to use as the Based on style. Then, when you open the Define Styles dialog box, you can take advantage of Word's suggested Based on style. If you don't position the insertion point properly, you can speed up the process of defining the new style by copying and pasting the instructions for an existing style into the instructions for that new style. We'll discuss that technique in detail in a few pages.

FIGURE 9-22

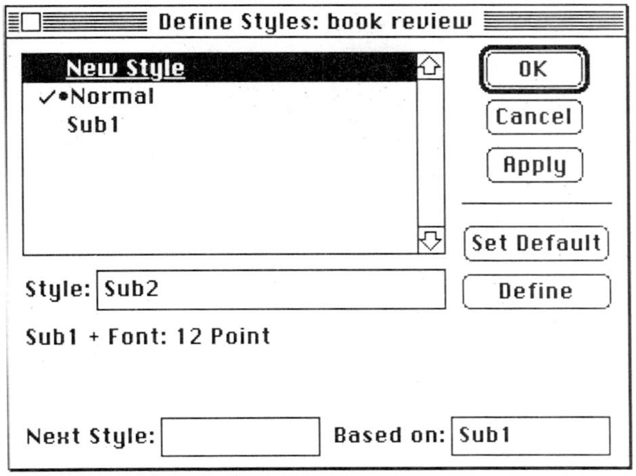

After you issue the appropriate formatting commands, Word will alter the instructions for the new style that you're creating.

Creating a new style that is not based on an existing style

There may be times when you want to create a style that is completely independent of other styles in your style sheet. To do this, you can simply erase the contents of the Based on edit bar in the Define Styles dialog box as you are creating the new style.

For instance, suppose you're defining the *Figure Caption* style that we described in the examples on pages 374-378. When you open the Define Styles dialog box, you'll see that the style's instructions begin with *Normal* + and that the word *Normal* appears in the Based on edit bar in the lower-right corner of the dialog box. If you want to make the *Figure Caption* style independent of the *Normal* style, all you have to do is erase the word *Normal* from the Based on edit bar and then click the Define button or click anywhere on the Style edit bar. After you do this, the Define Styles dialog box will look like Figure 9-23 on the next page.

As you can see, the instructions are the same as those that appear in Figures 9-15 and 9-18, with a couple of exceptions. First, the instructions no longer begin with *Normal* +. Another difference is that the instructions now specify the New York font. When you eliminate the Based on style, the style that you're defining will retain all the formatting characteristics of the Based on style. However, these characteristics will now be stated explicitly in the style's instructions instead of being implicit in the name of the Based on style.

FIGURE 9-23

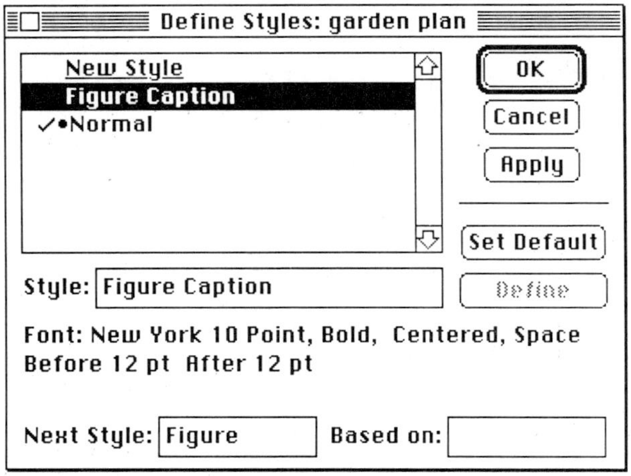

If you break the link to the Based on style, the formatting instructions for the dependent style will specify all of the characteristics of the former Based on style.

A word of warning

Although it's possible to create an "independent" style—that is, a style not based on any other style—in most cases, you'll want to avoid this. We can best illustrate why by using an example.

Suppose you are creating the style named *Figure Caption*, as we have described in our previous examples. When you click on the ruler icon for centered paragraph alignment, Word will use the left and right indents for that paragraph to determine the center point on the line. Since this style is based on the *Normal* style, the left and right indents are 0 and 6 inches. In other words, the left edge of each line of text will be aligned with the 0 mark on the ruler, and the right edge of the text will be aligned with the 6 inch mark (assuming you're using Word's default settings in the Page Setup dialog box). As a result, the center of each line will be the 3 inch mark on the ruler.

If you eliminate the link between the *Figure Caption* style and the *Normal* style, the left and right indents for *Figure Caption*—which determine the center point on each line—will no longer be tied to the indents for the *Normal* style. If you do not make any changes to the *Normal* style, this should be of no consequence. Suppose, however, you decide to modify the *Normal* style by dragging the right indent marker to the 5 inch point on the ruler. Word will change the right margin on the main body text in your document by one inch. However, since the *Figure Caption* style is no longer linked to *Normal*, any text that was formatted with that style will still be centered as though the right indent marker were at the 6 inch point on the ruler. In other words, all of your figure captions will no longer appear centered on the main body text.

This is just one example of a problem that you might encounter when you create a style that is not based on any other style. We chose to use the right indent in this example because of the way Word handles indents in a style's instructions. Earlier in our discussion of styles, we pointed out that Word often will not specify a certain formatting feature in a style's instructions if that feature conforms to the program's defaults. If you don't move the indent markers, for example, then a style's instructions will not say anything about indents. Unfortunately, when a formatting feature is not specifically stated in the instructions, it can be easy to disregard the way that feature affects not only the current style but also any dependent styles.

By the way, the best way to change margins in a document is to use the Page Setup dialog box instead of moving indent markers. This can help prevent the type of problem we just described. For more on the Page Setup dialog box and document margins, see Chapter 7.

Notes on linked styles

One style can be indirectly linked to several different styles. However, a style can be *directly* based on only one other style. For example, you might have a document in which *Style3* is based on *Style2*, which is based on *Style1*, which is based on *Normal*. In this case, *Style3* is indirectly linked to two styles, *Style1* and *Normal*, but it is directly based on only one style, *Style2*.

Word will not allow you to create circular style references. For example, suppose that *Style3* is based on *Style2*, which is based on *Style1*. If you then try to make *Style3* the Based on style for *Style1*, Word will beep and display the message, *Circular style references or too many levels of "Based on:" reference.*

You will also see this message if you try to create too many levels of linked styles. Word will allow you to have as many as nine levels of linked styles but no more than that. For example, you can create a style sheet in which *Style8* is based on *Style7*, which is based on *Style6*, which is based on *Style5*, and so forth, through *Style1*, which is based on *Normal*. However, if you try to create a *Style9* that uses *Style8* as its Based on style, Word will not allow it.

Of course, this does not mean that you cannot have more than nine styles that are indirectly linked to one another. For example, Figure 9-24 shows a diagram that illustrates how you might set up 14 styles in a style sheet that are all directly or indirectly linked to *Style1*, which is directly linked to *Normal*. Notice, however, that this style sheet contains only five levels of linked styles.

FIGURE 9-24

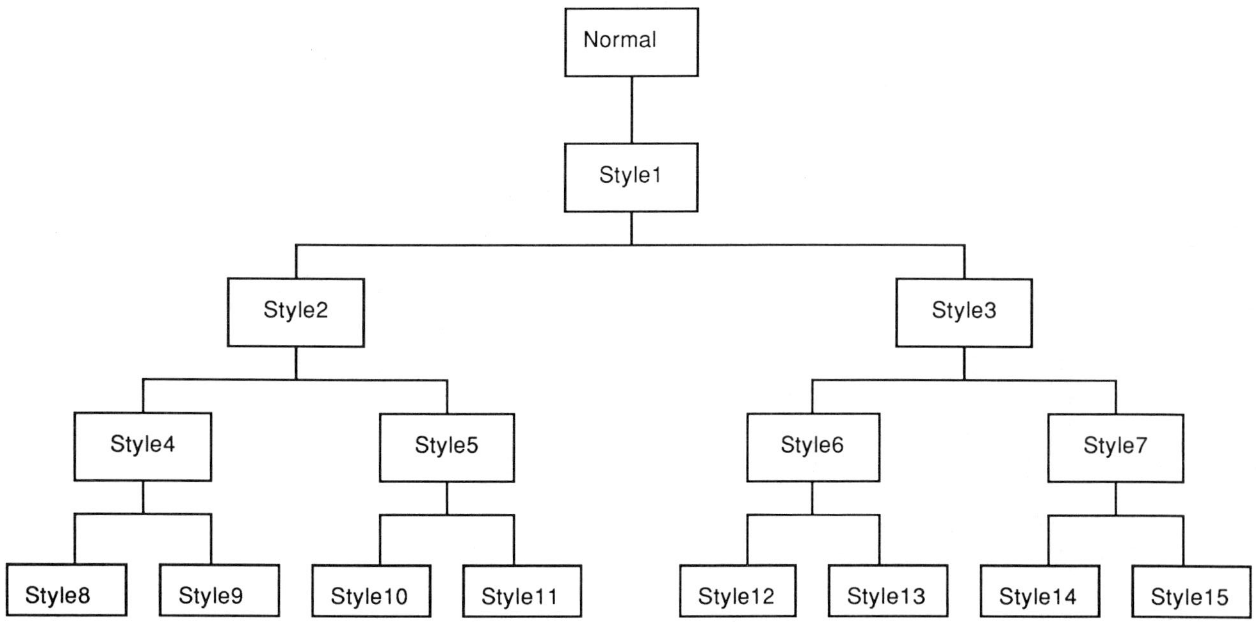

This diagram shows how you might set up links between Style1 *and 14 other styles on the style sheet.*

Copying and Pasting Style Instructions

When you're creating a new style, you can copy the instructions for an existing style into the instructions for the new style. Here's how it works. Suppose that your document's style sheet contains a style named *Figure Caption*. You would like to create a new style, named *Table Caption*, which has similar or identical formatting characteristics to the *Figure Caption* style. First, you would open the Define Styles dialog box, and with New Style selected, enter the style name *Table Caption* and click Define. Next, click on the name of the style whose instructions you want to "borrow"—in our example, this would be *Figure Caption*. With that style selected, choose Copy from the Edit menu. Then click on the name of the new style that you just created (*Table Caption*), and choose Paste from the Edit menu. Word will then copy the style instructions for the *Figure Caption* style into the instructions for the *Table Caption* style. If the style whose instructions you're copying has a Based on style, then the name of that Based on style will also be copied into the Based on edit bar of the dialog box.

After you copy the style instructions, you can use menu commands and ruler icons to make changes and additions to these style instructions. When the instructions are complete, just click Define again to lock them in.

When you copy instructions from one style to another, it's important that you perform the copy and paste *before* you issue commands and click on ruler icons. When you issue the Paste command, Word will overwrite any existing style instructions with the instructions of the style that you've copied. As a result, you cannot copy and paste the instructions for more than one style. If you try to do this, the instructions for the second style will completely overwrite the instructions for the first style.

The Next Style

When you open the Define Styles dialog box, you will see a Next Style edit bar in the lower-left corner of the dialog box. You use this edit bar to specify which named style you want to apply immediately after the style that you're defining. To enter a style name in the Next Style edit bar, simply click anywhere on the edit bar, and then type the name. Then click Define, Apply, or OK to lock in your Next Style specification.

For example, suppose that you are defining a style named *Figure Caption*, which will be used to format the figure captions in your document. You probably will want to follow each caption with a paragraph that is formatted according to the *Normal* style. Therefore, as you are defining the *Figure Caption* style, you should enter *Normal* in the Next Style edit bar.

The Next Style comes into play only when you press Return to end a paragraph. In our example, suppose that you apply the style *Figure Caption* to a line of text in your document. When you press Return at the end of that line, Word will begin a new paragraph, which is formatted with the *Normal* style. On the other hand, if you were to place the insertion point marker in the middle of the figure caption text and press Return, Word would break that text into two separate paragraphs, but the second paragraph would *not* assume the Next Style format. Instead, it would also be formatted with the *Figure Caption* style.

As you're defining a new style, if you do not enter a style name in the Next Style edit bar, Word will use the style that you are defining as the next style. For example, if you define the style named *Figure Caption*, but you don't specify a Next Style, Word will assume that the paragraph following the figure caption text should also be formatted according to the *Figure Caption* style.

Taking advantage of the Next Style

By carefully specifying the Next Style for each style on a style sheet, you can make one style automatically flow into another throughout a document. Each time you press Return to begin a new paragraph, Word will use a different style to format that paragraph. This can be especially helpful when you're creating a document in which you must frequently switch from one style to another. For example, suppose that you want to create a list of names and addresses, like that shown in Figure 9-25.

FIGURE 9-25

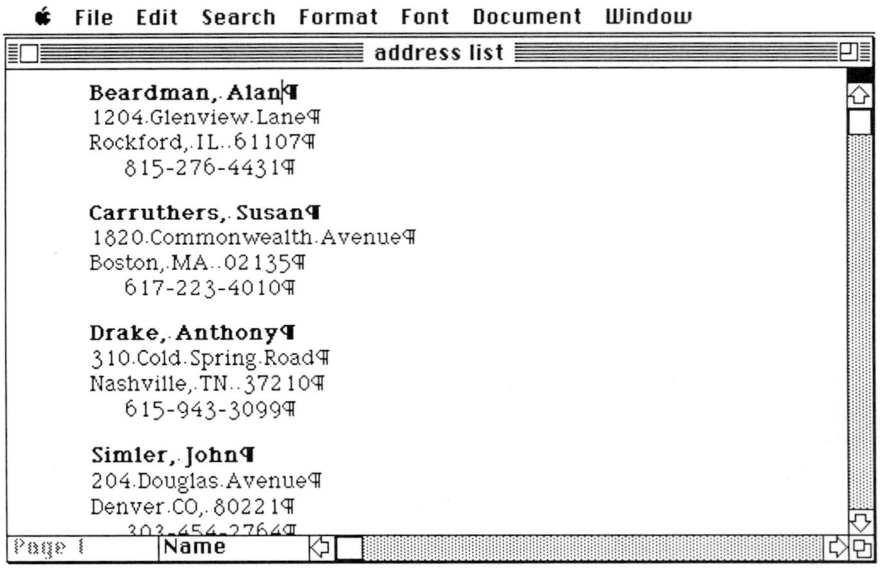

A list of names and addresses might be formatted with several different styles.

One way you can greatly speed up the process of creating this list is to set up a style sheet with four styles: *Name*, *Address1*, *Address2*, and *Phone*. As you might guess, the *Name* style will be used to format each person's name; the *Address1* style will be used to format the first line of each person's address; the *Address2* style will be used to format the second line of each address; and the *Phone* style will be used to format each phone number. To help speed up your text entry, you should ensure that the *Name* style uses *Address1* as its Next Style; the *Address1* style uses *Address2* as its Next style; and the *Address2* style uses *Phone* as its Next Style. Finally, to complete the "loop," the style named *Phone* should specify *Name* as its Next Style.

Once you have set up the style sheet as we have described, you will not need to do anything else to format the list of names and addresses. Just start with the *Name* style as you're entering the first name in the list, and, each time you press Return, Word will automatically cycle into *Address1*, *Address2*, *Phone*, and back to *Name*.

By the way, there's one minor constraint that you need to keep in mind as you are specifying the Next Style. You must enter a valid style name in the Next Style edit bar. This can present a problem if you haven't yet created the style that you want to use as the Next Style. For example, if you are defining the *Name* style, but you haven't yet created the style named *Address1*, Word will not allow you to enter *Address1* in the Next Style edit bar. To get around this problem, you may need to modify a style after you've created it in order to specify the correct Next Style. (In the next section, we talk about how you can modify an existing style.) Another way to work around this constraint is to define your styles in reverse order. In other words, the first style that you define should be the last style that you plan to use in your sequence of styles. In our example, you might begin by defining the *Phone* style. Then you would define *Address2*, then *Address1*, and finally, *Name*. As you're defining *Address2*, *Address1*, and *Name*, the style that you want to use as the Next Style will already exist, so you shouldn't have any problem entering its name in the Next Style edit bar.

Style Names

As you have seen, entering a style name is an essential step in creating a custom style. However, there are some rules about style names that you need to keep in mind when you do this. Word will accept a style name of virtually any length, but in general, shorter names are easier to work with. One problem with extremely long names is that you may not be able to see the full style name in the Styles or Define Styles dialog boxes. Word displays only about 20 characters of a style's name in the Style edit bar, and even fewer characters can appear in the Next Style and Based on edit bars.

Each style on a style sheet must have a unique name. If you enter a name of a new style that is identical to the name of an existing style, Word will alert you with the message, *Style already exists. Change its definition to match New Style?* If you click OK when you see this message, Word will replace the existing instructions for the named style with the formatting instructions that you have entered in the process of defining the new style. In other words, Word will delete from the style sheet the style that originally was assigned the name that you're using for the new style.

Interestingly, Word does make a distinction between upper- and lower-case letters in a style name. For example, a style sheet can include two completely different styles named *Paragraph1* and *paragraph1*.

You can assign two or more names to a style. As you're creating a new style, just enter the different names in the Style edit bar, separating the names from one another with commas. Why might you want to assign two names to a style? One name could be relatively long and descriptive to help you remember what the style does, while another name could be extremely short, perhaps only one or two letters. As we will explain later, the shorter style name can speed up the process of applying that style in your document.

When you've assigned more than one name to a style, Word will display both names on the same line in the list of style names in the dialog box. In other words, Word will not treat a style with two different names as though it were two different styles. For example, suppose you assign the names *Figure Caption* and *FC* to a style. Figure 9-26 shows how Word will display those names in the Styles dialog box.

FIGURE 9-26

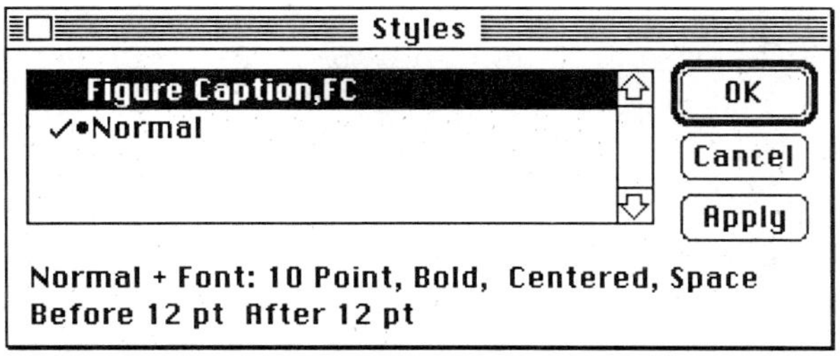

When you assign two or more names to a style, those names will appear on the same line in the style sheet, separated by a comma.

Because Word uses a comma to separate style names, you cannot include a comma as part of a style name. However, you can use any other character in a style name, including the special characters that are created by Option-key combinations (such as ¶ and §).

MODIFYING STYLES

After you have started to work with named styles, chances are you will need to make at least a minor change to one or more of them. Earlier in this chapter, we explained briefly how you can modify the *Normal* style. Modifying Word's other styles—both automatic styles and custom styles—is really no different.

To modify a style, just choose Define Styles... from the Format menu, and then click on the name of the style that you want to change. With the style name selected, issue the formatting commands and click on the appropriate ruler icons to alter the style as you wish. As you issue commands and click on ruler icons, Word will record all your changes in the instructions for the selected style. When you've completed your changes, you can lock them in by clicking Define.

For example, suppose that you've used the automatic style named *level 1* to format some of the subheadings in a document, and you decide that you want to change the appearance of those subheadings. The default instructions for the *level 1* style specify the *Normal* style with boldfacing added and a 12-point line space above the subheading. In order to make the subheadings stand out more from the body text of your document, you might want to change both the font and the point size. For instance, you may want your first-level subheadings to appear in 14-point Helvetica bold type with a 10-point line space above the subheading and a 6-point line space below.

For this example, we'll also assume that the *Normal* style has been modified so that it specifies a $^1/_4$ inch first-line indent and justified paragraph alignment. Since the *level 1* style is based on the *Normal* style, it also will specify a first-line indent and justified alignment. Therefore, as you're modifying the *level 1* style, you probably will want to remove the first-line indent and change its alignment to flush left.

To make these changes, first issue the Define Styles... command and click on the name *level 1* in the dialog box. Word will then display the instructions for *level 1* in the dialog box, as shown in Figure 9-27.

FIGURE 9-27

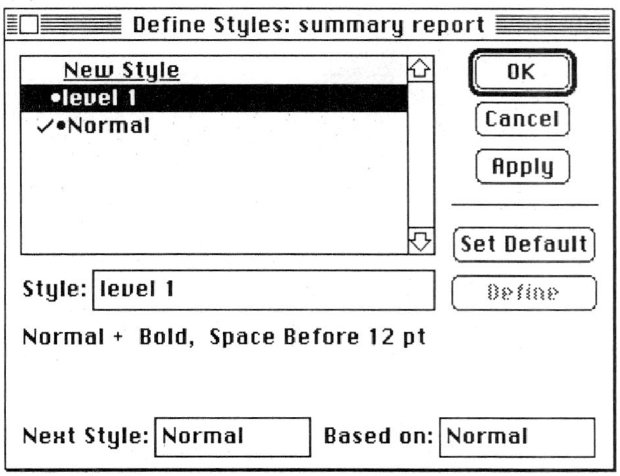

To modify a style, begin by opening the Define Styles dialog box and clicking on the style's name.

To modify this style, open the Character dialog box and click on Helvetica in the list of font names. Then type 14 in the Font Size list box and click the Bold format option. To change the line spacing above and below the subheading, open the Paragraph dialog box and replace the *12 pt* in the Before edit bar with 10. Then enter 6 in the After edit bar. With the Paragraph dialog box still open, move the first-line indent marker to the 0 position on the ruler and click the flush-left alignment icon on the ruler. Finally, click OK to close the Paragraph dialog box. At this point, the Define Styles dialog box will display the altered instructions for the *level 1* style as shown in Figure 9-28.

FIGURE 9-28

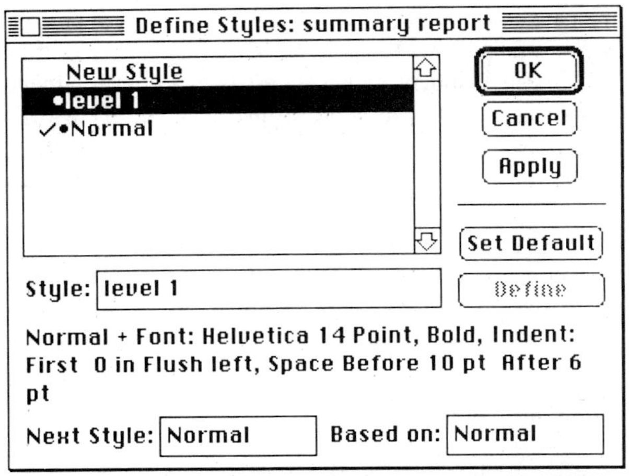

As you issue commands and manipulate ruler icons, Word will alter the style instructions to reflect your changes.

To complete the process of modifying this style, you should click OK, Apply, or Define. If you click OK, Word will redefine the *level 1* style in the style sheet, apply it to the current paragraph in your document, and close the dialog box. Word also will reformat any text in your document that has been formatted with the *level 1* style. The Apply button will have the same effect as OK except that Word will not close the dialog box. If you click Define, Word will redefine the *level 1* style and apply its new formatting instructions only to text that has been assigned that style. Word will not close the dialog box or apply the *level 1* style to the current paragraph if that paragraph has not already been assigned the *level 1* style.

Shortcuts

Word offers a couple of keyboard shortcuts that can help you modify a style's instructions. If you want to delete all of the instructions for a style except the names of the Based on style and the Next Style, click on the style name in the Define Styles dialog box and press ⌘-Shift-p. For example, suppose you want to alter the instructions for the *level 1* style that are displayed in Figure 9-28. Figure 9-29 shows how Word will alter the instructions for this style if you press ⌘-Shift-p.

FIGURE 9-29

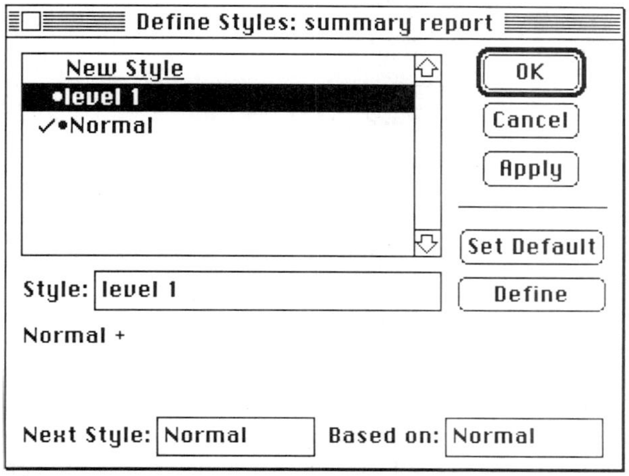

When you press ⌘-Shift-p, Word will delete all the instructions for the selected style except the names of the Next Style and Based on style.

You can use a similar shortcut to delete only the character formatting instructions for a style. After you open the Define Styles dialog box and click on the name of the style you want to modify, press ⌘-Shift-Spacebar. Word will then delete such characteristics as underlining, font, and point size from the style instructions. For example, Figure 9-30 on the next page shows what the Define Styles dialog box from Figure 9-28 would look like if we pressed ⌘-Shift-Spacebar.

Other Modifications

In the example we just presented, we showed how you can modify the formatting instructions for one of Word's automatic styles. To modify the formatting instructions for a custom style, you would follow the same procedure.

In most cases, when you modify a style, you'll change that style's formatting instructions, as we described in the preceding example. However, there are other modifications you may want to make as well, such as changing a style's name, specifying a different Based on style, and specifying a different Next Style. Let's take a look at how you might implement these other style modifications.

FIGURE 9-30

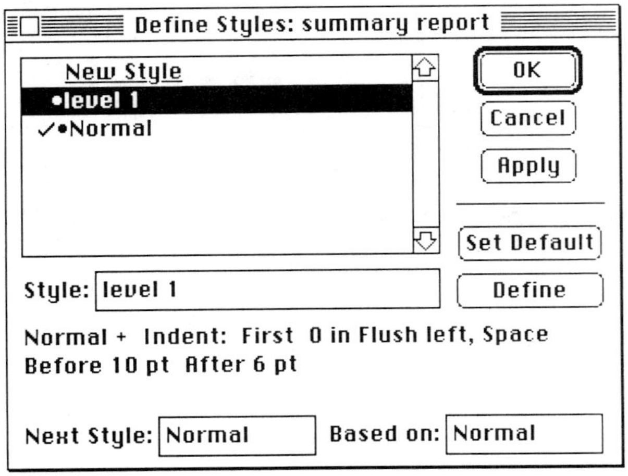

When you press ⌘-Shift-Spacebar, Word will delete all the character formatting instructions for a style.

Changing a style's name

To change the name of a style, open the Define Styles dialog box, and click on the name that you want to change. Word will place that name in the Style edit bar. Use the Backspace key to delete the name, then type a new name and click Define. Word will then display an alert box like the one shown in Figure 9-31. If you click OK in this alert box, the new name (in this case, *Line2*) will replace the old name. In addition, all references to the former style name—in the Based on or Next Style edit bars, for example—will be changed so that they refer to the new name.

FIGURE 9-31

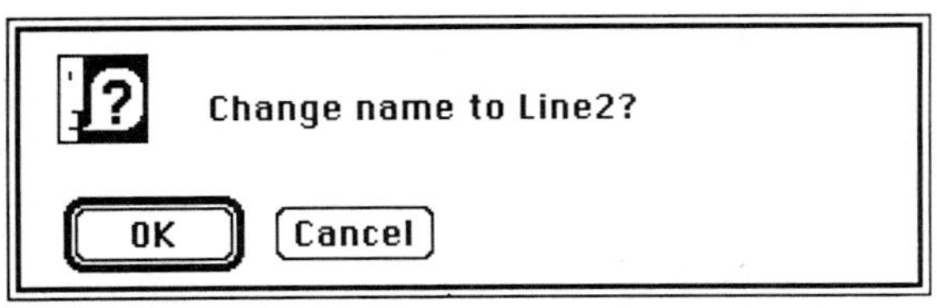

Word will display this alert box when you change the name of a style.

When you enter a new name in the Style edit bar, be sure that you do not type a name that already exists. If you do this, Word will display the somewhat ambiguous message shown in Figure 9-32. If you click OK in this alert box, Word will simply eliminate the style whose name you were changing. It will not "merge" that style or any of its characteristics with the style whose name appears in the alert box.

For example, suppose that your style sheet contains two styles named *Style1* and *Style2*. The instructions for *Style1* specify the *Normal* style plus boldfacing, while the instructions for *Style2* specify *Normal* plus underlining. Let's assume that you open the Define Styles dialog box and click on the name *Style1* to select it. Then you delete the *1* at the end of the style name and replace it with a 2—in other words, you change the name of *Style1* to be *Style2*. When you click Define, Word will display the message shown in Figure 9-32. If you click OK in this alert box, *Style1* will be eliminated from the style sheet. *Style2* will still exist, and its instructions will not change in any way—they will still specify the *Normal* style plus underlining.

FIGURE 9-32

If you enter an existing style name when you're changing the name of a style, you will see this alert box.

Specifying a different Based on style

To change the Based on style, choose Define Styles... from the Format menu, and in the Define Styles dialog box, click on the name of the style whose Based on style you want to change. Then, drag through the style name in the Based on edit bar to select it, and type the name of the style you want to use as the new Based on style. Finally, you should click Define to lock in the change.

For example, suppose that your style sheet contains a style named *Paragraph2*, which is based on a style named *Paragraph1*. *Paragraph2* uses all the same formatting characteristics as *Paragraph1* except for different indents. You'd like to change the Based on style for *Paragraph2* to *Normal*. To do this, first open the Define Styles dialog box and click on the style name *Paragraph2*. Figure 9-33 on the following page shows how the Define Styles dialog box will look at this point.

Next, drag through the name *Paragraph1*, which appears in the Based on edit bar. (Since this style name consists of only one word, you also can double-click on the name to select it.) Then type *Normal* as the name of your new Based on style, and click Define.

As soon as you click Define, Word will alter the instructions for the selected style so that they specify the new Based on style. This is shown in Figure 9-34. Notice that, in addition to specifying the new Based on style, the instructions now specify several other formatting characteristics of *Paragraph2*. It wasn't necessary to include these characteristics when *Paragraph2* was based on

Paragraph1 since these styles are almost identical. However, now that *Paragraph2* is based on *Normal*, all the differences between *Paragraph2* and *Normal* must be spelled out in the style instructions.

FIGURE 9-33

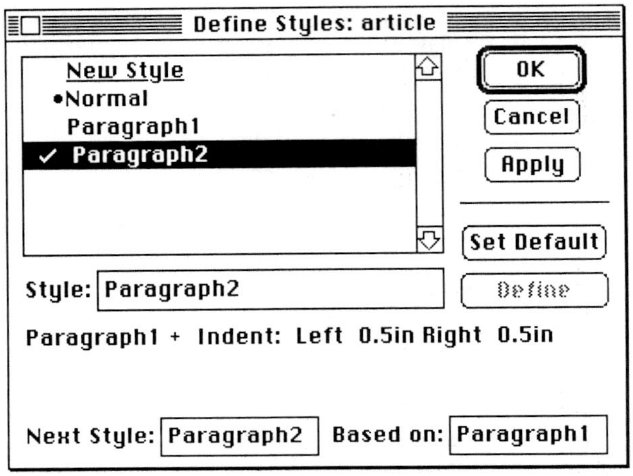

To specify a different Based on style, first select the name of the style that you want to modify.

FIGURE 9-34

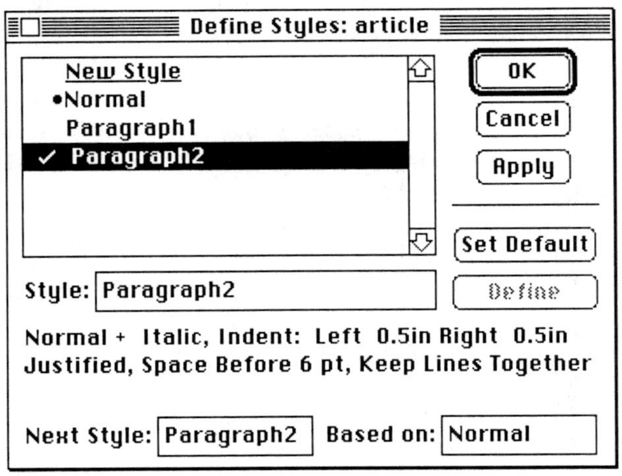

After you change the Based on style, Word will alter the instructions for the dependent style.

This example also illustrates another fact about changing the Based on style: Initially, that change will not affect the formatting characteristics of the dependent style. In our example, if you apply *Paragraph2* to some text in your document *after* you change its Based on style, the effects will be the same as when you applied it before you changed the Based on style. In other words, no matter what style *Paragraph2* is based on, when you apply it in your document, it will always format text to appear in italics with a left and right indent of $^1/_2$ inch, justified alignment, and a 6-point line space before each paragraph.

So what purpose is there in specifying a different Based on style? As we've described, any changes that you make to a Based on style may be carried over into the instructions for the dependent style (or styles). If your document contains two styles that specify similar formatting characteristics, then you may want to make sure that one of those styles is dependent on the other one. This can help you to maintain consistency between the instructions of the two styles. In the section called "Modifying a Based on Style," we explain more about how changes to one style may or may not affect other styles on the style sheet.

Breaking the link to the Based on Style

Instead of changing the Based on style, you can delete it altogether if you want. After you've opened the Define Styles dialog box and clicked on the name of the style that you want to modify, drag through the style name in the Based on edit bar to select it. Then press Backspace to delete that name. Finally, press Define to lock in this change.

You might recall from our earlier discussion that, in general, it's not a good idea to have a style on your style sheet that is not based on another style. However, if you want to ensure that certain style formats remain unchanged, no matter what style changes you make to other text in your document, Word allows you to do so by eliminating the Based on style.

Specifying a different Next Style

Another modification you may want to make to a style is to specify a different Next Style. To do this, first open the Define Styles dialog box. Then drag through the style name in the Next Style edit bar to select it. Finally, type a new name and click Define.

When you specify a different Next Style, your existing text will *not* be reformatted. The new Next Style will affect only text that you enter after the change has been made.

By the way, Word will not let you simply delete the Next Style. If you erase the contents of the Next Style edit bar without typing a replacement, Word will beep and display the message, *Valid style name is required.*

The Effects of Modifying a Style

Once you have made changes to a named style, those changes will affect any text in your document that already was formatted with the style that you changed. That text does *not* have to be selected at the time you modify the style in order to be reformatted. For example, suppose that your style sheet includes the automatic style named *level 1*, which you've used to format several different subheadings throughout your document. If you change the style instructions for *level 1*—to specify a different font, for example—Word will automatically reformat all of the *level 1* subheadings so that they are displayed in the new font. Of course, this automatic reformatting is one of the most important features of Word's style sheets. Since Word applies style sheet changes throughout the entire document, you are saved the time and trouble of reformatting individual sections of the document manually.

When you save a document after you've modified a style, the changes in the instructions for that style will be saved along with the document text. This is true for both automatic and custom styles. Of course, as we've mentioned before, if you modify one of Word's automatic styles, your modifications will *not* affect the default instructions for that style. If you create a new document that uses that automatic style, then Word will return to its default instructions for that style. However, you can change the default instructions for an automatic style, as we'll explain in the section called "Changing Defaults."

Modifying a Based on Style

If you make changes to a style that serves as the Based on style for other styles, then your changes may affect those other styles. For example, earlier in this chapter, we explained how any changes that you make to the instructions for the *Normal* style can affect the other styles that are based on *Normal*. Of course, it's possible to make some changes to a Based on style without affecting any dependent styles.

For example, suppose that your style sheet includes two custom styles, *First* and *Title*, both of which are based on the *Normal* style. *First* is used to format the first paragraph under each subheading in a document, and *Title* is used to format the text of the document's main title. We'll assume that the *Normal* style in this document specifies 10-point Times type with justified paragraph alignment and a $^1/_4$ inch first-line indent. Let's also suppose that the only difference between *First* and *Normal* is that *First* specifies no indent on the first line of each paragraph. Similarly, *Title* is almost identical to *Normal*, except that it specifies centered alignment, no indents, and 12-point type. Figures 9-35 through 9-37 show the Styles dialog box with each of these styles selected so you can view their instructions.

FIGURE 9-35

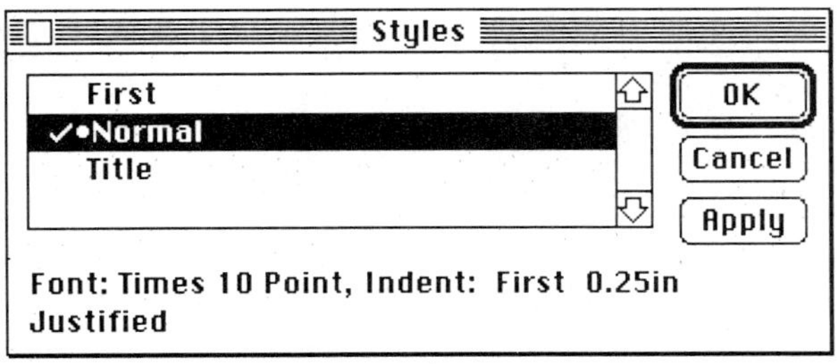

This dialog box displays the formatting instructions for the Normal *style.*

FIGURE 9-36

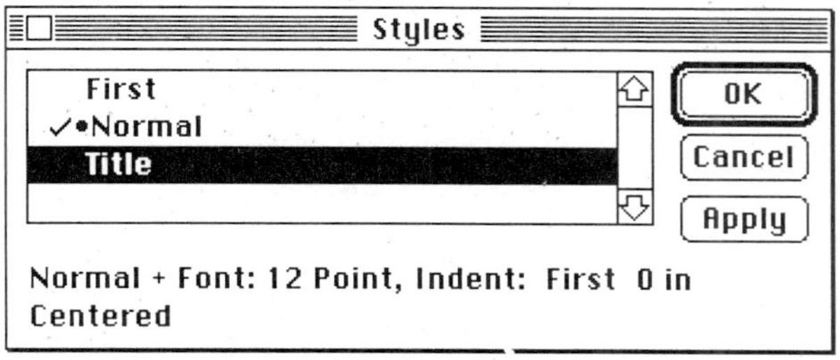

In this dialog box, we've selected the style named Title.

FIGURE 9-37

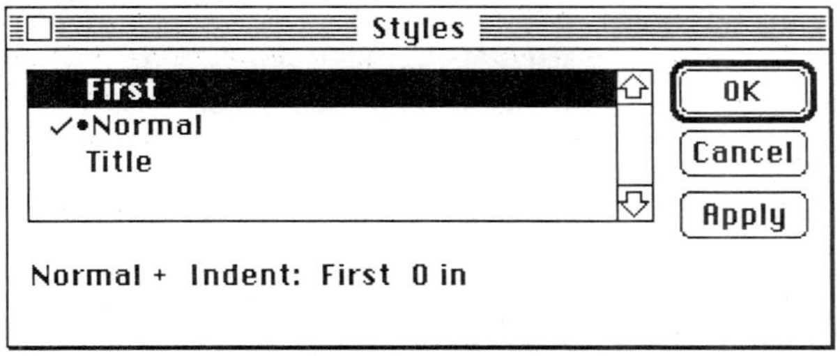

In this dialog box, you can see the formatting instructions for the style named First.

What will happen if you modify the *Normal* style? Some changes that you make will affect *First* or *Title* (or both), whereas other changes will not have any effect on these styles. For example, suppose that you alter *Normal* so that it uses flush-left paragraph alignment instead of justified alignment. This change will affect the style *First*, which uses the same alignment as *Normal*, but it will have no effect on *Title* since that style's instructions specifically call for centered alignment. On the other hand, suppose that you change the font for *Normal* from Times to Courier. This change will affect both the *First* and *Title* styles since the instructions for these styles do not specify a font different from that used in the *Normal* style.

Just remember that the instructions for a dependent style always spell out the *differences* between that style and its Based on style. If the change that you make to a Based on style affects one of these areas of specific difference, then that change will *not* be reflected in the dependent style's format. On the other hand, if the change involves a characteristic that is shared between the Based on style and a dependent style, then the dependent style's instructions will be affected by the change.

DELETING STYLES

To delete a named style from a style sheet, just choose Define Styles..., and then click on the name of the style that you want to delete. With that name selected, choose Cut from the Edit menu. Word will then display an alert box that asks if you really want to delete the selected style. If you click OK, there will be a pause of a few seconds, and then that style will be eliminated from the style sheet.

Once you delete a named style, any text that was formatted with that style will lose its special formatting. However, Word will automatically assign the *Normal* style to all of the paragraphs that previously were associated with the deleted style.

By the way, Word allows you to delete any style on the style sheet—custom or automatic—except the *Normal* style. Of course, since *Normal* is the style that Word uses whenever a paragraph has not been assigned another style, it should come as no surprise that Word insists on keeping this one style on the style sheet. When you delete one of the other automatic styles—such as the *level 1* style—from a particular style sheet, you do not, of course, delete that style from Word's library of automatic styles.

Deleting a Based on Style

If you delete a style that serves as the Based on style for another style, the dependent style will retain all of the formatting characteristics of the deleted style. Of course, any formatting characteristics that were derived from the Based on style will now be stated specifically in the style instructions. In addition, Word also will automatically make *Normal* the Based on style in place of the style that was deleted.

For example, suppose that your document contains a style named *Figure Caption*, whose instructions read *Normal + Font: Helvetica, 9 Point, Bold, Centered.* You've also created a style named *Table Caption*, with instructions that specify *Figure Caption + Flush right.* If you delete the style named *Figure Caption*, any text that was formatted with this style will be assigned the *Normal* style. However, any text that was formatted with the *Table Caption* style will not be affected by the deletion. In addition, Word will alter the instructions for the *Table Caption* style so that they now read, *Normal + Font: Helvetica, 9 Point, Bold, Flush right.*

Deleting a Next Style

If you delete a style that is used as the Next Style for one or more styles, then Word will automatically use *Normal* as the Next Style in place of the style that you deleted. Of course, Word also will reformat any existing text that was formatted with the deleted style. For example, suppose that your document's style sheet contains the style named *level 1*, which you've used to format several subheadings. *Level 1* specifies a style named *First* as its Next Style. If you delete *First* from the style sheet, Word will alter the paragraphs that were formatted with the *First* style so that they appear in the *Normal* style. In addition, when you next format a subheading using the *level 1* style, Word will apply the *Normal* style as soon as you press Return.

USING STYLE SHEETS

Now that we have covered all of the ins and outs of creating and modifying named styles, we've come to the heart of our subject: how you can use a style sheet to format a document. In this section, we'll show you how you can apply existing styles in a document, make global changes with a style sheet, and copy styles from one document to another.

Applying Named Styles in a Document

To apply a named style to a paragraph, first position the insertion point any anywhere on that paragraph. Then choose Styles… or Define Styles… from the Format menu. In the Styles or Define Styles dialog box, click on the name of the style that you want to apply to the current paragraph, and click Apply or OK. (OK will apply the style and close the dialog box, whereas Apply will apply the style without closing the dialog box.) Instead of clicking the OK button, you can press Return or Enter, which will have the same effect.

Notice that you do not have to select the entire paragraph where you want to apply a style—it's sufficient just to place the insertion point anywhere on that paragraph before you choose Styles… or Define Styles… from the Format menu. However, if you want to apply a style to more than one paragraph in a single step, then you do need to select all of those paragraphs before you choose Styles… or Define Styles….

Applying styles from the keyboard

If you can remember the name of the style that you want to use, there's a shortcut available for applying that style in your document. Instead of opening the Styles… or Define Styles… dialog box, just press ⌘-Shift-s, type the name of the style you wish to use, and press Return. When you press ⌘-Shift-s, Word will display the word *Style* in the lower-left corner of your window (where the page number usually appears), as shown in Figure 9-38. As you type, the style name that you enter will appear in this area, replacing the word *Style*.

FIGURE 9-38

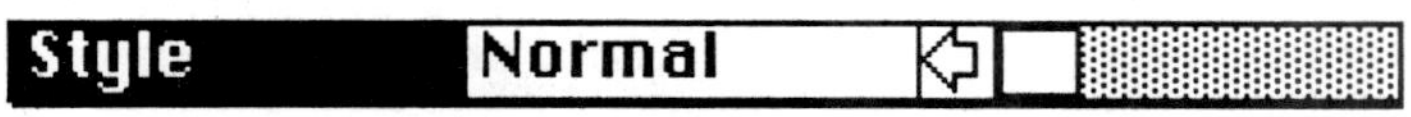

When you press ⌘-Shift-s, Word will display the word Style *in the lower-left corner of the current window.*

When you use this shortcut, you do not need to type the full name of the style that you want to apply. You can type only enough letters in the style's name to distinguish it from any other name on the style sheet. You also don't have to use correct case when you're typing a style name, unless you've created two styles whose names are identical except for case.

If you have assigned more than one name to a style, you can type any of those names when you're applying the style. You might recall that in our discussion of style names we suggested that you try to assign relatively short names to styles and, if you assign multiple names to a style, that you make at least one of those names extremely short—perhaps only one or two letters. By sticking to short style names as much as possible, you'll find it easier to apply styles using the keyboard method we've just described.

Reverting to the Normal style

Word offers another built-in shortcut for applying the *Normal* style. At the far-right edge of the ruler, you'll see a symbol that looks like an x with a vertical bar on either side (|x|). If you click on this symbol, Word will apply the *Normal* style to the current paragraph in your document (the paragraph on which the insertion point marker is positioned).

There's one minor drawback to accessing this shortcut: You cannot see the |x| symbol on your screen unless you're using a full-width window. If you've decreased the width of your document window so that the |x| isn't visible, you can bring the |x| back into view only by widening the window. You cannot bring it into view by clicking the horizontal scroll bar.

Applying styles from the Work menu

By far, the easiest and fastest way to apply a style in a document is to place that style name on the Work menu. The Work menu is a custom menu that you create, which can include style names, glossary terms, and file names. In fact, until you add at least one item to the Work menu, you won't even see the Work menu choice in the menu bar at the top of your screen. In Chapter 11, we discuss the Work menu in detail, and explain how you can add a style name and other items to that menu. For now, however, you just need to be aware that you can place style names on the Work menu. Once you've done this, all you need to do to apply a style is click on the paragraph that you want to format, then choose the style name from the Work menu. Unlike other techniques for applying styles, the Work menu allows you to bypass dialog boxes and doesn't require that you remember a style's name. Once you start using styles extensively, we would strongly recommend that you add the names of frequently applied styles to your Work menu.

Note

In our explanations of how to apply styles, we assumed that you had already entered some text that you wanted to format. However, you can select a style *before* you type the text to which you want to apply the style. With the insertion point marker positioned at the beginning of a new paragraph, select a style from the style sheet. Word will apply that style as you begin typing.

Manual Formatting Versus Style Sheet Formatting

As you're formatting a document, you can combine manual format changes with style sheet formatting. In most cases, Word will simply add your manual changes to the formatting features that are specified by the named styles. For example, suppose that your document's style sheet includes a style named *Style1* that specifies 12-point, Courier, bold type. Figure 9-39 shows some text with this style.

FIGURE 9-39

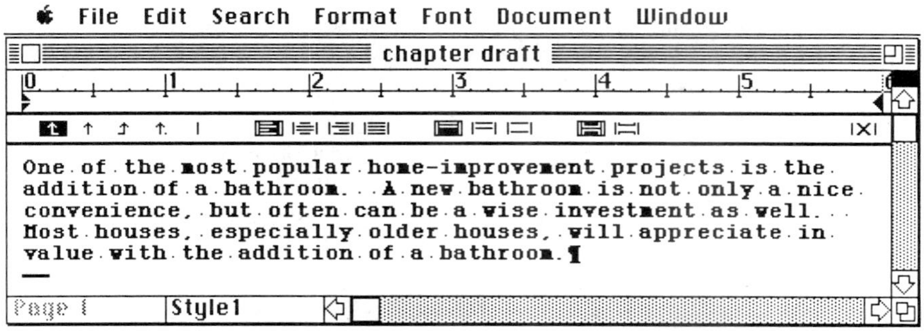

This screen shows some text that has been formatted with Style1.

If you select a paragraph where you've applied this style and then choose Italic from the Format menu, that paragraph will display italic formatting in addition to the boldfacing and other features specified by *Style1*. Furthermore, you can change the indents, margins, and other paragraph formatting features of this paragraph. Figure 9-40 shows a paragraph that has been formatted with both *Style1* and italics. We've also changed the first-line indent of this paragraph from the 0 position on the ruler to the $^1/_4$ inch position, and we've changed the alignment from flush left to justified.

FIGURE 9-40

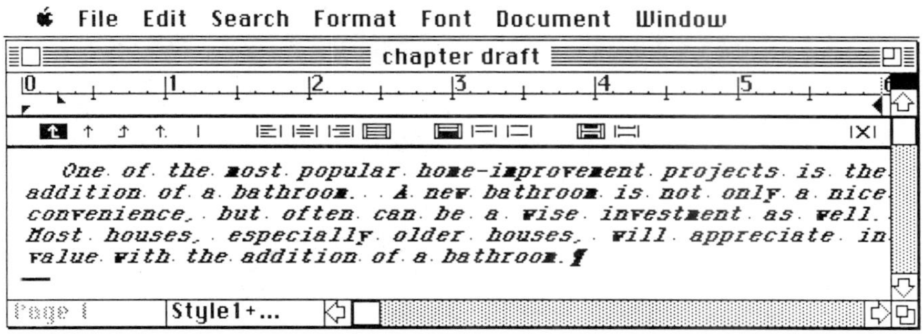

This text has been formatted with Style1 *and italics, which we've added manually.*

When you change the paragraph formatting of some text—for example, when you change the indents or alignment—Word will signify this by adding a plus sign and ellipsis to the style name designation that appears at the bottom of the window. For example, in Figure 9-40, because we changed the first-line indent and alignment of the paragraph, the style name designation *Style1+...* appears at the lower edge of the window. On the other hand, if you make only character formatting changes (such as assigning a new font, italics, etc.), Word will *not* change the style name designation that you see in the style status box.

Keep in mind that manual format changes will usually take precedence over style sheet formatting. If you manually assign a formatting characteristic to some text, and that characteristic conflicts with the formatting instructions of the style that you've applied to the text, then your manual formatting will override the style instructions. Going back to our example, suppose that after you've applied *Style1* to a paragraph, you select that paragraph and choose New York from the Font menu. Word will then apply the New York font to the text, instead of the Courier font, as specified by the style instructions.

Applying a named style after making manual format changes

So far, we've described what will happen when you make manual format changes *after* applying a style. If you format some text manually before you apply a named style to that text, the rules change a bit. When your manual format changes involve only character formats, then Word will again combine the formatting characteristics of the named style with any formats that you assigned manually. If one of the characteristics specified in the style instructions—font or point size, for example—conflicts with a character format that you've assigned manually, then the manual formatting will take precedence.

Manual changes to paragraph formats work differently. If you change the paragraph formatting characteristics of some text (indents, line spacing, etc.), and then assign a style to that text, the style's formatting instructions will take precedence over your manual paragraph formatting.

Returning once more to our example, suppose that your document contains some text that is formatted with Word's default *Normal* style (New York, 12-point, plain, flush left, and single spaced). Let's say that you make some manual changes—both character format changes and paragraph format changes—to that text. First, you select Italic from the Format menu, then you click on the ruler icon for centered alignment. Your text would now look like the one that is shown in Figure 9-41.

FIGURE 9-41

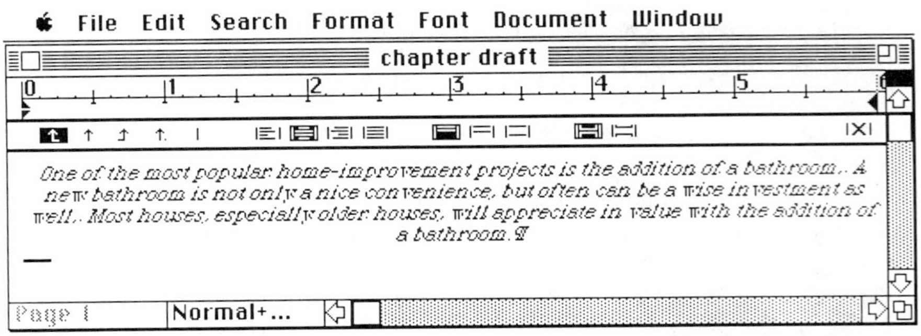

This text has been formatted to display in 10-point italic type with centered alignment.

If you now apply the *Style1* style to that paragraph, Word will alter the text so that it looks like Figure 9-42. Notice that the paragraph now appears in Courier, bold, italic type. The size of the text has not changed to 12 points, as specified in the *Style1* instructions, but instead, it remains at 10 points. In other words, Word altered the font, which was determined by the *Normal* style definition, but it did not alter the italicizing or point size since these were changes that were made manually. However, Word did change the paragraph alignment from centered (which was assigned manually) to flush left, according to the *Style1* instructions.

FIGURE 9-42

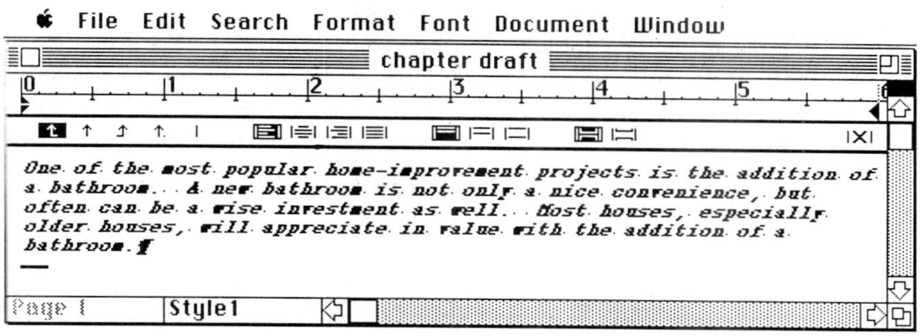

After applying Style1 *to the paragraph, the text retains its size and italic formatting but no longer appears with centered alignment.*

As we've just shown, whenever you decide to apply a new style to a paragraph, Word does not alter any character format changes that you've made manually. This is true even when you apply the *Normal* style. In other words, Word will continue to apply your manual character format changes in addition to the formatting characteristics specified by the *Normal* style.

The Plain Text option

When you choose Plain Text from the Format menu, you'll notice another difference between character format changes that you've implemented manually and style sheet format changes. The Plain Text option will remove the manual format changes, but it will *not* affect the format changes implemented by a named style. Going back to our example, suppose that you've formatted some text with the *Style1* style and also added italics, as shown in Figure 9-40. You then select that text and choose Plain Text from the Format menu. Word will remove the italics but will not remove the style characteristics of the *Style1* style: Courier font, 12 point size, and boldfacing. In other words, the definition of "Plain Text" will vary, depending on which style has been applied to the text that you're formatting.

Making Global Changes with a Style Sheet

Once you've applied named styles throughout a document, you can make significant format changes to that document merely by changing the instructions of one or more styles. When you change the style sheet, Word will reformat your document text according to those changes. You don't need to select any text before you modify a style's instructions—Word will automatically change any text where that style has been applied. We've already seen examples of what can happen in a document when you modify the instructions for one style. Let's consider an example that shows how you might make even more extensive formatting changes by modifying several styles.

Figure 9-43 shows part of a document in which three styles have been applied. The title has been formatted with a style named *Title* that specifies 14-point, New York, bold type, flush-left alignment, no indents, and a 9-point space after the text. The subheading has been formatted with a style named *Subheading*, which uses *Title* as its Based on style but specifies 12-point size and a 4-point line space above and a 2-point line space below the subheading. Finally, the body text in this document has been formatted with the *Normal* style, which specifies 10-point New York type, a $^1/_2$-inch first-line indention, and flush-left alignment.

FIGURE 9-43

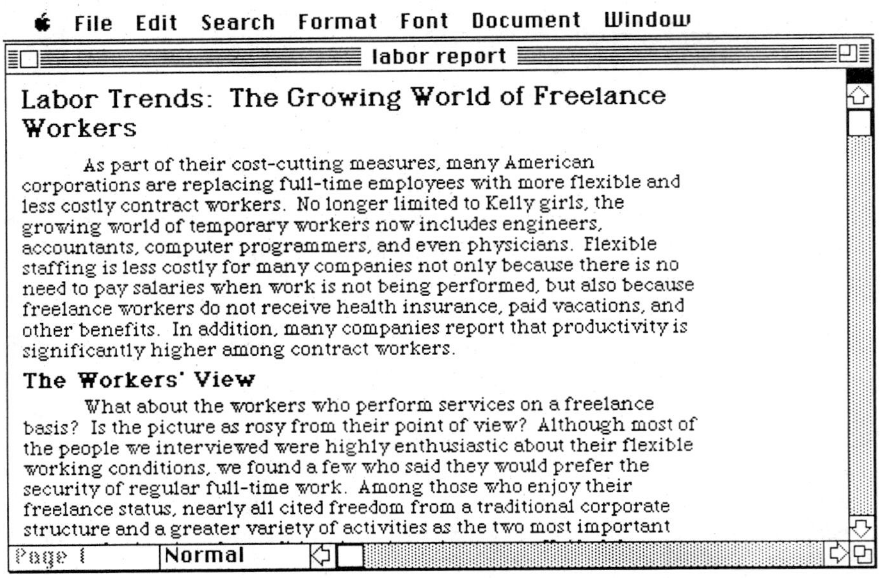

This document has been formatted with three styles: Title, Subheading, *and* Normal.

Let's suppose that you want to change the formatting of this document. You would like the title and subheading to appear in the Times font with centered alignment. Since the Times font is somewhat smaller than the New York font, you would like to change the size of the title text to 18 points and the subheading text to 14 points. You also want to change the main body text so that it appears in 12-point Helvetica type with justified paragraph alignment. In just a few easy steps, you can apply all of these formatting changes throughout the entire document.

Begin by opening the Define Styles dialog box and clicking the style name *Normal*. Open the Character dialog box, then choose Helvetica from the list of fonts and 12 from the list of sizes. Click OK to close the Character dialog box, then choose Show Ruler from the Format menu (assuming the ruler is not already displayed). On the ruler, click the justified alignment icon. Next, click Define in the Define Styles dialog box to lock in these changes to the *Normal* style. Now, select the *Title* style in the Define Styles dialog box, choose Times and 18 Point from the Font menu, then click the centered paragraph alignment icon on the ruler. Again, click Define to lock in these changes. Since the *Subheading* style is based on the *Title* style, the only formatting change you need to make for this style is to choose 14 Point from the Font menu. When you change the font and alignment for the *Title* style, those changes will be carried over into the instructions for the *Subheading* style as well.

After altering all the style instructions, click the close box of the Define Styles dialog box. Figure 9-44 on the next page shows how your document will appear at this point.

As we've mentioned before, one of the nicest advantages offered by style sheets is that you don't need to select any text before you make your formatting changes. When you alter a style's formatting instructions, Word will automatically change *any* text in your document where that style has been applied. If your insertion point marker is currently on a paragraph that uses another style, however, you'll want to make sure that you use the Define button to lock in your style-setting changes. If you use OK or Apply in the Define Styles dialog box, Word will change the format of the current paragraph to use your altered style instructions as well.

Importing Styles from Another Document

Word allows you to "borrow" styles from other documents and import them into your current document. You can borrow styles one at a time, or you can import all the styles on another document's style sheet into your current document. Either way, the ability to copy style definitions from document to document can save you the time of redefining styles for each new document, and it also can provide a quick and easy way to reformat text.

FIGURE 9-44

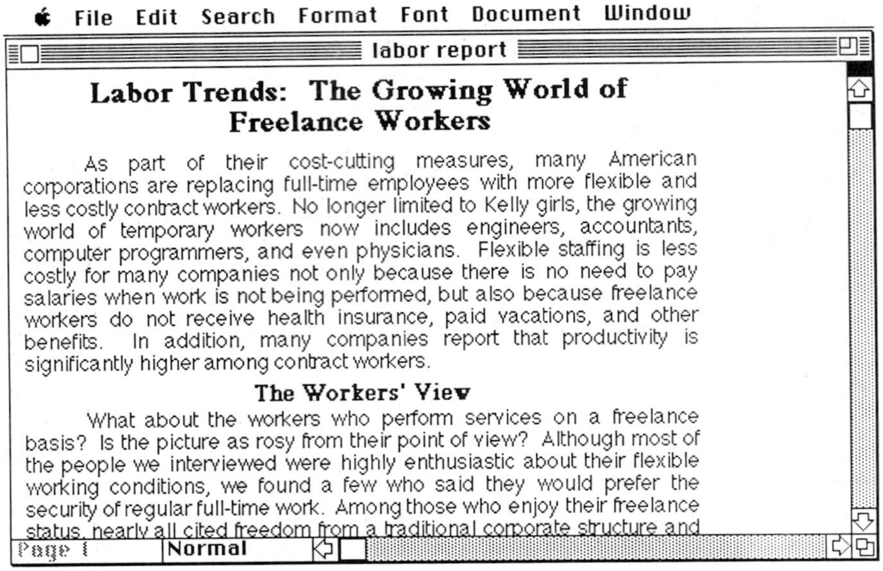

A few simple changes to the style sheet can significantly alter the appearance of a document.

Copying one style

If you want to copy a style from one document to another, you simply copy some text that has been formatted with that style. When you paste the formatted text into a document window, Word will also add the style name and style definition to that document's style sheet. For example, suppose you're working on a document named Intro in which you've created a style named *First ¶*. You would like to use this same style in a document named Summary. Begin by selecting some text that has been formatted with the *First ¶* style in the document named Intro. Then, choose Copy from the Edit menu. Next, open the Summary file and with that document window active, choose Paste from the Edit menu. Word will copy the text that you selected in Intro—with all of its formatting—into the Summary document window. If you then choose Styles... or Define Styles... from the Format menu, you will see that the style named *First ¶* is now part of the Summary style sheet.

When you use this technique, there are a couple of things you must keep in mind. First, the text that you select and copy must be a full paragraph (be sure that you select the ¶ symbol at the end of the paragraph). If you copy less than a full paragraph, Word will not transfer any of the text formatting or the style name to the other document. As soon as you paste the text in the second document, it will be formatted according to that document's *Normal* style.

Second, you need to be aware of how Word handles duplicate style names. Going back to our example, suppose that the style sheet for the Summary document already contained a style named *First ¶*. When you paste the *First ¶* text from Intro into Summary, Word will use the existing style instructions for *First ¶* to format that text, rather than importing the new style instructions from the Intro file. In other words, in cases of identical style names, the instructions for the style in the destination file will always take precedence over the instructions for the style with that same name in the file from which you are copying.

Third, if the style instructions for the paragraph that you are copying include a Based on style, unexpected results can occur. Word may use the definition of that Based on style in the destination file to format your copied paragraph. For example, suppose you have created a custom style called *Sub1* that is based on the *Normal* style. In this document, *Normal* carries the default 12-point, New York, plain character format. *Sub1* is identical to *Normal* except that it appears in bold, italic type. In other words, the definition of *Sub 1* reads *Normal + Bold Italic*. Now, suppose you decide to copy a paragraph that has been assigned the *Sub1* style to another document in which you have defined the *Normal* style as 10 point, Helvetica, plain. When you paste your *Sub1* paragraph into this document, Word will change the pasted text to appear in 10-point Helvetica, bold, italic type, instead of 12-point, New York, bold, italic, type. In other words, Word will not change the style's definition; however, because the *Sub1* style is based on *Normal*, Word will change the format of the paragraph to reflect the *Normal* settings in the current document. Only those character formats that you have explicitly stated in your *Sub1* style instructions (in this case, boldfacing and italics) will carry over to the second document.

Unfortunately, Word does not apply this rule about duplicate Based on style names consistently. If the style that you paste into another document has only different character formatting from its Based on style, then you will get the result we just described. After pasting some text, Word will use the definition of the Based on style in the destination document to determine the style characteristics of that text.

On the other hand, if the style that you copy to another document has different paragraph formatting from its Based on style, Word will *not* change that style's characteristics. Going back to our example, suppose that the *Sub1* style, in addition to bold italic character formatting, also has centered alignment. In other words, the definition for the *Sub1* style reads *Normal + Bold Italic, Centered.* Again, let's assume that you copy some *Sub1* text to a document in which the definition of the *Normal* style calls for 10-point Helvetica type. When you paste the *Sub1* text into this new document, Word will change none of the text formatting. The text that you paste will appear in 12-point New York, bold, italic type—just as it does in the original file. Furthermore, if you check the *Sub1* style definition in the destination document, you'll see that it reads *Normal + Font: New York 12 Point, Bold Italic, Centered.*

Finally, if the paragraph that you copy is based on a style that is not defined in your target document, Word will change the Based on setting for that style to *Normal.* However, Word will still retain all of the character and paragraph formats that you assigned to that paragraph in the original source document by creating a more specific set of instructions for that style. (Word handles this situation in the same way it handles the deletion of a Based on style, which we described earlier.) In other words, Word will analyze the paragraph you are copying and automatically add any necessary changes to its style instructions.

If all this sounds confusing, don't worry—it is. The best way to avoid having to wonder about what results might occur when you copy some formatted text from one document to another is to make sure that you don't have duplicate style names. Of course, you can't avoid having a *Normal* style in each of your documents. Thus, one of your first steps in setting up a new document should be to alter the *Normal* style to suit that particular document. Then, as you copy styles based on *Normal* from one document to another, you'll need to watch carefully for any unwanted format changes and handle these as they occur.

Copying one style at a time can be useful in many instances, but you often will find that it's more efficient to import an entire style sheet, rather than copying individual styles. Let's take a look at how you can do this.

Importing a complete style sheet

To import a style sheet from a file on disk, you must begin by issuing the Define Styles... command. Then, with the Define Styles dialog box open, choose Open... from the File menu. Word will present a list of all the Word document files on the current disk, as shown in Figure 9-45.

If the file containing the style sheet that you want to use is not on the current disk, you can click the Drive button to access another disk drive, or you can click Eject and insert a different disk. Once you see the name of the file that contains the style sheet you want to import, click on that name to select it, and then click Open (or double-click the file name). Word will automatically add the styles from that file to your current style sheet. (Your style sheet will contain *both* its original styles and all the styles from the style sheet of the disk file.)

If the style sheet on disk contains one or more styles with the same name as one of the styles in your current document, then the style from the disk file will overwrite the existing style. As you might expect, any text in your document that has been formatted with that style will be reformatted according to the instructions of the new style from the disk file.

For example, every document's style sheet contains the *Normal* style, but the formatting instructions for *Normal* will likely vary from document to document. Suppose you're working in a document where the *Normal* style specifies 12-point New York type (Word's default), and you import a style sheet whose *Normal* style specifies 10-point Courier type. Word will replace the instructions for the *Normal* style on your style sheet with the new instructions from the disk file. In addition, the main body text in your current document will be reformatted to display 10-point Courier type.

FIGURE 9-45

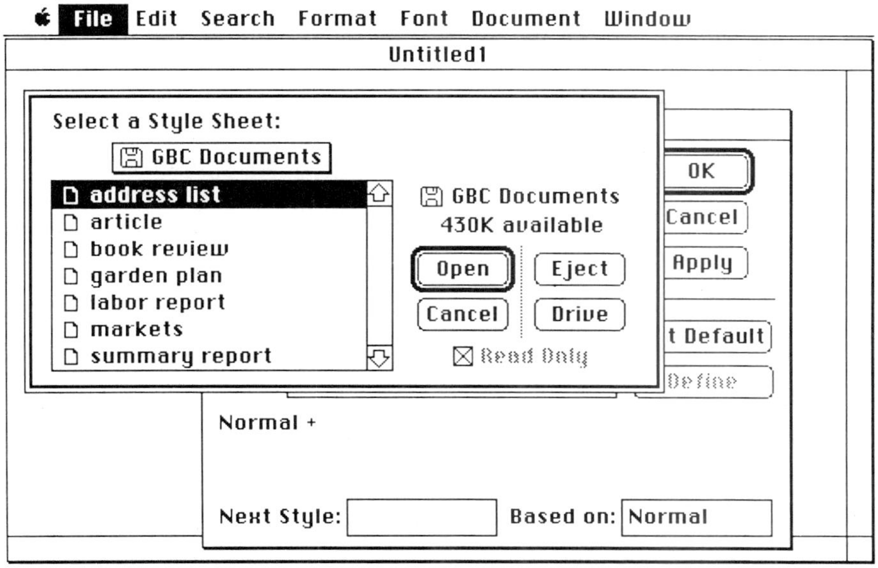

To import a style sheet from another document, choose Open… from the File menu while the Define Styles dialog box is open.

Of course, if the names of all or most of the styles on your current style sheet are identical to the style names that you import from disk, then your document may be radically reformatted. In some cases, this may be exactly what you want. Borrowing another document's style sheet offers an excellent way to rapidly reformat an entire document.

Creating a style sheet template

If you plan to use similar formats in several different documents, then you may want to store those formats in a style sheet template. A style sheet template is simply a blank document file in which you've defined a number of named styles. Such a template file will typically require only about 2K of disk space, so you can keep a copy of it on each disk where you store your document files or perhaps on your Word system disk. Each time you begin a new document, you can set up the style sheet for that document by choosing Define Styles… from the Format menu, then choosing Open… from the File menu and opening the template file. Word will automatically place all of the style names from that template file onto your new document's style sheet.

For example, suppose you must write a report every week that summarizes the activities of your department and lists the goals for the upcoming week. To format this report, you use three styles: *Title* (for the report title), *Normal* (for the main body text), and *List* (for the list of goals). By storing these styles in a style sheet template and placing the style names on your Work menu, you can speed up the process of formatting your report each week.

Let's say that you've just completed one of your reports, which you've saved in a file named Jun10Rpt. To create your style sheet template, begin by opening a new, blank document file. With this new document active, choose Define Styles... from the Format menu. Then choose Open... from the File menu. In the File Open dialog box, double-click the name Jun10Rpt. Word will then load the styles *Title*, *Normal*, and *List*—which are on the Jun10Rpt style sheet—into the style sheet for the new document. (The instructions for the *Normal* style in Jun10Rpt will overwrite Word's default instructions for the *Normal* style in the new document.) Now, all you need to do is save the blank document under a name such as Styles or Template. Then, each week as you begin a new report, your first step should be to load the styles from this file into a new document window where you plan to write your report.

Of course, you could load the styles directly from the Jun10Rpt file instead of creating a separate template file. However, as we mentioned before, the template file has the advantage of being small, so you can store copies of it on several different disks with your document files. In addition, by keeping a template file, you don't need to worry about discarding your regular document files when you're through with them. You can create several different template files if you want. For example, you might have one template file for letters, another for formal reports, and a third one for formatting tabular information.

CHANGING DEFAULTS

If there are certain styles that you use over and over in different documents, then you may want to change the default style sheet so that those styles are automatically available each time you start a new document in Word. In addition, you might want to change the default characteristics of some of Word's automatic styles, particularly the *Normal* style. In this section, we'll explain how to change Word's defaults and how you can recover the original default settings if you want.

Modifying the Default Style Sheet

As we explained at the beginning of our discussion of style sheets, initially, the only style on the default style sheet is the *Normal* style. Once you've added other styles—whether custom or automatic—to any document's style sheet, you can place any of those additional styles on the default style sheet. To add a style to the default style sheet, first open the Define Styles dialog box, then click on the style name that you want to place on the default style sheet. Next, click Set Default. Word will then display the alert box shown in Figure 9-46.

FIGURE 9-46

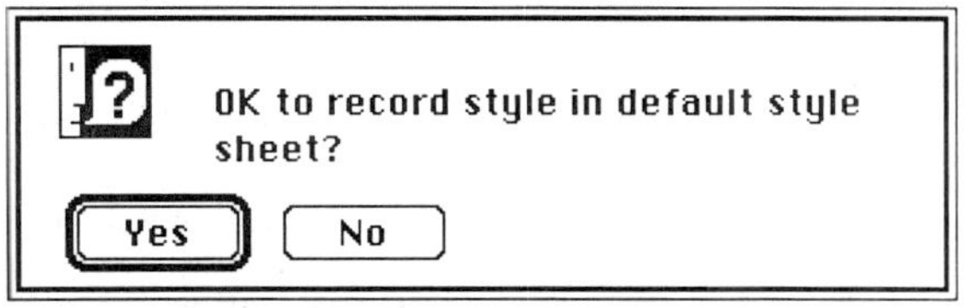

As you are adding a style to the default style sheet, you will see this alert box.

If you click Yes in this box, then Word will add the selected style to the default style sheet. Then, each time you open a new Word document, that style will automatically appear on the style sheet for that document.

Modifying the Default Characteristics of Automatic Styles

We've already seen an example of how you can change the formatting instructions for an automatic style on a document's style sheet. Suppose, however, you want to make a permanent change to one of Word's automatic styles. In other words, suppose that you want to modify the instructions for an automatic style so that every time you use that style in any document, the modified instructions will be in effect. For example, you may want to modify the default *Normal* style. Instead of beginning each new document with a *Normal* style of 12-point New York type with flush-left paragraph alignment, you would like to use a *Normal* style of 10-point Times type with justified paragraphs and a $^1/_2$ inch indent on the first line of each paragraph. First, you should choose Define Styles... from the Format menu and click on the style name *Normal* to select it. Then, choose Times and 10 Point from the Font menu. Next, click on the ruler icon for justified alignment and drag the first-line indent marker to the $^1/_2$ inch position. After you've made all of these changes, click the Set Default button in the Define Styles dialog box. Word will then display the alert box shown in Figure 9-45.

If you click Yes in the alert box, Word will alter the *Normal* style both in your current document and in any new documents that you create. Any text that you have formatted in your current document using the *Normal* style will be reformatted according to the new formatting instructions. Also, since the other automatic styles are all based on the *Normal* style, any text that has been formatted according to one of these other automatic styles may also be reformatted.

Of course, documents that were formatted in the old default *Normal* style and saved to disk will retain their original formatting.

Returning to the Original Defaults

Word stores the default style sheet and all of the instructions for automatic styles in the Word Settings file on your startup disk. If you want to restore the default style sheet and return the automatic styles to their original forms, you can delete or rename the Word Settings file. Word will then automatically recreate the Word Settings file using the original defaults: *Normal* will be the only style on the default style sheet, and the instructions for each of the automatic styles will return to their defaults.

Of course, if you delete or rename the Word Settings file, you'll affect more than just style sheets. You also will return the Font and Format menus to their original configurations. (For more on the Word Settings file, see Chapter 17.)

PRINTING A STYLE SHEET

To print a list of all the styles on a style sheet, choose Define Styles... from the Format menu, then choose Print... from the File menu. Word will then print a list like the one shown in Figure 9-47. Notice that it includes the style names in boldface and, under each name, the formatting instructions for that style. (For more information on printing, see Chapter 7.)

FIGURE 9-47

level 1
Normal + Font: 18 Point, Bold, Indent: First 0 in, Space Before 12 pt

level 2
Normal + Font: 14 Point, Bold, Indent: First 0 in, Space Before 6 pt

level 3
Normal + Font: 14 Point, Italic, Indent: First 0 in

level 4
Normal + Bold, Indent: First 0 in

level 5
Normal + Italic, Indent: First 0 in

Normal
Font: Helvetica 12 Point, Indent: First 0.25in Flush left

Word can produce a printed list of all the named styles on the current style sheet and their formatting instructions.

THE GLOSSARY 10

You've probably seen many books that include a glossary, or listing of special terms and their definitions. In Word, the glossary serves a slightly different purpose from what you might expect. Instead of containing definitions for special terms, the Word glossary stores frequently used terms or other text and abbreviations for those terms. Word's glossary feature gives you access to several shortcuts for inserting glossary text into your documents. The entries that you store in the glossary might include words that require special formatting or just long terms that are difficult to spell. A glossary item can be as short as a single character or as long as several pages of text. Word even allows you to store graphics in a glossary.

In this section, we will begin with an overview of how the Word glossary functions. Then we will move on to discussions of changing the glossary, creating and updating glossary files, and using the glossary.

HOW THE GLOSSARY WORKS

Whenever you load Word, the glossary is activated automatically. You might think of the glossary as a special "memory bin" for storing glossary terms. When you load Word—either by starting a new document or by opening an existing document file—the glossary initially will contain only the entries that are stored in the Standard Glossary file. This file is delivered on your Word disk and includes two entries that cannot be removed: *date* and *time*. It also includes the term *Index*, which can be used to mark index entries in your document. (Indexes are discussed in Chapter 13.) We will talk more about the Standard Glossary file later in this chapter and in Chapter 17.

One Glossary, Many Glossary Files

It's important to note that Word has only one glossary, which resides in RAM when Word is loaded. However, you can create many special disk files that store glossary entries. The entries in these files can be loaded into Word's glossary whenever you need them. For purposes of our discussion, we will use the term *glossary* when we refer to the one glossary or "memory bin" that you can access in Word, and we will use the term *glossary file* when we refer to one of the special files on disk that store glossary terms.

Changing the Glossary

After you open a document file or start a new document, you can change the contents of the glossary in several different ways. First, you can create your own entries and add them to the glossary. Second, you can delete entries from the glossary. Third, you can revise the entries in the glossary. Finally, you can retrieve a glossary file from disk and add its entries to the glossary.

Any changes you make to the glossary—creating and deleting entries or loading entries from another glossary file on disk—will remain in effect until you quit from Word. If you close one document and then open another without quitting from Word, the glossary entries that you used with the first document will still be active when you open the second document. Similarly, when you have two or more documents open at one time on your DeskTop, you can access only one glossary, no matter which document you are working in. Therefore, if you need to use different glossary entries for different documents that are open on your DeskTop, make sure that *all* those entries are loaded into the glossary.

Once you have made changes to the glossary, you may want to save the glossary to disk either in a new glossary file or in an existing glossary file. (If you don't save your changes, they will be lost when you quit from Word.) For example, suppose you have just started a new document by opening Word from the Finder level. Initially, the only entries in the glossary will be the entries from the Standard Glossary file, which Word loads automatically. If you create new entries and add them to the glossary, then the glossary will contain a combination of your new entries and the original Standard Glossary entries. You can save this combination either in a new glossary file or in the file named Standard Glossary.

If you save the glossary entries in the file named Standard Glossary, then each time you open a document, Word will automatically load those entries as it loads the Standard Glossary file. In other words, in each new document, your glossary will contain the combination of the initial Standard Glossary entries and the new entries that you created and saved. In Chapter 17, we describe how you can create multiple Standard Glossary files so that you can use a different "automatic" glossary in each Word session.

Glossary Files Are Not Attached to Documents

It's important to remember that no glossary file is "attached" to a particular document file. If you are working in a document, and you make changes to the glossary, you can save both the document and the revised glossary. However, Word will save the document and the glossary entries in separate disk files. The next time you open that document, Word will *not* automatically load the entries from the glossary file, unless you stored your changes in the file named Standard Glossary. You must open all other glossary files manually.

Now that we've seen an overview of how the glossary functions, let's take a look at the basics of working with the glossary.

GLOSSARY BASICS

To use the glossary in Word, you choose Glossary... from the Edit menu. This will bring up the dialog box shown in Figure 10-1. Most of the Glossary dialog box is taken up with a list box, which displays glossary terms. The first entry in the list is always New. You use New only when you want to define a new glossary entry. After New, the list box displays all the other glossary terms in alphabetical order. If there are more terms than can be displayed in the list box, you can click the scroll bar or scroll arrows to view additional glossary terms. In Figure 10-1, the only entries in the list box besides New are those that are loaded from the Standard Glossary file: *date*, *time*, and *index*.

FIGURE 10-1

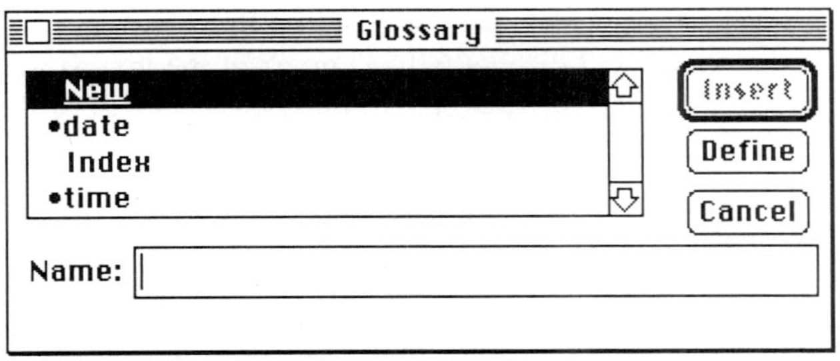

When you choose Glossary... from the Edit menu, Word will display the Glossary dialog box, which lists all the terms that currently are in the glossary.

At the beginning of our discussion of the glossary, we mentioned that Word's glossary is used to store frequently used terms and their abbreviations. The list box that you see in the Glossary dialog box shows only the abbreviations. For purposes of our discussion, we will use the word *glossary term* when we refer to one of the items in this list. The term *glossary text* will refer to the longer text that a glossary abbreviation represents. Finally, the term *glossary entry* will be used to denote a complete glossary item—both the glossary term and the text that that term represents.

If you want to see what a particular glossary term stands for, you can open the Glossary dialog box and click on that term in the list box. Word will then display the glossary text that the selected term represents in the lower-left corner of the dialog box. For example, suppose you want to see what the term *time* represents. When you click this term, the dialog box will look like Figure 10-2.

FIGURE 10-2

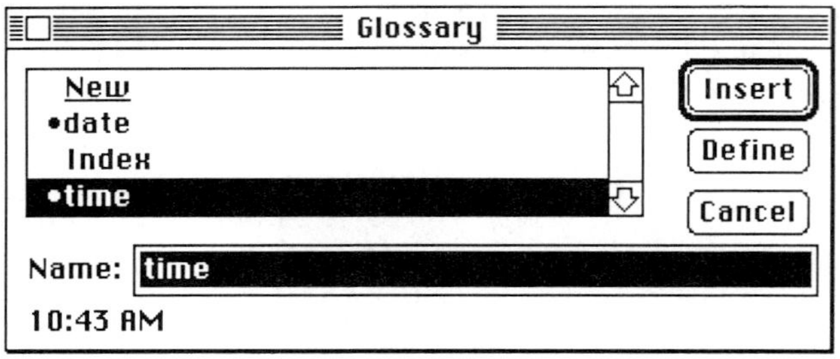

When you click a term in the Glossary dialog box, Word will display the text for that term in the dialog box.

Notice that the term you click—in this case, *time*—appears in the Name edit bar. Notice also that the time *10:43 AM* appears in the lower-left corner of the dialog box. This tells you that the glossary term *time* represents the current time in HH:MM AM/PM format.

Sometimes the text for a glossary term will be too long to be displayed in the dialog box. In that case, Word will display only as much of the text as will fit in the dialog box, followed by an ellipsis (...). If you want to see all of the text, you must click the Insert button to paste it into your document. Then you can use the Undo or Cut command to remove the text from your document.

Since the entries that are loaded from the Standard Glossary file are not really typical glossary entries, let's walk through a quick example of creating, using, and saving a typical glossary entry. We will talk more specifically about the *date* and *time* entries later in this chapter.

A QUICK EXAMPLE

Suppose you are creating a document in which you must frequently type the name of your company, International Consolidated Systems, Inc. Since this is a long name that you need to use over and over, it makes sense to add it to the glossary. To do this, first type the full company name anywhere in your document. Then drag through that name to select it. Next, choose Glossary**...** from the Edit menu to open the Glossary dialog box. With New selected in the list box, type an appropriate abbreviation in the Name edit bar. For example, you might type the abbreviation ICS. Then click the Define button. At this point, the dialog box will look like Figure 10-3.

FIGURE 10-3

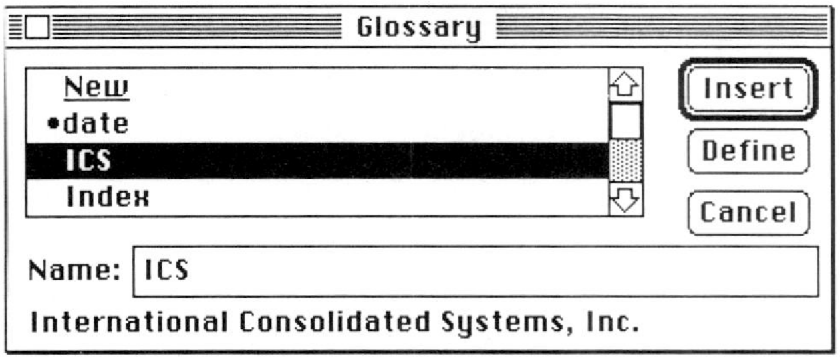

After you define a new glossary entry, Word will display the glossary term both in the Name edit bar and in the list of glossary terms.

To return to your document, just click the Cancel button or the close box, or click anywhere on your document window.

The next time you need to use the company name in your document, you can insert it with the Glossary... command instead of typing the full name. Once the Glossary dialog box is open, just click on the term ICS in the list box and then click the Insert button. Word will insert the full text for the glossary entry—*International Consolidated Systems, Inc.*—into your document at the current insertion point location and automatically close the Glossary dialog box. By the way, there are a couple of other methods for inserting glossary text in a document, which are even faster than the method we just described. We explain these other methods later on in the section called "Inserting Glossary Text in Your Document."

After you have added an entry to the glossary, you probably will want to save the glossary with that new entry. Continuing with our example, suppose that you want your company name to become a permanent part of the Standard Glossary file so that it will be loaded into the glossary each time you use Word. To save the glossary with this new entry, you must first issue the Glossary... command. Then, with the Glossary dialog box open, choose Save from the File menu. Word will display the dialog box shown in Figure 10-4. As you can see, Word suggests the name *Standard Glossary* as the file name for the glossary you are saving. All you have to do is click the Save button to save the current contents of the glossary into the Standard Glossary file.

FIGURE 10-4

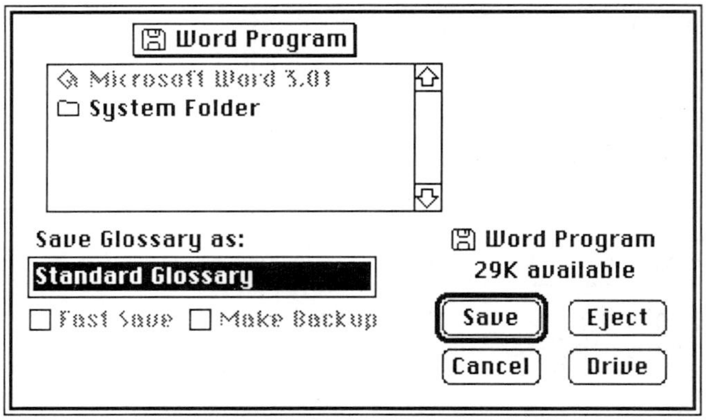

When you save glossary entries in a glossary file, Word will display this dialog box.

The example we just presented describes some of the most basic glossary-related tasks. However, using the glossary can be quite a bit more complicated than what we have described here. In the remainder of this section, we will talk about the specifics of working with the glossary and glossary files.

CHANGING THE GLOSSARY

We've just seen a quick example of how you can change the glossary by adding an entry. You also can change the glossary by revising entries, deleting entries, and merging glossary files. In other words, you can customize the glossary to suit any document. Keep in mind that any changes you make to the glossary are only temporary—they remain in effect only until you quit from Word. If you want to make a permanent change—for example, if you want to create a new glossary entry that you can use in later Word sessions—then you must be sure to save the revised glossary in a glossary file. In the section called "Creating and Updating a Glossary File," we explain how to save your glossary changes to disk.

Adding a New Glossary Entry

To add a new glossary entry, first type the text for that entry anywhere in your document. Then select the text you typed and choose Glossary**...** from the Edit menu. Word will automatically highlight <u>New</u> in the Glossary dialog box. You simply type the abbreviation that you want to use as the glossary term in the Name edit bar and then click the Define button.

As soon as you click Define, Word will place the abbreviation that you typed in the list of glossary terms and highlight it. (However, the abbreviation will still appear in the Name edit bar.) The text that your new entry represents will appear in the lower-left corner of the dialog box. You can return to your document by clicking the Cancel button, clicking the close box, or clicking anywhere on your document.

For example, suppose that you are creating a document in which you frequently must insert the notice, *COMPANY CONFIDENTIAL: For internal use only.* By placing this text in the glossary, you can use a shortcut to insert it in your document whenever you need it. Begin by typing the full notice anywhere in your document. Then drag through that text to select it and choose Glossary... from the Edit menu. With New highlighted in the list box, type the abbreviation CC (for "company confidential") in the Name edit bar, and click the Define button. Figure 10-5 shows the dialog box at this point. You can click either the Cancel button or the close box to complete the procedure.

FIGURE 10-5

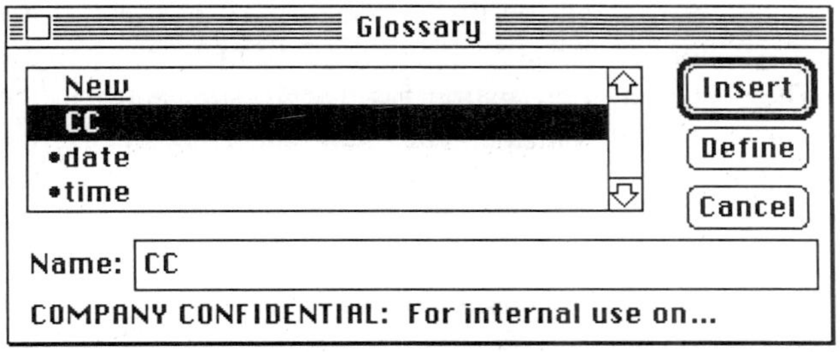

This is what the Glossary dialog box will look like immediately after defining the term CC.

Rules for glossary terms

When you type the glossary term in the Name edit bar, there are a few rules that you need to keep in mind. First of all, Word will not allow you to enter an existing glossary term when you are creating a new glossary entry. If you type a term in the Name edit bar that already has been defined, Word will beep and display the message, *That name is already defined.* In determining which terms have already been used, Word does not consider case. For example, a lower-case *g* is considered to be the same as an upper-case *G*. As you'll see in a minute, the fact that Word does not distinguish case in glossary terms can make the glossary easier to use.

You can use any characters that you want in a glossary term, including punctuation marks and various special characters produced with Option-key combinations. Interestingly, even though Word does not distinguish case in glossary terms, it does distinguish a character created with an Option-key combination from a regular alphanumeric character. For example, suppose you want to use the symbol © to represent the text for a copyright notice. You can create the glossary term © by typing the Option-c combination in the Name edit bar. After you've defined this entry, Word will also let you use the simple letter *g* (or *G*) to define another glossary term. By the way, when you use a special character such as © as a glossary term, Word will place that term at the end of the list of terms in the Glossary dialog box.

The maximum length for a glossary term is 31 characters, and a glossary term can consist of two or more words. Chances are, however, you'll want to keep each glossary term as short as possible so that you can type it quickly and so it will be easy to remember.

If you do not enter a term in the Name edit bar, but simply click the Define button, Word will supply a name, like *Unnamed1*. If you want to use a different name, you can replace the *Unnamed* term with the name you want to use and click Define once more.

Pasting glossary text from the Clipboard

Word allows you to use the contents of the Clipboard as your glossary text. Here's how it works. As you know, after you have cut or copied some text in your document, Word will store that text on the Clipboard. To use this as the text in a glossary entry, first choose Glossary... from the Edit menu to open the Glossary dialog box. Then type an abbreviation for the glossary entry in the Name edit bar. Next, choose Paste from the Edit menu and click the Define button in the Glossary dialog box. This tells Word that you want to use the contents of the Clipboard as your glossary text. As soon as you define the glossary term in this manner, Word will display the text (or the first few words of the text) in the lower-left corner of the Glossary dialog box.

Formatted glossary text

When you select text for a new glossary entry, Word stores the formatting for that text in the glossary. Going back to our previous example, suppose that you add bold formatting to the *COMPANY CONFIDENTIAL* notice before you create the glossary entry. Each time you use the glossary entry *CC*, the full notice—including bold formatting—will be inserted into your document.

In addition to bold formatting, Word will store different fonts, point sizes, superscripting, italics, and any other character formatting you may have assigned to your glossary text. If your glossary text is a complete paragraph (or several paragraphs), Word will store the paragraph formatting as well—including margins, line spacing, indentation, and so forth.

Although Word stores the formatting for your glossary text, it will not display that formatting when you view the glossary text in the dialog box. As with any other dialog box, Word displays all the text in the Glossary dialog box in 12-point Chicago.

There's one situation where Word will not store the formatting for your glossary text as you might expect. If you have used a named style to format a paragraph, and then you select all or part of that paragraph as your glossary text, Word will store the formatting of that selection *only* if the selection includes the ¶ at the end of the formatted paragraph. If you don't include this ¶, Word will store the text that you select in the glossary but will not store any of the special formatting that's specified by the named style. When you insert the glossary text into a document, it will appear in the *Normal* style.

Of course, if you include the ¶ in your text selection and then you insert the glossary text in the middle of a paragraph, Word may change the formatting of the paragraph in which you insert that glossary text. In general, if you want to create a formatted glossary entry, we recommend that you format the text manually, rather than using a named style, before you define the glossary entry. For more information on named styles and style sheets, see Chapter 9.

Revising an Existing Glossary Entry

After you have added entries to the glossary, you may need to change one or more of those entries. Word allows you to change both the glossary term and glossary text, though the procedure is different for each one. To change a glossary term (the abbreviation), first choose Glossary... from the Edit menu to open the Glossary dialog box. Then click the term in the glossary list that you want to change. When a term is selected, it will appear in the Name edit bar as well, as shown in Figure 10-6.

FIGURE 10-6

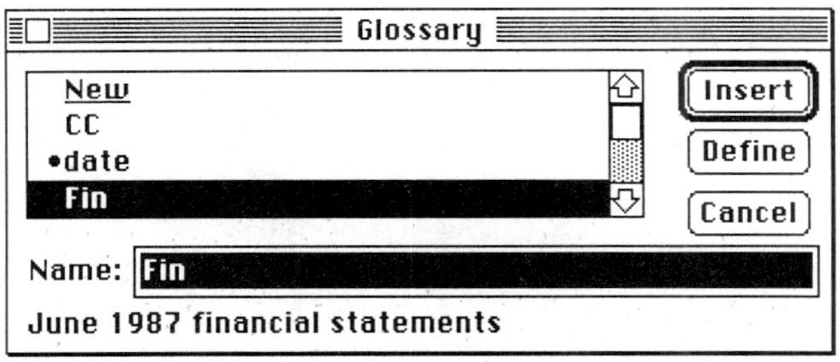

To revise a glossary term, open the Glossary dialog box and click on that term so that it appears in the Name edit bar.

If you begin typing at this point, Word will use the characters that you type to replace the existing term in the Name edit bar. After you have typed a new term, click the Define button to lock in your change. Word will then place your new term in the list box and remove the original term. To return to your document, click the Cancel button, click the close box, or click anywhere on your document window.

Instead of typing a new term from scratch, you can edit an existing glossary term using any of Word's normal editing techniques. For example, suppose you have created a glossary entry with the term *Fin*, which stands for the text *June 1987 financial statements*. To make the term a little more understandable, you might change it to be *JuneFin*. You can do this by opening the Glossary dialog box and clicking on the term *Fin* in the list box. Then click at the beginning of this term in the Name edit bar and type *June*. Click Define to lock in the change, and then click the close box to return to your document.

Changing the text for a glossary entry is similar to creating a new glossary entry. Word will not allow you simply to edit the existing glossary text; instead, you must replace it with new text. First, type the word or phrase that you want to use as your replacement text in an open document window (if those words do not already exist in your document). Then select that text and choose Glossary... from the Edit menu. In the Glossary dialog box, click on the term whose text you want to replace. Word will display that term in the Name edit bar and display all or part of the glossary text for that term in the lower-left corner of the dialog box. To complete the replacement, click the Define button. Word will then display all or part of your new glossary text in the dialog box. You can return to your document by clicking the Cancel button, clicking the close box, or clicking anywhere on your document window.

For example, suppose that your glossary includes the term *2EU*, which stands for *2nd Edition Update*. You would like to change the text for this glossary entry to *Current Edition Update*. First type the words *Current Edition Update* anywhere in your document. Then, select that text and choose Glossary... from the Edit menu. In the Glossary dialog box, click the term *2EU* to select it, then click Define. Immediately, Word will replace the existing text for that term—*2nd Edition Update*—with the text that you've selected in your document—*Current Edition Update*.

Deleting a Glossary Entry

Deleting a glossary entry is very easy. Just choose Glossary... from the Edit menu and click on the glossary term that you want to delete. Then choose Cut from the Edit menu. Word will display an alert box that asks *Delete glossary entry?* If you click Yes, Word will remove the selected glossary entry from the glossary. The Glossary dialog box will remain open on your screen, so you can insert or delete new entries if you like.

Word will not allow you to delete the standard glossary entries *date* and *time*. If you try to delete one of these entries, Word will beep and display an alert box that says *Can't cut a standard glossary entry*. Word also will not allow you to delete more than one glossary entry at a time. If you need to get rid of a lot of entries in the glossary, you must delete them one at a time. However, there is a quick way to remove *all* the entries from your glossary except the standard *date* and *time* entries. We'll talk about that in just a minute.

By the way, if the entry that you delete is part of a glossary file stored on disk, Word will *not* delete that entry from the glossary file when you choose Cut from the Edit menu. The next time you open that glossary file, the entry that you deleted will be loaded into the glossary. If you want to delete an entry from a glossary file, you must open that file and load its contents into the glossary, delete the entry from the glossary, and then save the revised glossary to disk. In a few pages, we'll explain in more detail how to revise a glossary file.

Deleting All Nonstandard Glossary Entries

Occasionally, you may need to clean out all entries from the glossary. For example, before you load the glossary entries from a file on disk, you may want to remove all existing entries from the glossary. With one command, you can delete all entries from the glossary except the standard *date* and *time* entries. Just choose Glossary... from the Edit menu, then choose New from the File menu. Word will display a dialog box that asks, *Delete all nonstandard glossary entries?* If you click Yes, Word will delete every glossary entry except *date* and *time*. Keep in mind, however, that any changes you have made to your glossary will be lost when you issue the New command, unless you save your changes first.

WORKING WITH GLOSSARY FILES

So far, we've explained how you can change the glossary by creating new entries, revising existing entries, and deleting entries. There's one more way to make changes to the glossary, and that is by merging entries from two or more glossary files. In order to do this, however, you must first have created a glossary file by saving glossary entries to disk. Therefore, before we talk about merging glossary files, let's examine how you go about saving glossary entries to disk.

Creating and Updating a Glossary File

After you have made changes to the glossary—particularly when you've created new glossary entries—you may want to save those changes to disk so you can use them in a later Word session. When you save the entries in the current glossary to disk, you can either create a new glossary file, or you can save the entries in an existing glossary file. At the Finder level, glossary files are represented by a special icon, which is shown in Figure 10-7.

FIGURE 10-7

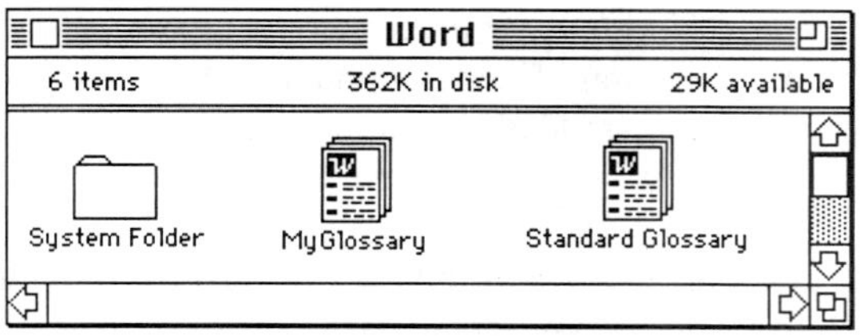

At the Finder level, glossary files are represented by a special type of icon.

Creating a new glossary file

To save your glossary entries, you must first choose Glossary... from the Edit menu. Then, with the Glossary dialog box open on your screen, choose Save or Save As... from the File menu. Word will then display the dialog box shown in Figure 10-8. If you have not opened a glossary file in the current Word session, the Save Glossary as edit bar will display the file name, *Standard Glossary*, as shown in Figure 10-4. If you have opened a glossary file in the current Word session, this edit bar will be blank.

FIGURE 10-8

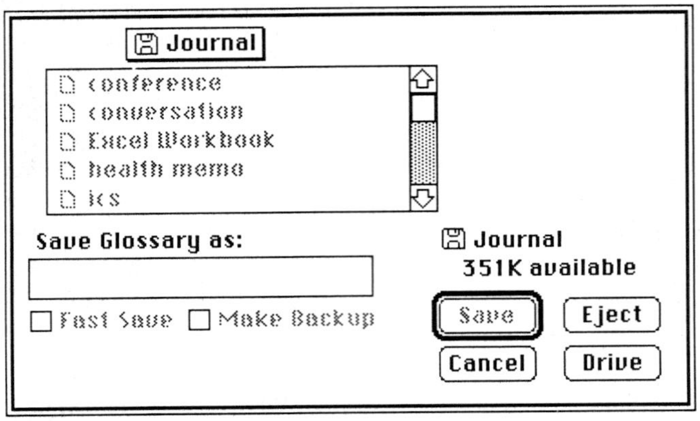

When you save glossary entries to disk, Word will display this dialog box.

If you want to create a completely new glossary file to store the entries in your current glossary, then you should type a name for that file in the Save Glossary as edit bar. (If Word is displaying the name *Standard Glossary* in the edit bar when you open the dialog box, you can simply type the file name you wish to use, and that name will replace *Standard Glossary*.) After you've entered the name of the file in which you want to store the glossary entries, just click the Save button. (By the way, the Make Backup and Text Only options are not available when you're saving a glossary file.)

Before you save a glossary to disk, you may want to delete some of the entries in that glossary—particularly if you have loaded entries from several glossary files during the current Word session. Keep in mind, however, that you cannot delete the *date* and *time* entries that are loaded from the Standard Glossary file. Therefore, any new glossary file that you create must always contain these two entries.

If you make any changes to the glossary and then try to quit from Word without saving the glossary, Word will display the message, *Save changes to glossary?* If you click Yes, Word will open the Glossary dialog box, then open the Save dialog box shown in Figure 10-8. You can then follow the standard procedure for saving the glossary entries to disk. If you click No in the Save Changes alert box, Word will quit to the Finder level without saving your glossary revisions. By clicking Cancel in the alert box, you can abort the Quit command.

If, in addition to glossary changes, you also have made changes to one or more documents and haven't saved those changes, Word's warning procedure will be somewhat different when you choose Quit from the File menu. First, you'll see a message asking whether you want to save changes in the current document. For example, you might see the message, *Save changes to Untitled2?* Whether you click Yes or No, Word will then display the message *Save changes to glossary?* If you click Yes, Word will display the Save dialog box shown in Figure 10-8, where you can enter the name of the file in which you want to save your glossary entries.

Updating an existing glossary file

Instead of saving the entries in the current glossary into a completely new file, you may want to save those entries into an existing glossary file. To do this, you open the Glossary dialog box, choose Save or Save As... from the File menu, and then type the name of the existing file in the Save Glossary as edit bar. (Word will display in dim video the names of all files on the current disk in the File Save dialog box.) After you type the name and press Return, you'll see a message asking if you want to replace the existing glossary file on disk. If you click Yes, Word will overwrite that file with the entries in your current glossary. Word will *not* merge the entries in your current glossary with the entries in the glossary file on disk.

One of the best reasons for saving the glossary into an existing file is to update that file with new entries. For example, suppose that you have opened a document and you have loaded into the glossary the entries from a file named MyGlossary. You then create several new glossary entries so that your glossary contains *both* the entries from MyGlossary and these new entries. If you want, you can replace the MyGlossary file on disk with the expanded set of entries in your current glossary. First, choose Glossary... from the Edit menu, then choose Save or Save As... from the File menu. Type the name *MyGlossary* in the edit bar. Word will beep and display a dialog box that asks *Replace existing "MyGlossary"?* Click Yes if you want to proceed. Word will then overwrite the contents of MyGlossary on disk with the entries currently in the glossary.

Opening Glossary Files

To open a glossary file from within Word, just choose Glossary... from the Edit menu; then, while the Glossary dialog box is displayed, choose Open... from the File menu. Word will display the dialog box shown in Figure 10-9, which lists all the glossary files on the current disk.

FIGURE 10-9

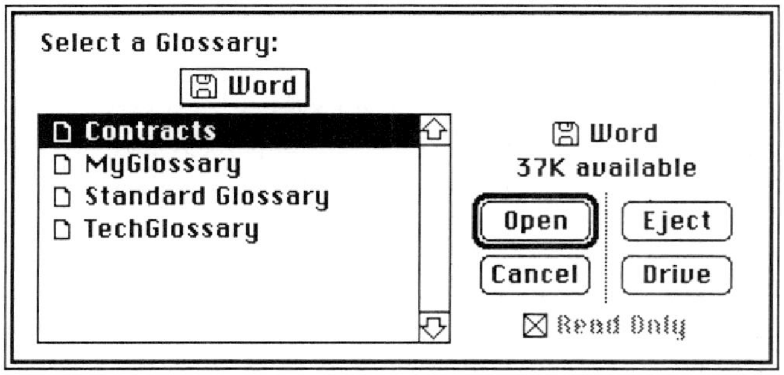

As you open a glossary file, Word will display this dialog box.

To open a glossary file, just click on the file name to select it, and then click the Open button. (You also can just double-click the name of the glossary file you want to open.) As with other File commands in Word, you can access other disks if the glossary file that you want to open is not on the current disk. For instance, you would click the Drive button if you want to search another disk drive for a glossary file, and you would click the Eject button if you want to eject the disk in the current drive and read a different disk.

When you open a glossary file, you won't actually see that file on your screen. However, the glossary terms from the file will appear in the list in the Glossary dialog box as Word adds those terms to the current glossary contents.

Merging glossary files

To merge two or more glossary files, you simply load those files into Word's glossary. Word will expand the glossary to accommodate the entries from all the glossary files that you open (RAM permitting). For example, suppose that you have created a glossary file named Contracts and you would like to merge the entries from this file with the entries in the Standard Glossary file. Of course, as soon as you open a document or start a new document in Word, the entries from the Standard Glossary file will be loaded into the glossary. To merge the entries from the Contracts glossary file, all you have to do is open that file, using the procedure we just described.

If any term in the glossary file you are merging is identical to a term that already exists in the glossary, Word will overwrite the existing term with the term from the new file. For example, suppose that you have created a glossary entry consisting of the term *mw*, which represents the text *Microsoft Word.* Now, suppose that you open a second glossary file which also contains the term *mw*. In the file, however, *mw* represents the text *Michael Williams*. After you open the glossary file, your glossary will contain only one *mw* glossary term, which will stand for *Michael Williams*. The text that was in your glossary before you opened the file—*Microsoft Word*—will no longer be in the glossary.

By the way, Word does not warn you when a glossary entry from a file is about to replace an existing entry. Therefore, before you open a glossary file, it's probably a good idea to save your existing glossary entries to disk so that you do not risk losing any of them.

Opening a glossary file from the Finder

Word allows you to start a new document and open a glossary file in one step. At the Finder level, just double-click on the icon for the glossary file that you want to use. This will load the Word program and open a new, blank document window (just as if you had double-clicked the disk icon for the Word program file). In addition, however, if you open the Glossary dialog box, you'll see that Word has automatically loaded all of the entries from the glossary file that you selected at the Finder level. You can use this technique to load the entries from several glossary files, if you want. At the Finder level, press the Shift key, and click on the icon for each glossary file that you want to use.

Then, choose Open... from the File menu. Again, the Word program will be loaded, and you'll see a new, blank document window. When you check the glossary, you'll see that it contains all of the entries from the files you selected at the Finder level.

Opening a glossary file by itself

At times you will want your glossary to contain only the entries from a particular file. In these cases, you must clean out the glossary of any other entries before you open that file. To delete all the entries in the glossary except *date* and *time* (which cannot be deleted), just choose Glossary... from the Edit menu, then choose New from the File menu. When you see the box shown in Figure 10-10, click Yes. After deleting your existing glossary entries, you can choose Open... from the File menu while the Glossary dialog box is still open and select the name of the glossary file you want to open.

FIGURE 10-10

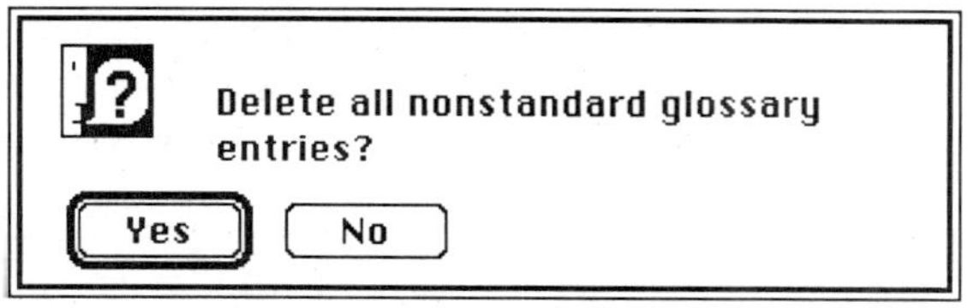

When you're cleaning out all entries from the glossary, Word will display this alert box.

Deleting a Glossary File

If you want to delete a glossary file from within Word, you can do so, but only if that file has not been opened during the current Word session. To delete the file, just choose Delete... from the File menu. Then, in the Delete dialog box, click on the name of the glossary file that you want to delete and click the Delete button. Word will ask you to confirm the deletion before it gets rid of the file.

Once you have opened a glossary file, Word will not let you delete it. In fact, the file name will not even appear in the Delete dialog box. The only glossary file names that will appear in the dialog box are files that have not been opened during the current Word session. Even if you clear the glossary of all the entries that were loaded from a particular glossary file, Word still won't let you delete it. If you want to get rid of a glossary file that you've opened during the current Word session, you must quit from Word and delete that file at the Finder level by dragging it into the trash. (Of course, you can always use the Delete... command to get rid of the file the next time you load the Word program.)

By the way, if you delete the Standard Glossary file by dragging it into the Trash at the Finder level, Word will still load the *date* and *time* entries into the glossary each time you open a document. However, any other glossary entries that you may have stored in the Standard Glossary file will be lost.

INSERTING GLOSSARY TEXT IN YOUR DOCUMENT

In the example on pages 418 through 419, we explained one method for inserting glossary text into a document: First, you position the insertion point marker at the location where you want to insert the text. Then choose Glossary... from the Edit menu. Next, click on the glossary term whose text you want to insert. (Recall that you will see the text for that term in the lower-left corner of the Glossary dialog box—or as much text as will fit in the dialog box.) Finally, click the Insert button to place the glossary text in your document and close the dialog box.

Inserting Glossary Text from the Keyboard

Unless you need to view the text for a glossary entry or you cannot remember a glossary term, opening the Glossary dialog box and clicking the Insert button is *not* the most efficient way to insert glossary text into a document. Word offers a much easier way to enter glossary text. First, position the insertion point marker at the location where you want to insert the text. Then, press ⌘-Backspace. You'll see a *Name* prompt in the lower-left corner of your document window (where the page number normally appears), as shown in Figure 10-11. Type the glossary term (the abbreviation) for the text that you want to insert in your document and press Return. As soon as you press Return, Word will insert the full glossary text into your document.

FIGURE 10-11

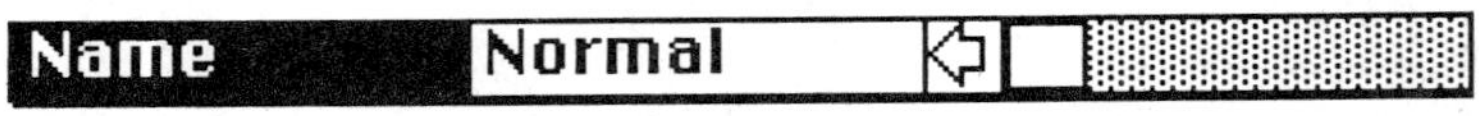

When you press ⌘-Backspace, Word will display a Name *prompt in the lower-left corner of the current window.*

Of course, in order to use this technique, you must remember the correct glossary term so that you can type it at the *Name* prompt. Case does not matter when you enter a glossary term. If you cannot remember the correct term or if you decide that you do not want to insert the glossary text in your document, you can cancel this procedure by pressing the ⌘ and period keys (⌘-.) or by clicking anywhere on your screen.

Inserting Glossary Text from the Work Menu

Although using ⌘-Backspace offers a significant shortcut for inserting glossary text, the fastest way to access a glossary entry is to place the glossary term on the Work menu. The Work menu is a custom menu that you can create in Word to speed up several kinds of tasks. The Work menu does not appear on your screen unless you have created at least one custom menu item. Once you've added one or more glossary terms on the Work menu, all you have to do to insert glossary text is select the appropriate term from the Work menu. You don't need to open the Glossary dialog box or type a glossary term. In Chapter 11, we discuss the Work menu in detail and explain how to add glossary terms and other items to that menu.

Using ⌘-a to Repeat a Glossary

Sometimes you may need to insert glossary text into your document at several different locations. Once you have used the Glossary... command or pressed ⌘-Backspace to enter that term, you can insert it in different locations throughout your document by using the ⌘-a key combination. After inserting your glossary text for the first time, just click at the next spot where you want to insert that text and press ⌘-a. Of course, since Word always repeats the last command that you issued when you press ⌘-a, you can use this technique only as long as you do not issue another command or make any editing changes to your document.

Inserting Glossary Text from the Clipboard

You can also place your glossary text on the Clipboard and then use the Paste command to insert the text at different locations throughout your document. To place glossary text on the Clipboard, first open the Glossary dialog box and click on the glossary term you want to use. Then choose Copy from the Edit menu to place a copy of that text on your Clipboard. Next, close the Glossary dialog box. Now you can click anywhere in your document where you wish to insert the text and choose Paste from the Edit menu. Word will insert the Clipboard text at that location, and, of course, the text will remain on the Clipboard so you can paste it in additional locations. To make the procedure even faster, type ⌘-v instead of pulling down the Edit menu and choosing Paste.

Undoing a Glossary Insertion

After you've inserted some glossary text—using the Glossary... command, the Work menu, the ⌘-Backspace technique, or the ⌘-a method—you can delete that text by choosing Undo Expand Glossary from the Edit menu. As with any other Undo procedure, the Undo Expand Glossary option will only be available immediately after you insert the glossary text, before you do anything else. We find Word's Undo message to be rather confusing; in fact, it's actually a throwback to an earlier version of Word in which the process of inserting glossary text worked somewhat differently. (In earlier versions, you had to type an abbreviation into your document, then select it and press ⌘-Backspace to "expand" it into the full glossary text.) Nevertheless, it's nice to know that Word offers an Undo option for getting rid of unwanted glossary text.

If you're pasting glossary text from the Clipboard, then you can remove any text that you insert by choosing Undo Paste from the Edit menu. Again, you must choose Undo immediately after you paste. This is no different from using the Undo command to remove any other text that you've pasted in a document.

WORKING WITH *DATE* AND *TIME* ENTRIES

At the beginning of our discussion of the Word glossary, we talked about the *date* and *time* entries that are stored in the Standard Glossary file. Since Word always loads the entries from the Standard Glossary file into the glossary, and since you cannot remove the *date* and *time* entries, any glossary file that you create will contain a *date* entry and a *time* entry.

Whenever you insert the *date* glossary entry, Word will place the current date into your document in M/D/YY form. Similarly, whenever you insert the *time* entry, Word will place the current time in your document in HH:MM AM/PM form. These are your "system" date and time, which are controlled by the Macintosh's internal clock. You can adjust the date and time by using the Alarm Clock desk accessory.

When you use the glossary to place either the date or time in a document, Word will format the date or time like the surrounding text where you insert it. For example, if you insert the current date between two words that have bold formatting, the date will also appear in bold. Once in your document, the date and time are simply characters, just like those you type from the keyboard. They are not dynamic date and time values. As a result, you can edit the date and time in your document just as you would edit any other characters.

Dynamic Date and Time Entries

Word allows you to create a glossary entry consisting of a dynamic date or dynamic time. When you use such an entry in your document, Word will update that date or time each time you print the document. A dynamic date or dynamic time entry will *not* replace the standard date or time glossary entry. The dynamic entries must be created in addition to the standard entries.

To create a dynamic date entry, first open the header or footer window. (Just choose Open Header… or Open Footer… from the Document menu.) Figure 10-12 shows a blank header window in Word.

FIGURE 10-12

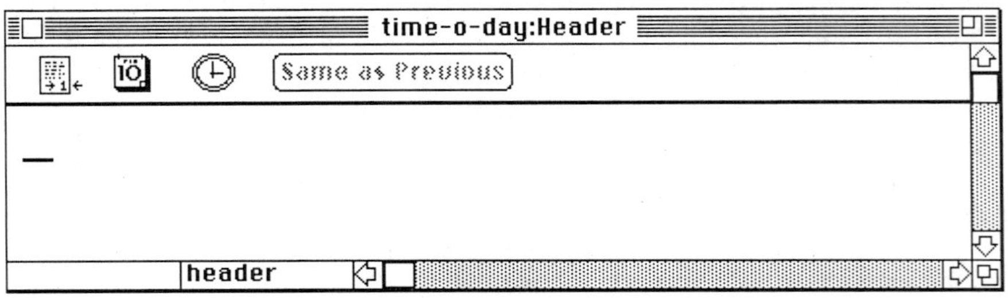

Word displays both a date icon and a time icon at the top of a header window.

After you open the header or footer window, click on the date icon at the top of the window. When the date appears in the header or footer window, select it and then format it in the font and style that you wish to use in your document. (Initially, the date will appear formatted in the *Normal* style for the current document.) Then, with the date still selected in the header window, choose Glossary... from the Edit menu and type an abbreviation for the dynamic date entry. Since Word will not let you use the standard glossary term, *date*, you must type a new term, such as *date2*. Click the Define button and then close the Glossary dialog box to complete the procedure.

The steps for adding a dynamic time entry to the glossary are identical, except that you click the time icon in the header or footer window instead of clicking the date icon. Again, Word will not let you use the standard glossary term, *time*, to define the dynamic time entry. Instead you must use a new term such as *time2* or *dytime*.

Inserting a dynamic date or dynamic time entry into your document is no different from inserting any other glossary text. You can use the Glossary... command or the ⌘-Backspace key combination. You can even place the dynamic date or time entry on the Work menu or on the Clipboard.

How can you distinguish a dynamic date or time from a regular date or time? When Word inserts a dynamic date or time into your document, it draws a dotted-line box around that date or time, as shown in Figure 10-13. This box appears only when Show ¶ is activated.

FIGURE 10-13

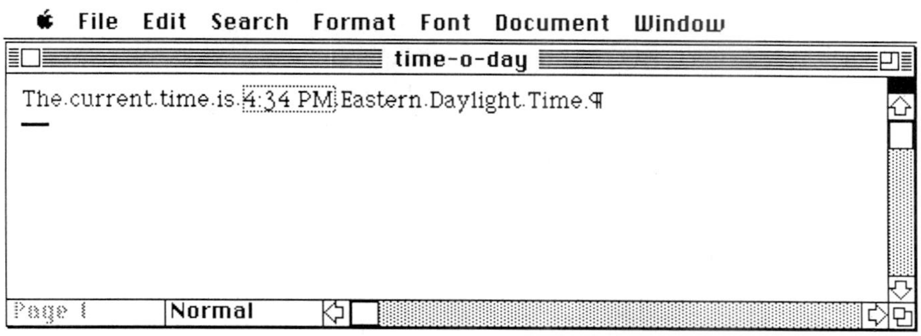

When you insert a dynamic date or time into a document, Word draws a dotted-line box around the date or time.

Because Word treats these dynamic date and time entries as single characters, you cannot edit a dynamic date or time as you can a regular date or time, or any other text in a document. Although you can cut, copy, or paste the entire date or time, you cannot cut, copy, or paste only part of the date or time. For instance, you cannot replace the month in a dynamic date with a different month. However, you can format the dynamic date or time using various fonts or any of Word's formatting commands. As you might expect, you must format the entire date or time, not just a portion of it.

STORING GRAPHICS IN THE GLOSSARY

Although you'll probably use the glossary mainly to store text, you also can use it to store graphics. As we explain in Chapter 16, most graphics consist of a picture or chart created in another Macintosh program, then inserted into a Word document. Word considers each graphic to be a single character, which you can cut, copy, or paste, just as you would regular characters.

To add a graphic to the glossary, you must first paste that graphic into a Word document. (We explain how to do this in Chapter 16.) Then, the procedure that you use to add the graphic to the glossary is the same procedure that you would follow to add any other glossary entry. First, click on the graphic to select it. (You'll be able to tell that the graphic is selected by the small black boxes or "handles" that appear on the frame of the graphic.) With the graphic selected, choose Glossary… from the Edit menu. Then type a name for the glossary entry in the Name edit bar, and click the Define button. Finally, close the Glossary dialog box to complete the procedure. (By the way, if you change the size of the graphic before you add it to the glossary, Word will store the graphic in its new size.)

Once a graphic is stored in the glossary, you can use all the techniques that we have described to paste that graphic into your document. You can open the Glossary dialog box, click on the glossary term for the graphic, and then click the Insert button. Or, you can type ⌘-Backspace, enter the graphic name at the *Name* prompt, and press Return. Finally, you can add the glossary term for the graphic to the Work menu or copy it to the Clipboard.

After you have added a graphic to the glossary, you can, of course, save the glossary to disk in a glossary file. This allows you to access the graphic very easily by simply opening the glossary file in which it is stored. In fact, if you want to use a graphic in multiple documents, probably the easiest way to do so is to store that graphic in a glossary file. That way, you don't have to keep track of the various Scrapbook files that contain graphics.

PRINTING THE GLOSSARY

If you want to get a printout of the contents of the glossary, first choose Glossary… from the Edit menu. Then, with the Glossary dialog box open, choose Print... from the File menu. Word will print a listing of each glossary term and the text for that term. Figure 10-14 shows a sample glossary listing.

FIGURE 10-14

CC
    COMPANY CONFIDENTIAL: For internal use only.

date
    5/13/87

dydate
    5/13/87

dytime
    4:40 PM

ICS
    International Consolidated Systems, Inc.

JuneFin
    June 1987 financial statements

MW
    Microsoft Word 3.01

time
    4:40 PM

This figure shows a typical printout of glossary contents, with glossary terms on the left and glossary text on the right.

CUSTOM MENUS 11

One of the most useful features of Word 3 is its ability to create custom menus. Word allows you to customize the selections on both the Format and Font menus. In addition, you can create a special custom menu called the Work menu, which can be used to apply styles, insert glossary items, and open files.

The main benefit of custom menus is that they greatly speed up certain tasks that normally require you to open a dialog box. With custom menus, you often can bypass dialog boxes since the option you need to use is available as a menu item.

For example, normally the process of superscripting text involves the following steps: First, you select the text that you want to appear in superscripted format. Then, you choose Character… from the Format menu. When the Character dialog box is open, you click the Superscript option and enter the number of points for superscripting in the By edit bar (or you can use the default By setting of 3 points). Finally, you click OK to apply the superscript format and close the dialog box.

Instead of performing all of these steps, you can make Superscript an option on your Format menu. (The menu item will specify by how many points you want to superscript, such as *Superscript 3 pt.*) Then, to apply superscripting, all you have to do is select the text that you want to format and choose *Superscript* from the Format menu.

Most of the options in the Character and Paragraph dialog boxes can be made into Format menu options. You also can add to the Format menu some of the paragraph format settings that are controlled by ruler icons—paragraph alignment, line spacing, paragraph spacing, and the Normal paragraph setting. You can even add one option from the Section dialog box—namely, the number of columns of text on a page.

The Font menu, like the Format menu, can be customized to include any font that's listed in the Character dialog box, as well as any point size.

The third custom menu, the Work menu, is different from the Font and Format menus in a couple of important ways. First, the Work menu does not appear on your screen until you have placed at least one item on that menu. Second, the options that you add to the Work menu are not items that appear in Word's standard dialog boxes. Instead, the Work menu includes items that you have created: glossary terms, named styles from the style sheet, and file names. Therefore, before you can add anything to the Work menu, you must first create a glossary entry, define a style, or save a file. In previous chapters, we've explained how to do each of these things.

Before we talk about the Font, Format, and Work menus individually, we need to cover a few basic concepts that apply to all three. As you'll see, the process of adding and deleting custom menu options is virtually the same, no matter which menu you're working with. After we cover these basic concepts, we'll explain how to customize the Font and Format menus and how you can create and use the Work menu.

CUSTOM MENU BASICS

Before you can take advantage of custom menus in Word, you must select Full Menus from the Edit menu. Until you activate the Full Menus setting, you won't be able to add or delete menu items, nor will you be able to view any custom menu items that you added previously. Interestingly, if you've removed one of Word's default selections from a menu, that selection will reappear when you select Short Menus from the Edit menu.

Adding a Menu Option

No matter which menu you want to customize, the process of adding and deleting items is the same. First, you press the Option and ⌘ keys as you type an equal sign (Option-⌘-=). This will cause the I-beam pointer temporarily to assume the shape of a bold plus sign (**+**). Using this special pointer, you perform all of the steps that you normally would in executing a certain task. Generally, this will involve opening a dialog box and clicking a selection. Once you've done this, the pointer will resume its normal shape, and a new menu item will appear on your Font, Format, or Work menu. (If you've used software with macro programming capability, you might find it helpful to think of Word's custom menu items as macros. Like macros, each of these menu items represents a series of steps that has been recorded.)

By the way, the Word manual instructs you to press the Option, ⌘, and + keys when you want to add an item to a menu. Although + and = occupy the same key on your keyboard, the + requires that you hold down the Shift key. If you press Shift, Word will not accept your keystrokes and convert the pointer to the bold plus shape. Therefore, to avoid confusion, we tell you to type Option-⌘-= when you need to add a menu option.

If, after you press Option-⌘-=, you decide that you do *not* want to add a menu item, press the ⌘ and period keys to cancel (⌘-.). The pointer will then return to its normal appearance.

It's possible to add so many items to a menu (particularly the Format menu) that not all of the options will be visible when you click on that menu choice. If this happens, you can view the options at the bottom of the menu by dragging the pointer beyond the lower edge of your screen. Of course, if a menu gets quite lengthy, you may want to delete some of the options.

A shortcut

If you want to add two or more similar items to a menu, you don't need to close and reopen a dialog box for each item. After you've added one item, you can press Option-⌘-= while the dialog box is still open. When the pointer assumes the bold plus shape, click on the next item that you want to add to a menu. This technique can be especially helpful when you're adding several Character formatting options to the Font and/or Format menus or when you want to add several style names to the Work menu.

For example, suppose you want to add the options Small Caps and All Caps to your Format menu. You can press Option-⌘-=, issue the Character... command, and click the All Caps option. Then, without closing the dialog box, you can press Option-⌘-= again and click the Small Caps option. Both options will now appear on your Format menu.

Deleting a Menu Option

To remove an item from a custom menu, you press the Option, ⌘, and minus keys simultaneously (Option-⌘--). The pointer will then assume the shape of a bold minus sign (▬). Just use this pointer to select the menu option that you want to delete. As soon as you've deleted a menu item, the pointer will resume its normal appearance. After you press Option-⌘--, if you decide that you do not want to follow through with deleting a menu item, you can press ⌘-period to cancel.

By the way, in customizing the Font or Format menu, you are not limited to deleting only the menu options that you have added. You also can delete any of Word's default options from these menus except, of course, menu items that are used to open dialog boxes, such as the Section... command. For example, you can remove one of Word's default font options, such as Geneva, from the Font menu. When you remove a menu item, you can, of course, still access that option through a dialog box. For example, if you remove Geneva from the Font menu, that font will still be available through the less convenient Character dialog box.

CUSTOMIZING THE FONT MENU

As we explained in our introduction, Word allows you to add fonts and font sizes to the Font menu. When you first open Word, the Font menu (in Full Menus) offers seven font choices and five size options, as shown in Figure 11-1. (Of course, your Font menu may vary according to the printer drivers and fonts that you have installed on your startup disk.)

FIGURE 11-1

Word's default Font menu offers seven font choices and five different sizes.

Typically, additional fonts and sizes are available through the Character dialog box, which is shown in Figure 11-2. As you can see, a list of fonts and a list of font sizes appear in the lower-left corner of this dialog box.

FIGURE 11-2

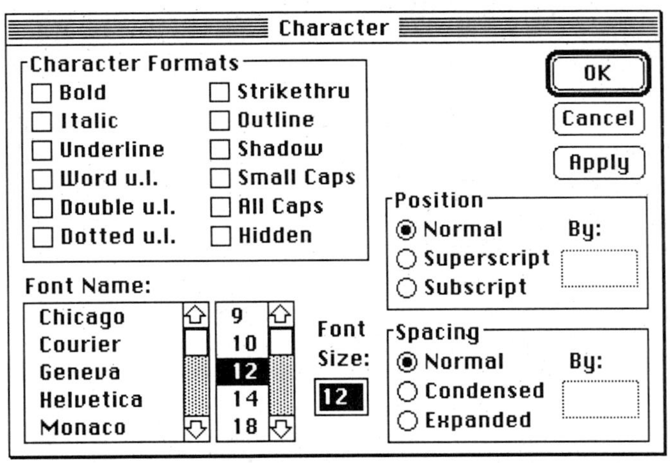

The Character dialog box lists all the available fonts and font sizes.

Let's consider how you might add a font and font size to the Font menu. Suppose you're starting out with Word's default Font menu and you want to add both a new font name—Courier—and a new size—24 Point—to that menu.

Word requires that you add the font name and font size separately, so we'll begin by adding the name. First, press Option-⌘-= to tell Word that you want to record a new menu option. Then, use the bold plus pointer to select Character... from the Format menu. In the Character dialog box, click on the Courier option in the list of fonts. Once you have selected Courier, the pointer will change to the arrow shape that you normally see when a dialog box is open. You can then click Cancel, Apply, or OK to complete the procedure. If you click Cancel, Word will simply close the Character dialog box. If you click OK, Word will close the dialog box and apply the selected font in your document. (As you begin to type, the characters will appear in the Courier font.) If you click the Apply button, Word will apply the new font in your document, without closing the dialog box. Then you can apply additional formats, such as superscripting, without closing and reopening the dialog box.

In any case, once you've closed the Character dialog box, if you click on the Font menu, you'll notice that Courier is now an option on that menu, as shown in Figure 11-3 on the next page.

The procedure for adding a new point size to the Font menu is similar. First, press Option-⌘-=. Then, use the bold plus pointer to select Character... from the Format menu. In the Character dialog box, click on 24 in the list of Font sizes. Finally, click OK or Cancel to complete the procedure. As you can see, Figure 11-4 on the following page shows the Font menu from Figure 11-3 with the new size added.

Adding a Nonstandard Font Size

As we explain in Chapter 5, different fonts in Word have different "standard" sizes. Each time you click on a font name in the Character dialog box, the list of font sizes will be adjusted to show only the standard sizes for the selected font. For example, if you click on the name *Monaco* in the Character dialog box, Word will display only two standard sizes, 9 and 12. When you choose to use a particular font, however, you can specify a size other than one of the standard sizes. To do this, you must type the size that you want to use in the Font Size edit bar of the Character dialog box. For instance, if you want to create 11-point Monaco type, you would open the Character dialog box, select Monaco from the list of fonts, and type 11 in the Font Size edit bar.

As you might expect, you can add "nonstandard" font sizes to the Font menu. In other words, if a particular size does not appear in the list of font sizes in the Character dialog box, you still can add that size to the menu. The procedure is only slightly different from adding a standard font size. Begin by pressing Option-⌘-= and opening the Character dialog box. In the Font Size edit bar, type the font size that you want to add to the menu. Next, click this edit bar with the plus sign pointer, and then, to complete the procedure, press Return, or click OK, Apply, or Cancel.

FIGURE 11-3

This Font menu has been customized to include Courier.

FIGURE 11-4

We've added the 24 Point size option to the Font menu.

CUSTOMIZING THE FORMAT MENU

As we mentioned earlier, you can alter the Format menu to include a variety of options, including character formats, paragraph formats, and even one option from the Section dialog box. Although you follow the standard procedure for adding most options to the Format menu, there are a couple of tricky situations that you need to be aware of. Let's walk through a few examples that illustrate how to add various kinds of options to the Format menu.

Adding Character Format Options

As we explained earlier, to add an option like All Caps to your Format menu, you would begin by pressing Option-⌘-=. Then, with the bold plus pointer, choose Character... from the Format menu. In the Character dialog box, you would click the All Caps option, then click OK or Cancel to close the dialog box. When you pull down the Format menu, you'll see that it now includes a Caps option, as shown in Figure 11-5 on page 444. (By the way, when you add an option to the Format menu, you may see slightly different wording than in the dialog box, as has happened in this example.)

Adding Position and Spacing options

When you apply one of Word's character Position options (Superscript and Subscript) or one of the character Spacing options (Condensed or Expanded), you must specify a numeric argument that tells Word exactly how you want to apply the option. For example, when you superscript a character, you must specify by how many points you want that character to be superscripted.

Word has a default numeric argument for each of its Position and Spacing options. The default argument for superscripting is 3 points, and the default argument for subscripting is 2 points. The Condensed option uses a default numeric argument of 1.5 points, while the Expanded option uses a default argument of 3 points. (By the way, a point is equal to $^1/_{72}$nd of an inch.)

When you add a Position or Spacing option to the Format menu, Word will include a numeric argument as part of the new menu item. For example, if you add the Subscript option to the Format menu, the menu item will specify by how many points you want to subscript, such as *Subscript 3 pt.*

If you want to create a Position or Spacing menu item that uses Word's default numeric argument, then you can follow the standard procedure for adding that option to the Format menu. For example, suppose that you want your Format menu to include an option that will superscript text by 3 points. You would press Option-⌘-=, open the Character dialog box, and click the Superscript option. As soon as you click Superscript, Word will enter *3 pt* in the By edit bar, next to the Superscript option. Also, the pointer will resume its normal shape, which indicates that the option you clicked—and its default numeric argument—have been added to the Format menu. You can complete the procedure by pressing Return or by clicking OK, Apply, or Cancel.

If you want to add to the Format menu a Position or Spacing option that uses a numeric argument other than Word's default, then you must follow a slightly different procedure. Open the Character dialog box *before* you press Option-⌘-=. Then, in the dialog box, click the option that you want to add to the menu. Next, replace Word's default numeric argument in the By edit bar with the number that you wish to use. Without closing the dialog box, press Option-⌘-=, and use the bold plus pointer to click the option once more. Then, click OK or Cancel to close the dialog box.

For example, suppose that you want to create a menu item for superscripting text by 4 points. First choose Character... from the Format menu. Then, in the Character dialog box, click the Superscript option and type 4 in the By edit bar. Now, press Option-⌘-=, and click the Superscript option once more. The pointer will resume its normal shape, and you can click OK or Cancel to complete the procedure. When you pull down the Format menu, you'll see that it includes the option *Superscript 4 pt*, as shown in Figure 11-6.

FIGURE 11-5

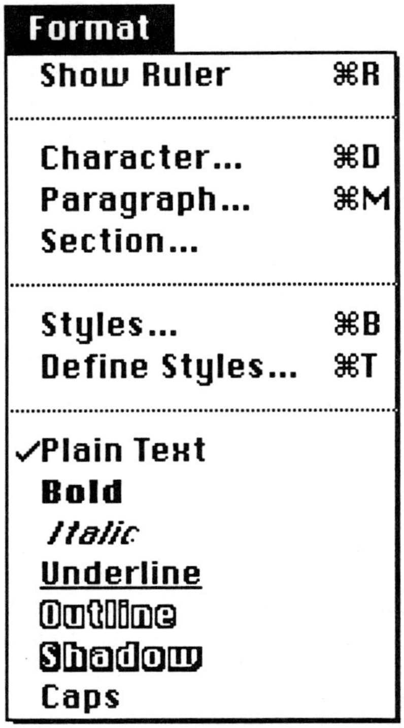

This Format menu now includes the Caps option.

FIGURE 11-6

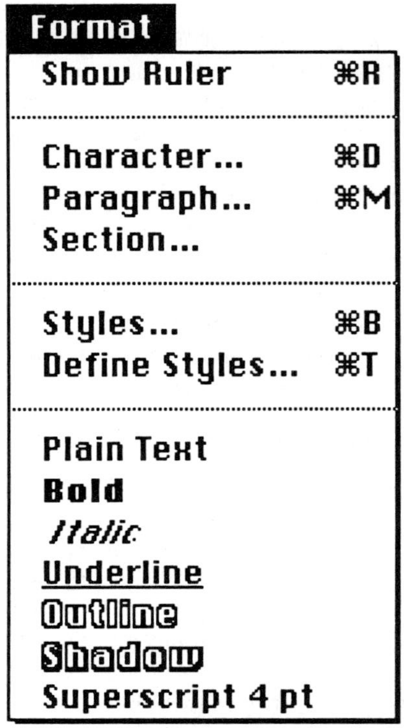

This custom Format menu includes an item for superscripting text by 4 points.

Adding Paragraph Format Options

Adding Paragraph format options to the Format menu is very similar to adding Character format options. However, there are a couple of special considerations that you need to keep in mind. First, some Paragraph formatting options are controlled by ruler icons rather than by the Paragraph dialog box. Most of these options can be added to the Format menu, where they will appear as words, not icons. For example, Word's paragraph alignment options (flush left, centered, flush right, or justified), which are controlled by ruler icons, can be placed on the Format menu. When you do this, the new menu items will appear as *Left*, *Centered*, *Right*, and *Justified*.

Why might you want to create a new menu item when it's so easy to click a ruler icon? First, adding Paragraph formatting options to the Format menu allows you to hide the ruler and free up more space on your screen for text display. In addition, if you're using a narrow window, you may not be able to view all of the icons on the ruler without expanding the window. (Clicking the horizontal scroll bar will not bring more ruler icons into view.) To avoid the inconvenience of having to change your window size in order to access a ruler icon, you can add an option to the Format menu that will accomplish the same purpose as clicking on the ruler icon.

Keep in mind that you cannot create a menu item out of every option in the Paragraph dialog box or every ruler icon. In the Paragraph dialog box, you can create a menu item from each of the Border options and from each of the check box options except Line Numbering. (The check box options that *can* be placed on the menu are Side-by-Side, Page Break Before, Keep With Next ¶, and Keep Lines Together.) You cannot create menu items from the Spacing Before and After settings, nor can you create menu items to control the type of tab leader.

On the ruler, each of the alignment icons, the line-spacing icons, and the open/close paragraph spacing icons can be made into menu options. You also can create a menu item from the Normal paragraph symbol (|x|) that appears at the right edge of the ruler. You cannot create a menu item to control tab placement and type or to control the placement of the vertical line.

An example

Suppose you want the Format menu to include the Side-by-Side option and the Left alignment option. Begin by pressing Option-⌘-=, and, with the bold plus pointer, choose Paragraph... from the Format menu. In the Paragraph dialog box, click the Side-by-Side option, then click OK or Cancel.

To add Left alignment to the menu, again start by pressing Option-⌘-=. Choose Show Ruler from the Format menu, and click the Left alignment icon on the ruler. When you click this icon, Word not only will add the Left option to your Format menu, it also will apply left alignment to your current paragraph. If this is not what you want, you can issue the Undo command or click on a different alignment icon when the pointer resumes its normal shape. Figure 11-7 on the next page shows the Format menu with the two new paragraph formatting options added.

Adding the Number of Columns Option

As we mentioned in the introduction to this chapter, Word allows you to create a menu item from one of the options in the Section dialog box—the Columns Number option. The procedure for adding this option to the Format menu is similar to the procedure for adding one of the Position or Spacing character options since you must include a numeric argument that specifies the number of columns.

As we explain in Chapter 8, when you format text to appear in more than one column, you also must enter a numeric argument that specifies the amount of space that you want to appear between columns. Unfortunately, Word does not seem to be able to "store" this spacing option as part of the menu item for columnar formatting. Therefore, when you've created a menu option for columnar formatting, that option will include the number of columns but it will not tell you how much space will appear between columns. For example, a new menu option might be *Columns 2*. When you apply this option, Word will, of course, format the text in the current section into two columns. The amount of space between the columns, however, will be determined by the current setting in the Spacing edit bar of the Section dialog box.

You can change the Spacing setting manually by opening the Section dialog box and entering a number (such as .5 for $^1/_2$ inch) in the Spacing edit bar. You also can create a default Spacing setting so that whenever you use two or more columns, Word will automatically allow a certain amount of space between columns. This is probably the best course of action if you want to add the Columns option to your Format menu. Let's walk through an example that demonstrates the procedure for adding the Columns option and applying that option in a document.

Suppose you would like to create a menu item that allows you to set up a three-column layout. Begin by choosing Section... from the Format menu. In the Section dialog box, replace the 1 in the Number edit bar with a 3. Next, press Option-⌘-= to convert the pointer to a bold plus sign. Using this special pointer, click on the Number edit bar. Immediately, the pointer will resume its normal shape, and you can click OK or Cancel to complete the procedure. When you check the Format menu, you'll see that it now includes the option *Columns 3*, as shown in Figure 11-8.

FIGURE 11-7

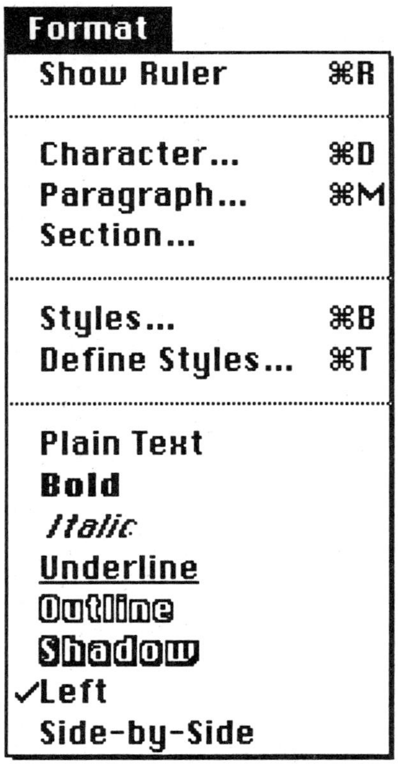

This Format menu includes two paragraph formatting options.

FIGURE 11-8

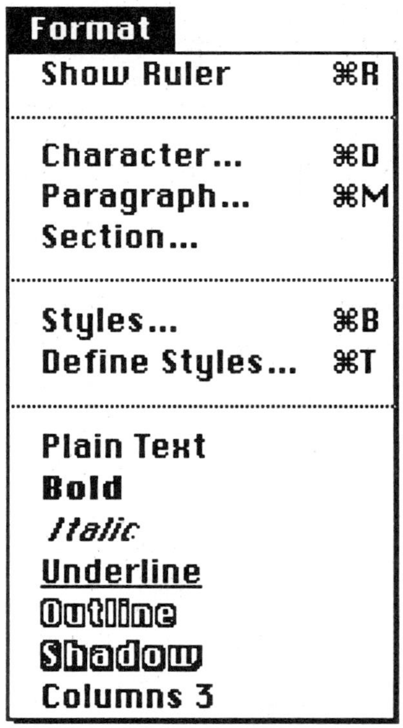

This Format menu now includes an option for columnar formatting.

Now let's suppose that you're working in a document that uses Word's default Page Setup settings so that each line of text is six inches long. If you were to apply the *Columns 3* menu option in this document, the result would look like Figure 11-9.

FIGURE 11-9

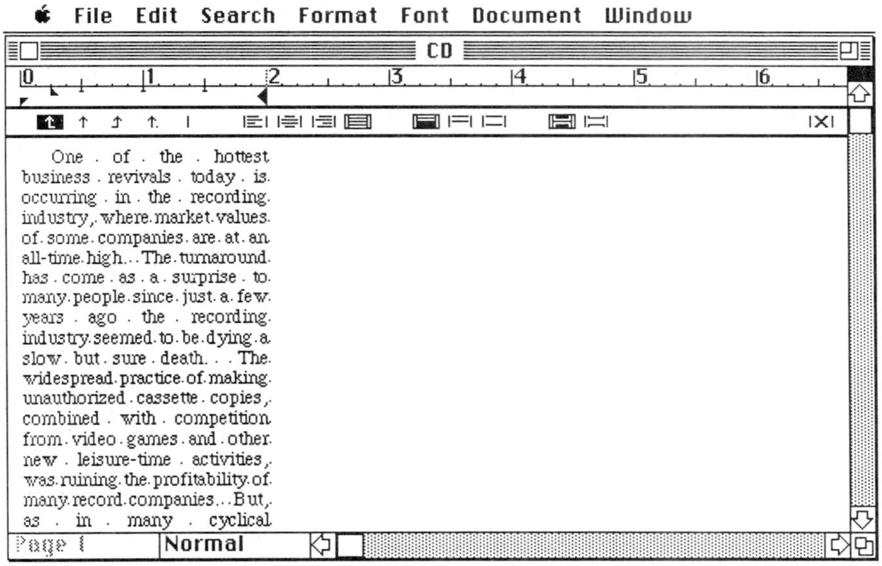

We've applied the Columns 3 *menu option in this document.*

As you can see from the ruler setting at the top of the screen, the columns of text in this document will be two inches wide. However, since you have only six inches of space between your left and right margins, a two-inch column width means that Word has not allotted any space between columns. You can confirm this by looking at the Page Preview screen or by opening the Section dialog box, where you'll see that the Spacing edit bar is blank. To create $^1/_4$ inch of space between columns, you must open the Section dialog box and enter .25 in the Spacing edit bar. When you close the dialog box, your screen will look like Figure 11-10. Notice that the column width is now about 1 $^3/_4$ inches instead of two inches. (For more on multicolumn documents, see Chapter 8.)

FIGURE 11-10

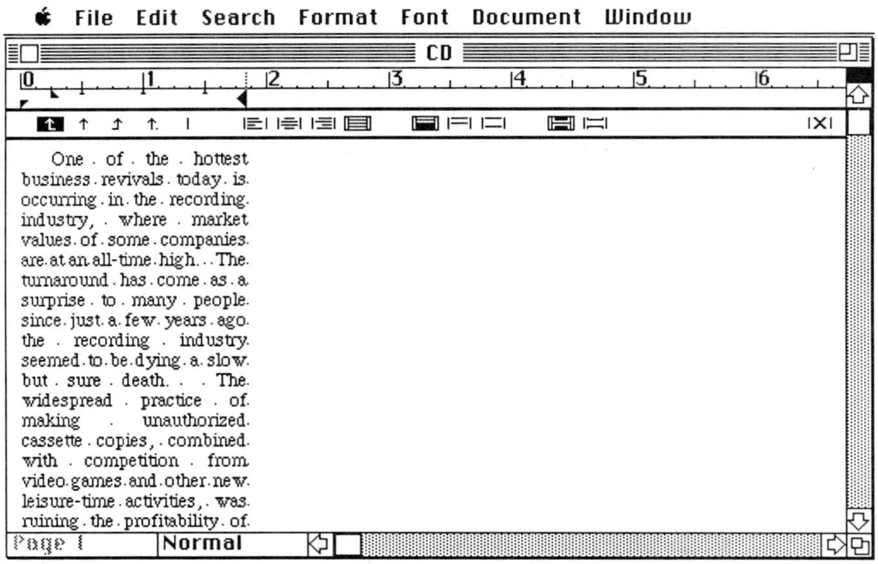

After entering a Spacing setting in the Section dialog box, Word decreases the width of each column.

THE WORK MENU

The Work menu is a special menu that you can create to help speed up the processes of inserting glossary text, applying styles, and opening files. It may include only one item, such as a glossary term, or it may contain many items, including file names, glossary terms, and style names. If your Work menu contains at least one of each possible option, Word will display those menu options in three sections, with file names at the top, glossary terms next, and style names below that. A gray line separates the three sections, and within each section, the menu items will be organized alphabetically. For example, Figure 11-11 shows a Work menu that includes three file names and several glossary terms and style names.

The procedures for adding style names, glossary terms, and file names to the Work menu are quite similar. To add a style name, you should begin by pressing Option-⌘-= (of course!) and choosing Styles... or Define Styles... from the Format menu. In the dialog box, use the bold plus pointer to click on the style name that you want to place on the menu. As soon as you do this, the pointer will resume its normal shape, indicating that the style name you selected is now part of the Work menu. You can click OK or Cancel to close the dialog box and complete the procedure.

To add a glossary term to the Work menu, press Option-⌘-=, then choose Glossary... from the Edit menu. In the Glossary dialog box, click on the term that you want to add to the Work menu, then click Cancel or Insert.

FIGURE 11-11

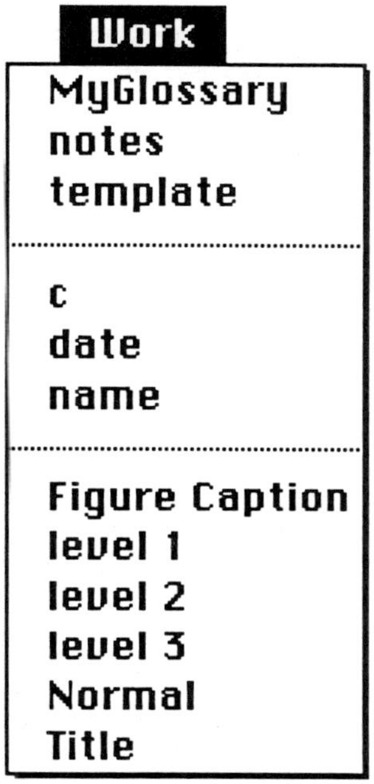

Word separates the items on the Work menu into three sections, placing file names on top, glossary terms next, and style names at the bottom of the menu.

To add a file name, begin by pressing Option-⌘-=, then choose Open... from the File menu. Click on the name of the file that you want to place on the Work menu, then click the Open button. As soon as you do this, the pointer will resume its normal shape and Word will close the Open dialog box. Word will not open the file that you select at this time but will place its name on your Work menu.

In addition to document files, Word allows you to add glossary files to the Work menu. To do this, press Option-⌘-=, then choose Glossary… from the Edit menu. With the Glossary dialog box open, choose Open... from the File menu, click on the name of the glossary file you want to add to the menu, and click the Open button. Word will close the File Open dialog box, and the pointer will resume its normal shape. However, the Glossary dialog box will remain open, so you'll need to click Cancel or click the close box to close it.

Using the Work Menu

When you select an item from the Work menu, the results will be different, depending on whether you've chosen a file name, glossary term, or style name. If you select a file name, Word will open that file. If Word cannot find the file on one of your current disks, it will display a message like the one shown in Figure 11-12.

FIGURE 11-12

If you choose a file name from the Work menu and that file is not on one of your current disks, Word will display this dialog box.

If the disk containing that file has been inserted in a disk drive during the current Word session, you won't see this alert box. Instead, Word will display a message that prompts you to insert the correct disk.

If you select from the Work menu the name of a document file that's already open, Word will simply create a new window for that document. For example, suppose your Work menu contains a file named *Essay*. If that file is already open and you select Essay from the Work menu, Word will create a new full-screen window named *Essay:2*.

When you select a glossary term from the Work menu, Word will "type" the text for that term at the current insertion point location. For example, suppose that your glossary contains the term *FY88*, which represents the text *Fiscal year 1988*, and you've added this term to your Work menu. When you select FY88 from the Work menu, Word will insert the text *Fiscal year 1988* at the current insertion point location, just as if you'd opened the Glossary dialog box, clicked on the term, and clicked the Insert button.

Similarly, when you select a style name from the Work menu, Word will apply that style to the current paragraph, just as if you had opened the Styles dialog box, clicked that style name, and clicked OK.

Unfortunately, you cannot "attach" differents sets of customized menus to different documents. Your Work menu will display the same commands, no matter what document is active on the Word DeskTop. However, some of the items on this menu may be disabled in certain documents. Specifically, you cannot use a glossary term that appears on the Work menu unless you've opened the glossary file that contains that term. Similarly, you cannot use the Work menu to apply a style unless that style is on your current document's style sheet. If you select an item from the Work menu that Word is unable to use (such as a style name that's not on the current style sheet), Word will just beep.

Because the Work menu will be the same in all documents, you may want to use identical style names in different documents and identical glossary terms in different glossary files. That way, you can get more mileage out of fewer menu options since the style names and glossary terms on your Work menu will have different effects, depending on which document you're working in and which glossary file (or files) you've opened.

For example, suppose you've added the glossary term *im* to your Work menu. You've also created two different glossary files that contain this term. In one of the glossary files, this term represents the text *international markets*, while in another glossary file, the term *im* stands for *interesting mistake*. When you choose *im* from the Work menu, Word will look at the entries in your current glossary to determine what text to insert in your document. If you've loaded the first glossary file, Word will insert the words *international markets*. If you've loaded the entries from the other glossary file, however, Word will insert the words *interesting mistake*. Of course, if you open both of these glossary files during the same Word session, the text that's represented by *im* will be the glossary text from the most recently opened glossary file. (See Chapter 10 for more on glossary files.)

Similarly, suppose that the style sheet in several different documents includes a style named *Title*, and you've added this style name to your Work menu. When you choose *Title* from the Work menu, Word will look at the definition of that style on your current style sheet in order to determine what set of formatting attributes to apply. In one document, the *Title* style might call for 18-point, Times, bold text with centered alignment. In another document, the definition of *Title* might specify 14-point, Helvetica, bold, italic type with flush-left alignment. In both documents, however, the *Title* style can be applied quickly from the Work menu, without having to open a dialog box.

SAVING CUSTOM MENUS

When you quit from Word, your custom menus will be stored in the Word Settings file. This file also stores the default style sheet and the default Page Setup settings. In Chapter 17, we discuss the Word Settings file in detail, and we explain how you can use multiple Word Settings files to access different sets of defaults as you need them. For example, with different Word Settings files, you can create several sets of custom menus and use the particular set that's appropriate for a given document.

By the way, if you don't quit to the Finder level at the end of a Word session—in other words, if you simply turn off your computer or you accidentally crash—Word will not record to disk any custom menu changes you've made during the current session of Word. When you next load Word, your menus will be the same as they were at the beginning of the last session.

OUTLINING 12

Sometimes when you create a document, you know exactly what you want to say and how you want to say it. At other times, however, you just can't seem to get started, or you have so much information that structuring it seems overwhelming. Word 3 comes to your rescue with a powerful new outliner facility that can help you organize your thoughts and build a document from the ground up.

Though Word's outliner is quite easy to use, it is really very sophisticated. As you'll see, the outliner works in conjunction with many of the program's other special features to help you create, edit, and organize your text. The combined power of the outliner and style sheets lets you format your document quickly and easily. In addition, you can use the Outlining command to create a table of contents for your document (more on this topic in Chapter 13), to navigate through long documents quickly, and to rearrange blocks of text with just a few keystrokes.

To access the outliner, make sure that the Full Menus setting is active, then select the Outlining command from the Document menu. You'll see a window like the one in Figure 12-1 on the next page. To return to your document window, simply choose Outlining again. You can easily toggle back and forth between the outline and document windows at any time by pressing ⌘-u.

As you can see in Figure 12-1, a new set of icons appears when you issue the Outlining command. As you assemble your outline, you'll use these icons to organize and prioritize information and to expand and collapse your view of the document. In addition to these new icons, Word gives new definitions to many of your special function keys. We'll look at each of these features as we walk through the process of creating and editing text in the outline window.

FIGURE 12-1

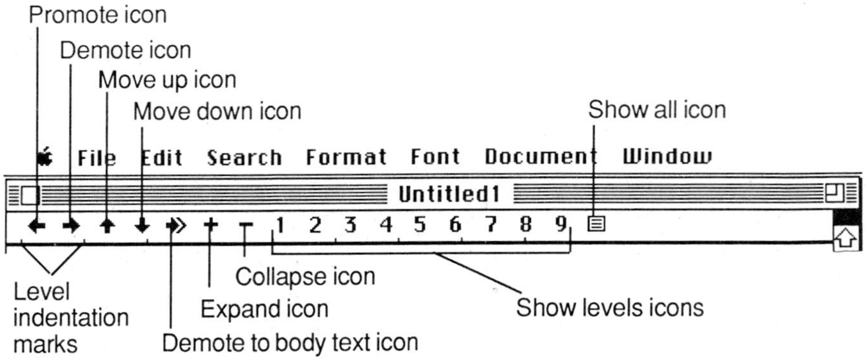

When you issue the Outlining command, Word will display a window like this one.

Word's outliner divides your document text into two different categories: headings and body text. Generally, you'll enter your headings in the outline window and then return to the document window to enter your body text. Each heading is assigned a level, numbered from 1 to 9.

Level 1 headings represent your broadest or most important categories of ideas, while levels 2 through 9 represent subordinate levels of ideas under your main headings. You can use level 1 through level 9 entries as headings in your finished document, or you can opt to hide them from view once you have completed your document.

Word helps you visualize the relationships between outline topics by assigning different levels of indention to the text that appears in your outline window. Major thoughts—level 1 headings—start at the left margin, while subordinate headings are indented. The level 2 headings will appear indented $^1/_2$ inch, level 3 headings are indented 1 inch, and so forth—with each new level being indented an additional $^1/_2$ inch. Any body text that you enter into your document will appear indented $^1/_4$ inch from the preceding heading. (Actually, the amount of indention that Word uses for the different levels in the outline window corresponds to the default tab stops on your document ruler. If you change the Default Tab Stops setting in the Page Setup dialog box, Word will change the amount indention for each level of text in the outline window.)

To help simplify your view of the outline, Word ignores any character or paragraph formatting that you may have applied to your text in the document window. The text in an outline window will display the character formats that are specified by the document's *Normal* style. In fact, the ruler is deactivated when you are in outline view, and the commands on your Font and Format menus are dimmed. Therefore, you won't be able to format text in an outline window. You can, however, use the Show ¶ command to see the special markup characters in your document while you are viewing your text in the outline window. You may find the Show ¶ command helpful when you're selecting text to edit.

BUILDING AN OUTLINE

The easiest way to learn to use the outliner is to walk through the creation of a sample document. To illustrate, we'll create an article entitled *Freelancing: A Beginner's Guide*. We'll use the outliner to rough out our ideas, then we'll build on this outline to create a finished document. If you'd like to follow along with our example, begin by opening a new document. Choose Full Menus from the Edit menu, if that setting is not already active, then select the Outlining command from the Document menu.

Figure 12-2 shows a portion of the outline for our sample article. To create this outline, start by typing the first heading, *Cutting loose*, then press the Return key to start a new paragraph. Whenever you begin a new outline, Word assumes that your first paragraph will be a level 1 heading. It also assumes that all subsequent paragraphs should be entered at the same level as the previous entry until you indicate otherwise.

FIGURE 12-2

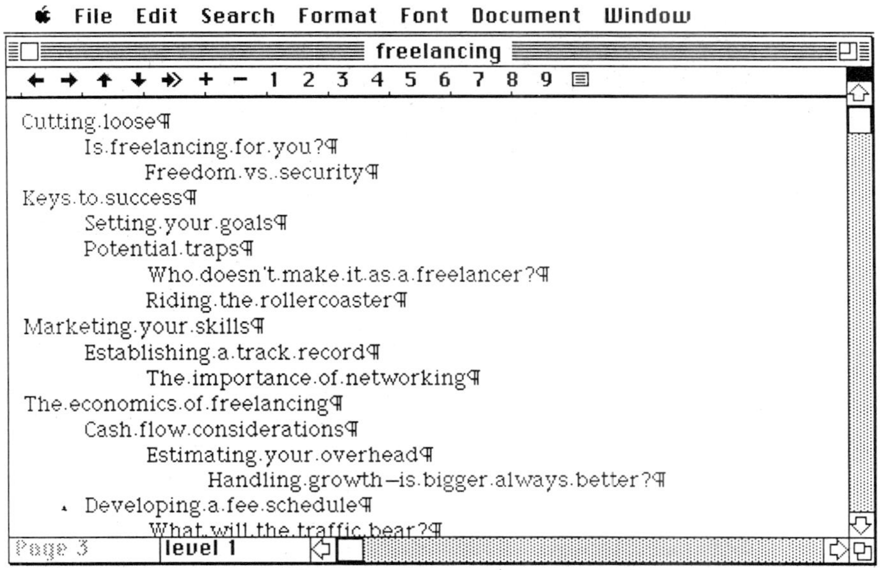

We'll start by entering our ideas in the outline window and assigning priority levels to each idea.

To create the subordinate heading that appears in the second line of the sample outline window, click on the ➡ icon at the top of the window and type the phrase *Is freelancing for you?* You will notice that your second paragraph has been "demoted" to a level 2 heading, as indicated in the style status box at the bottom of the screen. Word also indents the paragraph $^1/_2$ inch to the right of the first line to indicate that this heading is subordinate to the first heading. Press Return again to begin the third paragraph, then click the ➡ icon to indent this level 3 heading an additional $^1/_2$ inch.

After you type the text for the third heading, you're ready to move on to your next major topic: *Keys to success.* Notice that this paragraph appears at the same level as the first heading in Figure 12-2. When you press the Return key at the end of the third paragraph to enter this heading, however, Word will assume that you want this new paragraph to appear as a level 3 heading. Click the ⬅ icon twice to "promote" the fourth paragraph to a level 1 heading.

To complete the outline, continue typing the sample text shown in Figure 12-2, clicking the ➡ and ⬅ icons to promote and demote each heading as needed. If you have a Macintosh with an expanded keyboard, you can also use the ➡ and ⬅ keys to assign your heading levels. (Though our sample outline uses only four heading levels, Word allows you to create as many as nine levels. Generally, the more detailed your outline, the greater the number of levels you will use.)

As you enter your outline text, keep in mind that the outline window is just another type of window—another view of the document, as far as Word is concerned. Any actions you take in the outline window will also affect the contents of your document window—and vice versa. For example, when you press ⌘-u to return to your document window, after typing the sample outline shown in Figure 12-2, your screen will look like the one in Figure 12-3.

FIGURE 12-3

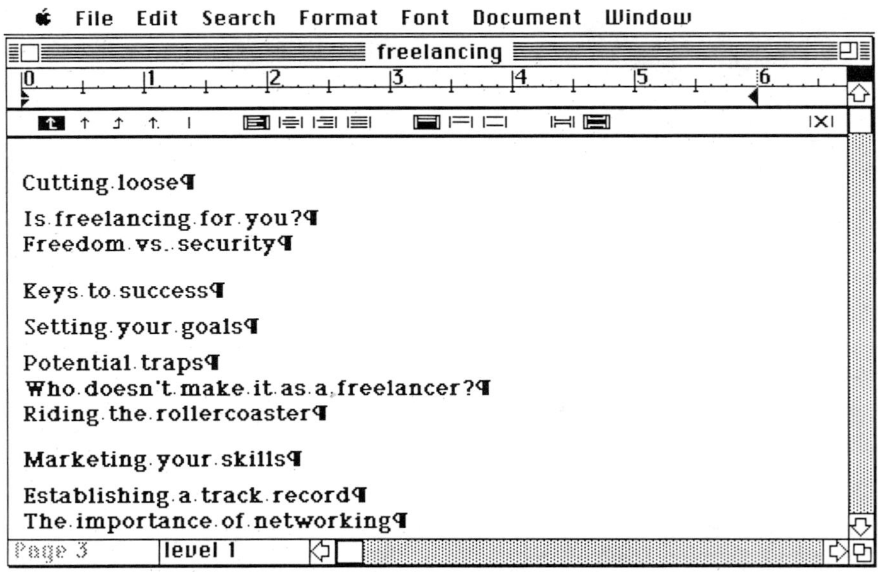

When you toggle back to the document window, the outline text will look like this.

Adding the Body Text

When you return to the document window, all of your headings are now aligned with the left side of your screen. Each heading also appears in bold type, with little distinction other than the different amounts of white space that appear above each paragraph. However, if you keep your eye on the style status box at the lower-left corner of the screen as you click on the various headings, you'll see that Word has remembered the level that you assigned to each heading.

While you were creating your outline, Word was busy behind the scenes creating a style sheet for your document. For each heading level that you entered into the outline window, Word created a corresponding set of style specifications for that heading. We'll show you how to use these automatic styles to format your document later in this chapter. First, let's add some substance to our outline and explore some techniques for editing our document through the outline window.

After the bare bones of the outline are in place, you can flesh out your document by adding your body text. In the document window, begin by clicking at the end of the first paragraph, then press the Return key to begin a new paragraph. As you begin typing the body of the document, part of which is shown in Figure 12-4, notice that Word will automatically format your body text to appear in the default *Normal* style—12 point, New York, plain.

FIGURE 12-4

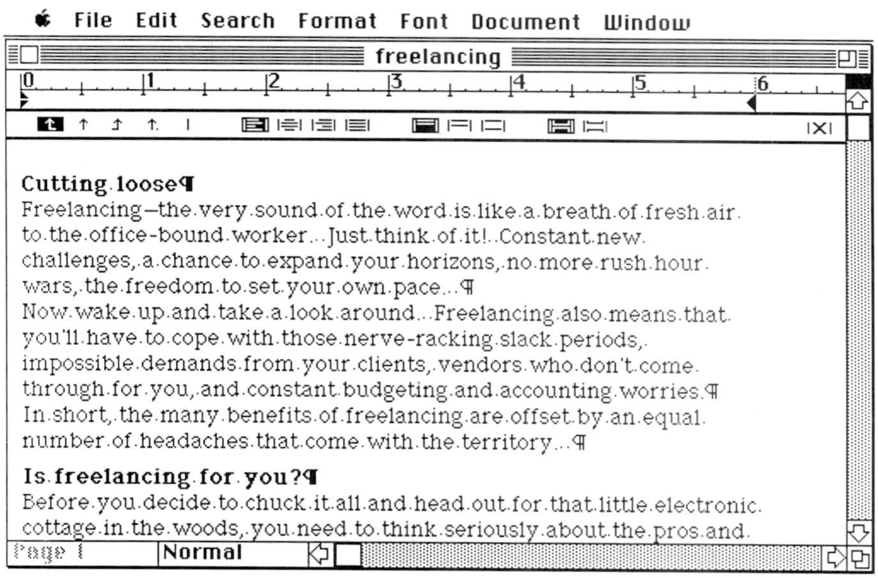

When you click at the end of a heading paragraph and press Return, Word will automatically assign the Normal *style to your body text paragraph.*

Now that we have entered some body text, let's toggle back to the outline window and see what has happened to our outline. As shown in Figure 12-5, when you return to the outline window, a number of changes will have taken place. First of all, your indentions reappear to give you a clear view of the relationship between each heading in the document. Second, Word has condensed each paragraph of your body text to only one line—just enough text to remind you of the topic of each paragraph. An ellipsis appears at the end of these lines to indicate that additional text follows. Also, notice that each body text paragraph is indented $^1/_4$ inch to the right of the heading under which it falls. This half-level indention gives you another visual clue as to the organizational structure of your document.

FIGURE 12-5

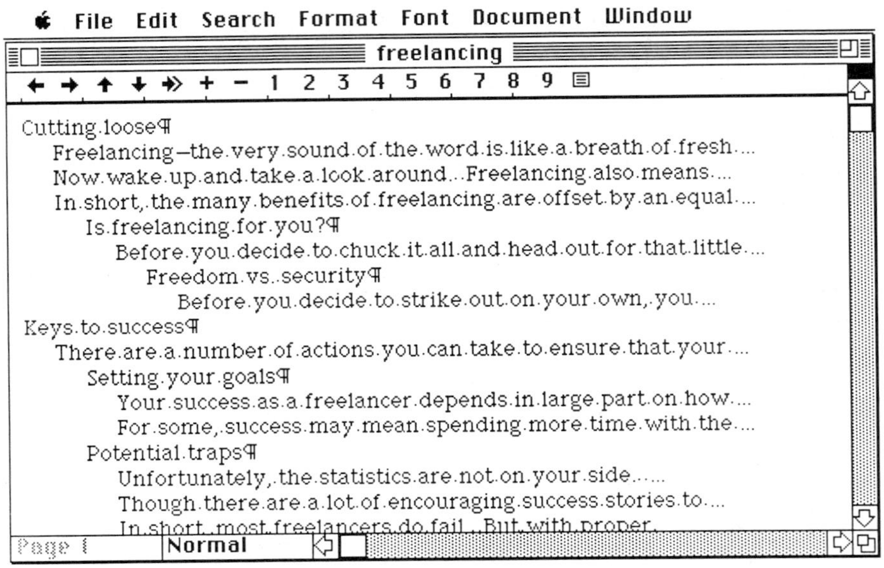

When you return to the outline window, Word displays only the first line of your body text paragraphs.

Selection Techniques

Once you have entered your headings and drafted your body text, you'll probably need to make some changes and reorganize some information in your document. Word offers a lot of shortcuts for editing your document in the outline window. As in the document window, however, before you can do any editing, you must first select the text that you want to work with. Let's take a look at some of the special selection techniques that Word makes available in the outline window.

When you are working within a single paragraph of an outline, you can use Word's standard selection techniques (described in Chapter 4) to select the text you want to work with. For example, to select an entire word, you can double-click on that word. To select an entire sentence, press the ⌘ key and double-click on that sentence.

In the document window, when you want to select an entire paragraph, double-click in the selection bar next to that paragraph. In the outline window, things work a little differently. You need only click once in the selection bar on the left side of the outline window to select an entire heading. (Keep in mind that each heading occupies one paragraph.) When you double-click in the selection bar, Word highlights not only the current heading but all of the subordinate text under that heading. By subordinate text, we mean all of the headings and body text between the current heading and the next heading at an equal or higher level.

For example, if you click once in the selection bar to the left of the level 1 heading *Cutting loose* at the top of the outline window in Figure 12-5, Word will highlight that entire paragraph, including the ¶ marker at the end. If you double-click next to this heading, however, your outline window will look like the one in Figure 12-6. As you can see, Word highlights the paragraph that contains the text *Cutting loose*, as well as all of the subordinate text up to the next level 1 heading.

FIGURE 12-6

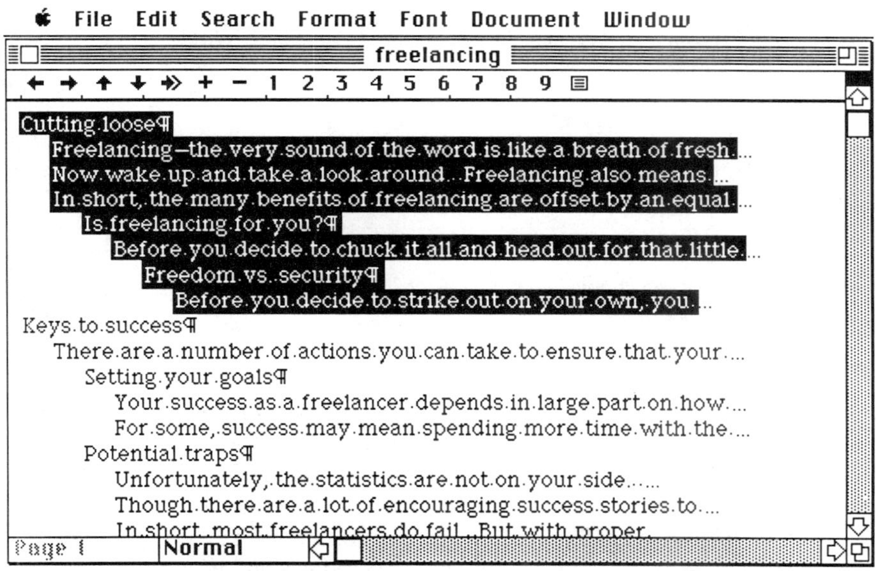

To highlight a heading and all of its subordinate text, just double-click next to the heading.

Collapsing and Expanding the Outline

Even though Word displays only the first line of each paragraph of body text in the outline window, your outline can get pretty lengthy once you've created several levels of subheadings and inserted body text under each. If you lose the big picture, you can eliminate some of this clutter by collapsing the outline to hide selected headings and body text from view.

For example, suppose you want to see only the level 1 headings in your outline. Just click on the 1, which is the show level 1 icon at the top of the outline window, to collapse the outline. As you can see in Figure 12-7, all of the body text and headings under your level 1 headings will disappear. Word displays a gray line under each level 1 entry to indicate that additional text appears below those headings.

FIGURE 12-7

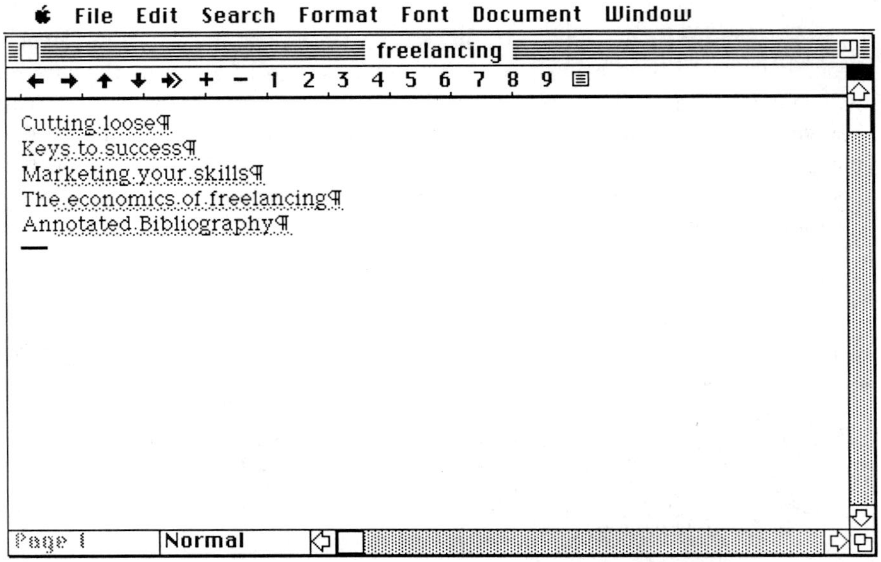

When you click on the show level 1 icon, Word will collapse your outline to show only your level 1 headings.

To expand the outline again, just click on another show level icon. For example, if you click on the show level 3 icon, Word will expand the outline to display all of your level 1, 2, and 3 headings. Your body text will remain hidden from view. To bring all of your headings and the first line of each body text paragraph back into view, click on the show all icon that appears to the right of the show level 9 icon. If you have a numeric keypad, you can also press the * key to redisplay all of your outline headings and body text.

Collapsing and expanding selected portions of the outline

While the show level icons affect the display of your entire outline, the expand and collapse icons—represented by the + and - symbols at the top of the outline window—affect only selected portions of your outline display. If you have a numeric keypad, you can also use the + and - keys to expand or collapse portions of your outline.

Returning to the fully expanded outline shown in Figure 12-5, suppose you want to collapse the headings and body text that appear under the second level 1 heading. Simply click on that heading, then click on the collapse icon, or press the - key on your numeric keypad. As you can see in Figure 12-8, Word will collapse all of the body text that originally appeared under that heading. If you click on the collapse icon or press the - key again, Word will collapse all of the level 3 headings that appear under that heading, then all of the level 2 headings.

FIGURE 12-8

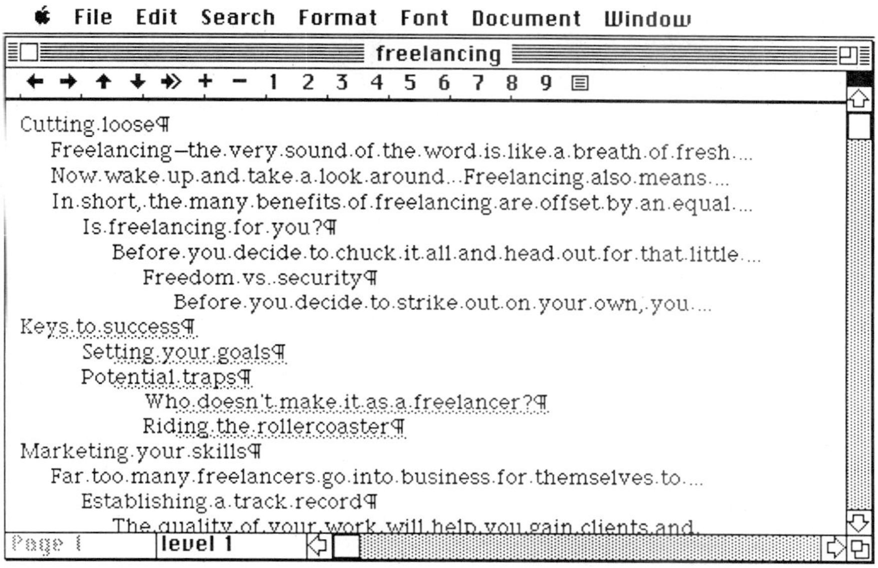

Use the collapse icon or the - key on your numeric keypad to collapse selected portions of the outline.

To reverse this process, just click on the heading again, then click on the expand icon, or press the + key on your numeric keypad. The first time you click on the expand icon or press the + key, your level 2 headings will reappear, then your level 3 headings, then your body text.

When you use these expand and collapse techniques, Word will not collapse any of the other text in your outline—only the text that falls between the current heading and the next heading at an equal or higher level will be affected. In our example, only the text that appears between the second and third level 1 headings is affected. You could also click on the level 2 heading *Setting your goals* to collapse all of the subtext between that heading and the next heading of equal or higher value, *Potential traps.*

To expand or collapse all of the subordinate text under a heading in one step, click in the selection bar to highlight the entire heading paragraph, rather than clicking on the heading. For example, to collapse all of the headings and body text under the heading *Keys to success* in our sample outline, you would click in the selection bar on the left side of the outline window to highlight the heading and the ¶ marker in the ninth line. Then you would click the collapse icon to hide all of the headings and body text between that heading and the next level 1 heading, *Marketing your skills*. Figure 12-9 shows the results.

FIGURE 12-9

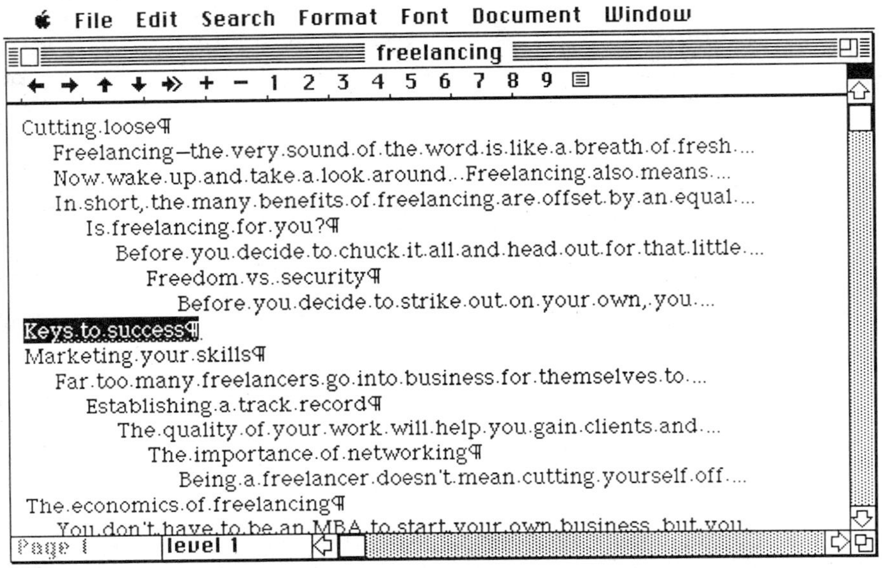

To collapse all of the subordinate text under a heading, select the entire heading paragraph before you click the collapse icon.

As you might have guessed, you can reselect the entire paragraph that contains the heading *Keys to success*, and click on the expand icon, or press the + key on your numeric keypad to redisplay all of the text between that heading and the next level 1 heading.

A navigation tip

When you are working with a long document and want to move to another area, you can use the outline to navigate quickly through your document. Just toggle to the outline window, then collapse the outline by clicking one of the show level icons. If the level 1 headings are too obscure to help you find your place, keep expanding the outline until you locate the spot you want. Now, highlight the heading or body text that represents the section you want to work with. When you press ⌘-u to return to your document window, Word will bring the highlighted text into view.

EDITING IN THE OUTLINE WINDOW

You can use any of the editing techniques described in Chapters 4 and 6 to edit text in your Word outline. However, when you use the Find... and Change... commands in the outline window, Word will operate only on the text that is visible on the screen.

For example, when you issue the Find... command, Word will not find any occurrences of your find text that are located in a collapsed portion of the outline. If you want to search through all of the text in your document, you'll probably find it easier to perform the Find operation in the document window. However, if you want to search for or change occurrences of a text string only in your document's headings, you may be able to streamline your search and replace procedures by working in the outline window.

In addition to these standard document editing techniques, Word offers a number of special editing features to help you edit text in the outline window. Let's take a look at some of these features.

Changing a Heading Level

You can easily change the level of any heading in your outline at any time. Begin by clicking on that heading or by selecting the paragraph that contains the heading, then click on the promote or demote icon. If you have a Macintosh with an expanded keyboard, you can also use the ➡ or ⬅ keys to promote or demote a heading.

In addition to changing the level number of the selected heading, Word will change the indention of that paragraph to reflect its new level. Word will also adjust the indention of any body text that appears immediately under the selected heading to indicate that it still "belongs to" that heading.

Unless you specifically instruct it to do so, however, Word will not change the levels of any other subordinate text in the outline. If you want to promote or demote a heading and all of its subordinate text, you must double-click in the selection bar to select the heading and all of its subordinate text before you click on the promote or demote icon.

For example, suppose you want to demote the level 1 heading *Keys to success* in the sample outline to a level 2 heading. If you simply click on that heading and click the demote icon, the outline will look like Figure 12-10 on the following page.

However, if you double-click in the selection bar to select the heading and all of its subordinate text and then click the demote icon, your outline will look like the one in Figure 12-11 on the next page. As you can see, Word has also demoted all of the subordinate headings and body text between the *Keys to success* heading and the next level 1 heading, *Marketing your skills*. In effect, the *Keys to success* heading and all of its subtext now fall under the first level 1 heading, *Cutting loose*.

FIGURE 12-10

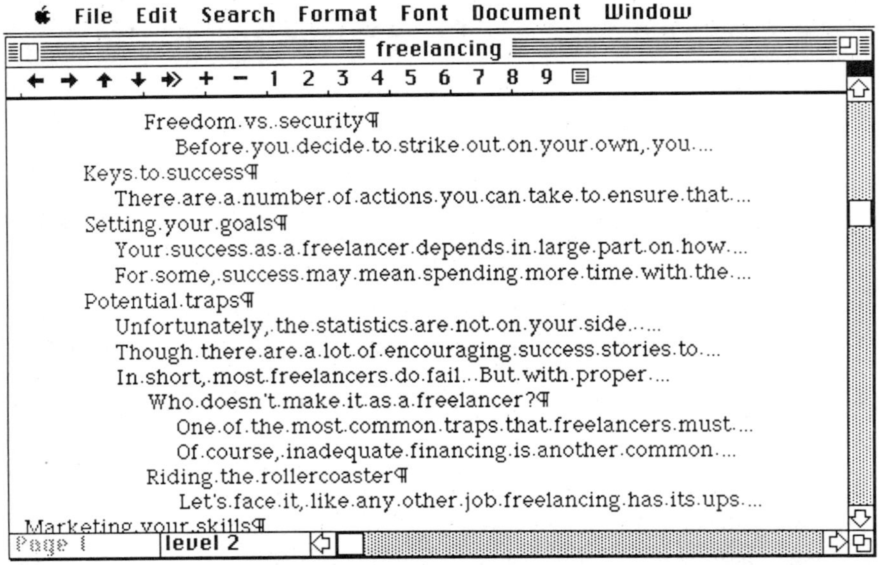

If you click on a heading before you click the promote or demote icon, Word adjusts the level of the heading and its body text.

FIGURE 12-11

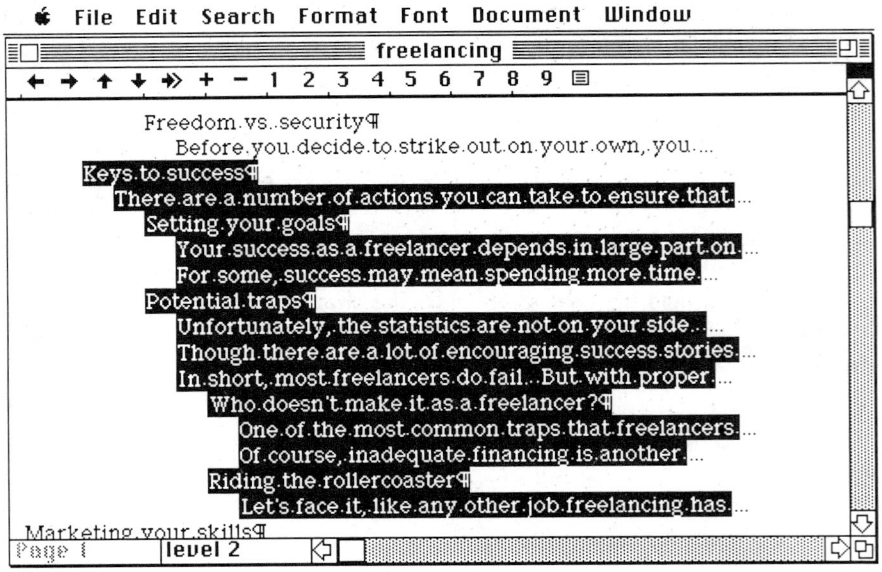

To promote or demote a heading and all of its subordinate text, double-click in the selection bar before you click the promote or demote icon.

Promoting Body Text

If you click on a body text paragraph in the outline window and then click the promote icon or press the ← key on your expanded Macintosh keyboard, Word will convert your body text to the same level as its immediate superior heading. For example, if you click on the body text paragraph that begins *Freelancing—the very sound* in the second line of our sample outline, and click the promote icon, Word will promote that entire paragraph to a level 1 heading. As you can see in Figure 12-12, when you promote the paragraph to a heading, Word will display the entire contents of that heading, rather than only the first line. Naturally, you might use this technique when you want to see the contents of a body text paragraph in the outline window.

FIGURE 12-12

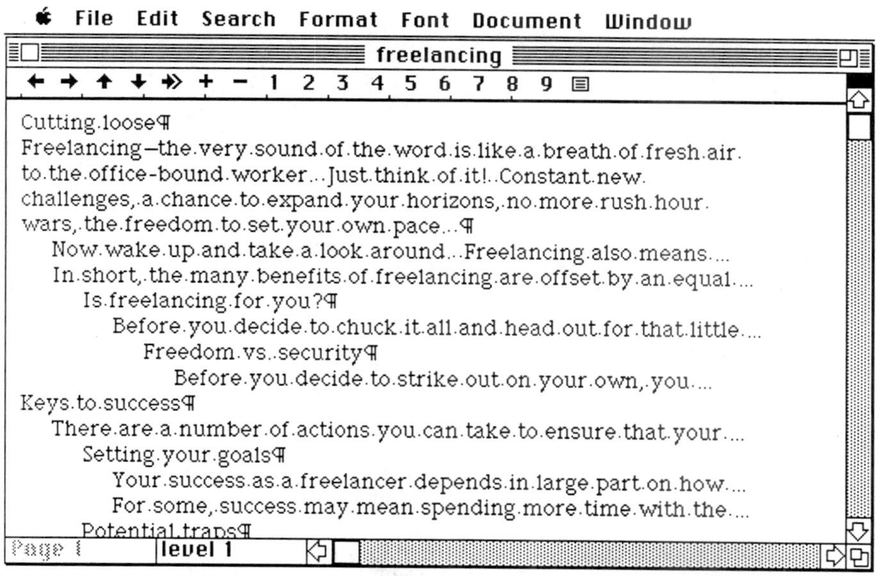

We've used the promote icon to convert the first paragraph of body text to a level 1 heading.

By the same token, if you select this body text paragraph and click the demote icon or press the → key, Word will convert the selected body text to the next subordinate heading level—level 2. Again, Word will display the entire contents of the body text paragraph. Word also will indent the heading $^1/_2$ inch to the right of the preceding level 1 heading.

Converting a Heading to Body Text

To convert a heading to body text, just click on the heading you want to work with and click the demote to body text icon (the double arrow that appears immediately after the ↓ icon). Alternatively, if you have a Mac Plus keyboard, you can press ⌘-→ to convert the heading to body text.

When you demote a heading to body text, Word will change the indention of that heading—and any subordinate body text that appears immediately below the heading—to appear $^{1}/_{4}$ inch to the right of the heading immediately preceding it. In short, your heading and any body text that may have been attached to it become part of the subordinate body text for the preceding heading.

For example, if we select the level 2 heading *Is freelancing for you?* in our sample outline and click the demote to body text icon, our outline window will look like the one in Figure 12-13. Notice that the body text that was formerly attached to this level 2 heading now carries the same indention as the rest of the body text for the level 1 heading *Cutting loose*. Also, notice that Word now displays the style notation *Normal* in the status box at the bottom-left corner of the screen.

FIGURE 12-13

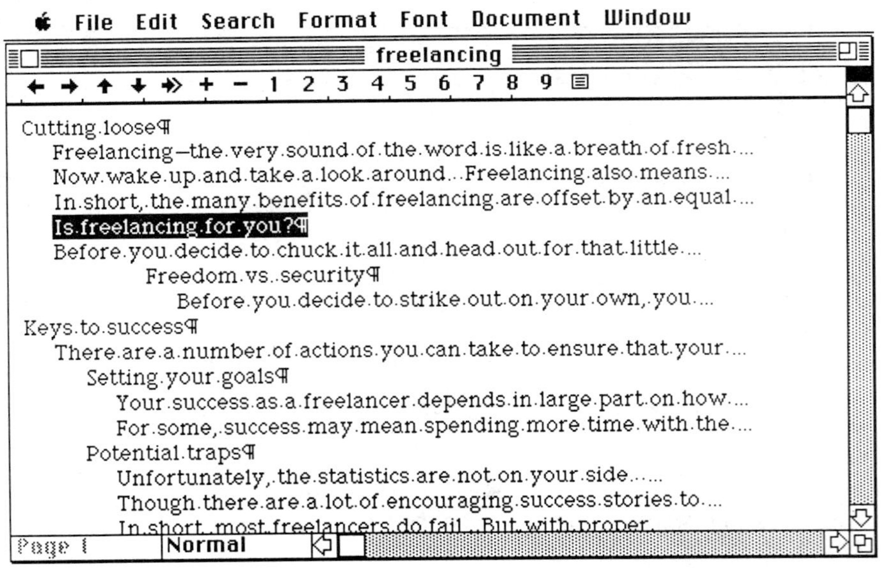

You can use the demote to body text icon to convert any heading in your outline to standard body text.

Inserting a New Heading

The easiest way to insert a new heading into your outline is to click in front of the paragraph immediately below the spot where you want your new heading to occur and press ⌘-Option-Return. When you press ⌘-Option-Return, Word will insert a new ¶ marker to the left of the current insertion point. However, your insertion point marker will not jump to the next line but will remain on the same line as the new ¶ marker.

Initially, your new heading will appear at the same level of the heading that you clicked on before pressing ⌘-Option-Return. Of course, you can use the promote and demote icons to change the heading level if you like.

Continuing with our sample outline, suppose we want to add a new level 2 heading—*Success stories*—between the level 3 heading *Freedom vs. security* and the level 1 heading *Keys to success.* If you were to click at the end of the level 3 heading and press Return, your new heading would appear between the *Freedom vs. security* heading and the text paragraph that begins *Before you decide.* If you try clicking at the end of the text paragraph and pressing the Return key, Word will break that text paragraph into two paragraphs instead of inserting a new blank paragraph after the text paragraph.

To get around these problems, just click in front of the level 1 heading *Keys to success,* and press ⌘-Option-Return. As you can see in Figure 12-14, Word will push the level 1 heading down a line and insert a new ¶ marker for you. Now all you need to do is click the demote icon to change this paragraph to a level 2 heading and type your new text. Figure 12-15 shows the results.

FIGURE 12-14

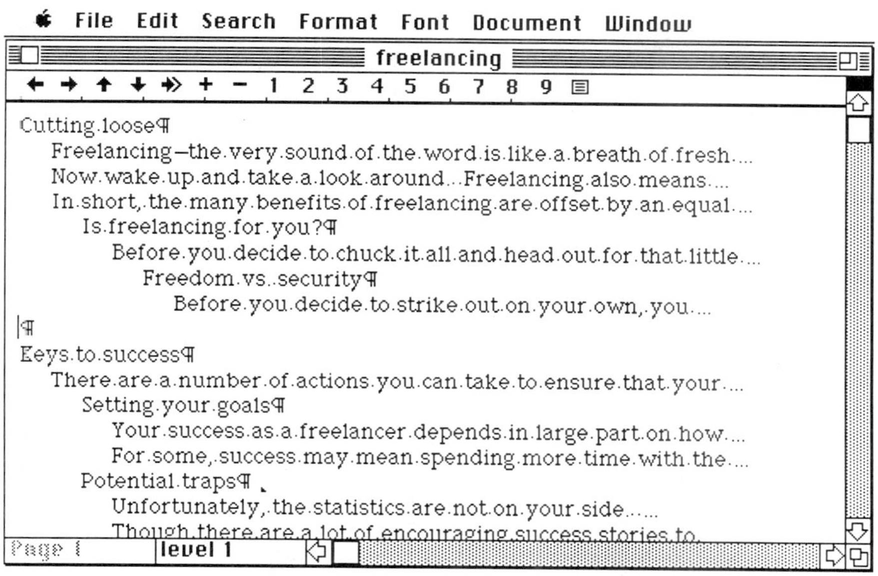

To insert a new heading, click in front of the paragraph immediately below the spot where you want your new heading to occur, and press ⌘-Option-Return.

FIGURE 12-15

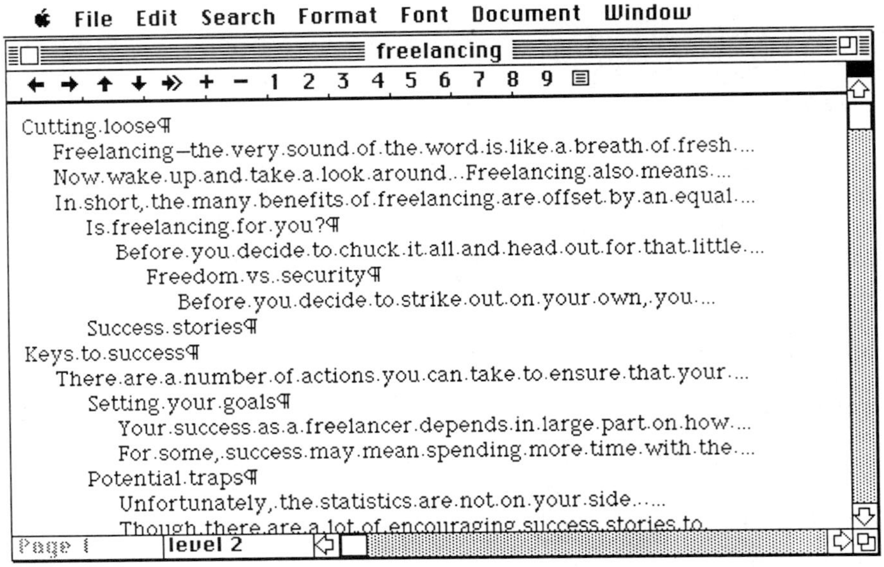

After you create your new blank paragraph, assign the appropriate level, and type the new heading text.

Deleting a Heading

If you decide to delete a heading from your outline, be sure to expand the outline before you begin. Otherwise, you may inadvertently delete all of the subordinate text for that heading as well. It is important to remember that when you select a heading in a collapsed outline, you also select all of the subordinate text for that heading.

For example, if you were to select the level 1 heading *Cutting loose* in Figure 12-7 and then click the show all icon, you would see that Word has highlighted all of the subtext between the first and second level 1 headings in the outline window. In short, any changes you make to a heading while the outline is collapsed will affect all of the subtext below that heading.

Once you have expanded the outline and selected the heading or body text paragraph that you want to delete, you can simply press the Backspace key or issue the Cut command to remove that heading from its current location.

Moving a Heading

There are two ways to move blocks of text in the outline window. The first is the standard Cut and Paste technique—just select the heading and any subordinate text that you want to move; issue the Cut command; then click on the spot where you want to place the text, and issue the Paste command.

As we mentioned just a moment ago, when you use the Cut command to delete or move text in an outline window, keep in mind that your changes may affect more than the text that is visible on your screen. When you select a heading with collapsed subtext, you are selecting all of that subtext as well. If you don't want this subordinate text to move along with the heading, you will need to expand your outline before you issue the Cut command. However, if you do want the subtext to be included in your selection, you may find it easier to collapse the outline before you begin the Cut and Paste procedure.

Similarly, when you select your Paste area, you may want to expand any collapsed text in that area to ensure that you are not inserting text between a heading and its subordinate text.

In addition to the Cut and Paste commands, you can use the move up and move down icons in the outline window to rearrange blocks of text. For example, suppose you decide to move the level 2 heading *Setting your goals* and all of its subtext. You want this text to appear just below the body text paragraph that reads *Before you decide to chuck it all.* If the portion of your outline that you want to move is collapsed, all you need to do is click on the heading to select it and all of its subordinate text. If your outline is not collapsed, you'll need to double-click on the heading to make your selection.

Now, click the move up icon to move the selected text block toward the beginning of the document. (If you have a Macintosh with an expanded keyboard, you can also use the ⬆ and ⬇ keys to move blocks of text up and down through the outline window.) When you click the move up icon, Word will move the selected block up through the outline window one heading at a time. The program will skip past any body text paragraph. Keep clicking the move up icon or pressing the ⬆ key until the text block is in the desired position. (If you need to move the text block a long distance, you may want to collapse some or all of the outline text before you begin in order to save time.) Figure 12-16 on the next page shows the results.

By the way, notice that when you move a block of text up in the outline window, you simply change the order of those paragraphs; you do not change your heading levels or the relationship between your headings and body text.

THE OUTLINER AND STYLE SHEETS

As we hinted at the beginning of this chapter, Word's built-in outliner is designed to work hand-in-hand with the style sheet facility. When you begin a document in an outline window, Word assumes that you will want to use each topic in the outline as a subheading in your document. As you switch from the outline window to a document window, Word automatically sets up a style sheet, assigning a different style name to each level of the outline.

To illustrate, let's continue with our sample freelancing article. As you know, when you switch from the outline window to a normal document window, Word no longer indents the different levels of outline text. However, if you place the insertion point on any line in the document window, you'll see the level for that text in the style status box in the lower-left corner of the screen.

Each of the levels that you use in the outline window now has a corresponding style name on the document's style sheet. If you choose Styles... or Define Styles... from the Format menu, you'll see that the style sheet in our sample document includes the style names *level 1, level 2, level 3,* and *level 4.* Like every other document style sheet, this style sheet will also include the style named *Normal*, as shown in Figure 12-17.

FIGURE 12-16

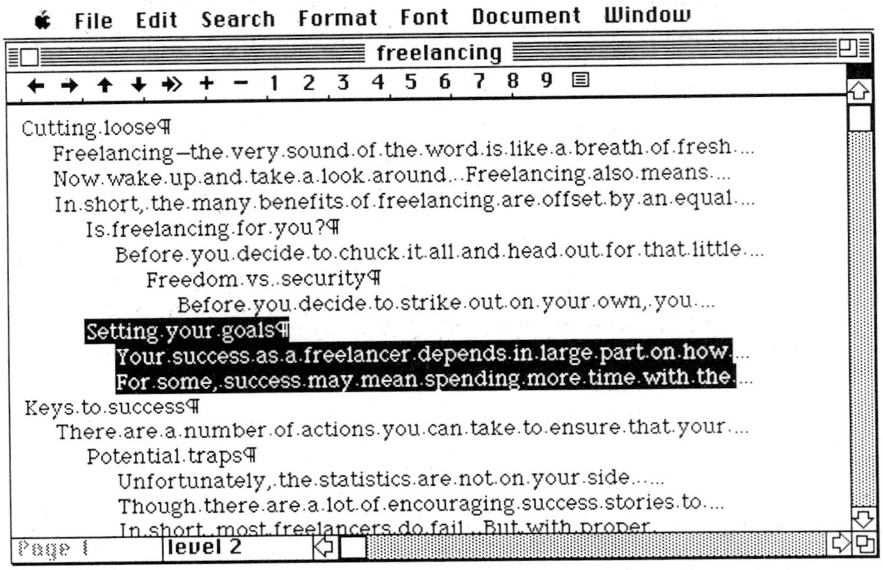

To reposition a selection in the outline window, you can click the move up and move down icons or press the ↑ and ↓ keys.

Although Word gives you a helpful headstart by setting up the styles named *level 1, level 2,* and so forth, Word does not provide much distinction in the formatting of each of these *level* styles. The default formatting instructions for the *level 1* style are *Normal + Bold, Space Before 12 pt.* The instructions for *level 2* are *Normal + Bold, Space Before 6 pt.* Finally, the instructions for the *level 3* through *level 9* styles all read *Normal + Bold.* In other words, the various level styles all have identical formatting instructions, except for the extra line spacing before the *level 1* and *level 2* styles.

If you plan to use the text from your outline as subheadings in a document, you probably will want to alter the style instructions so that there will be more distinction in the appearance of the different subheadings. Before you begin altering the style instructions for each of the *level* styles, however, you should think about how you want to format the document's *Normal* style. Because each of the *level* styles is based on the *Normal* style, any changes that you make to the formatting instructions for *Normal* will affect the appearance of text that is formatted with the *level* styles. Therefore, *Normal* should be the first style that you modify.

FIGURE 12-17

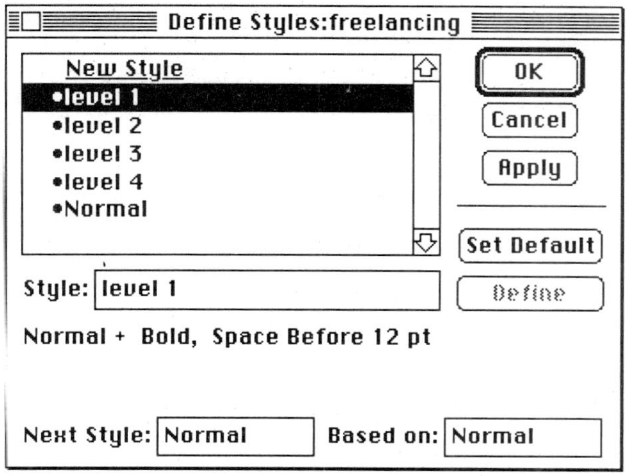

Each level from the outline is now a style name on the style sheet.

Let's suppose that you want the main body text in your document to be formatted with 12-point Helvetica type, with a 1/4 inch indent on the first line of each paragraph. To alter the *Normal* style to meet these specifications, choose Define Styles... from the Format menu, and click the name *Normal* to select it. Then open the Character dialog box and choose Helvetica in the list of fonts, then click 12 in the list of sizes. Next, drag the first-line indent marker to the 1/4 inch position on the ruler. Finally, click Define to lock in these changes, and click Cancel to close the dialog box. Figure 12-18 on the next page shows how the screen from Figure 12-4 will appear after you have modified the *Normal* style as we have described. Notice that all of the text from the outline now appears in Helvetica with a 1/4 inch indent. (By the way, Word will also use your new *Normal* character format specifications to display the characters in the outline window.)

Once you've modified the *Normal* style, you can make additional changes to the instructions to each of the *level* styles. Continuing with our example, suppose you would like the level 1 subheadings to appear in 18-point bold, the level 2 subheadings to appear in 14-point bold, the level 3 text to appear in 14-point italic, and finally, you want the level 4 text to appear in 12-point bold. You also want each of the subheadings to be aligned with the left margin, instead of being indented like the *Normal* text, and you want to retain the existing Space Before settings for the level 1 and level 2 headings.

FIGURE 12-18

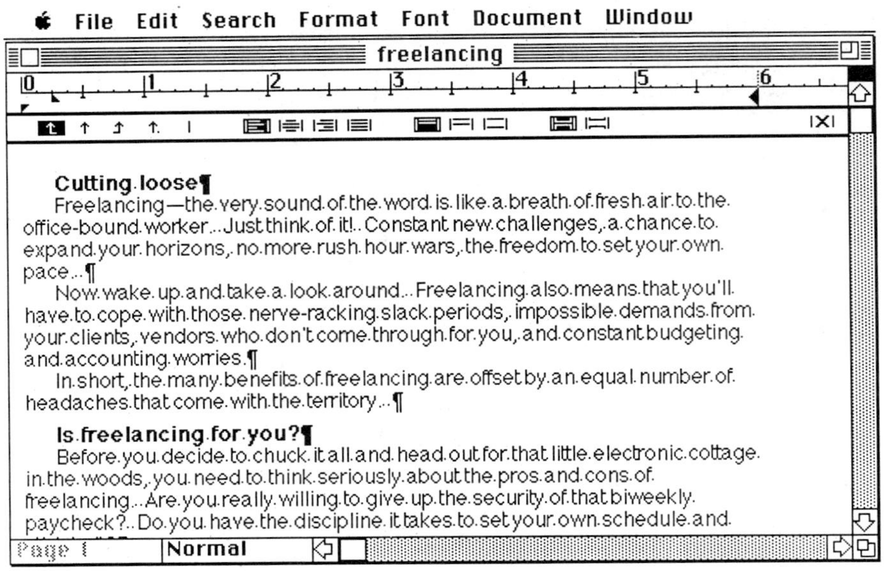

When you modify the Normal *style, Word will also change the formatting of each of the* level *styles that are based on* Normal

To modify each of these styles, you would follow the standard procedure described in Chapter 9. Click on one of the headings that belong to the level that you want to format, then choose Define Styles... from the Format menu. In the Define Styles dialog box, click on the name of the style that you want to modify, then select the character and paragraph formats for this heading level. When you click OK, Apply, or Define in the Define Styles dialog box, Word will apply the specified formats to all of the headings in your document that carry that *level* style. Figure 12-19 shows the first few headings in our sample document after we modified the *level* styles.

By the way, if you decide that you don't want all of your headings to appear in your finished document, just apply the Hidden character format to the level that you want to hide. Word will hide all of the headings at those levels in your document window, but it will still display them in your outline window.

As you're changing the formatting instructions for each of the *level* styles, you may want to change the Based on style as well. Instead of using *Normal* as the Based on style for each of the *level* styles, you might want to base each *level* style on the next highest *level* style. Specifically, the *level 5* style could be based on *level 4,* which could be based on *level 3,* which could be based on *level 2,* which could be based on *level 1*, which would be based on *Normal.* That way, when you make format changes to the *level 1* style—new indention settings, for example—those changes will affect all of your subheadings.

FIGURE 12-19

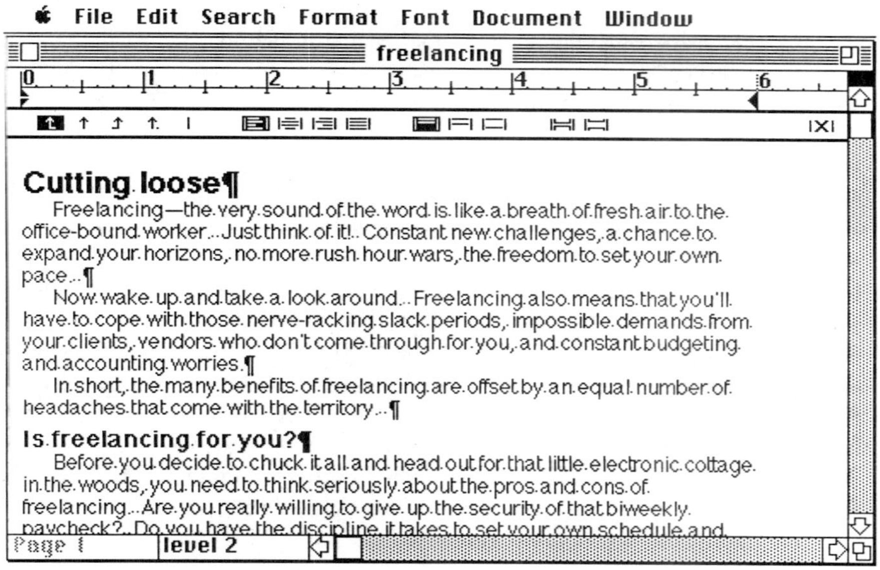

After you modify the instructions for each of the level *styles, Word will apply those new formatting instructions to your document.*

Also, notice that Word uses the Next Style specification *Normal* for all of the *level* styles. As you saw earlier, when you click at the end of a heading paragraph in your document window and press the Return key to begin a new paragraph, Word assumes that you want that text to appear in the *Normal* style. You can change this Next Style setting for any of your headings if you want to use a special format for the text that appears immediately below your headings.

For example, you might create a style called *First ¶* to format the first paragraph after each heading. Then you could use the style name *First ¶* in the Next Style edit bar for each of your *level* styles. Word will treat your *First ¶* paragraphs like standard body text when you return to the outline window. In fact, any text that does not carry the *level 1* through *level 9* style names will be treated as body text in the outline window.

As you already know, while you're viewing the document in the outline window, you can change the level of any subheading by placing the insertion point marker on that subheading and clicking the ➡ or ⬅ icon. Word will, of course, change the indention and level number of the text in the outline window. In addition, when you switch to the normal document view, you'll see that Word has reformatted that text by applying a different style.

For example, suppose that you decide to change the subheading *Freedom vs. security* in Figure 12-16 from a level 3 topic to a level 2 topic. In the outline window, you would place your insertion point marker anywhere on this subheading and click the ⬅ icon once. When you switch back to the document window, you will see that this subheading is now formatted with the *level 2* style instead of the *level 3* style.

You can also change the level of any heading in the document window with the Define Styles... or Styles... command. When you return to the outline window, your heading will be demoted or promoted to the appropriate level.

PRINTING THE OUTLINE

To print your document outline, just activate the outline window and issue the Print... command as usual. You can print the entire outline or collapse it to print only certain levels. Word will print the outline exactly as it appears in the outline window, with one exception: If the first line of any body text paragraphs are visible in your outline window, Word will print those paragraphs in their entirety.

Even though it ignores any character or paragraph formats that you may have assigned to the text in your document window, Word does recognize your Page Setup and Section dialog box settings when you print the outline. Any headers, footers, section breaks, or manual page breaks that you may have created will also be included in your printed outline. Figure 12-20 shows the printed version of the outline, collapsed to show only level 1, 2, and 3 headings.

FIGURE 12-20

- Cutting loose
  - Is freelancing for you?
    - Freedom vs. security
  - Setting your goals
- Keys to success
  - Potential traps
    - Who doesn't make it as a freelancer?
    - Riding the rollercoaster
- Marketing your skills
  - Establishing a track record
    - The importance of networking
- The economics of freelancing
  - Cash flow considerations
    - Estimating your overhead
      - Handling growth—is bigger always better?
  - Developing a fee schedule
    - What will the traffic bear?
      - Service options
      - Incentive pricing
- Annotated Bibliography

If you activate the outline window before you issue the Print... command, Word will print your outline exactly as it appears on the screen.

ADDING A TABLE OF CONTENTS, AN INDEX, AND FOOTNOTES 13

One of the most time-consuming and boring tasks in creating a document is developing reference aids, such as indexes, footnotes, and tables of contents. Word 3 has taken much of the tedium out of these tasks by adding special index, footnote, and table of contents facilities.

The steps you follow to create indexes and tables of contents are quite similar. You simply enter special hidden identification codes into the body of your document to flag the entries you want to include. Then you can use the Index... or Table of Contents... command to compile these entries.

Footnotes, on the other hand, are entered in a separate window that is saved to disk with your document (much like a header or footer window). Word will print your footnotes automatically when you print your document.

Since it's the simplest of the three reference aid features, let's start with the table of contents; then we'll look at Word's indexing and footnoting capabilities.

CREATING A TABLE OF CONTENTS

Word gives you two ways to build entries for a table of contents. First, you can enter special codes into your document to flag the entries that you want to include in your table of contents. Second, if you have used the outliner facility (described in Chapter 12) to create your document, you can instruct Word to compile a table of contents directly from the headings that you have entered into the outline. We'll take a look at the coding technique first.

Defining Your Table of Contents Entries

A table of contents entry has three parts: a hidden code that identifies the start of the entry, the entry text, and an end-of-entry marker. The three-character code that identifies the start of the entry consists of a period, the letter *c*, and another period (.c.). You must assign the Hidden character format to this code; otherwise Word will not recognize it as a table of contents marker.

Your end-of-entry marker may be a paragraph marker (¶), an end-of-line marker (↵), or a semicolon (;). If you decide to use a semicolon, you'll probably want to assign the Hidden format to that character so that it will not appear in your document text.

The text that you use for a table of contents entry can be either existing text in your document or new text that you type specifically for the entry. Generally, you'll want to use existing document headings and subheadings for your entry text, rather than typing new text. However, in order to create a special table of contents entry, you may need to enter new text. If you type some text in your document specifically for a table of contents entry, you'll probably want to assign the Hidden format to that text so that it doesn't appear in your printed document.

We've created three table of contents entries in the sample document shown in Figure 13-1. The first entry, in the title, takes advantage of an existing heading. Notice that the *.c.* flag appears with a gray underline, indicating that we have assigned the Hidden format to that code. The ¶ marker at the end of the heading serves as our end-of-entry marker.

FIGURE 13-1

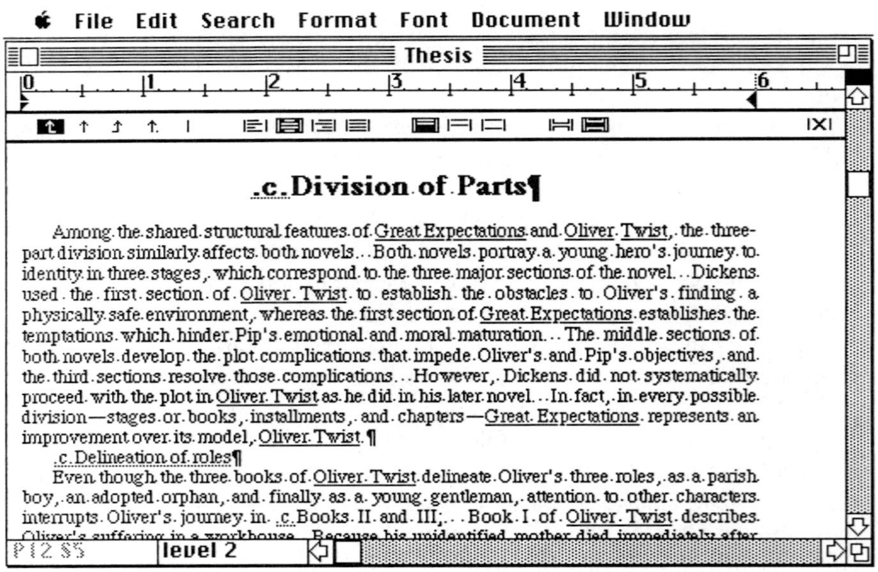

We created three table of contents entries in this sample document.

The second table of contents entry, *Delineation of roles*, appears just after the first paragraph of body text. This entry, like the first entry, occupies an entire paragraph, but it is not part of our document text. For that reason, we have assigned the Hidden format to the entire entry, including the ¶ marker. (As we explained in Chapter 7, if you don't hide markup characters, like blank spaces and ¶ markers, you'll find extra white space in your document when you print.)

The third entry, which appears in the last line shown on the screen, also takes advantage of existing body text. Therefore, we assigned the Hidden format only to the *.c.* and *;* portions of the entry to prevent them from appearing in our printed document.

Multilevel table of contents entries

You can create as many as nine levels of entries for your tables of contents by including a numeric level argument in your .c. code. As you'll see when we compile a table of contents, Word will indent the entries according to the level you have assigned to them. To assign a level to an entry, enter a value from 1 to 9 after the *c* character, like this: .c2., .c3., .c4., and so forth. (Be sure to include the period after the level number.) You can enter your first-level table of contents entry codes as .c1., if you like, but the level code is not necessary for first-level entries.

For example, in the sample screen shown in Figure 13-2, we used a first-level table of contents code to flag the major heading at the top of the screen. We used the .c2. code to mark the text *Delineation of roles* as a second-level entry under *Division of Parts*, and we used a third-level code to define the inline entry *Books II and III*.

FIGURE 13-2

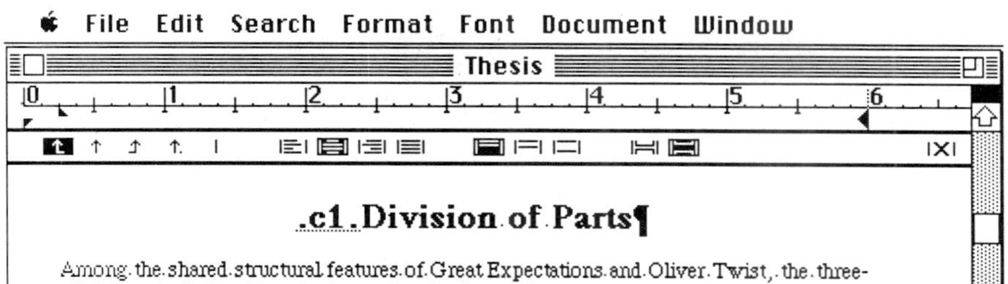

We've created three levels of table of contents entries on this screen.

Collecting table of contents entries from your outline

If you use the outliner facility to create a document, you won't have to enter any special codes into that document in order to create your table of contents. As we explained in Chapter 12, when you enter headings into your document through the outline window, Word automatically assigns style names to each level. Major headings are assigned the style *level 1*; subheadings are formatted with the styles named *level 2*, *level 3*, and so forth. (You may remember that your document can contain as many as nine levels of styles—the same number of levels available for table of contents entries.)

If you instruct Word to compile the table of contents from your outline, it will search through your document to locate all of the paragraphs that carry the style names *level 1* through *level 9*. These headings will become the text for your table of contents. As you might guess, your *level 1* headings will become first-level table of contents entries; your *level 2* headings will become second-level table of contents entries; and so forth.

Compiling the Table of Contents

Once you have defined the entries that you want to use in your table of contents, you can use the Table of Contents... command on the Document menu to compile the table of contents. (This command is available only when the Full Menus setting is in effect.) When you issue the Table of Contents... command, you'll see a dialog box like the one in Figure 13-3.

FIGURE 13-3

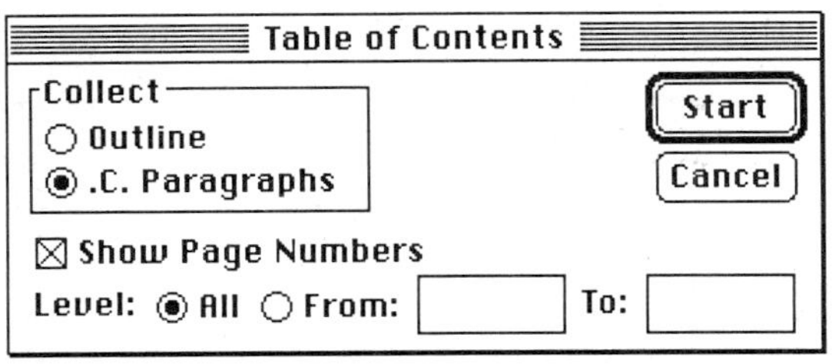

This dialog box appears when you issue the Table of Contents... command.

The option you select in the Collect section of the dialog box tells Word where to look for the table of contents entries. If you want to use the heading levels from your outline, click the Outline option. If you don't have (or don't want to use) outline headings as your table of contents entries, click the .C. Paragraphs option. Word will gather its table of contents entries from the text marked with the .c. codes that you inserted in your text.

Next, you need to tell Word how many entry levels you want to include in your table of contents. Just click All if you want to include all of the entries in the table of contents. Alternatively, you can enter the levels you want to use in the From and To edit bars. If you want to include page numbers in the table of contents, select the Show Page Numbers option. Finally, click the Start button to begin compiling the table. If you need to halt the compilation for any reason, you can press the ⌘ and period keys (⌘-.) to cancel the procedure.

When you click the Start button in the Table of Contents dialog box, Word repaginates the entire document, searches for the table of contents entries, compiles the table of contents, and inserts the table text in a new section at the beginning of the document.

If you've already compiled a table of contents for your document, Word asks if you want to replace the existing table. Click Yes to replace your old table of contents with a new one. If you click No, Word will place the new table of contents in another new section at the beginning of the document, right in front of the old one. You may want to use this technique to create separate tables for different types of information in your document, such as diagrams, illustrations, and so forth. We'll talk more about creating other types of tables of contents in a moment.

Figure 13-4 shows a sample table of contents that we compiled in Word. As you can see, each entry contains the entry text, followed by a tab marker, the page number (since we have opted to display page numbers), and a paragraph marker to end the entry. Word also has inserted a section marker at the end of the table of contents. Because the table of contents appears in its own section, you can change its page layout and page numbering scheme without affecting the rest of your document.

FIGURE 13-4

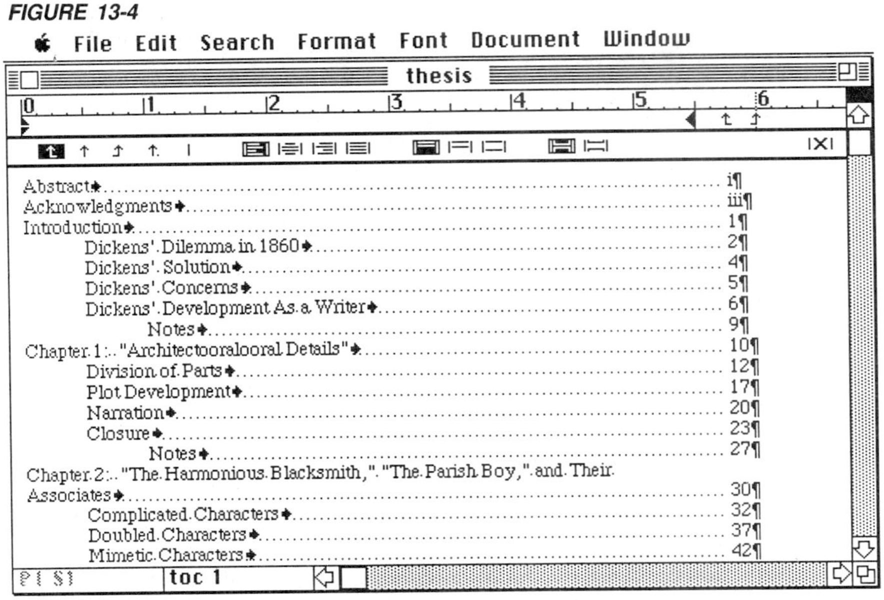

Your compiled table of contents will look like this.

By the way, the best time to compile the table of contents is right before you print the final version of your document. Word automatically repaginates your document when you issue the Table of Contents... command to ensure that your page numbers are accurate. However, if you edit or reorganize the document after compiling the table of contents, your page numbers may change, causing the table of contents entries to be incorrect.

We also recommend that you deselect the Show Hidden Text option in the Preferences dialog box before you compile your table of contents. If you don't plan to include this hidden text in your printed document, you'll need to hide it in the document window so that your document will be repaginated correctly when Word compiles the table.

Formatting the Table of Contents

As we mentioned above, the table of contents initially appears in a new section at the very beginning of your document. In addition, the character formatting of the table of contents will match the *Normal* style for your document. For example, if you're using Word's default *Normal* style, your table of contents will appear in 12-point, New York, plain type. (See Chapter 9 for more on style sheets and defining the *Normal* style.) Although Word does not assign any special character formatting to a table of contents, it does assign certain paragraph formats to each entry in the table. This paragraph formatting determines the amount of indention for each level of entries, as well as the tabs and dot leaders that are used to position the page numbers in the table.

Of course, once you've created a table of contents, you can change the character and paragraph formats of that text. You also can use the Cut and Paste commands to move the table to another part of your document. The easiest way to reformat your table of contents text is to redefine the style definitions that Word has applied to the table. Let's take a look at the relationship between the table of contents and Word's style sheet facility.

Using the style sheet

Like the outliner that we discussed in Chapter 12, Word's table of contents facility is designed to work hand-in-hand with the style sheet facility. For each table of contents entry level you create, Word adds a style name to the document's style sheet. If you choose Styles… or Define Styles… from the Format menu after creating a table of contents, you'll see that your document's style sheet includes the style names *toc 1*, *toc 2*, *toc 3*, and *toc 4*. Like every other document style sheet, this style sheet will also include the style named *Normal*, as shown in Figure 13-5. If you have used the outliner to build your document, you'll also see the style names *level 1*, *level 2*, and so forth.

Table 13-1 on page 482 lists the default style instructions for each level of entries in a table of contents. As you can see, all of these styles are based on the *Normal* style—that's why your table of contents will display the same character formats as the main body text in your document. However, as you can tell from the style definitions, Word assigns different amounts of left indention to each level in the table of contents.

FIGURE 13-5

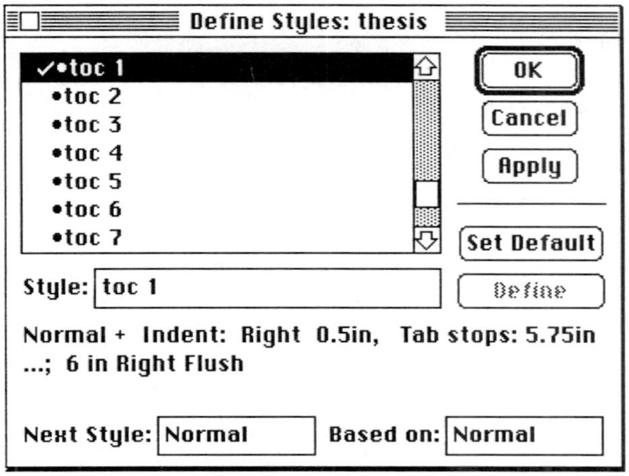

Each level from the table of contents is now a style name on the style sheet.

To modify one of your *toc* styles, just click on one of the table of contents entries that belong to the level that you want to format, then choose Define Styles… from the Format menu. In the Define Styles dialog box, click on the name of the style that you want to modify (a check mark should appear next to that style name), then select the character and paragraph formats that you want to use for this level. When you click OK or Apply in the Define Styles dialog box, Word will apply your new format selections to all table of contents entries in your document that carry that style name.

For example, in the sample document that we used to create the table of contents shown in Figure 13-4, our *Normal* style specifies 12-point, Times, plain type. As a result, our table of contents also appears in 12-point, Times, plain type. Suppose that we decide we want the first-level headings in this table of contents to appear in 14-point, Times, bold type. We can change the format of all the first-level entries by modifying the *toc 1* style on the style sheet. First, we would click anywhere on one of the first-level table of contents entries in the document and select the Define Styles… command from the Format menu. Then, we would click on the name *toc 1* in the list that appears in the dialog box. Next, we would choose Bold from the Format menu and 14 Point from the Font menu. When we click OK to lock in these style changes and return to the document window, our table of contents will look like Figure 13-6.

TABLE 13-1

Style Name	Style Definition
toc 1	*Normal* plus 5 $^1/_2$ inch right indent, left-aligned tab with dot leader at 5 $^3/_4$ inches, right-aligned tab at 6 inches
toc 2	*Normal* plus $^1/_2$ inch left indent, 5 $^1/_2$ inch right indent, left-aligned tab with dot leader at 5 $^3/_4$ inches, right-aligned tab at 6 inches
toc 3	*Normal* plus 1 inch left indent, 5 $^1/_2$ inch right indent, left-aligned tab with dot leader at 5 $^3/_4$ inches, right-aligned tab at 6 inches
toc 4	*Normal* plus 1 $^1/_2$ inch left indent, 5 $^1/_2$ inch right indent, left-aligned tab with dot leader at 5 $^3/_4$ inches, right-aligned tab at 6 inches
toc 5	*Normal* plus 2 inch left indent, 5 $^1/_2$ inch right indent, left-aligned tab with dot leader at 5 $^3/_4$ inches, right-aligned tab at 6 inches
toc 6	*Normal* plus 2 $^1/_2$ inch left indent, 5 $^1/_2$ inch right indent, left-aligned tab with dot leader at 5 $^3/_4$ inches, right-aligned tab at 6 inches
toc 7	*Normal* plus 3 inch left indent, 5 $^1/_2$ inch right indent, left-aligned tab with dot leader at 5 $^3/_4$ inches, right-aligned tab at 6 inches
toc 8	*Normal* plus 3 $^1/_2$ inch left indent, 5 $^1/_2$ inch right indent, left-aligned tab with dot leader at 5 $^3/_4$ inches, right-aligned tab at 6 inches
toc 9	*Normal* plus 4 inch left indent, 5 $^1/_2$ inch right indent, left-aligned tab with dot leader at 5 $^3/_4$ inches, right-aligned tab at 6 inches

Word uses these default style instructions to format your table of contents.

As you're changing the formatting instructions for each of the *toc* styles, you may want to change the Based On style as well. Instead of using *Normal* as the Based On style for each of the level styles, you might want to base each *toc* style on the next-highest level *toc* style. This can help you maintain formatting consistency among the different levels in a table of contents. Specifically, *toc 5* could be based on *toc 4*, which could be based on *toc 3*, which could be based on *toc 2*, which could be based on *toc 1*, which would be based on *Normal*. That way, when you make a format change to the *toc 1* style, your change will affect all of the other *toc* styles as well.

FIGURE 13-6

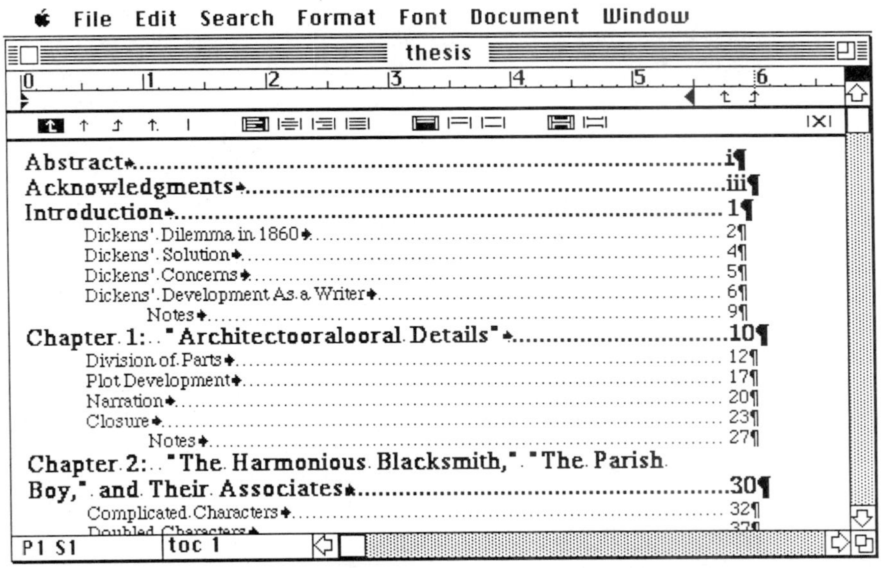

We used the Define Styles... command to format the first-level table of contents entries in this document.

Numbering the table of contents pages

As you already know, Word creates a new section for each of your tables of contents. Since the table of contents is generally considered part of your document's front matter, you'll probably want to create special page numbers for your table of contents pages (and any other front matter items like the title page, acknowledgments, and so forth). The lower-case Roman numbering scheme (i, ii, iii) is commonly used for this part of a document.

To number your table of contents pages, click anywhere in that section, issue the Section... command, and click the Page Numbering option. Select the page number style you want to use, and specify the position for your page numbers in the From Top and From Right edit bars.

To use a different page numbering style for the body of your document, click in the first section of the main document and issue another Section... command. Select the numbering scheme you want to use, and click the Restart at 1 option.

If you do want your table of contents pages to be numbered with the rest of your document, you'll need to reserve page numbers for the table before you issue the Table of Contents... command. Otherwise, your page numbers in the table of contents will be inaccurate. To reserve page numbers for your table of contents, just insert a manual page break or section break at the spot where your table will appear. You may need to include two or more page breaks if your table will be more than a page long. When you compile the table, Word will include the extra blank pages that you have created in its page count as it compiles page numbers for your table of contents.

Creating Other Tables

You can use the Table of Contents... command to compile other types of tables, such as a list of illustrations or a list of tables. You can accomplish this in one of two ways. If you've used Word's outliner in creating your document, you can compile your main table of contents from the different levels of outline text. Then, you can type .c. codes in your document window to flag the entries for your secondary tables. If you did not use the outliner, you can reserve separate .c. entry levels for each of the tables that you plan to build.

Let's start with the latter case: If you didn't use the outliner to create your document, you'll need to reserve different .c. levels for each of the tables that you want to create. For example, suppose you have created a document that contains several diagrams and illustrations. For easy reference, you want to create a list of these items that is separate from your main table of contents.

Since you will need to use .c. codes to define both your table of contents entries and your illustration table entries, you need first to decide which level of detail you want to use in your main table of contents. Let's say you want to include four levels of entries in your main table of contents. Use the entry codes .c1. (or simply .c.) through .c4. to define your table of contents entries. Now, use the entry code .c5. to define your illustration table entries.

When you're ready for Word to compile the tables, issue the Table of Contents... command and type the level number *5* in the From Level edit bar. When you click Start, Word will compile your table of illustrations entries and place them at the beginning of the document. Now, to compile the main table of contents, issue another Table of Contents... command, and enter the level number 1 in the From edit bar and the level number *4* in the To edit bar. Remember to click No when Word asks whether you want to replace the existing table of contents. Word will then compile the second table and insert it in a new section in front of the illustration table. Once you've compiled both tables, you can use the style sheet to format the different levels in each table.

If you created your document using Word's outliner, the process for setting up multiple tables is even easier. You can compile your main table of contents by issuing the Table of Contents… command and choosing the Outline option. After compiling the main table of contents, you can insert .c. codes in your document window to define the entries for your second table. To compile this table, issue the Table of Contents… command and choose the .C. Paragraphs option in the dialog box. Again, remember to click No when Word asks whether you want to replace your existing table of contents. Word will compile the second table and insert it in front of any existing tables.

When you use this technique, keep in mind that Word will apply the same *toc* level styles to both of your tables. If you use the style sheet to change one of your *toc* style definitions, Word will apply your changes to any table where an entry is formatted with that style. For example, if you've created two tables, both of them will have at least first-level entries. Therefore, if you alter the definition of the *toc 1* style, you will affect the format of the first-level entries in both tables. If you want to use different formats for the two tables, you may want to format one of the tables manually or create a new set of style names for the entries in that table.

BUILDING AN INDEX

Though the process is a bit more complex, building an index is much like building a table of contents. Index entries—like table of contents entries—contain three main parts: a hidden code that identifies the start of the entry, the entry text, and an end-of-entry marker. You also can add a number of optional arguments to define subentry levels and to format page number references.

The code that identifies the start of an entry consists of three characters: a period, the letter *i*, and another period (.i.). You must assign the Hidden character format to this code, or Word will not recognize your index entry. Your end-of-entry marker may be a paragraph marker (¶), an end-of-line marker (↵), or a semicolon (;). If you decide to use a semicolon, you'll probably want to assign the Hidden format to that character so that it will not appear in your document text.

The text that you use for an index entry can be either existing text in your document or new text that you enter specifically for the entry. If you decide to type new index text into your document, you'll probably want to assign the Hidden format to that text so that it doesn't appear in your printed document.

For example, we have created three index entries in the sample document shown in Figure 13-7 on the next page. The first entry at the top of the screen (*Division of Parts*) takes advantage of existing text. Notice that the *.i.* flag appears with a gray underline, indicating that we have assigned the Hidden format to that marker. The ¶ marker after the heading serves as our end-of-entry marker.

The second index entry, *Delineation of roles*, occurs just after the first paragraph of body text. Since it is not part of our document text, we assigned the Hidden format to the entire entry, including the ¶ marker. (As we explained in Chapter 7, if you don't hide demarcation characters, like blank spaces and ¶ markers, you'll find extra white spaces in your document when you print.)

The third entry, which appears near the beginning of the eighteenth line, also takes advantage of existing text. We assigned the Hidden format to the *.i.* and *;* portions of the entry to prevent them from appearing in our printed document.

FIGURE 13-7

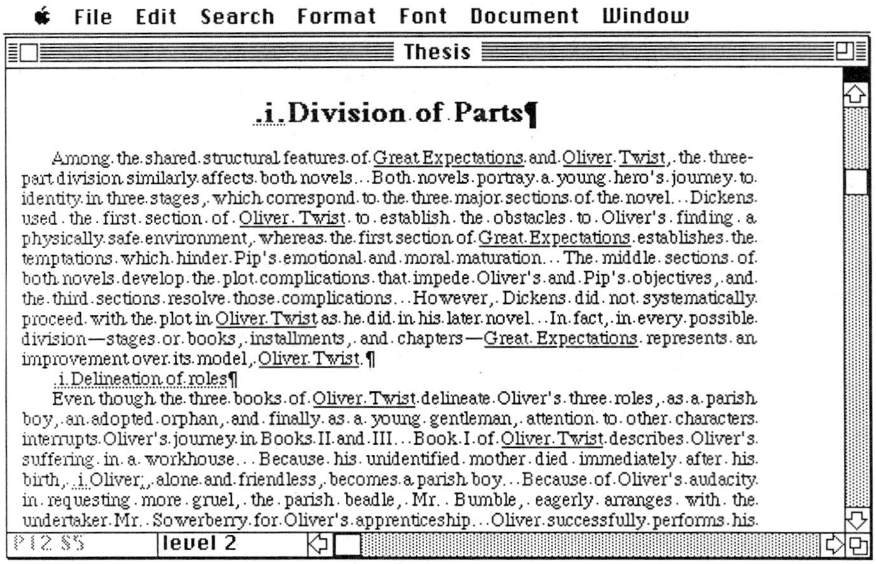

We created three index entries in this sample document.

Defining Subentries

You can create as many as seven levels of index entries by adding subentry text to your index entries. Just type the index code, the main index entry, and a colon. Then add the subentry text and an end-of-entry code. For example, in the sample document shown in Figure 13-7, you might define the second and third index entries as subentries under the main heading *Division of Parts* by typing

.i.Division of Parts:Delineation of roles¶

and

.i.Division of Parts:Delineation of roles:Oliver¶

(Of course, you don't actually type the ¶ marker after each entry; we've included it here simply to indicate that, when you press Return after creating each entry, a ¶ marker will appear to serve as your end-of-entry marker.)

Notice that every time you type a subentry, you also must type its main entry. Also, keep in mind that you must use a colon to separate each subentry level. Finally, remember to assign the Hidden format to these entries so that they won't clutter your printed document. Figure 13-8 shows our sample document with the first-, second-, and third-level index entries in place.

FIGURE 13-8

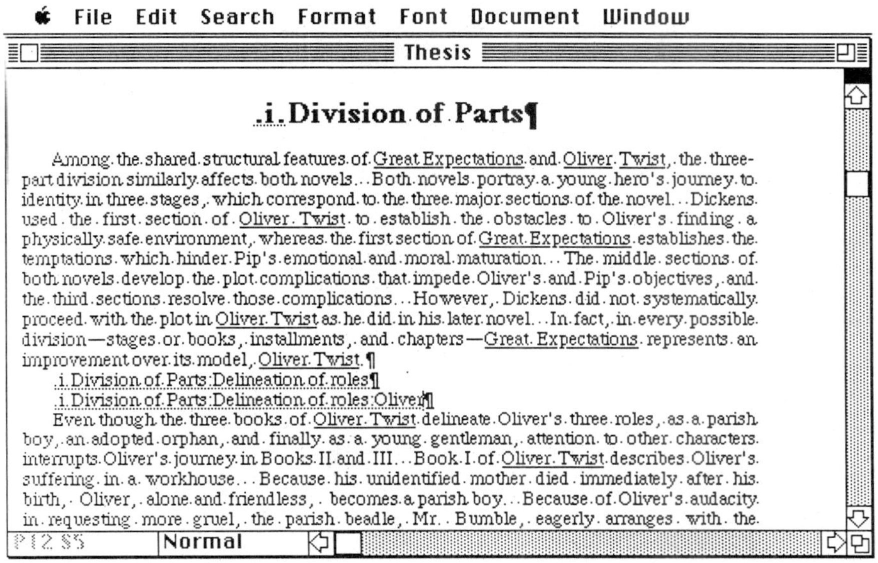

We added a pair of second- and third-level subentries under the main entry, Division of Parts.

The Index... Command

Once you have defined all your index entries, Word can take over the indexing task. When you issue the Index... command, Word will gather and alphabetize your entries, sniff out any duplicate entries and merge them, throw out any duplicate page references for an entry, compile the index, insert the correct page numbers, and add the index to the end of your document.

Before you issue the Index... command, however, you need to select Preferences... from the Edit menu and make sure that the Show Hidden Text option is deselected. If you skip this step, your document may not be paginated correctly, and you'll end up with inaccurate page number references in the finished index.

After removing the hidden text from your screen, select the Index... command from the Document menu. (This command is available only when the Full Menus setting is in effect.) You will see a dialog box like the one in Figure 13-9.

FIGURE 13-9

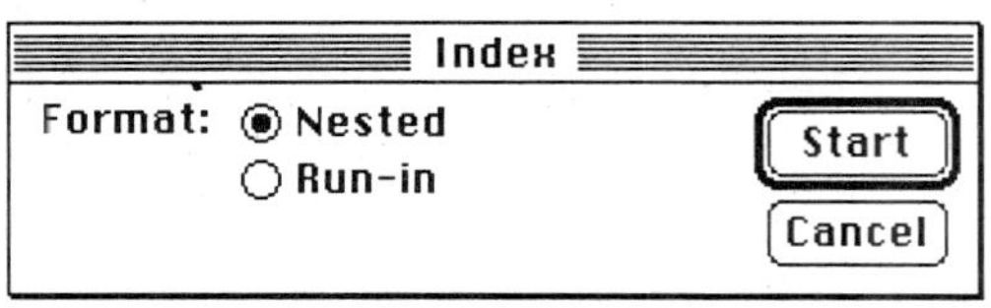

Word presents this dialog box when you issue the Index... command.

If you click the Nested option, Word will indent each of your subentries on a new line under the main entry, as shown in Figure 13-10.

FIGURE 13-10

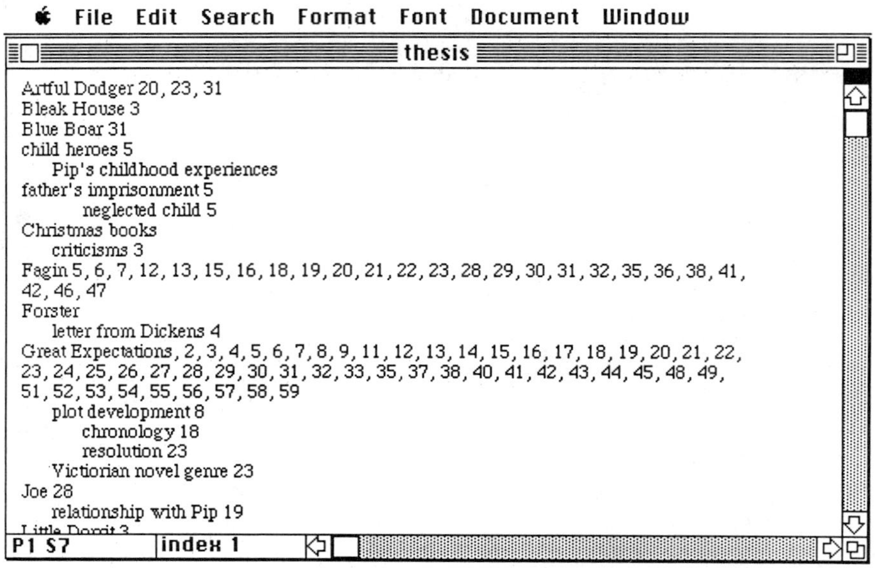

When you use the Nested option, Word will indent each subentry on a new line under the main entry.

If you use the Run-in option, Word will include each subentry in the same paragraph as its main entry. The subentries will be separated from the main entry and from other subentries by a semicolon, as shown in Figure 13-11.

Word will create a new section at the end of your document to hold the finished index. (Thus, you'll be able to format it separately from the rest of your document.) If you have already compiled an index for the document, Word will ask whether you want to replace the existing index. If you click No, Word will add the new index in another new section following the existing index. If you click Yes, Word will replace the old index with the new one.

FIGURE 13-11

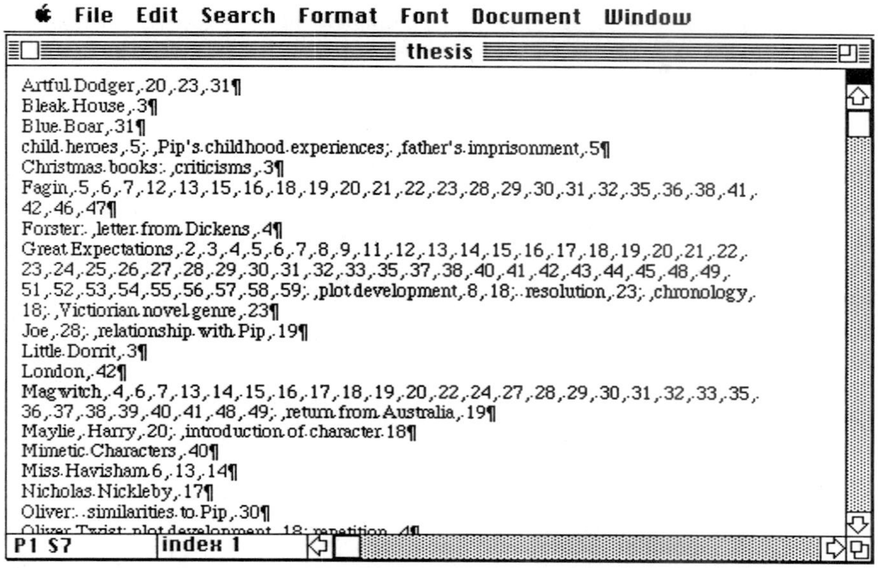

When you use the Run-in option, Word will include your subentries in the same paragraph as the main entry.

Index Arguments

Word offers a number of optional index arguments that let you control the the format of the page numbers in index entries, add notes to your entries, and create multipage references. For example, you can format your page numbers to appear in bold type by adding the character *b* to your index code. Just place the formatting code directly after the character *i* but before the period, like this:

.ib.Division of Parts;

In your finished index, this entry will appear like this:

Division of Parts **1**

Similarly, you can add an *i* to your index code to format page numbers in italics. For example, if you enter

.ii.Division of Parts;

your index entry will look like this in the finished index:

Division of Parts *1*

If you add both the b and i codes to your index entry, Word will format the page number to appear in bold italic type. Thus, the index entry

.iib.Division of Parts;

would result in

Division of Parts ***1***

Sometimes an index entry needs to refer to a range of pages rather than a single page. To let the reader know that a particular topic is discussed on several consecutive pages, add a left parenthesis character to the first index entry code and a right parenthesis to the last index entry code. For example, if you type

.i(.Division of Parts;

on page 5 of your document, then move to page 10 and type

.i).Division of Parts;

Word will create an index entry like this:

Division of Parts 5-10

Rather than using a page number reference in your index, you'll sometimes want to refer the reader to another part of the index for further information. For example, rather than creating a separate set of entries and page numbers for the topic *Delineation of roles*, you might want to enter a note to refer the reader to the main topic *Division of Parts*. To replace the page number with text, type a # symbol after the index entry text, then type your cross-reference text. For example, the entry

.i.Delineation of roles#(see Division of parts);

will appear like this in your finished index:

Delineation of roles (see Division of parts)

If you like, you can add an i or b code to format the cross-reference portion of the entry and help separate it from the main entry text. For example, you might add an italic code like this:

.ii.Delineation of roles#(see Division of parts);

to create the entry

Delineation of roles *(see Division of parts)*

Combining Index and Table of Contents Entries

Often, you'll want the same entry to appear in both your table of contents and your index. If you are creating a first-level index entry, you can string together the index and table of contents codes. For example, suppose you want the heading *Division of Parts* in Figure 13-7 to be included in both your index and table of contents. You can set up the entry like this:

.c..i.Division of Parts;

When you want to include a subentry in an index entry, however, you'll need to type a separate entry for the table of contents and for the index. If you don't, Word will include the subentry text in your table of contents, as well as in your index. For example, rather than using the combined entry

.c..i.Division of Parts:Delineation of roles;

you should enter the table of contents and index entries separately like this:

.c.Division of Parts;
.i.Division of Parts:Delineation of roles;

Remember to assign the Hidden format to your index entry so that it does not appear in your printed document.

Formatting the Index

Initially, the character and paragraph formats of your first-level index entries will match the *Normal* style for your document. Subentries are identical to first-level entries, except that Word indents each subentry $^1/_4$ inch.

Of course, once you've created an index, you can assign it any character and paragraph formats you like. You can also use the Cut and Paste commands to move the index to another part of your document. The easiest way to reformat your index text is to redefine the style definitions that Word has applied to the index. Let's take a look at the relationship between the index and Word's style sheet facility.

Using the style sheet

Like the outliner and table of contents, Word's index facility is designed to work hand-in-hand with style sheets. If you used the Nested option to compile your index, Word will create a style name for each index level in your document. These index styles, which are named *index 1*, *index 2*, and so forth, correspond to the various entry levels that you have created for your index. Each of these styles is based on the *Normal* style. If you choose the Define Styles... command from the Format menu after creating an index, you'll see a dialog box like the one in Figure 13-12.

FIGURE 13-12

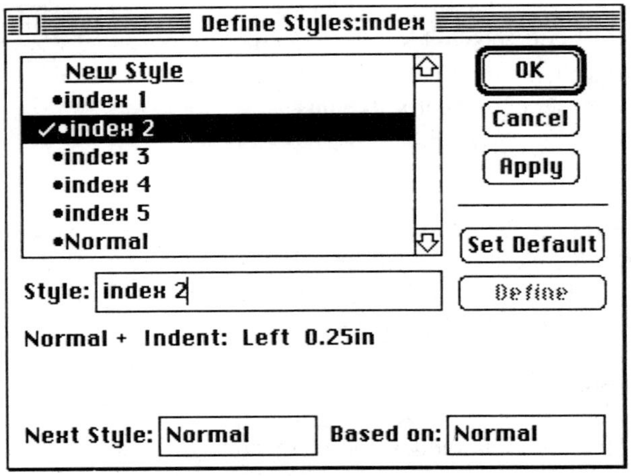

Each level from the index is now a style name on the style sheet.

If you used the Run-in option to include all of your index subentries in the same paragraph as your main entry (as shown in Figure 13-11), Word will create only one index style—*index 1*. Since each main entry appears in the same paragraph as all of its subentries, there is no need to create special formatting instructions for different index levels.

You can modify any of the index styles by changing the style instructions on the style sheet. Just click on one of the index entries that belong to the level that you want to format, then choose Define Styles... from the Format menu. In the Define Styles dialog box, click on the name of the style that you want to modify, then select the character and paragraph formats for that index level. When you click OK or Apply in the Define Styles dialog box, Word will apply the specified formats to all of the index entries in your document that carry that style name. (For a detailed discussion of modifying styles, see Chapter 9.)

For example, in the sample document that we used to create the index shown in Figure 13-10, our *Normal* style, which formats the main body text of the document, specifies 12-point, Times, plain type. As a result, our index also appears in 12-point, Times, plain type. Suppose that you decide that you want the first-level headings in the index to appear in bold type. Just click on one of the first-level index entries in the document and issue the Define Styles... command. In the Define Styles dialog box, click on the style name *index 1*, then choose the Bold option from the Format menu. When you click OK to lock in this change and return to the document window, your index will look like the one in Figure 13-13. Notice that any formatting change you make to an index style affects the entire index entry—both the text portion and the page number reference.

FIGURE 13-13

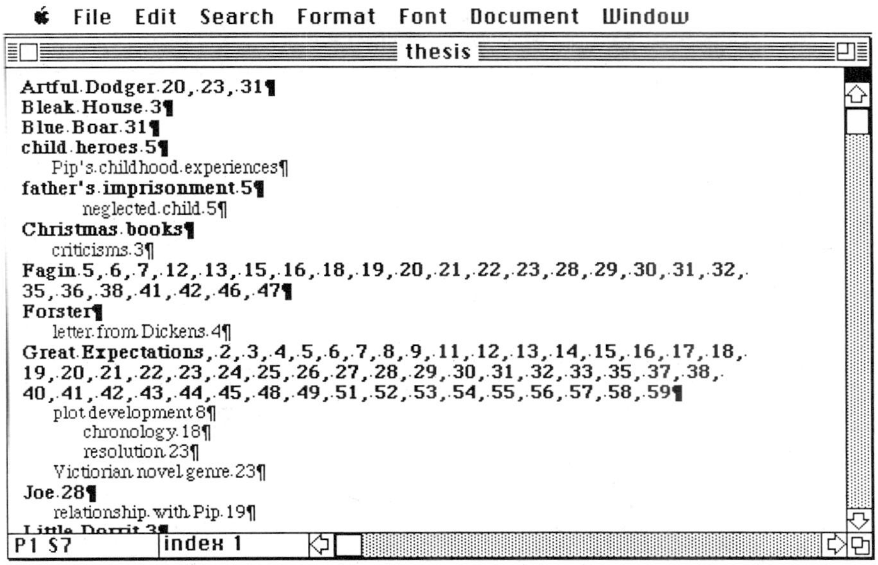

We used the Define Styles... command to format the first-level index entries in this document.

As you're changing the formatting instructions for an index style, you may want to change the Based on style as well. Instead of using *Normal* as the Based on style for each of the *index* styles, you might want to base each *index* style on the next-highest *index* style. Specifically, *index 5* could be based on *index 4*, which could be based on *index 3*, which could be based on *index 2*, which could be based on *index 1*, which would be based on *Normal*. That way, when you make a format change to the *index 1* style, that change will affect not only the first-level index entries, but also all of the subsequent levels of index entries.

ADDING FOOTNOTES

The mere mention of footnotes strikes fear in the heart of anyone who has ever struggled through a term paper. But with Word, footnotes don't have to be frightening. Word's footnoting facility allows you to enter your footnote text as you create your document (while the information is still fresh in your mind and at your fingertips). Word will automatically number and track the sequence of your footnotes for you—even if you modify the document by adding and deleting footnotes. Then, when you are ready to print the document, you can tell Word where to place the footnotes and choose how the footnotes will be separated from the rest of the text on a page.

Creating Footnotes

Let's start by showing how you would create a footnote in the sample document shown in Figure 13-14. The first step is to place your insertion point marker at the spot where you want your footnote reference marker to appear. In this example, we want to add our sample footnote reference at the end of the first paragraph in the main body of the document.

FIGURE 13-14

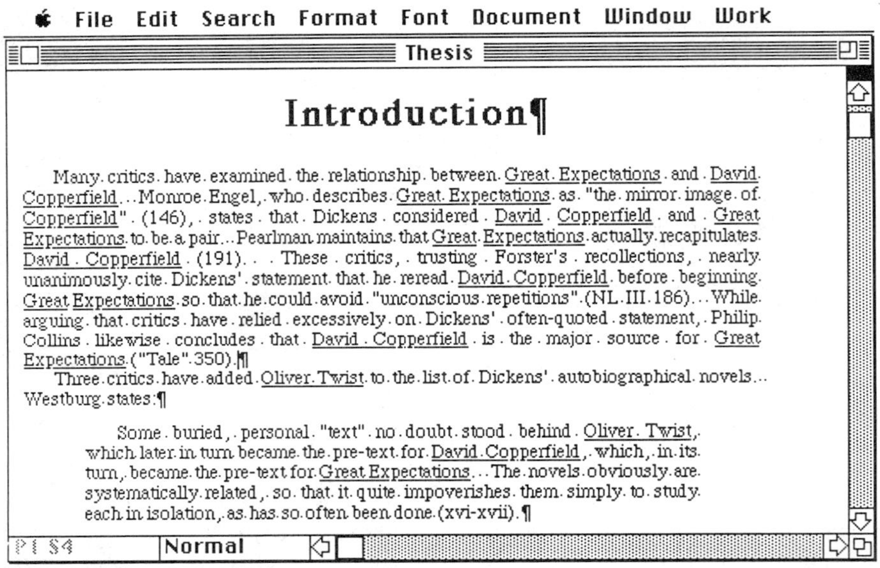

We'll insert a sample footnote reference into this document.

Once you've clicked at the spot where you want to place your footnote reference, choose Footnote... from the Document menu. If you're using the Short Menus setting, you'll see a dialog box like the one in Figure 13-15. If you're using the Full Menus setting, you'll see a dialog box like the one in Figure 13-16. We'll take a look at the Separator, Cont. Separator, and Cont. Notice options in a few moments. First, let's take a look at the reference mark options that appear in both dialog boxes.

FIGURE 13-15

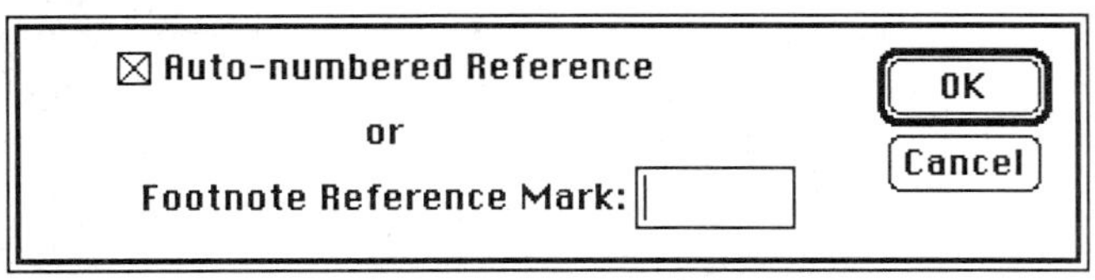

If you use Short Menus, you'll see this dialog box when you issue the Footnote... command.

FIGURE 13-16

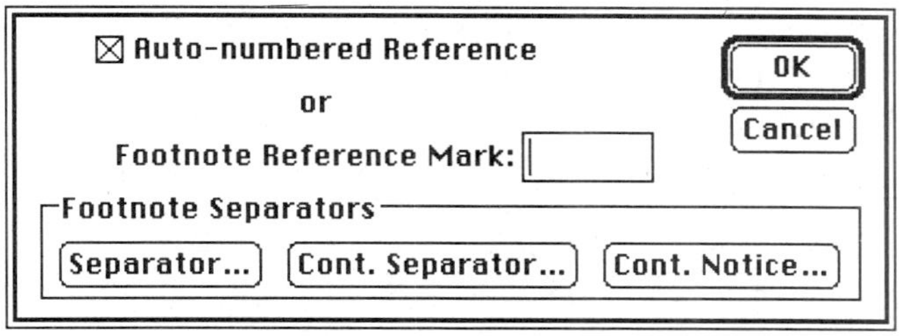

When the Full Menus setting is in effect, you'll see this dialog box when you issue the Footnote... command.

If you want Word to number your footnotes automatically, click the Auto-numbered Reference option in the Footnote dialog box. If you'd rather use your own reference marker, such as an * or † symbol, just type the marker you want to use in the Footnote Reference Mark edit bar. You can enter as many as ten characters. Word will automatically deselect the Auto-numbered Reference option when you type an entry in the Footnote Reference Mark edit bar.

When you click OK, Word will insert the correct footnote number or other reference marker just to the right of the current insertion point in your document. Word also will split your document window into two panes, as shown in Figure 13-17, and display a corresponding reference marker in the bottom window pane.

FIGURE 13-17

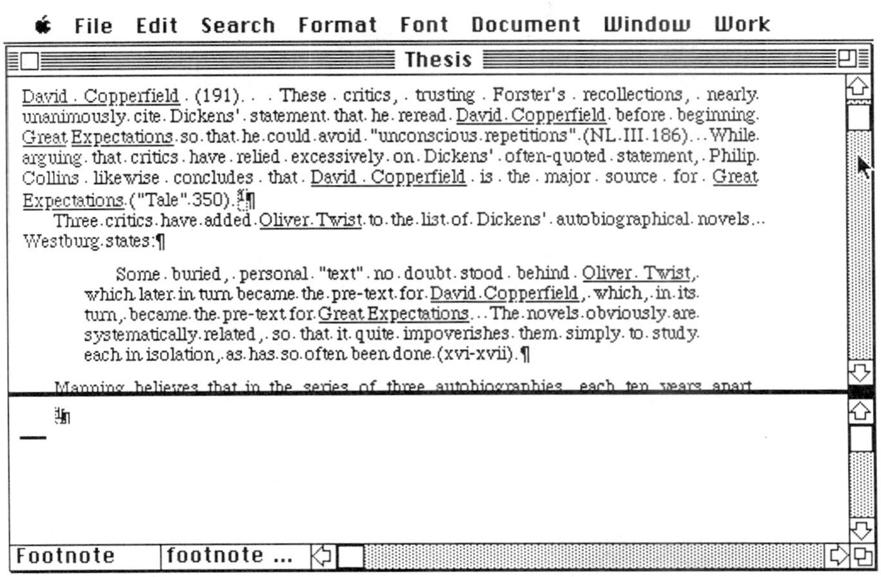

When you click OK in the Footnote dialog box, Word will add a footnote reference marker and split your document window into two panes.

At this point, all you need to do is type your footnote text after the reference marker in the bottom pane. Figure 13-18 shows the text for our sample footnote. There is no limit to the length or number of paragraphs that you can include in a footnote. If your footnote text is too long to view in the bottom portion of the split screen, you can use the vertical scroll bar in the lower pane to bring additional text into view, or you can drag the split bar up to make the bottom pane larger. To drag the split bar, just point to the black rectangle that appears between the two vertical scroll bars on the right side of the window.

FIGURE 13-18

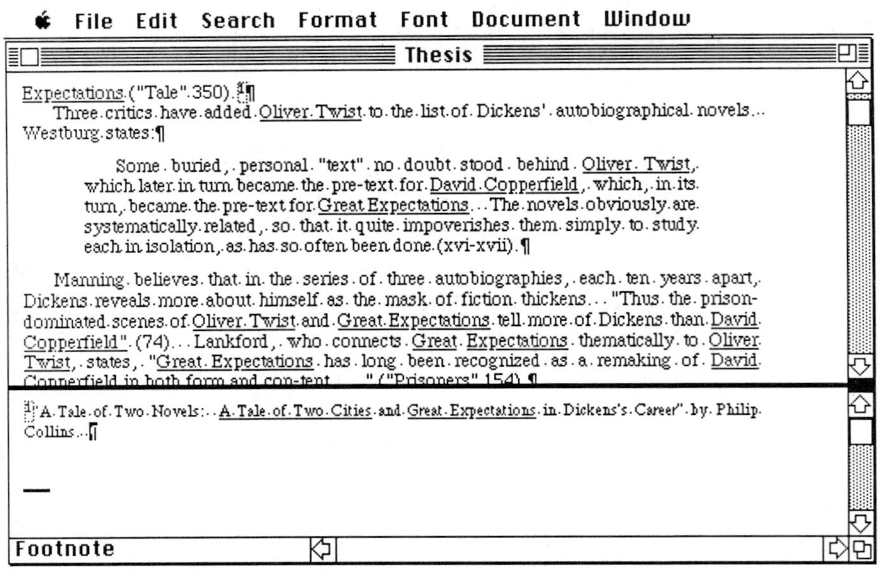

We have entered our footnote text in the bottom window pane.

When you're through entering your footnote text, you can click anywhere in the document window above the split bar to resume working in your document. Word will continue to display the footnote pane at the bottom of the screen.

The document and footnote panes that you see in Figure 13-18 look very similar to the window panes that you create by dragging the split bar in your document window. (We explained this technique in Chapter 2.) However, the footnote pane is actually a separate entity. Though footnotes are saved to disk along with your document, Word does not consider footnotes to be a part of the body of the document.

Why did Microsoft choose to use this split-pane format, rather than creating a new window for your footnotes as it does for headers and footers? Notice the vertical scroll bars that appear in the document and footnote panes. These scroll bars allow you to move through your document and footnote text quickly and easily. As you scroll through the document window, Word will automatically scroll the contents of the footnote window pane, as well, in order to display the footnote text that corresponds to the first footnote reference on your screen. By the same token, when you scroll through your footnote entries in the bottom window pane, Word will scroll the corresponding parts of your document text into view in the upper pane.

To expand your view of the document window, you can drag the split bar down toward the bottom of the screen. To hide the footnotes altogether, you can drag the split bar past the top or bottom of the document window.

When the Full Menus setting is in effect, you can quickly bring your footnote text back into view by pressing the Shift key as you drag down the split bar. (When your document window is not split into panes, the split bar will appear at the top of the vertical scroll bar.) You also can press ⌘-Option-Shift-s to toggle the footnotes into and out of view.

Shortcuts

To add a new footnote reference to your document, you can access the Footnote dialog box quickly, by pressing ⌘-e instead of selecting the Footnote… command from the Document menu. If you are using the Auto-Numbered Reference option (rather than typing your own footnote reference markers), you can bypass the Footnote dialog box altogether by pressing the Return key immediately after you press ⌘-e. Word will automatically insert the appropriate reference number into your document and footnote pane. All you'll need to do is start typing your footnote text.

By the way, after you've finished inserting or editing footnote text in the footnote window, you can return to your previous place in the document window by pressing ⌘-Option-z. If you have a numeric keypad, just press the 0 key to move back to your previous location in the document.

Inserting and Deleting Footnotes

You may have noticed that a dotted border appears around the automatic footnote reference numbers in the sample document shown in Figure 13-18. This border indicates that your footnote references are dynamic—that is, Word will adjust all of your footnote references whenever you insert or delete an automatically-numbered footnote from your document. (By the way, the dotted border is visible only when you've chosen Show ¶ from the Edit menu.)

To delete a footnote, just delete the footnote reference marker in your document window. Word will automatically delete the corresponding footnote text as well. Even better, Word will also renumber all subsequent footnote references for you automatically.

To insert a new footnote between existing footnotes, click at the spot in the document window where you want the footnote reference number to appear, select Footnote... (or press ⌘-e), and then press Return. Word will insert the correct footnote reference number in the document, move the insertion point marker to the correct location in the footnote pane, and open a new paragraph so you can enter the footnote text. Again, all subsequent footnotes will be renumbered automatically, both in your document and in your footnote text.

Editing Footnotes

If you have entered your own footnote reference marker (such as a † symbol), and you decide you want to use a different reference marker, you'll need to edit the marker both in your document and footnote panes. In changing the reference marker in your document, you should not attempt to edit it directly. Otherwise, Word will delete your footnote reference and text. Instead, select the footnote reference marker in your document, issue the Footnote... command and type a new reference marker in the Footnote Reference Mark edit bar. Word will change the entry in your document window but will not automatically change the reference marker in your footnote pane. You'll need to select the reference marker in the footnote pane and overtype it with the new reference marker.

Once you have created a footnote, you can use Word's standard editing techniques to edit the footnote text. For example, you can insert, delete, cut, copy, and paste text just as you would in the document window. You can also use the Find..., Change..., Hyphenate..., and Spelling... commands to edit your footnote text. Word will not automatically check your footnote text when you issue one of these commands from the document window. However, you can check your footnote text separately by clicking in the footnote window pane before issuing the Find..., Change..., Hyphenate..., or Spelling... command. (See Chapter 6 for more information about these editing techniques.)

Copying footnotes

Here's a handy shortcut for repeating a footnote entry in two or more locations in your document. If you select a footnote reference marker in your document, issue the Copy command, and then paste that reference marker in another part of the document, Word will automatically copy the corresponding text for that footnote as well. The copied footnote text will appear in the appropriate location in the footnote window, and—if you copied an automatically numbered reference marker—when you paste, Word will also change that number to reflect its new position in the document. As when you insert any new automatically numbered footnote reference, Word will renumber any subsequent reference markers as well.

Formatting Footnotes

When you insert a footnote into your document, Word automatically adds two new style names to your style sheet: *footnote reference* and *footnote text*. As you can see in Figure 13-19, the *footnote reference* style will format your footnote reference markers to appear in 9-point type, superscripted 3 points. The *footnote text* style will format your footnote text to appear in 10-point plain type. Both styles appear in the font you have specified for your document's *Normal* style.

FIGURE 13-19

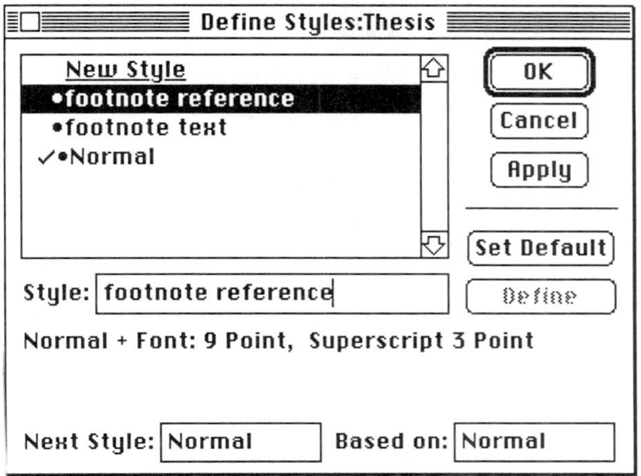

When you create a footnote, Word adds the footnote reference *and* footnote text *styles to the style sheet.*

The easiest way to change the format of your footnote text or reference markers is to change the style definition of *footnote reference* or *footnote text* in the Define Styles... dialog box. When you do this, Word will apply the new formatting instructions to all of the footnote text or reference markers in your document. (For a discussion of modifying named styles, see Chapter 9.)

By the way, Word will not allow you to select a reference marker in your document. For that reason, you won't be able to change the formatting of one or more reference markers manually.

Changing Footnote Separators

When you print your document, Word will automatically print your footnotes as well. As you can see in Figure 13-20, Word uses a short horizontal line between your document text and footnote text to separate the two elements on the printed page. When a footnote is too long to fit on one page, Word will automatically place part of the text on the following page. To indicate that the footnote text on the next page is a continuation, Word uses a horizontal rule that extends from margin to margin.

FIGURE 13-20

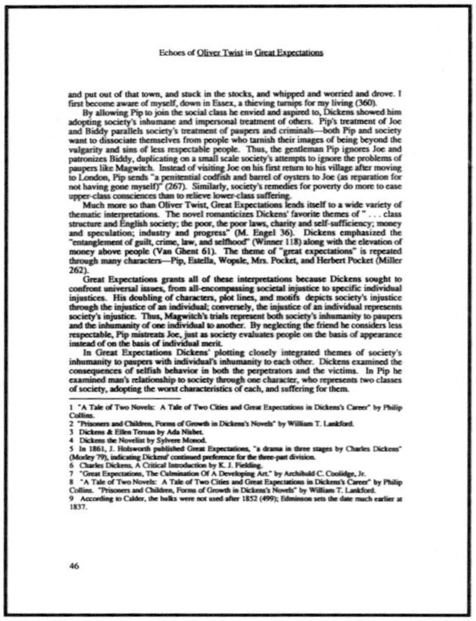

Echoes of Oliver Twist in Great Expectations

and put out of that town, and stuck in the stocks, and whipped and worried and drove. I first become aware of myself, down in Essex, a thieving turnips for my living (360).

By allowing Pip to join the social class he envied and aspired to, Dickens showed him adopting society's inhumane and impersonal treatment of others. Pip's treatment of Joe and Biddy parallels society's treatment of paupers and criminals—both Pip and society want to dissociate themselves from people who tarnish their images of being beyond the vulgarity and sins of less respectable people. Thus, the gentleman Pip ignores Joe and patronizes Biddy, duplicating on a small scale society's attempts to ignore the problems of paupers like Magwitch. Instead of visiting Joe on his first return to his village after moving to London, Pip sends "a penitential codfish and barrel of oysters to Joe (as reparation for not having gone myself)" (267). Similarly, society's remedies for poverty do more to ease upper-class consciences than to relieve lower-class suffering.

Much more so than Oliver Twist, Great Expectations lends itself to a wide variety of thematic interpretations. The novel romanticizes Dickens' favorite themes of " . . . class structure and English society; the poor, the poor laws, charity and self-sufficiency; money and speculation; industry and progress" (M. Engel 36). Dickens emphasized the "entanglement of guilt, crime, law, and selfhood" (Winner 118) along with the elevation of money above people (Van Ghent 61). The theme of "great expectations" is repeated through many characters—Pip, Estella, Wopsle, Mrs. Pocket, and Herbert Pocket (Miller 262).

Great Expectations grants all of these interpretations because Dickens sought to confront universal issues, from all-encompassing societal injustice to specific individual injustices. His doubling of characters, plot lines, and motifs depicts society's injustice through the injustice of an individual; conversely, the injustice of an individual represents society's injustice. Thus, Magwitch's trials represent both society's inhumanity to paupers and the inhumanity of one individual to another. By neglecting the friend he considers less respectable, Pip mistreats Joe, just as society evaluates people on the basis of appearance instead of on the basis of individual merit.

In Great Expectations Dickens' plotting closely integrated themes of society's inhumanity to paupers with individual's inhumanity to each other. Dickens examined the consequences of selfish behavior in both the perpetrators and the victims. In Pip he examined man's relationship to society through one character, who represents two classes of society, adopting the worst characteristics of each, and suffering for them.

1 "A Tale of Two Novels: A Tale of Two Cities and Great Expectations in Dickens's Career" by Philip Collins.
2 "Prisoners and Children, Forms of Growth in Dickens's Novels" by William T. Lankford.
3 Dickens & Ellen Ternan by Ada Nisbet.
4 Dickens the Novelist by Sylvere Monod.
5 In 1861, J. Holsworth published Great Expectations, "a drama in three stages by Charles Dickens" (Morley 79), indicating Dickens' continued preference for the three-part division.
6 Charles Dickens, A Critical Introduction by K. J. Fielding.
7 "Great Expectations, The Culmination Of A Developing Art." by Archibald C. Coolidge, Jr.
8 "A Tale of Two Novels: A Tale of Two Cities and Great Expectations in Dickens's Career" by Philip Collins. "Prisoners and Children, Forms of Growth in Dickens's Novels" by William T. Lankford.
9 According to Calder, the hulks were not used after 1852 (499); Edminson sets the date much earlier at 1837.

46

10 "'The Parish Boy's Progress': The Evolving Form of Oliver Twist" by William Lankford.
11 Adrain, Arthur A. Dickens and the Parent-Child Relationship. Athens, Ohio: Ohio University Press, 1984.
12 Axton, William F. Circle of Fire, Dickens' Vision & Style & the Popular Victorian Theater. Lexington: University of Kentucky Press, 1966.
13 "Great Expectations Yet Again." Dickens Studies Annual 2 (1971): 278-93.
14 "'Keystone' Structure in Dickens' Serial Novels." University of Toronto Quarterly 37 (1967): 31-50.
15 Bailey, Paul. "Reflections on Great Expectations. Listener 104 (1980): 330-31.
16 Barfoot, C. C. "Great Expectations: The Perception of Fate." Dutch Quarterly Review of Anglo-American Letters 6 (1976): 2-33.
17 Barnes, John. A Critical Commentary on Dickens's Great Expectations. London: Macmillan, 1966.
18 Booth, Wayne C. The Rhetoric of Fiction. 2nd ed. Chicago: The University of Chicago Press, 1983.
19 Briggs, Asa. The Making of Modern England 1783-1867, The Age of Improvement. 1959. New York: Harper Torchbooks, 1965.

Word uses a short horizontal line to separate your footnotes from your body text and a margin-to-margin line to indicate that a footnote continues from one page to the next.

If you like, you can create your own separators by using the Separator and Cont. Separator options in the Footnote dialog box. (Remember, these options are available only when you have selected the Full Menus setting.) To access these options, choose Footnote… from the Document menu. Then, rather than clicking OK to start a new footnote entry, click the Separator button. Word will close the Footnote dialog box and present a new window, like the one shown in Figure 13-21.

FIGURE 13-21

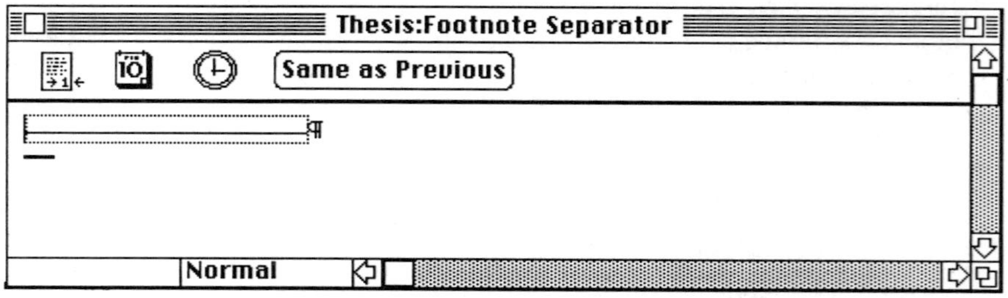

Use this Separator window to customize the separator line that divides your footnotes from your body text.

Notice that Word displays a horizontal line about 1 $^1/_2$ inches long in the Footnote Separator window. Though you cannot change the size or format of this line, you can add characters to the Separator window, or you can delete the line altogether and insert your own separator characters. (We'll show an example of this in a moment.) You also can use the icons at the top of the Separator window to add a dynamic date, time, and/or page number to your separator.

When you click Cont. Separator... in the Footnote dialog box, Word will display the window shown in Figure 13-22. As you can see, this window contains the margin-to-margin line that Word uses as the default separator between document and footnote text when a footnote continues from one page to another. (This window is identical to the Footnote Separator window except for the length of the separator line.) Again, you can insert additional characters or overwrite the separator line if you like.

FIGURE 13-22

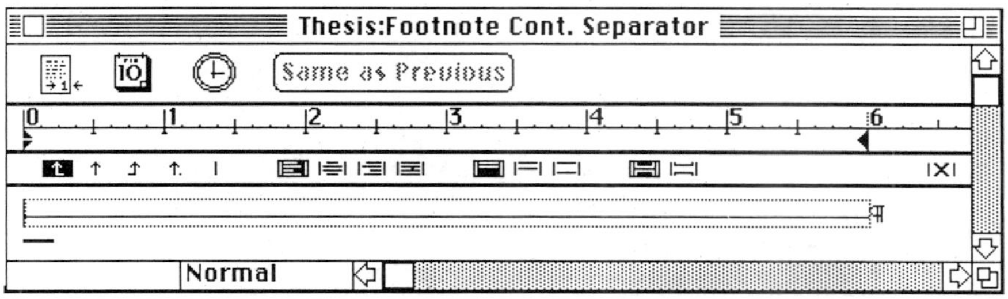

You can enter your own separator characters in the Cont. Separator window.

In addition to customizing your separators, Word allows you to place a notice at the end of your footnotes on one page to let the reader know that the footnote text continues on the next page. To do this, click Cont. Notice... in the Footnote dialog box. You will then see a blank Cont. Notice window like the one in Figure 13-23. In this window, you can enter a phrase like *(continued on next page)*. Of course, Word will print the contents of the Cont. Notice window only when a footnote entry flows from one page to the next.

FIGURE 13-23

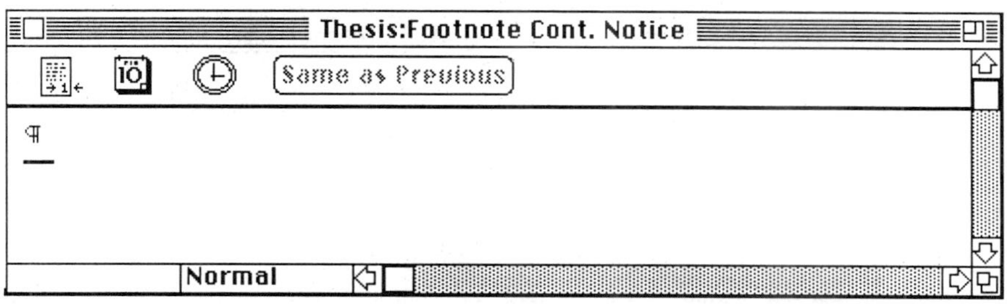

You can use this window to notify the reader that a footnote continues on the next page.

To illustrate how you might use the Separator, Cont. Separator, and Cont. Notice windows, let's customize the footnote separators and create a continuation notice for the sample pages in Figure 13-20. First, make sure that the Full Menus setting is in effect. Then, select the Footnote... command from the Document menu. Next, click on the Separator... button to access the window shown in Figure 13-21. Now, let's suppose you'd like to replace the default line separator with the word *Footnotes*. You want this word to appear in 12-point, Helvetica, underlined type, and you want to center the separator between your document margins.

Just double-click on the existing separator line to select it, then type the word *Footnotes*. (Word will overwrite the line when you begin typing.) Next, double-click on the word you just typed, issue the Character... command, and choose the Helvetica font and 12 Point size, then click the Underline and Bold options. Finally, choose Show Ruler from the Format menu and click on the centered alignment icon. (You also may want to click the open space icon to create some extra white space between the last line of body text and your footnote separator.) Figure 13-24 shows the Separator window at this point.

FIGURE 13-24

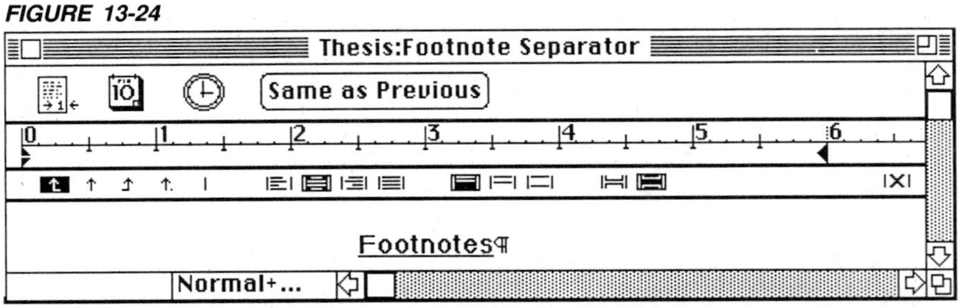

We replaced Word's default line separator with the word Footnotes.

Now, to format the continuation separator, follow the same steps described above, except type the text *Footnotes (Continued)* in the Cont. Separator window. Also, be sure to format the word *(Continued)* in italics. Figure 13-25 shows this window after we typed the new text.

FIGURE 13-25

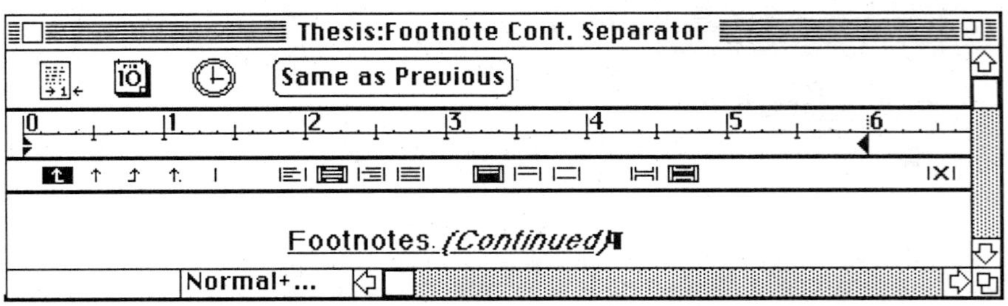

We modified our continuation separator to display the words Footnotes (Continued).

Finally, to create a continuation notice, open the Cont. Notice window and enter a message like *(continued on next page).* Format your continuation notice to appear in 10-point, Helvetica, plain text, as shown in Figure 13-26.

FIGURE 13-26

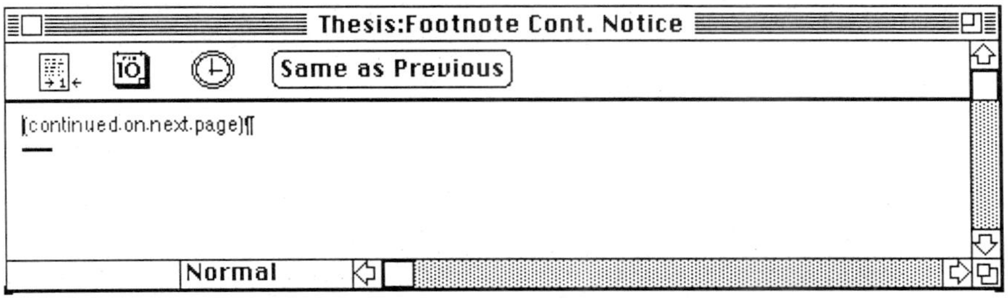

We've added a message to the Cont. Notice window.

Now, when you print your document, Word will use your new separators and print the continuation notice where necessary, as shown in Figure 13-27.

FIGURE 13-27

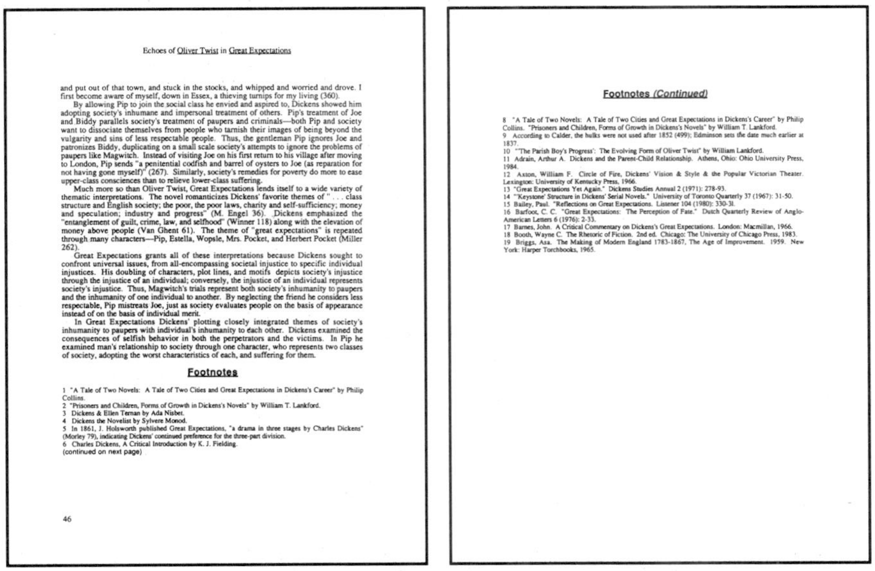

Echoes of Oliver Twist in Great Expectations

and put out of that town, and stuck in the stocks, and whipped and worried and drove. I first become aware of myself, down in Essex, a thieving turnips for my living (360).

By allowing Pip to join the social class he envied and aspired to, Dickens showed him adopting society's inhumane and impersonal treatment of others. Pip's treatment of Joe and Biddy parallels society's treatment of paupers and criminals—both Pip and society want to dissociate themselves from people who tarnish their images of being beyond the vulgarity and sins of less respectable people. Thus, the gentleman Pip ignores Joe and patronizes Biddy, duplicating on a small scale society's attempts to ignore the problems of paupers like Magwitch. Instead of visiting Joe on his first return to his village after moving to London, Pip sends "a penitential codfish and barrel of oysters to Joe (as reparation for not having gone myself)" (267). Similarly, society's remedies for poverty do more to ease upper-class consciences than to relieve lower-class suffering.

Much more so than Oliver Twist, Great Expectations lends itself to a wide variety of thematic interpretations. The novel romanticizes Dickens' favorite themes of " . . . class structure and English society; the poor, the poor laws, charity and self-sufficiency; money and speculation; industry and progress" (M. Engel 36). Dickens emphasized the "entanglement of guilt, crime, law, and selfhood" (Winner 118) along with the elevation of money above people (Van Ghent 61). The theme of "great expectations" is repeated through many characters—Pip, Estella, Wopsle, Mrs. Pocket, and Herbert Pocket (Miller 262).

Great Expectations grants all of these interpretations because Dickens sought to confront universal issues, from all-encompassing societal injustice to specific individual injustices. His doubling of characters, plot lines, and motifs depicts society's injustice through the injustice of an individual; conversely, the injustice of an individual represents society's injustice. Thus, Magwitch's trials represent both society's inhumanity to paupers and the inhumanity of one individual to another. By neglecting the friend he considers less respectable, Pip mistreats Joe, just as society evaluates people on the basis of appearance instead of on the basis of individual merit.

In Great Expectations Dickens' plotting closely integrated themes of society's inhumanity to paupers with individual's inhumanity to each other. Dickens examined the consequences of selfish behavior in both the perpetrators and the victims. In Pip he examined man's relationship to society through one character, who represents two classes of society, adopting the worst characteristics of each, and suffering for them.

Footnotes

1 "A Tale of Two Novels: A Tale of Two Cities and Great Expectations in Dickens's Career" by Philip Collins.
2 "Prisoners and Children, Forms of Growth in Dickens's Novels" by William T. Lankford.
3 Dickens & Ellen Ternan by Ada Nisbet.
4 Dickens the Novelist by Sylvere Monod.
5 In 1861, J. Holsworth published Great Expectations, "a drama in three stages by Charles Dickens" (Morley 79), indicating Dickens' continued preference for the three-part division.
6 Charles Dickens, A Critical Introduction by K. J. Fielding.
(continued on next page)

46

Footnotes *(Continued)*

8 "A Tale of Two Novels: A Tale of Two Cities and Great Expectations in Dickens's Career" by Philip Collins. "Prisoners and Children, Forms of Growth in Dickens's Novels" by William T. Lankford.
9 According to Calder, the hulks were not used after 1852 (499); Edminson sets the date much earlier at 1837.
10 "'The Parish Boy's Progress': The Evolving Form of Oliver Twist" by William Lankford.
11 Adrain, Arthur A. Dickens and the Parent-Child Relationship. Athens, Ohio: Ohio University Press, 1984.
12 Axton, William F. Circle of Fire, Dickens' Vision & Style & the Popular Victorian Theater. Lexington: University of Kentucky Press, 1966.
13 "Great Expectations Yet Again." Dickens Studies Annual 2 (1971): 278-93.
14 "'Keystone' Structure in Dickens' Serial Novels." University of Toronto Quarterly 37 (1967): 31-50.
15 Bailey, Paul. "Reflections on Great Expectations. Listener 104 (1980): 330-31.
16 Barfoot, C. C. "Great Expectations: The Perception of Fate." Dutch Quarterly Review of Anglo-American Letters 6 (1976): 2-33.
17 Barnes, John. A Critical Commentary on Dickens's Great Expectations. London: Macmillan, 1966.
18 Booth, Wayne C. The Rhetoric of Fiction. 2nd ed. Chicago: The University of Chicago Press, 1983.
19 Briggs, Asa. The Making of Modern England 1783-1867, The Age of Improvement. 1959. New York: Harper Torchbooks, 1965.

These printed pages show our customized separators and continuation notice.

The Same as Previous button

Oddly enough, Word will not allow you to create different separators and continuation notices for different pages in your document. In fact, you cannot even change the separators or continuation notice from one section to another. Any changes you make in these windows will affect your entire document. That being the case, you may wonder what purpose the Same as Previous button serves in these three windows.

The Same as Previous button that appears in the Separator, Cont. Separator, and Cont. Notice windows does not serve the same purpose as the Same as Previous button that you saw in the header and footer windows in Chapter 7. When you're working with footnotes, the Same as Previous button is used to return the contents of the current window to the default. For example, if you were to click this button in the window shown in Figure 13-24, Word would remove the *Footnotes* notice and replace it with its default line separator.

Positioning and Numbering Footnotes

Word gives you a number of choices for positioning your footnotes: You can print each footnote on the same page where its footnote reference marker appears; you can group your footnotes at the end of a document section; or you can print all of your footnotes at the end of your document. If you want each footnote to appear on the same page as its reference marker, you can tell Word to place the footnotes either at the bottom of the page or directly beneath the last paragraph on the page. (In some cases, the last paragraph on a page may occur in the middle of the page or somewhere other than the bottom of the page.) You also can control whether your footnotes will be numbered consecutively throughout a document or separately on each page or in each section.

You control the positioning of your footnotes through both the Page Setup and Section dialog boxes. The Page Setup dialog box offers three options for positioning footnotes: Bottom of Page, Beneath Text, and Endnotes. This dialog box also includes a check-box option, Restart Numbering, that determines whether your footnotes will be numbered consecutively throughout a document, or numbered separately on each page or in each section. Finally, the Page Setup dialog box also includes a Start Footnote Numbers at edit bar, which allows you to begin your footnote numbers at something other than Word's default of 1. We'll talk about this edit bar in the last section of this chapter, "Working with Long Documents."

If you click the Bottom of Page option in the Page Setup dialog box, each footnote will appear at the bottom of the page on which its reference marker occurs, as shown in Figure 13-28. If you click Beneath Text, your footnotes will appear on the same page as their reference markers, but Word will print them directly under the last paragraph on the page, as shown in Figure 13-29 on page 506.

When you choose the Bottom of Page or Beneath Text option, you can number your footnotes separately on each page, or you can number them continuously throughout the document. If the Restart Numbering option is activated in the Page Setup dialog box, Word will use a different set of footnote numbers on each page. If you deselect this option, Word will number your footnotes continuously from page to page.

FIGURE 13-28

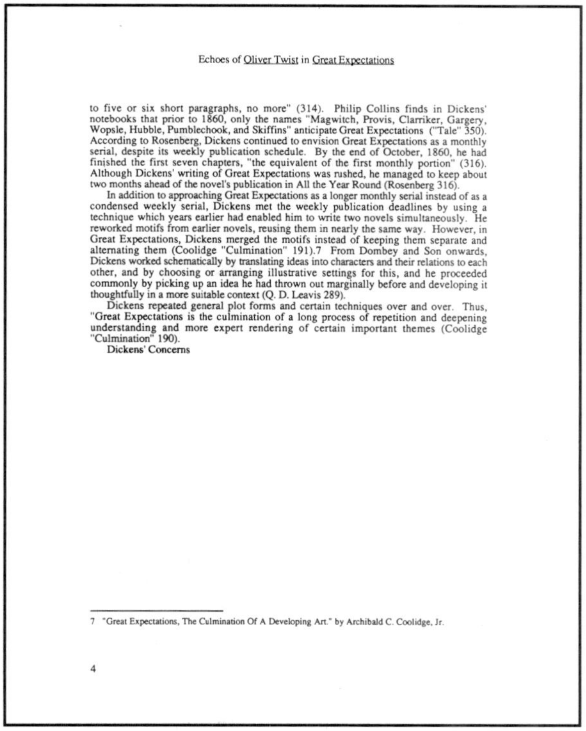

Echoes of Oliver Twist in Great Expectations

to five or six short paragraphs, no more" (314). Philip Collins finds in Dickens' notebooks that prior to 1860, only the names "Magwitch, Provis, Clarriker, Gargery, Wopsle, Hubble, Pumblechook, and Skiffins" anticipate Great Expectations ("Tale" 350). According to Rosenberg, Dickens continued to envision Great Expectations as a monthly serial, despite its weekly publication schedule. By the end of October, 1860, he had finished the first seven chapters, "the equivalent of the first monthly portion" (316). Although Dickens' writing of Great Expectations was rushed, he managed to keep about two months ahead of the novel's publication in All the Year Round (Rosenberg 316).

In addition to approaching Great Expectations as a longer monthly serial instead of as a condensed weekly serial, Dickens met the weekly publication deadlines by using a technique which years earlier had enabled him to write two novels simultaneously. He reworked motifs from earlier novels, reusing them in nearly the same way. However, in Great Expectations, Dickens merged the motifs instead of keeping them separate and alternating them (Coolidge "Culmination" 191).7 From Dombey and Son onwards, Dickens worked schematically by translating ideas into characters and their relations to each other, and by choosing or arranging illustrative settings for this, and he proceeded commonly by picking up an idea he had thrown out marginally before and developing it thoughtfully in a more suitable context (Q. D. Leavis 289).

Dickens repeated general plot forms and certain techniques over and over. Thus, "Great Expectations is the culmination of a long process of repetition and deepening understanding and more expert rendering of certain important themes (Coolidge "Culmination" 190).

Dickens' Concerns

7 "Great Expectations, The Culmination Of A Developing Art." by Archibald C. Coolidge, Jr.

4

If you use the Bottom of Page option, the footnote text will appear at the bottom of the page on which its reference marker appears.

To group your footnotes at the end of each section in a document, select the Endnotes option in the Page Setup dialog box. Of course, if your document contains only one section, this option will place your footnotes at the end of the document. If your document contains more than one section, you must be sure that the Include Endnotes option is selected in the Section dialog box for each section. (Word's default for Include Endnotes is active.) This tells Word to include the footnotes for that section at the end of the section. If you do not select Include Endnotes for one or more sections, Word will place the footnotes for those sections at the end of the next section for which the Include Endnotes option is active (or at the end of your document, if you've deselected Include Endnotes in the remainder of your sections.) This can be helpful in situations where you've created separate sections for formatting purposes only.

When you group your footnotes at the end of each section, you can choose to number your footnotes sequentially throughout the entire document, or you can number the footnotes separately in each section. Again, the Restart Numbering option in the Page Setup dialog box determines whether you will have continuous footnote numbering. If you activate this option, Word will number the footnotes in each section separately. When this option is deselected,

FIGURE 13-29

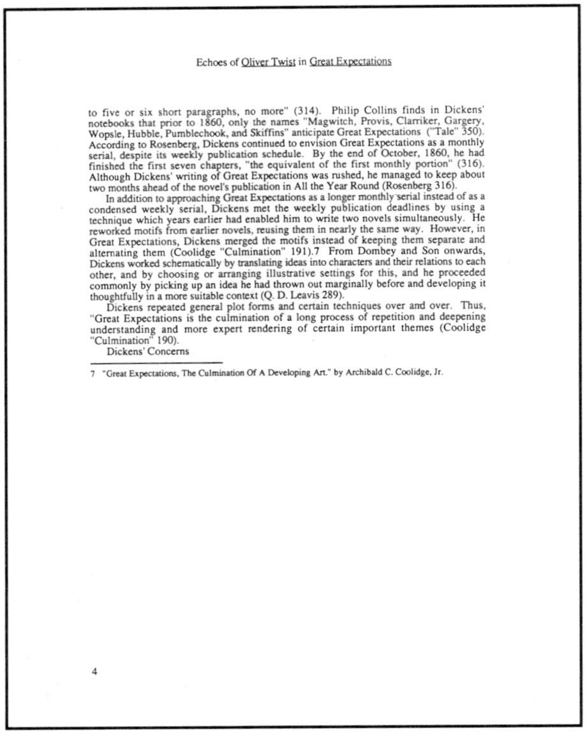

Echoes of Oliver Twist in Great Expectations

to five or six short paragraphs, no more" (314). Philip Collins finds in Dickens' notebooks that prior to 1860, only the names "Magwitch, Provis, Clarriker, Gargery, Wopsle, Hubble, Pumblechook, and Skiffins" anticipate Great Expectations ("Tale" 350). According to Rosenberg, Dickens continued to envision Great Expectations as a monthly serial, despite its weekly publication schedule. By the end of October, 1860, he had finished the first seven chapters, "the equivalent of the first monthly portion" (316). Although Dickens' writing of Great Expectations was rushed, he managed to keep about two months ahead of the novel's publication in All the Year Round (Rosenberg 316).

In addition to approaching Great Expectations as a longer monthly serial instead of as a condensed weekly serial, Dickens met the weekly publication deadlines by using a technique which years earlier had enabled him to write two novels simultaneously. He reworked motifs from earlier novels, reusing them in nearly the same way. However, in Great Expectations, Dickens merged the motifs instead of keeping them separate and alternating them (Coolidge "Culmination" 191).7 From Dombey and Son onwards, Dickens worked schematically by translating ideas into characters and their relations to each other, and by choosing or arranging illustrative settings for this, and he proceeded commonly by picking up an idea he had thrown out marginally before and developing it thoughtfully in a more suitable context (Q. D. Leavis 289).

Dickens repeated general plot forms and certain techniques over and over. Thus, "Great Expectations is the culmination of a long process of repetition and deepening understanding and more expert rendering of certain important themes (Coolidge "Culmination" 190).

Dickens' Concerns

7 "Great Expectations, The Culmination Of A Developing Art." by Archibald C. Coolidge, Jr.

4

If you use the Beneath Text option, the footnote text will appear directly under the last paragraph on the page.

Word will number all of the footnotes in the document sequentially. By the way, when you choose the Endnotes option in the Page Setup dialog box, Word will always print your footnotes immediately after the last paragraph in a section. Word will not place the footnotes at the bottom of the last page or on a separate page.

If you would like to place all of your footnotes at the end of a document that contains multiple sections, then you must perform the following steps. First, select the Endnotes option in the Page Setup dialog box. Then, click on each section, open the Section dialog box, and make sure that the Include Endnotes option is deselected. (Of course, you can select some text in several sections—or your entire document—then open the Section dialog box and deselect Include Endnotes.) Word will "save up" your footnotes until it reaches a section in which you have selected the Include Endnotes setting or until it reaches the end of your document. Word will then print the footnotes just below the last paragraph in the document. When your footnotes appear at the end of a document, Word will always number them sequentially from the beginning of the document, even if you've clicked the Restart Numbering option in the Page Setup dialog box.

WORKING WITH LONG DOCUMENTS

As we explained in Chapter 8, it is possible to use the Next File option in the Page Setup dialog box to link two or more document files for printing. When you use this technique to consolidate several smaller documents into one long document, Word can also consolidate your table of contents, index, and footnote entries.

To create a master table of contents or master index, you follow a few simple steps. First, make sure that you've entered the correct file name in the Next File edit bar for each document that you want to link. Also, be sure that you've entered the correct page number in the Start Page Numbers at edit bar of the Page Setup dialog box for each document. (If you don't number the pages of your linked documents sequentially, the page references in your index and table of contents will be incorrect.) Now, just open the first document in the series and issue the Table of Contents... or Index... command. Word will repaginate your current document, then repaginate each of the linked documents on disk. Then, if you're creating a table of contents, Word will place that table of contents in a new section at the beginning of your current document. If you're compiling an index, Word will open the last document in your series of linked documents and place the index in a separate section at the end of that document. That's all there is to it!

Numbering Footnotes in Long Documents

If you want Word to group all of your footnotes at the end of the last document in a linked series, you'll need to select the Endnotes option in the Page Setup dialog box for each document to indicate that you want to group your footnotes, rather than placing them at the bottom of each page. Then you must issue the Section... command and deselect the Include Endnotes option for each section of every document—except for the last section in the last document.

You'll also need to give Word a starting footnote reference number for each document in the series, except the first. To determine the correct starting footnote number for each document, begin by opening the first document in the series and scrolling to the bottom of your footnotes list in order to determine the last footnote reference number for that document. Then, open the next document in the series, issue the Page Setup... command and type the starting reference number for that document in the Start Footnote Numbers at edit bar. Word will immediately renumber all of the footnotes in that document. Now, take a look at the last footnote in this document to determine the starting footnote reference number for the next document. Follow these steps for each of the remaining linked documents. When you print the linked documents, your footnotes will be numbered sequentially, and Word will print all of the footnotes at the end of the linked series.

MERGING DOCUMENTS 14

If you're like most people, a great deal of the business writing that you perform each day is dull and repetitive—sending out billing notices to your clients or churning out dozens of "personal" invitations to the grand opening of your company's new production facility, for example. If you find yourself stuck with these jobs very often, you'll be thrilled to know that Word's merge facility can take the time and tedium out of these repetitive tasks.

The merge facility is a powerful feature that lets you combine data from two or more files to create any number of customized documents. You provide the standardized text in one document and the variable information in another document. When you issue the Print Merge... command, Word will print multiple versions of the standard text document, automatically customizing each version with a name, address, account balance—or other information—from a second document.

For example, in your grand opening invitations, you might enter the text of your letter in one document and the names and addresses of each invited guest in another. When you merge the two files, Word will create a personal letter of invitation for each guest. Similarly, when you send out billing notices, you might store the text of the notice in one document and the names, addresses, and amounts due for each of your clients in another document. Then you can merge the information in these two files to create all of your billing statements with just a few keystrokes.

You commonly hear Word's merge facility referred to as a form letter facility since it is used so often to customize business letters. However, there are dozens of equally useful applications for the merge facility, such as mailing labels and management reports, to mention only a couple. For that reason, we prefer the term *merge facility* rather than *form letter facility*.

USING THE MERGE FACILITY

As we hinted in our introduction, you'll need to create at least two files in order to generate a series of merge documents: a main document and a data document. The main document contains your standard text, which will remain constant for each of your merge documents. The data document contains the text that you want to vary from one merge document to the next. Word combines the information from the data document and the main document to create a series of customized merge documents.

Although only two documents are required to use the merge facility, you can also set up a whole series of subdocuments and have Word combine the text from those documents into your merge documents as well. We'll show you how to do this in a few pages.

Why Bother?

If you've ever dealt with a cantankerous word processor that made your form letters look like glued-together bomb threats from an illiterate terrorist, you may be dubious about using the merge facility. For example, how many times have you received a computer-generated letter in which half of your name was truncated on the mailing label? Or you may have found your name floating in the middle of a moth-eaten line of text because it didn't fill the allotted space. Thus, Catherine Hammerschmidt is rechristened Catherine Hammers (or, even worse, Catheri Hammersc) and Ann Lee gets lost in the middle of a sentence like

```
Just for you, Ann Lee        , we've reserved a...
```

Well, you can set these doubts to rest. Word has gone a step beyond most other programs to let you develop truly professional merge documents. Because the merge facility includes a number of sophisticated capabilities for extracting and formatting variable information, your form letters don't have to *look* like form letters. Word automatically adjusts the text in every merge document to accommodate variable-length entries. You can even choose to exclude blocks of text from selected merge documents without leaving gaping holes in your printed document.

There are a number of other advantages to using Word's merge facility to create variable documents. The most obvious advantage is that you can compile and print all of your merge documents with a single command—no more typing different names and addresses for each version of a form letter. This not only saves time but also helps you to avoid typographical errors and inconsistencies. You will save even more time—and disk space—by letting Word fill in the blanks for you as it prints, rather than creating and saving each version of your document to disk.

Though your main document and data document may take a little time and planning to develop, once you set them up, you can use those files again and again. In addition, Word lets you mix and match information any way you like. That is, you can use the same data document to "feed" any number of main documents, and you can draw information from any number of data documents into a main document by directing Word to the files that you want to use.

SETTING UP THE DATA DOCUMENT

Before we can put the merge facility through its paces, we need to create a pair of main and data documents. Let's begin by setting up our data document, then we'll set up our main document and show you how to merge the information from the data document into the main document text.

If you've ever worked with a computerized data base program, you should have no trouble mastering data documents in Word. A data document is nothing more than a specially structured collection of entries that are stored in a standard Word file. This file can contain any kind of information—from inventory numbers and prices to names, addresses, and telephone numbers.

Every data document consists of three elements: records, fields, and field headers. Each paragraph in a data document is a record, and each column is a field. When you merge the data and main documents, each record provides the variable data needed to create one new merge document. The field header paragraph, which appears at the top of the data document, identifies the information that is stored in each field. As you'll see in a moment, these field headers are the key link between your data document and your main document.

Figure 14-1 shows the sample data document that we'll be using to create our merge documents throughout this chapter. The first line in this document contains our field headers: LastName, FirstName, Address1, Address2, City, ST, ZIP, and Sign. Each line of text after this first one is a separate record, containing information on one individual.

FIGURE 14-1

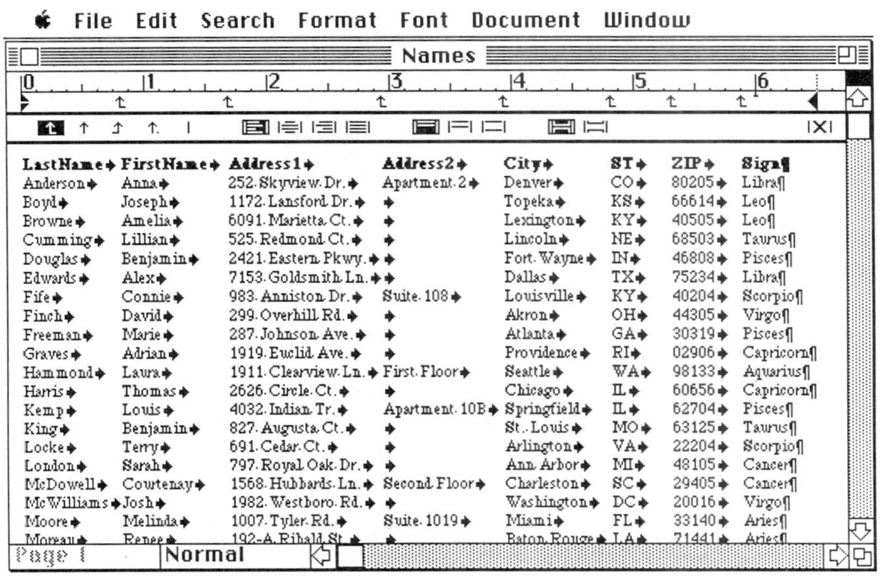

LastName	FirstName	Address1	Address2	City	ST	ZIP	Sign
Anderson	Anna	252 Skyview Dr.	Apartment 2	Denver	CO	80205	Libra
Boyd	Joseph	1172 Lansford Dr.		Topeka	KS	66614	Leo
Browne	Amelia	6091 Marietta Ct.		Lexington	KY	40505	Leo
Cumming	Lillian	525 Redmond Ct.		Lincoln	NE	68503	Taurus
Douglas	Benjamin	2421 Eastern Pkwy.		Fort Wayne	IN	46808	Pisces
Edwards	Alex	7153 Goldsmith Ln.		Dallas	TX	75234	Libra
Fife	Connie	983 Anniston Dr.	Suite 108	Louisville	KY	40204	Scorpio
Finch	David	299 Overhill Rd.		Akron	OH	44305	Virgo
Freeman	Marie	287 Johnson Ave.		Atlanta	GA	30319	Pisces
Graves	Adrian	1919 Euclid Ave.		Providence	RI	02906	Capricorn
Hammond	Laura	1911 Clearview Ln.	First Floor	Seattle	WA	98133	Aquarius
Harris	Thomas	2626 Circle Ct.		Chicago	IL	60656	Capricorn
Kemp	Louis	4032 Indian Tr.	Apartment 10B	Springfield	IL	62704	Pisces
King	Benjamin	827 Augusta Ct.		St. Louis	MO	63125	Taurus
Locke	Terry	691 Cedar Ct.		Arlington	VA	22204	Scorpio
London	Sarah	797 Royal Oak Dr.		Ann Arbor	MI	48105	Cancer
McDowell	Courtenay	1568 Hubbards Ln.	Second Floor	Charleston	SC	29405	Cancer
McWilliams	Josh	1982 Westboro Rd.		Washington	DC	20016	Virgo
Moore	Melinda	1007 Tyler Rd.	Suite 1019	Miami	FL	33140	Aries
Moreau	Renee	192-A Ribald St.		Baton Rouge	LA	71441	Aries

We'll use this data document to create some sample merge documents.

Rules of the Game

Although creating a data document is quite easy, there are a number of rules that you must follow as you set up this file. First of all, your field headers must occupy the very first paragraph of the data document. Otherwise, Word will not be able to locate the correct field entries when you merge the main and data files. Each field name can be as long as 65 characters, and you can create as many as 256 fields in each data document. For readability and ease of use, we recommend that you use short, easy-to-remember field names.

Although Word allows you to include blank spaces in your field names, we recommend that you avoid them. As you'll see in a moment, when you're setting up your main document, you'll have to remember to type any blank spaces that you've included in your field names. Therefore, you might be better off avoiding blanks altogether.

We mentioned earlier that each record occupies a single paragraph. Word uses the ¶ marker to signal the end of each record. If your data document contains a lot of fields or if some of your field entries are very long, then your records may wrap into two or more lines. This is fine—Word will be able to interpret the data in each record as a unit as long as that information appears in a single paragraph and in the same order as the information in the field header row.

As you're entering records, be sure that you do not leave any blank lines in your data document. These will cause error messages when you create your merge documents.

You must also be sure that your field entries are typed exactly as you want them to appear in your merge documents. For example, any extra blank spaces that you include in a field entry will also appear in the merge documents and may cause your text to be misaligned. You should be sure to use the correct case for your field entries—for example, you'll want to capitalize the first letter of each first name, last name, city, and street entry. If you're using standard two-digit postal abbreviations, you'll also want to type your state field entries in upper-case letters—KY, LA, and MO, for example.

Field separators

Notice that the field headers in our sample data document are separated by a tab marker. In addition, we've separated the field entries in each record with tabs. If you wish, you can use commas instead of tabs to separate the fields in each data record and in the names in your field header row. Whether you choose to use commas or tabs, for consistency, you should use the same delimiters in your field header row and in each of your data records.

We recommend strongly that you use tabs instead of commas to separate the fields in your data document. For one thing, tab-delimited files are much easier to read and, consequently, much easier to edit. As you'll see through the course of this chapter, when you use tabs to separate fields, you can also take better advantage of Word's sorting capabilities.

If you have imported your data records from another program, those records may be delimited automatically with commas between the field entries. If this is the case, you can easily use the Change… command, described in Chapter 6, to replace the commas with tab markers. Just enter a single comma (,) in the Find What edit bar, and then type ^t in the Change to edit bar. Then click the Change All button to make the switch. We'll talk more about sharing data with other programs in Chapter 16.

Record length

Another important rule to remember is that every data record must contain exactly the same number of fields. Even if you choose to leave some fields blank, you must enter a tab or comma as a placeholder in that field. For example, notice that many of the Address2 fields in the sample data base shown in Figure 14-1 are empty. However, we inserted extra tab markers as placeholders for these empty fields.

If we had not included these extra separator characters, all of our subsequent field entries would have been out of order. Then, when we tried to access the information from those records later, Word would pull information from the wrong fields—using the information in the City field in place of the Address2 data, using information from the ST field in place of the City data, and so forth. As you might guess, this could lead to havoc when we create our merge documents.

Literal text

Since Word interprets tab markers and commas as field separators, you may be wondering how you can enter commas and tabs into your data records. Here's the trick: If you want to include a comma or tab within a field entry, you must enclose that entire field entry in quotation marks. For example, you would enter the company name *MegaCorp, Incorporated* as *"MegaCorp, Incorporated."* The quotation marks around this field entry indicate that you want the contents to be interpreted as literal characters, ignoring any field separator markers.

You now may be wondering how you can include quotation marks within one of your fields. To do this, you must enclose both the field entry and the quotation marks within another set of quotation marks. For example, suppose you have a client who insists on calling himself *Jim "Pop" Stallone*. You would enter his name into the field like this: *"Jim ""Pop"" Stallone."* The outer set of quotation marks tells Word that you want to enter literal characters, while the double quotation marks around the word *Pop* let Word know that you want to place literal quotation marks around that word.

The only characters that are completely off limits for field entries (or field headers) are the guillement symbols (« and »)—also called international quotation marks. As you'll see in a moment, Word reserves these characters for the merge instructions that you include in the main document.

Formatting and Organizing Your Data Document

We warned you earlier that you should type your field entries exactly as you want them to appear in your merge document, using the correct capitalization, spelling, spacing, and so forth. However, the formats that you assign to the entries in your data document have absolutely no effect on the way that information will appear when you create your merge documents. You'll assign the formatting specifications for the merge documents when you create your main document. (This means that the same field entries can take on different formats in different merge documents. You even can format the same field entry in different ways within the same merge document.) Nevertheless, as you are creating a data document, you may want to use certain character, paragraph, Page Setup, and Section formats to make the data records easy for you to read and edit.

For example, you may have noticed in Figure 14-1 that we entered a series of manual tab stops on our ruler. These ensure that the entries in each column are aligned properly and allow us to make certain that no information is missing. The tabs will also help us in editing our field entries and make it easier to extract information from the data document later. However, formatting our fields with tabs is not required at all. It makes no difference to Word whether your data document is aesthetically pleasing, as long as all of the information is in place and in order.

Organizational tips

Your data document will be much more useful if you organize your information carefully. As you set up your fields, think about how you will use the information when you create your merge documents. Then try to design the fields so that you can access any piece of information quickly and easily. For example, you may be tempted to type your clients' names in a single field. Instead, consider using three separate fields to hold each person's first name, middle initial, and last name. You may also want to create additional fields for titles like Dr., Mr., and Ms. and for professional designations like C.P.A. and Vice President.

Though it may seem like a lot of trouble to create a separate field for every piece of information in your data document, the importance of this organizational issue will become clearer as you begin sorting data and extracting information from the data document. For example, in the sample data document shown in Figure 14-1, notice that we split our address information into five separate fields: Address1, Address2, City, ST, and ZIP. As we'll demonstrate in a few pages, this technique will allow us to sort and select records on the basis of key information like state and zip code.

Data header documents

If you have imported the text for your data document from another program into Word, your data document may not automatically include a field header paragraph like the one shown in Figure 14-1. To get around this problem, you can either manually edit the imported file to create your field headers, or you can store your header paragraph in a separate header document.

To create a header document, just type your field entries into a Word file. Separate the field names with tabs or commas as usual—just as if you were entering your headers into a standard data document. A little later on, we'll show how you can use the information from a data header document when you create your merge documents.

SETTING UP THE MAIN DOCUMENT

Once you have created your data document, you're ready to build your main document. You create, edit, and format this document exactly as you would any other Word file, except that you add placeholders in those spots where you want Word to fill in variable information later. Figure 14-2 shows a sample main document that we have created to extract information from the FirstName, LastName, and Sign fields of our sample data document.

FIGURE 14-2

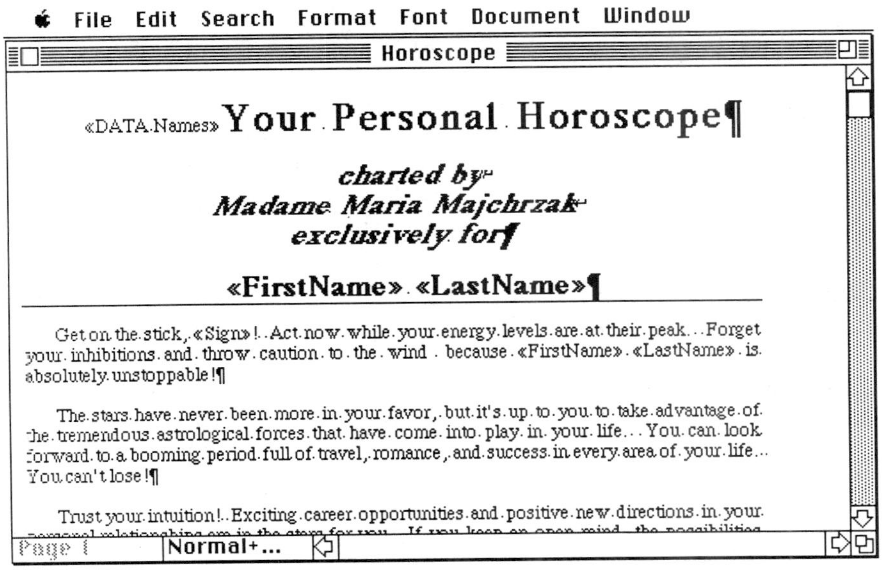

The main document contains special instructions that let you extract information from the data document.

Notice the *«DATA Names»* instruction that appears in the first line of this document. This instruction tells Word the name of the data document that contains the information needed to create the merge documents. This DATA instruction will not appear when you print your merge documents, nor will it affect the line or character spacing for the document heading.

The fifth line of our main document contains two field name instructions, *«FirstName»* and *«LastName»*, which tell Word to extract the entries from the FirstName and LastName fields of our data document and place them into the main document. Thus, when Word prints our first merge document, it will plug in the FirstName entry *Anna* and the LastName entry *Anderson* where these field name instructions occur. In printing our second merge document, Word will plug in the FirstName entry *Joseph* and the LastName entry *Boyd*. Unless we specify otherwise, Word will create a new merge document for each record in our data document, plugging in the appropriate FirstName and LastName entries for each new version of the merge document.

Our main document includes three more field name instructions in the first paragraph of body text. In the sixth line, we use the field name instruction *«Sign»* to extract the individual's astrological sign from the data document. Then, in the seventh line, we use the field name instructions *«FirstName»* and *«LastName»* again. As you might expect, when we create our merge documents, Word will again extract the appropriate information from each record and plug it in where these instructions occur.

Before we see how our finished merge documents appear, let's take a look at some of the rules for entering instructions into the main document file and for formatting the variable text.

Merge Instruction Basics

The sample document in Figure 14-2 uses the two most common types of merge instructions—the DATA instruction and the field name instruction. A little later in this chapter, we'll show you some additional merge instructions that you can use to vary the contents of your merge documents. No matter what type of instructions you are entering, however, the basic rules remain the same.

To separate your instructions from the standard text in your main document, use a pair of guillement characters (« and »). To enter the opening « character, press Option-\. To enter the closing » character, press Shift-Option-\.

You can also use an end-of-paragraph marker as a delimiter for your merge instructions. As you'll see in a few pages, the ¶ marker can help you avoid awkward line breaks in your merge documents.

The DATA instruction

The first instruction in your main document must be the DATA instruction, which takes the form

«DATA document»

This instruction tells Word where to find the variable information it will use to "fill in the blanks" in your printed merge documents. For example, the DATA instruction *«DATA Names»* tells Word to look in the data file named Names for the variable information.

When you type your DATA instruction, be sure to enter a blank space between the word DATA and the beginning of your data document name. Otherwise, Word will not be able to locate your data document file. If your file name contains blank characters, you should include those blank characters in your argument as well.

Word does not distinguish between upper- and lower-case letters in your DATA instructions. For example, you can enter the first word of your DATA instruction as *data*, *DATA*, or *Data*. However, we generally find it easier to distinguish our merge instructions from the rest of the text in our main document when we use upper-case letters.

Similarly, the document names that you enter into your DATA instructions may appear in either upper- or lower-case letters. For example, in the sample document shown in Figure 14-2, we could have entered our document name argument as *Names*, *names*, or *NAMES*.

Referring to a data header document

In our discussion of organizing a data document, we explained how, in some cases, you may store your field headers in a separate document. When you have created and saved a data header document, you'll need to add an additional argument to your DATA instruction to direct Word to this header file.

For example, suppose you have stored the headers for a data document called Clients in a file named Client Headers. To let Word know where your header text is stored, you would enter your DATA instruction like this:

«DATA Client Headers,Clients»

Keep in mind that the same header document can apply to any number of data documents. For this reason, you may find it convenient to store a set of headers in a separate file when the information in your data documents must be updated frequently or when you have created several data documents that use the same headers. That way, you can be sure that all of your data documents contain correct header information.

The field name instructions

As we hinted earlier, the field names at the top of your data document provide the link between your main document and the information stored in your data documents. To plug in text from a specific field in your data document, all you need to do is type the field header, enclosed in guillement characters. No other arguments are required for this instruction.

You can refer to the same field as many times as you like in your main document, and you can enter your field name instructions in any order. As long as the field names in your main document match exactly your field headers in the data document, Word will be able to extract the needed information from the appropriate field in each record.

Unlike the DATA instruction, Word does consider case in your field name instructions. For example, we used the field header *FirstName* to identify our first name fields in the sample data documents shown in Figure 14-1. If we use a field name instruction like *«firstname»* or *«Firstname»*, Word will not be able to locate the appropriate field when we merge the documents.

Although Word will accept blank spaces in the field headers of your data document, you must be sure to enter these spaces correctly when you type your field name instructions into the main document. Otherwise, Word will not recognize your instructions.

Rather than trying to remember whether or not a field name should contain a blank space, we generally prefer to avoid blank spaces altogether. For example, in our sample data document we used the field names *FirstName* and *LastName*, rather than *First Name* and *Last Name*. Though this is entirely a matter of preference, you'll run into fewer errors if you develop some rules for consistent field name references.

Formatting Your Merge Text

You may have noticed that the two sets of *«FirstName»* and *«LastName»* field instructions in lines 5 and 7 of Figure 14-2 carry different character formats. In the heading near the top of the document, we used 18-point, Times, bold text; in the body text, we used 12-point, Times, plain. As you might guess, Word will apply these character formats to our variable text when it creates the merge documents. As this illustrates, you can perform character-level formatting of your variable text simply by applying the desired formats to your field name instructions. In fact, Word will use the character formats that you assign to the first character in the field name instruction to format all of the text that replaces that instruction in the merge documents.

For example, if you want the individual's astrological sign, which appears in the fifth line of our sample document, to appear in italic type, you can assign the Italic format to the letter *S* in the field name instruction sign, like this: «*S*ign». For readability, you may prefer to italicize the entire field name instruction, like this: *«Sign»*.

In addition to character formatting, Word will use all of the Page Setup, Section, and paragraph settings that you assign in your main document to format your merge documents. We'll show you some examples of how your Section and Page Setup dialog box settings affect your merge document formats when we talk about creating mailing labels in Word.

MERGING THE DOCUMENTS

Once you have created your data and main documents, you're ready to use the Print Merge... command to merge the two files. To create your merge documents, make sure that the main document is active on the Word DeskTop, then select Print Merge... from the File menu.

Your data document does not have to be open on the Word DeskTop when you issue the Print Merge... command. Word can read the data from that file on disk. However, your data document should be located on the same disk—and in the same folder, if you are using folders—as your main document. If Word cannot find your data document, it will present an Open dialog box and ask you to locate the needed file. You'll have to access the disk (or folder) on which the document is located before you can continue with the merge procedure. If your data document is located on another disk, you may have to do quite a bit of disk-swapping as Word builds each of your merge documents.

When you issue the Print Merge... command, Word will display a dialog box like the one in Figure 14-3. If you want to print your documents, just click the Print button or press the Return key.

FIGURE 14-3

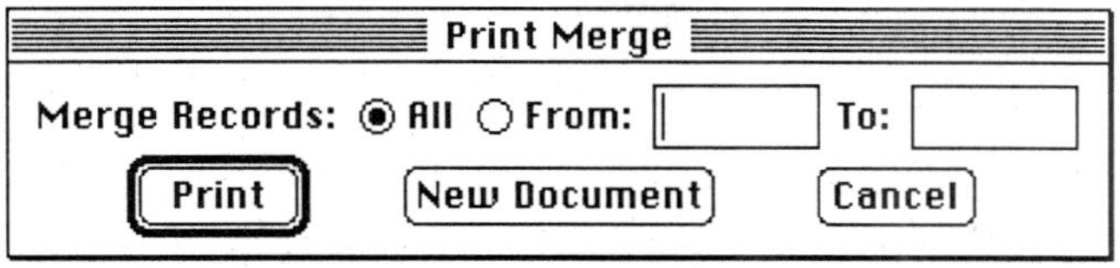

You'll see a dialog box like this one when you issue the Print Merge... command.

The From and To options in the Print Merge dialog box let you control which data records you want to use in your merge documents. If you want to create merge documents for every record in your data document, leave the default All option selected. If you want to print only some of the records, enter the start and end ranges in the From and To edit bars. For example, if you want to merge the data from the fourth, fifth, and sixth data records, you would type the value *4* in the From edit bar and the value *6* in the To edit bar.

When you click on the Print button in the Print Merge dialog box, Word will present you with a Print dialog box exactly like the one you see when you issue the Print... command to print a standard Word document. (See Chapter 7 for a complete description of the Print dialog box.)

All of the options in the Print dialog box work just as they do when you print a standard Word document. Keep in mind, however, that the Pages options in the Print dialog box refer to the number of document pages you want to print, not the number of records—that setting is controlled in the Print Merge dialog box. If you specify a From and To value in the Print dialog box, Word will print the specified range of pages once for each record in your data document. In other words, if you have a four-page document, and you use From and To values of 2 and 3, Word will print pages 2 and 3 of the merge document for every record in your data document. (Of course, if you've instructed Word to merge only a subset of your data records, then the page range will be printed once for each record you've selected.)

Similarly, the Copies option refers to the number of copies of each merge document you want to print, not the total number of documents you want to print. For example, if you use a Copies setting of 3, Word will print three copies of your merge document for each record in the data document. (Again, if you've chosen to merge a range of records from the data document, instead of all the records, Word will print the specified number of copies for each record.)

Figures 14-4 and 14-5 show the first two merge documents that Word will create when you merge the Names data document with the Horoscope main document shown in Figures 14-1 and 14-2. As you can see, Word has printed the text of the Horoscope file, substituting the text from the FirstName, LastName, and Sign fields of the first and second records in our data document for each of the field name instructions in our main document.

FIGURE 14-4

Your Personal Horoscope

charted by
Madame Maria Majchrzak
exclusively for

Anna Anderson

Get on the stick, Libra! Act now while your energy levels are at their peak. Forget your inhibitions and throw caution to the wind because Anna Anderson is absolutely unstoppable!

The stars have never been more in your favor, but it's up to you to take advantage of the tremendous astrological forces that have come into play in your life. You can look forward to a booming period full of travel, romance, and success in every area of your life. You can't lose!

Trust your intuition! Exciting career opportunities and positive new directions in your personal relationships are in the stars for you. If you keep an open mind, the possibilities are endless! Plan to spend some time on those creative endeavors you've been avoiding lately. You may discover an untapped well of energy and insight.

The adage "He who hesitates is lost" has never been more true in your case, Anna! The Mercury-Pluto opposition makes all things possible, but when Saturn enters Capricorn, Libra may be left out in the cold! So think fast and don't resist those sudden flashes of inspiration!

To create this merge document, Word extracted information from the first record in our data document.

After you click OK in the Print dialog box, if Word doesn't recognize one of the field names in your main document, it will display the alert message *Unknown field name.* You will have the option of stopping the merge procedure or continuing. You must remember that if you choose to continue, Word will insert the error message in each of your merge documents.

Creating a Merge File

Rather than routing your merge text directly to a printer, you can use the New Document button in the Print Merge dialog box to "print" your merged text to a Word file. When you use this option, Word will open a new Word document called Form Letters1. Like the Untitled documents that Word creates when you issue the New command, each Form Letters file that you create during a Word session will be numbered sequentially—Form Letters2, Form Letters3, and so forth.

FIGURE 14-5

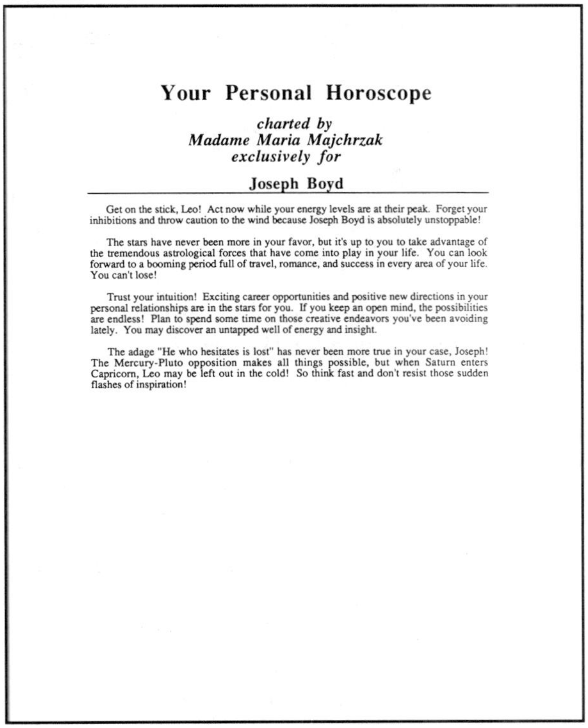

Your Personal Horoscope

charted by
Madame Maria Majchrzak
exclusively for

Joseph Boyd

Get on the stick, Leo! Act now while your energy levels are at their peak. Forget your inhibitions and throw caution to the wind because Joseph Boyd is absolutely unstoppable!

The stars have never been more in your favor, but it's up to you to take advantage of the tremendous astrological forces that have come into play in your life. You can look forward to a booming period full of travel, romance, and success in every area of your life. You can't lose!

Trust your intuition! Exciting career opportunities and positive new directions in your personal relationships are in the stars for you. If you keep an open mind, the possibilities are endless! Plan to spend some time on those creative endeavors you've been avoiding lately. You may discover an untapped well of energy and insight.

The adage "He who hesitates is lost" has never been more true in your case, Joseph! The Mercury-Pluto opposition makes all things possible, but when Saturn enters Capricorn, Leo may be left out in the cold! So think fast and don't resist those sudden flashes of inspiration!

To create this merge document, Word extracted information from the second record in our data document.

Instead of creating a new file for each of the records in your data document, Word places all of the merge text into a single Form Letters file. A section break will appear between the text for each record. For instance, if we were to click the New Document button as we merged the files in our example, Word would create the document shown in Figure 14-6 on the next page. As it creates this document, Word creates the merge text for Anna Anderson, then inserts a section break marker and creates the merge text for Joseph Boyd. (By the way, as you might have guessed, you will not see the Print dialog box when you use the New Document option.)

You can save these Form Letters documents, if you like, or you can use them as temporary files to see the results of your merge instructions before you print. In order to get a better idea of how the printed merge documents will appear, you may want to use the Page Preview... command, discussed in Chapter 7. If your data document contains many records, you may want to use the From and To options in the Print Merge dialog box to preview only a few of the merged documents. This spot-checking technique can save you a lot of time, frustration, and paper before you begin printing a series of merge documents.

FIGURE 14-6

You can save your merge text in a file rather than printing it.

If you decide to save your Form Letters document, keep in mind that the file is not dynamic. That is, a Form Letters file is not linked in any way to your main document or data file. If you change the information in either of those files, you'll have to use another Print Merge... command to create a new, updated merge file.

SPECIAL INSTRUCTIONS

In addition to the DATA and field name instructions, Word offers a number of special instructions that let you vary the contents of your merge documents. You can use these instructions to create logical criteria, to update selected information manually each time you issue the Print Merge... command, to combine data from two or more records in the same merge document, and to insert text from other Word files into your merge documents.

The INCLUDE Instruction

The INCLUDE instruction lets you extract text from another Word file into your merge documents. This instruction takes the same form as the DATA instruction that we discussed earlier:

«INCLUDE document»

To use this instruction, all you need to do is type the INCLUDE instruction at the spot where you want the "included" text to appear. If any additional main document text appears after the INCLUDE instruction, Word will print that text immediately after the "included" text. If you want a page or section break to occur before the "included" text, just insert a manual page or section break marker directly in front of the INCLUDE statement. Similarly, if you want a page or section break to occur after the "included" text, you can insert a manual break after the INCLUDE instruction.

As with the data document, any files that you want to include in your merge document should be located on the same disk and in the same folder as your main document. Otherwise, you'll need to locate the file for Word when you issue the Print Merge... command.

For example, suppose we want to include a "sun sign profile" after the text from our sample Horoscope document. This additional text is located in a file called Profile, shown in Figure 14-7. To include the text from this document in your merge documents, all you need to do is type the instruction

«INCLUDE Profile»

at the end of your main document text, as shown in Figure 14-8. When you merge the main, data, and include documents, Word will create a series of merge documents like the one shown in Figure 14-9.

FIGURE 14-7

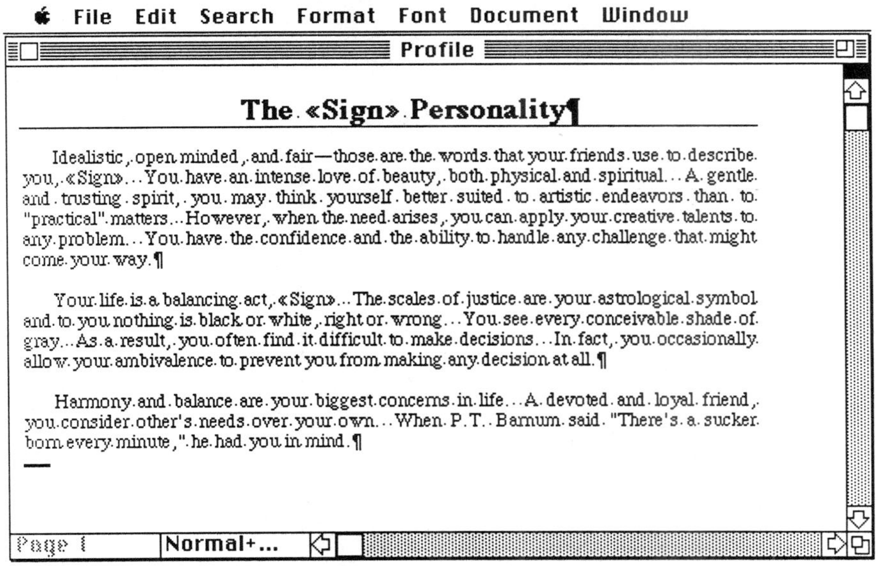

This file contains our sun sign profile text.

FIGURE 14-8

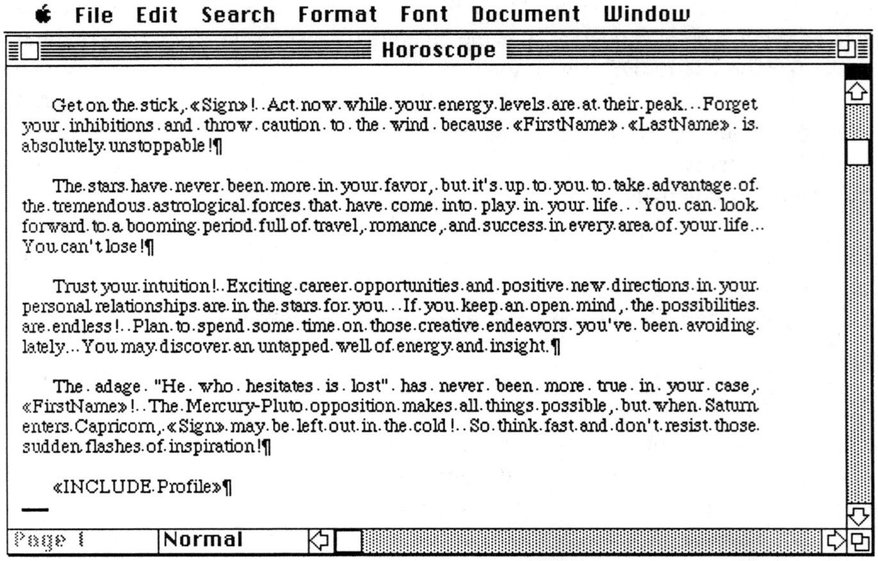

Get on the stick, «Sign»! Act now while your energy levels are at their peak. Forget your inhibitions and throw caution to the wind because «FirstName» «LastName» is absolutely unstoppable!¶

The stars have never been more in your favor, but it's up to you to take advantage of the tremendous astrological forces that have come into play in your life. You can look forward to a booming period full of travel, romance, and success in every area of your life. You can't lose!¶

Trust your intuition! Exciting career opportunities and positive new directions in your personal relationships are in the stars for you. If you keep an open mind, the possibilities are endless! Plan to spend some time on those creative endeavors you've been avoiding lately. You may discover an untapped well of energy and insight.¶

The adage "He who hesitates is lost" has never been more true in your case, «FirstName»! The Mercury-Pluto opposition makes all things possible, but when Saturn enters Capricorn, «Sign» may be left out in the cold! So think fast and don't resist those sudden flashes of inspiration!¶

«INCLUDE Profile»¶

Type the INCLUDE instruction where you want the additional text to appear.

FIGURE 14-9

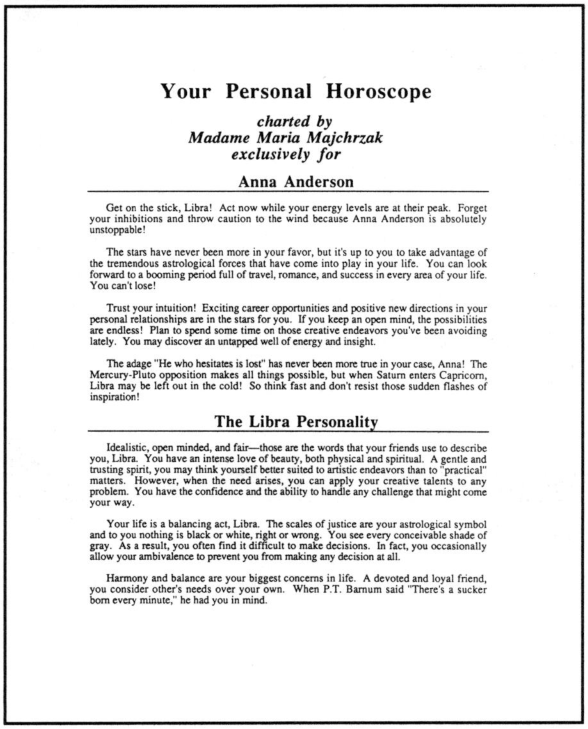

Your Personal Horoscope

charted by
Madame Maria Majchrzak
exclusively for

Anna Anderson

Get on the stick, Libra! Act now while your energy levels are at their peak. Forget your inhibitions and throw caution to the wind because Anna Anderson is absolutely unstoppable!

The stars have never been more in your favor, but it's up to you to take advantage of the tremendous astrological forces that have come into play in your life. You can look forward to a booming period full of travel, romance, and success in every area of your life. You can't lose!

Trust your intuition! Exciting career opportunities and positive new directions in your personal relationships are in the stars for you. If you keep an open mind, the possibilities are endless! Plan to spend some time on those creative endeavors you've been avoiding lately. You may discover an untapped well of energy and insight.

The adage "He who hesitates is lost" has never been more true in your case, Anna! The Mercury-Pluto opposition makes all things possible, but when Saturn enters Capricorn, Libra may be left out in the cold! So think fast and don't resist those sudden flashes of inspiration!

The Libra Personality

Idealistic, open minded, and fair—those are the words that your friends use to describe you, Libra. You have an intense love of beauty, both physical and spiritual. A gentle and trusting spirit, you may think yourself better suited to artistic endeavors than to "practical" matters. However, when the need arises, you can apply your creative talents to any problem. You have the confidence and the ability to handle any challenge that might come your way.

Your life is a balancing act, Libra. The scales of justice are your astrological symbol and to you nothing is black or white, right or wrong. You see every conceivable shade of gray. As a result, you often find it difficult to make decisions. In fact, you occasionally allow your ambivalence to prevent you from making any decision at all.

Harmony and balance are your biggest concerns in life. A devoted and loyal friend, you consider other's needs over your own. When P.T. Barnum said "There's a sucker born every minute," he had you in mind.

When we issue the Print Merge... command, Word combines the text from all three documents.

Notice in Figure 14-7 that our profile document also contains field name instructions to fill in the client's sign. Your include document can contain any of the special instructions that you use in your main document, except for the DATA instruction. Word allows you to use only one DATA instruction at a time, and that DATA instruction must be the first instruction in your main document file.

Why would you want to use the INCLUDE instruction to place additional text into your merge documents, rather than simply entering that text into the main document? First of all, you can refer to the same include file in any number of main documents, thus saving yourself the time, effort, and disk space required to enter the "included" text in several files.

In addition, as you'll see in a few pages, you can set up criteria that instruct Word to extract data from different include files, depending on the results of certain conditional instructions.

The SET Instruction

If you need to vary only a few words from one document to the next, you'll probably find it more efficient to use a SET instruction, rather than using the INCLUDE instruction to extract your variable text from a separate file. The SET instruction lets you manually change the contents of selected fields in your merge documents each time you create a new set of merge documents.

The SET instruction can take three forms:

«SET field name=text»
«SET field name=?»
«SET field name=?message»

You use the *field name* argument to define the name of the field that you want to vary each time you create a new set of merge documents. Then, you enter that field name into the desired locations in your main document text in order to flag the spots where you want Word to insert your text.

The *field name* argument for your SET instruction should be different from all of the field names that appear in your data document's field header row. Like the field names from your data document, your SET instruction field names will be typed into your main document at each place where you want to vary some text. However, instead of extracting text from the data document, when Word encounters a field name from a SET instruction, it will use text that you have provided. If you use a field name in your SET instruction that matches one of the field names in your data document, you'll see the alert message *SET name is also the name of a DATA field.* when you issue the Print Merge... command. This same message will appear in your merge documents at each spot where the duplicate field name appears.

The text option

If you use the first form of the SET instruction, you'll type the text that you want to use for the variable field directly into your main document before you issue the Print Merge... command. For example, we mentioned at the beginning of this chapter that you might want to use the merge facility to create a series of personalized invitations to your company's grand opening. Suppose your grand opening party is going to be so big that you must spread it over three days in order to accommodate all of your guests.

In order to create three different sets of form letters that carry different invitation dates, you could insert into your main document a SET instruction with a *field name* argument called *Date*, like this

«SET Date=March 1»

Then, to vary the definition of the Date field, you would edit this SET instruction each time you issued the Print Merge... command so that it specifies a different date.

For example, Figure 14-10 shows an invitation letter in which this SET instruction appears immediately after the DATA instruction. After entering the SET instruction to define the Date field, we typed the instruction *«Date»* in the first and third lines of the body text of our letter.

FIGURE 14-10

We used the SET instruction to vary our invitation dates in the form letter.

To divide our invitations into three different groups (with a different invitation date for each group), we would issue three separate Print Merge... commands. Using the From and To options in the Print Merge dialog box, we would specify a different range of data records for each merge procedure. For example, suppose our data document contains 300 records. We might use From and To arguments of 1 and 100 to print the first batch of invitations, 101 and 200 to print the second batch, and 201 and 300 to print the last batch.

To vary the invitation date from one group of letters to the next, we would simply change the text in the SET instruction before issuing the Print Merge... command. In the second batch, for example, our SET instruction might read

«SET Date=March 2»

while the SET instruction in the third batch would specify March 3.

SET prompts

Rather than entering your SET text directly into the main document, you can have Word prompt you for the new date information each time you issue the Print Merge... command. To create a prompt, you use either the second or third form of the SET instruction. If you use the question mark for the SET function,

«SET Date =?»

you'll see a dialog box like the one in Figure 14-11 when you issue the Print Merge... command. All you need to do is type the text that you want Word to insert at each «Date» instruction in your document and click OK or press Return.

FIGURE 14-11

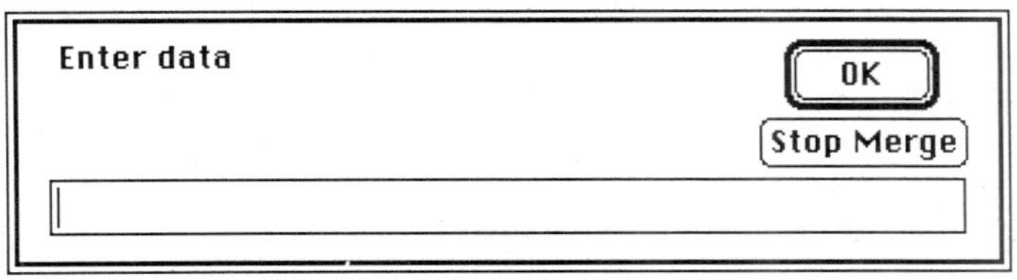

If you use the question mark for the SET instruction, Word will prompt you for the text to enter into your SET fields.

If you have entered more than one SET instruction into your main document, Word's generic *Enter data* message won't be of much help to you since you can't tell for which field you're supposed to be entering the data. If you would like to see a more descriptive message in this dialog box, you can use the third form of the SET instruction. This form includes a custom message that you create to remind yourself of what kind of data you're supposed to be entering. For example, if you use a SET instruction like

«SET Date =?Enter the invitation date.»

Word will present a dialog box like the one in Figure 14-12.

FIGURE 14-12

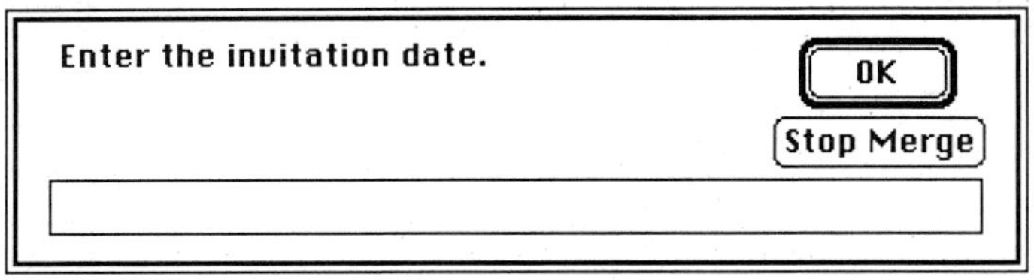

You can also create your own prompts for the SET dialog box.

The ASK Instruction

The ASK instruction is similar to the SET instruction except that it allows you to vary a field entry for each of your merge documents. Instead of varying a field for each Print Merge... command, the ASK instruction will vary one or more fields for each merge document that you create with a single Print Merge... command. The ASK instruction can take two forms:

«ASK field name=?»
«ASK field name=?message»

As with the SET instruction, the question mark form of the ASK instruction tells Word to present a dialog box like the one in Figure 14-11. This dialog box will appear once for each record in your data document to let you define the field entry you want to use for that record.

To help you remember what type of data you want to enter, Word also lets you specify a prompt message to appear in your ASK dialog box. To create this message, you use the second form of the ASK instruction.

For example, suppose you decide that you want to create a personalized greeting for each of the guests that you plan to invite to your grand opening. You might set up a form letter like the one in Figure 14-13. The ASK instruction in the letter's salutation will cause Word to prompt you for a greeting for each letter.

Unfortunately, as you respond to each of these ASK prompts, you will have no way of knowing which record is being processed. You won't be able to see the merge documents as they are created, and Word gives you no record number prompt or other indication of which invitation letter you are working with. As you might imagine, this limitation makes it pretty difficult to personalize each of your merge documents.

FIGURE 14-13

You can use the ASK instruction to vary a field entry for each of your merge documents.

Here's an easy way to get around that problem: Nest one or more field name instructions in your ASK message to identify the record that is currently being processed. For example, rather than using the instruction

«ASK Greeting=?Enter a greeting.»

in Figure 14-13, you could use an instruction like

«ASK Greeting=?How do you want to greet «FirstName» «LastName»?»

When you issue the Print Merge... command, Word will present a dialog box like the one in Figure 14-14 as it creates the merge text for each record in your data document.

FIGURE 14-14

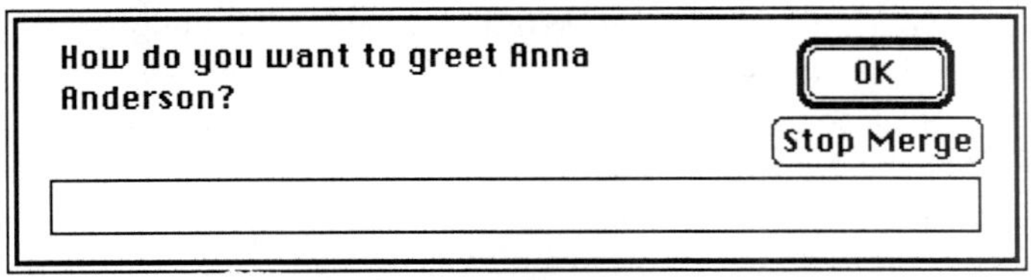

You can embed field name instructions in your ASK messages to keep track of which record is being processed.

The IF and ENDIF Instructions

In many instances you'll want to create variations in your merge documents that can't be handled with a simple ASK or SET instruction. For example, you may need to insert special text into your merge documents that is dependent on the information in one of the fields in your data document. Word's IF and ENDIF instructions let you handle these situations by setting up conditional tests in your Main document file.

The simplest form of the IF instruction is

«IF field name»text«ENDIF»

This instruction tells Word to check the contents of the specified field in the current record to determine whether that field contains an entry. If there is an entry, then the conditional test is true, and Word will print the text that appears between the IF and ENDIF instructions. If the field is empty (that is, if you have inserted an extra comma or tab to skip past a field in the data document), then the conditional test is false, and Word will omit the text from your merge documents.

The text that you enter between the IF and ENDIF instructions can be any length and may even contain more than one paragraph or document section. In short, Word considers *anything* between the IF and ENDIF instructions to be conditional on the result of the IF comparison.

Continuing with the sample invitation letter created in Figure 14-10, suppose you want to include a note to your married clients to invite their spouses to the grand opening celebration as well. You have included a field in your data document that contains the name of each client's spouse—if he or she is married. For those who are not married, this field is blank.

You could set up a conditional instruction like the one that is shown in Figure 14-15 to test for the presence of an entry in the Spouse field of your data document. If that field contains an entry, Word will print the text *Of course, we'd also be thrilled if «Spouse» would like to accompany you to our celebration as well! The more, the merrier!* (In printing this text, Word will, of course, substitute the name from the Spouse field for the *«Spouse»* field instruction.) If the Spouse field is empty, Word will omit this paragraph.

You may have noticed that we included our ENDIF instruction after the ¶ marker at the end of our conditional text—just in front of the word *Sincerely* in the closing of our invitation letter. In doing so, we were able to avoid any unwanted blank lines in our merge documents. Remember, when you enter conditional text into your main document, Word considers everything between your IF and ENDIF instructions—including end-of-paragraph markers—to be conditional. Thus, by placing your ENDIF instruction at the beginning of the next paragraph—after the ¶ marker—you can ensure that no blank lines will appear in your merge text when the IF condition proves false.

FIGURE 14-15

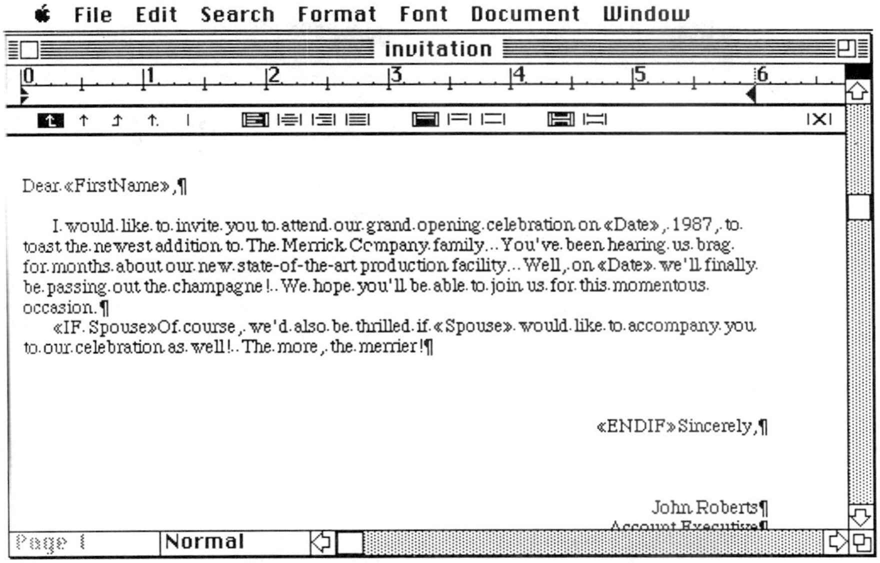

This conditional text will appear only if there is an entry in the Spouse field for this client.

Comparing text and numbers

Rather than simply testing for the presence of an entry in a field, you can use an IF instruction to compare the contents of a field to a string or value that you specify. Word lets you compare text entries as well as numeric values with these two forms of the IF instruction:

«IF field name="comparison text"»text«ENDIF»
«IF field name=comparison value»text«ENDIF»

Notice that the comparison text in the first IF instruction appears enclosed in quotation marks. These are required. However, you should not include quotation marks around comparison values. If you place quotations marks around numeric values, Word will treat those values as text rather than numbers.

Returning to our sample Horoscope document, suppose we want to include a birthday greeting to those persons on the mailing list whose birthdays are approaching. Let's assume that you will be mailing these letters in mid-September, so the Libras are the next group of clients with birthdays on their astral horizons. You could create an IF instruction like the one in Figure 14-16 to include a birthday greeting for clients with the Sign field entry *Libra*.

FIGURE 14-16

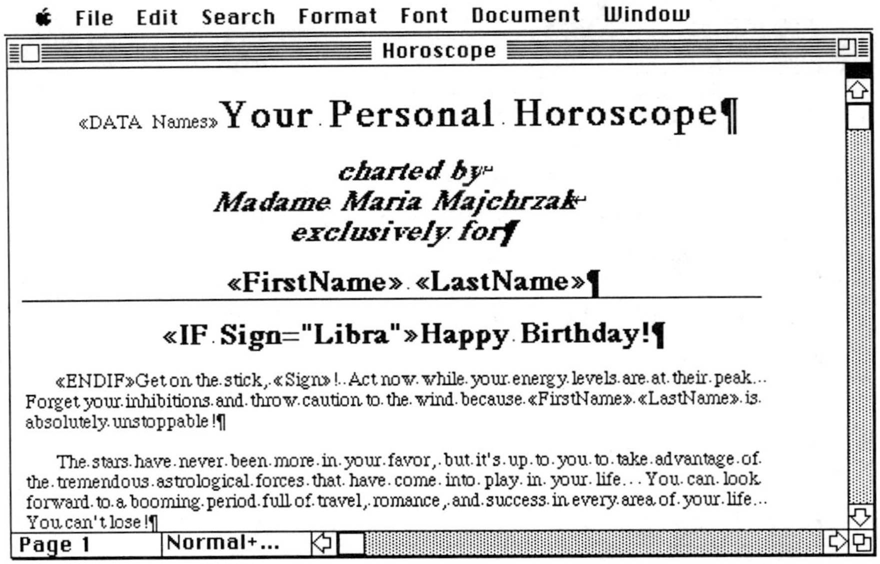

This IF instruction tells Word to print a birthday greeting for all of the Libras on our mailing list.

When you're using the IF instruction to test numeric field entries, you can use the < and > signs to determine whether a field entry is greater than or less than your comparison value. For example, suppose you need to send a series of billing notices to some of your clients. We'll assume that your client data document includes an OD field that lists the number of days that each payment is past due.

Now, suppose you want to issue a particularly strong message to those people whose payments are more than 15 days late. You could use an IF instruction like the one shown in Figure 14-17 to determine whether the value in the OD field is greater than 15. If the logical test OD>15 is true, then Word will include the sentence *Your bill is seriously past due!* in the billing notice for that client. If payment is 15 days overdue or less, this sentence will not appear in the merge document.

FIGURE 14-17

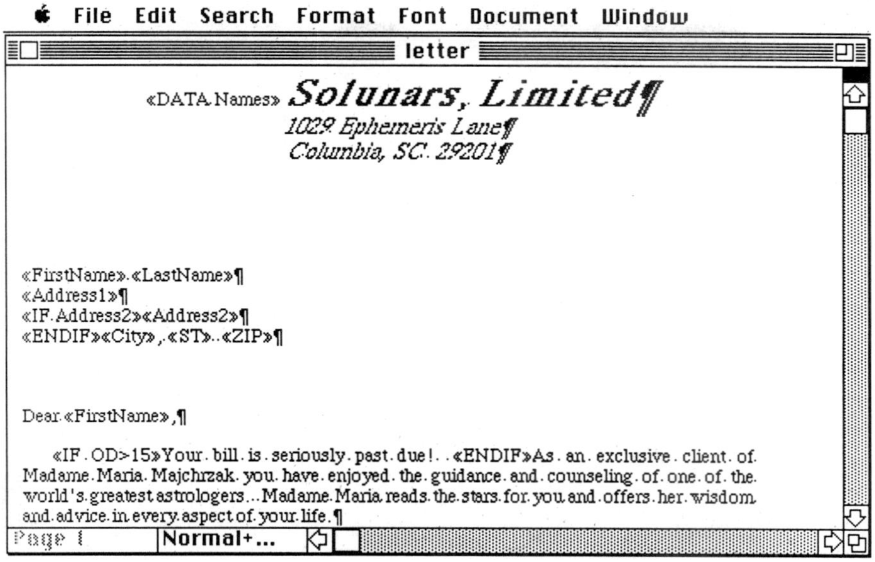

You can use a comparison value in an IF instruction to determine whether each client's payment is more than 15 days overdue.

The ELSE instruction

Thus far, all of our conditional tests have instructed Word to enter a text block into our merge document only if a given condition is true. However, there may be occasions when you want to print alternative text in your merge document when a condition is false. Word's ELSE instruction works hand-in-hand with the IF instruction to let you accomplish just that.

The ELSE instruction, which takes no arguments of its own, is designed to be nested within the IF instruction like this:

«IF field name»text«ELSE»alternative text«ENDIF»

Continuing with the sample invitation letter shown in Figure 14-15, suppose you want to add an alternative line of text for your unmarried clients (those with no entry in the Spouse field), inviting them to bring along a guest. You could accomplish this by changing your IF instruction to look like the one in Figure 14-18.

FIGURE 14-18

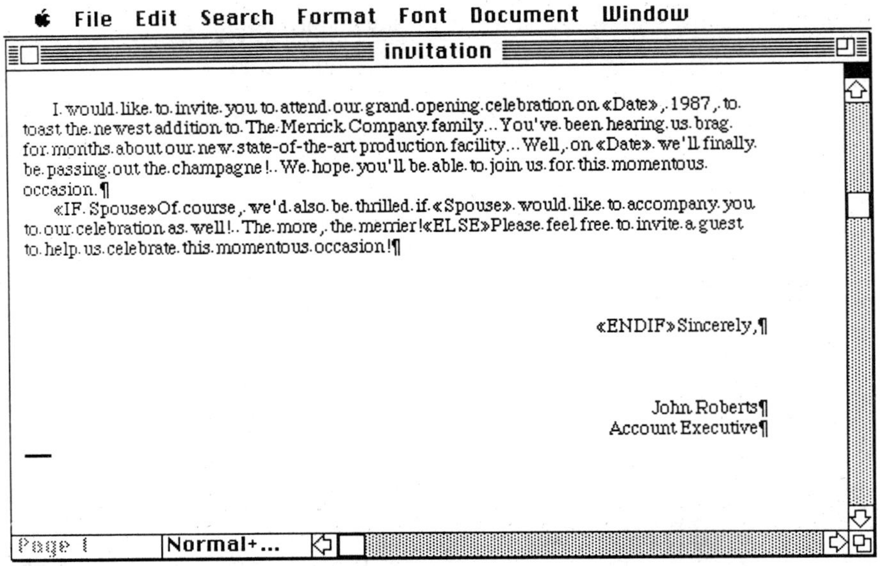

We used the ELSE instruction to add alternative text for unmarried clients.

As you can see, to create the alternative text, you simply add the nested instruction *«ELSE»Please feel free to invite a guest to help us celebrate this momentous occasion!* to your IF instruction.

Using IF to control blank lines

You may have noticed in the sample overdue letter in Figure 14-17 that we used the conditional instruction *«IFAddress2»«Address2»* to create the second address line of our address block. We placed the ENDIF instruction just before the *«City»* field instruction in the next line. As you may remember, in the sample data document that we showed you in Figure 14-1, only some of the records contain entries in the Address2 field. The others simply contain extra tab markers or commas as placeholders for this empty field.

To keep from printing a blank line in the address block whenever the Address2 field is empty, we defined the *«Address2»* field instruction as conditional text. As with the conditional text in Figures 14-15 and 14-18, in Figure 14-17 we chose to place our ENDIF statement after the ¶ marker for the Address2 block to ensure that no extra paragraph break occurs at this point when the Address2 field is empty.

Nesting IF instructions

You've already seen several examples of nested instructions as we've created our sample merge documents throughout this chapter. For instance, we showed how you could nest a field name instruction within an ASK instruction, and we showed how to nest a field name instruction within an IF instruction. As you might have guessed, you can also nest two or more IF instructions in your main document to test for a number of possible conditions. In fact, by stringing together a group of IF instructions, you can create a fairly sophisticated series of conditional tests.

When you string together two or more conditional tests, you must make sure that you include a matching ENDIF instruction for each IF instruction. Thus, your nested IF instructions would look something like this:

«IF field name1="comparison text"»text«IF field name2="comparison text2"»text2«IF field name3="comparison text3"»text3 «ENDIF» «ENDIF»«ENDIF»

Of course, you can also embed other instructions, like INCLUDE, ELSE, ASK, and SET, within your IF instructions These nested instructions will generally serve as text arguments.

For example, in the sample document shown in Figure 14-8, we showed how you could create an INCLUDE instruction to extract text from a file named Profile. Suppose you decide to create 12 separate profile documents—one for each astrological sign. We have named these documents Aries, Taurus, Gemini, and so forth. To select the appropriate profile for each of your clients, you could string together a series of 12 IF instructions like this:

«IF Sign="Aries"»«INCLUDE Aries»«ELSE»«IF Sign="Taurus"» «INCLUDE Taurus»«ELSE»«IF Sign="Gemini"»«INCLUDE Gemini» «ELSE»«IF Sign="Cancer"»«INCLUDE Cancer»«ELSE»«IF Sign="Leo"» «INCLUDE Leo»«ELSE»«IF Sign="Virgo"»«INCLUDE Virgo»«ELSE»«IF Sign="Libra"»«INCLUDE Libra»«ELSE»«IF Sign="Scorpio"»«INCLUDE Scorpio»«ELSE»«IF Sign="Sagittarius"»«INCLUDE Sagittarius»«ELSE»«IF Sign="Capricorn"»«INCLUDE Capricorn»«ELSE»«IF Sign="Aquarius"» «INCLUDE Aquarius»«ELSE»«IF Sign="Pisces"» «INCLUDE Pisces» «ENDIF»«ENDIF»«ENDIF»«ENDIF»«ENDIF»«ENDIF»«ENDIF»«ENDIF» «ENDIF»«ENDIF»«ENDIF»«ENDIF»

Notice that the text argument for each of our IF instructions is an INCLUDE instruction that directs Word to the appropriate profile document.

The NEXT Instruction

As we have already explained, when you use the Print Merge... command to create a new Form Letters file, Word inserts a section break marker between the end of the merge text for one record and the beginning of the merge text for the next record. When you print your merge documents, Word again inserts a section break between the merge text for different records, and, because the default Section Start setting is New Page, Word automatically starts a new page as it begins printing the text for each new record.

If you would like to omit these page and section breaks, you can insert a series of NEXT instructions in your main document. The NEXT instruction tells Word to extract the information from another record in the data document and continue merging—without starting a new document or inserting a section break. Therefore, after each NEXT instruction, you will also need to enter another copy of your main document text. The NEXT instruction takes no arguments of its own—you insert it in front of other merge instructions to tell Word to extract information from the next record in your data document.

For example, suppose you want to create a list of your clients' names, with ten names printed on a page. If you were to create a main document with the simple field instructions

«FirstName» «LastName»

Word would print only one client name on each page. In order to print ten names on a page, you would set up your main document so that it contains these field instructions repeated ten times. After the first *«FirstName» «LastName»* sequence, you would include a NEXT instruction in front of each additional field instruction sequence, like this:

«NEXT»«FirstName» «LastName»

Each time Word encounters a NEXT instruction, it will extract the first and last name information from another record in the data document and merge it into the main document where the next *«FirstName» «LastName»* sequence appears.

MAILING LABELS

Our discussion of merging would be incomplete without covering the topic of mailing labels. You might use Word's print merge capabilities to create mailing labels as often as you use it do any other kind of merging. In this section, we'll cover the basics of creating mailing labels in Word.

In fact, you already know most of what you need to know to create mailing labels. The first step in creating mailing labels is to set up a data document like the one in Figure 14-1 that contains the names and addresses of the people you want to print labels for. Next, you must create a main document that defines the form of the mailing labels. Finally, you use the Print Merge... command to print the labels.

Setting Up the Main Document

Setting up the main document for mailing labels is very similar to setting up the main document for other print merge applications: You just need to enter the instructions that define the labels in a new document. For instance, Figure 14-19 shows a sample main document that you could use to print single-column mailing labels. As you can see, the DATA instruction at the beginning of the document refers to the data document Names. The document includes the fields

FirstName, LastName, Address1, Address2, City, State, and ZIP. Notice that we've used the *«IF Address2»«Address2»«ENDIF»* instruction sequence (which we described earlier) in this document. As before, these instructions ensure that none of the printed labels will contain an extra blank line.

FIGURE 14-19

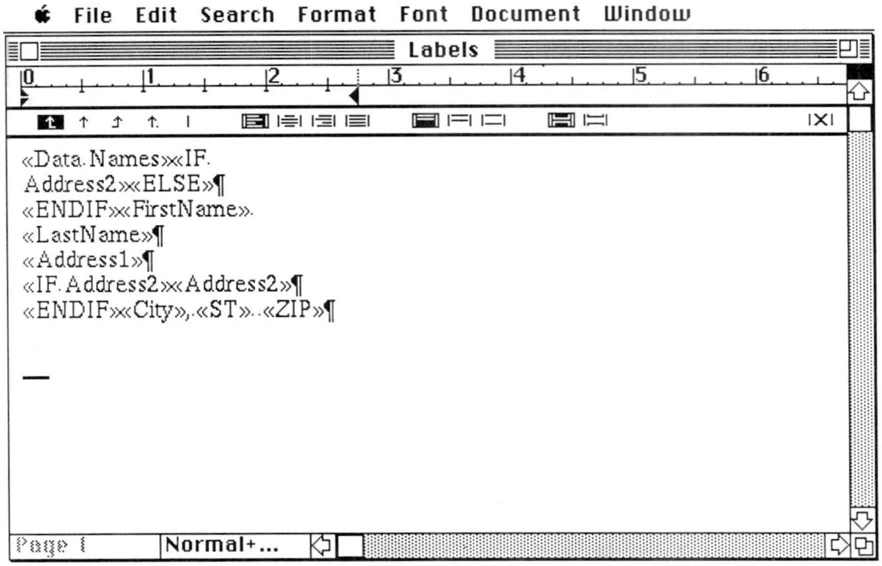

This is the main document you can use to create mailing labels.

After you've entered the instructions that define your labels, you need to use the Page Setup... command to change the default page layout. In the Page Setup dialog box, first enter the dimensions of your labels in the Paper Width and Height edit bars. Assuming you are printing on continuous-feed labels, the Height setting should match the height of your labels (usually 1 inch or 1 $^{1}/_{2}$ inches). The Width setting should equal the width of your labels. (As we'll explain in the next section, you will need to use a different Width setting if you are printing multiple columns of labels.)

Changing the Height setting to match the size of your labels tells Word to treat each label as a page. To make sure that Word will start a new page after it prints each label, you should also change the Section Start option in the Section dialog box to New Page before you begin to print.

In order to position your information correctly on the labels, you also need to change your Left, Right, Top, and Bottom margin settings in the Page Setup dialog box. You'll probably want to enter a value of about .25 for each margin setting since mailing labels typically don't allow much extra room for margins.

Multicolumn Labels

Word also allows you to print multiple-column mailing labels—labels that appear two, three, or four across each page. In general, the process of creating multiple-column labels is similar to that of creating single-column labels. To generate multiple-column labels, however, you'll need to create an additional instruction set in the main document for each column of labels. Each additional instruction set must begin with a NEXT command. For example, if you're printing labels three across, you would have three instruction sets, with a NEXT instruction preceding each of the last two sets. If you're printing labels two across, you would have only two instruction sets, with a NEXT instruction preceding the second set. The NEXT instructions tell Word to pull another record from the data document without inserting a section break. By setting up your main document to include more than one set of instructions, and by using the NEXT instruction as we've described, you tell Word to insert a section break after each group of labels. For example, if you're printing labels three across, Word will insert a section break after each group of three labels.

In addition to adding instruction sets to the main document, you need to set up columnar formatting in the main document. To do this, enter a Number setting in the Section dialog box that corresponds to the number of labels you want to print side-by-side. If you are printing labels three across, then you would change the Number setting to 3. For two-across labels, you would enter 2 in the Number edit bar.

The section breaks that Word inserts after every group of labels, combined with the columnar formatting that you establish in the Section dialog box, will give you the multiple-across format. As we explained in Chapter 8, when you use columnar formatting, Word will "wrap" your columns separately in each section of a document. This causes each group of labels (between section breaks) to be printed across the page instead of in a single column. In other words, each label in a group will appear in its own column on the page. (For more on section breaks and columnar formatting, see pages 336-338.)

After setting up columnar formatting in your main document, you need to open the Page Setup dialog box and enter the dimensions of your label forms in the Paper Width and Height edit bars. As before, the Height setting should be equal to the height of a single label. The Width setting that you specify should be equal to the width of the combined multiple-across labels. For example, if you're printing labels two across and each label measures 1.5 inches by 3.5 inches, then your Width setting should be 7. (In this example, the Height setting would be 1.5.) If you are printing three-across labels, you would triple the Width setting from 3.5 to 10.5.

Finally, if you are printing to continuous-form labels, you should change the Section Start option in the Section dialog box to New Page. Changing this setting ensures that Word will start a new page after it prints each set of labels.

Using the LaserWriter

If you are fortunate enough to have access to a LaserWriter or LaserWriter Plus, you may want to print your labels using that printer. In general, the process of setting up and printing mailing labels using a LaserWriter is identical to that of printing labels with any other printer. However, there are a couple of differences. First, because the LaserWriter cannot accommodate form-feed labels, you're likely to use label sheets to create your mailing labels. For this reason, you'll usually print labels three across on your LaserWriter. You can use the instructions in the previous section to set up your main document for three-across labels.

In order to position your label information correctly on the label sheet, you'll need to open the Page Setup dialog box and change the Height and Width options to match the size of the label sheets you'll be using. For example, if you will be printing to 8 1/2 inch x 11 inch label sheets, you should change the Width setting to 8.5 and the Height setting to 11. You'll also need to change the Left, Right, Top, and Bottom margin settings. You'll probably want to enter a value of about .5 for each margin setting since mailing labels typically don't allow much extra room for margins.

Finally, you must change the Section Start option in the Section dialog box to No Break. Changing this setting ensures that Word will not start a new page after it prints each group of labels. This step is essential if you are planning to print to label sheets.

An Example

To see how the whole process works, let's consider an example. Suppose you want to print the sheet of mailing labels shown in Figure 14-20 on the next page by extracting the name and address information from the sample data document in Figure 14-1. We'll assume that you'll be printing this label sheet on a LaserWriter. To create these labels, you would set up a main document like the one shown in Figure 14-21 on the next page.

Although you cannot see the entire contents of the main document on the screen in Figure 14-21, it contains three sets of instructions for extracting name and address information from the data document—corresponding to the three columns of labels on the page. Each set of instructions will extract the name and address from one record in the data document. Notice that the second instruction set begins with a NEXT instruction (the third set also begins this way). The NEXT instructions tell Word to pull another record from the data document without inserting a section break.

FIGURE 14-20

Anna Anderson 252 Skyview Dr. Apartment 2 Denver, CO 80205	Joseph Boyd 1172 Lansford Dr. Topeka, KS 66614	Amelia Browne 6091 Marietta Ct. Lexington, KY 40505
Lillian Cumming 525 Redmond Ct. Lincoln, NE 68503	Benjamin Douglas 2421 Eastern Pkwy. Fort Wayne, IN 46808	Alex Edwards 7153 Goldsmith Ln. Dallas, TX 75234
Connie Fife 983 Anniston Dr. Suite 108 Louisville, KY 40204	David Finch 299 Overhill Rd. Akron, OH 44305	Marie Freeman 287 Johnson Ave. Atlanta, GA 30319
Adrian Graves 1919 Euclid Ave. Providence, RI 02906	Laura Hammond 1911 Clearview Ln. First Floor Seattle, WA 98133	Thomas Harris 2626 Circle Ct. Chicago, IL 60656
Louis Kemp 4032 Indian Tr. Apartment 10B Springfield, IL 62704	Benjamin King 827 Augusta Ct. St. Louis, MO 63125	Terry Locke 691 Cedar Ct. Arlington, VA 22204
Sarah London 797 Royal Oak Dr. Ann Arbor, MI 48105	Courtenay McDowell 1568 Hubbards Ln. Second Floor Charleston, SC 29405	Josh McWilliams 1982 Westboro Rd. Washington, DC 20016
Melinda Moore 1007 Tyler Rd. Suite 1019 Miami, FL 33140	Renee Moreau 192-A Ribald St. Baton Rouge, LA 71441	Mary Paulson 375 Southside Dr. New York, NY 10016
Betty Penn 566 Manhattan Dr. Lexington, KY 40505	Jim Ray 1432 Brook St. c/o Ann Ray Modesto, CA 95350	Howard Roberts 1617 Baxter Ave. San Francisco, CA 94121
Edward Shearer 728 Jessamine Ln. Phoenix, AZ 85032	John Smith 8918 Central Ave. Memphis, TN 38107	Gary Springer 5091 Bardstown Rd. Birmingham, AL 35261
Michael Stevens 1391 Fern Creek Rd. Nashville, TN 37214	Janet Stroud 2223 Keane Ave. St. Paul, MN 55117	Anne Taylor 560 Bluegrass Ave. Frankfort, KY 40620

You can use the print merge facility to print a sheet of labels like this one.

FIGURE 14-21

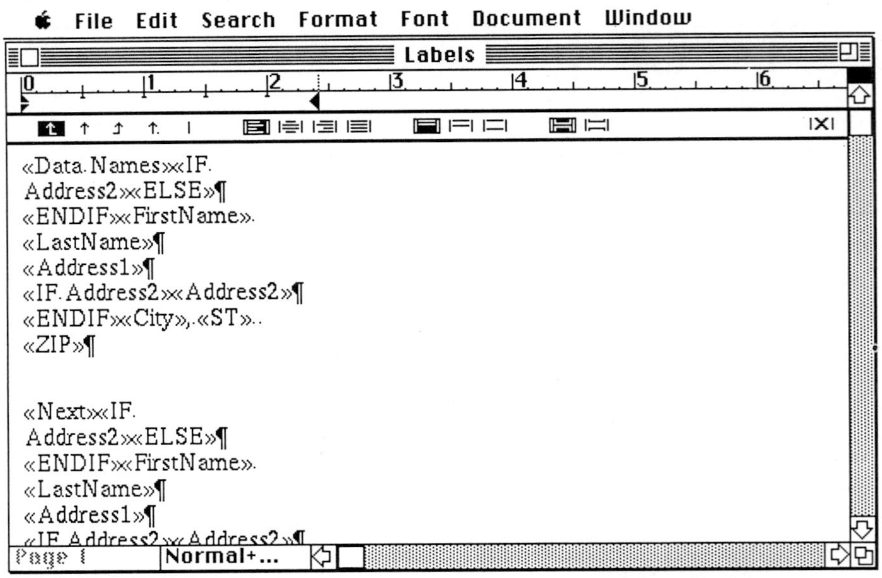

This is the main document you can use to create the sheet of printed labels.

Also notice that in this document we have used the instruction sequence *«IFAddress2»«Address2»«ENDIF»* (which we described earlier) to ensure that none of our printed labels will contain an extra blank line. Since we're printing a sheet of labels, however, eliminating any extra blank lines that might crop up solves only half the problem. In addition, you must make sure that each label begins at the proper position on the label sheet. When you print one group in which all three labels contain only three lines of text (that is, none of the labels in that group include an Address2 line), the next group of names and addresses may begin too high on the sheet. When this happens, that group of names and addresses—and all subsequent groups on the sheet—may be printed incorrectly. To avoid this problem, you must insert an extra blank line above or below the labels in the "short group" so that the next group will be properly positioned.

You can tell Word to create these extra blank lines by including the instructions

«IF Address2»«ELSE»¶
«ENDIF»

at the beginning of each set of instructions. Notice in Figure 14-21 that no text appears after the ELSE instruction in the second line of each instruction set but that a ¶ marker does appear. This indicates that Word should add a blank line whenever the IF condition is false. Stated in English, these instructions tell Word, "If the current data record contains an entry in the Address2 field, then print the label with no changes. If the Address2 field does *not* contain an entry, then insert a blank line before printing the name and address information."

After entering the instructions in this main document, we made a couple of changes to its settings. First, we changed the Number setting in the Section dialog box to 3. This tells Word to print the document in three-column format. Next, we clicked the US Letter option to set the Height and Width settings in the Page Setup dialog box to 8.5 and 11. These settings match the dimensions of the label sheets we're printing to. We also changed the Left, Right, Top, and Bottom margin settings to .5. Finally, we changed the Section Start option in the Section dialog box to No Break. Changing this setting ensures that Word will not start a new page after it prints each row of labels.

After setting up the main document as we've described, we printed our labels. To do this, we simply chose the Print Merge... command and clicked the Print option. When the Print dialog box came into view, we clicked OK. Figure 14-20 shows the resulting labels.

OTHER SPECIAL FEATURES 15

As you've seen, Word 3 offers a number of special features and capabilities that are designed to make your work easier and faster. In previous chapters, we've looked at the most important of these special features, including style sheets, the glossary, and the outliner. In this chapter, we'll show you how to take advantage of several more of Word's special capabilities. We'll begin with discussions of line numbering and paragraph numbering, then we'll move into sorting paragraphs and performing calculations in Word. We'll wrap up with a look at Word's ability to create mathematical and scientific formulas and other special symbols with character formulas.

NUMBERING LINES

You can create line numbers in your printed documents by activating the Line Numbering option in the Section dialog box. When you choose Section... from the Format menu, you'll notice this option in the upper-right corner of the dialog box. (See Figure 15-1 on the next page.) If you click the Line Numbering option, then click OK, Word will number all the lines in the current section of your document. Of course, if your document contains only one section, then Word will number all the lines in the entire document.

FIGURE 15-1

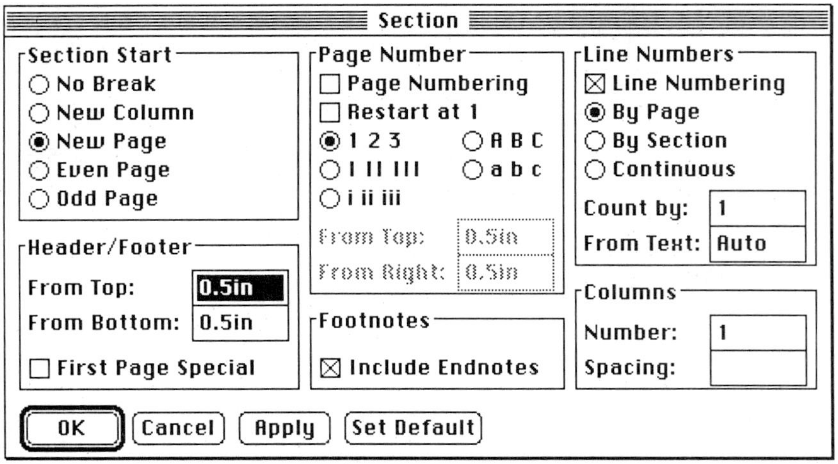

To number lines in your document, click the Line Numbering option in the Section dialog box.

Line numbers do not appear on your screen unless you use the Page Preview... command to preview your printed document. However, Word will always include the line numbers in your printed document. For example, Figure 15-2 shows part of a printed document with line numbers.

If your document contains a blank line that you created by pressing Return or Enter, Word *will* number that line. However, if you've formatted a paragraph to have double line spacing or one-and-one-half line spacing, Word will not number the blank lines between the lines of text in that paragraph. Similarly, if a paragraph's format specifies a certain amount of space before and/or after the paragraph text, Word will not assign a line number to these before and after spaces. Word does not number the lines in a footnote, nor does it number the lines of your header or footer text.

Numbering Options

When you activate the Line Numbering option, you can control certain features about your line numbers. First, you can specify how often Word should restart its line numbers. You can restart the line numbers at the top of each new page, at the beginning of each new section, or you can choose to number all the lines in a document continuously. Word's default is to restart line numbering on each page.

You can also control how frequently Word prints a line number. For example, you can choose to print a number next to every line (this is the default), or you can choose to display line numbers only on every fifth or every fifteenth line. Whatever interval you choose, Word will still include each line in its line count; however, it will print only those line numbers that fall at the interval you specify.

FIGURE 15-2

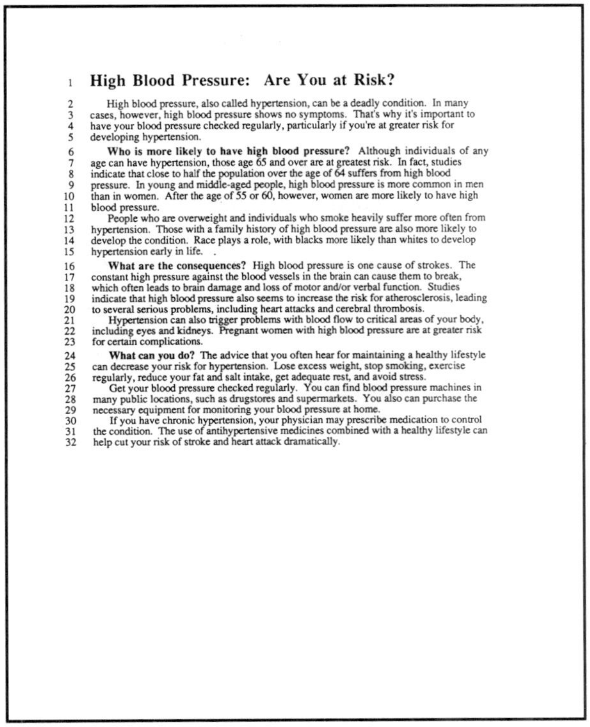

High Blood Pressure: Are You at Risk?

High blood pressure, also called hypertension, can be a deadly condition. In many cases, however, high blood pressure shows no symptoms. That's why it's important to have your blood pressure checked regularly, particularly if you're at greater risk for developing hypertension.

Who is more likely to have high blood pressure? Although individuals of any age can have hypertension, those age 65 and over are at greatest risk. In fact, studies indicate that close to half the population over the age of 64 suffers from high blood pressure. In young and middle-aged people, high blood pressure is more common in men than in women. After the age of 55 or 60, however, women are more likely to have high blood pressure.

People who are overweight and individuals who smoke heavily suffer more often from hypertension. Those with a family history of high blood pressure are also more likely to develop the condition. Race plays a role, with blacks more likely than whites to develop hypertension early in life.

What are the consequences? High blood pressure is one cause of strokes. The constant high pressure against the blood vessels in the brain can cause them to break, which often leads to brain damage and loss of motor and/or verbal function. Studies indicate that high blood pressure also seems to increase the risk for atherosclerosis, leading to several serious problems, including heart attacks and cerebral thrombosis.

Hypertension can also trigger problems with blood flow to critical areas of your body, including eyes and kidneys. Pregnant women with high blood pressure are at greater risk for certain complications.

What can you do? The advice that you often hear for maintaining a healthy lifestyle can decrease your risk for hypertension. Lose excess weight, stop smoking, exercise regularly, reduce your fat and salt intake, get adequate rest, and avoid stress.

Get your blood pressure checked regularly. You can find blood pressure machines in many public locations, such as drugstores and supermarkets. You also can purchase the necessary equipment for monitoring your blood pressure at home.

If you have chronic hypertension, your physician may prescribe medication to control the condition. The use of antihypertensive medicines combined with a healthy lifestyle can help cut your risk of stroke and heart attack dramatically.

Line numbers appear in your printed document but are not displayed on screen unless you use the Page Preview... command.

Finally, Word lets you control the placement of line numbers relative to your document text. Default placement is $^1/_4$ inch from the left edge of each line of text. Let's take a look at each of these Line Numbering options in detail.

Restarting line numbers

Word's default selection for restarting line numbers is By Page. This option tells Word to number the lines on each page separately, beginning with 1. If you would prefer to number all of the lines in each section continuously without restarting the numbers on each new page, click the By Section option. Actually, this option allows you to restart your line numbers anywhere you want—you simply enter a section break (by pressing ⌘-Enter) whenever you want to restart your line numbering at 1. Of course, if your document contains only one section, the By Section option will cause all the lines in that document to be numbered continuously.

You can use the third option, Continuous, to achieve continuous line numbering in documents with more than one section. When you choose this option, Word will number every line in your document without restarting the line count at sections or pages. In order for this option to work properly, you must be sure that you've activated line numbering in every section in your document and that you've clicked the Continuous option for each section.

Keep in mind that when you select the By Page, By Section, or Continuous option, your selection will apply only to the current section (the section on which the insertion point marker is positioned when you open the Section dialog box). This allows you more flexibility in numbering lines. For example, suppose that your document contains three sections. You would like to number the lines in the first section independently, then number the lines in the last two sections continuously. To achieve this, you would click the By Section option for both the first and the second sections. Then, in the third section, click the Continuous option. This tells Word that you want the line numbers in the third section to be continued from the line numbers in the second section, rather than restarting at 1.

As another example, suppose that you want your line numbers to restart at the beginning of each new section *and* at the beginning of each new page. Use the By Page option in those sections that cross from one page to the next and the By Section option in the rest of the sections.

In some cases, you may want to begin your numbering in the first section of a document with some number other than 1. For example, if you're printing a set of linked documents, you may want the line numbers to continue in sequence from one document to the next, rather than starting with 1 at the beginning of each document. You can change the first line number in your document from 1 (Word's default) to any other value by entering a beginning line number in the Line Numbers at edit bar of the Page Setup dialog box. For example, suppose that you would like the first line number in a document to be 463. Choose Page Setup... from the File menu and enter *463* in the Line Numbers at edit bar, as shown in Figure 15-3. (For more on linking documents, see Chapter 8.)

FIGURE 15-3

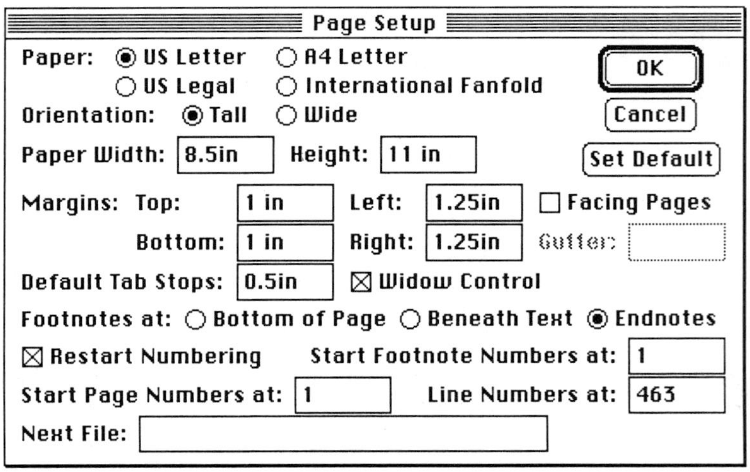

To begin the line numbers in a document at some number other than 1, enter the starting line number in the Page Setup dialog box.

By the way, if you've clicked the By Page or By Section option in the Section dialog box, Word will begin numbering each page or section after the first one with 1, no matter what you've entered in the Line Numbers at edit bar.

Line number frequency

As we mentioned earlier, you can also control how frequently line numbers are printed in your document. The entry in the Count by edit bar determines the frequency of your printed line numbers. Word's default Count by setting is 1; if you do not change this, Word will print a line number next to every line in your document, as shown in Figure 15-2. If you would like to print line numbers at wider intervals, then you should replace the 1 in the Count by edit bar with a different number.

For example, suppose you want your line numbers to appear only on every fifth line. In that case, you should enter a *5* in the Count by edit bar. As you can see, Figure 15-4 shows the document from Figure 15-2 after we changed the Count by value to 5. Notice that the first line number that appears in this document is 5.

FIGURE 15-4

High Blood Pressure: Are You at Risk?

High blood pressure, also called hypertension, can be a deadly condition. In many cases, however, high blood pressure shows no symptoms. That's why it's important to have your blood pressure checked regularly, particularly if you're at greater risk for developing hypertension.

Who is more likely to have high blood pressure? Although individuals of any age can have hypertension, those age 65 and over are at greatest risk. In fact, studies indicate that close to half the population over the age of 64 suffers from high blood pressure. In young and middle-aged people, high blood pressure is more common in men than in women. After the age of 55 or 60, however, women are more likely to have high blood pressure.

People who are overweight and individuals who smoke heavily suffer more often from hypertension. Those with a family history of high blood pressure are also more likely to develop the condition. Race plays a role, with blacks more likely than whites to develop hypertension early in life.

What are the consequences? High blood pressure is one cause of strokes. The constant high pressure against the blood vessels in the brain can cause them to break, which often leads to brain damage and loss of motor and/or verbal function. Studies indicate that high blood pressure also seems to increase the risk for atherosclerosis, leading to several serious problems, including heart attacks and cerebral thrombosis.

Hypertension can also trigger problems with blood flow to critical areas of your body, including eyes and kidneys. Pregnant women with high blood pressure are at greater risk for certain complications.

What can you do? The advice that you often hear for maintaining a healthy lifestyle can decrease your risk for hypertension. Lose excess weight, stop smoking, exercise regularly, reduce your fat and salt intake, get adequate rest, and avoid stress.

Get your blood pressure checked regularly. You can find blood pressure machines in many public locations, such as drugstores and supermarkets. You also can purchase the necessary equipment for monitoring your blood pressure at home.

If you have chronic hypertension, your physician may prescribe medication to control the condition. The use of antihypertensive medicines combined with a healthy lifestyle can help cut your risk of stroke and heart attack dramatically.

By changing the Count by value to 5, you can print line numbers on only every fifth line.

When you enter a Count by value other than 1, the results can sometimes be confusing because you can't see where one set of numbers ends and another begins. For example, suppose that your document contains several sections and you've activated line numbering in each section. If a new section starts in the middle of a page, Word will restart the line numbers at the section break. However, because your printed document does not show every line number, you won't be able to tell where the new section—and the new set of line numbers—starts. For instance, in the document shown in Figure 15-5, a new section begins at the headline in the middle of the page (*Philosophy and Learning*). Notice that, because we've chosen to display line numbers on only every tenth line, there is a significant area of unnumbered lines around the section break. To make matters more difficult, there are two lines numbered 10—one in the first section and one in the second section.

FIGURE 15-5

Perspectives on Learning

Learning is such an important phenomenon that intelligence itself is often measured in terms of the capacity to learn. However, we should not confuse intelligence and learning since learning ability is only one component of intelligence. Nevertheless, studies have shown that the ability to learn is closely tied to other measures of intelligence, such as the ability to reason and the ability to think creatively. For this reason, studying learning ability offers one of the best proxies for studying individual intelligence.

Because of the far-reaching importance of learning, many researchers have studied this subject from many different perspectives. This paper is an overview of different ways that scholars have thought about learning. In the first section, I will present the philosophical foundations on which the study of learning is based, and cover various definitions of learning. In the second section, I will present the perspectives that several different scholars have taken on four major areas of learning: memory, purposeful instruction, purposeful study, and incidental experience. The third section of this paper will cover briefly several topics that are related to learning, including discovery and instinct. I will also give several researchers' observations on the factors that can enhance learning.

Philosophy and Learning

Hilgard and Bower claim that scientific inquiry into the question of learning was long predated by philosophers' views on learning.[1] Interestingly, most modern research on the subject of learning tends to follow a particular philosophical viewpoint. Thus, we will begin by looking at the major philosophical foundations for viewing the learning process.

The philosophy of learning can be divided into two major branches: the analysis of knowledge (epistemology) and the nature and organization of mental life. In this paper, I will deal with the former branch, the analysis of knowledge. In the field of epistemology, there are two camps, the empiricists and the rationalists. Empiricists tend to be interested in external, measurable behavior, while rationalists tend to concern themselves with the internal workings of the mind. Empiricists include such philosophers as Hobbes, Locke, Hume, and Mill.

There are four major points in the empiricist view: sensationalism, reductionism, associationism, and mechanism. Sensationalism assumes that all knowledge comes through the senses. Reductionism assumes that all knowledge is built out of a few fundamental building blocks. Associationism is the view that we remember events along with the context in which they occur. Mechanism assumes that thought is a mechanical process, which if understood, would be totally predictable. Of these four points, associationism is the one most emphasized by the empiricist philosophers.

The rationalist viewpoint was put forth by such philosophers as Descartes and Kant. They tend to disagree with every major tenant of the empiricist view. In fact, the rationalists say that the mind, before any experience, has its own preconceived notions and thoughts. Experience is unstructured chaos, which must be fit into our preconceived reason. As Kant said, "Although all our knowledge begins with experience, it by no means follows that it all originates from experience."[2] According to Kant, the form in which matter (experience) is organized into memory is *a priori* to that matter (experience) coming to be stored in memory. Thus Kant classified matter or experience as *a posteriori*.

If you choose not to show all line numbers, you won't be able to see when a new set of line numbers begins at a section break.

Line number position

As we mentioned above, Word's default position for line numbers is 1/4 inch from the left edge of each line of text. If you'd like to change this, enter a number in the From Text edit bar. For example, to position your line numbers 1/2 inch from the left edge of your text, you'd enter .5 in the From Text edit bar.

In positioning line numbers, Word assumes that the left edge of your text is determined by your Left margin setting in the Page Setup dialog box. If, in fact, you've indented your text by moving the indent markers on the ruler, Word won't take this into account in positioning line numbers. For example, suppose that your Left margin setting is 1.25 (Word's default). Suppose also that you've formatted every paragraph in your document by moving the first-line and left indent markers to the 1 inch position on the ruler. This will create a total margin space of 2 $^1/_4$ inches in your printed document. If you activate line numbering in this document and enter .5 in the From Text edit bar, your line numbers will actually be printed 1 $^1/_2$ inches from the left edge of your text.

The number that you enter in the From Text edit bar must be less than the width of the Left margin setting in the Page Setup dialog box. Otherwise, Word will not be able to fit your line numbers on the printed page.

If you would like to position your line numbers at the right edge of each line, enter a negative number in the From Text edit bar. For example, suppose that your document is set up with Word's default 1 $^1/_4$ inch left and right margins. If you haven't moved the left and right indent markers, each line of text will be six inches long. To position your line numbers $^1/_2$ inch from the right edge of your text, enter -6.5 in the From Text edit bar. You can calculate this number by adding the line length (6 inches) to the amount of space that you want between the text and each line number ($^1/_2$ inch), then using the negative of this value. As you might expect, if you enter a negative number whose absolute value is less than the length of your lines of text, such as -1, Word will print your line numbers on top of your text.

Selective Line Numbering

In some cases, you may want to assign line numbers only to certain parts of your document. There are a couple of ways you can number lines selectively. First, if you want to number the lines in only a small part of your document—say, a single paragraph or a few paragraphs—then you should place a section break both before and after that part of your document. To insert a section break, just press ⌘-Enter. Word will display a double dotted line on your screen to mark the boundary of the new section. (If you don't want the new section to be printed on a separate page, be sure to click the No Break Section Start option in the Section dialog box.) Figure 15-6 on the next page shows a document in which we've inserted section breaks both before and after a couple of paragraphs.

After you've "sectioned off" a part of your document, position your insertion point marker anywhere within the section that you want to number, choose Section... from the Format menu, and click the Line Numbering option to activate it.

Another way you can control line numbering in a document is by "turning off" the line numbers on selected paragraphs. After you've clicked the Line Numbering option in the Section dialog box, select the paragraph or paragraphs whose lines you do *not* want to number. Then choose Paragraph... from the

Format menu to open the Paragraph dialog box. As you can see in Figure 15-7, when you first open this dialog box, the Line Numbering option will already be selected. Click this option to turn off line numbering for the selected paragraph(s), then click OK to close the dialog box.

FIGURE 15-6

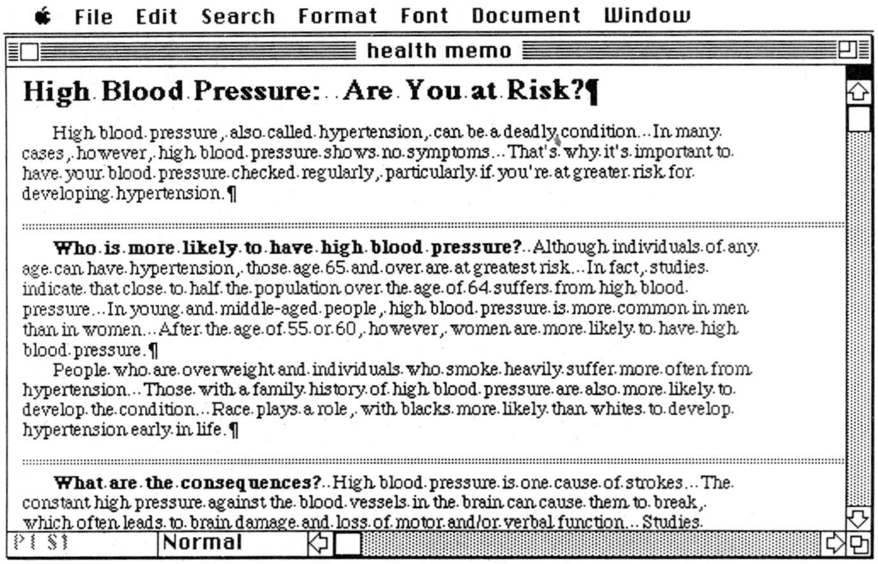

To number the lines only in a small portion of your document, place a section break both before and after that text.

FIGURE 15-7

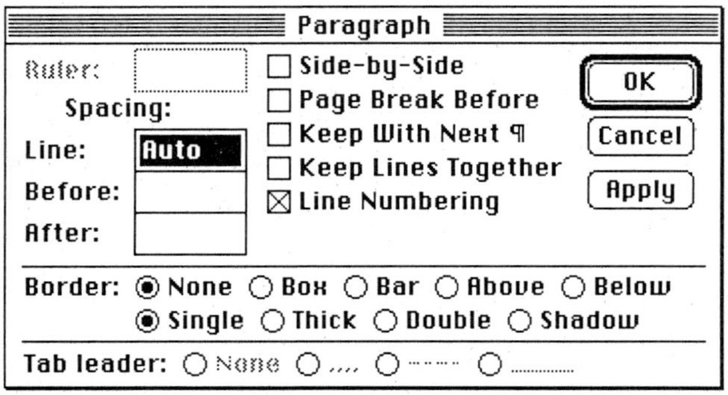

If you have activated line numbering in a section, Word will activate the Line Numbering option in the Paragraph dialog box as well.

As we demonstrated, when you select the Line Numbering option for a section, Word will initially activate the Line Numbering option in the Paragraph dialog box. Though you can deselect this option for certain paragraphs, you can't apply the Line Numbering option to any paragraph until you have activated that option in the Section dialog box. If you do not select Line Numbering in the Section dialog box, the Line Numbering option in the Paragraph dialog box will be dimmed.

When you "turn off" the line numbers for a selected paragraph, Word will not print line numbers next to that text, nor will it include those lines in its line number count. For example, Figure 15-8 shows part of a printed page from a document in which we've numbered all of the lines except those in the second paragraph. Notice that the last line before the unnumbered paragraph is numbered 8, while the first line after the unnumbered paragraph picks up the count again with the number 9.

FIGURE 15-8

The Clark School Opens in Fairfield

The Clark School, a new private, nonprofit school for young children, opened its doors this week. The school, which is located in the old Gardner High School building on Bern Road, offers preschool and elementary education through the third grade. According to Susan Ballard, the school's director, children from ages two through eight are considered to be in the "early childhood" years, and thus it is logical to provide a special learning environment for them.

The stated purpose of the Clark School is "to provide a unique, creative, educational experience in which each child can develop at an individual rate to his or her full potential." Classes are small, with a 12-to-2 student-teacher ratio for children ages two and three, and a 15-to-2 ratio for children ages four and five. In the first through third grades, the student-teacher ratio is 25 pupils per two teachers.

Tuition for one school term varies from $500 for a two-day-per-week program to $2000 for children in the primary school program. Payments are due three times per year, in September, November, and February. Most classes for the upcoming school year are filled, though there are a few openings in the second and third grades.

Educational Philosophy

All of the classrooms at the Clark School are organized according to the "learning centers" concept. Children are offered a variety of creative activities in different areas of the room. In a preschool classroom, you might find wooden blocks in one corner, books in another corner, an art activity at a table, and several other activities available in other areas of the room. A typical elementary classroom will include a reading center, a table for manipulating math objects, and an area devoted to a special topic, such as dinosaurs.

We interviewed the director of the Clark School and several teachers in order to get a more detailed picture of the educational environment they hope to provide. All the people we spoke with emphasized that the school is designed to help children grow emotionally and socially, as well as intellectually. "A child must feel good about himself if he is to reach his maximum potential in learning to relate to other people and his environment," said Linda Phillips, a preschool teacher. According to Ms. Phillips, the school's educational philosophy is based on the research of such psychologists as Eric Erickson and Jean Piaget, as well as on the ideas of well-known educators, such as Dorothy Cohen and Maria Montessori.

Another important element of the Clark School's educational philosophy is the idea that children should be allowed to pursue their own pace in learning. "Forced learning is inappropriate—if not impossible—for young children," said Mrs. Ballard. "Studies have shown that children who are pushed into subjects before they are ready may develop a negative attitude toward school in general and almost certainly will lose some of their natural creativity."

Although the Clark School will allow children to learn at their own rate, the curriculum will revolve around structured activities and planned schedules. Teachers will send a weekly newsletter to parents, informing them about the activities of the current and upcoming weeks. Ann Willard, a kindergarten teacher, said that the weekly newsletter, plus scheduled conferences, will allow her to maintain regular contact with parents, which she hopes will further their support and involvement with the school.

When you eliminate line numbers from a selected paragraph, Word will not include that paragraph in its line count.

Special situations

If you're using a multicolumn page design, and you have selected the Line Numbering option, Word will number the lines in each column. For example, Figure 15-9 shows a two-column document with numbered lines. Notice that the line numbering is continuous from the bottom of the first column to the top of the second column.

FIGURE 15-9

The Clark School Opens in Fairfield

The Clark School, a new private, nonprofit school for young children, opened its doors this week. The school, which is located in the old Gardner High School building on Bern Road, offers preschool and elementary education through the third grade. According to Susan Ballard, the school's director, children from ages two through eight are considered to be in the "early childhood" years, and thus it is logical to provide a spetial learning environment for them.

The stated purpose of the Clark School is "to provide a unique, creative, educational experience in which each child can develop at an individual rate to his or her full potential." Classes are small, with a 12-to-2 student-teacher ratio for children ages two and three, and a 15-to-2 ratio for children ages four and five. In the first through third grades, the student-teacher ratio is 25 pupils per two teachers.

Tuition for one school term varies from $500 for a two-day-per-week program to $2000 for children in the primary school program. Payments are due three times per year, in September, November, and February. Most classes for the upcoming school year are filled, though there are a few openings in the second and third grades.

Educational Philosophy

All of the classrooms at the Clark School are organized according to the "learning centers" concept. Children are offered a variety of creative activities in different areas of the room. In a preschool classroom, you might find wooden blocks in one corner, books in another corner, an art activity at a table, and several other activities available in other areas of the room. A typical elementary classroom will include a reading center, a table for manipulating math objects, and an area devoted to a special topic, such as dinosaurs.

We interviewed the director of the Clark School and several teachers in order to get a more detailed picture of the educational environment they hope to provide. All the people we spoke with emphasized that the school is designed to help children grow emotionally and socially, as well as intellectually. "A child must feel good about himself if he is to reach his maximum potential in learning to relate to other people and his environment," said Linda Phillips, a preschool teacher. According to Ms. Phillips, the school's educational philosophy is based on the research of such psychologists as Eric Erickson and Jean Piaget, as well as on the ideas of well-known educators, such as Dorothy Cohen and Maria Montessori.

Another important element of the Clark School's educational philosophy is the idea that children should be allowed to pursue their own pace in learning. "Forced learning is inappropriate—if not impossible—for young children," said Mrs. Ballard. "Studies have shown that children who are pushed into subjects before they are ready may develop a negative attitude toward school in general and almost certainly will lose some of their natural creativity."

Although the Clark School will allow children to learn at their own rate, the curriculum will revolve around structured activities and planned schedules. Teachers will send a weekly newsletter to parents, informing them about the activities of the current and upcoming weeks. Ann Willard, a kindergarten teacher, said that the weekly newsletter, plus scheduled conferences, will allow her to maintain regular contact with parents, which she hopes will further their support and involvement with the school.

When you use columnar formatting in a document, Word will number the lines in every column.

When you number the lines in a multicolumn document, be sure that you allow enough space between columns to display the line numbers. You also should be careful that the From Text setting for your line numbers is less than the Spacing setting for your columns. Otherwise, your line numbers will not fit in the gutter between columns.

Side-by-side paragraph formatting is, unfortunately, incompatible with line numbering. If you assign the Side-by-Side format to one or more paragraphs in a document, Word will simply skip those paragraphs as it assigns line numbers. Not only will Word fail to print line numbers next to side-by-side paragraphs, it won't even consider those paragraphs in its line number count. For example, Figure 15-10 shows the document from Figure 15-8 after we assigned the Side-by-Side format to the subheading *Educational Philosophy* and to the first paragraph after the subheading. Notice that the line numbers skip from 23, at the end of the paragraph immediately before the subheading, to 24, at the beginning of the first paragraph after the side-by-side paragraphs.

FIGURE 15-10

The Clark School Opens in Fairfield

The Clark School, a new private, nonprofit school for young children, opened its doors this week. The school, which is located in the old Gardner High School building on Bern Road, offers preschool and elementary education through the third grade. According to Susan Ballard, the school's director, children from ages two through eight are considered to be in the "early childhood" years, and thus it is logical to provide a special learning environment for them.

The stated purpose of the Clark School is "to provide a unique, creative, educational experience in which each child can develop at an individual rate to his or her full potential." Classes are small, with a 12-to-2 student-teacher ratio for children ages two and three, and a 15-to-2 ratio for children ages four and five. In the first through third grades, the student-teacher ratio is 25 pupils per two teachers.

Tuition for one school term varies from $500 for a two-day-per-week program to $2000 for children in the primary school program. Payments are due three times per year, in September, November, and February. Most classes for the upcoming school year are filled, though there are a few openings in the second and third grades.

Educational Philosophy

All of the classrooms at the Clark School are organized according to the "learning centers" concept. Children are offered a variety of creative activities in different areas of the room. In a preschool classroom, you might find wooden blocks in one corner, books in another corner, an art activity at a table, and several other activities available in other areas of the room. A typical elementary classroom will include a reading center, a table for manipulating math objects, and an area devoted to a special topic, such as dinosaurs.

We interviewed the director of the Clark School and several teachers in order to get a more detailed picture of the educational environment they hope to provide. All the people we spoke with emphasized that the school is designed to help children grow emotionally and socially, as well as intellectually. "A child must feel good about himself if he is to reach his maximum potential in learning to relate to other people and his environment," said Linda Phillips, a preschool teacher. According to Ms. Phillips, the school's educational philosophy is based on the research of such psychologists as Eric Erickson and Jean Piaget, as well as on the ideas of well-known educators, such as Dorothy Cohen and Maria Montessori.

Another important element of the Clark School's educational philosophy is the idea that children should be allowed to pursue their own pace in learning. "Forced learning is inappropriate—if not impossible—for young children," said Mrs. Ballard. "Studies have shown that children who are pushed into subjects before they are ready

Word will not number paragraphs that have been assigned the Side-by-Side format.

NUMBERING PARAGRAPHS

Word's Renumber… command on the Document menu allows you to number paragraphs automatically throughout all or part of a document. When you issue this command without selecting any text, Word will assign a number to every paragraph in the current document. If you select one or more paragraphs before you choose Renumber…, then Word will assign numbers only to the paragraphs in your selection. (By the way, if you select less than a full paragraph of text—say, a word or two—before you choose Renumber…, then Word will assume that you want to assign a number only to the paragraph that contains your selection.) In numbering paragraphs, Word doesn't recognize section breaks; the paragraphs before and after a section break will be numbered continuously.

You can control many different features of your paragraph numbers, including their alignment in relation to your text, the type of numbering scheme used, and the Start number for a sequence of paragraphs. If you decide to add, delete, or rearrange paragraphs, Word's Renumber... command makes it very easy to get your paragraph numbers back in order.

Automatic paragraph numbering is particularly useful in documents with multiple levels of paragraphs—such as legal documents or outlines. In these cases, Word lets you control the numbering scheme of each level. For example, your first-level paragraphs might be numbered *1.*, *2.*, *3.*, and so forth, while your second-level paragraphs are numbered *1-A.*, *1-B.*, and so forth. Before we talk about numbering multiple levels of paragraphs, however, let's examine some of the basics of paragraph numbering. These basic concepts will apply whether your document contains only one level of paragraphs or several levels.

Numbering Basics

To number all of the paragraphs in a document, just choose Renumber... from the Document menu. Word will then display the dialog box shown in Figure 15-11.

FIGURE 15-11

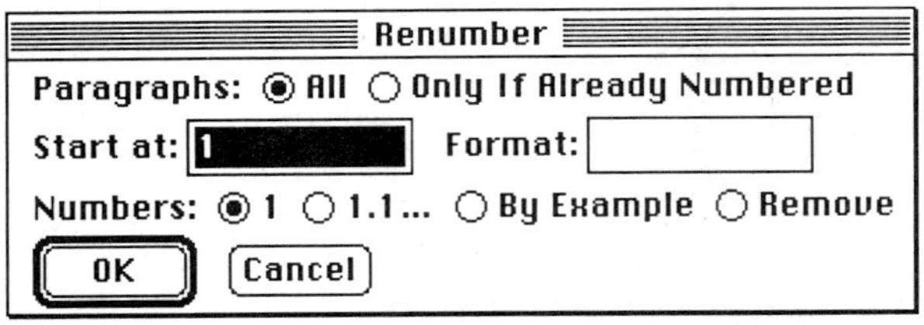

You'll see this dialog box when you choose Renumber... from the Document menu.

When you see this dialog box, all you have to do is click OK. Word will then close the dialog box and place an Arabic numeral followed by a period (*1.*, *2.*, *3.*, and so forth) at the beginning of each paragraph. Figure 15-12 shows an example of a document after we've issued the Renumber... command.

Notice that Word aligns each paragraph number with the first-line indent marker on the ruler. In this example, the first-line indent marker for each paragraph is positioned at the $^{1}/_{4}$ inch mark on the ruler. Therefore, each paragraph number is indented by $^{1}/_{4}$ inch. Notice also that Word inserts a tab space between the paragraph number and the paragraph text. This causes the first character of text to be positioned at the first tab after the initial indent. Since we have not changed Word's default tab stops, the first character of each paragraph in our example is aligned with the default tab stop that occurs at the $^{1}/_{2}$ inch position on the ruler. As we'll explain in just a minute, you can change the alignment of paragraph numbers and text by manipulating your indent markers and tabs.

FIGURE 15-12

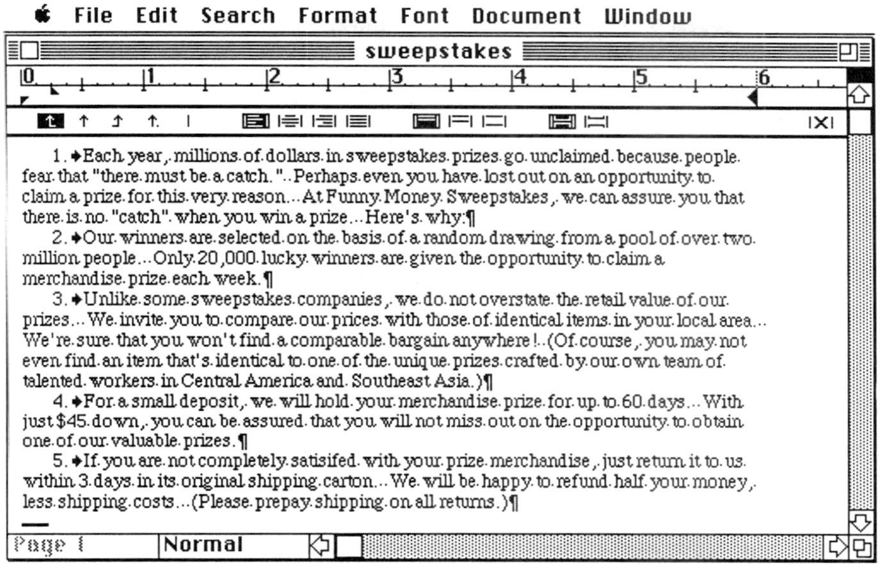

Word's default numbering scheme will place an Arabic number followed by a period at the beginning of each paragraph.

Choosing a numbering scheme

As we showed in the above example, Word's default numbering scheme for paragraphs uses Arabic numerals. If you would prefer to use Roman numerals or alphabetic characters, you can specify your preference in the Renumber dialog box. Just enter the type of character that you want to use in the Format edit bar. For example, if you want to use Roman numerals, you can enter an *I* in the Format edit bar. To use alphabetic characters in your numbering scheme, you can enter an *A*. To specify Arabic numerals, you can type a *1* in the edit bar. (Since Arabic numerals are Word's default, you don't need to enter anything in the edit bar unless you are converting existing numbers from another format into Arabic numerals.)

The first time you issue the Renumber... command, you'll notice that the Format edit bar is blank. In fact, this edit bar will always be blank unless the first paragraph in your document (or the first paragraph in your selection) has been numbered. After you've numbered some paragraphs, however, the Format edit bar will display an example of the line numbering scheme for the first paragraph in your document or selection. For instance, if you select some paragraphs that have been numbered with Roman numerals, then choose Renumber..., Word will display an *I.* or *i.* in the Format edit bar.

If you want to use a numbering scheme other than the one that Word suggests in the edit bar, you can just replace the characters in the Format edit bar. For example, suppose you want to change the Arabic numerals in a document to Roman numerals. Issue the Renumber... command, then, in the Format edit bar, drag through the *1.* to select it, and type an *I.* or *i.* as a replacement. When you click OK, all your paragraph numbers will be converted to Roman numerals

As you're specifying a numbering scheme, you don't have to use the first letter of the alphabet, the Roman numeral I, or a 1. You can type any Arabic number to specify an Arabic numbering scheme, and you can enter any letter (except I, V, or X) to indicate that you want to use an alphabetic numbering scheme. Similarly, you can enter almost any Roman numeral to specify a Roman numeral numbering scheme. Interestingly, if you type a high Roman numeral that's only a single character—such as L, C, or M—Word will interpret your entry as an alphabetic character. However, if you enter a high Roman numeral that is made up of two or more characters—such as LIX or CM—Word will correctly interpret your entry as a Roman numeral.

If you choose an alphabetic or Roman numeral numbering scheme, Word allows you to select either upper-case or lower-case for your paragraph "numbers." The case that you use for the entry in the Format edit bar will determine the case of the "numbers" in your document. For example, if you want to use a lower-case alphabetic numbering scheme, then you should enter a lower-case letter—such as *c*—in the Format edit bar. Similarly, if you want to use a lower-case Roman numeral numbering scheme (i, ii, iii, and so forth), then you should enter a lower-case Roman numeral in the edit bar, as we've done in Figure 15-13.

FIGURE 15-13

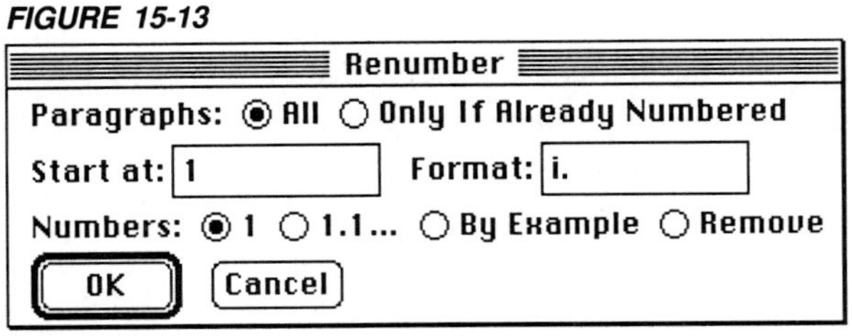

The entry in the Format edit bar tells Word what kind of numbering scheme you want to use for your paragraphs.

Choosing the separator characters

As we've already shown, Word's default separator character is a period after each paragraph number. If you would like to use a different separator character, then you must enter that character—along with a number or letter—in the Format edit bar. For example, suppose you want to use a right parenthesis (with lower-case Roman numerals) as your separator character. In that case you would enter *i)* in the Format edit bar, as shown in Figure 15-14.

FIGURE 15-14

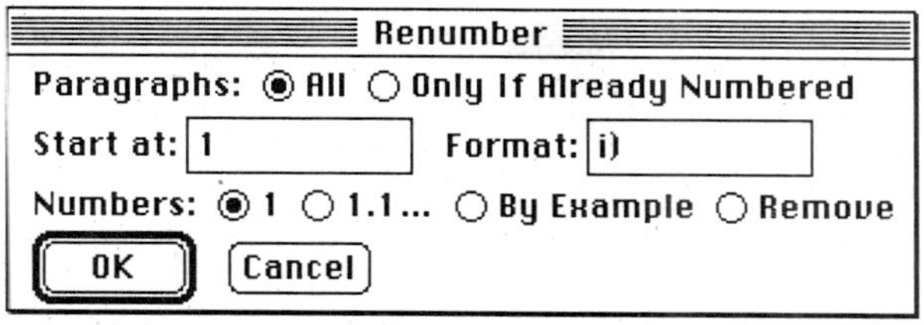

Your entry in the Format edit bar can also specify a separator character.

Word allows you to use any of the standard nonalphanumeric characters as separator characters. For example, all of the characters that are produced with the shifted numeric keys are valid separator characters, including #, *, and -. The characters that are produced with the Option-key combinations (such as § and •) are *not* considered valid separator characters.

You can place a separator character both before and after each paragraph number. If you do this, Word allows you to use two different characters. For example, you might want to enclose each paragraph number in parentheses, in which case you would enter *(i)* in the Format edit bar.

Interestingly, Word will not allow you to place a separator character before a number without also placing a character after the number. For example, *-1-* and *<i>* are both valid entries for the Format edit bar, but *>1* is not. Word also will not allow any "extra" separator characters. For example, if you type two separator characters before the number in the Format edit bar (such as ***1*), Word will beep and display the message, *Invalid number*. If you place two or more separator characters after the number, such as *1***, Word will simply ignore all separator characters after the first one.

When you're numbering multiple levels of paragraphs, Word allows you to use a different separator character between each level number. For example, third-level paragraphs might be numbered 2.1-a). We will discuss the format of multiple-level paragraph numbers later on in the section, "Numbering Multiple Levels of Paragraphs."

Specifying a Start number

When you first issue the Renumber… command for a document or a selection, Word will number each paragraph in sequence, starting with 1, A, or I (depending on the kind of numbering scheme you've chosen). If you want to use a different Start number, you must specify this in the Start at edit bar in the Renumber dialog box. For example, if you would like the first paragraph in the document or selection to be numbered 14, then you should enter a *14* in the Start at edit bar, as shown in Figure 15-15. Word will then number the second paragraph 15, the third paragraph 16, and so forth.

FIGURE 15-15

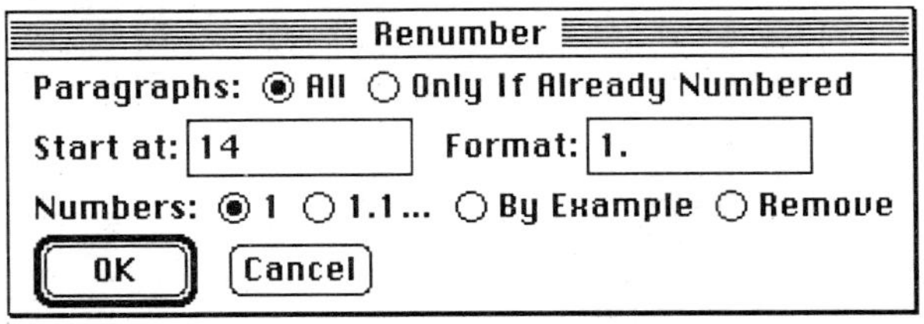

The entry in the Start at edit bar indicates the first paragraph number in your document or selection.

If you select some paragraphs before you issue the Renumber... command, and the first paragraph in your selection has already been assigned a number, then Word will display that number in the Start at edit bar. The same thing will happen when you're renumbering an entire document and the first paragraph of the document has already been assigned a number. Of course, you can still replace Word's suggested Start number with a different number.

Interestingly, your Start number does not have to be stated in the same format as your chosen numbering scheme. For example, suppose that you want to use an alphabetic numbering scheme, and you would like to begin "numbering" your paragraphs with the letter *d.* When you open the Renumber dialog box, you would enter *a.* in the Format edit bar to specify an alphabetic numbering scheme, and you could enter either *d.* or *4.* in the Start at edit bar (since *d* is the fourth letter of the alphabet).

As you'll see in a few pages, specifying a Start number in a document with multiple levels of paragraphs is a little more complicated. We'll cover that topic in the section on numbering multiple levels of paragraphs.

Formatting your paragraph numbers

Word uses the formatting features of the first character in each paragraph to determine the format of that paragraph's number. In other words, Word will match the character formatting of each paragraph's number—font, size, boldfacing, and so forth—to the format of the first character in the paragraph. This automatic formatting can be especially helpful in documents in which you've used character formatting to distinguish different kinds of topics. For example, Figure 15-16 shows a document with different kinds of formatting. Figure 15-17 shows this same document after we've issued the Renumber... command. Notice that some of the numbers appear in Times bold type, while others appear in Helvetica italic.

After you have numbered your paragraphs, you can change the format of your paragraph numbers if you want. If you reformat the numbers, and then issue the Renumber... command again, Word will not alter your manual format changes. (By the way, if your paragraph numbers are arranged in a column, keep in mind that you can use the Option key to make a block selection and reformat all of the numbers at once. Chapter 5 describes this block selection technique in more detail.)

FIGURE 15-16

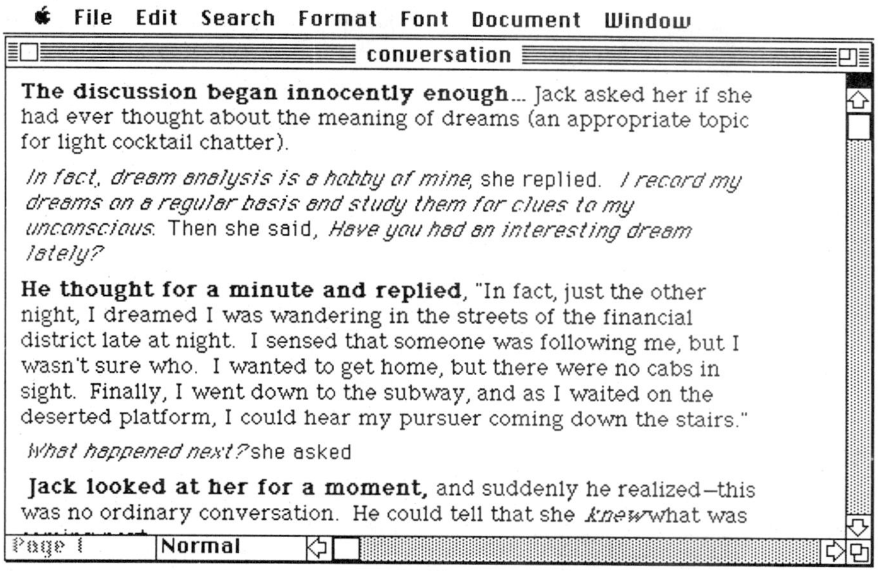

This document contains paragraphs with different character formatting.

FIGURE 15-17

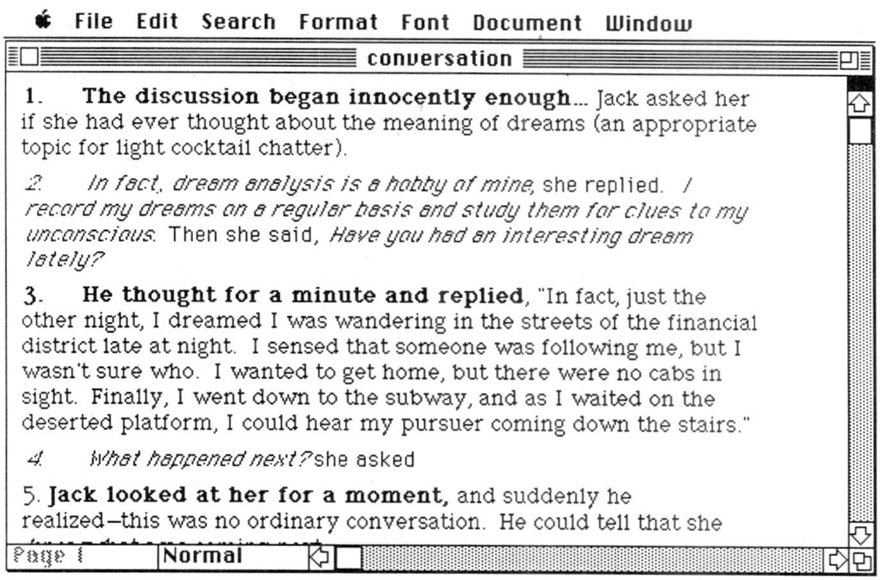

Word uses the formatting characteristics of the paragraph text to determine the format of each paragraph number.

Aligning numbers and text

As we explained at the beginning of this section, Word aligns each paragraph number with the first-line indent marker on the ruler. Word also inserts a tab space after each paragraph number so that the first character of paragraph text is aligned with the first tab after the indent. (Of course, the position of the first-line indent marker and the first tab can change from paragraph to paragraph in your document.)

If you would like to change the amount of space between a paragraph number and the first character of paragraph text, then all you have to do is place a tab at the appropriate place on the ruler. For example, Figure 15-18 shows some numbered paragraphs in which each number is aligned at the left edge of the screen (since the first-line indent marker is at the 0 position on the ruler), while the first character of text in each paragraph is aligned with the $^1/_2$ inch position on the ruler.

FIGURE 15-18

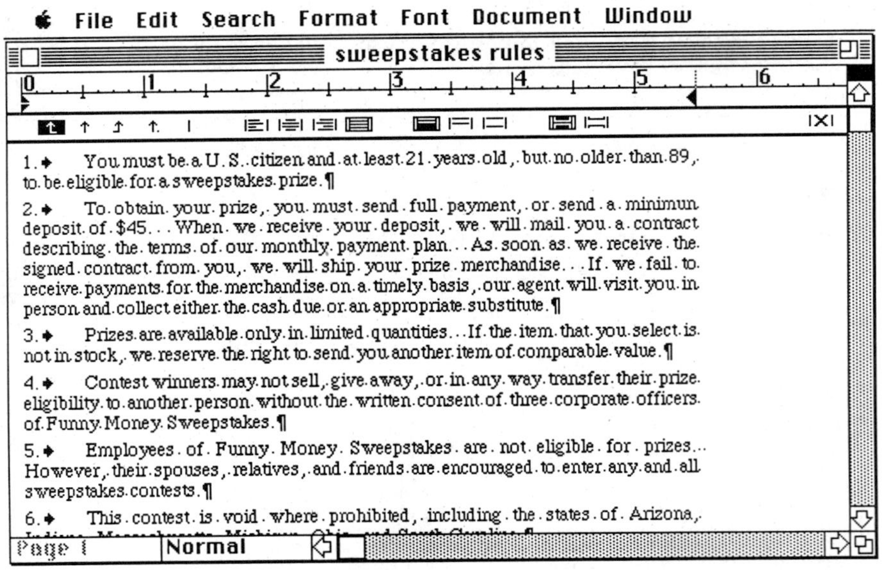

In these paragraphs, the numbers are aligned at the 0 position on the ruler, while the first character of text is aligned at the $^1/_2$ inch position.

Let's say that you would like to indent the first character of text by an additional $^1/_4$ inch. First, select these paragraphs, then click on the left tab stop icon to select it, and click on the $^3/_4$ inch position on the ruler. The result will look like Figure 15-19.

FIGURE 15-19

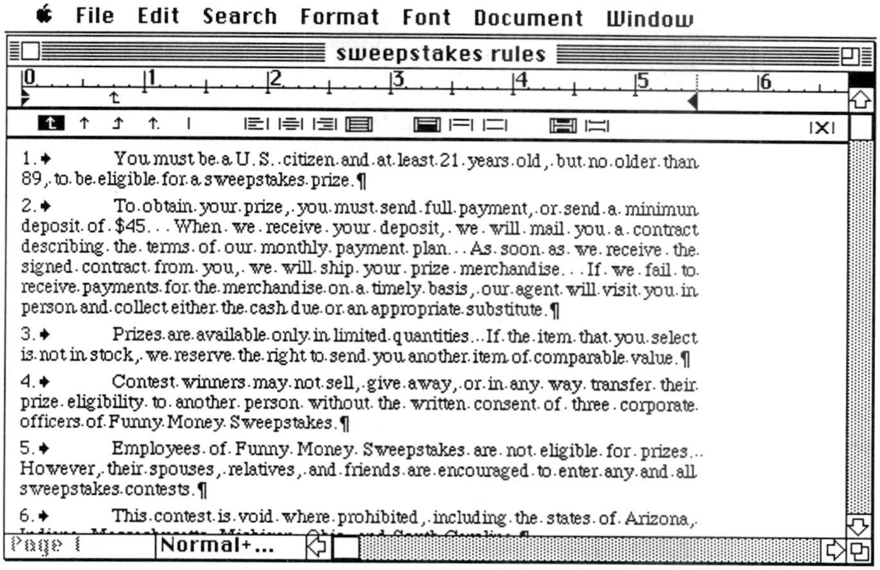

By inserting a tab, you can change the alignment of the first line of paragraph text.

By moving the left indent marker, you can change the alignment of the paragraph text (after the first line) in relation to the paragraph number. For example, you can "hang" paragraph numbers outside of the paragraph text. Figure 15-20 on the next page shows the paragraphs from Figure 15-19 after we moved the left indent marker to the $^1/_2$ inch position on the ruler.

Notice in Figure 15-20 on the next page that the first line in each paragraph is no longer aligned with the tab stop at the $^3/_4$ inch position. Instead, it is aligned with the left indent marker at the $^1/_2$ inch position. In deciding where to align the first line of text, Word looks for the first "stopping place" on the ruler after the first-line indent. In many cases, the first stopping place will occur at a tab—either one of Word's default tabs or a tab that you insert manually. However, if you move the left indent marker to the right of the first-line indent marker, you may create a "stopping place" *before* a tab, as we've done in Figure 15-20. In that case, Word will align the first character of text with the left indent marker.

If you were to move the left indent marker to the right of the tab, then your paragraphs would look like Figure 15-21. Notice that the first line of text in each paragraph is aligned at the tab that we've inserted at the $^1/_4$ inch position, while subsequent lines are aligned at the left indent marker, which occurs at the $^1/_2$ inch position. As a result, both the paragraph numbers and the initial text in each paragraph hang outside the left margin.

FIGURE 15-20

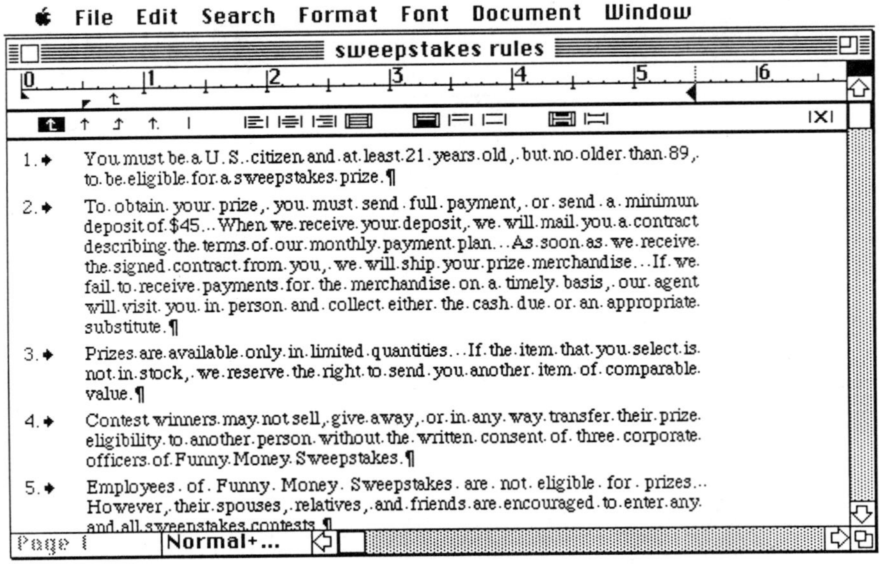

By moving the left indent marker, you can create "hanging" paragraph numbers.

FIGURE 15-21

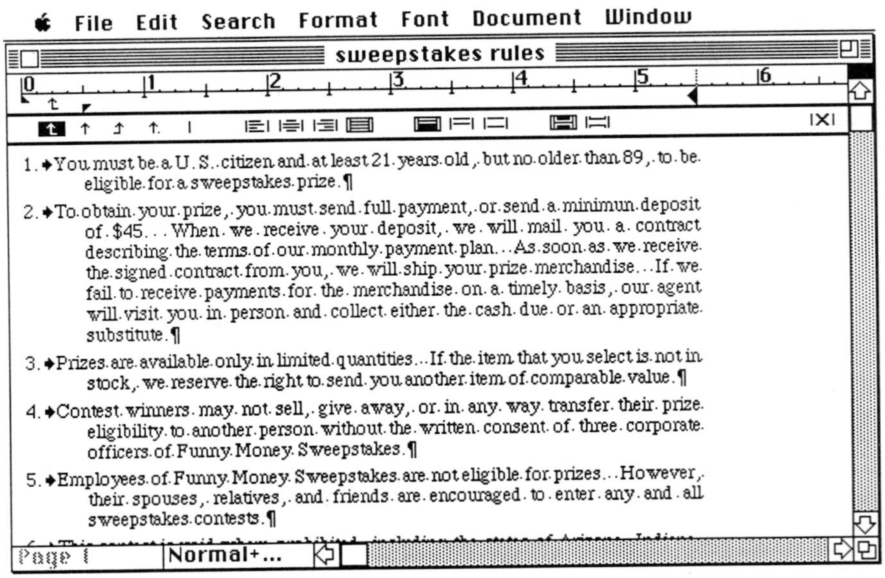

If you move the left indent marker to the right of the first tab, Word will align the first line of text in a paragraph with the tab stop.

Finally, by moving the left indent marker to the left of the first-line indent marker, you can cause the paragraph numbers to appear indented. For example, in Figure 15-22, we've moved the left indent marker to the $-^1/_2$ inch position on the ruler.

FIGURE 15-22

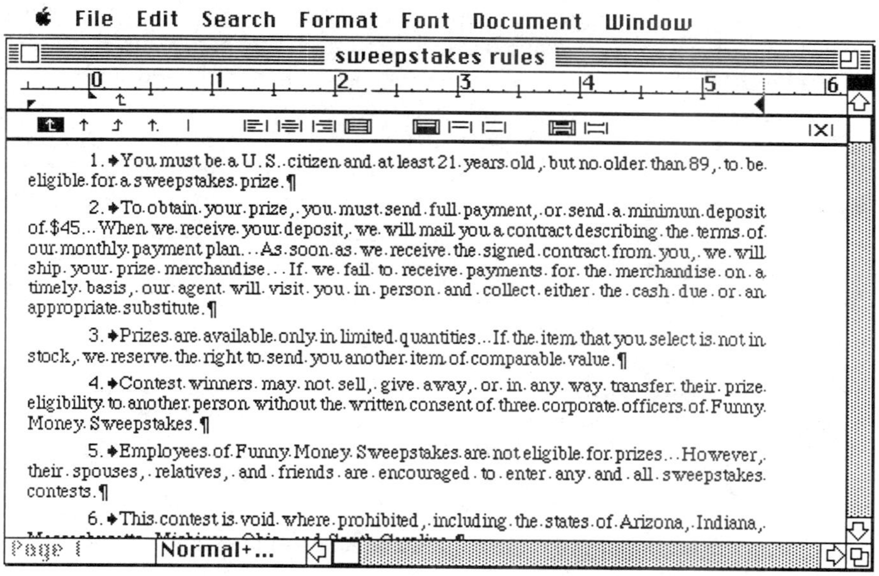

By moving the left indent marker to the left of the first-line indent marker, you can indent your paragraph numbers.

In the examples that we've presented so far, we have assumed that you want to change the alignment of only a few numbered paragraphs. In these cases, you must select those paragraphs before you move the indent markers or insert tab stops. If you would like to change the alignment of *all* the paragraphs in a document, then you must select the entire document before you make your ruler changes. A more efficient way to change the alignment of all the paragraphs in your document—or even a few paragraphs—is to alter the style definition (or definitions) for those paragraphs on the style sheet. For information on how to use named styles to format paragraphs, see Chapter 9.

Selective numbering

Chances are, when you number the paragraphs in a document, you will want to exclude certain paragraphs, such as the title, subheadings, figure captions, and so forth. Unfortunately, there's no automatic way to exclude certain paragraphs from the effects of the Renumber... command. However, there are a couple of techniques you can use to achieve selective paragraph numbering.

First, you can number your document a few paragraphs at a time, selecting only the paragraphs to which you want to assign a number. For example, you might begin by selecting all the paragraphs after the main title and before the first subheading, then issue the Renumber... command. After you number these paragraphs, you might select another group of paragraphs between the first and second subheadings, and again issue the Renumber... command. When you number this second group of paragraphs (and all subsequent paragraph groups), be sure to enter the correct number in the Start at edit bar of the Renumber dialog box. Otherwise, your paragraph numbers won't appear in sequence.

Another technique you can use to achieve selective numbering is to number *all* of the paragraphs in your document and then manually remove each unwanted number. After removing the numbers, you can issue the Renumber... command once more and click the Only If Already Numbered option. Word will then renumber your document, ignoring the paragraphs that don't already have numbers. In other words, the second time you issue the Renumber... command, Word will place all the remaining paragraph numbers in the correct order.

Numbering blank paragraphs

Whenever you number the paragraphs in a document, Word skips over blank paragraphs—that is, paragraphs which consist of a ¶ with no associated text. However, there may be instances where you want to number these blank paragraphs, perhaps so you can add text to these locations later. To do this, you must manually enter a number for each of these blank paragraphs. These numbers, which are simply temporary placeholders, do not have to be in proper sequence, nor do they have to use the same numbering scheme as the rest of your paragraph numbers.

After you type a number in front of each blank paragraph, you can use the Renumber... command to make Word replace these placeholder numbers with correct numbers. The Renumber... command will number the blank paragraphs in sequence, using the same numbering scheme (Arabic, Roman, or alphabetic) as the rest of your paragraph numbers.

For example, suppose that you would like to number each of the blank paragraphs (along with the rest of the document) shown in Figure 15-23. Before you issue the Renumber... command, type a 1 followed by a period and a tab space at the beginning of each blank paragraph. (The period is not absolutely necessary in this case. However, if you use an alphabetic character for your placeholder instead of a numeral—which is perfectly acceptable—you must be sure to type a separator character so that Word can distinguish your "number" from the paragraph text.) Figure 15-24 shows the document with the placeholder numbers.

FIGURE 15-23

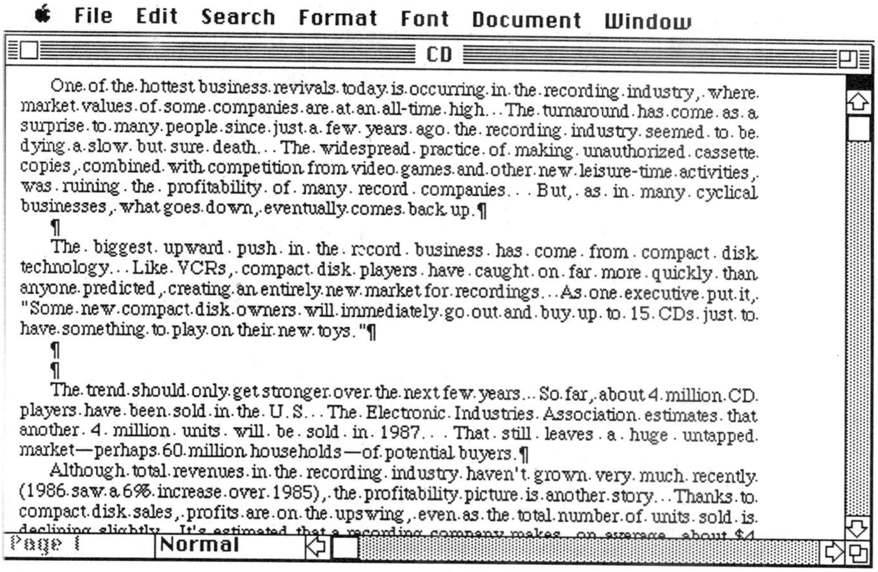
File Edit Search Format Font Document Window

CD

One of the hottest business revivals today is occurring in the recording industry, where market values of some companies are at an all-time high... The turnaround has come as a surprise to many people since just a few years ago the recording industry seemed to be dying a slow but sure death... The widespread practice of making unauthorized cassette copies, combined with competition from video games and other new leisure-time activities, was ruining the profitability of many record companies... But, as in many cyclical businesses, what goes down, eventually comes back up.¶

¶

The biggest upward push in the record business has come from compact disk technology... Like VCRs, compact disk players have caught on far more quickly than anyone predicted, creating an entirely new market for recordings... As one executive put it, "Some new compact disk owners will immediately go out and buy up to 15 CDs just to have something to play on their new toys."¶

¶

¶

The trend should only get stronger over the next few years... So far, about 4 million CD players have been sold in the U.S... The Electronic Industries Association estimates that another 4 million units will be sold in 1987... That still leaves a huge untapped market—perhaps 60 million households—of potential buyers.¶

Although total revenues in the recording industry haven't grown very much recently (1986 saw a 6% increase over 1985), the profitability picture is another story... Thanks to compact disk sales, profits are on the upswing, even as the total number of units sold is

Page 1 Normal

Word normally will not number blank paragraphs like those shown in this document.

FIGURE 15-24

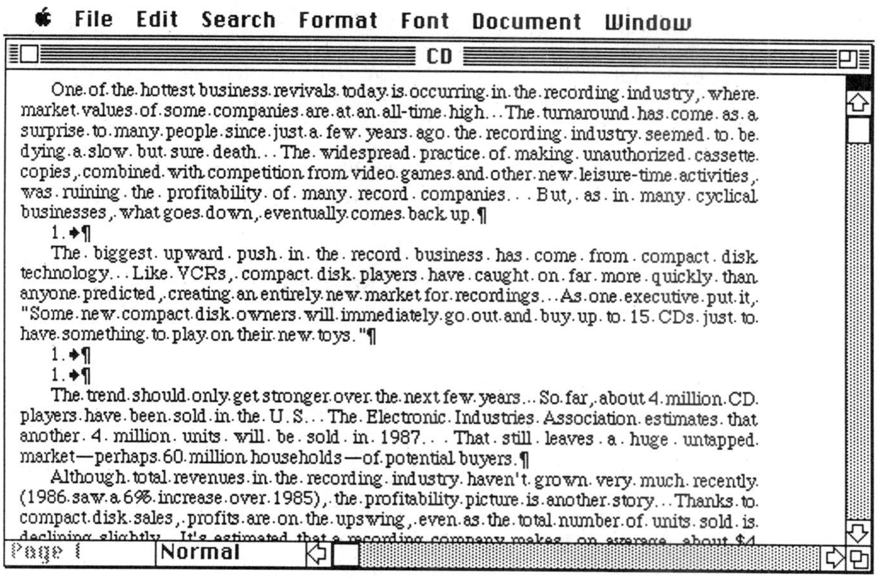
File Edit Search Format Font Document Window

CD

One of the hottest business revivals today is occurring in the recording industry, where market values of some companies are at an all-time high... The turnaround has come as a surprise to many people since just a few years ago the recording industry seemed to be dying a slow but sure death... The widespread practice of making unauthorized cassette copies, combined with competition from video games and other new leisure-time activities, was ruining the profitability of many record companies... But, as in many cyclical businesses, what goes down, eventually comes back up.¶

1.→¶

The biggest upward push in the record business has come from compact disk technology... Like VCRs, compact disk players have caught on far more quickly than anyone predicted, creating an entirely new market for recordings... As one executive put it, "Some new compact disk owners will immediately go out and buy up to 15 CDs just to have something to play on their new toys."¶

1.→¶

1.→¶

The trend should only get stronger over the next few years... So far, about 4 million CD players have been sold in the U.S... The Electronic Industries Association estimates that another 4 million units will be sold in 1987... That still leaves a huge untapped market—perhaps 60 million households—of potential buyers.¶

Although total revenues in the recording industry haven't grown very much recently (1986 saw a 6% increase over 1985), the profitability picture is another story... Thanks to compact disk sales, profits are on the upswing, even as the total number of units sold is

Page 1 Normal

To number blank paragraphs, begin by entering a placeholder number and tab before the ¶.

The next step is to issue the Renumber... command as you normally would. In this example, let's assume that you enter *A.* in the Format edit bar to specify an upper-case alphabetic numbering scheme. When you click OK, your document will look like Figure 15-25. Notice that Word has replaced each placeholder number with the correct letter for that paragraph.

FIGURE 15-25

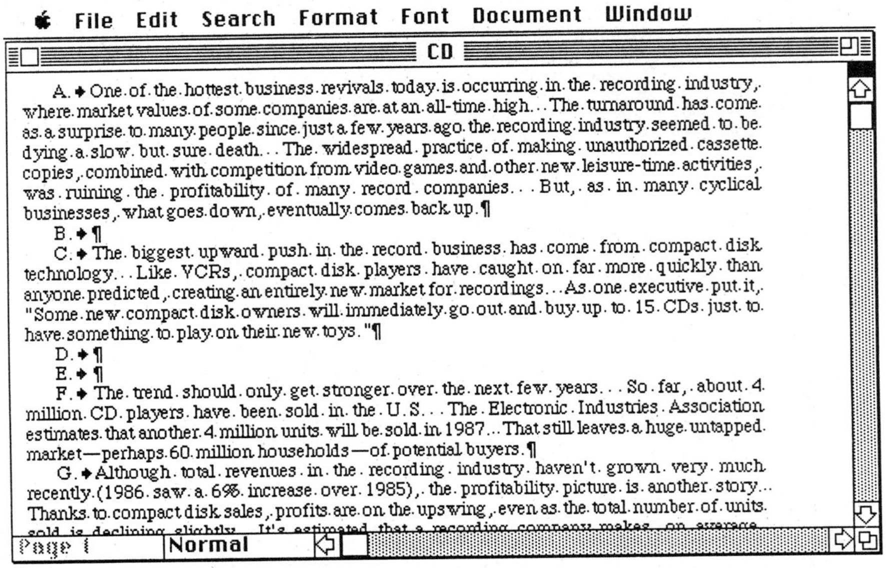

When you issue the Renumber... command, Word will replace each placeholder number with a properly formatted number or letter in the correct sequence.

By the way, you can use this same technique to number blank paragraphs in documents that have multiple levels of paragraphs. When you issue the Renumber... command, just be sure that you enter in the Format edit bar the type of numbering scheme that you want to use for each paragraph level. Word will then assign the correct number to each blank paragraph, no matter at what level it occurs.

Numbering Multiple Levels of Paragraphs

As we mentioned in the introduction to this section, paragraph numbering is perhaps most useful in documents that contain multiple levels of superior and subordinate paragraphs, such as legal documents or teaching materials. When you issue the Renumber... command, Word is able to recognize different levels of paragraphs and assign a different set of numbers to each level. For example, Figure 15-26 shows a document with three different levels of numbered paragraphs. Notice that Word uses a different set of numbers for each level.

FIGURE 15-26

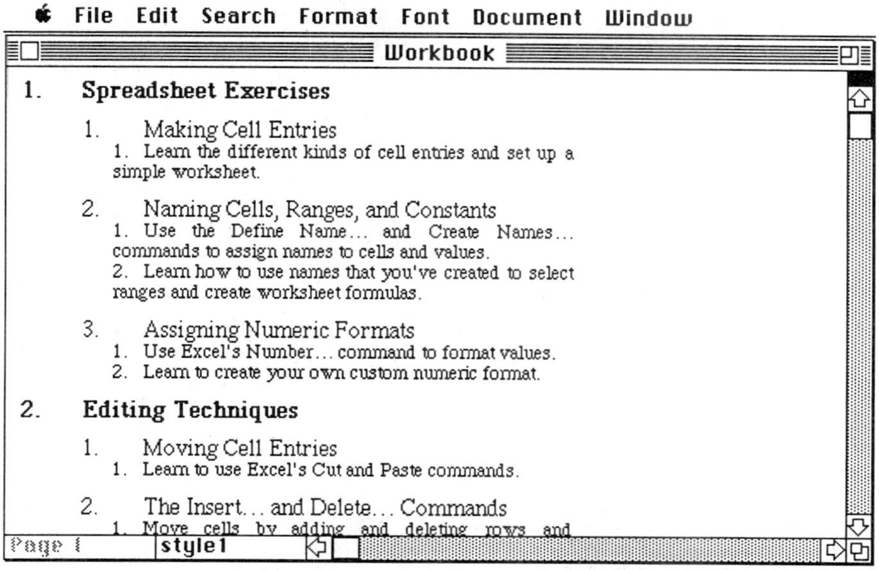

Word is able to assign a different set of numbers to each level of paragraphs in a document.

Not only is Word able to number each level separately, it also can use a different numbering scheme and different separator characters for each level. For example, Figure 15-27 on the following page shows the document from Figure 15-26 in which we've specified a different numbering scheme for each of the three levels of paragraphs. Notice that the first level uses Arabic numerals, while the second level uses upper-case alphabetic characters, and the third level returns to Arabic numerals.

How can Word distinguish the different levels of paragraphs in a document? The amount of indention on the first line of each paragraph indicates the level of that paragraph. The further to the right a paragraph is indented, the more subordinate its level. For example, suppose you have a document in which the first line of some of the paragraphs is not indented at all. In other paragraphs, the first line is indented by $^{1}/_{4}$ inch. If you were to issue the Renumber... command, Word would recognize two different levels of paragraphs in this document. All of the paragraphs with no first-line indention would be considered first-level paragraphs, and Word would number these sequentially. The paragraphs with the $^{1}/_{4}$ inch first-line indention would be considered second-level paragraphs. Each consecutive group of these second-level paragraphs would be numbered sequentially. However, when Word reaches a first-level paragraph, that would be its signal to start over in numbering the next set of second-level paragraphs. In other words, Word assumes that each group of second-level paragraphs "falls under" a particular first-level paragraph.

FIGURE 15-27

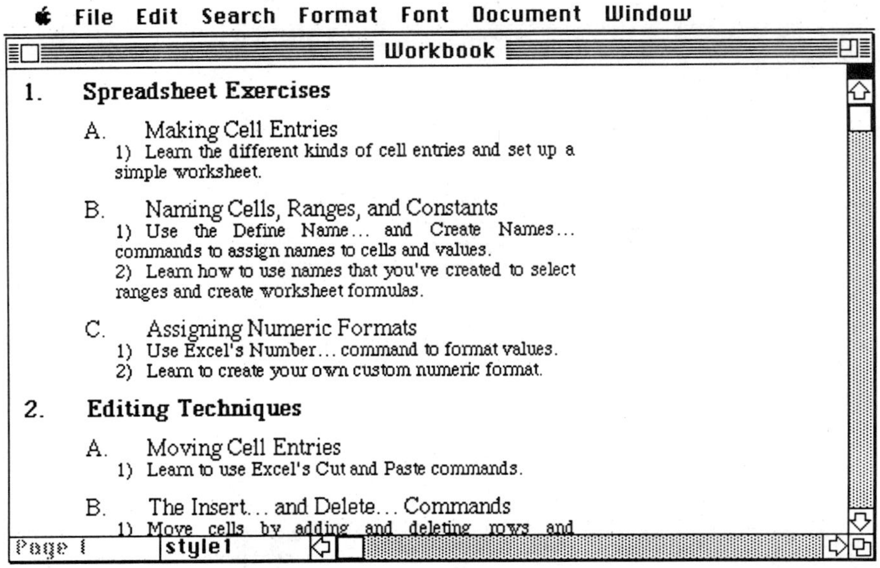

Word can use a different numbering scheme and different separator characters for each level of paragraphs.

By the way, a paragraph's indention *must* be created with the first-line indent marker on the ruler—not a tab or spaces—in order to differentiate paragraph levels. If you move the first-line indent marker for one or more paragraphs, Word won't automatically change your numbers. However, when you choose Renumber... again, Word will recognize your new indentions and change the paragraph numbering accordingly. Because even a small difference in indention ($^1/_{16}$ inch) can signal a new level, we recommend that you use a style sheet to define the formatting of your different paragraph levels. That way, you can be sure that every paragraph at the same level will have the same amount of first-line indention.

In addition to indention, Word is able to use the different parts of an outline created in the Outliner to distinguish various paragraph levels. We'll discuss in detail the relationship between Word's Outliner and the Renumber... command later in this chapter. First, let's consider the numbering options that are available for multilevel documents.

Specifying a numbering scheme for each level

As we illustrated in Figure 15-27, you can use a different numbering scheme for each level of paragraphs in a document. In other words, you can mix Arabic numerals, Roman numerals, and alphabetic characters among the different levels. You also can use different separator characters for each level.

You don't need to issue a separate Renumber... command for each level of paragraphs in order to specify different numbering schemes. You simply enter in the Format edit bar the type of characters that you want to use in numbering each document level. For example, suppose that you have a document with three levels of paragraphs in which you want to use a standard outline numbering scheme. Figure 15-28 shows the entry you might make in the Format edit bar of the Renumber dialog box to specify this kind of paragraph numbering. Figure 15-29 shows the results in a document.

FIGURE 15-28

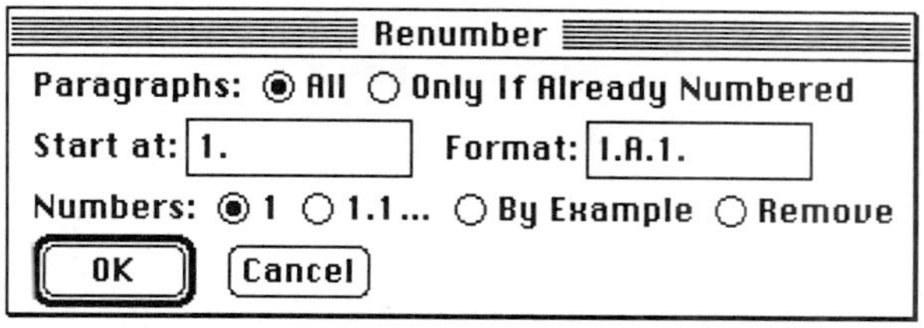

In the Format edit bar, enter the type of characters that you want to use in numbering each of the different paragraph levels in your document.

FIGURE 15-29

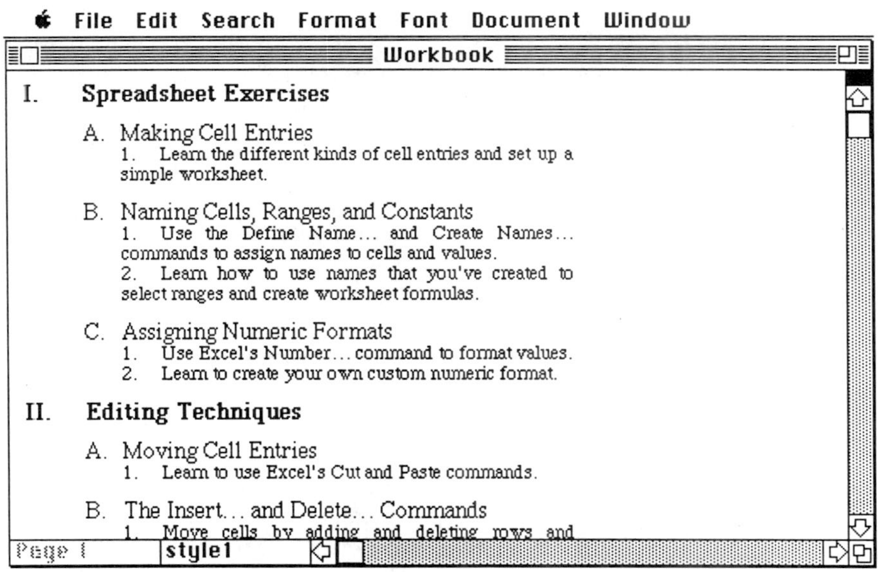

This screen shows the effects of the numbering scheme specified in the dialog box of Figure 15-28.

As with single-level documents, if you do not specify a particular numbering scheme for one or more levels, Word will number the paragraphs at that level with simple Arabic numbers. For example, suppose that you're numbering a document with three levels of paragraphs, but you specify only one kind of character in the Format edit bar, a Roman numeral. Word will use Roman numerals to number the first level of paragraphs, but use the default Arabic numerals to number the second- and third-level paragraphs.

If you've previously numbered the paragraphs at a subordinate level, then you don't have to specify a numbering scheme when you next issue the Renumber... command. The numbering scheme that already appears in your document will override Word's default; that is, if you do not specify a particular numbering scheme in the Format edit bar, Word will *not* automatically convert the numbers on previously numbered paragraphs to the default Arabic numerals.

Of course, you do not have to specify the format of all your paragraph numbers with one command—though that's usually the easiest approach. If you want to specify the numbering scheme for only one level of paragraphs, select those paragraphs, issue the Renumber... command, and type in the Format edit bar a character representing the kind of numbering you want to use. This technique may require that you issue the Renumber... command several times since all the paragraphs in a single level are not likely to be adjacent to one another in a document.

Using different separator characters at each level

When you type an entry in the Format edit bar, you must use the same separator character for all paragraph levels. In other words, you must enter something like *I)A)1)a)* or *I-A-1-a-*. If you try to specify different separator characters for different levels—for example if you enter *I.A.1)a>* —the results will be unpredictable. In most situations, Word will choose one of the separator characters that you enter and use it for all paragraph levels, rather than using a different separator character for each level. Word also requires that your separator character appear only after each level's number. For example, if you enter something like *(I)(A)(1)(a)* in the Format edit bar, Word will display the message *Invalid number*.

If you want to use a different separator character for each paragraph level, you must perform a couple of extra steps. Here's the technique. Suppose that you want to number the paragraphs in your document using a standard outline numbering scheme (I, A, 1, a). However, instead of displaying a period after each paragraph number, you would like to use a variety of separator characters: a period after the first-level Roman numerals, a right parentheses after the second-level upper-case alphabetic characters, a period after the third level of Arabic numbers, and another parenthesis after the fourth level of alphabetic characters.

Begin by issuing the Renumber... command, then enter *I.A.1.a.* in the Format edit bar, click the 1 Numbers option, and click OK. When Word has numbered your paragraphs, as shown in Figure 15-30, select the first number at each level and add the appropriate separator character. For example, you would select the first second-level *A.* in line 2 and replace it with *A)*. Then you would select the first fourth-level *a.* in line 13 and replace it with *a)*. After you've created one "example" paragraph number at each level, your screen will look like Figure 15-31.

FIGURE 15-30

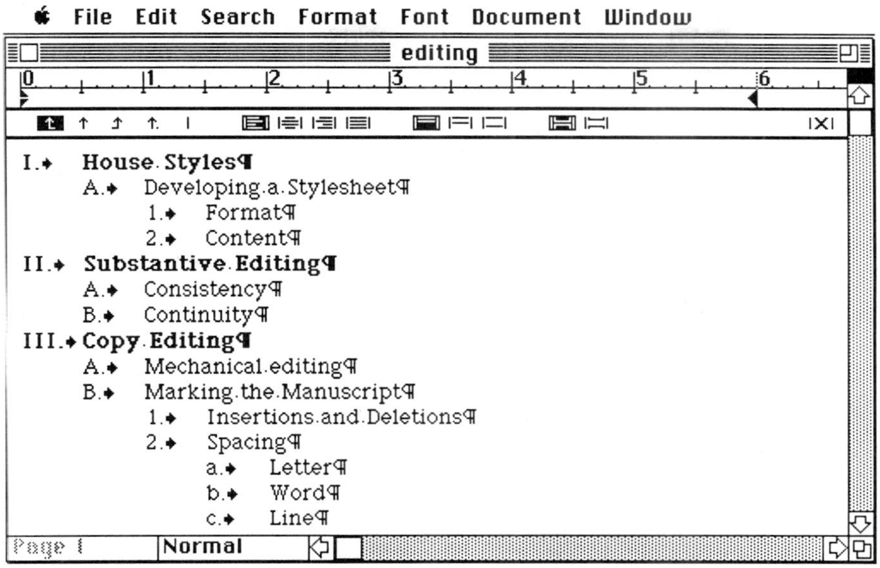

We used the I.A.1.a. numbering scheme to number these paragraphs.

FIGURE 15-31

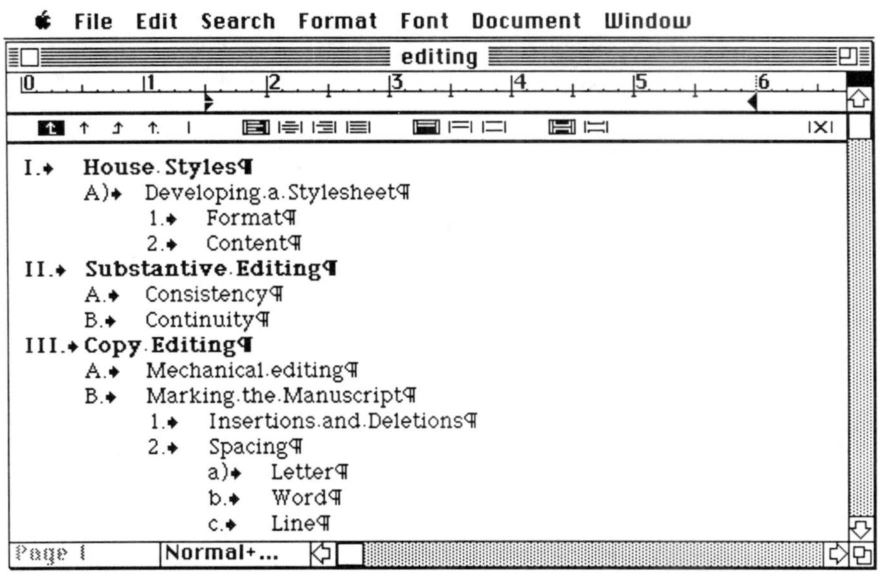

We added our own separator characters to the first number at the second and fourth levels.

Now, issue the Renumber… command once more. In the dialog box, erase the contents of the Format edit bar and click the By Example option, then click OK. The results will look like Figure 15-32.

FIGURE 15-32

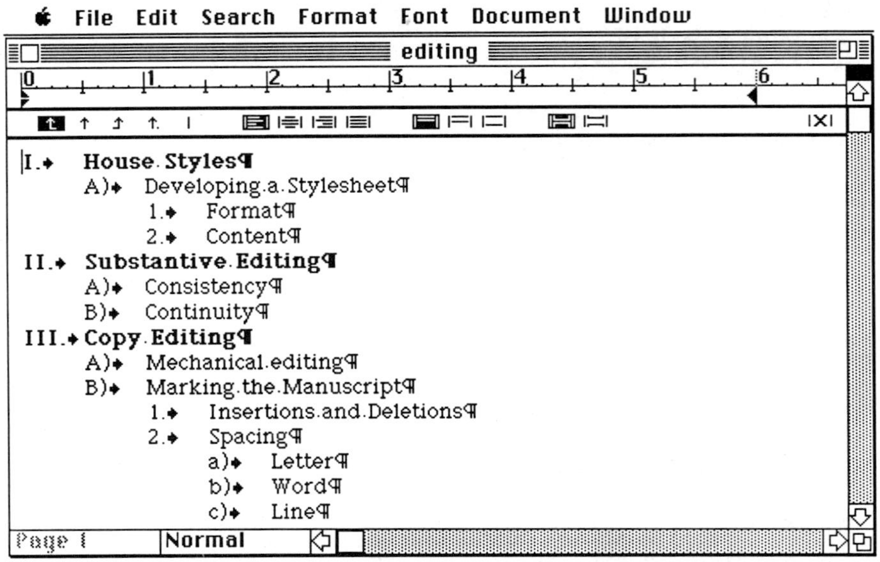

When we reissue the Renumber… command, Word uses our manual numbering scheme to renumber the paragraphs.

Displaying the numbers of superior levels

Word allows you to include in your paragraph numbers the numbers of all superior levels of paragraphs. To display superior levels, click the 1.1... Numbers option in the Renumber dialog box. For example, going back to Figure 15-29, if you were to open the Renumber dialog box and click the 1.1... option, the result would look like Figure 15-33. Notice that, for each paragraph level, Word displays the number of all superior levels. By the way, when you're displaying superior levels, you can use the method we described above to display a variety of separator characters between the number of superior levels—for example, I.A)1.a).

There may be times when you would like the numbers for some of your paragraphs to display their superior levels, while the numbers for other paragraphs do not. Using the By Example option in the Renumber dialog box, you can control the display of superior level numbers on a level-by-level basis throughout your document.

FIGURE 15-33

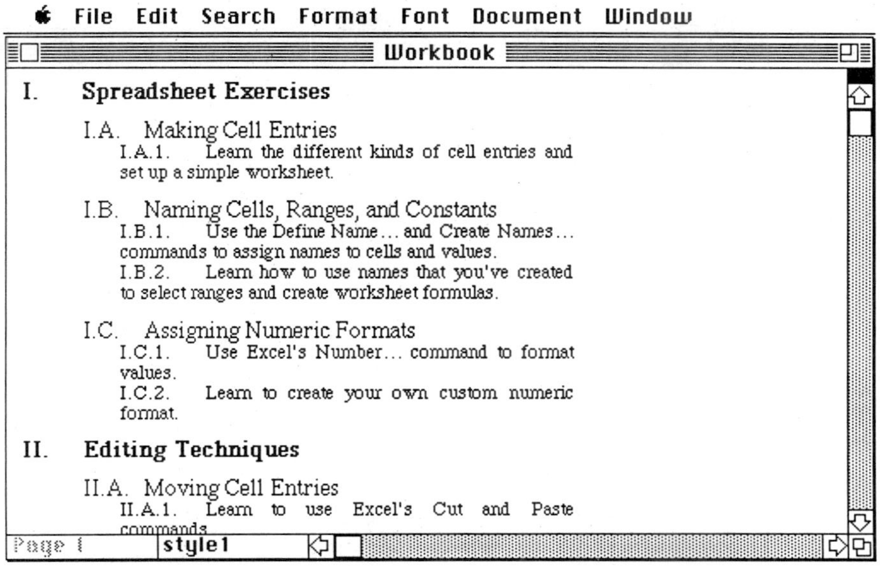

When you click the 1.1... Numbers option in the Renumber dialog box, Word will display all superior levels in each paragraph's number.

For instance, in the document shown in Figure 15-33, suppose that you would like to display the numbers of superior levels only on the second-level paragraphs. On the first- and third-level paragraphs, you want to display only the number of the current level. Begin by displaying the numbers of superior levels on *all* your paragraphs (as we've done in Figure 15-33). Then, for each level on which you do *not* want to display the numbers of superior levels, edit the number on the first paragraph in that level so that it no longer displays the superior levels. In our example, you must edit the number for the first third-level paragraph (which begins, *Learn the different kinds*).

After editing the paragraph number, issue the Renumber... command, and in the dialog box, click the By Example option. When you click OK, Word will change the paragraph numbers so that the format of each number at a given level matches the format of the first paragraph number in that level. Figure 15-34 shows our sample document with the numbers of superior levels displayed only on the second-level paragraphs.

FIGURE 15-34

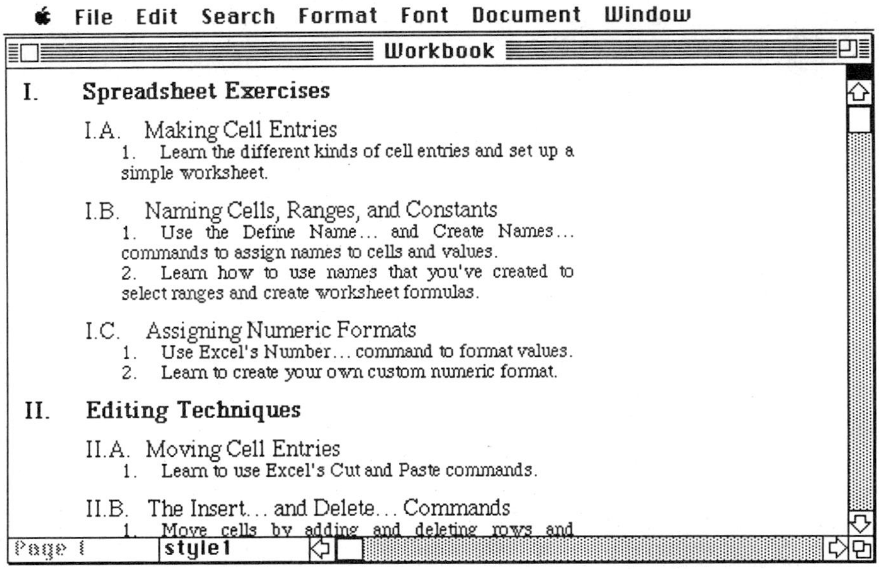

In this document, only the second-level paragraph numbers display the numbers of superior levels.

Specifying a Start number

When you're working with a document that contains multiple levels of paragraphs, specifying a Start number can be a bit tricky. The number that you enter in the Start at edit bar *must* include the number of all superior paragraph levels, but it must *not* include the numbers of subordinate levels. For example, Figure 15-35 shows a document with three levels of paragraphs that are numbered with a standard outline numbering scheme. As you can see, a new second-level topic has been inserted between paragraph A (*Software Issues*) and paragraph B (*Hardware Issues*). In addition, we've added a couple of third-level topics under the new second-level paragraph.

To renumber this document, you would begin by selecting all of the text beginning with the new second-level paragraph. (Select *AI Issues* and the following text.) Then choose Renumber... from the Document menu, and in the Renumber dialog box, enter *I.A.1.* in the Format edit bar. In the Start at edit bar, enter *III.B* or *3.2*, then click the 1 Numbers option. Also, be sure that the All option is activated at the top of the dialog box. Figure 15-36 shows the screen after we selected the text to be numbered and made the appropriate entries in the Renumber dialog box. Figure 15-37 shows the result.

FIGURE 15-35

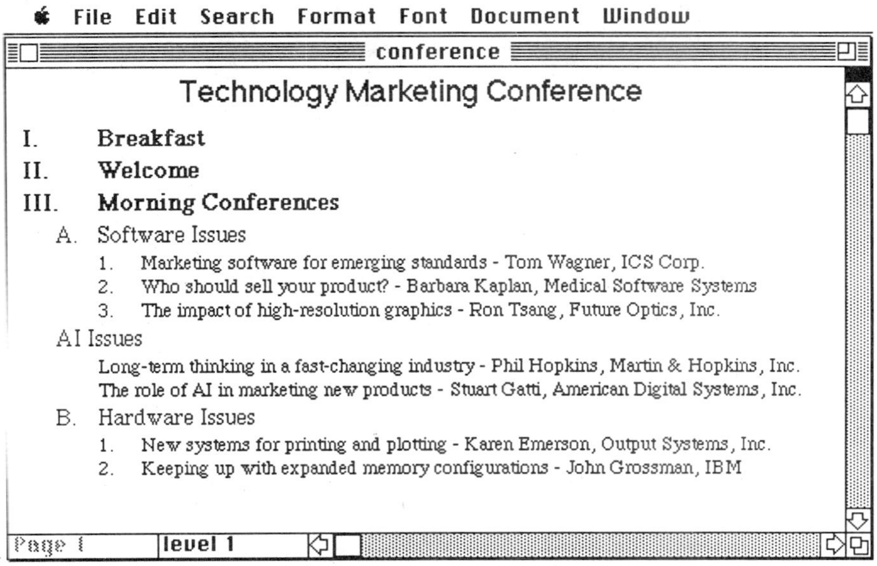

We've inserted some new paragraphs in this three-level document.

FIGURE 15-36

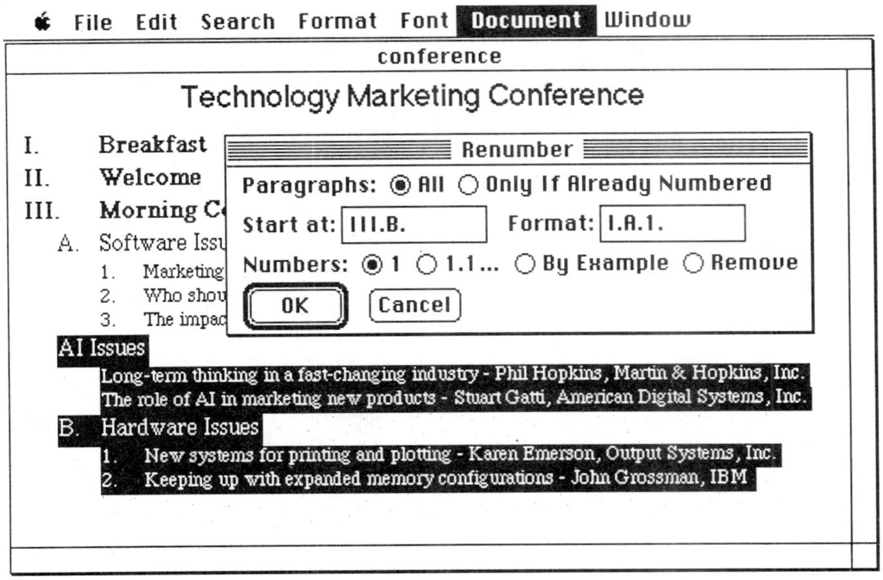

In renumbering paragraphs in a multiple-level document, the Start number should include the number of any superior paragraph levels.

FIGURE 15-37

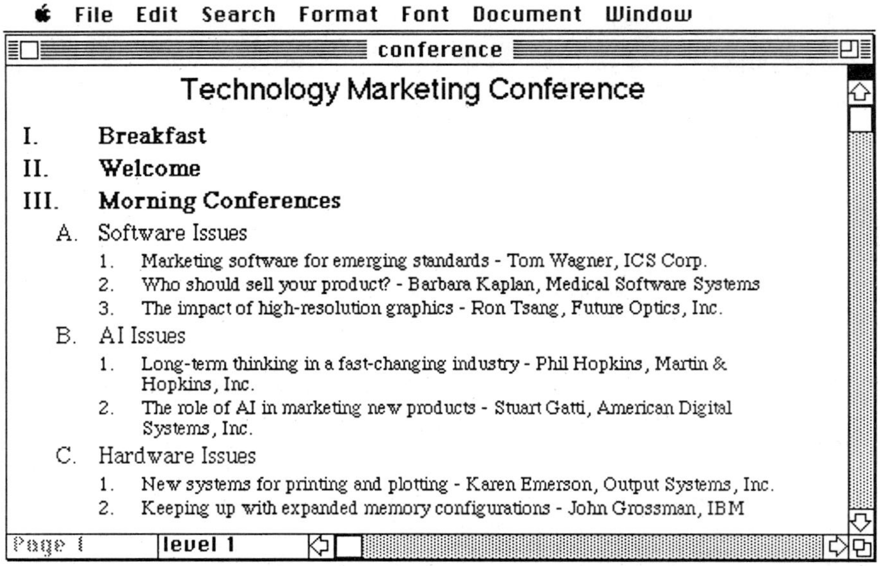

This screen shows the result of renumbering the document in Figure 15-35 with the dialog box settings shown in Figure 15-36.

Although we chose to enter our Start number as *III.B.*, we could just as easily have entered it as *3.2*. Remember, the entry in the Format edit bar tells Word what kind of numbering scheme you want to use at the different paragraph levels (Roman numerals, Arabic numerals, or alphabetic characters). The entry in the Start at edit bar simply indicates *where* in this numbering scheme you want to start numbering your paragraphs. A Start number of *3.2*, like *III.B*, indicates that you want to start numbering with the second second-level paragraph after the third first-level paragraph.

Notice that, even though we want the first paragraph in our selection to be numbered with *B.*, our Start number includes the *III* of the immediately superior paragraph. Had we entered simply a *B* as our Start number, Word would have misinterpreted our intentions. Word considers a *B* in the Start at edit bar to be the same as a *2*; both indicate that you want to begin numbering with the second number in the particular numbering scheme that you've chosen. In our example, a *B* in the Start at edit bar would have caused the first paragraph in the selection to be numbered with a II since our entry in the Format edit bar specifies a standard outline numbering scheme, where the second first-level paragraph is always numbered II.

Revising Your Paragraph Numbers

Word's ability to update paragraph numbers is very flexible. Once you've numbered some or all of the paragraphs in a document, you can easily update the numbers to reflect any changes that you make, such as adding, deleting, or moving text. If you want to maintain the format of all your numbers as you update them, be sure that the By Example option is selected in the Renumber dialog box and that the first paragraph number at each level is formatted appropriately.

Adding, deleting, and rearranging paragraphs

If you add new paragraphs to your document, delete some paragraphs, or rearrange your existing paragraphs, you can easily update your paragraph numbers by issuing the Renumber... command. Just be sure that no text is selected when you choose Renumber... so that Word will be able to change all the numbers in your document and not just the numbers of selected paragraphs. Of course, there may be times when the changes that you make affect only a limited area of your document. In that case, you'll probably find that it's faster to select just the affected area before you issue the Renumber... command.

When you add or rearrange selected paragraphs, you may need to enter a new Start at number in the Renumber dialog box. If you do this, just keep in mind how Word interprets the entry in the Start at edit bar.

Removing paragraph numbers

Immediately after you issue the Renumber... command and click OK, you can undo your numbering by selecting Undo Renumber from the Edit menu. If you have just numbered your document for the first time, then Word will delete all of the paragraph numbers. If you issued the Renumber... command to reformat or update your paragraph numbers, then Undo will cancel only your latest change.

You can remove paragraph numbers at any time by clicking the Remove option in the Renumber dialog box. If you don't select any text before you do this, Word will remove all of the paragraph numbers in your document. If you want to remove the numbers on only some of the paragraphs in your document, you can select those paragraphs before you choose Renumber... and click the Remove option.

Paragraph Numbers and the Outliner

The Renumber... command offers a handy way to number an outline that you've created with Word's Outliner facility. In fact, whenever you need to create an outline with numbered points, you'll find that it's much easier to enter your outline text and then use the Renumber... command to number all the outline points, rather than type the number for each outline point manually. As you might expect, Word is able to recognize the different levels of an outline and number each level appropriately.

Let's consider a simple example of how you might use the Renumber... command in an outline window. As you learned in Chapter 12, the first step in creating an outline is to choose Outlining from the Document menu. This will switch your screen from a normal document view to the outline view. Once you're in an outline window, type the text of your outline and use the ➡ and ⬅ icons to specify the level of each part of the outline. Figure 15-38 shows a completed outline before we've added any numbers.

FIGURE 15-38

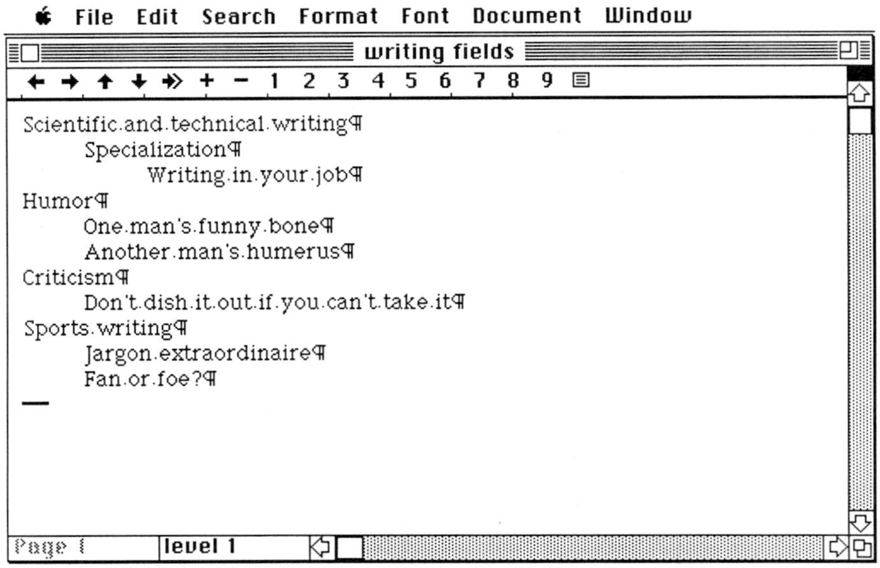

To create a numbered outline, begin by entering your outline text in a blank outline window.

To number the outline, choose Renumber... from the Document menu. In the Renumber dialog box, enter the numbering scheme that you want to use in the Format edit bar. For standard outline numbering, you would enter *I.A.1.a.i.* (Of course, if your outline contains fewer than five levels, you would not need to enter as many characters in the Format edit bar.) Make sure that your Start at number is 1 and that you have clicked the 1 Numbers option. When you click OK, Word will number each point of the outline so that the outline looks like Figure 15-39.

In this example, Word numbered all of the outline text since we had not chosen to collapse any part of the outline. If you collapse the outline before you number it, Word will assign numbers only to the visible parts of the outline. For example, going back to the unnumbered outline shown in Figure 15-38, if you were to click on the 2 icon at the top of the screen, Word would collapse the outline so that all text below level 2 is not visible on the screen. If you then issue the Renumber... command, Word would number only the level 1 and level 2 text that is visible on your screen.

FIGURE 15-39

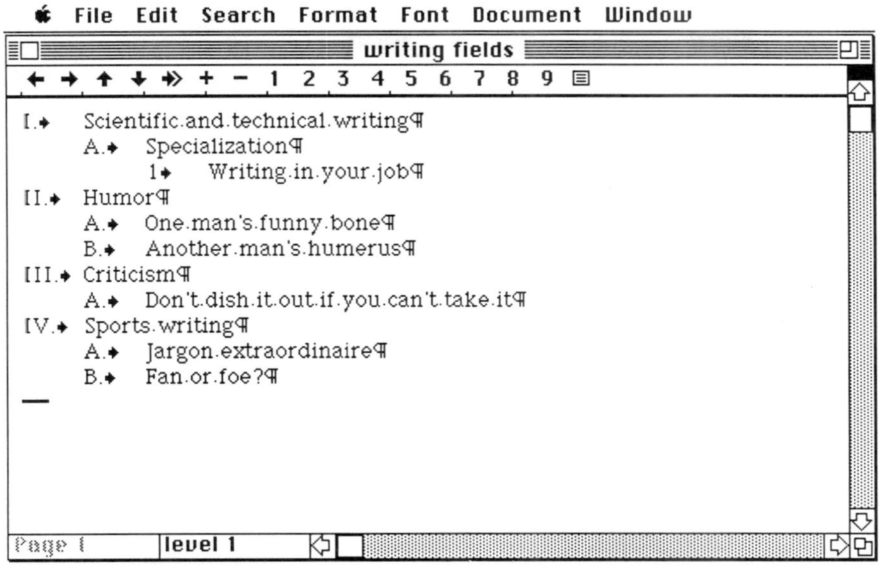

You can use the Renumber... command to number the text in an outline window.

By the way, collapsing the outline and choosing Renumber... will *not* remove existing numbers from the lower levels in the outline. For example, suppose that after you number the entire outline (as shown in Figure 15-39), you decide to click the 2 icon so that all level 3 text is collapsed out of view. If you then choose Renumber... once more, Word will update the numbers of the visible outline text. However, when you expand the outline to bring the level 3 text back into view, you'll see that that text still retains the numbers that were assigned by the first Renumber... command.

Once you've used Word's Outliner to create your outline text, you don't have to number that text in the outline window. If you want, you can switch to the document window before you issue the Renumber... command. Interestingly, even though your outline text does not display different amounts of indentation in the document view, Word is still able to recognize the outline levels and number the paragraphs appropriately. For example, suppose that you've just created the outline shown in Figure 15-38. If you choose Outlining from the Document menu, Word will return to a normal document view and your screen will look like Figure 15-40.

FIGURE 15-40

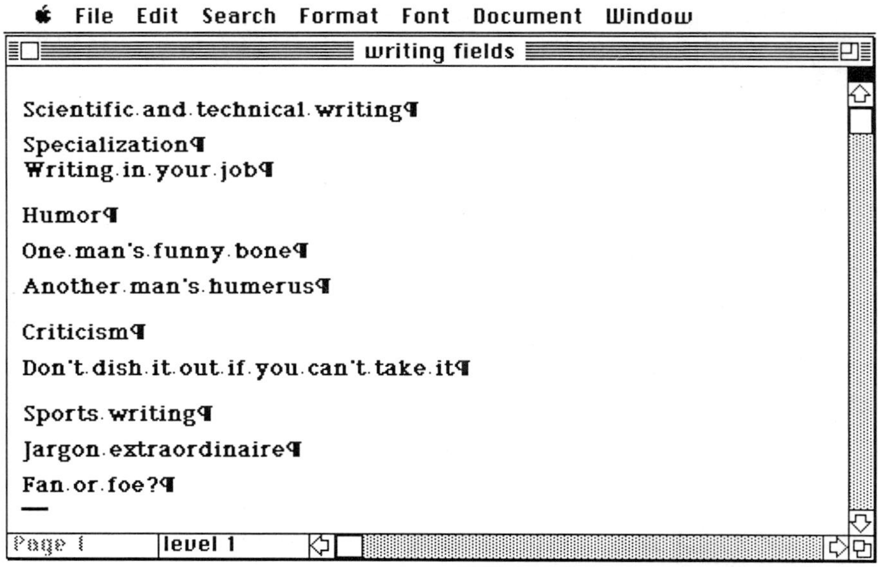

When you switch to the normal document view, your outline will no longer be displayed with different amounts of indentation.

Once in the document view, you can select Renumber... from the Document menu to number the different parts of the outline. Figure 15-41 shows how your screen will appear after you issue the Renumber... command and specify a standard outline numbering scheme for this document.

SORTING

Word's Sort command allows you to rearrange lists, paragraphs, and tables quickly and easily. You can choose to sort in either ascending or descending order. When you select the Sort command from the Document menu, Word will sort paragraphs according to the first character or first few characters in each paragraph. (There are a few cases where Word will ignore the first character in each paragraph. We'll cover those cases later in this section.)

If you don't select any text before you issue the Sort command, Word will sort *all* the paragraphs in your document. In sorting the paragraphs, Word will ignore section boundaries. If you want to sort only a portion of a document, you can select the text that you want to sort before you issue the Sort command. For example, if you want to rearrange five paragraphs, you can select those paragraphs before you choose Sort from the Document menu.

One of the most powerful features of Word's Sort command is its ability to sort a table of information based on a single "key column." We'll demonstrate this technique in a few pages. First, however, let's consider a few basic facts about sorting with Word.

FIGURE 15-41

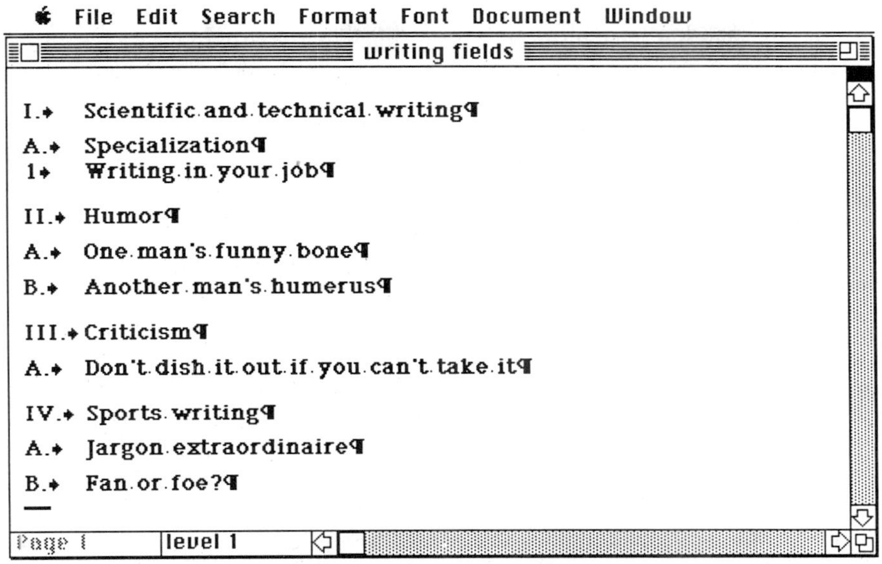

The Renumber... command is able to recognize the different levels created in the Outliner and number your text accordingly.

Sorting Basics

Word 's default sort order is ascending. However, you can sort in descending order by pressing the Shift key as you choose Sort from the Document menu. Once you've issued the Sort command, you can undo your sort by choosing Undo Sort from the Edit menu. (Like other Undo commands, this one must be issued immediately after you sort, before you do anything else.)

When you're sorting into ascending order, the general priority of characters is as follows: Punctuation marks and other nonalphanumeric characters precede numbers, and numbers precede letters. However, Word will place some nonalphanumeric characters *after* numbers, but before letters. Specifically, the characters

: ; < > = ? @ [ ] ^ _ `

have a lower priority in the sort order than numbers.

If a paragraph begins with an indent, tab, or blank space, Word will ignore the space and sort the paragraph according to the first character after the tab, indent, or space. Similarly, if a paragraph begins with a quotation mark ("), Word will sort that paragraph according to the first character after the quotation mark. (This rule does not apply to the single quotation mark, '.)

Completely blank paragraphs—that is, paragraphs that consist of a ¶ with no text—will be ignored in the sort. In other words, when you sort text, Word will not change the location of any blank lines that you may have created by pressing the Return key. Another rule of sorting is that upper-case letters precede lower-case letters. For example, a paragraph that begins with *G* will precede one that begins with *g*. Both paragraphs will precede one that begins with an *H*. If two or more paragraphs begin identically, Word will scan the text in each paragraph until it finds differing characters and sort on that basis.

In addition to these basic rules of sorting, there are some special rules that apply to sorting by numbers. We'll address these next, as we talk about sorting numbered paragraphs and lists of numbers.

Sorting by Number

When Word sorts numbers, it considers each string of digits to be a numeric value; it does not simply look at the first digit in the series. For example, in sorting numbers, Word knows that the number 6 comes before the number 10, even though the first digit in 10, 1, is less than 6. Word is also able to evaluate number-letter combinations correctly. For example, if you're sorting paragraphs that are numbered 1-A, 1-B, 1-C, and so forth, Word will be able to evaluate the numbers properly.

There are a couple of situations that you need to avoid when sorting numbered paragraphs. These are likely to occur if you've used the Renumber... command to number paragraphs. First, Word is *not* able to evaluate Roman numerals correctly in sorting numbered paragraphs. Word will sort Roman numerals as though they were strings of normal alphabetic characters. Thus, the sorted order of the numbers will be I, II, III, IV, IX, VI, and so forth. Of course, if your paragraph numbers do not go beyond Roman numeral VIII, then you're okay. In general, however, if you want to sort numbered paragraphs, we recommend that you use Arabic numerals or alphabetic characters.

You also need to be cautious about sorting documents with multiple levels of numbered paragraphs. In some cases, Word cannot keep track of the different levels. Figure 15-42 shows what would happen if you sorted the document from Figure 15-37 on page 576, which contains three levels of paragraphs. This figure also illustrates a problem you can encounter with Roman numerals.

If you want to sort a document with multiple levels of paragraphs, then you should be sure to include the number of all superior levels in each paragraph's number. For example, to sort the document from Figure 15-37 without encountering the kinds of problems shown in Figure 15-42, you would want to number the second-level paragraphs *III.A.*, *III.B.*, and *III.C*. Then, your third-level paragraphs would be numbered *II.A.1*, *III.A.2*, *III.B-1.*, and so forth. When you display the numbers of superior levels like this, Word will be able to keep the different paragraph levels straight when it sorts. (For more on automatic paragraph numbering and displaying superior levels, see the section earlier in this chapter entitled "Numbering Paragraphs.")

FIGURE 15-42

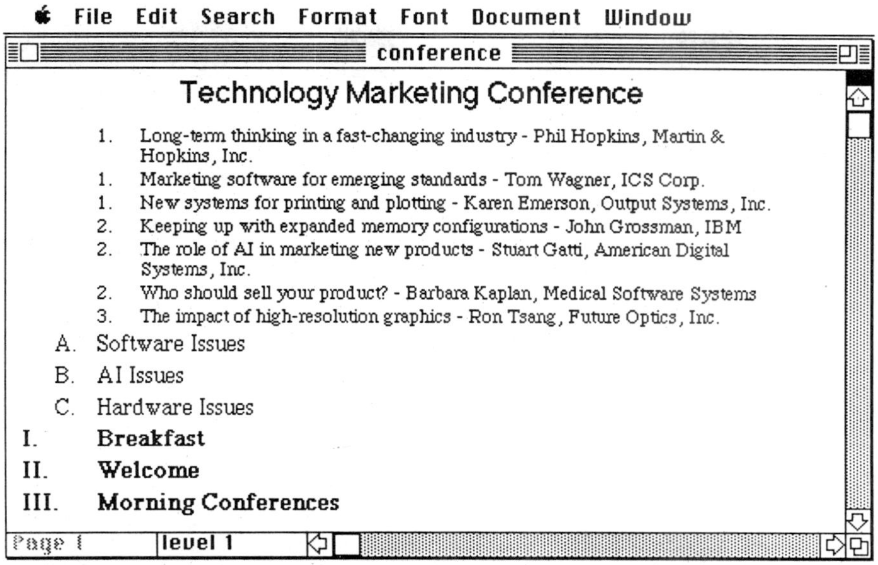

If your document contains multiple levels of numbered paragraphs, the Sort command may not work as you expect.

Using numbered paragraphs to rearrange a document

Word's ability to sort by number offers a quick and easy way to rearrange several paragraphs in a document. Here's how it works. Suppose you've written a document in which you would like to rearrange several paragraphs. You could cut and paste each paragraph until they're all in the correct order. A faster method, however, is to type a number at the beginning of each paragraph, which indicates where you want to place that paragraph relative to the other paragraphs. For example, Figure 15-43 on the next page shows a document in which we've typed numbers at the beginning of several paragraphs. Be sure that you include at least one blank space between the number and the paragraph text—as you'll see in a moment, this will speed up the process of removing the numbers after you've rearranged the paragraphs.

Once you've numbered the paragraphs, select them, and choose Sort from the Document menu. Word will then automatically rearrange the paragraphs according to their numbers, as shown in Figure 15-44 on the following page.

You can now remove the numbers, either with manual editing techniques or by using Word's Renumber... command. To remove the numbers with the Renumber... command, select Renumber... from the Document menu, and in the dialog box, click the Remove option and click OK. This technique will work only if you've included at least one blank space between each number and the first character of paragraph text.

FIGURE 15-43

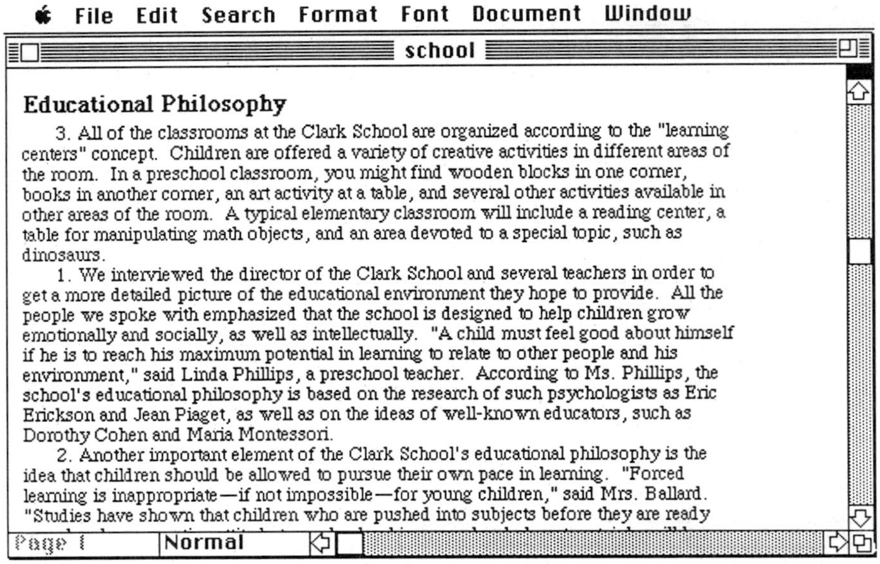

Educational Philosophy

3. All of the classrooms at the Clark School are organized according to the "learning centers" concept. Children are offered a variety of creative activities in different areas of the room. In a preschool classroom, you might find wooden blocks in one corner, books in another corner, an art activity at a table, and several other activities available in other areas of the room. A typical elementary classroom will include a reading center, a table for manipulating math objects, and an area devoted to a special topic, such as dinosaurs.

1. We interviewed the director of the Clark School and several teachers in order to get a more detailed picture of the educational environment they hope to provide. All the people we spoke with emphasized that the school is designed to help children grow emotionally and socially, as well as intellectually. "A child must feel good about himself if he is to reach his maximum potential in learning to relate to other people and his environment," said Linda Phillips, a preschool teacher. According to Ms. Phillips, the school's educational philosophy is based on the research of such psychologists as Eric Erickson and Jean Piaget, as well as on the ideas of well-known educators, such as Dorothy Cohen and Maria Montessori.

2. Another important element of the Clark School's educational philosophy is the idea that children should be allowed to pursue their own pace in learning. "Forced learning is inappropriate—if not impossible—for young children," said Mrs. Ballard. "Studies have shown that children who are pushed into subjects before they are ready

To rearrange paragraphs quickly, begin by placing a number at the beginning of each paragraph to indicate its placement.

FIGURE 15-44

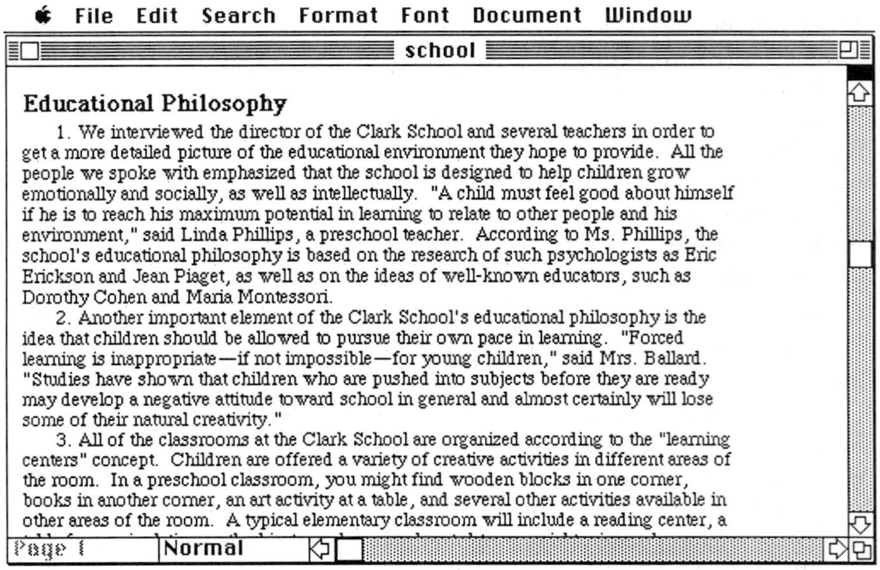

Educational Philosophy

1. We interviewed the director of the Clark School and several teachers in order to get a more detailed picture of the educational environment they hope to provide. All the people we spoke with emphasized that the school is designed to help children grow emotionally and socially, as well as intellectually. "A child must feel good about himself if he is to reach his maximum potential in learning to relate to other people and his environment," said Linda Phillips, a preschool teacher. According to Ms. Phillips, the school's educational philosophy is based on the research of such psychologists as Eric Erickson and Jean Piaget, as well as on the ideas of well-known educators, such as Dorothy Cohen and Maria Montessori.

2. Another important element of the Clark School's educational philosophy is the idea that children should be allowed to pursue their own pace in learning. "Forced learning is inappropriate—if not impossible—for young children," said Mrs. Ballard. "Studies have shown that children who are pushed into subjects before they are ready may develop a negative attitude toward school in general and almost certainly will lose some of their natural creativity."

3. All of the classrooms at the Clark School are organized according to the "learning centers" concept. Children are offered a variety of creative activities in different areas of the room. In a preschool classroom, you might find wooden blocks in one corner, books in another corner, an art activity at a table, and several other activities available in other areas of the room. A typical elementary classroom will include a reading center, a

When you issue the Sort command, Word will sort the paragraphs according to their numbers.

Sorting a Table by Key Column

Word's ability to sort tables of information is similar to that of many simple data base programs. Word can sort all of the entries in one column (or field) of a table and rearrange the rest of the table according to that sorted column. Word even has a limited ability to use multiple sort keys. Let's consider a simple example that demonstrates Word's table-sorting capability.

Suppose your document contains the table of data shown in Figure 15-45 You would like to sort this information into ascending order by sales representative. You should begin by selecting the Sales Rep names in the second column of the table. This column is called your "sort key." To select the column, press the Option key, then click in front of the first name in that column and drag down until you've selected the entire column, as shown in Figure 15-46 on the next page.

FIGURE 15-45

Account Name	Sales Rep	Volume
Movers & Shakers, Inc.	Anderson	$249,300
Constructors & Builders, Inc.	Chilton	$365,200
Razers & Wreckers, Inc.	Chilton	$ 64,000
Sellers & Traders, Inc.	Nichols	$ 84,500
Rebels & Renegades, Inc.	Anderson	$102,430
Authors & Writers, Inc.	Chilton	$ 68,300
Lookers & Watchers, Inc.	Anderson	$ 98,400
Sweepers & Cleaners, Inc.	Nichols	$221,000
Publishers & Printers, Inc.	Nichols	$167,200
Packagers & Distributors, Inc.	Anderson	$ 49,800
Designers & Planners, Inc.	Anderson	$ 59,400
Dreamers & Visionaries, Inc.	Nichols	$ 32,300
Diggers & Drillers, Inc.	Chilton	$243,590
Ranchers & Farmers, Inc.	Chilton	$ 74,450
Teachers & Trainers, Inc.	Nichols	$189,900
Porters & Carriers, Inc.	Chilton	$ 21,345
Butchers & Bakers, Inc.	Nichols	$ 75,540
Plumbers & Carpenters, Inc.	Anderson	$101,100

You can use Word's Sort command to sort a table like this one.

Once you've selected the information on which you want to base your sort, just choose Sort from the Document menu. Figure 15-47 on the following page shows the result.

As we mentioned above, Word's Sort command offers a limited ability to use multiple sort keys—that is, you can sort on more than one column of data. In order to do this, the sort keys or columns must be adjacent to one another in the table and arranged in order of priority from left to right. For instance, in our example, you could sort the table in Figure 15-45 on the basis of *both* sales rep and volume. In this case, the Sales Rep column would be your primary sort key

FIGURE 15-46

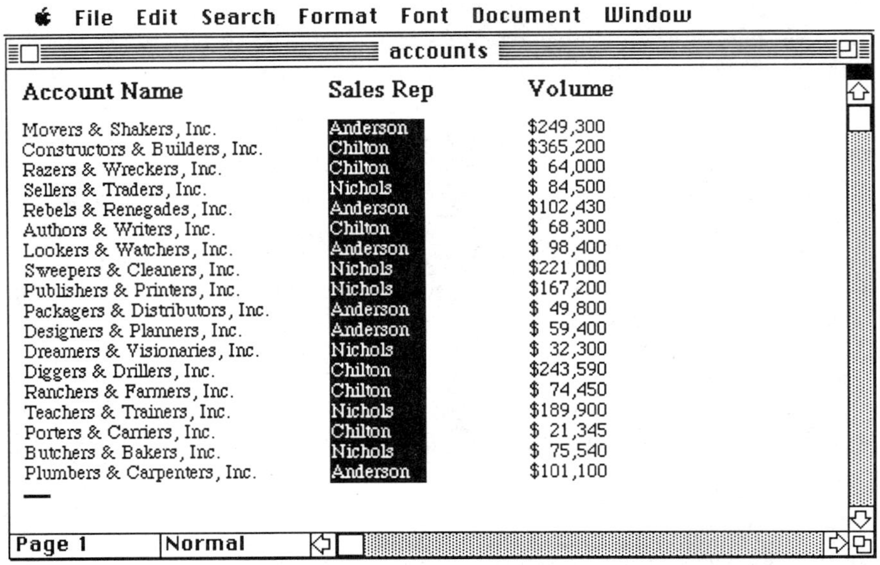

Account Name	Sales Rep	Volume
Movers & Shakers, Inc.	Anderson	$249,300
Constructors & Builders, Inc.	Chilton	$365,200
Razers & Wreckers, Inc.	Chilton	$ 64,000
Sellers & Traders, Inc.	Nichols	$ 84,500
Rebels & Renegades, Inc.	Anderson	$102,430
Authors & Writers, Inc.	Chilton	$ 68,300
Lookers & Watchers, Inc.	Anderson	$ 98,400
Sweepers & Cleaners, Inc.	Nichols	$221,000
Publishers & Printers, Inc.	Nichols	$167,200
Packagers & Distributors, Inc.	Anderson	$ 49,800
Designers & Planners, Inc.	Anderson	$ 59,400
Dreamers & Visionaries, Inc.	Nichols	$ 32,300
Diggers & Drillers, Inc.	Chilton	$243,590
Ranchers & Farmers, Inc.	Chilton	$ 74,450
Teachers & Trainers, Inc.	Nichols	$189,900
Porters & Carriers, Inc.	Chilton	$ 21,345
Butchers & Bakers, Inc.	Nichols	$ 75,540
Plumbers & Carpenters, Inc.	Anderson	$101,100

The first step in sorting the table is to select the column that you want to use as your "sort key."

FIGURE 15-47

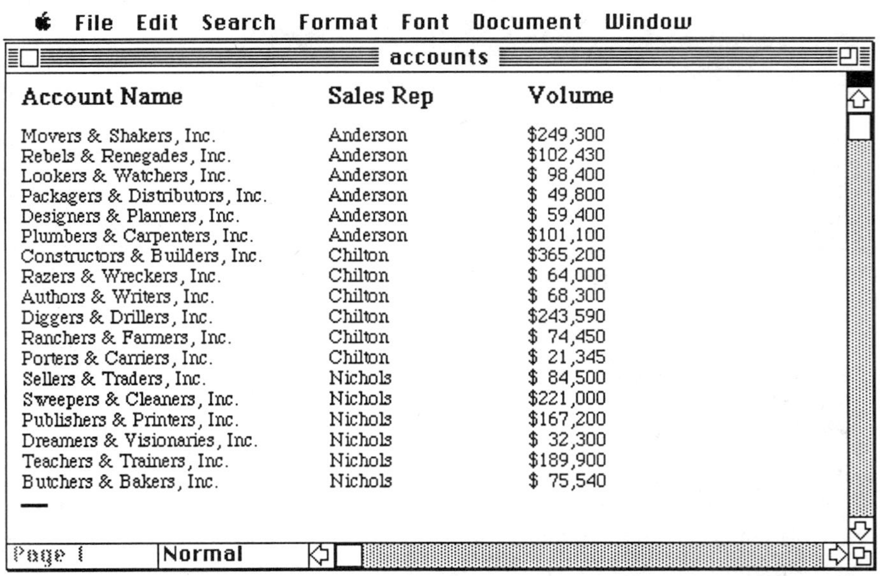

Account Name	Sales Rep	Volume
Movers & Shakers, Inc.	Anderson	$249,300
Rebels & Renegades, Inc.	Anderson	$102,430
Lookers & Watchers, Inc.	Anderson	$ 98,400
Packagers & Distributors, Inc.	Anderson	$ 49,800
Designers & Planners, Inc.	Anderson	$ 59,400
Plumbers & Carpenters, Inc.	Anderson	$101,100
Constructors & Builders, Inc.	Chilton	$365,200
Razers & Wreckers, Inc.	Chilton	$ 64,000
Authors & Writers, Inc.	Chilton	$ 68,300
Diggers & Drillers, Inc.	Chilton	$243,590
Ranchers & Farmers, Inc.	Chilton	$ 74,450
Porters & Carriers, Inc.	Chilton	$ 21,345
Sellers & Traders, Inc.	Nichols	$ 84,500
Sweepers & Cleaners, Inc.	Nichols	$221,000
Publishers & Printers, Inc.	Nichols	$167,200
Dreamers & Visionaries, Inc.	Nichols	$ 32,300
Teachers & Trainers, Inc.	Nichols	$189,900
Butchers & Bakers, Inc.	Nichols	$ 75,540

When you choose Sort from the Document menu, Word will sort the table according to the column that you selected.

since it is in the leftmost column, and the Volume column would be the secondary sort key. To set up this sort, you must select both columns before you issue the Sort command. Figure 15-48 shows the table with these two columns selected.

FIGURE15-48

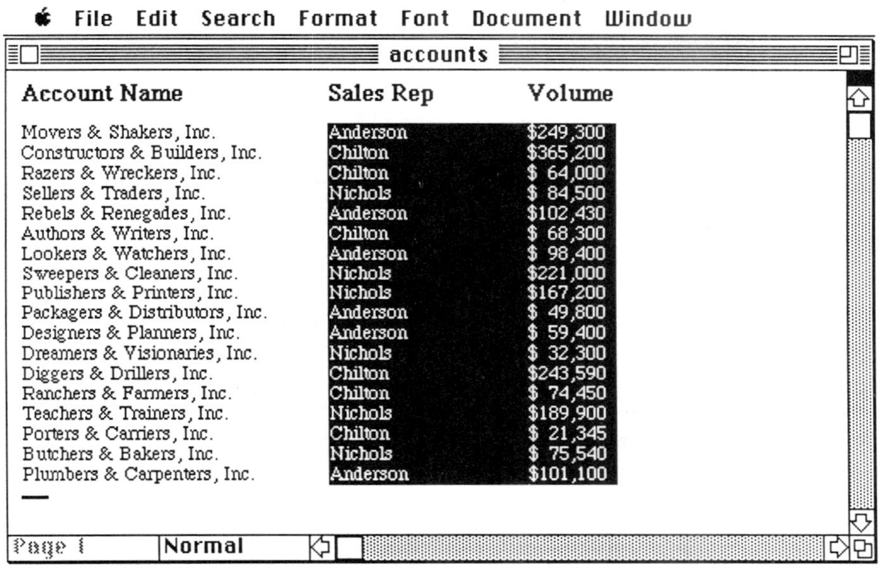

Account Name	Sales Rep	Volume
Movers & Shakers, Inc.	Anderson	$249,300
Constructors & Builders, Inc.	Chilton	$365,200
Razers & Wreckers, Inc.	Chilton	$ 64,000
Sellers & Traders, Inc.	Nichols	$ 84,500
Rebels & Renegades, Inc.	Anderson	$102,430
Authors & Writers, Inc.	Chilton	$ 68,300
Lookers & Watchers, Inc.	Anderson	$ 98,400
Sweepers & Cleaners, Inc.	Nichols	$221,000
Publishers & Printers, Inc.	Nichols	$167,200
Packagers & Distributors, Inc.	Anderson	$ 49,800
Designers & Planners, Inc.	Anderson	$ 59,400
Dreamers & Visionaries, Inc.	Nichols	$ 32,300
Diggers & Drillers, Inc.	Chilton	$243,590
Ranchers & Farmers, Inc.	Chilton	$ 74,450
Teachers & Trainers, Inc.	Nichols	$189,900
Porters & Carriers, Inc.	Chilton	$ 21,345
Butchers & Bakers, Inc.	Nichols	$ 75,540
Plumbers & Carpenters, Inc.	Anderson	$101,100

To sort on two columns, select both columns before you choose Sort from the Document menu.

When you choose to sort on two columns, Word will first sort the table according to the information in the leftmost column—the primary sort key. Then, Word will sort each group of rows with a common entry in the primary sort column according to the information in the second selected column—the secondary sort key. Of course, you won't see any indication on your screen that Word is performing a "double sort," as we've described. All you'll see is the result. For example, Figure 15-49 on the next page shows the table from Figure 15-48 after issuing the Sort command. Notice that the information in this table is not only grouped by the names of the sales reps, but within each sales rep's grouping, the accounts appear in ascending order by volume.

When you use two or more sort keys, Word must apply the same sort order—either ascending or descending—with each of the sort keys. If you would like to get around this limitation, you must perform separate sort procedures. For example, suppose that you would like to sort the table in Figure 15-45 according to the sales reps' names and according to account volume. However, within each sales rep grouping, you would like the accounts to be listed in descending order according to volume.

FIGURE 15-49

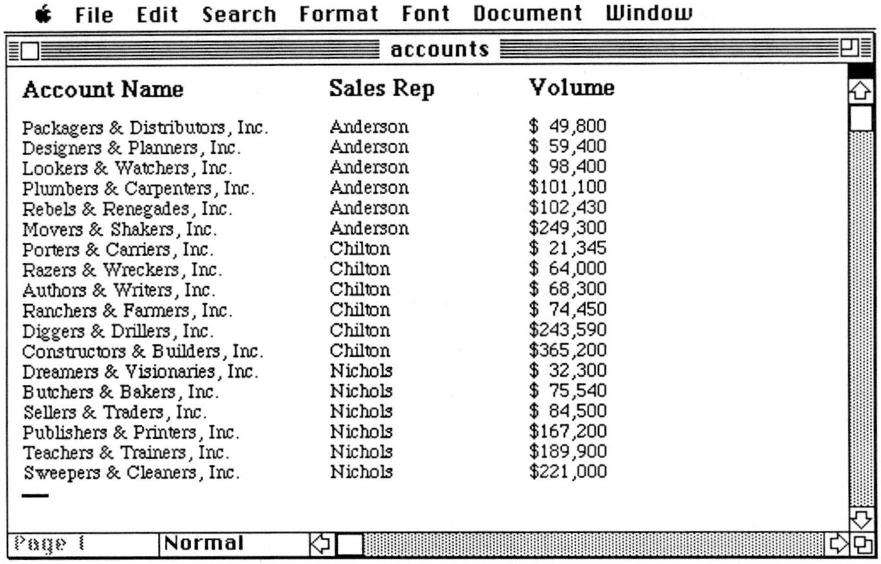

Account Name	Sales Rep	Volume
Packagers & Distributors, Inc.	Anderson	$ 49,800
Designers & Planners, Inc.	Anderson	$ 59,400
Lookers & Watchers, Inc.	Anderson	$ 98,400
Plumbers & Carpenters, Inc.	Anderson	$101,100
Rebels & Renegades, Inc.	Anderson	$102,430
Movers & Shakers, Inc.	Anderson	$249,300
Porters & Carriers, Inc.	Chilton	$ 21,345
Razers & Wreckers, Inc.	Chilton	$ 64,000
Authors & Writers, Inc.	Chilton	$ 68,300
Ranchers & Farmers, Inc.	Chilton	$ 74,450
Diggers & Drillers, Inc.	Chilton	$243,590
Constructors & Builders, Inc.	Chilton	$365,200
Dreamers & Visionaries, Inc.	Nichols	$ 32,300
Butchers & Bakers, Inc.	Nichols	$ 75,540
Sellers & Traders, Inc.	Nichols	$ 84,500
Publishers & Printers, Inc.	Nichols	$167,200
Teachers & Trainers, Inc.	Nichols	$189,900
Sweepers & Cleaners, Inc.	Nichols	$221,000

This screen shows the result of sorting on both the sales reps' names and account volume.

The way to accomplish this is to sort only by sales rep initially so that your table looks like Figure 15-47. Then, select the volume numbers within each sales rep's grouping and sort into descending order. For example, after you've sorted by sales rep, you would select all of the volume information for Anderson, as shown in Figure 15-50.

After you've selected the information, hold down the Shift key as you choose Sort from the Document menu. When you've repeated this procedure for each of the three sales rep groupings, the table will look like Figure 15-51.

Sorting in an Outline Window

The Sort command is available in the outline view, but you should use it with caution. First, Word does not distinguish the different levels of an outline when you sort (just as it does not distinguish different levels of numbered paragraphs). If you're not careful, the Sort command can destroy the structure of superior and subordinate outline levels. For example, Figure 15-52 on page 590 shows what happened when we sorted the outline from Figure 15-30. (We issued the Sort command before numbering the outline.) Notice that Word has moved some of the subordinate outline sections to the beginning of the outline.

FIGURE 15-50

File Edit Search Format Font Document Window

accounts

Account Name	Sales Rep	Volume
Movers & Shakers, Inc.	Anderson	$249,300
Rebels & Renegades, Inc.	Anderson	$102,430
Lookers & Watchers, Inc.	Anderson	$ 98,400
Packagers & Distributors, Inc.	Anderson	$ 49,800
Designers & Planners, Inc.	Anderson	$ 59,400
Plumbers & Carpenters, Inc.	Anderson	$101,100
Constructors & Builders, Inc.	Chilton	$365,200
Razers & Wreckers, Inc.	Chilton	$ 64,000
Authors & Writers, Inc.	Chilton	$ 68,300
Diggers & Drillers, Inc.	Chilton	$243,590
Ranchers & Farmers, Inc.	Chilton	$ 74,450
Porters & Carriers, Inc.	Chilton	$ 21,345
Sellers & Traders, Inc.	Nichols	$ 84,500
Sweepers & Cleaners, Inc.	Nichols	$221,000
Publishers & Printers, Inc.	Nichols	$167,200
Dreamers & Visionaries, Inc.	Nichols	$ 32,300
Teachers & Trainers, Inc.	Nichols	$189,900
Butchers & Bakers, Inc.	Nichols	$ 75,540

Page 1 Normal

To sort the accounts into descending order by volume, select the information in the third column for one sales rep, and issue the Sort command while you hold down the Shift key.

FIGURE 15-51

File Edit Search Format Font Document Window

accounts

Account Name	Sales Rep	Volume
Movers & Shakers, Inc.	Anderson	$249,300
Rebels & Renegades, Inc.	Anderson	$102,430
Plumbers & Carpenters, Inc.	Anderson	$101,100
Lookers & Watchers, Inc.	Anderson	$ 98,400
Designers & Planners, Inc.	Anderson	$ 59,400
Packagers & Distributors, Inc.	Anderson	$ 49,800
Constructors & Builders, Inc.	Chilton	$365,200
Diggers & Drillers, Inc.	Chilton	$243,590
Ranchers & Farmers, Inc.	Chilton	$ 74,450
Authors & Writers, Inc.	Chilton	$ 68,300
Razers & Wreckers, Inc.	Chilton	$ 64,000
Porters & Carriers, Inc.	Chilton	$ 21,345
Sweepers & Cleaners, Inc.	Nichols	$221,000
Teachers & Trainers, Inc.	Nichols	$189,900
Publishers & Printers, Inc.	Nichols	$167,200
Sellers & Traders, Inc.	Nichols	$ 84,500
Butchers & Bakers, Inc.	Nichols	$ 75,540
Dreamers & Visionaries, Inc.	Nichols	$ 32,300

Page 1 Normal

The information in this table has been sorted into alphabetical order by sales rep, and within each rep's grouping, the accounts are arranged in descending order by volume.

FIGURE 15-52

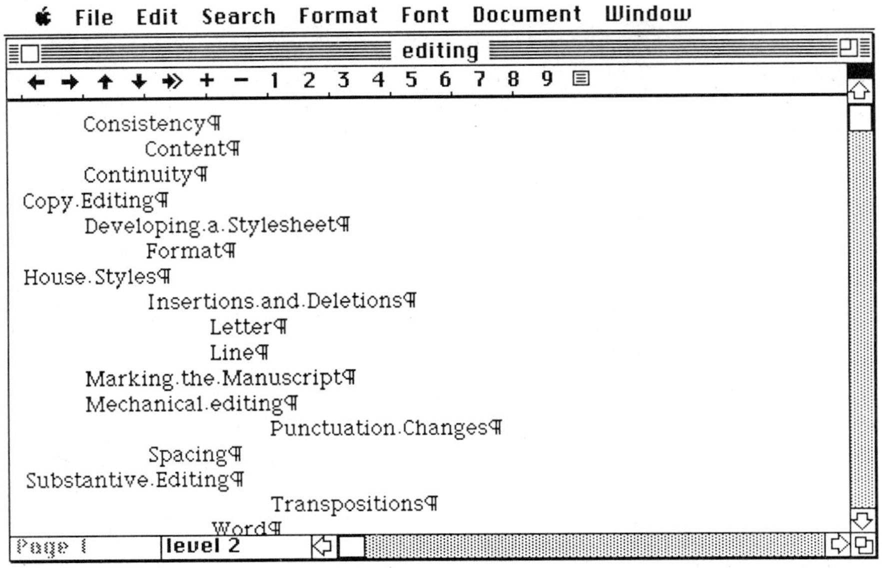

Sorting in an outline window can destroy your outline levels.

The best way to avoid this kind of problem is to number the outline, using a numbering scheme in which each outline number includes the number of its superior levels. For example, in Figure 15-52, we might label the paragraphs in our sample document *I.*, *I.A.*, *I.A.1.*, and so forth. (For more on numbering an outline and various numbering schemes, see the section in this chapter entitled "Numbering Paragraphs.")

You can use the Sort command in an outline window to rearrange large portions of a document. Here's how it works. Suppose that you created an outline using Word's outliner, then you switched to the document view and filled in the document text. Next you switched back to the outline view, where Word displays only your document subheadings and the first line of each paragraph of body text, as shown in Figure 15-53.

This "bird's-eye" view can be very helpful in checking the organization and flow of your document. Then, if you decide that you want to rearrange your document, you can do so very easily in the outline view. For example, in the outline view, you can move one subheading, and in so doing, move all of the body text under that subheading as well. The Sort command can be a handy tool for rearranging various parts of a document in an outline window. If you want to use the Sort command, however, you must be sure to collapse out of view any portions of your document that you do not want to sort.

FIGURE 15-53

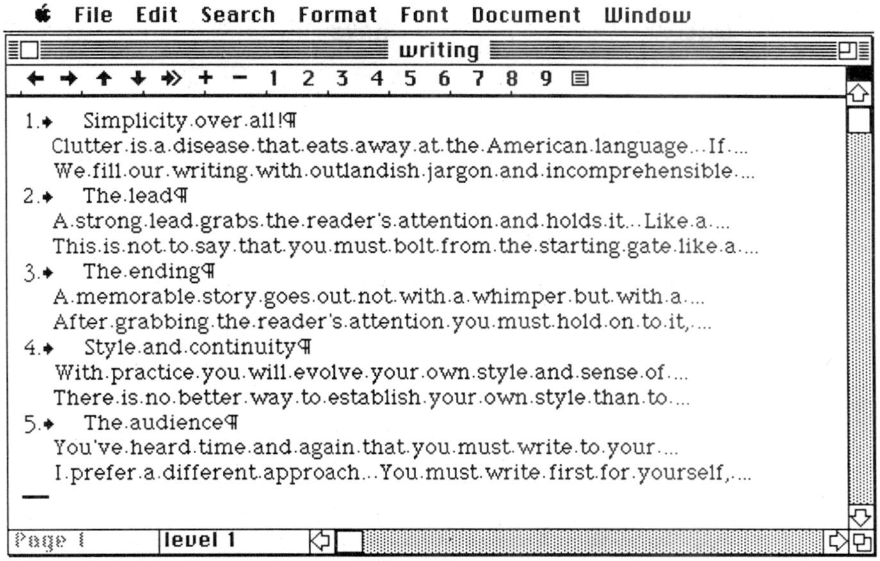

When you switch from a document view to an outline view, Word displays each heading and the first line of each paragraph of body text.

For example, suppose you would like to reverse the order of Sections 2 and 3 in the document shown in Figure 15-53. You can do this by changing the number in front of each section's heading, selecting those headings, and then issuing the Sort command. Before you choose Sort, however, be sure that you collapse the body text out of view. If you do *not* collapse the body text, the result of the Sort command will look like Figure 15-54 on the next page.

Notice that Word has rearranged the outline so that the headings for Sections 2 and 3 appear together, with all the body text for both headings underneath. In addition, Word has sorted the body text according to the first word in each paragraph, resulting in a meaningless flow. To correct this problem, you should select Undo Sort immediately.

To avoid this kind of problem, you should click the 1 icon at the top of the outline window so that only the headings that you want to sort are visible. Figure 15-55 on the following page shows the outline after collapsing the body text out of view.

FIGURE 15-54

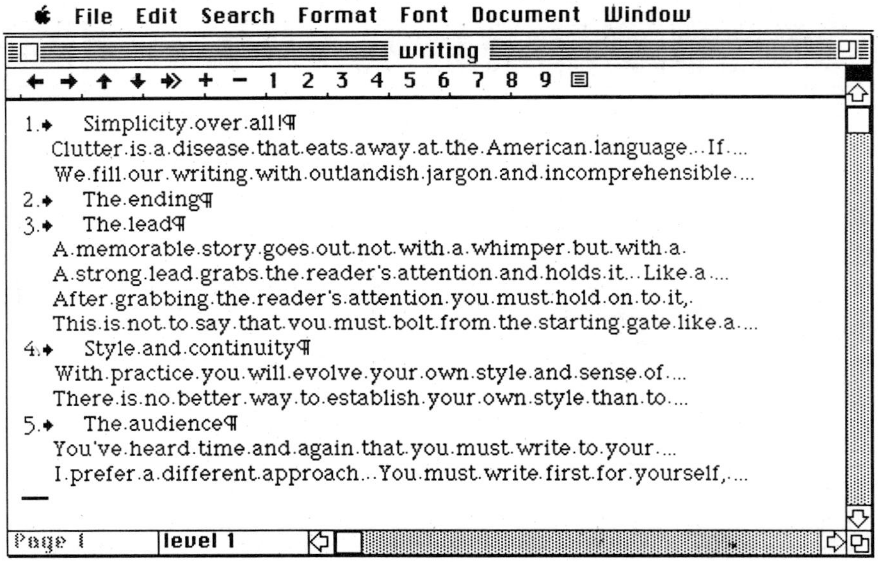

If you do not collapse the body text in an outline window before you sort, Word will sort that text as well as your headings.

FIGURE 15-55

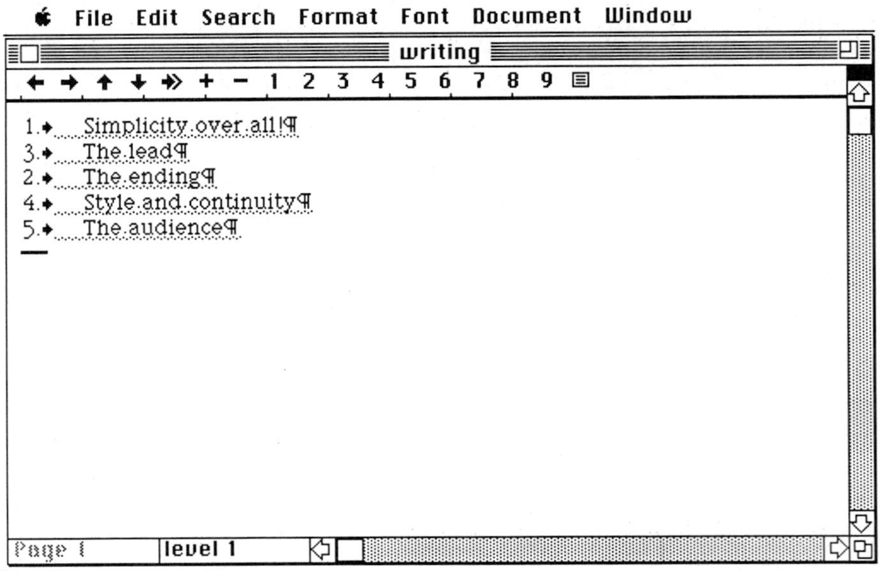

Before using the Sort command to rearrange a document in the outline view, you should collapse the outline so that the body text is no longer visible.

Once you've collapsed the outline, select the headings that you want to sort and choose Sort from the Document menu. After sorting the headings, you can click the Show All icon to see what happened in your body text. Figure 15-56 shows the result.

FIGURE 15-56

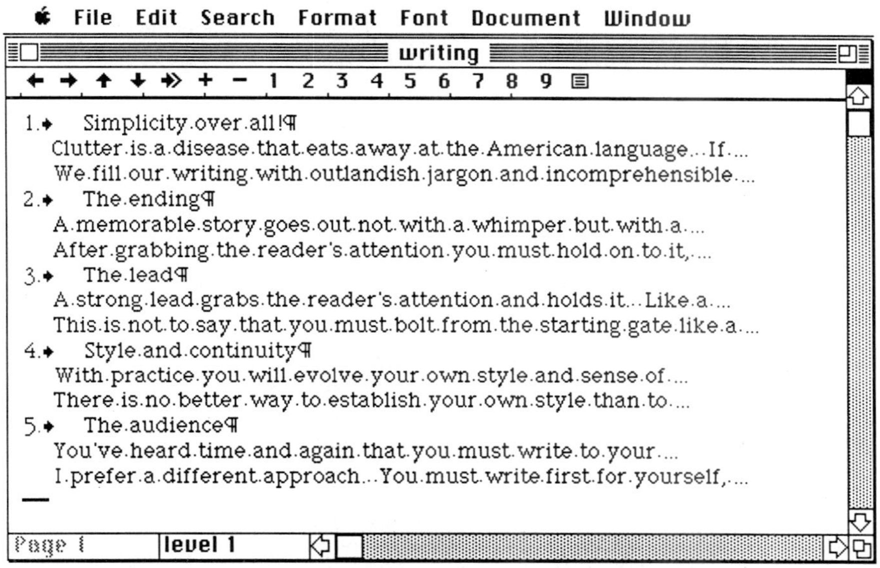

After sorting the selected headings, click the Show All icon to see how the Sort command affected the body text in your document.

As you can see, Word not only changed the order of the headings but also moved the body text so that it falls under the correct heading.

In a simple situation like the one we've just described, you probably would be better off just selecting the text that you want to move and using the Cut and Paste commands. However, in a longer document that requires more serious revisions, using the Sort command in the outline window can save time.

PERFORMING MATHEMATICAL CALCULATIONS

Another special feature of Word 3 is its ability to perform basic mathematical calculations. With this capability, you can perform quick calculations and then plug the results of those calculations into your document. Word can add, subtract, divide, and multiply values, and calculate percentages.

For example, suppose that you have created a table of cash receipts like the one in Figure 15-57. You want to compute your total receipts for the week and insert that total value in the table. Begin by highlighting all the lines in the table, then press ⌘-=. As you can see in Figure 15-58, Word displays the total value 6025.09 in the status box at the lower-left corner of the screen.

FIGURE 15-57

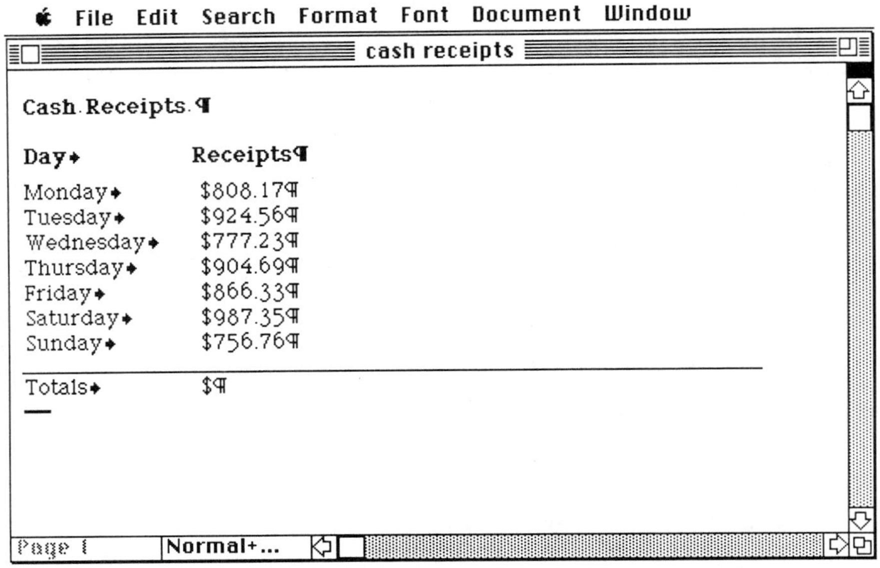

Word can total a column of numbers like the cash receipts shown in this table.

FIGURE 15-58

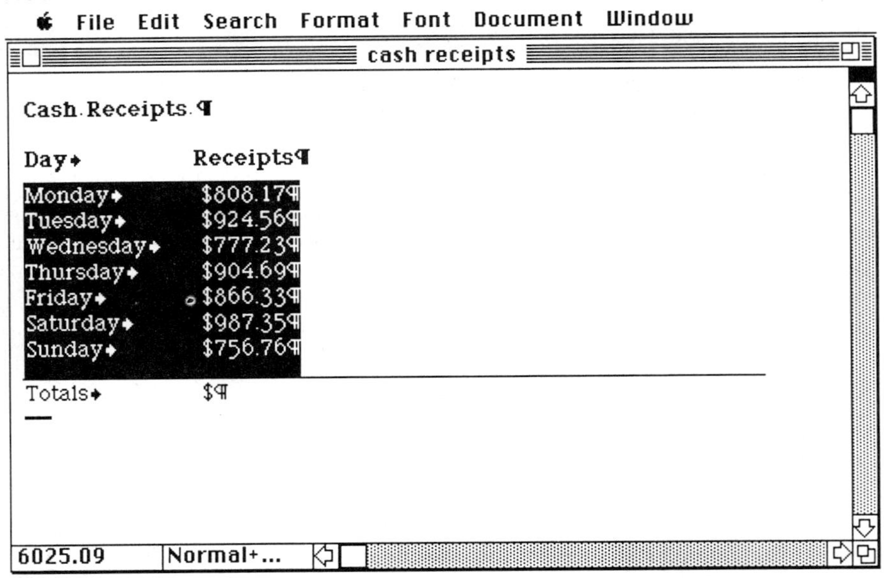

Word displays the results of its calculation in the status box at the bottom-left corner of the screen.

Word also places a copy of this total value on your Clipboard so that you can issue the Paste command (or press ⌘-v) to enter the results of your calculation into your document. For example, if you click to the right of the dollar sign in the Totals line and then select Paste from the Edit menu, Word will paste the value 6025.09 to the right of the insertion point. Figure 15-59 shows our table after we pasted the calculated value into the Totals line.

FIGURE 15-59

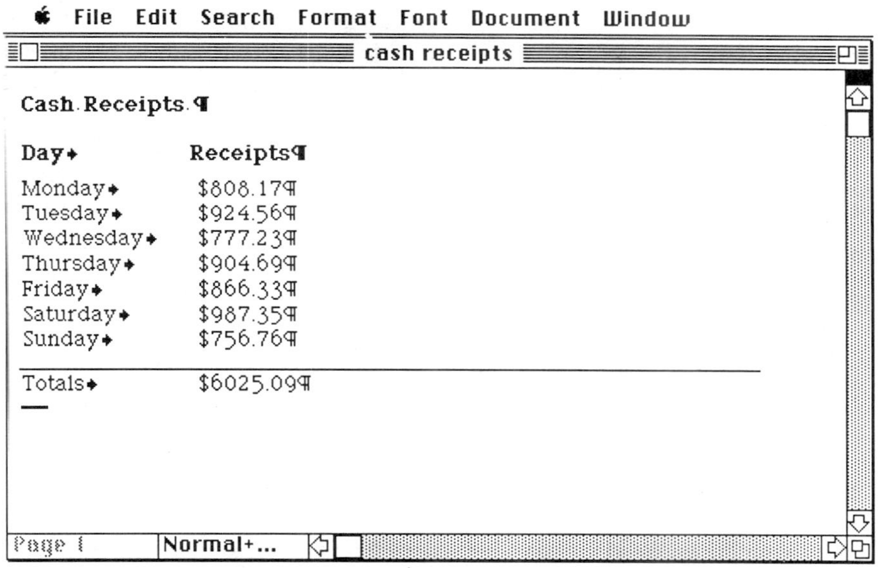

You can paste the result of your calculations into the worksheet.

When you add a series of values, as we did in the previous example, Word does not require that you use any mathematical operators. Unless the text you select includes a mathematical operator, Word assumes that you want to add the values in that selection.

Also, notice that you can highlight entire lines of text and numbers, rather than selecting only the individual values that you want to total. (As you'll see in a moment, if you want to select individual columns from a table of values, you can use the Option key to narrow your selection.) When you use the ⌘-= technique, Word ignores any alphabetic characters in your selection. It treats the numbers on either side of the alphabetic characters as separate values. For example, if you make an entry like *10x9* in your document, Word will treat this string as two separate values—10 and 9.

Word also ignores blank spaces and most punctuation and special markup characters like ?, #, @, ¶, and ↵. There are a few exceptions to this rule, including commas, periods, and the +, -, *, /, and % characters. For example, if a value is enclosed in parentheses—(100), for instance—Word treats that value as a negative number.

If you include commas between numbers—as in 100,100—Word will consider those numbers to be a single value. That's because Word treats commas as separators, dividing hundreds from thousands, thousands from millions, and so on. If a space appears before or after a comma, however, Word will treat the numbers as two separate values.

Similarly, if you include a period between two numbers—as in 100.25—Word will interpret the numbers as a single value since it recognizes the period as a decimal point. Again, if you enter a space before or after the decimal point, Word will ignore the period character and treat the numbers as two separate values. By the way, if any of the values that you are using in your calculations contain commas and/or decimal points, Word will display commas and/or decimal points in the result as well.

The +, -, *, /, and % characters serve as mathematical operators when you are performing calculations in Word. As you might have guessed, the + character, which is optional, tells Word that you want to add a series of values, while the - sign tells Word that you want to subtract. The * and / signs indicate multiplication and division, respectively. The % operator tells Word that you want to calculate a percentage.

Adding Individual Rows and Columns of Data

We've already shown how you can total the values in a table that contains only one column of numbers. However, if you're working with a table that contains two or more columns of numbers, Word also allows you to total each column individually and to total the numbers across each row. To illustrate, let's add two columns to the table that we started in Figure 15-57. As you can see in Figure 15-60, we have added another column of values and a Totals column to the table. Although the Totals column is blank right now, setting it up in advance will allow us to paste our calculation results quickly. We'll begin by calculating the total values in each line or row of this sample table.

Calculating the totals for each line of the table is easy. All you need to do is click in the invisible selection bar next to the first line of the table to select the entire line. (You can drag through the values in the 6/1 Receipts and 6/8 Receipts columns if you like, but since Word will ignore any alphabetic characters, it's faster to just select the entire line.) After selecting the value in the first line, press ⌘-=. When you see the total value in the status box at the bottom-left corner of your screen, click just to the left of the ¶ marker at the end of that line and press ⌘-v. Figure 15-61 shows how the screen will appear just after we select the first line and press ⌘-=. Repeat this process for each line in the table.

FIGURE 15-60

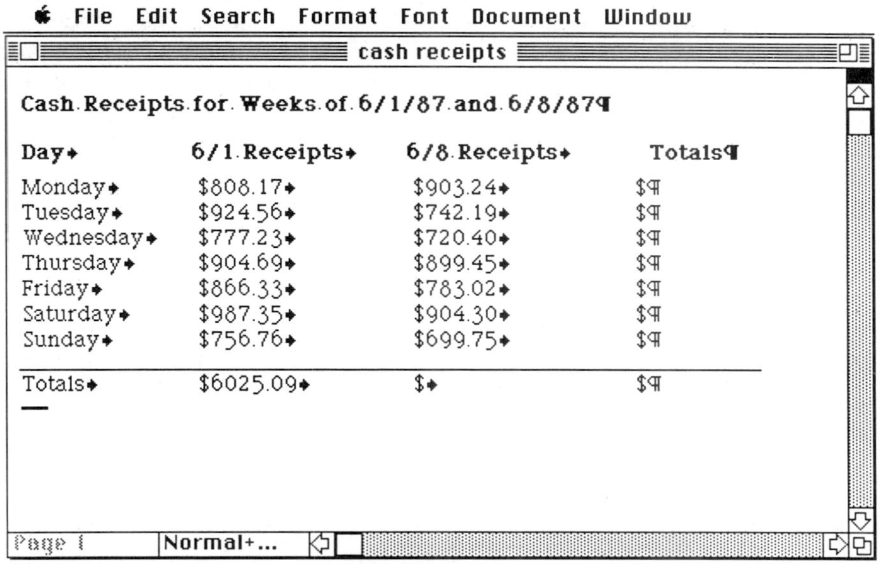

We've added some additional data to our table.

FIGURE 15-61

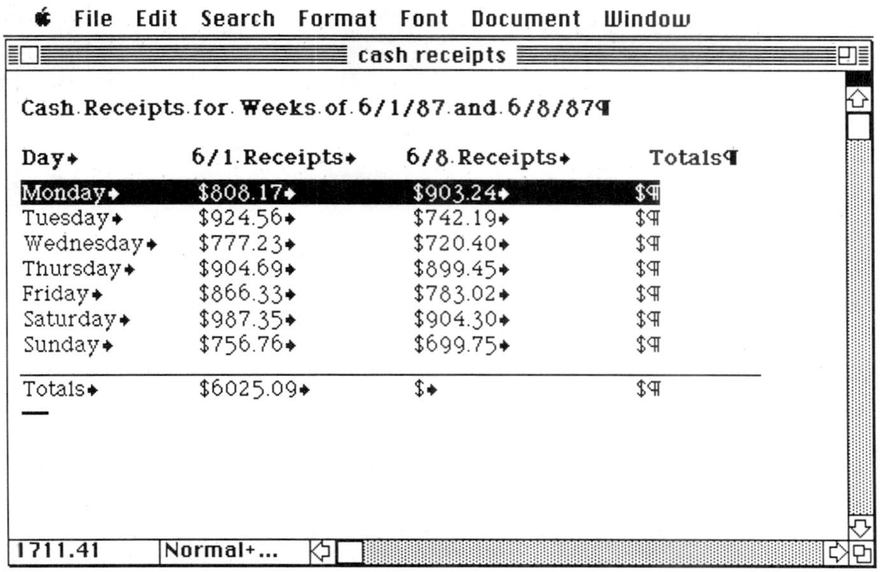

We used the ⌘-= technique to calculate the total for the first line.

Since we have already calculated the totals for the 6/1 Receipts column, our next task is to calculate the totals for the 6/8 Receipts column. The first step is to select the column that we want to total. (If we were to select two or more columns of numbers in the table, Word would add all the values in the selection.) As you learned in Chapter 4, you can select a column in Word by using the Option key. In our example, press the Option key, then click just to the left of the first value in the second column and drag down and to the right until the values for Monday through Sunday are highlighted, as shown in Figure 15-62. Now, just press ⌘-= to total the highlighted values, then click to the right of the dollar sign in column two of the Totals line and press ⌘-v. Figure 15-63 shows the table at this point.

FIGURE 15-62

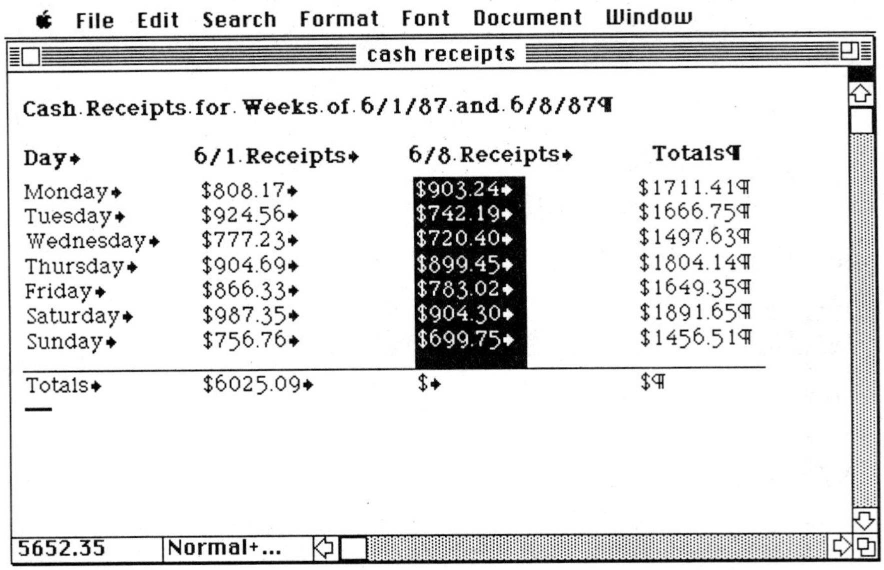

Press the Option key and drag to select an individual column in the table.

Finally, to calculate the grand total for the table, you can highlight either the Totals line at the bottom of the table or the Totals column on the right side of the table and press ⌘-=. Though either technique will yield the same result, keep in mind that the first character in your selection determines the format for your calculation result. So, if you want your grand total to appear in bold type, you should highlight the last column of the table, including the bold heading at the top of the column, and press ⌘-=. When you paste the calculation result at the end of the last row in the table, Word will format your grand total to appear in bold type. (You may want to apply the Bold format to the $ symbol that appears next to the grand total as well.) As you can see, Figure 15-64 shows the completed table.

FIGURE 15-63

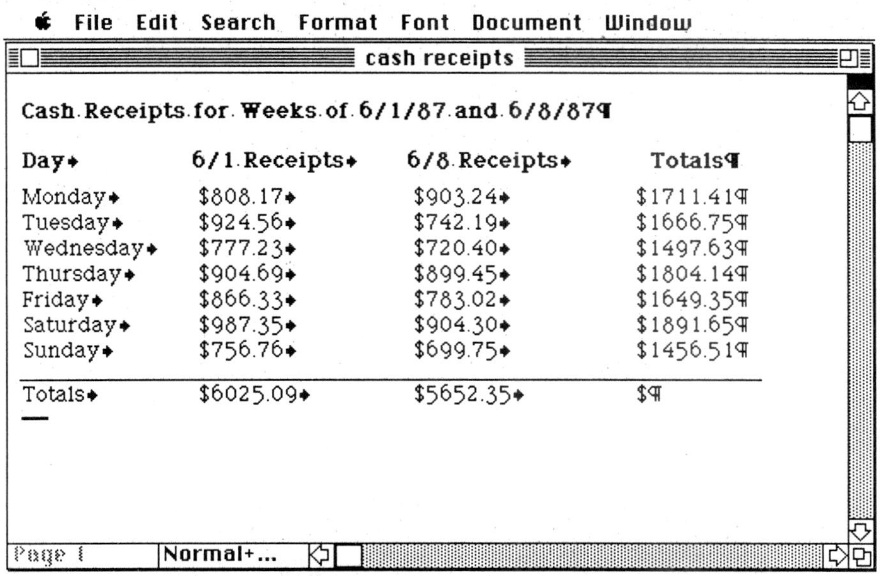

Cash Receipts for Weeks of 6/1/87 and 6/8/87¶

Day◆	6/1 Receipts◆	6/8 Receipts◆	Totals¶
Monday◆	$808.17◆	$903.24◆	$1711.41¶
Tuesday◆	$924.56◆	$742.19◆	$1666.75¶
Wednesday◆	$777.23◆	$720.40◆	$1497.63¶
Thursday◆	$904.69◆	$899.45◆	$1804.14¶
Friday◆	$866.33◆	$783.02◆	$1649.35¶
Saturday◆	$987.35◆	$904.30◆	$1891.65¶
Sunday◆	$756.76◆	$699.75◆	$1456.51¶
Totals◆	$6025.09◆	$5652.35◆	$¶

We have pasted the results of our columnar calculation into the Totals line of the table.

FIGURE 15-64

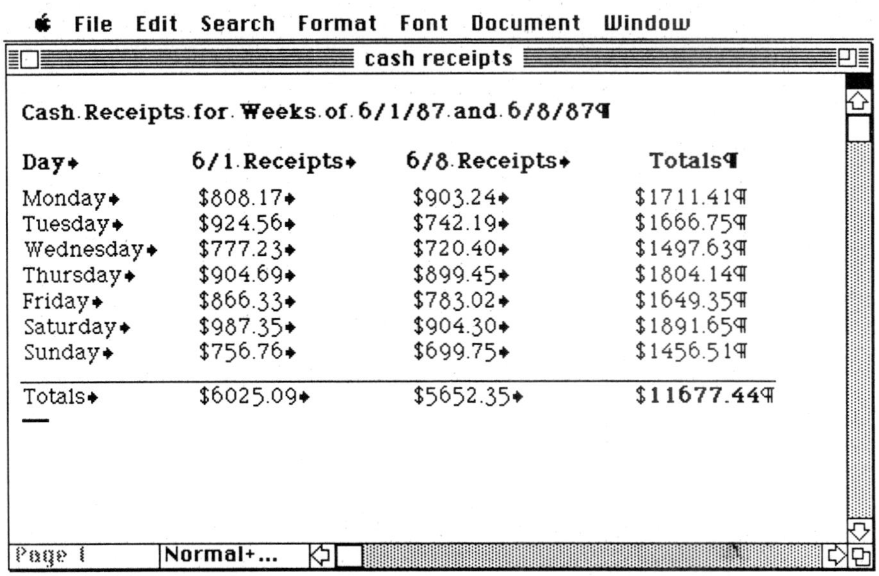

Cash Receipts for Weeks of 6/1/87 and 6/8/87¶

Day◆	6/1 Receipts◆	6/8 Receipts◆	Totals¶
Monday◆	$808.17◆	$903.24◆	$1711.41¶
Tuesday◆	$924.56◆	$742.19◆	$1666.75¶
Wednesday◆	$777.23◆	$720.40◆	$1497.63¶
Thursday◆	$904.69◆	$899.45◆	$1804.14¶
Friday◆	$866.33◆	$783.02◆	$1649.35¶
Saturday◆	$987.35◆	$904.30◆	$1891.65¶
Sunday◆	$756.76◆	$699.75◆	$1456.51¶
Totals◆	$6025.09◆	$5652.35◆	**$11677.44**¶

Our completed table displays both line and column totals.

Other Calculations

If you would like to perform calculations other than addition, you must enter mathematical operators into your document window. For example, to multiply 10 times 2, you would type

10*2

in your document, select those characters, and press ⌘-=. Word will display the result, 20, in the bottom-left corner of your window. As with addition calculations, Word also will place the result on the Clipboard so that you can paste it anywhere in your document by clicking on that spot and selecting Paste from the Edit menu or typing ⌘-v.

When you use the +, -, *, /, and % operators in your calculations, keep in mind that Word performs its calculations from left to right and from top to bottom. The program does not assign any precedence to the different mathematical operators. For example, if you were to use the ⌘-= technique to calculate the result of an entry like

10-8*2+15

in your document, you might expect Word to multiply the values 8 and 2 first, thereby reducing the formula to

10-16+15

to return the value 9. Instead, Word will perform the operations in the order of their appearance and return the value 19. In other words, the program simply takes the calculation arguments in order, like this:

10 - 8 = 2
2 * 2 = 4
4 + 15 = 19

You might be tempted to enclose parts of your formulas in parentheses or brackets to control the order of operations. Unfortunately, Word will ignore any separator characters like these when you use them to break apart portions of your formulas. For example, Word will ignore your parentheses in the formula

10-(8*2)+15

As we mentioned earlier, however, when you place constant numeric values (rather than mathematical formulas) in parentheses, Word will treat the value in parentheses as a negative number. Therefore, Word will recognize the parentheses in the formula

10+(8)*2+15

The result of this formula will be identical to the result of the formula

10-8*2+15

To give you a feel for Word's calculation techniques, Table 15-1 shows some sample formulas that you might enter into your Word documents and the result of each.

TABLE 15-1

Formula	Result
5*4+3	23
4+3*5	35
3+4*5	35
10*(9)	-90
10*9	90
10+(9)	1
10-9	1
10%*6	0.6
10%+6	6.1
10%+10%	.2

This table lists sample formulas and the results of Word's calculations.

Notice that you enter the +, -, *, and / operators in front of the number that you want to add, subtract, multiply, or divide by. However, you enter the % sign directly after the number that you want it to apply to. Thus, you would use the formula

18%*70

to determine that 18 percent of the value 70 is equal to 12.6. When you place a % sign after a value, Word converts that value to a decimal by dividing by 100. Thus, the formula above is equivalent to

.18*70

Similarly, the formula

20%+5

is equal to

.2+5

CHARACTER FORMULAS

Another exciting and unique feature of Word is its ability to create special characters using "character formulas." With character formulas, you can create complex scientific and mathematical formulas, such as

$$\int \frac{dx}{x^2\sqrt{27x^2 + 6 - 1}}$$

that are integrated right into your document. Character formulas can be useful to nearly any writer, not just those with a technical or scientific bent. With a little imagination, you can use character formulas to create a tremendous variety of special symbols and to present ordinary text in an unusual way.

The General Form of Character Formulas

Each character formula begins with a special character, \, which tells Word that the next few characters should be interpreted as a formula, instead of literal characters. You create the \—which looks like a backslash with a period under it—by pressing Option-⌘-\. The \ is followed by one or more commands. Each command requires one or more arguments. The commands tell Word what action you want to perform, and the command arguments indicate the character or characters to be acted upon. A command's argument or arguments must always be enclosed in parentheses.

For example, the Box command is represented by \ and the letter *X*. This command draws a box or border around the character or characters that you specify in the command's argument. Figure 15-65 shows an example of the Box command on screen. In the upper screen of this figure, you see the actual formula, while the lower screen displays the formula result.

FIGURE 15-65

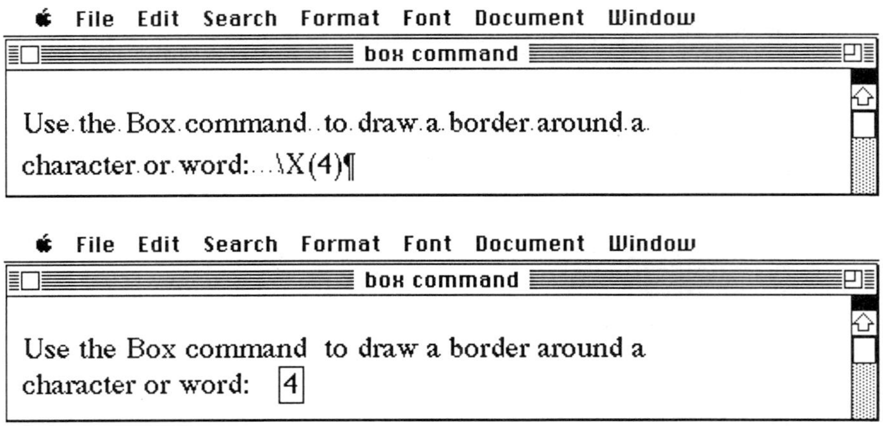

This screen shows an example of a simple character formula. Notice that the command \X is followed by an argument, 4, which is enclosed in parentheses.

You can include options with some commands that affect how the command is carried out. When you use an option with a command, that option must be entered between the command name and the command argument. In addition, you must precede the option with the formula character \. If you use more than one option, then each option must be preceded with a \.

For example, when you use the Box command, you can include options that tell Word to draw only the top, bottom, right, or left edge of the box. You also can combine these options so that Word draws just the parts of the box that you specify, such as the top edge and right edge. In a few cases, an option will require its own "argument"—a character that precisely defines how that option should affect the formula. We will describe these "option arguments" where appropriate as we explain each of Word's formula commands.

To summarize, then, the basic form of a character formula is

\C\O*n*(a1,a2,...an)

where \ is a special formula character; *C* is the command itself; *O* is the command option; *n* is the option's argument; and *a1*, *a2*, and so forth are the command's arguments.

Character formula rules

You can enter a character formula anywhere in a document. Begin by typing the special character \, then enter the formula's components. You can use either upper- or lower-case letters for the formula commands and options. When you enter your command arguments, however, be sure that you use the case and formatting that you want to appear in the final result. For example, if you want your formula result to display a superscripted character, then you must apply the Superscript format to that character as you're creating the formula.

Word will not display any formula results on your screen until you choose Hide ¶ from the Edit menu. As long as Show ¶ is active, you will see only character formulas, not results. In Figure 15-65, we chose Show ¶ to create the upper screen where the formula is displayed. We used Hide ¶ to display the formula result in the lower screen.

If you enter a formula incorrectly, Word will not be able to evaluate the formula and, therefore, will not display the formula result, whether or not you've chosen Hide ¶. When you print a document that includes formulas, Word will always print formula results.

While Show ¶ is active, you can edit and format any of the individual components of a formula. For example, you can select one of the arguments and assign it a different font or size. Of course, any changes like this will affect the appearance of the formula result.

Although you can edit the individual characters in a formula while Show ¶ is active, Word generally considers the formula result to be a single character. Therefore, when you choose Hide ¶, it's usually not possible to cut, copy, or otherwise alter only part of the formula result. In addition, Word requires that a formula's displayed result fit on a single line. (The formula itself can be as long as you want; Word will wrap the formula from one line to another if necessary.) If the displayed result is too long to fit on a single line, then Word will not be able to evaluate the formula. There are a couple of simple ways to get around this length limitation, should you encounter it. First, you may want to enter extremely long formulas as individual paragraphs, rather than integrating them into your text. When you do this, you can change the right indent of any formula paragraphs, as needed. Another solution is to break up a long formula into two or more separate formulas so that each formula's result occupies no more than one line.

Character Formula Commands

Word offers ten commands that you can use to build character formulas. Although you often will use only a single command to achieve a certain result, you can combine different commands in a single formula, and you can embed one command within the argument of another command. In our examples, we will show you each command in a "stand-alone" situation, except in cases where a command is designed specifically to be used with another command.

The Overstrike (\O) command

The Overstrike command, \O,causes two or more characters to appear in the same space. The form of this command is

\O(a1,a2,...an)

where *a1, a2*, and so forth, represent the characters that you want to appear "on top of" one another. Each argument can be as short as a single character or as long as several words.

As an example of the Overstrike command, suppose you want to represent the "short" *e* sound, as in the word *pet*. You would like to print a lower-case *e* with a breve symbol (˘) over it. (In some fonts, such as Times and Helvetica, the breve symbol can be created by typing Shift-Option-period. It is not available in all fonts.) Figure 15-66 shows how you can use Word's Overstrike command to achieve the desired result.

The Overstrike command offers three options: AR, AL, and AC. These options, which stand for align right, align left, and align center, determine the placement of the character represented by the second argument relative to the character represented by the first argument. If you do not use one of these options, Word will assume you want centered alignment (AC).

The Box (\X) command

The Box command, \X, draws a border around the argument that you specify. Unlike the Border options in the Paragraph dialog box, you can apply the Box command to single characters. The Box command has the form

\X(a1)

where *a1* is the character or characters that you want to draw the box around.

FIGURE 15-66

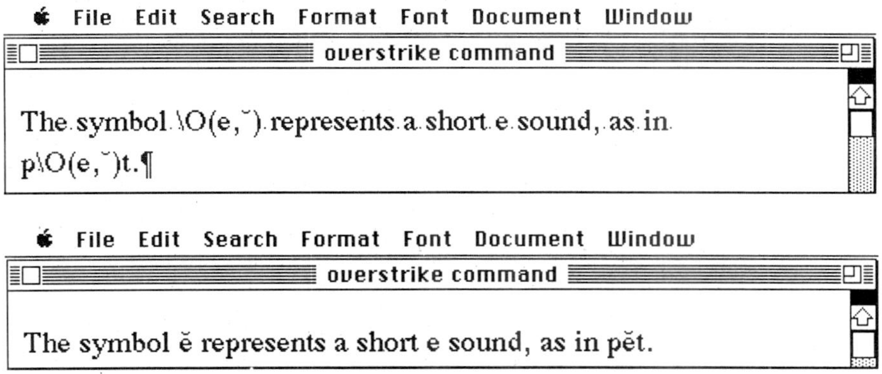

Use the \O command to position two or more characters in the same space. In these screens, we've used this command to position a breve symbol over the letter e.

For example, suppose you want the name of your company, National Systems Corporation, to appear in Helvetica 14-point type with a border around it. Figure 15-67 shows a formula that achieves this result.

FIGURE 15-67

You can use the \X command to draw a border around several words.

The Box command can accept only one argument. If you want the argument to include a comma, you must precede that comma with the \ symbol. Otherwise, Word will think that you are trying to enter more than one argument and will not be able to evaluate the formula. In cases where your argument must contain a lot of commas, you would be better off embedding the List (\L) command within your argument for the Box command, rather than typing a separate \ for each comma. We'll explain the List command on page 613.

The Box command can accept four options: TO, BO, LE, and RI. These stand for Top border, Bottom border, Left border, and Right border, respectively. You use one or more of these options when you want to draw only a partial border around your argument. You can combine these options in any way.

The Fraction (\F) command

The Fraction command does exactly what you would expect: It creates a fraction using the arguments you specify as the numerator and denominator. The form of the Fraction command is

\F(a1,a2)

where *a1* is the numerator and *a2* is the denominator. The Fraction command does not accept any options. Figure 15-68 shows an example of this command.

FIGURE 15-68

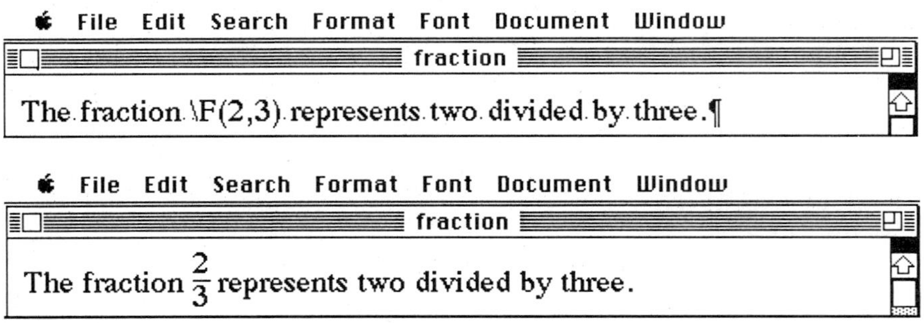

The .\F command creates a fraction using the arguments you specify for the numerator and denominator.

The numerator and denominator arguments do not have to be simple whole numbers, like those used in Figure 15-68. You can use complex formulas, such as $4x^2+12y-23$, or even text as either the numerator or denominator.

The Radical (\R) command

The Radical command, \R, draws a radical or "square root" symbol. The form of the command is

\R(a1,a2)

The second argument is optional. If you use only one argument, then that argument will be placed inside the radical to create a square root. If you use two arguments, then Word will place the second argument (*a2*) inside the radical and will place the first argument (*a1*) above the radical to indicate the root being computed. For example, Figure 15-69 shows a formula that displays the square root of 100 and another formula that displays the cube root of 100.

FIGURE 15-69

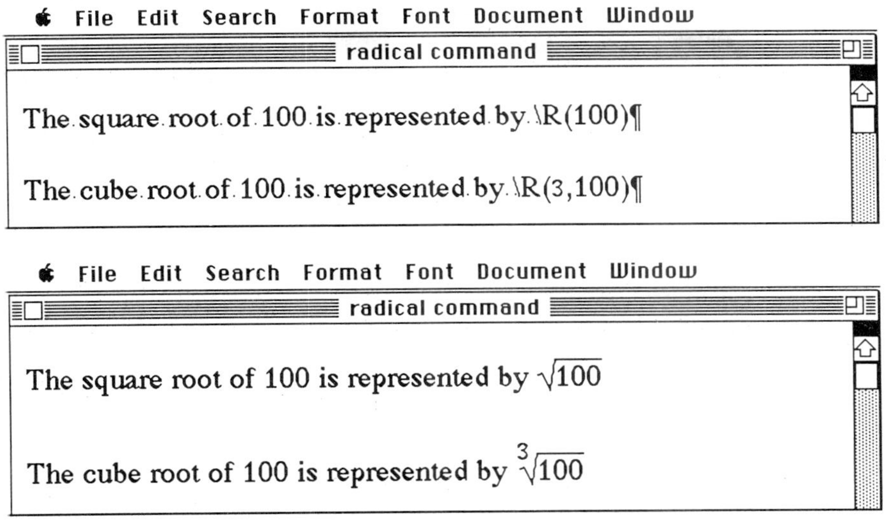

Use the \R command to display the radical symbol in a mathematical formula.

When you use the second argument with the Radical command, you may want to change the point size of the first argument so that the exponent outside the radical symbol is smaller than the number inside the radical.

The Array (\A) command

The Array command creates a two-dimensional array using the arguments that you specify. In its simplest form, the Array command has the form

\A(a1,a2,a3,...an)

The arguments, *a1*, *a2*, and so forth, are the elements of the array that you want to create. The simple form of the Array command creates a one-column array with the elements centered on top of one another. Figure 15-70 on the following page shows an example of the Array command. Notice that Word stacks the elements, one on top of another, with the first argument, *10*, at the top of the stack.

There are several options you can use with the Array command to control the number of columns in an array and to control the spacing and alignment of array elements. If you want to create a multicolumn array, you must use the CO*n* option, where *n* is a number that indicates how many columns you want to include in the array.

FIGURE 15-70

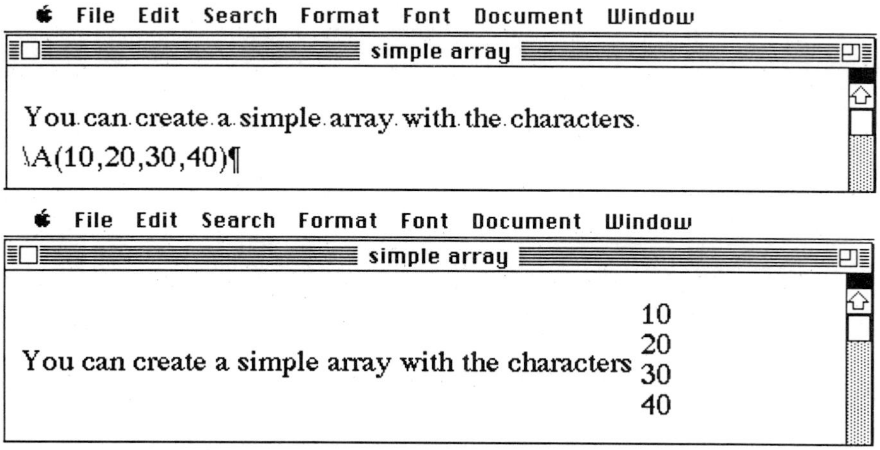

In its simplest form, the \A command will create a one-column array.

There also are options you can use with the Array command to control both the horizontal and vertical spacing of the array elements. Normally, Word does not place any space between the columns of an array. In addition, the amount of space between the rows in an array is equal to the leading of normal lines of text. The HS*n* option controls horizontal spacing and the VS*n* option controls vertical spacing. In both cases, *n* is a whole number that indicates the amount of space, in points, that you want to add between the rows or columns of the array. For example, if you use the HS1 option, Word will add one point of space between the columns of the array. This one point is in addition to the normal space that appears between characters. Similarly, if you use the VS1 option, Word will add one point of space between the rows of the array.

There are three more options that you can use with the Array command to control the alignment of characters within the columns of the array: AL, AR, and AC. AL stands for Align Left, AR stands for Align Right, and AC stands for Align Center. If you do not use an alignment option, Word will create an array with centered alignment.

The Integral (\I) command

The Integral command, \I, is used to draw integrals, summations, products, or any other formulas that take a similar form. The simplest form of this command is

\I(a1,a2,a3)

where *a1* is the lower limit, *a2* is the upper limit, and *a3* is the integrand character. Figure 15-71 shows a simple example of the Integral command. To enhance the appearance of the resulting integral formula (in the lower screen), we assigned a smaller point size to the first two arguments of the command.

FIGURE 15-71

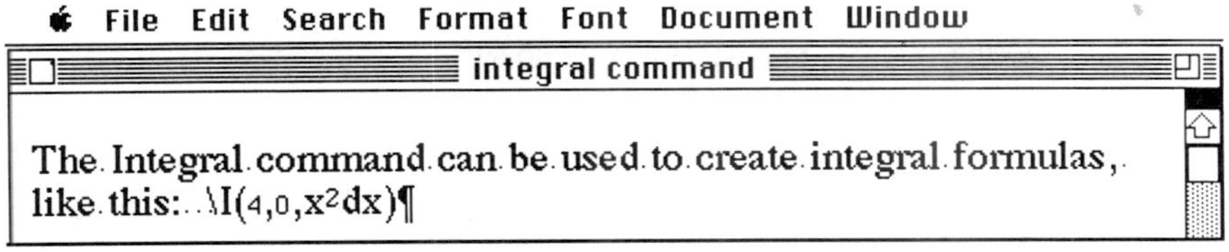

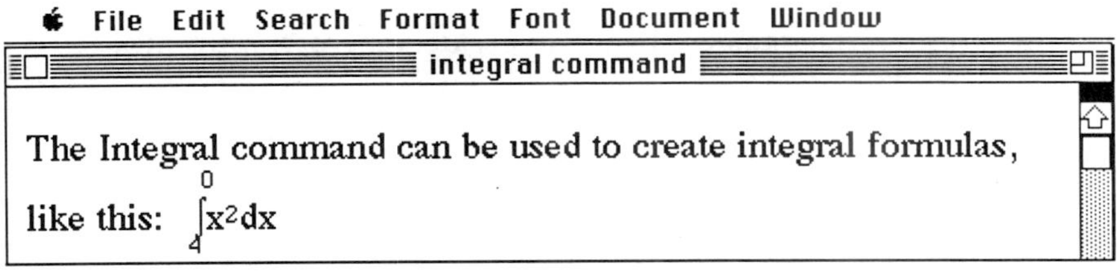

These screens show the \I command in its simplest form.

The Integral command offers a couple of options that allow you to display a summation symbol, Σ, or a product symbol, π, instead of the integral symbol, ∫. To create a summation formula, you use the SU option in your integral formula. To create a product formula, you use the PR option.

You are not limited to the ∫, Σ, and π symbols when you use the Integral command. By adding the FC or VC option to your formula, you can use any character on the keyboard in place of the default ∫ symbol. The FC option indicates a character of fixed height: Whatever character you type in the formula is the character Word will use in the resulting formula display. The VC option, on the other hand, indicates a character of variable height. Word will change the size of the character that you type to correspond to the size of the third argument in the formula. This option is particularly appropriate in cases where the third argument of the \I command is a fraction. When you use either the FC or VC option, you must type a \ before the option, then type another \ before the character that you want to substitute for the ∫ symbol.

There's one more option that you can use with the \I command: IN. This option changes the placement of the first two arguments in the formula result. Instead of the first two arguments appearing above and below the integral symbol (or whatever other symbol you use in the formula), the IN option causes them to appear to the right of the integral symbol in "inline" format.

The Superscript/Subscript (\S) command

In its simplest form, the Superscript/Subscript (\S) command has the form:

\S(a1)

This command positions the single argument that you specify as a superscript. For example, Figure 15-72 shows a formula in which we've created a superscripted 2. In this example, the 10 at the beginning of the formula is not really part of the formula; it merely serves as the "base" for the superscripted 2. (By the way, we lowered the point size of the argument, 2, in order to enhance the appearance of the formula result.)

FIGURE 15-72

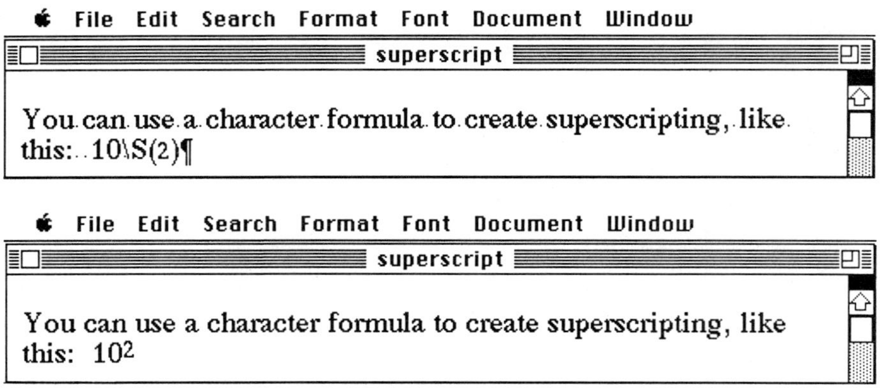

You can use the \S command to create superscripting.

When you use the \S command with no options, Word will superscript the argument you specify by three points. If you want to superscript the argument by a different number of points, you can insert an UP*n* option in the formula, where *n* is a number of points by which you want to superscript the argument.

The DO*n* option allows you to create a subscript instead of a superscript. Again, *n* is the number of points by which you want to subscript the argument.

Whenever you use either the UP*n* or the DO*n* option, you must specify an *n* value. Otherwise, Word will assume an *n* value of zero and will not superscript or subscript your argument.

You probably are wondering why anyone would ever use the Superscript/Subscript command instead of simply choosing Character... from the Format menu and clicking the Superscript or Subscript option. There's really only one difference between using the Superscript/Subscript command and assigning the Superscript or Subscript format from the Character dialog box. The \S command can accept more than one argument, and when you use two or more arguments, Word will superscript the first argument and then "stack" the additional arguments in a column under the first argument. When you use multiple arguments with the \S command, the command will not recognize any UP*n* and DO*n* options. Therefore, there's no point in using the UP*n* and DO*n* options when your \S command has more than one argument.

The Displace (\D) command

The Displace (\D) command allows you to move characters forward or backward by a specified number of points. The Displace command is different from other commands in two important ways. First, it does not accept any arguments. Instead of acting upon an argument, this command always displaces the characters that immediately follow the command. Nevertheless, you must place a pair of parentheses after the Displace command.

Another important feature of the Displace command is that it *requires* an option. There are three possible options that you can use with this command: FO*n*, BA*n*, and LI. The FO*n* option moves characters forward on the line by *n* points. Similarly, the BA*n* command moves characters backward by *n* points. The LI option draws a line between the character just before the \D command and the character just after the \D command. The LI option must always be used with either the FO*n* or BA*n* option.

The main purpose of the Displace command is to give you precise control over the placement of characters on a line. For example, suppose that you want to create exactly $^{1}/_{4}$ inch (or 18 points) of space between two words on a line. Figure 15-73 shows a formula that does this. Notice that we used the FO18 option with this formula to create the 18 points of space.

FIGURE 15-73

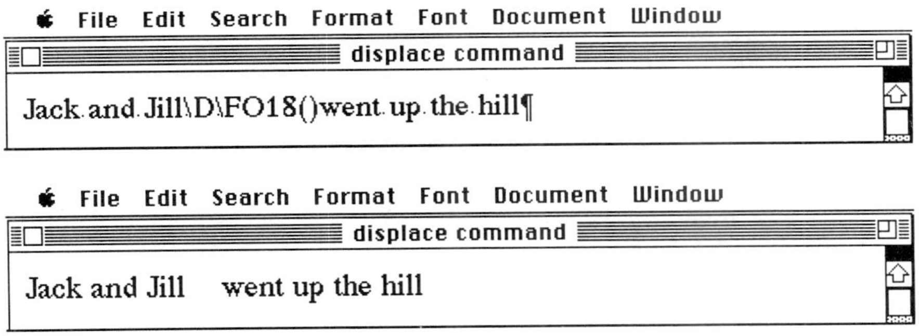

Use the \D command with the FOn option to insert a precise amount of horizontal space on a line.

The FO option moves *all* characters that follow the Displace command in the current paragraph forward (to the right) *n* points. If the *n* value for the FO option is large enough, some characters on the current line will wrap to the next line. This may cause characters on the next line to wrap to another line as well.

The BA*n* option moves all characters that follow the Displace command in the same paragraph backward (to the left) *n* points. Because the Displace command does not affect the characters that come before the command, the displaced characters will probably write over other characters on the same line. If the *n* value that you specify is large enough, Word will displace characters beyond the beginning of the line. However, the displaced characters will not "wrap up" to the previous line. Instead, they will be placed in the blank area of your screen beyond the left margin. If you want to view the displaced characters, you must drag the indent marker on your ruler to the left so that this part of your screen comes into view.

The LI option simply draws a line in the space that you create with the Displace command. When you use the LI option with the FO option, Word underlines the space created by the FO option. If you use the LI option with the BA*n* option, Word will draw the line under the characters that have been displaced by the BA option.

The Bracket (\B) command

The Bracket (\B) command brackets its argument with any character you specify. In its simplest form, the Bracket command looks like this:

\B(a1)

This command places parentheses around the argument, *a1*. For example, the command \B(ABC) will enclose the string ABC in parentheses, like this: (ABC).

You probably are wondering why you would use the Bracket command instead of simply typing parentheses. This command is essential when you are building a formula and you want one of your arguments to appear in parentheses in the formula result. If you simply type the parentheses, you could confuse another command in the formula. For example, suppose you want to create the fraction $^{3}/_{4}$, surrounded by parentheses. If you type the parentheses as part of the argument for the \F command, you'll create an invalid formula. Figure 15-74 shows the correct way to create the fraction $^{3}/_{4}$ surrounded by parentheses. Notice that in the formula result, Word altered the size of the parentheses to be compatible with the height of the fraction.

FIGURE 15-74

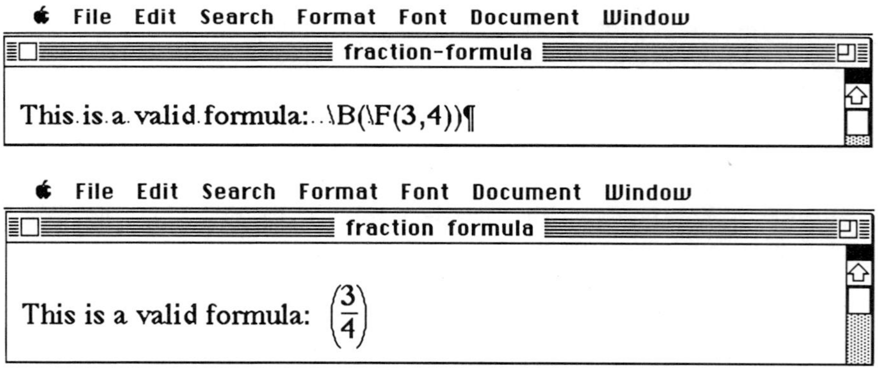

The \B command allows you to display parentheses in a formula result.

The BC option allows you to use characters other than parentheses as bracketing characters. The BC option is always followed by \ and the character that you wish to use for bracketing. When you use this option, you need to specify only the opening (or left bracket) character—such as { or [—and Word will supply the closing bracket character.

The LC and RC options allow you to place a bracket character on only the left or only the right of the argument. The LC option places the bracket character you specify on the left side of the argument. Similarly, the RC option places the bracket character you specify on the right side of the argument. As with the BC option, each of these options must be followed by a \ and the character that you want to use.

The List (\L) command

The List command, like the Bracket command, is designed to be used with other commands. This command simply creates a list, separated by commas, of the arguments that you specify. In its simplest form, the List command looks like this:

\L(a1,a2,...an)

and its result is simply a list of items separated by commas. When might you use this command? Since Word normally interprets a comma as an argument separator, the List command comes in handy whenever you want to use a list of items as a single argument. For example, suppose that you want to create a list of numbers with a box drawn around the list. Since the Box (\X) command can accept only one argument, the formula \X(10,20,30,40,50) is invalid. As you can see, Figure 15-75 shows how the List command can be used to overcome this limitation.

FIGURE 15-75

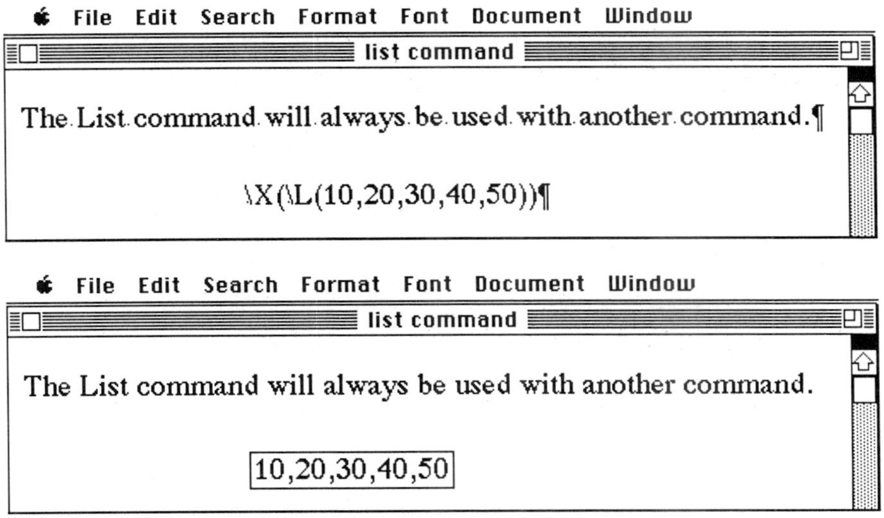

You can use the \L command when your formula result must display items separated by commas.

16 SHARING DATA WITH OTHER PROGRAMS

If you're like most Word users, your Mac does a lot more for you than word processing. You probably use a spreadsheet program like Microsoft Excel for its number-crunching capabilities or a graphics package like MacPaint or MacDraw to create illustrations and charts. If you do a great deal of desktop publishing, you may use a page layout application such as PageMaker as well.

In this chapter, we'll show you some techniques for combining the power of Word with other applications. We'll cover a wide range of topics, including using the Switcher to run two or more programs concurrently; adding graphics to your Word documents; and sharing data with other word processing programs, worksheet programs, and desktop publishing packages.

THE SWITCHER

The Switcher application lets you operate two or more Macintosh programs concurrently. With just a click of the mouse, you can easily move back and forth between your Word documents and documents created in other programs. Because you can also use the Switcher to transfer information via the Clipboard, Switcher is a great timesaver when you need to move data from one Macintosh program to another.

Preparing to Use the Switcher

Though you can use the Switcher with a 512K Mac, you'll find that your memory and disk space limitations make it difficult to run two or more applications concurrently. We recommend that you use a Mac Plus with at least one 800K disk drive and one 400K disk drive if you plan to use Switcher. Preferably, you'll want two 800K drives or a Mac installed with a hard disk.

To use the Switcher, place your 800K Word startup disk—which contains your Word program file, your System folder, and the Switcher application—in the internal 800K drive as usual. Then, place the program files that you plan to use on a disk in your external drive. (Keep in mind that you need only one set of System files when you use the Switcher. All of the programs that you open will operate under the System that you used to boot your Macintosh.) You'll also want to reserve some space on your second disk for the data files that you plan to work with and, if space permits, for your Main Dictionary file, Hyphenation file, and any other utility files that you might need.

Loading Programs with Switcher

In order to load two or more programs simultaneously, you must use a Switcher document. Microsoft has already done much of the setup work for you by providing you with five ready-made Switcher documents: Word/Excel, Word/File, Word/Works, Word/MacDraw, and Word/MacPaint. These files are located on the utility disk. To use one of these Switcher sets, just copy it to the disk that contains the application programs you plan to use with Word. Then, double-click on the Switcher set icon to load Word and the selected applications simultaneously.

If you don't find the Switcher set you need on your Word utility disk, you can easily build your own Switcher document. To begin, double-click on the Switcher application icon at the Finder level. When you do this, you'll see a dialog box like the one in Figure 16-1. To load the programs you want to use, double-click on the generic application icons on the left side of the dialog box. When you double-click one of these icons, Switcher will present an Open dialog box much like the one you use to open Word files. This box will display the application programs available on your internal and external disk drives. To load one of these programs, double-click on the name of the program. When you do this, Word will replace the generic application icon with the icon for the program you have loaded. You can repeat this process to load other applications. For example, Figure 16-2 shows our screen once we have used the Switcher to load the Word and Excel programs.

If you plan to reuse a Switcher combination you have created, you can use the Save Set... command on the Switcher File menu to save the Switcher set to disk. Then, the next time you want to load that group of programs, you can simply click on the icon for this Switcher file at the Finder level.

By the way, you can also use the Attach Document... command on the Switcher File menu to attach documents to your Switcher sets so that those files will be loaded automatically when you load the program. You can even attach Word glossary files via the Switcher to load those glossaries automatically when you load Word.

Once you have loaded Switcher, you can use the double arrows at the top-right corner of your screen to move from one application to another. To make the switch even more quickly, just press ⌘-]. To bring the Switcher screen back into view, click on the center of the double arrow icon.

FIGURE 16-1

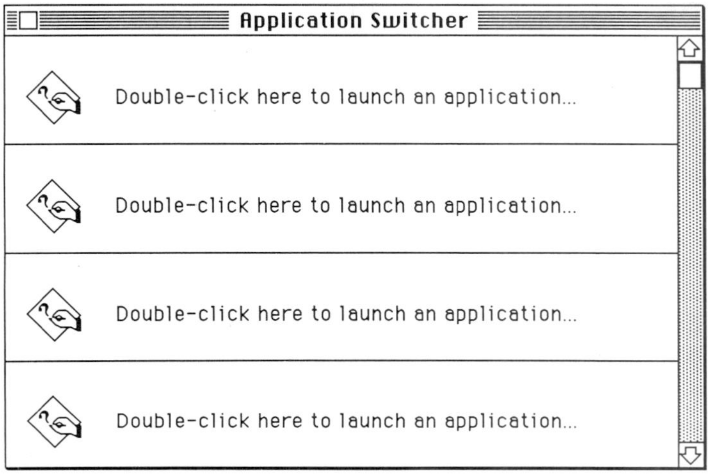

You can use this dialog box to create your own Switcher files.

FIGURE 16-2

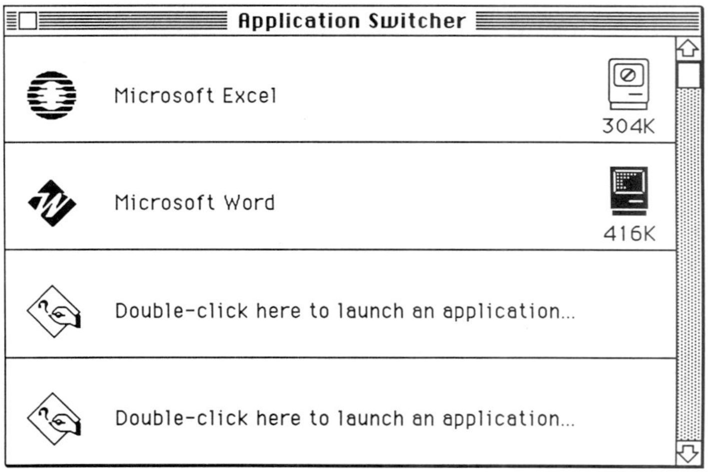

If you use the Switcher to load Word and Excel, your Switcher screen will look like this one.

Using QuickSwitch

The QuickSwitch facility works hand in hand with Switcher to let you define links between your Word documents and documents created in compatible programs, including Excel, MacDraw, and MacPaint. In order to use QuickSwitch, you'll need to copy the QuickSwitch application file from the Switcher Sets folder on the Word utility disk to your Word program disk or the disk that contains the other applications you plan to use. (By the way, if you use Excel Version 1.03 or later, you won't need to use the QuickSwitch application file. QuickSwitch is already installed in your Excel program.)

We'll talk more about QuickSwitch when we show you how to copy MacPaint graphics and Excel data into your Word documents.

GRAPHICS

One of the Mac's greatest selling points is its ability to integrate high-quality graphics and text images. Microsoft has taken advantage of this ability with a number of special tools to let you insert graphics into your Word document files. Word lets you integrate graphics into your documents, flow text around these graphics, and even size and crop graphics to fit your layout needs. You can also convert text into graphics and insert blank graphics frames into your Word documents as placeholders for photographs or illustrations that will be manually pasted in later. Word treats your graphic as a single character, which can be cut, copied, and pasted just like a text element.

Importing Graphics with the Switcher

If you're using the Switcher, the fastest way to insert a graphic into your Word document is to copy the graphic to the Clipboard, then switch to Word and paste it into the desired location in your document. That's all there is to it!

For example, Figure 16-3 shows a MacPaint screen in which we've drawn the logo for a hypothetical company. Let's suppose that we now want to insert this logo into a Word document. To do this, we select the graphic, issue the Copy command, press ⌘-] to switch to our Word document, click at the spot where we want the graphic to appear, and issue the Paste command. Word will then copy the graphic from the Clipboard into the document window, as shown in Figure 16-4.

Whenever you paste a graphic into a Word document, Word will place a graphic frame around the graphic. Though this frame is not visible when the Hide ¶ setting is in effect, when you Choose Show ¶ from the Edit menu, Word will display a dotted border around the graphics frame, as shown in Figure 16-5 on page 620. As you'll see in a moment, you can use the frame to change the size and scale of your graphic.

If you want to place a border around this graphic, just assign the Outline character format to the graphic as you would any other text element. You can also use the Shadow and Bold character formats to format the graphic border.

Updating your graphics with QuickSwitch

Once you've copied a graphic from MacPaint or MacDraw into Word, you can use the QuickSwitch facility to make a change to that graphic at any time. To take advantage of this capability, the QuickSwitch application file must be on the same disk as your MacPaint file, and you must have already loaded Word and your graphics program (MacPaint or MacDraw) with the Switcher. Let's assume that you've done these things and that you want to update a graphic that you've pasted into a Word document. To begin, select the graphic in your Word document, press ⌘-, to switch to MacPaint or MacDraw, and paste the graphic into an empty MacPaint or MacDraw document. Once the graphic is in

FIGURE 16-3

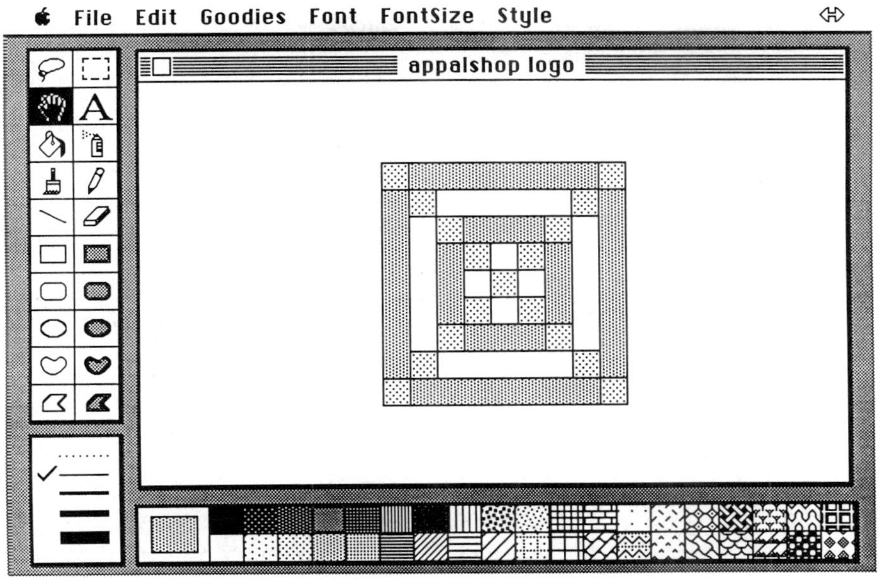

This is a graphic that we created in MacPaint.

FIGURE 16-4

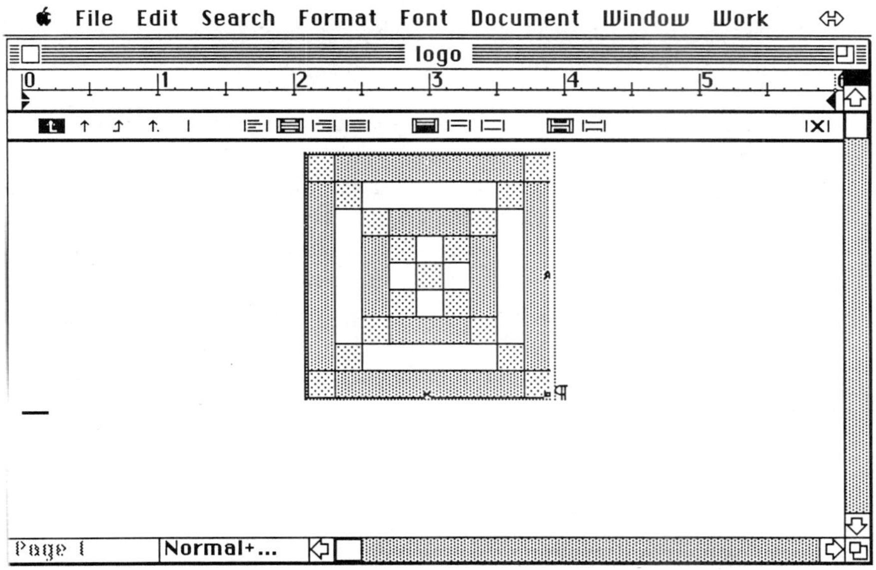

We've pasted our graphic into our Word document.

FIGURE 16-5

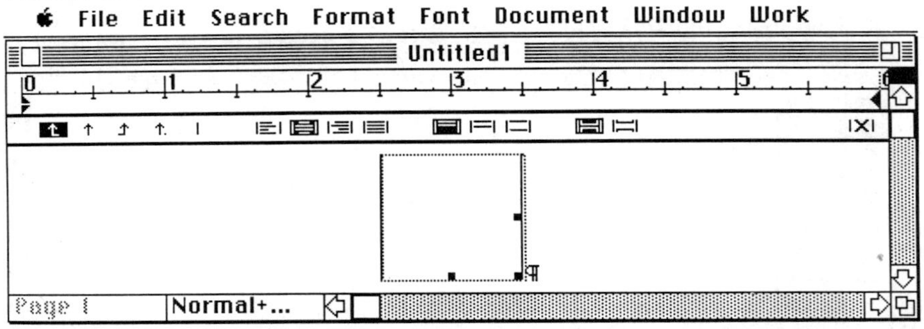

Use the Insert Graphics command to insert a blank frame in your document.

MacPaint or MacDraw, you can make any needed changes. After you've made your changes, just press ⌘-, again to move back to your Word document. QuickSwitch will automatically update the graphic in your document to incorporate your changes.

One note of warning: Word will recognize only that portion of the MacPaint or MacDraw window where you orginally pasted the graphic. If you move or resize the graphic, the entire graphic may not be returned to your document window. Thus, if you need to make substantial changes to a MacPaint or MacDraw image, it will probably be easier to start over by pasting an entirely new graphic over the existing graphic in your document window.

Using the Scrapbook

If you don't have the memory capacity or the desire to use the Switcher to copy graphics into Word, you can always use the Scrapbook to make the transfer. Once you've drawn the graphic, the first step in transferring a graphic to a Word document is to copy it from your graphics program (MacPaint or MacDraw) into the Scrapbook file. To do this, open the graphic into your graphics program, select the graphic, and issue the Copy command. Then choose Scrapbook from the menu to open the Scrapbook, and select Paste from the Edit menu to place the graphic in the Scrapbook.

After you quit from the graphics program, you'll need to copy the Scrapbook file that contains the graphic from your MacPaint or MacDraw startup disk onto your Word startup disk (the disk that contains the System files that you use with Word). If the Scrapbook file on your Word startup disk contains some items that you want to keep, you'll need to rename that file before you copy the Scrapbook file from your MacPaint startup disk. Otherwise, the Scrapbook file you're copying will overwrite the original file. (See Chapter 6 for more on creating and using multiple Scrapbook files.)

Once you've copied the Scrapbook file, you can open a new or existing Word document as you normally would. Once the document is open, choose Scrapbook from the menu. If your Scrapbook contains more than one graphic, you may need to click on the scroll bar at the bottom of the Scrapbook window to bring the graphic you want to use into view. Only one graphic will be visible at a time in the Scrapbook window.

When the graphic you want to use is in view, choose Copy from the Edit menu. Then position the insertion point in your Word document where you want the graphic to appear, and choose Paste from the Edit menu. Word will then copy the graphic from your Scrapbook into the document window.

Sizing Graphics

Word lets you resize a graphic in two ways: by cropping or by scaling. To crop a graphic—that is, to resize the graphic without changing its original scale—just click on the graphic to display the handles around its borders, then change the size of its frame to suit your layout needs. As you might have guessed, you can use the bottom handles to change the height of the graphic and the right handle to adjust the width. To change the size of the frame without altering its original proportions, drag the corner handle.

If your frame is larger than the graphic, Word will center the graphic within the frame. To shrink the frame again to the smallest size that holds the graphic, just double-click anywhere on that graphic.

When you crop, keep in mind that Word will not change the actual size of the picture you have pasted into the document. Instead, Word will display only as much of the graphic as it has room for in the frame. For example, if we click on the graphic shown in Figure 16-4 and drag the corner handle up and to the left, Word will display only part of the original image, as shown in Figure 16-6.

FIGURE 16-6

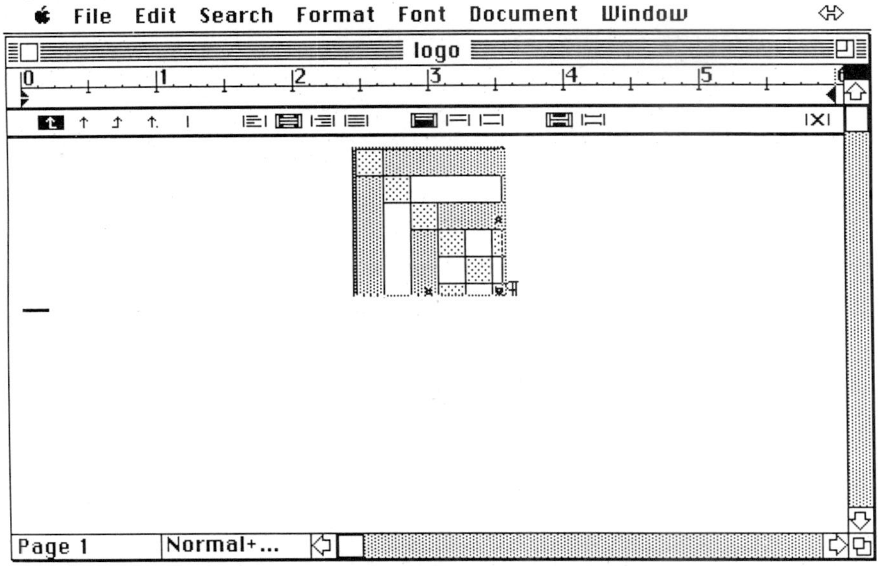

When you crop a graphic frame, Word displays only as much of the graphic as it has room for in the frame.

To rescale the graphic—that is, to change the actual size of the image rather than just the frame—you can press the Shift key as you drag the frame handles. For example, returning to the sample graphic shown in Figure 16-4, if we press the Shift key as we drag the corner handle, Word will reduce the size of the entire graphic image, as shown in Figure 16-7.

FIGURE 16-7

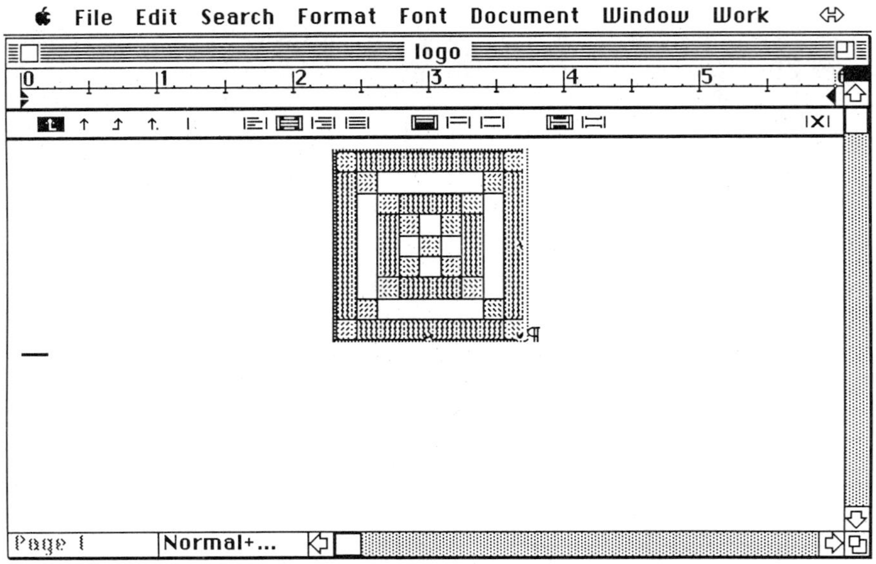

When you scale a graphic, Word will change the size of the graphic image.

Positioning Your Graphics

As we mentioned earlier, you can use several of Word's character formatting commands and options to create borders for your graphics. If you place a ¶ marker after the graphic so that it occupies its own paragraph, you can also assign paragraph formats to your graphics to control how they are positioned in your text. For example, you can use the ruler alignment icons to align your graphics to the left, right, and center margins of your document, and you can use the Paragraph... command to add space above and below your graphic.

One of the easiest ways to wrap text around your graphic is to assign the Side-by-Side format to the paragraph that holds your graphic. Then you assign the Side-by-Side format to the text that you want to place next to your graphic to align the text and graphic on the page. (For more on using the Side-by-Side paragraph format, see Chapter 8.)

The Insert Graphics Command

There may be times when you'll want to add an empty graphic frame to your Word document. An empty frame can serve as a placeholder for an illustration to be pasted in later. You can use the Insert Graphics command to create a blank graphics frame. When you issue this command, Word places a blank frame at the current insertion point. You can size and scale this frame any way you like, just as you would resize a frame that contains a graphic.

Converting Text into a Graphic

Some of the text in your Word documents cannot be read by other programs. For example, the character formulas you create using the technique described in Chapter 15 will not translate to other word processors or to desktop publishing programs like PageMaker.

To get around this problem, you can convert your text into a graphic. To do this, first highlight the text that you want to convert in your Word document, then press Option-⌘-d. When you do this, Word will place a copy of your selection on your Clipboard in graphic form. You can now use the Paste command as usual to paste this text picture onto the Scrapbook or directly back into your document.

EXCHANGING DATA WITH EXCEL

You can import data from almost any spreadsheet application into your Word documents either by copying that data directly to Word or by saving that data in a text format that Word can read. Since Excel is one of the most compatible spreadsheet programs for use with Word, we'll show you how to transfer information between Word and Excel documents first. Then we'll take a look at some other spreadsheet programs that you can use with Word.

Importing Spreadsheet Data

If you use Excel, from time to time you will probably want to import some data from an Excel spreadsheet into a Word document. In general, all you have to do is copy the information you want to import from the Excel worksheet and then paste that information into your Word document. Of course, the whole process works more smoothly if you use Switcher to load both programs simultaneously. You can also use QuickSwitch to create links between the copy data in the Word document and the original data in the Excel worksheet.

An example

Let's look at an example. Suppose you have created an Excel sales projections worksheet like the one in Figure 16-8, and you want to import the data from cells A4:F9 into a Microsoft Word document. Begin by using the Switcher to load Excel and Word. (Microsoft provides you with an Excel/Word Switcher on your Word utility disk, or you can create your own.) Once you've loaded the two programs, open the Word document and the Excel spreadsheet that you want to work with.

FIGURE 16-8

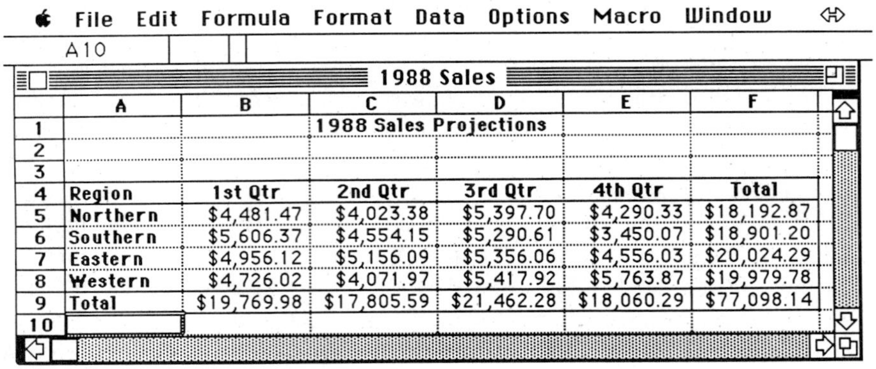

We want to copy the data from cells A4:F9 into a Word document.

Next, in the Excel worksheet highlight the range of cells that contain the information you want to include in your Word document, issue the Define Name... command, and assign a name to the range. (We'll use the name *Summary*.) You'll see why this range name is important in a moment.

Now, while the range of cells is still highlighted, issue the Copy command. Then switch to your Word document by pressing ⌘-] or by clicking on either side of the Switcher arrow that appears on the right side of your menu bar. In your Word document, place your insertion point marker at the spot where you want to insert the Excel data, and click. Then, issue the Paste command to place a copy of the Excel data into your document. Figure 16-9 shows the results.

FIGURE 16-9

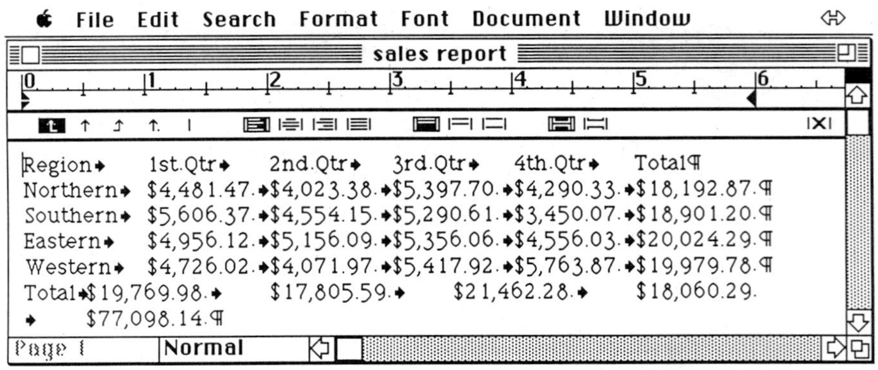

We have pasted our Excel data into our Word document.

As you can see, when you copy the contents of a worksheet to Word, the data from the worksheet will appear in Word's default *Normal* style. Though any numeric formats that you have asigned to your worksheet entries will carry over into Word, any font specifications, bold face or italic formats you may have assigned in Excel will be lost. For instance, in the example, the currency format we assigned to the values in Excel are transferred to Word, but the bold formatting is not. Also, notice that Word places a ¶ marker at the end of each row of data that we imported and a tab marker after each column of data. We'll talk more about these markers in a few pages when we tell you how to use an Excel data base as a Word data document.

Once you've imported information from Excel into Word, you'll probably want to change the tab settings and reformat the data to create a more attractive display, as we've done in Figure 16-10.

FIGURE 16-10

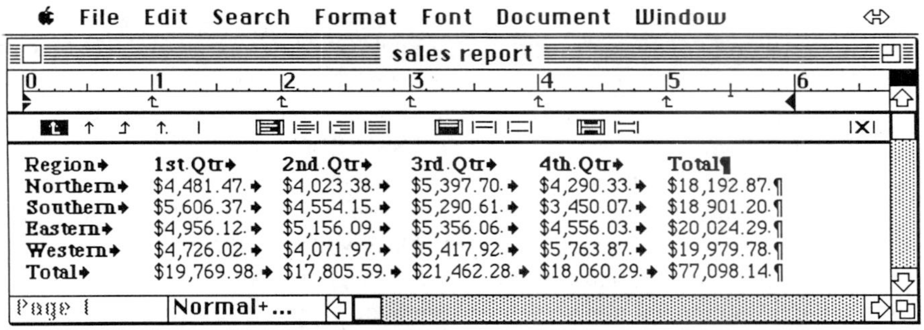

We have formatted the copied worksheet values to create a table in Word.

Building links

As we explained earlier, the QuickSwitch facility works with the Switcher to let you set up links between your Word documents and documents created in compatible programs, including Excel. That means that you can draw information from an Excel worksheet, plug it into your Word document, and automatically update your Word document whenever you make changes to your worksheet. If you have Excel Version 1.03 or a later version, the QuickSwitch capability is built into your Excel program. If you have an older version of Excel, you'll need to use the special QuickSwitch application file that comes with your Word 3 package.

To link the data you've imported into Word to the original data in Excel, you need to add an instruction line to your Word document that identifies the source of the data. This instruction line must include the name of the program from which the data was drawn, the name of the Excel worksheet file, and the range in which the data is located. Each element must be separated by an exclamation point (!), like this:

Program!File!Area

Since we have assigned the name *Summary* to the range in the Excel worksheet that contains the original data, we'll type this instruction line immediately above the table:

Excel!Sales Report!Summary

Once you have entered the instruction line in your Word document, you must assign the Hidden format to the instructions.

By the way, although we used a range name in the instructions in the example, you can also use cell references in the R1C1 form to specify the address of the original data. You'll probably find it easier to name the source range and use the name as the Area argument in your instructions.

Once you've linked the data in your Word document to the data in the Excel worksheet, you can use that link to simplify the process of updating your Word document. For example, suppose you want to make some changes to your Excel worksheet, then add those changes to your Word table. Rather than repeating the copying, pasting, and formatting process described above, you can simply highlight the Word table and press the ⌘ and comma keys (⌘-,) to move back to your Excel worksheet. (Pressing ⌘-, automatically switches you to Excel and invokes QuickSwitch.) QuickSwitch will automatically select the source range from which your table data was drawn.

At this point, you can move through the selected range in the Excel worksheet and make any needed changes. Once you've made your changes, just press ⌘-, again to move back to the Word document. Word will automatically update the document without changing any of the character formats, tab stops, or border specifications that you assigned earlier.

Using Excel Data Bases with Word

If you wish, you can use Excel data base files as data documents for your Word merge files. This makes it easy to create mailing labels, form letters, and so forth, from the data in your Excel data base.

Since the structure of Excel data bases is very similar to that of Word merge print data documents, the chances are good that your Excel data base is already set up to be used as a data document. In fact, all you need to do to use your Excel data base as a merge document is save the data base worksheet as a text file so that it is readable by Word. To do this, just issue the Save As... command and choose the Text Only option in Excel's Save As dialog box.

Once you have saved the Excel data base as a text file, you can load it into Word as you would any other document. When you load the data base text, you'll see that each data base record will occupy one paragraph, and each field will be separated by tab markers. Your field names will appear above the data base text to serve as your field header row.

As we explained in Chapter 14, if any of the field entries in a data record contain commas, you must place quotation marks around those fields. Otherwise, Word will interpret the comma as a field separator. Fortunately, when you save your Excel data base as a text file, Word automatically places quotation marks around any fields that contain commas.

By the way, if you are using the Switcher, you can also copy records from your data base directly into an open Word file, using the same techniques we described above for copying standard worksheet entries. If you are copying a lot of records, however, we think you'll find it more convenient simply to save the worksheet as a text file.

Importing Excel Charts

You can also import graphs that you've created in Excel into Word. All you have to do is issue the Copy Chart command in the Excel chart window. When you do this, Excel will give you the option of copying the chart as it is shown on the screen or as it will appear in print—that is, in the proportions you have specified in Excel's Page Setup... dialog box. Simply select the option you want, then switch to your Word document, and paste the chart picture into the desired location.

You can use QuickSwitch to set up a link between a chart that you created in Excel and a picture of that chart in your Word document. For the most part, the procedure for linking a Word graphic to an Excel chart is the same as that for linking numbers and text to an Excel worksheet. The form of the formula you use to link a Word graphic to an Excel chart is

Excel!File!

Notice that there is no need for an area name reference in this formula. However, although this argument is not needed, we have found that you must still include the exclamation point that divides the File argument from the Area argument.

Let's look at an example. Suppose you've created a chart like the one in Figure 16-11, and you want to copy that chart into a sales report that you've created in Word 3. To begin, issue the Copy Chart command in the Excel chart window. Excel will then give you the option of copying the chart as it is shown on the screen or as it will appear when printed. Just select the option you want, switch to your Word document, and paste the chart picture where you want it to appear. Then, immediately above the chart picture, type the instruction line

Excel!Sales Report!

Remember to assign the Hidden format to the instruction line. Figure 16-12 shows the chart as it will look in the Word document.

FIGURE 16-11

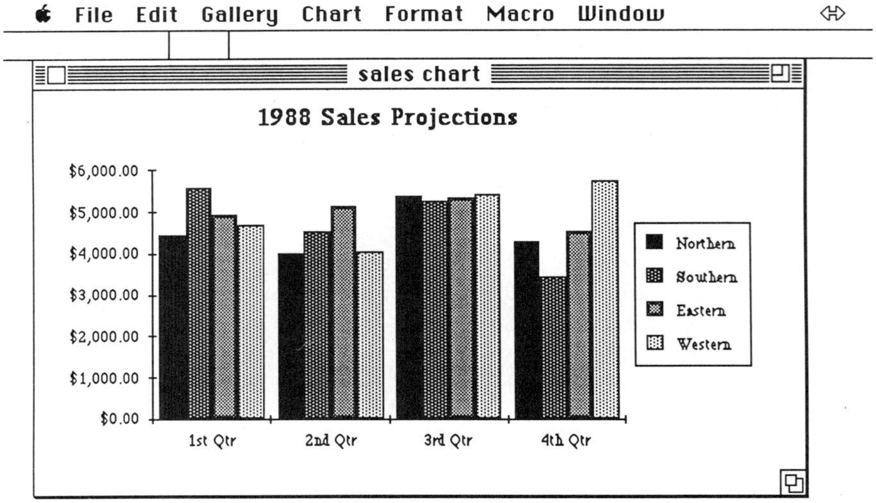

We want to place a copy of this Excel chart in a Word document.

FIGURE 16-12

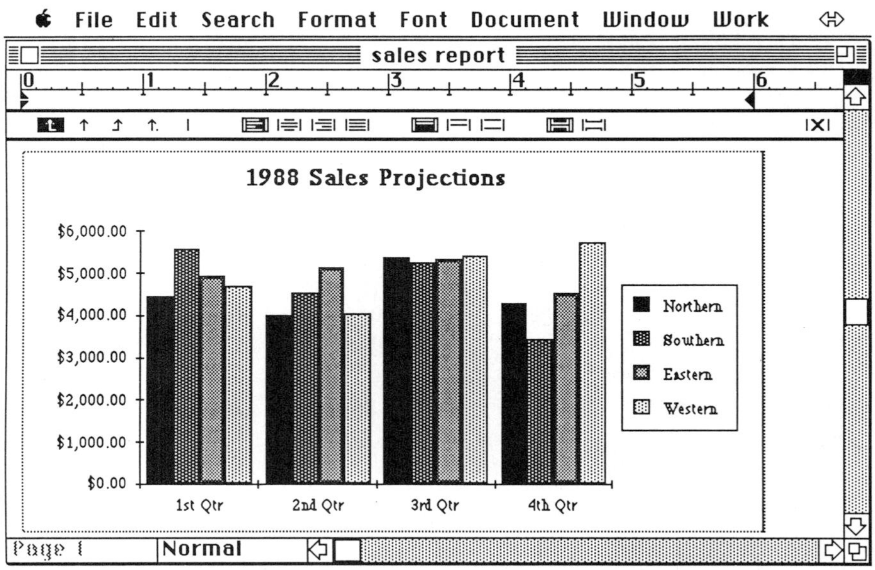

We have pasted the chart into our Word document as a graphic.

From now on, you can update the chart picture by clicking on the graphic and pressing ⌘-,. When you do this, QuickSwitch will automatically switch to Excel and activate the chart window if it is not already active. Once you are in Excel, you can make a change to your Excel chart, either by reformatting the chart itself or by making a change to the supporting Excel worksheet. Once you have made the desired changes to the chart, press ⌘-, again to move back to Word and update the chart picture.

The Copy Picture Command

Excel also offers a Copy Picture command that lets you copy any portion of your worksheet as a graphic. You can use the Scrapbook or the Switcher to transfer a graphic image created with this command to Word, using the same techniques outlined above.

Exporting Data to Excel

As you might expect, you can also transfer data from Word to Excel, although you won't export data to Excel as often as you'll import data from Excel. All you have to do to export data to Excel is copy the information you want to export from the Word document and then paste that information into your Excel worksheet. Of course, the whole process works more smoothly if you use Switcher to load both programs simultaneously.

If you're exporting tabular data to Excel, you will need to use tabs to separate the data that you want to appear in different columns in the Excel worksheet. Otherwise, the data will not be divided correctly into the columns of the Excel worksheet. In general, the format we described in Chapter 14 for print merge data documents is exactly the format you should use to prepare your files for transfer from Word to Excel.

OTHER SPREADSHEET PROGRAMS

In the preceding section, we showed you how to use the Switcher and the Scrapbook to exchange data between Word and Excel. You also can use either the Switcher or the Scrapbook to exchange data between Word and other Macintosh spreadsheets and data base programs, including Microsoft Multiplan, Microsoft File, and the Microsoft Works spreadsheet and data base. Just follow the instructions we gave when we showed you how to exchange information with Excel.

Multiplan

In addition to using the Copy and Paste commands to copy data between Multiplan and Word, you can save your Multiplan files into a SYLK file format. You can then open that SYLK file directly into Word.

PC-based Progams

If you want to exchange data between Word and one of the PC-based spreadsheet or data base programs, the process is a little more complicated. The key to this kind of data exchange is the ASCII file format. Before you save a Word document to ASCII format, however, you should check the manual for your PC program to see what special characters that program uses as field delimiters. Unlike the Macintosh programs we've addressed, some PC programs do not recognize tabs as field delimiters. For example, Lotus 1-2-3 requires that you separate the information in different fields using commas and that you enclose the contents of each text field in quotation marks. (For a complete discussion of importing ASCII files into 1-2-3, we recommend *Douglas Cobb's 1-2-3 Handbook*, published by The Cobb Group, Inc., and Bantam.)

Once you have set up your Word document with the correct field delimiters, you should save that document in the Text Only or Text Only with Line Breaks format. If you pressed Return to insert a ¶ marker at the end of each line in your document (or if your paragraphs are all quite short), then you can safely use the Text Only option. The ¶ markers will separate your document into discrete lines in the ASCII file, and when you load this file into your PC program, each line will appear in a separate row. On the other hand, if you are transferring a block of text from Word that does not include ¶ markers at the end of each line, you should save the file using the Text Only with Line Breaks option.

After saving your document as an ASCII text file, you will need to transfer that file to a 5 $^{1}/_{4}$ inch IBM PC diskette. To do this, you must connect your Mac to the PC using a specially configured cable or a modem, then use communications software to transfer the file or files.

SHARING DATA WITH OTHER WORD PROCESSORS

Word makes it easy for you to share data with a number of other word processing programs. You can use the File Format... option in the Save As dialog box to save a Word document into one of several different file formats, which then can be loaded into another program. When you click the File Format... button in the Save As dialog box, you'll see the list of format options shown in Figure 16-13.

FIGURE 16-13

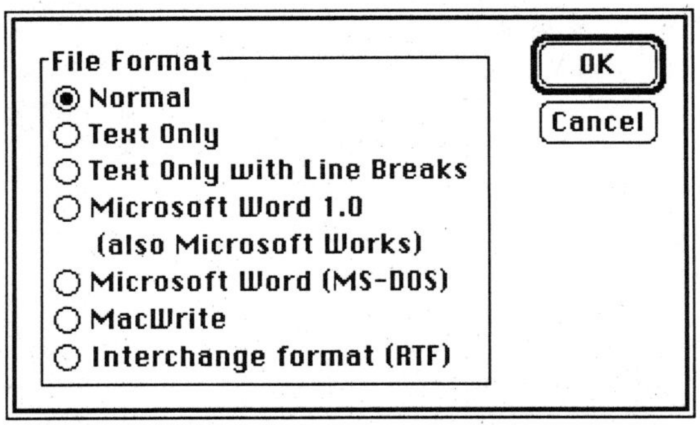

To save a Word document in a different file format, choose Save As... from the File menu, then click the File Format... button to see this list of options.

Notice that you can save a Word document into files that can be read by MacWrite, Word 1.0, Microsoft Works, and Word for the IBM PC (Microsoft Word MS-DOS). You also can save a Word document into an ASCII text file by selecting the Text Only or Text Only with Line Breaks option. (More on the ASCII format in a moment.) Finally, you can save a Word document into a Rich Text Format file, also called an RTF or Interchange format file.

In addition to saving documents into various kinds of file formats, Word can open files created by many other word processing programs. To open a file created by another word processor, you choose the Open... command from the

File menu and select the name of the file you want to open. (Sometimes you'll have to press the Shift key as you choose Open... in order to see the name of the file in the dialog box.) Word performs the translation automatically as it opens the file.

Word can also read ASCII text files. Since nearly every word processing program can save documents into ASCII format, you can use this feature to load documents from a number of different word processors (and other programs as well) into Word.

Of course, if the word processor that you're exchanging files with runs on an IBM PC or compatible (or another machine that requires a different disk format), being able to create compatible files is not enough. You also will need to transport the files between your Macintosh and the IBM PC across a special cable or via modem before you can load them into the other program.

Exchanging Documents with Other Programs

As we mentioned earlier, Word allows you to save documents into files that can be read by Word 1.0, MacWrite, or Microsoft Works. To save a document into one of these formats, you select Save As... from the File menu, then click the File Format... button in the Save As dialog box. When the list of file formats appears, click the one you want to use, then click OK. After you save a Word document in one of these special formats, you'll be able to load that document directly into another word processing program. In most cases, Word will transfer your character and paragraph formats along with the document text. Of course, special features that are available only in Word 3—such as side-by-side paragraphs—will not transfer to the new format.

You also can open a Word 1.0, MacWrite, or Microsoft Works word processing document into Word. To do this, choose Open... from the File menu, then double-click on the name of the file that you want to open. As Word is opening the file, you'll see a message like *Converting a MacWrite file. Document will appear in a new untitled window.* in a box on your screen. You can click the Cancel button that you'll see in this message box if you want to stop the file conversion.

When the converted document appears on your screen, it will display all of the character formatting that you assigned to it in the other word processing program. Your paragraph formats, however, may not be transferred properly. Of course, after you load the document, you can use Word to edit and format it just as you would any other text.

Exchanging files with the MS-DOS version of Word is somewhat more complicated since the two programs use different disk formats. After you save a Word document in Microsoft Word (MS-DOS) format, you will need to import that file to a 5 $^{1}/_{4}$-inch disk via modem or special cable before you can load it on your PC. Your computer dealer or consultant can help you with this process.

Exchanging Documents via the ASCII Format

As we've mentioned, most word processing programs, including Word, can save documents to disk in the ASCII file format. In addition, nearly every word processing program and many spreadsheet and data base programs can read ASCII files. ASCII stands for American Standard Code for Information Interchange. The ASCII system uses a three-digit code to represent each number, letter, and symbol. For example, your computer knows the character *e* as 101.

You might think of the ASCII file format as the "lowest common denominator" format. When you save a Word file in this format, you create a pure text file without any special character or paragraph formats. Similarly, when you load an ASCII file into Word, you will see plain text on your screen with no special character or paragraph formatting. It's the "plain jane" nature of ASCII files that makes them useful for moving documents from one program into another.

Saving Word documents in ASCII format

If you want to save a Word document into an ASCII file, choose Save As... from the File menu, then click on the File Format... button. Word will present the list of format options shown in Figure 16-13. Click the Text Only or the Text Only with Line Breaks option. Then, click OK in the File Format box to return to the Save As dialog box. Finally, you may want to enter a new file name in the Save Current Document as edit bar. When you've finished, click OK to save the document in ASCII format.

As soon as you execute the Save As... command, Word will replace the document on your screen with the ASCII version of the document. All of your character, paragraph, and section formatting will be gone. However, you won't lose your paragraph breaks. If you selected the Save Text Only with Line Breaks option, you'll see additional paragraph breaks at the end of every line.

If you had previously saved the document to disk in the normal Word file format (and you didn't overwrite that file with the Save As... command), you'll be able to recover all of your formatting simply by opening that document.

If your purpose in saving your document in ASCII format is to read it into another word processing program, then you probably will want to use the Text Only option, not the Text Only with Line Breaks option. This second option is designed primarily for transferring information from Word to spreadsheet and data base programs. However, there are some cases where you will want to choose the Text Only with Line Breaks option. For example, if you want to transfer a Word document into a format that can be loaded into the Lotus Symphony word processor, you should choose Text Only with Line Breaks. Later in this chapter, we'll talk more about transferring Word documents into a format that can be read by spreadsheet and data base programs.

Opening an ASCII file in Word

To open an ASCII format file into Word, first press the Shift key, then choose Open... from the File menu. (If you do not press the Shift key as you select the Open... command, Word may not display the names of the ASCII files in the File Open dialog box.) Next, open the ASCII file just as you would open any other file: Double-click on the file name, or click on the file name and then click the Open button. When the file is open, you'll see plain text on your screen. However, you can edit and format this text just as you would any other document. (Sometimes you may also see some stray coding characters when you import an ASCII file from another program. These can easily be deleted with common editing techniques.) After you've edited and formatted the text to suit your needs, you can save the document in Word format. To do this, just issue the Save or Save As... command as you normally would. (If you don't want to overwrite the plain ASCII file on disk, use the Save As... command, and type a different file name for your new version of the document.)

RTF/DCA Exchanges

The Rich Text format (RTF) allows you to transfer files between Word and other programs without losing formats. When you save a Word document into an RTF file, Word converts every formatting characteristic of the document into an alphanumeric code. If you view an RTF document on your screen, you'll see a rather confusing combination of document text and lots of code text. Microsoft's goal in creating the RTF—also called the Interchange format—was to provide a way to exchange documents between Word and numerous other word processing programs without losing any formatting. Right now, you can use the DCA Conversion program to convert an RTF file into DCA format. The DCA—or Document Content Architecture format—is a file structure used by many IBM word processors, including DisplayWrite, and a number of mainframe word processors.

To convert a Word document into DCA format, you must first save that document in the Interchange format. To do this, issue the Save As... command, click the File Format... button, then select the Interchange format option, and click OK. When you click OK to save the document in the new format, Word will replace the document on your screen with the new Rich Text Format document. You can then quit from Word and run the DCA Conversion program to transfer this RTF file into DCA format.

You also can use the DCA Conversion program to convert a DCA file into an RTF file. Once you've done this, you can load the RTF file into Word. To do this, choose Open... from the File menu as you normally would, and double-click on the name of the RTF file that you want to open. Word will then display an alert box that asks *Interpret RTF text?* If you click Yes, Word will then display the message *Converting an Interchange format (RTF) file. Document will appear in a new untitled window.* You can click Cancel if you want to halt the conversion procedure. When the file appears on your screen, it will display the character and paragraph formats that were assigned in the other word processing program.

If you click No when you see the *Interpret RTF text?* message, Word will load the file directly and display on screen the combination of plain text and RTF format codes.

SHARING DATA WITH PAGEMAKER

With all of its sophisticated page design and formatting capabilities, Word 3 does have a few limitations when it comes to performing full-fledged desktop publishing. If you create a lot of publications, you may want to take advantage of one of the many desktop publishing packages available for the Macintosh.

Most of these programs are able to read your Word files directly from disk, with no copying or pasting between applications. To give you an idea of how you can use Word with desktop publishing software, we'll look briefly at the PageMaker program, which is the most sophisticated and most popular desktop publishing package on the market.

Working with PageMaker

PageMaker, developed by Aldus Corporation, has the look and feel of an electronic layout board. Pagemaker gives you a great deal of control over the layout, placement, and format of your documents. You can use this program to place documents in predefined master page templates that you design with PageMaker's special tools.

Exporting files to PageMaker

Version 2 of PageMaker can read Word 3 files directly from disk, eliminating the need for the Switcher or any copying and pasting between programs. When you import a Word file into a PageMaker document, PageMaker recognizes most of your character and paragraph formatting characteristics. However, it does not carry over your Page Setup or Section dialog box specifications. This is logical, since PageMaker is specifically designed to perform these page layout tasks. Table 16-1 shows the formatting characteristics that PageMaker will carry over when you load a Word file into PageMaker.

TABLE 16-1

Format	Effect in PageMaker
Type faces	Type faces do carry over into PageMaker, as long as that type face is installed on your PageMaker System file; otherwise, PageMaker will use its default Times type face.
Type sizes	PageMaker accepts only whole point sizes; if you have specified any fractional point sizes, such as 11.5, PageMaker will round the type size to the next whole point size—12, for example.
Character formats	All formats carry over except for the Hidden format and some Underline formats. PageMaker converts any Word u.i., Double u.i., and Dotted u.i. formats to standard unbroken underlines. Hidden text will not appear in PageMaker documents.
Carriage returns	All paragraph and line breaks carry over into Word.
Page and section breaks	Manual page breaks and section breaks do not carry over into PageMaker, nor do the Page Break Before, Keep lines together, or Keep with Next ¶ Paragraph formats.

Line and Paragraph spacing	These do carry over into PageMaker.
Line numbers	Line numbers do not carry over into PageMaker.
Paragraph numbers	These do carry over into PageMaker.
Tabs	All tab formats carry over except for the vertical bars you create with the vertical line icon.
Borders	The Borders options that you apply in the Paragraph dialog box do not appear in PageMaker.
Indents	Your first line, left, and right indents do carry over, but PageMaker uses the margins settings you supply for your PageMaker document, rather than the ones you developed in Word. As a result, your line widths may vary from Word to PageMaker.
Alignment	Your left, right, centered, and justified alignment settings do carry over.
Multicolumn and Side-by-Side format	These do not carry over into PageMaker.
Headers, Footers, and Page Numbers	These do not carry over into PageMaker.
Indexes, Footnotes, and Tables of Contents	PageMaker will read the text for these elements, but it will strip away the hidden codes you have used to define your index and table of contents entries. Similarly, all footnotes carry over, but PageMaker groups them at the end of your document.
Outlines	Since PageMaker does not recognize your style sheet specifications, it will transfer the text from your outline to PageMaker, but it will not recognize the heading levels you have assigned to that text. Your style specifications for these elements will remain intact, however.
Graphics	Any graphic that you have placed in your Word documents will appear in PageMaker, but any text that you have wrapped around the graphic will appear before or after the graphic. In other words, if you have placed a graphic in the middle of a paragraph, PageMaker will insert a paragraph break before and after the graphic. Of course, you can easily position the graphic in PageMaker and flow your text around it.

Most of your Word formats carry over to PageMaker.

Importing files from PageMaker

PageMaker offers an export feature that allows you to write PageMaker files back into Word 3 format. This tool removes any special features that PageMaker has applied to the document but which are not supported by Word. It also adds back a few features that were removed from the document when it was first imported into PageMaker. For example, if you have used Word's Border option to draw a box or border around a paragraph, PageMaker will ignore those settings when it imports your Word 3 document. However, when you export that document back to Word 3, your border formats will reappear. The same is true of the word-only underlining character format.

There is one important exception to this rule. Since PageMaker strips any hidden characters from your Word files, any codes you have entered for your document index, footnotes, or table of contents will not be reestablished when you convert a PageMaker document back into Word 3 format. Of course, the text for the index, table of contents, and so on, will still be a part of the file.

DEFAULTS 17

Like other software programs, Word 3 comes with certain preset defaults. These default settings control such things as the page layout, the appearance of your screen, character and paragraph formatting, glossary entries, and print settings. Of course, when you begin a new document, you are not stuck with using Word's default settings. If a particular setting is not suitable for the document you're working on, you can change it. In most cases, your change will not affect Word's default setting. For example, you can change the margins in any document by altering the entries in the Page Setup dialog box. However, when you open a new document, Word will return to its default margin settings.

If you find that you're changing one or more of Word's default settings each time you start a new document, then you should consider making a permanent change to that setting. For example, if you're always changing the Left and Right margin settings in the Page Setup dialog box from 1.25 to 1, then you probably should change Word's default settings for the left and right margins.

Although we've already discussed many of Word's defaults in previous chapters of this book, we will summarize that information in this chapter. In some cases, we'll refer you to a previous chapter for more specific instructions on how to change a particular default setting. In this chapter, we'll also talk about the Word Settings file, which stores most of Word's default settings, and we'll explain how you can create multiple Word Settings files to store several different sets of defaults. Similarly, we'll show you how to create more than one file for storing standard glossary entries (those glossary entries that Word loads automatically each time you open a document). Finally, this chapter will offer some tips on creating and using document templates. Let's begin, however, with a look at Word's default settings.

SCREEN DISPLAY DEFAULTS

Word has a number of default settings that affect various elements of your screen display each time you use the program. These settings include the unit of measure on the ruler and the display of hidden text. Let's look at how you can change these default settings.

Menus

As we explained in Chapter 2, Word's initial default menu configuration is Short Menus. You can change this by selecting Full Menus from the Edit menu. Once you change from Short Menus to Full Menus (or vice versa) and quit from Word, your change becomes the new default. Any document that you open—even one previously saved to disk—will display Full Menus. Figure 2-3 on page 26 shows the different menu selections that are available in Short Menus and Full Menus.

If you choose to use Full Menus, Word allows you to customize the selections on the Font and Format menus and create a special menu called the Work menu. In Chapter 11, we explained how you can add options to and delete options from the Font and Format menus and how to create the Work menu. Like the Full/Short Menus setting, your custom menus are stored in the Word Settings file. Therefore, once you make a change to the Font or Format menu or create the Work menu, your custom menus will appear in all of your Word documents. If you discard or rename the Word Settings file, Word will return automatically to its original default menu configuration. (Figure 2-3 shows the default options available when Full and Short Menus are in effect.)

Ruler Display

When you begin a new document or open an existing document, you will not see the ruler displayed at the top of the window. You must choose Show Ruler from the Format menu (or press ⌘-r) to bring the ruler into view. The ruler will show up only in the document that's active when you select the Show Ruler command. Any other documents that are open on your DeskTop will not be affected. Similarly, if you close a document with the ruler displayed and then reopen that document, the ruler will no longer appear. You cannot change Word's default hidden ruler. In other words, there's no way to force Word to display the ruler automatically each time you open a document.

Unit of measure

The default unit of measure on Word's ruler is inches. If you want, you can change the unit to be centimeters or points. To make a change, just choose Preferences... from the Edit menu. Word will then display the dialog box shown in Figure 17-1. All you have to do is click on the Measure option that you want to use.

Once you select a different unit of measure, Word will change the ruler appearance in *all* of your documents, even documents that previously were saved to disk with a different ruler measure. As you might guess, the unit of measure that you select is stored in the Word Settings file. If you discard or rename this file, Word will automatically return to its default unit of measure, inches. Figure 17-2 shows the same screen with the three different types of rulers.

FIGURE 17-1

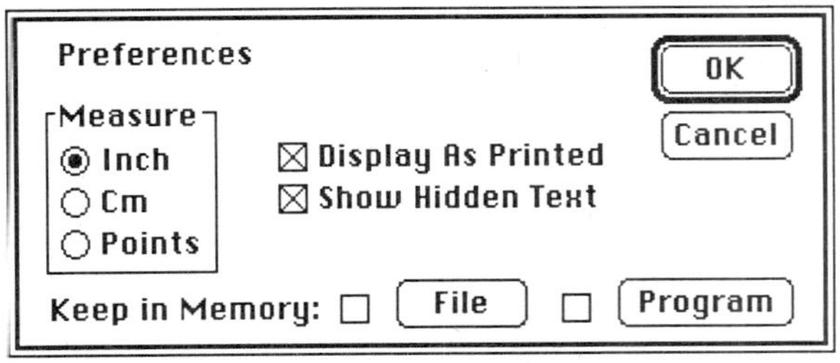

To change the unit of measure on the ruler, open the Preferences dialog box, and click on your choice.

FIGURE 17-2

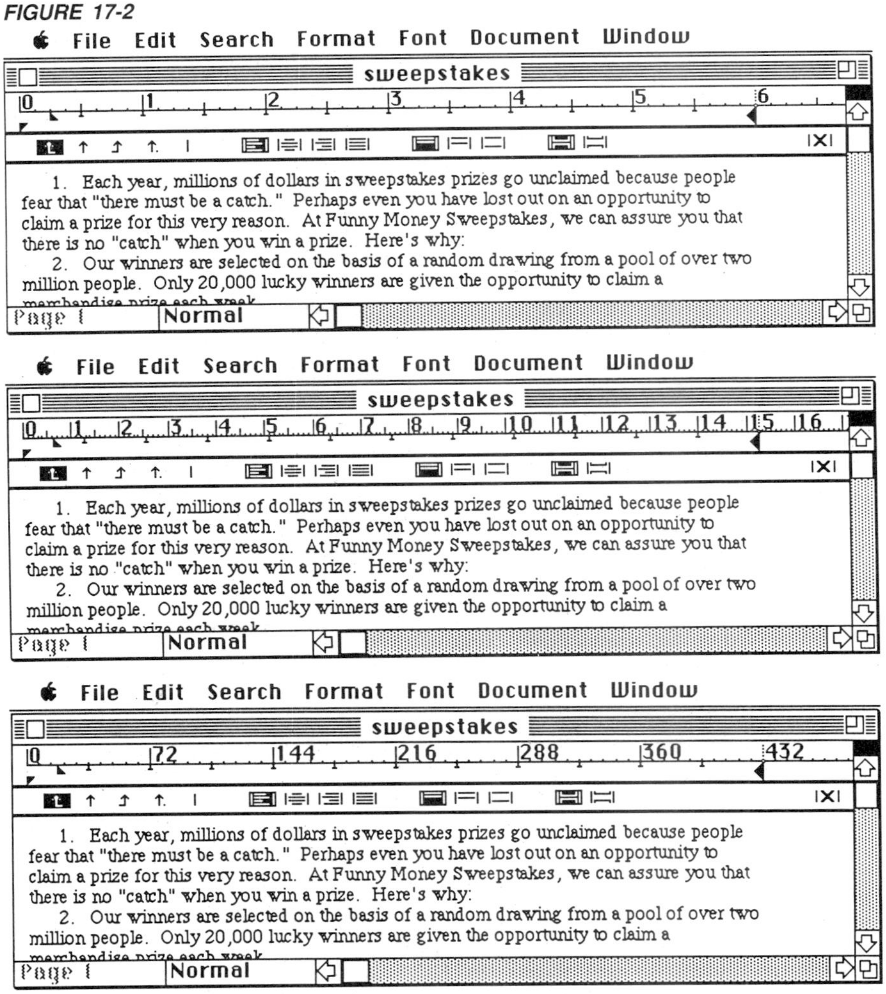

Word allows you to specify one of three different units of measure on the ruler: Inches, Centimeters, or Points.

You might notice that Word does not change the alignment of text on the screen when you change the ruler measure. All the indents and tabs occur at the same positions. In other words, when you change the Measure option in the Preferences dialog box, Word does not merely change the markings on the ruler; it also converts the position of each indent and tab to the new unit of measure. For example, in Figure 17-2 the first-line indent marker appears at the $^{1}/_{4}$ inch mark on the inch ruler, at the .6 centimeter mark on the centimeter ruler, and at the 18-point mark on the point ruler.

In addition to changing the appearance of rulers, the Measure option in the Preferences dialog box will determine the unit of measure in some of the edit bars in your dialog boxes. For example, Figure 17-3 shows the Page Setup dialog box after changing the unit of measure to centimeters. Notice that the paper width and height, as well as all the margins, are now stated in centimeters. Other dialog boxes that will be affected by a change in the ruler measure are the Paragraph dialog box and the Section dialog box.

FIGURE 17-3

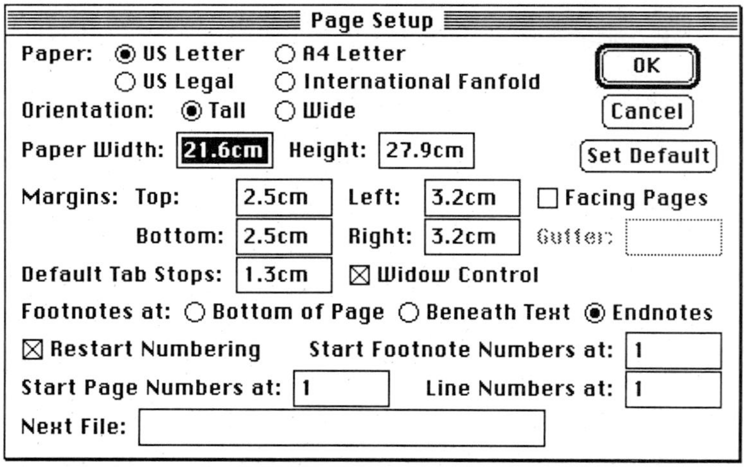

When you change the ruler measure from inches to centimeters, Word will use centimeters in dialog boxes as well.

Besides dialog boxes, the Measure option can affect your style definitions. Any named style that specifies one or more indents or tabs will use the new unit of measure in its style definition.

Finally, when you change the ruler measure, you'll notice a difference on the Page Preview screen. If you click the Margins icon (the third icon from the top) and then click on one of the margin "handles" that Word displays, you'll notice that the margin measurement that appears in the lower-left corner of your window will be displayed in the same units that you've specified for the ruler. Similarly, Word will display the position of your page numbers, headers, footers, and page-break markers in the same units that you have chosen to display on the ruler.

Display of Hidden Text

When you choose to apply the Hidden format to some text, Word will not actually hide that text until you print your document. On your screen, the hidden text will appear with a dotted underline. (See Chapter 5 for more on using the Hidden format. See Chapter 7 for more on printing hidden text.) If you don't want to display hidden text on your screen, then you must change Word's default setting for displaying hidden text in the Preferences dialog box. As you can see in Figure 17-1, the Preferences dialog box includes a Show Hidden Text option, which initially is activated. To suppress the display of hidden text, click on this option to deactivate it. When you turn off the Show Hidden Text setting, Word not only suppresses the display of hidden text but also closes up the space that that text occupied and reforms the paragraph.

Once you turn off the Show Hidden Text option, you won't be able to view hidden text in *any* document, even a document previously saved to disk. That's because the Show Hidden Text option—like other settings in the Preferences dialog box—is stored in the Word Settings file. If you discard or rename this file, Word will return to its default setting and display all hidden text on screen.

Display As Printed

The Preferences dialog box includes another option, Display As Printed, which can, in some circumstances, affect the appearance of text on your screen. When you're using Word's initial defaults, the Display As Printed option will be activated. In most cases, this is what you'll want since it allows you to be sure that "what you see is what you get." Like the Show Hidden Text setting, the Display As Printed setting affects all of your Word documents. If you deactivate this option in the Preferences dialog box, your change will become the new default. Again, Word stores this setting in the Word Settings file.

One of the few cases in which you might want to turn off Display As Printed is when you've chosen a printer, such as a daisy-wheel model, that does not support multiple fonts. If you've formatted your document with a font that is not available on your printer, then the Display As Printed option may cause the text on your screen to be difficult to read. In order to save some eye strain, you may want to turn off Display As Printed until you're actually ready to print.

By the way, your selections in the Print dialog box do *not* affect the results of the Display As Printed option. For example, if you're using an ImageWriter and you select Draft quality in the Print dialog box, you won't see "draft" text on your screen when Display As Printed is activated. Similarly, the Smoothing and Font Substitution options in the LaserWriter Print dialog box do not affect the text on your screen, regardless of whether Display As Printed is activated. Finally, the Print dialog boxes for both the ImageWriter and the LaserWriter include a Print Hidden Text option. Again, this option does not affect the appearance of hidden text on your screen, even when Display As Printed is activated. To remove hidden text from your screen display, you must turn off the Show Hidden Text option in the Preferences dialog box.

PAGE LAYOUT DEFAULTS

There are a number of settings which control the default layout of any new document that you begin in Word. These settings appear in the Page Setup and Section dialog boxes, which are shown in Figures 17-4 and 17-5.

FIGURE 17-4

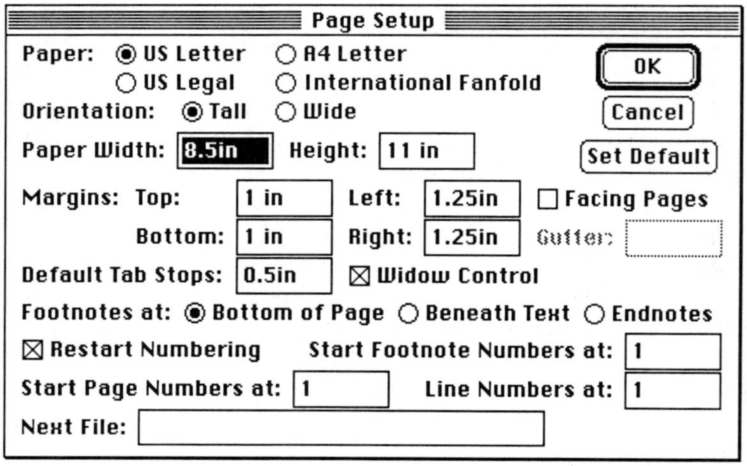

This Page Setup dialog box shows Word's initial default settings.

FIGURE 17-5

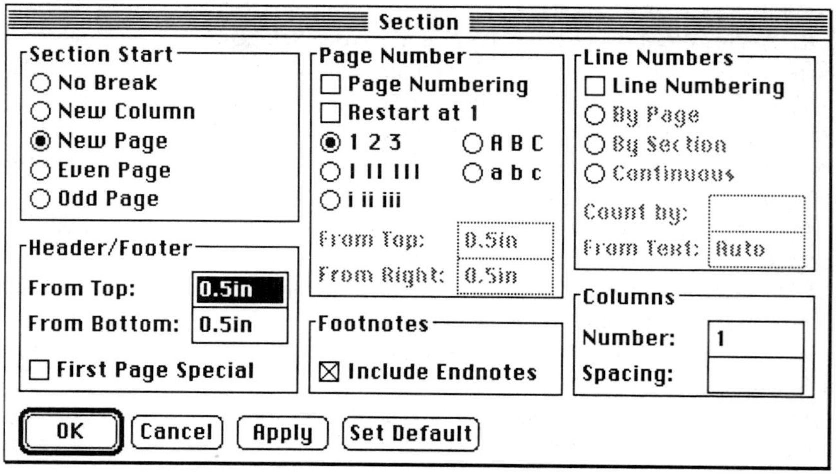

This Section dialog box shows Word's initial default settings.

You can change the default for any of the settings in these dialog boxes just by entering a new value for that setting or clicking a new option and then clicking the Set Default button. Keep in mind that when you click Set Default, Word will replace the defaults for *all* of the settings represented in that dialog box with the current settings. For example, to change Word's default margins, you simply enter new margin measurements in the Top, Bottom, Left, and/or Right edit bars of the Page Setup dialog box and click Set Default. Word will save your new default margins in the Word Settings file. In addition, if you've made any other changes in the Page Setup dialog box, Word will save those changes as well when you click Set Default.

You can change Word's default page layout settings without affecting any documents previously saved to disk and without altering any documents open on your DeskTop that you haven't yet saved. In fact, you can even make a change to one of Word's default page layout settings without affecting your current document. (In this regard, the default page layout settings are unlike the default screen display settings, which typically affect all documents, including documents previously saved to disk.) For example, suppose that you have entered new margin measurements in the Top and Bottom edit bars of the Page Setup dialog box and have clicked Set Default. If you do not want these new defaults to affect your current document, click Cancel to close the dialog box. If you do want to apply the new margins to your current document, click OK. In either case, once you change the margins and click Set Default, any new document will display your new margin settings. However, any document saved to disk with the "old" default margins will still have those margins.

Of course, you can change any of the page layout settings for a particular document without affecting the default settings. All you have to do is change the value in the Page Setup or Section dialog box for the setting you want to change and click OK. As long as you don't click Set Default, the default value for that setting will not change.

Margins

As we explained in Chapter 7, your document margins are controlled in the Page Setup dialog box. Initially, Word's default margin measurements are 1 inch for the top and bottom margins and 1 $^1/_4$ inches for the left and right margins. If you want to change Word's default margin measurements, you just enter the new measurements in the Top, Bottom, Left, and/or Right edit bars of the Page Setup dialog box and click the Set Default button.

Text Area

While the margin measurements determine the amount of white space surrounding the text area on a page, the actual dimensions of the text area depend not only on your margin measurements but also on your selection of paper size and whether you have chosen Tall or Wide orientation. Word's default orientation for text is Tall. Word's default paper choice is US Letter. (For more on determining the size of the text area, see Chapters 7 and 8.)

If you want to change the default paper choice to something other than US Letter (such as US Legal), just click on that option in the Page Setup dialog box, then click Set Default. If you want to specify a custom paper size as your default (instead of selecting one of Word's predefined options), enter the paper dimensions in the Paper Width and Height edit bars, then click Set Default. You can change the default orientation from Tall to Wide by clicking the Wide option and then clicking Set Default.

Number of Columns

Normally, Word assumes that every new document will contain only one column of text. If you want to create a document with two, three, or even more columns, you must choose Section... from the Format menu and enter the number of columns in the Number edit bar in the lower-right corner of the dialog box. You also must enter a measurement in the Spacing edit bar to tell Word how much gutter space to allow between columns. (For more on columnar formatting, see Chapter 8.)

If you want to change the default number of columns from 1 to 2 (or more), just enter the number of columns in the Section dialog box and the spacing value in the Spacing edit bar and then click the Set Default button. Word will then store both the current number of columns and the entry in the Spacing edit bar as its new defaults. (Like many other default settings, the number of columns is stored in the Word Settings file.) Any time you begin a new document, it will automatically appear in your new default columnar format. Documents saved to disk in the single-column format (or another format that's different from the default) will not be affected by the new default.

Page Numbers

Word's initial default settings do not call for automatic page numbering in documents. If you want to change this default, just open the Section dialog box and click the Page Numbering option to activate it, then click the Set Default button. Word will record the active Page Numbering setting in your Word Settings file. Word also will store any special page numbering options that you've selected, such as the numbering scheme you've chosen (1, 2, 3; A, B, C; etc.) and the position of page numbers relative to the top and right edges of each page. Once you've changed the default, the Page Numbering feature will be activated automatically each time you begin a new document. Changing the default will not, however, affect documents previously saved to disk or unsaved documents that are open on your DeskTop.

Although you probably will want to start your page numbers with 1, Word allows you to start with any number. To change the starting page number, open the Page Setup dialog box, and enter the new number in the Start Page Numbers at edit bar. If you want this starting number to become your new default, then click the Set Default button. As usual, this new default will be stored in the Word Settings file, and it will not affect any documents already saved to disk with a different starting page number. However, any new documents that you open will have your new default starting page number in the Start Page Numbers at edit bar of the Page Setup dialog box.

Line Numbers

Line numbering, like page numbering, is controlled in the Section dialog box. If you want to number the lines in a document, open the Section dialog box and click on the Line Numbering option. (For a complete explanation of numbering lines in a document, see Chapter 15.)

If you want numbered lines to be the default in each new document, then you should click the Set Default button in the Section dialog box after you activate the Line Numbering feature. As with page numbering, Word will record not only the activated Line Numbering setting, but also all of the related line numbering options as its new defaults. As you might expect, these new defaults will be recorded in the Word Settings file.

As with page numbers, Word assumes that your line numbers should begin with 1. If you want to start with a different number, you must enter the starting number in the Line Numbers at edit bar of the Page Setup dialog box. If you want to make this new starting line number your default for all new documents, just click the Set Default button in the Page Setup dialog box. Again, Word will store the new default setting in the Word Settings file.

Headers and Footers

Headers and footers are controlled by settings in your Section and Page Setup dialog boxes and by style definitions on the style sheet. Word's initial default settings assume that you want to use the same header and/or footer on every page of your document and position that header/footer $^1/_2$ inch from the edge of your paper. However, by changing the First Page Special setting in the Section dialog box, you can place a special header/footer on the first page of your document (or on the first page of each section). By changing the Facing Pages option in the Page Setup dialog box, you can place different headers/footers on your right and left pages. (For a detailed discussion of headers and footers, see Chapter 7.)

As you might guess, you can change Word's default settings so that the First Page Special or Facing Pages option will be activated automatically in each new document. To change the First Page Special setting, just click that option in the Section dialog box and then click the Set Default button. Similarly, to change the Facing Pages setting, just click that option in the Page Setup dialog box and then click the Set Default button. When you do either of these things, Word will store the new defaults in the Word Settings file. Any documents previously saved to disk will not be affected by the new defaults.

To change the position of a header or footer, just enter a new measurement in the From Top or From Bottom edit bar of the Section dialog box. If you want to make the new measurement(s) the default for all new documents, just click the Set Default button in the Section dialog box. (Instead of typing new measurements in the From Top or From Bottom edit bars of the Section dialog box, you can change the position of your header and/or footer on the Page Preview screen. Word will then record the numeric measurement of the new position(s) in the Section dialog box. Again, you can make the measurement(s) your new default by clicking the Set Default button.)

You can alter other features of your headers and footers by changing the definitions of the *header* and *footer* styles on the style sheet. To do this, choose Define Styles... from the Format menu, then click on the style name *header,* or *footer* to select it. With the style name selected, issue the appropriate commands to change the style instructions. (For a complete discussion of modifying styles on the style sheet, see Chapter 9.)

If you want the altered style instructions to become the new default instructions for the style named *header*, click the Set Default button in the Define Styles dialog box while the *header* style name is selected. When you see the message *OK to record style in default style sheet?* click Yes. Word will not only change the default instructions for the *header* style but also will add that style name to the default style sheet. Each time you open a new document, the style named *header*—with your modified instructions—will appear on the style sheet for that document.

Word does not offer any way to define default header or footer text. If you want to create a default header or footer, you'll need to create a template that includes the standard header or footer, then use that template as the basis for your documents. We'll show you how to create templates in a few pages.

Footnotes

Footnotes, like headers and footers, are controlled by settings in your Section and Page Setup dialog boxes, as well as by style definitions. The dialog box selections determine whether footnotes will appear at the bottom of each page, at the end of each section, or at the end of an entire document. These settings also determine whether your footnotes will be numbered separately on each new page, in each new section, or continuously throughout a document. (Chapter 13 explains footnotes in detail.)

Word's default settings in the Page Setup dialog box cause footnotes to appear at the bottom of each page, with a new set of footnote numbers on each page. Word's default starting number for the footnotes on each page is 1. If you want to change the default footnote settings, select your choices in the Page Setup dialog box, then click the Set Default button. As usual, Word will record your new default settings in the Word Settings file.

There's only one footnote-related setting in the Section dialog box—Include Endnotes. Word's default setting for this option is active. Include Endnotes comes into play only when your document contains more than one section and you've selected the Endnotes option in the Page Setup dialog box. When this is the case, the Include Endnotes setting in the Section dialog box instructs Word to print the footnotes for the current section at the end of that section, instead of printing them at the end of the entire document. If you want all of your footnotes to be printed at the end of the document, then you should deactivate the Include Endnotes option. To make the deactivated Include Endnotes option Word's new default, click Set Default in the Section dialog box.

As we explain in Chapter 9, whenever you use footnotes in a document, Word automatically adds two style names to that document's style sheet: *footnote reference* and *footnote text*. The *footnote reference* style is used to format the number or symbol in your document that calls out the footnote, while the *footnote text* style determines the format of the footnote itself. You can alter either one of these styles, if you wish. After you alter the instructions for one of the footnote-related styles, you can place those altered instructions on Word's default style sheet by clicking the Set Default button while the style name is selected in the Define Styles dialog box. When you see the message *OK to record style in default style sheet?*, click Yes. Word will not only change the default instructions for the selected style but also will add that style name to the default style sheet.

Section Start

The Section Start option in the Section dialog box tells Word whether or not to start a new page whenever it encounters a section break. Word's default selection for Section Start is New Page. If you want to change this default, click on one of the other options in the Section dialog box (No Break, New Column, Even Page, or Odd Page), and then click the Set Default button. Like other Section dialog box settings, this one will be stored in the Word Settings file. Therefore, you can expect your default selection to show up in all new documents, though your new default will not affect previously saved documents.

Default Tab Stops

The Default Tab Stops option controls the interval between Word's default tab stops. To change this setting, open the Page Setup dialog box, enter a new measurement in the Default Tab Stops edit bar, and click Set Default.

Widow Control

The other paragraph setting that appears in the Page Setup dialog box—Widow Control—prevents Word from placing one line of a paragraph on a page by itself. Normally, this setting is active. If you want to change Word's default so that the Widow Control setting is deselected, just open the Page Setup dialog box, click on the check box next to the Widow Control option, then click Set Default. Again, your changes to Word's default Page Setup settings will be stored in the Word Settings file.

FORMATTING DEFAULTS

In Chapters 6 and 9, we described Word's default paragraph and character formats. You may recall that the default format for a paragraph specifies flush-left alignment, single spacing, no indents, no tabs other than the defaults, no space before or after the paragraph (other than normal line spacing), no borders, and no special features (such as Side-by-Side or Keep Lines Together). Word's default character formatting calls for 12-point, New York, plain type.

As we explained in Chapter 9, Word's default character and paragraph formats are controlled by the definition of the default *Normal* style. In addition, however, a couple of paragraph features—namely, the placement of default tab stops and the treatment of widows—are controlled through settings in the Page Setup dialog box. If you want to change Word's default character and/or paragraph formats, you can do so by altering the instructions for the *Normal* style and clicking the Set Default button in the Define Styles dialog box. Chapter 9 offers a detailed discussion of the *Normal* style, including explanations and examples of how you can alter that style. Like most other Word defaults, the definition of the default *Normal* style is stored in the Word Settings file. If you discard or rename this file after you've altered the default *Normal* style, Word will return to its original defaults for character and paragraph formatting.

Although Word's default style sheet will initially contain only the *Normal* style, there are 32 other automatic styles available. In Chapter 9, we explained how you can modify the default instructions for any of these automatic styles. We also explained how you can add styles—both automatic styles and custom styles—to Word's default style sheet. As usual, the contents of Word's default style sheet will be stored in the Word Settings file. If you discard or rename this file, Word will return to its original default style sheet, which contains only the *Normal* style.

PRINTING DEFAULTS

Most of the settings that affect printing are—quite naturally—found in the Print dialog box. Figures 17-6 and 17-7 show Word's default selections in the Print dialog boxes for the LaserWriter and ImageWriter.

FIGURE 17-6

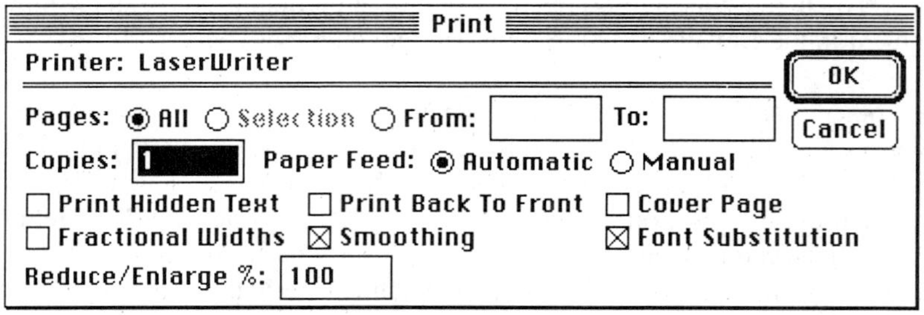

This Print dialog box shows Word's default selections for using the LaserWriter.

FIGURE 17-7

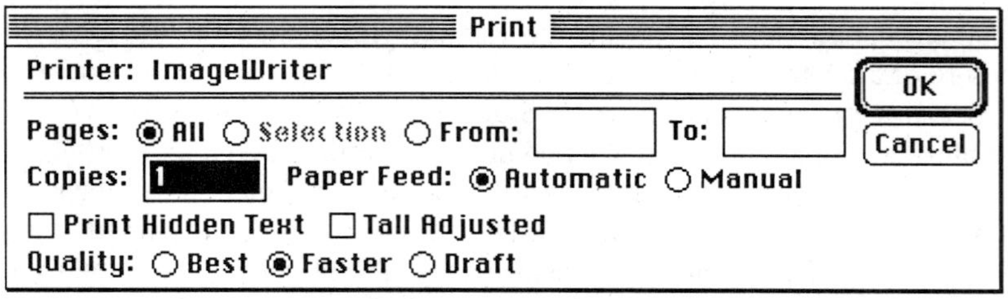

This Print dialog box shows Word's default selections for using the ImageWriter.

Changing Word's default print settings is not as straightforward as changing some of the other defaults. First, the Print dialog box does not contain a Set Default button, like the one found in the Page Setup, Section, and Define Styles dialog boxes. Nevertheless, when you change some of the settings in the Print dialog box, Word will save those settings as its new defaults. In some cases, your change will affect *all* Word documents—both new documents and all previously saved documents. In other cases, your change will affect only the current document. Let's examine each of the print settings, beginning with those in the LaserWriter Print dialog box.

LaserWriter Settings

The first two settings in the Print dialog box for the LaserWriter are Pages and Copies. As we explained in Chapter 7, the Pages setting allows you to control how much of your document will be printed—all of it, only a selected group of pages, or only the selection you've highlighted in the document window. The default Pages selection is All. The Copies setting determines how many copies of the document will be printed. Word's default for this setting is 1 copy. You cannot change the default for either the Pages or the Copies setting. In fact, if you change one or both of these settings, your change will affect only the current Print... command. The next time you need to print your document, you must respecify your Pages and Copies settings after you open the Print dialog box.

Word does allow you to change the default selections for the Paper Feed, Print Hidden Text, Print Back To Front, Cover Page, and Fractional Widths options. Initially, the Paper Feed selection is Automatic, and the Print Hidden Text, Print Back To Front, Cover Page, and Fractional Widths options are not active. If you change one or more of these default selections, your change will affect *all* Word documents, even those previously saved to disk. Like many other default settings, these are saved in the Word Settings file.

The last three options in the Print dialog box—Smoothing, Font Substitution, and Reduce/Enlarge %—are all document specific. With Word's default settings in effect, both Smoothing and Font Substitution will be activated, and the Reduce/Enlarge % setting will be 100. Any change that you make to these options will affect your current document only (and will be saved to disk with that document). You cannot change Word's default selections for these options.

ImageWriter Settings

As in the LaserWriter Print dialog box, Word's default setting for the Pages option in the ImageWriter Print dialog box is All. Similarly, Word's default Copies setting is 1. If you change one of these settings, your change will affect only the current Print... command in the current document. The next time you print your document, you'll have to respecify your Pages and Copies settings.

Word does allow you to change the default selections for the Paper Feed, Print Hidden Text, and Quality options. Initially, the Paper Feed setting is Automatic, Print Hidden Text is not active, and the Quality selection is Faster. As in the LaserWriter Print dialog box, any change you make to one of these selections will become your new default. All new documents and any documents previously saved to disk will reflect the new selection.

The one document-specific option in the ImageWriter Print dialog box is Tall Adjusted. Word's default for this option is deactivated. You cannot change this default setting. In other words, in any new document, this option will not be selected initially. However, if you want to change this setting for a particular document, you can do so by clicking the check box next to the Tall Adjusted option. When you save the document, Word will save the active setting.

Selected Printer

When you use the Chooser command on the menu to select a printer, your printer choice will become the default until you issue the Chooser command once more and make another selection. The selected printer is a Macintosh setting—it's not controlled by Word. In fact, if you quit from Word and then load another program (such as MacPaint), you'll find that the printer you selected in Word will still be the default printer.

Next File

There's one setting in the Page Setup dialog box that can affect printing. When you enter a file name in the Next File edit bar, Word will automatically print that file after it prints the current document. Word does not allow you to specify a default Next File. Your entry in the Next File edit bar will affect the current document only, even if you click the Set Default button in the Page Setup dialog box.

MEMORY MANAGEMENT DEFAULTS

The Preferences dialog box includes two Keep in Memory settings, which allow you to control—to some extent—your computer's RAM utilization. Theoretically, the Keep in Memory options can speed up processing by loading disk information into RAM. In addition, the Keep in Memory File option can, in some situations, help 512K Mac users avoid some disk-switching by loading a document file into RAM. The effects of the Keep in Memory setting can be temporary, affecting only the current file and Word session, or they can be permanent, affecting each Word session and every document that you open.

If you want to load your current document into RAM, just click the Keep in Memory File button (not the check box) in the Preferences dialog box. Word will then load your document into RAM and close the dialog box. If you want *every* document that you open in Word to be loaded into RAM, click on the check box next to the File button. Once you've done this, Word will save the active setting in the Word Settings file, and each time you open a document, that document will be loaded entirely into RAM automatically. We have found that, after clicking the File button or checking the option box, Word still must read information from a document file on disk, at least occasionally. Therefore, you shouldn't consider this setting to be a panacea for your disk-switching woes.

The Program option under the Keep in Memory setting can be used to load the Word program into RAM. If you click the Program button, the option will be active only for the current Word session. If you click the check box next to the Program button, the option will be activated in every Word session. Again, we've found that, after activating the Keep in Memory Program setting, Word still will want to read information from disk once in a while.

THE WORD SETTINGS FILE

As we've mentioned in our introduction and throughout this chapter, the Word Settings file controls most of Word's defaults. When you make a change to one of Word's default settings, that change will be stored in the Word Settings file. The Word Settings file does not exist when you first begin to use Word. However, Word creates this file automatically the first time you open the program and quit to the Finder level. You'll find the Word Settings file stored in the System folder on your startup disk for Word. If you discard or rename this file—or even if you remove it from the System folder on your startup disk—Word will create a new Word Settings file with all settings returned to their original defaults. Table 17-1 summarizes the various settings that are controlled by the Word Settings file. (By the way, the Word Settings file also controls all of the default settings displayed in the dialog boxes shown in Figures 17-1, 17-4, and 17-5.)

TABLE 17-1

Item	**Default**
Screen Display	
Short/Full Menus	Short Menus
Font menu selections	Chicago, Geneva, Monaco, New York, Venice (plus Boston and Times, when you select Full Menus)
Format menu selections	Plain Text, Bold, Italic, Underline, Outline, Shadow
Work menu	No Work menu appears
Unit of measure on ruler	Inches
Display of hidden text	Hidden text is displayed with a dotted underline
Display As Printed	Activated so that "What you see is what you get."
Page Layout	
Paper dimensions	US Letter, 8.5 inches wide, 11 inches high
Text orientation	Tall
Left margin	1.25 inches
Right margin	1.25 inches
Top margin	1 inch
Bottom margin	1 inch
Number of columns	1
Automatic page numbering	Deactivated
Line numbering	Deactivated

Continued on next page

Item	Default
Headers and footers	Single header/footer throughout document, printed 1/2 inch from edge of paper
Footnotes	Appear at the bottom of each page; Word uses a different set of numbers for the footnotes on each page.
Section start	New page
Formats	
Paragraph format	Flush-left alignment, single spacing, no indents, default tab stops every 1/2 inch, no space before or after, no borders or other special features
Character format	12-point, New York, Plain
Normal style	Displays all the characteristics of Word's default paragraph and character formats
Style sheet	Contains only the default *Normal* style
Widow Control	Activated
Print Settings	
Paper Feed	Automatic
Print Hidden Text	Deactivated
Print Back To Front	Deactivated
Cover Page	Deactivated
Fractional Widths	Deactivated
Memory Management	
Keep in Memory File	Deactivated
Keep in Memory Program	Deactivated

These are the default settings that are controlled by the Word Settings file.

Creating multiple Word Settings files

If you often work with documents that use different settings, then you should consider creating more than one Word Settings file. This will allow you to access multiple sets of defaults, such as different custom menus and different default Page Layout settings. For example, suppose that you work with two basic document formats most of the time. The two formats use different margins, a different style sheet, and different font and size options. By storing the default settings for these two formats in two separate settings files, you can save yourself considerable time in setting up new documents.

You already know how to save one set of defaults: After establishing your Page Layout and Section settings, you just click the Set Default button in each of these dialog boxes to store your settings as Word's new defaults. To save any custom styles on the default style sheet, you open the Define Styles dialog box, click each of the style names you want to save, and click Set Default. To save any custom menus, you just quit from Word—the program will automatically store the menus with the other defaults in the Word Settings file.

In order to create your second Word Settings file, you must first either rename the original Word Settings file or copy it to another disk or folder. (If you skip this step, the second settings file you create will overwrite the first file.) Then you load Word and specify your new defaults using the techniques we've described in this chapter. When you quit from Word, your new default dialog box settings, styles, and menu options will be stored in the file named Word Settings. At this point, you'll have two sets of defaults: The first set, which is stored in the Word Settings file that you copied to another disk or renamed, and the second set, which is stored in the Word Settings file that currently is in your System folder.

As you might expect, you can create as many sets of defaults as you want. However, at any given time there can be only one file named Word Settings in your System folder. Even if you have created several files to store other settings, when you load Word, it reads only the settings stored in the file named Word Settings. Before you open Word, you need to be sure that the file named Word Settings in your System folder contains the defaults that you want to use for that Word session. If the settings you want to use are in a different file, you'll need to change the name of the current Word Settings file (to something like *Alternative Settings*) or move that file out of the System folder to another folder or disk. Then you'll have to copy the other settings file into the System folder (if it is not already there) and change its name to Word Settings.

CREATING MULTIPLE STARTUP DISKS

Although it's fairly easy to create multiple Word Settings files, you may find that moving and renaming these files can be a hassle or, at best, confusing. One way to avoid this problem is to create separate Word startup disks for each set of defaults. For example, you might have one disk named Word Format1, which contains your Word program and a System folder containing one Word Settings file. Another disk, named Word Format2, would contain the Word program and a System folder containing another Word Settings file. (If you're using a 512K Macintosh with two single-sided disk drives, then you would create two system or startup disks, each containing a different Word Settings file, along with the other System files.)

Once you have created your different startup disks, just insert the appropriate disk for the document that you want to work with when you load Word. When you are ready to use another set of defaults, you will need to quit from Word, issue the Shut Down command, and then reload the program, using another startup disk.

One advantage to creating two or more different Word startup disks is that you can use different printer drivers, fonts, desk accessories, and so forth, on each disk—in addition to your different Word Settings files. This allows you to customize each Word startup disk even further. You also may want to store a different Standard Glossary file on each disk so that your glossary will automatically contain different entries, depending on which Word startup disk you've chosen to use. Let's take a look at how you go about creating multiple Standard Glossary files.

Multiple Standard Glossary Files

As we explained in Chapter 10, whenever you open Word, the entries from the Standard Glossary file are loaded automatically into the glossary. Word's default Standard Glossary file contains the terms *date*, *time*, and *Index*. Word makes it possible for you to store additional entries in the Standard Glossary file, if you want. Of course, any new terms that you add to the Standard Glossary file will be loaded into the glossary automatically each time you open a document.

If you want Word to load different sets of terms into the glossary each time you open the program, you can create multiple Standard Glossary files. Once you've done this, you'll be able to access a particular Standard Glossary file by copying that file to the startup disk you use with Word (the disk that contains your System folder).

To create a custom Standard Glossary file, just add the desired terms to the glossary as you are working in Word. Before you quit from Word, you can save the contents of the glossary into the file named Standard Glossary. Then, at the Finder level, copy the first Standard Glossary file to another disk or folder and discard that file. Now, to create another Standard Glossary file, load Word again. At this point, the glossary will contain only the Standard Glossary terms *date* and *time*. You can now add to the glossary any terms you want to include in the second Standard Glossary. Then, before you quit from Word, you should save the contents of the glossary into the file named Standard Glossary. You will now have two Standard Glossary files: one on your current startup disk and a second file on another disk (or in another folder).

Before you begin a Word session, you should be sure that the file named Standard Glossary on your startup disk contains the glossary entries that you want to use in that session. Of course, if you open Word and then realize that you've used the wrong Standard Glossary file, you can always load the entries from the other file on disk. Chapter 10 explains how to open glossary files.

DOCUMENT TEMPLATES

Using multiple Word Settings files and multiple Standard Glossary files can be very useful. Chances are, however, you won't want to create a new set of defaults for every different document configuration you use. You will find it more practical to change some settings on a document-by-document basis. However, even this process often can be speeded along through the use of document templates—blank document files in which you've preset certain settings, such as margins and styles. You can create document templates that contain predefined settings for each of the different types of documents you create: memos, letters, reports, and so on.

To create a document template, you first open a new, blank document window. Once the document is open, you issue commands to define the margins, styles, and other settings that you want to include in the template. If you're creating a template for documents that will use virtually identical text (such as certain kinds of contracts), you also may want to enter some standard text in the template file. After setting up your formats and entering any text you want to include, you're ready to save the document. To do this, issue the Save or Save As... command and choose a name for the file that identifies the type of template you've created. (You might use the name *Memo* for a template you would use to create memos, *Report* for a report template, and so on.)

Once you've created a template for a specific kind of document, you can use that template whenever you need to create that kind of document. You begin by opening the template file from the Finder level. When Word loads this file, you will see a blank document window (unless, of course, you've entered some standard text). However, all of your margins, styles, and other features for this new document will already be defined. You can just type the text of your document in the blank window, then use the Save As... command to save the text under a different name. (Be sure that you don't issue the Save command since this will cause Word to overwrite your template with the document you just created.)

By the way, some of Word's settings cannot be controlled with a document template. For example, as we explained earlier, such things as custom menus and the unit of measure on the ruler will show up in all of your Word documents. However, there are many document features that you can specify in a template file: Page Setup settings, the style sheet, Section parameters, headers, footers, and footnotes.

Although many of your templates will be quite simple, the settings in a blank template file can be as complex as the settings in your most intricate documents. For example, you could create a template with multiple sections and different Section dialog box settings in each section. Furthermore, each section of your document template might use a different header and/or footer. You may even want to save a number of footnote-related settings in a document template.

After you create one or more document templates, you may want to use each template with a different customized Word startup disk. For example, each template file will probably have certain style names stored on its style sheet. Before you open a template file, you may want to be sure that you're using a Word Settings file whose Work menu contains the style names that you've created in that template. That way, you'll be able to apply the styles directly from the Work menu as you're creating your document.

Similarly, different document templates are likely to require different glossary entries. To save yourself the trouble of opening glossary files from disk, you may want to make sure that the file named Standard Glossary on your Word startup disk contains the entries that you'll need when you use a particular template. Then, when you open the template, your glossary will already be loaded with the appropriate entries.

CONCLUSION

Of course, keeping track of multiple Word Settings files, Standard Glossary files, and various template files can get to be pretty confusing. We would suggest that you don't attempt to use the techniques we've described in this chapter until you're quite comfortable with Word. Then, you might begin by setting up a custom Word disk for your most common applications and, perhaps, create a template or two to use with that disk. As you become more familiar with Word, you'll be able to "automate" various settings with ease and even create entire turn-key document systems, if you want.

KEYBOARD AND MOUSE TECHNIQUES A1

Selection and Navigation: Expanded Keyboard

Select word	Double-click word
Select sentence	Press ⌘ and click on sentence
Select line	Click next to line in selection bar
Select paragraph	Double-click next to paragraph in selection bar
Select column	Press Option key, click next to first character in column, then drag down
Select document	Press ⌘-Option-m or press ⌘ and click in selection bar
Select a graphic	Click inside graphic frame or drag over graphic
Extend selection	Click at beginning of block, then press Shift and click at end of block
Extend selection to character	Press minus (-) on keypad then type character
Move up one line	Press ↑ or 8 on keypad
Move down one line	Press ↓ or 2 on keypad
Move left one character	Press ← or 4 on keypad
Move right one character	Press → or 6 on keypad
Move left one word	Press ⌘-← or ⌘-4 on keypad
Move right one word	Press ⌘-→ or ⌘-6 on keypad
Move to beginning of line	Press 7 on keypad
Move to end of line	Press 1 on keypad
Move to beginning of previous sentence	Press ⌘-7 on keypad
Move to beginning of next sentence	Press ⌘-1 on keypad

Move to beginning of previous paragraph	Press ⌘-↑ or ⌘-2 on keypad
Move to beginning of next paragraph	Press ⌘-↓ or ⌘-8 on keypad
Move to top left of screen	Press ⌘-5 on keypad
Move to beginning of document	Press ⌘-9 on keypad
Move to end of document	Press ⌘-3 on keypad
Move back to previous location	Press ⌘-Option-z or 0 on keypad

Selection and Navigation: Standard Keyboard

Select word	Double-click word
Select sentence	Press ⌘ and click on sentence
Select line	Click next to line in selection bar
Select paragraph	Double-click next to paragraph in selection bar
Select column	Press Option key, click next to first character in column, drag down and right
Select document	Press ⌘-Option-m or press ⌘ and click in selection bar
Select a graphic	Click inside graphic frame or drag over graphic
Extend selection	Click in front of first character, then press Shift and click after last character
Move up one line	Press ⌘-Option-o
Move down one line	Press ⌘-Option-,
Move left one character	Press ⌘-Option-k
Move right one character	Press ⌘-Option-l
Move left one word	Press ⌘-Option-j
Move right one word	Press ⌘-Option-;
Move to beginning of line	Press ⌘-Option-'-k
Move to end of line	Press ⌘-Option-'-l
Move to beginning of previous sentence	Press ⌘-Option-'-j
Move to beginning of next sentence	Press ⌘-Option-'-;
Move to beginning of previous paragraph	Press ⌘-Option-y
Move to beginning of next paragraph	Press ⌘-Option-b
Move to top left of screen	Press ⌘-Option-'-o
Move to beginning of document	Press ⌘-Option-'-p
Move to end of document	Press ⌘-Option-'-.
Move back to previous location	Press ⌘-Option-z

Windowing and Scrolling: Expanded Keyboard

Action	Keys
Activate another window	Press ⌘-Option-w
Make active window full-screen size or return to original size	Press ⌘-Option-]
Open/Close split window	Press ⌘-Option-s
Open/Close footnote window	Press ⌘-Option-Shift-s
Scroll up one screen	Press 9 on keypad
Scroll down one screen	Press 3 on keypad
Scroll up one line	Press ⌘-Option-[
Scroll down one line	Press ⌘-Option-/

Windowing and Scrolling: Standard Keyboard

Action	Keys
Activate another window	Press ⌘-Option-w
Make active window full-screen size or return to original size	Press ⌘-Option-]
Open/Close split window	Press ⌘-Option-s
Open/Close footnote window	Press ⌘-Option-Shift-s
Scroll up one screen	Press ⌘-Option-p
Scroll down one screen	Press ⌘-Option-.
Scroll up one line	Press ⌘-Option-[
Scroll down one line	Press ⌘-Option-/

Editing

Action	Keys
Nonbreaking hyphen	Press ⌘-~
Optional hyphen	Press ⌘--
Space	Press Spacebar
Nonbreaking space	Press ⌘-Spacebar
Tab	Press Tab
New line	Press Shift-Return
New paragraph	Press Return or Enter
New paragraph without moving insertion point marker	Press ⌘-Option-Return
New Page	Press Shift-Enter
New Section	Press ⌘-Enter
Delete character to right	Press ⌘-Option-f
Delete previous word	Press ⌘-Option-Backspace
Delete next word	Press ⌘-Option-g
Delete a selection	Press Backspace
Copy text	Press ⌘-Option-c
Copy formats	Press ⌘-Option-v
Move text	Press ⌘-Option-x
Paste special character	Press ⌘-Option-q
Insert glossary text	Press ⌘-Backspace, then type glossary term and press Return

Issuing Commands

Action	Keys
Calculate	Press ⌘-=
Change...	Press ⌘-h
Character...	Press ⌘-d
Close	Press ⌘-w

Copy	Press ⌘-c
Cut	Press ⌘-x
Define Styles...	Press ⌘-t
Find...	Press ⌘-f
Repeat Find	Press ⌘-Option-a
Font	Press ⌘-Shift-e, then type font name and press Return
Footnote...	Press ⌘-e
Glossary...	Press ⌘-k
Go To...	Press ⌘-g
Insert Graphics	Press ⌘-i
New	Press ⌘-n
Open...	Press ⌘-o
Outlining	Press ⌘-u
Paragraph...	Press ⌘-m
Paste	Press ⌘-v
Print...	Press ⌘-p
Quit	Press ⌘-q
Repaginate	Press ⌘-j
Save	Press ⌘-s
Show/Hide ¶	Press ⌘-y
Show/Hide Ruler	Press ⌘-r
Spelling...	Press ⌘-l
Styles...	Press ⌘-b
Undo	Press ⌘-z

Using Dialog Boxes

Move to next group of options	Press →
Move to previous group of options	Press ←
Move to next option	Press ⌘-Tab or decimal point on keypad
Move to previous option	Press ⌘-Shift-Tab
Move to next edit bar	Press Tab
Move to previous edit bar	Press Shift-Tab
Move up in list box	Press ↑
Move down in list box	Press ↓
Choose current item	Press ⌘-Spacebar or 0 on keypad
Choose item directly	Press ⌘-first letter of option
Open folder	Press ⌘-↑
Close folder	Press ⌘-↓

Formatting Paragraphs

Normal	Press ⌘-Shift-p or click |x| on ruler
Side-by-side	Press ⌘-Shift-g
Flush left	Press ⌘-Shift-l
Flush right	Press ⌘-Shift-r
Centered	Press ⌘-Shift-c
Justified	Press ⌘-Shift-j

Indent first line	Press ⌘-Shift-f
Nest	Press ⌘-Shift-n
Unnest	Press ⌘-Shift-m
Hanging indention	Press ⌘-Shift-t
Double-space	Press ⌘-Shift-y
Open Space	Press ⌘-Shift-o
Apply a style	Press ⌘-Shift-s, then type style name and press Return

Formatting Characters

All caps	Press ⌘-Shift-k
Bold	Press ⌘-Shift-b
Dotted underline	Press ⌘-Shift-\
Double underline	Press ⌘-Shift-[
Hidden	Press ⌘-Shift-x
Italic	Press ⌘-Shift-i
Outline	Press ⌘-Shift-d
Plain	Press ⌘-Shift-Spacebar
Shadow	Press ⌘-Shift-w
Small caps	Press ⌘-Shift-h
Strikethrough	Press ⌘-Shift-/
Subscript	Press ⌘-Shift-+
Superscript	Press ⌘-Shift--
Underline	Press ⌘-Shift-u
Word underline	Press ⌘-Shift-]
Font Change	Press ⌘-Shift-e, then type font name and press Return
Larger font size	Press ⌘-Shift->
Smaller font size	Press ⌘-Shift-<
Symbol font	Press ⌘-Shift-q

Using the Outliner: Expanded Keyboard

Promote selection	Press ←
Demote selection	Press →
Move selection up	Press ↑
Move selection down	Press ↓
Demote heading to body text	Press ⌘-→
Expand current paragraph	Press + (on keypad)
Collapse current paragraph and all subtext	Press - (on keypad)
Expand all hidden text	Press * (on keypad)

Using the Switcher

Switch right	Press ⌘-[
Switch left	Press ⌘-]
Return to Switcher	Press ⌘-\
QuickSwitch	Press ⌘-,

Other Techniques

Task	Technique
Repeat last command	Press ⌘-a
Cancel operation in progress	Press ⌘-.
Open a menu	Press decimal point on numeric keypad, then type first letter or number of menu. Press ← or → to move to adjacent menu after a menu has been opened.
Select item from open menu	Press ↓ or ↑
Add a command to a menu	Press ⌘-+, then issue command
Remove an item from a menu	Press ⌘--, then point to menu item
Move left indent marker only	Press Shift and drag bottom of marker
Move left or first-line indent marker past zero position	Press Shift and drag marker
Move both left and first-line indent markers past zero	Click on markers, then press Shift and drag
List all files on disk	Press Shift and choose Open…
Repaginate entire document	Press Shift and choose Repaginate
Search for formats	Press ⌘-Option-r
Perform descending sort	Press Shift and choose Sort
Move header or footer	Drag into place in Page Preview
Move header or footer into text area	Press Shift and drag into place in Page Preview window
Open/Close footnote window	Shift-⌘-Option-s
Open footnote window	Press Shift and drag split bar down
Access help	Press ⌘-? (pointer changes to a ?)
Convert selection to MacDraw picture and place in on the Clipboard	Press ⌘-Option-d

WORD ICONS A2

Pointer Icons

⌶	I-beam
↖	Left arrow
↗	Right arrow
+	Crosshair
🔍	Magnifying glass
?	Question mark
+	Plus sign
—	Minus sign
→1←	Page number
⌚	Watch

Document Window Icons

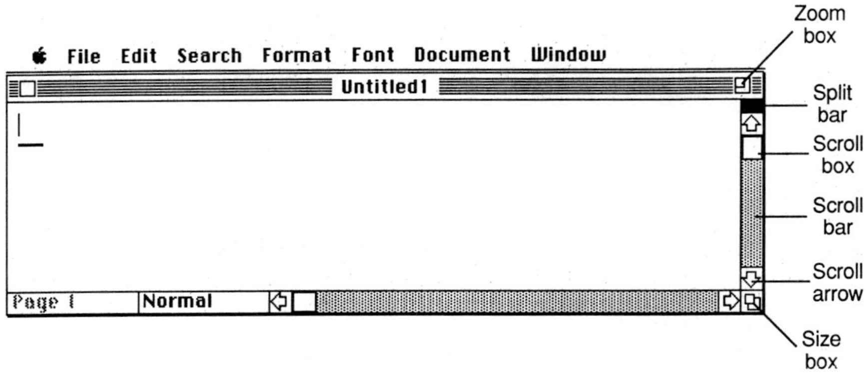

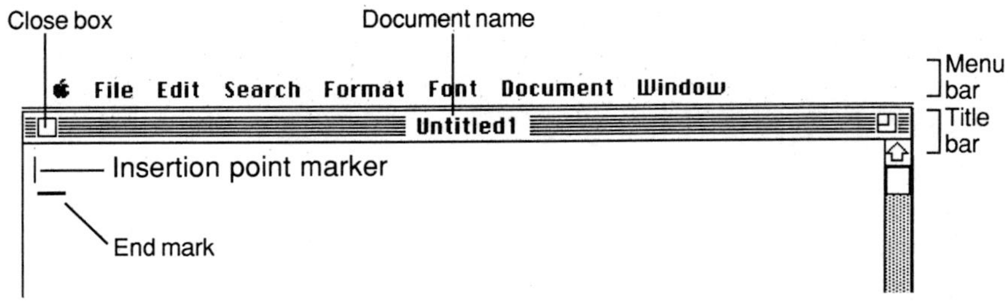

Dialog Box Icons

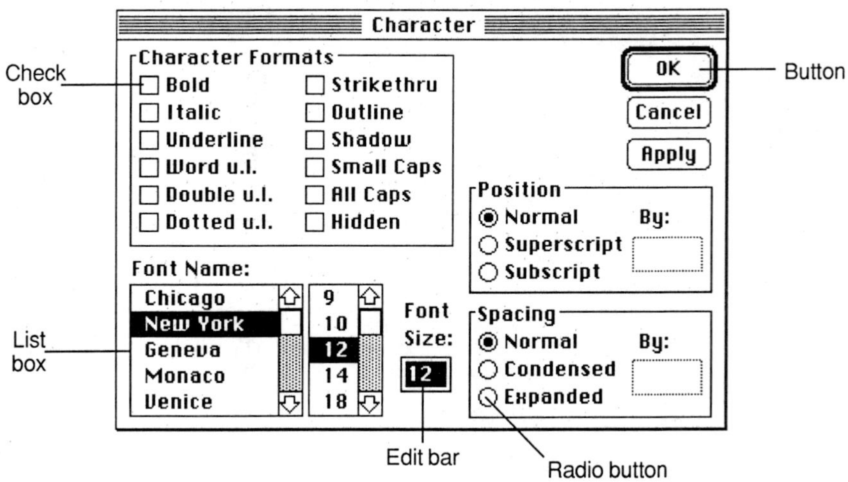

Ruler Icons

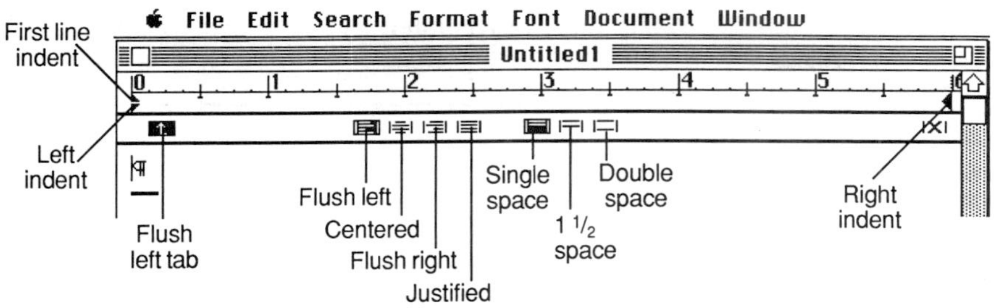

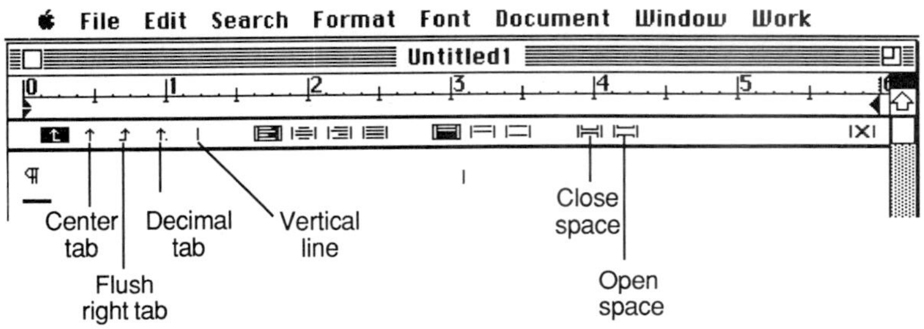

Page Preview Window Icons

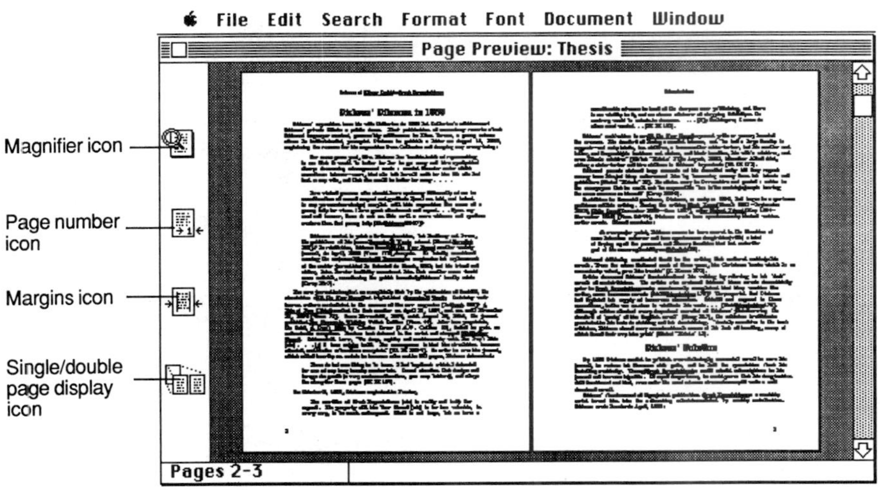

Header, Footer, and Footnote Window Icons

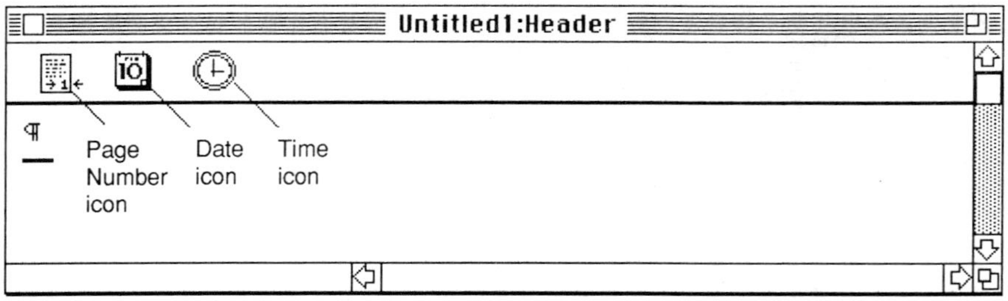

Outline Window Icons

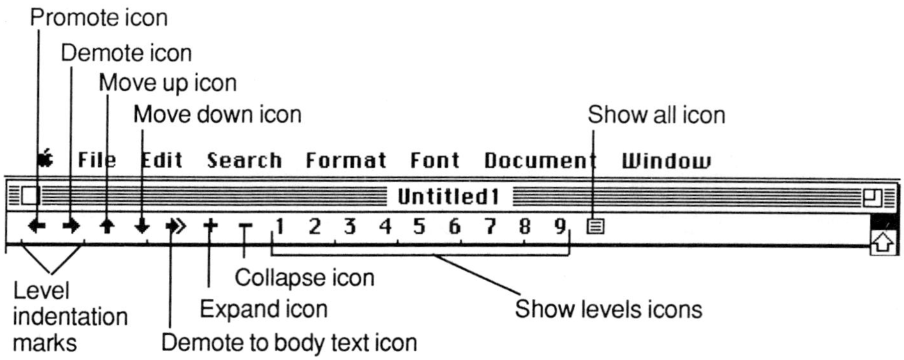

OTHER HARDWARE CONFIGURATIONS A3

Using Word on a Macintosh SE with a hard disk or on a Mac Plus installed with a hard disk is not much different from using Word on a Mac Plus with two 800K drives. That's not to say that the hard disk doesn't offer some significant advantages, which we'll address in a moment. In addition, the SE is noticeably faster than earlier versions of the Macintosh. Nevertheless, once you've loaded Word 3, the hardware differences are virtually transparent. All of your Word windows will look the same, and, of course, the commands and dialog boxes will not change.

GETTING STARTED

The first step in getting started with Word on a hard disk machine is to copy your Word program file from the master Word program disk onto your hard disk. After starting up your computer, insert your master Word program disk into the floppy disk drive. Then double-click the icon for the master Word program disk so you can view its contents. Next, drag the *Word Program* file icon from the master disk over the icon for your hard disk. You also should copy the Standard Glossary file and the Switcher program from your master Word program disk onto your hard disk. (In a moment, we'll talk about the various options for storing the Standard Glossary file on a hard disk.)

Your hard disk probably already contains a System folder with the System file, Finder, Clipboard, and various desk accessories and printer drivers. Therefore, you don't need to copy the System folder from your master Word program disk to your hard disk. (More on the System file in a moment.) If you need to install additional printer drivers, however, then you can do so.

After copying the Word program file and other files from your master Word program disk, the next step is to copy the appropriate files from your master Word utilities disk onto your hard disk. Eject the master Word program disk from your floppy disk drive and insert the master Word utilities disk. Then, if you want to copy the entire contents of the utilities disk onto the hard disk, just drag the icon for the master utilities disk over the icon for the hard disk. You will then see the alert message *The two disks are different types, so the contents of "Word Utilities" will be placed in a folder on "HARD DISK."*

When you click OK in the alert box, your Mac will automatically create a folder on the hard disk to store the utilities files. This folder will have the same name as the disk from which the files were copied. In a moment, we'll explain some tips on how to arrange the utilities files on your hard disk.

Even though you probably have plenty of storage space on the hard disk—especially if it's relatively new—you may want to conserve space by copying only selected files from the utilities disk instead of copying the entire disk. For example, you may not want to copy the UK Dictionary file or the DCA Conversion file.

After copying the appropriate files from your master Word program and utilities disks to your hard disk, you may want to create an additional floppy-disk backup of your master disks. If you have only one floppy disk drive in addition to your hard disk, you'll need to copy the entire contents of both the master Word program disk and the master utilities disk onto the hard disk, if you have not already done so. (On your Mac DeskTop, just drag each disk icon over the icon for the hard disk.) Word will automatically create a folder to hold the files on each disk, and you can copy these folders onto two blank floppy disks. Of course, if you have two floppy disk drives in addition to your hard disk, you can back up your master disks by following a procedure similar to the one that we described on pages 8 and 9 of Chapter 1.

After copying your master files onto your hard disk and making an additional backup, store the master disks and backups in a safe place. As we stressed in Chapter 1, never alter your master disks!

The System Files

Word 3 is shipped with Version 3.2 of the Apple System file and Version 5.3 of the Finder. If you've purchased a Macintosh SE, however, you'll have at least version 4 of the System file. Since this later version is specifically designed to take advantage of the SE, we would recommend that you use it instead of Version 3.2, which comes on your Word program disk. (That's why we did not tell you to copy the System folder from your master Word program disk to the hard disk.) One of the most noticeable differences between Version 4 of the system and earlier versions is the appearance of the icons that show up in alert boxes. Instead of seeing the impertinent face in profile, you see something akin to a traffic sign. For example, Figure A3-1 shows how some of Word's alert boxes will appear when you 're running the program under System 4.

One of the nicest benefits of using a hard disk is that you have plenty of room to install various fonts and desk accessories on your System file. We recommend that you go ahead and install all the fonts and desk accessories that you think you'll need to use in Word.

FIGURE A3-1

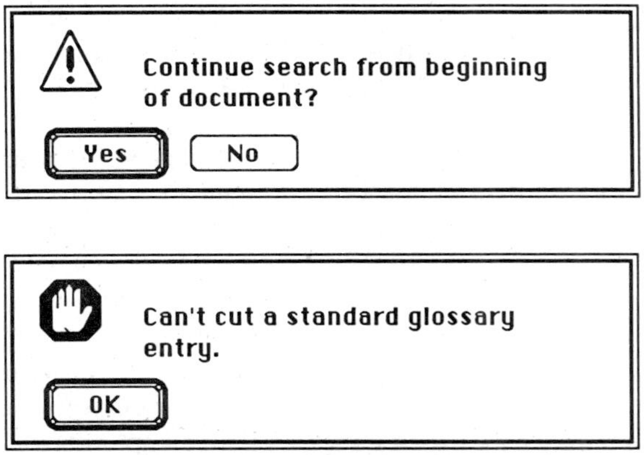

When you're running Word with System 4, you will see new icons in alert boxes.

By the way, do *not* attempt to keep two or more versions of the System file on your hard disk since this almost certainly will lead to errors. If, for some reason, you would like to use more than one version of the System (for accessing different fonts and desk accessories, for example), then you can store those different System files on various floppy disks. To access a particular System file, just boot your Macintosh with that file on the disk in your internal floppy drive. When you boot your computer, the Macintosh will look first to the internal floppy disk drive for the System and Finder files. Of course, if you want to boot from the version of the system that you've installed on your hard disk, just make sure that the internal floppy drive does not contain the system disk when you start up your computer.

Printer Resources

When you copy printer resource files from your master Word disks to the hard disk, you *must* place those files in the System folder. If a printer resource is not in the System folder, then you won't see that printer option when you open the Chooser dialog box. Of course, the storage space provided by a hard disk gives you the tremendous advantage of being able to keep multiple printer drivers readily accessible. You don't have to switch startup disks or rearrange files when you want to change from one printer to another. Nevertheless, we recommend that you do not consume space unnecessarily by copying printer resource files that you don't plan to use to your hard disk.

The Standard Glossary and Utilities Files

When you're setting up your hard disk with the various Word files, we recommend that you store the Standard Glossary, Word Help, Main Dictionary, and Word Hyphenation files in the System folder. When these files are in the System folder, Word will be able to access them automatically. That is, the entries in the Standard Glossary file will be loaded into the glossary automatically each time you open Word or open a document from the Finder level. Similarly, when you issue the Spelling... or Hyphenate... command, Word will automatically load the Main Dictionary or Word Hyphenation file, without asking you to locate it. Finally, when you choose About Microsoft Word... from the menu and click the Help button, Word will automatically load the Help file without asking you to locate it.

Word will also be able to locate each of these files automatically if they are on your hard disk but not stored in a folder. However, to reduce clutter in your hard disk window at the Finder level, we suggest that you place these files in the System folder. If you store one of these files in another folder, Word will not be able to locate it automatically. Of course, this does not mean that you won't be able to access the Main Dictionary, Word Hyphenation, Word Help, or Standard Glossary file. It merely means that you'll have to perform an extra step when you want to use the Spelling, Hyphenation, or Help facility or when you want to load the Standard Glossary entries into your glossary. For example, suppose that you've stored the Main Dictionary file in a folder named Word Utilities. When you issue the Spelling... command, Word will display a dialog box with the message *Please locate "Main Dictionary."* (You can see this dialog box in Figure 6-37.) Now, all you have to do is double-click on the folder name *Word Utilities* to open it, then double-click on the file name *Main Dictionary*.

There's one exception to this rule about folders and utilities files. If you've stored the Standard Glossary file or one of the utilities files in the same folder as the document you're working on, then Word will be able to access that file automatically. Of course, you probably won't want to do this since it will mean that Word will not be able to access the file automatically when you open a document in a different folder. We'll talk about document files and folders in the next section.

OTHER FILES AND FOLDERS

When you save files to a hard disk, folders become a necessity. How you organize your various files, however, will depend on your own individual computing preferences. If you use Word quite frequently, then you probably should keep the Word program icon visible within the window for your hard disk or even out on your Macintosh DeskTop, instead of tucking it away in a folder. That way, you can open the program quickly by double-clicking the icon at the Finder level.

Generally, you will use folders to store related files. However, all of the files that you keep in one folder won't necessarily be Word files. For example, if you integrate graphics into your documents, you may want to store some MacPaint files and Word document files in the same folder. Each folder might contain all of the files that are relevant to a particular project. If you keep the contents of each folder to less than 800K, then you'll be able to back up your work onto floppy disks easily by just copying the entire folder to a floppy disk each time you update the files.

Keep in mind that you can nest folders within folders. When you're using multiple levels of nested folders and you want to open a document from the

Finder level, you can prevent "window clutter" on your DeskTop by pressing the Option key each time you double-click a folder icon to view its contents. Pressing the Option key tells your Macintosh to "forget" that window after you open an application and then quit to the Finder level again. (You must be using Finder 5.1 or a later version in order to take advantage of this technique.)

As we explain in Chapter 3, you can open and close folders from within Word. Assuming you've organized your documents fairly logically, folders make it much easier to find a particular file since they limit the number of file (and folder) names that you see in the dialog box when you issue the Open... command. For example, in the File Open dialog box shown in Figure A3-2, you can see a list of the folders stored on the hard disk. If you double-click the folder name *Book*, you'll see the various folders and documents that are stored in that folder.

FIGURE A3-2

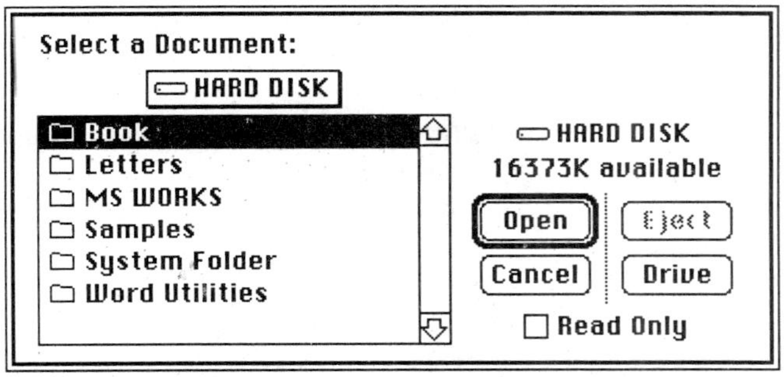

This File Open dialog box displays a list of the folders stored on the hard disk.

Similarly, when you issue the Save As... command, you'll see fewer file names in the dialog box if you've organized your files into folders. That way, it's easier to check and see if you've already used a certain file name before you type a name in the Save Current Document as edit bar.

By the way, if you open a document at the Finder level that's stored in a folder, Word will display the contents of that folder when you choose Open or Save As... from the File menu. In other words, the list that you see in the dialog box will always reflect the current "level" in your hierarchy of folders.

MANAGING DEFAULTS

In Chapter 17, we describe how you can create multiple Word Settings files in order to access different sets of defaults. We also explain how you can create multiple Standard Glossary files. You may recall that the Word Settings file controls such things as custom menus and Page Setup defaults, whereas the Standard Glossary file determines which glossary entries Word will load automatically. With a hard disk, creating and using multiple Word Settings files and multiple Standard Glossary files is easier than ever. With the extra storage space, you don't have to store your different files on different disks—they can all fit on your hard disk, if you want.

Multiple Word Settings Files

The first step in creating multiple Word Settings files is to create a folder in which to store the files. You might name this folder something like *Other Settings*. Next, open Word and set up some new defaults: Customize the menus, change the default style sheet, alter the Page Setup defaults, and so forth. After you've established one set of defaults from within Word, quit to the Finder level, then drag the Word Settings file into the Other Settings folder. Once you've done this, you should rename the file. You can change the name by simply appending a letter or number onto the end of the existing file name (*Word Settings2*, for example), or you might want to replace the name with something more descriptive, such as *Chapter Fonts*. When you next load Word, all your settings will be returned to their original defaults since the Word Settings file is no longer in the System folder. If you want, you can now create another set of defaults, quit from Word, and drag the new Word Settings file (which Word creates automatically) from the System folder into the Other Settings folder.

To use a particular set of defaults, move the appropriate file from your Other Settings folder into your System folder and rename it *Word Settings*. Then, the next time you load Word, the default settings that are stored in the current Word Settings file will be effective.

Multiple Standard Glossary Files

If you would like Word to load a different set of glossary entries automatically each time you start the program, then you should create multiple Standard Glossary files. As we explained in Chapter 17, creating multiple Standard Glossary files is simply a matter of saving glossary entries in different files and then renaming one of those files *Standard Glossary*. As with the Word Settings files, you may want to create a special folder on your hard disk with a name like *Glossaries*, to store your different glossary files.

Unlike the Word Settings file, the Standard Glossary file does not have to be in your System folder, although, as we described earlier, this is the recommended setup. The Standard Glossary file also can occupy the same folder as your Word program file, or you can keep it on your hard disk, not in a folder at all.

As we explained in Chapter 10, when you open Word, your glossary will always contain the two standard entries, *date* and *time*—whether or not Word has loaded the Standard Glossary entries. Of course, if Word has not loaded the Standard Glossary entries, you can access those entries, or the entries from any other glossary file, by opening the Glosssary dialog box, then choosing Open... from the File menu, and double-clicking the name of the glossary file you want to use.

INDEX

Command-Shift Z: strips styling from text without reverting to the Normal style's font.

D

E

F

G

H

M

N

O

P

T

U

V

W

Z